D0091872

teach yourself

gaelic dictionary

boyd robertson
and
ian macdonald

For over 60 years, more than 40 million people have learnt over 750 subjects the **teach yourself** way, with impressive results.

be where you want to be
with **teach yourself**

CALGARY PUBLIC LIBRARY

DEC / / 2004

For UK order enquiries: please contact Bookpoint Ltd., 130 Milton Park, Abingdon, Oxon OX14 4SB. Telephone: +44 (0) 1235 827720. Fax: +44 (0) 1235 400454. Lines are open 09.00–18.00, Monday to Saturday, with a 24-hour message answering service. Details about our titles and how to order are available at www.teachyourself.co.uk

For USA order enquiries: please contact McGraw-Hill Customer Services, PO Box 545, Blacklick, OH 43004-0545, USA. Telephone: 1-800-722-4726. Fax: 1-614-755-5645.

For Canada order enquiries: please contact McGraw-Hill Ryerson Ltd., 300 Water St, Whitby, Ontario L1N 9B6, Canada. Telephone: 905 430 5000. Fax: 905 430 5020.

Long renowned as the authoritative source for self-guided learning – with more than 30 million copies sold worldwide – the *Teach Yourself* series includes over 300 titles in the fields of languages, crafts, hobbies, business, computing and education.

British Library Cataloguing in Publication Data: a catalogue record for this title is available from The British Library.

Library of Congress Catalog Card Number: on file

First published in UK 2004 by Hodder Headline, 338 Euston Road, London NW1 3BH.

First published in US 2004 by Contemporary Books, a Division of the McGraw-Hill Companies, 1 Prudential Plaza, 130 East Randolph Street, Chicago, IL 60601, USA.

The 'Teach Yourself' name is a registered trade mark of Hodder & Stoughton Ltd.

Copyright © 2004 Boyd Robertson and Ian MacDonald

In UK: All rights reserved. No part of this publication may be reproduced or transmitted in any form or by any means, electronic or mechanical, including photocopy, recording, or any information storage and retrieval system, without permission in writing from the publisher or under licence from the Copyright Licensing Agency Limited. Further details of such licences (for reprographic reproduction) may be obtained from the Copyright Licensing Agency Limited, 90 Tottenham Court Road, London W1T 4LP.

In US: All rights reserved. Except as permitted under the United States Copyright Act of 1976, no part of this publication may be reproduced or distributed in any form or by any means, or stored in a database or retrieval system, without the prior written permission of Contemporary Books.

Typeset by Transet Limited, Coventry, England.
Printed in Great Britain for Hodder & Stoughton Educational, a division of Hodder Headline, 338 Euston Road, London NW1 3BH by Cox & Wyman Ltd., Reading, Berkshire.

Hodder Headline's policy is to use papers that are natural, renewable and recyclable products and made from wood grown in sustainable forests. The logging and manufacturing processes are expected to conform to the environmental regulations of the country of origin.

Impression number 10 9 8 7 6 5 4 3 2 1
Year 2010 2009 2008 2007 2006 2005 2004

contents

introduction

This *faclair* or dictionary was compiled in response to an invitation from the publishers to produce a publication that would complement the course book *Gaelic* in the Teach Yourself series and be useful to learners and to Gaelic speakers generally. The publishers were aware that there was a need and demand for a compact two-way dictionary of this kind.

One of the problems with a concise dictionary is that difficult decisions have to be taken as to what should be included and what left out. On occasion, therefore, there will be a noun here, but not the related adjective – and so on. This can be frustrating for the user, but within the constraints of the prescribed format we have tried to make the selection the most practically useful we could.

Anyone compiling a dictionary, whatever its length, must have recourse to the work of others, and we were grateful to have ready access to several existing dictionaries. The older Gaelic–English works by MacBain and Dwelly were consulted extensively, as were Derick Thomson's more recent *The New English–Gaelic Dictionary*, the all-Gaelic *Brìgh nam Facal* by Richard Cox and Clò Ostaig's *An Stòr-Dàta Briathrachais Gàidhlig*. We also drew on *Faclair na Pàrlamaid: Dictionary of Terms,* produced by the European Language Initiative and published by the Scottish Parliament, the Secondary Review Group's word list for schools, *Faclan Ùra Gàidhlig*, and two Irish dictionaries, Tomás de Bhaldraithe's *English–Irish Dictionary* and Séamus Mac Mathúna and Ailbhe Ó Corráin's *Pocket Irish Dictionary*.

Ian Quick read the dictionary in draft and contributed many useful suggestions. We are much obliged to him for his painstaking and perceptive commentary. Any shortcomings that remain are our responsibility. Katie Kennedy had the major task of keying in the text and formatting it onto disk. She has played a vital role in the production process, and we greatly appreciate her input and sustained commitment. We would also wish to acknowledge the support and encouragement given to us by Sheila Robertson and other members of our families, by John De Cecco of the University of Strathclyde and by Sue Hart and Ginny Catmur of the publishers, Hodder and Stoughton.

Detailed guidance on how to use the book is given in **the layout of the dictionary**. We hope it will prove a user-friendly work.

Tha sinn an dòchas gum bi am faclair feumail do luchd-labhairt na Gàidhlig, co-dhiù a tha iad fileanta no aig toiseach tòiseachaidh.

Boyd Robertson and Ian MacDonald

Selection and format of entries

For reasons of space, it has been possible to include only a small number of the many variants (including plurals) to be found in the language. These are indicated in the form used in 'Also **gàireachdaich**' under the main entry, **gàireachdainn.** Elsewhere, we have used oblique strokes, as in **neach-iùil/treòrachaidh.** In the case of hyphenated words like these, the oblique stroke indicates that the first element and the hyphen should also be added to the second word – ie, that the alternatives are **neach-iùil** and **neach-treòrachaidh.** Similarly, the oblique stroke in **gun toinisg/chiall** shows that the alternatives are **gun toinisg** and **gun chiall.**

We have also, to save space, usually given only the forms that are appropriate for the third person singular, masculine and feminine, in many phrases – eg, the translation of **awake** is given as **na d(h)ùisg,** *etc*, where the full paradigm would be **nam dhùisg, nad dhùisg, na dhùisg, na dùisg, nar dùisg, nur dùisg, nan dùisg.** Users should change the third person to another as required.

The language has more than one form of the prepositional pronouns that express 'to the, for the' etc and 'of the'/'off the', **don, dhan** and **dan** all being used for the first meaning and **den, dhen** and **dhan** for the second, but we have confined ourselves here to using only **dhan** for the first of these meanings and only **dhen** for the second.

We have used contractions throughout, as given in the **Abbreviations** section, and contracted forms of the headword are often used in entries. But the full headword is given where its form has changed – for example, where a consonant has been lenited (followed by h), and also if the word has fewer than four letters or if there may be ambiguity.

We have occasionally provided grammatical information – for instance, where a word or phrase should be followed by the genitive case – and short sections after the two main sections of the dictionary provide tabular information on the definite article, verbs and prepositional pronouns. These are intended to enable the user to have convenient access to basic forms, but it is not possible in any dictionary to provide the detailed guidance to be found in a grammar book. Similarly, the lists of personal and place names at the end are intended to be handy and useful, but they are necessarily selective.

A grammar book is also the best place in which to learn in detail where Gaelic greatly differs from English in the way certain meanings are expressed – for example, the fact that 'never' is not rendered by a separate word but is expressed by a negative form of a verb with one of the words used to render 'ever'. In such situations we have tried to give guidance as clear as space permitted, but we could not go into detail.

Nouns are nearly always listed before a related adjective, and an adjective before a related verb, but in cases in which, for example, an adjective is commoner than the noun, the adjective has been given first.

Headwords are in bold, translations are in roman and explanatory notes such as '+ *gen*' are in italics.

Current orthographic conventions are adopted throughout but earlier forms of spelling which users will encounter are provided as appropriate, and introduced by the term *Formerly*.

English words with one spelling but different meanings are included within one entry, but Gaelic ones are listed separately.

Layout of Gaelic–English section

All Gaelic text is in bold type.

Where a number of alternative translations of a Gaelic word are given, the order in which they appear aims to reflect currency and frequency of use.

When a Gaelic word has entirely distinct meanings, these are separated by semi-colons.

Some translations are glossed in brackets to clarify the context.

Alternative spellings of words are given either within the entry or as a separate entry:

eg **naoi** *n, a* nine *Also* **naodh**
maith *v See* **math**

Secondary forms of entries show the element to be added to the basic form:

eg **màileid** *n* **-e, -ean** *f* bag, suitcase

In many cases, the secondary form involves an internal adaptation of the primary form. The secondary form begins with the last unchanged letter of the original or, sometimes, the last unchanged letter before h:

eg **mòinteach** *n* **-tich, -tichean** *f* moor, moorland
easbhaidheach *a* **-dhiche** deficient, defective

The full secondary form is given in words where the primary form changes radically:

eg **sgian** *n* **sgeine, sgeinean** *f* knife

Where a secondary form of the word appears in the example, it is given in full.

Nouns

The gender of nouns is given after the last secondary form, usually the nominative plural. Some nouns can be feminine (*f*) in certain areas and masculine (*m*) in others.

Nouns are normally entered in their nominative singular form. The genitive singular and nominative plural forms are also indicated:

eg **faoileag** *n* **-eig, -an** *f* seagull

Where the genitive singular has the same form as the nominative singular, only the nominative plural form appears:

eg **slabhraidh** *n* **-ean** *f* chain

Where there are alternative forms of the genitive singular or nominative plural, these are given with an oblique:

eg **rathad** *n* **-aid/rothaid, -aidean/ròidean** *m* road, route, way

When nouns are normally accompanied by the definite article (*the* in English), the entry gives the full form:

eg **griùthrach** *n* **-aich** *f* **a' ghriùthrach** measles

In compound nouns, only the element that shows change from the basic form is shown in the genitive singular and nominative plural:

eg **ball-coise** *n* **buill-, buill-** *m* football

Where a noun and adjective have the same form, they are listed together under the same headword:

eg **ceithir** *n, a* four

Diùrach *n* **-aich, -aich** *m* someone from Jura *a* from, or pertaining to, Jura

Adjectives

The comparative/superlative form of the adjective is indicated along with the primary form except where the two are identical or in cases where they have little practical application.

Verbs

Verbs are entered in their root form, the second singular imperative or command form. The verbal noun (equivalent to the *-ing* ending in verbs in English) is also given where it differs from the root, but not otherwise:

eg **coisich** *v* **-seachd** walk

Where a verb is normally followed by a preposition, that is indicated thus:

eg **èist** *v* **-eachd** (+ **ri**) listen (to)

Common forms of irregular verbs are entered separately and most forms are listed in the **Grammar**.

Prepositions

Prepositions are usually followed by the dative case form of the noun. When the preposition is followed by the genitive case of the noun, this is indicated thus: (+ *gen*).

Prepositional pronouns

Each form of prepositional pronoun is included as a separate entry.

Layout of English–Gaelic section

The English headwords are in bold type.

Where a number of Gaelic words are given for an English headword, the order in which they appear reflects currency and frequency of use.

When an English word has entirely distinct meanings, these are separated by semi-colons and their sphere of application is specified in brackets.

Where a verb is intransitive, this is indicated thus: (*intrans*).

abbreviations

a	adjective
abb	abbreviation
acad	academic
ad	advertisement
adj phr	adjectival phrase
adv	adverb
adv phr	adverbial phrase
adv pref	adverbial prefix
abstr	abstract
agric	agriculture
anat	anatomical
atmos	atmosphere
aug conj	augmented conjunction
aug prep	augmented preposition
Bibl	Biblical
biol	biological
bot	botanical
caps	capital letters
coll	collective
colloq	colloquial
comp	comparative
comp a	comparative adjective
con	concrete
conj	conjunction
corresp	correspondence
contr	contraction
cult	cultural
dat	dative case
def art	definite article
def v	defective verb
dem a	demonstrative adjective
dem pron	demonstrative pronoun
descr	description
dom	domestic
eccl	ecclesiastical
educ	education(al)
emph (pron)	emphatic (pronoun)
exam	examination
exclam	exclamation
f	feminine
fig	figurative
fin	financial
gen	genitive case
geneal	genealogical
gen pl	genitive plural
geog	geography, geographical
geol	geology, geological
gram	grammar
impl	implement
ind	industry, industrial
infin part	infinitive particle
instit	institution

intens	intensive
interj	interjection
interr	interrogative
int part	interrogative particle
int pron	interrogative pronoun
intrans	intransitive
irreg v	irregular verb
jud	judicial
lang	language
leg	legal, legislation
len	lenition
ling	linguistics, linguistically
lit	literal(ly)
liter	literature, literary
m	masculine
math	mathematics
mech	mechanical
med	medical
met	metaphorical
metr	metrical
mil	military
mus	music(al)
n	noun
naut	nautical
neg	negative
neg conj	negative conjunction
neg part	negative particle
neg pref	negative prefix
nf	noun feminine
nm	noun masculine
nom	nominative case
num a	numerical adjective
num part	numerical particle
org	organization
past part	past participle
pej	pejorative
pers pron	personal pronoun
phil	philosophical
phot	photographic
phr	phrase
phys	physical
pl	plural
pol	polite
polit	politics, political
pop	population
poss pron	possessive pronoun
pref	prefix
prep	preposition
prep phr	prepositional phrase
prep pron	prepositional pronoun
pron	pronoun
punct	punctuation
rel	relative
rel part	relative particle
rel pron	relative pronoun
relig	religion, religious
sg	singular
stat	statistics
suff	suffix
sup a	superlative adjective
temp	temperature
topog	topographical
trad	traditional(ly)
trans	transitive
typ	typographical
v	verb
veg	vegetable
voc	vocative case
voc part	vocative particle
vn	verbal noun
v part	verbal particle
vulg	vulgar
+	followed by

Gaelic–English dictionary

A

a *num part* used before the numbers 1–19 in counting or when they are not followed by a noun **a h-aon, a dhà, a trì, a h-ochd, a h-aon deug, a dhà dheug, trithead 's a naoi, seachdad 's a ceithir**
a *voc part* when addressing someone **A Mhairead!** Margaret! **A Dhonnchaidh!** Duncan! **A Charaid/Bhanacharaid** Dear Sir/Madam (*at start of letter*)
a *prep* (*contraction of* **do**) to (+ *len*) **a' dol a Pheairt** going to Perth
a *prep* (*contraction of* **de**) of (+ *len*) **uair a thìde** an hour (*of time*)
a *rel part* who, whom, which, that **an tè a thachair rium** the one whom I met **an t-aodach a cheannaich sinn** the clothes that we bought
a *infin part* (*contraction of* **do**) to (+ *len*) **a bheil sibh a' dol a thadhal?** are you going to call? (*becomes* **a dh'** *before vowels*) **a' dol a dh'èirigh** going to get up
a *poss pron* her (*without len*); his (+ *len*) **a màthair 's a h-athair** her mother and father **a phiuthar is a bhràthair** his sister and brother
a' *def art* the (*See Forms of the article in Grammar*)
a' *v part* (*used before verbal nouns not beginning in vowels*) **a' ceannach** buying **a' suidhe** sitting
à *prep* from, out of
aba *n* **-chan** *m* abbot
abachadh *n* **-aidh** *m* ripening **gealach an abachaidh** the harvest moon *f*
abaich *v* **abachadh** ripen, mature
abaich *a* **-e** ripe, mature
abaid *n* **-e** *f* abbey
abair *irr v* **ràdh** say (*See irr v* **abair** *in Grammar*); used to give emphasis **a. sealladh!** what a sight!/some sight! **a. e!** indeed!/you can say that again!
abairt *n* **-e, -ean** *f* saying, expression, phrase
àbhachd *n f* fun, joking, mirth
àbhachdach *a* **-aiche** funny, given to joking
àbhachdas *n* **-ais** *m* fun, joking, mirth
abhag *n* **-aig, -an** *f* small dog, tyke
abhainn *n* **aibhne/-e, aibhneachan/aibhnichean** *f* river
àbhaist *n f* norm, custom, habit **'s à. dhomh ...** I usually ... **mar as à.** as usual
àbhaisteach *a* **-tiche** usual, normal
a-bhàn *adv* down, downward(s)
a bharrachd *adv phr* in addition, extra; either **fhuair mi £5 a bh.** I got £5 extra **chan eil sin fìor a bh.** that isn't true either *prep phr* (+ **air**) in addition to
abharsair *n* **-ean** *m* adversary **an t-A.** the Devil
a bhith *v* to be (*See verb* **to be** *in Grammar*)
a' bhòn-dè *adv phr* the day before yesterday
a' bhòn-raoir *adv phr* the night before last
a' bhòn-uiridh *adv phr* the year before last *Also* **a' bhèan-uiridh**
a-bhos *adv* (being) over here/on this side
abhsadh *n* **-aidh** *m* slackening **gun a.** non-stop, without halting
ablach *n* **-aich, -aich/-aichean** *m* carcase; person affected by illness or something suffering from wear and tear **tha e na a.** he is in poor shape **seann a. de chàr** an old wreck of a car
abstol *n* **-oil, -oil/-an** *m* apostle
aca(san) *prep pron* their; they **bha aca ri falbh** they had to go
acadamh *n* **-aimh, -an** *f* academy
acaid *n* **-e, -ean** *f* stabbing pain, stitch
acair(e) *n* **(-e), acraichean** *f m* anchor
acair(e) *n* **(-e), acraichean** *f m* acre
acarsaid *n* **-(e), -ean** *f* anchorage, harbour

acfhainn *n* **-(e), -ean** *f* equipment, instruments, tools **a. eich** horse harness
acfhainneach *a* **-niche** equipped; expert
ach *conj* but; (*after neg*) only, except **cha robh ann ach fathann** it was only a rumour
ach am/an *conj See* **feuch**
achadh *n* **-aidh/acha, -aidhean/ achannan** *m* field
a-chaoidh *adv* forever, always; (*after neg v*) never **cha tig iad a-ch.** they'll never come
achd *n* **-a, -an** *f* Act (*of Parliament*)
achdarra *a* skilful, expert, methodical
a-cheana *adv* already, previously
a-chianaibh *adv* recently, a short time ago
a chionn ('s) *adv phr* because, since **a ch. gu bheil mi sgìth** because I'm tired
achlais *n* **-(e), -ean** *f* armpit, oxter
achmhasan *n* **-ain, -ain** *m* rebuke, reprimand, reproach *v* **thoir a. do** rebuke, reprimand
a chum *prep phr* (+ *gen*) to **a chum an taighe** to the house *Also* **chum**
a chum is gu *conj* in order that **a chum is gum faic thu iad** in order that/so that you will see them
acrach *a* **-aiche** hungry
acraich *v* **-achadh** anchor
acras *n* **-ais** *m* hunger **a bheil an t-a. ort?** are you hungry?
actair *n* **-ean** *m* actor
ad(a) *n* **aide, -(a)n/-(a)ichean** *f* hat
adag *n* **-aig, -an** *f* haddock; stook (*eg of corn*)
a dh'aindeoin *prep phr* (+ *gen*) despite *adv phr* despite, even although, nevertheless **thig e a dh'. sin** he'll come despite that **a dheòin no (a) dh'.** willy-nilly/ like it or not
adha *n* **àinean** *m* liver
adhairc *n See* **adharc**
adhaltranach *a* **-aiche** adulterous
adhaltranas *n* **-ais** *m* adultery
adhar *n* **-air** sky *m*
adharc *n* **-airc(e), -an/-aircean** *f* horn
adhartach *a* **-aiche** progressive
adhartas *n* **-ais** *m* progress
adhbhar *n* **-air, -air/-an** *m* cause, reason **air an a. sin** for that reason, that being so, hence
adhbh(a)raich *v* **adhbh(a)rachadh** cause
a dh'ionnsaigh *prep phr* (+ *gen*) to, towards
adhbrann *n* **-ainn, -ainnean/-an** *f m* ankle
a dhìth *adv phr* needed; lost (forever) **tha sin a dh. orm** I need that **chaidh an streapadair a dh.** the climber perished
adhlacadh *n* **-aidh, -aidh/-aidhean** *m* funeral, burial, interment
adhlaic *v* **-acadh** bury, inter
adhradh *n* **-aidh, -aidhean** *m* worship, act of worship **a. teaghlaich** family worship **dèan a.** *v* worship
Afraganach *n* **-aich, -aich** *m* African *a* African
ag *v part* (*used before verbal nouns beginning in vowels*) **ag ithe 's ag òl** eating and drinking
agad(sa) *prep pron* your (*sg*) **a bheil càr agad?** do you have a car?
agaibh(se) *prep pron* your (*pl & pol*) **cò agaibh a bh' ann?** which of you were there?
againn(e) *prep pron* our **tha iad a' fuireach againne** they're staying with us
agair *v* **-t** petition, demand **ag agairt a chòraichean** demanding his rights
agallaich *v* **-adh/-achadh** interview; give abuse, quarrel with
agallaiche *n* **-an** *m* interviewer
agallamh *n* **-aimh, -an** *m* interview **dèan a.** *v* interview
agam(sa) *prep pron* my **cò th' agam an seo?** who's this?
agh *n* **aighe, aighean** *f m* heifer; hind

àgh *n* **àigh** *m* joy, bliss; good fortune **An ainm an Àigh!** For goodness's sake! **Gun sealladh an t-Àgh orm!** Goodness gracious me!
aghaidh *n* **(-e), -ean** *f* face (*human or geog*), facade **a. ri a.** face to face **nach ann ort a tha 'n a.!** what a cheek you've got! **bhithinn an a. sin** I'd be against that **air a.** forward **thug e an a. orm** *v* he (*verbally*) attacked/rebuked me
aghaidh-choimheach *n* **-coimhich, aghaidhean-coimheach** *f* mask, false-face
àghmhor *a* **-oire** happy; fortunate
a-ghnàth *adv* always (*past, present, future*), ever
agus *conj* and (*also contracted to* **is, 's**)
a h-uile *a* (*precedes n*) every, each, all **a h-uile h-oidhche** every night
àibheis *n* **(-e), -ean** *f* abyss, the deep; (*colloq*) large structure; ruin
àibheiseach *a* **-siche** large, huge; remarkable
aibidil *n* **-ean** *f* alphabet **òrdugh na h-a.** *m* alphabetical order
aice(se) *prep pron* her **an tèid aice air tighinn?** can she come?
àicheadh *n* **-eidh, -eidhean** *m* denial **rach às à.** *v* deny
àicheidh *v* **-eadh** deny
àicheil *a* negative
aideachadh *n* **-aidh, -aidhean** *m* admission, confession
aidh *excl* aye, yes
àidhear *n See* **èadhar**
aidich *v* **aideachadh** admit, confess
aidmheil *n* **(-e), -ean** *f* creed, faith
aifreann *n* **-rinn(e), -rinnean** *f m* Mass (*relig*)
aig *prep* at; (*also used to denote possession*) **tha càr aig Sìm** Simon has a car
aige(san) *prep pron* his **bidh fios aigesan** he'll know
àigeach *n* **-gich, -gich** *m* stallion
aigeann *n* **-ginn** *m* sea-bed *Also* **aigeal**
aigeannach *a* **-aiche** spirited, lively
aighear *n* **-eir** *m* joy, high spirits, merriment
aighearach *a* **-aiche** joyful, in high spirits, merry
aigne *n f* mind, consciousness, spirits
ailbhean *n* **-ein, -an** *m* elephant
àile *n m* air, atmosphere
àileadh *n m See* **fàileadh**
aileag *n* **-eig** *f* hiccups **bha an a. orm** I had the hiccups
àilgheas *n* **-eis** *f* will, inclination, desire
àilgheasach *a* **-aiche** choosy, fussy, fastidious, hard to please
ailisich *v* **-seachadh** criticize strongly
àill *n f* wish, desire **dè b' àill leibh?** what is your wish? **b' àill leibh?/bàillibh?** pardon?
àilleachd *n f* beauty, loveliness
àilleag *n* **-eig, -an** *f* jewel
àilleagan *n* **-ain, -ain** *m* little jewel, treasure
àillidh *a* **-e** beautiful, lovely
aillse *n f* cancer **tha a. air** he has cancer **a. sgamhain** lung cancer
ailm *n* **-e, -ean** *f* elm tree
ailtire *n* **-an** *m* architect
ailtireachd *n f* architecture
aimhleas *n* **-eis** *m* harm, hurt; misfortune
aimhleasach *a* **-aiche** harmful, hurtful; unfortunate
aimhreit *n* **(-e), -ean** *f* argument, dispute
aimhreiteach *a* **-tiche** argumentative, disputatious
aimlisg *n* **-e, -ean** *f* confusion, disorder; mischief **'s e a. a th' ann** he's a mischief
aimlisgeach *a* **-giche** mischievous
aimsir *n* **(-e), -ean** *f* time, era; weather **san t-seann a.** in days gone by
aimsireil *a* **-e** temporal, of this world; climatic
ain-deòin *n f* unwillingness, reluctance
ain-deònach *a* **-aiche** unwilling, reluctant

aineol *n* **-oil** *m* stranger, foreigner; lack of acquaintance **bha mi air m' a. sa bhaile** I was a stranger in the town
aineolach *a* **-aiche** ignorant, unaware, ill-informed
aineolas *n* **-ais** *m* ignorance
aingeal *n* **-gil, ainglean** *m* angel
aingidh *a* **-e** wicked, heinous
aingidheachd *n f* wickedness, iniquity
ainm *n* **(-e), -ean/-eannan** *m* name **a. sgrìobhte** signature **dè an t-a. a th' ort?** what's your name?
ainmeachadh *n* **-aidh** *m* nomination; mention
ainmear *n* **-eir, -an** *m* noun **a. gnìomhaireach** verbal noun
ainmeil *a* **-e** famous
ainmhidh *n* **-ean** *m* animal
ainmich *v* **ainmeachadh** name, mention; announce
ainmichte *a* designated, nominated
ainmig *adv* seldom, rarely
ainmneach *a* nominative **an tuiseal a.** the nominative case
ainneamh *a* **-eimhe** rare, infrequent **gu h-a.** rarely, infrequently
ainneart *n* **-eirt** *m* oppression, violence
ainneartach *a* **-aiche** oppressive, violent
ainnir *n* **(-e), -ean** *f* maiden
ainnis *n* **-e** *f* need, poverty
ainniseach *a* **-siche** needy, indigent
aintighearn(a) *n* **(-a), -an** *m* tyrant, oppressor, abuser of power
aintighearnas *n* **-ais** *m* tyranny, oppression, abuse of power
air *adv* on **tha an solas air** the light is on
air *prep* on; by; about; at; however, no matter; (*used to describe feelings and states*) **tha an t-acras/an t-eagal orm** I'm hungry/I'm afraid (*sometimes with len*) **air chuairt** on a trip **rug mi air chois air** I caught him by the foot **a' bruidhinn air na rudan sin** speaking about these things **bha sinn a' bruidhinn ort** we were speaking about you **air banais** at a wedding **math air ...** good at ... **air cho anmoch 's gum bi sinn** however late we are/will be
air *adv* after (*used before vn*) **tha iad air tilleadh** they've returned (*lit* they're after returning) **tha iad air an doras fhosgladh** they've opened the door
air(san) *prep pron* on him/it
air adhart *adv phr* ahead, forward(s), onwards **dol-air-adhart** *f* carry-on, undesirable behaviour
air aghaidh *adv phr* ahead, forward(s), onwards
air ais *adv phr* back, backwards **air ais 's air adhart** backwards and forwards
air ball *adv phr* at once, immediately
air beulaibh *prep phr* (+ *gen*) in front of **a. b. an taighe** in front of the house **air mo bheulaibh** in front of me
air bhog *adv phr* afloat **cuir a. b.** *v* launch
air bhonn *adv phr* in operation, up and running **cuir a. b.** *v* establish, set up
airc *n* **-e** *f* distress, want
àirc(e) *n* **(-e), -ean** *f* ark **À. Nòah** Noah's Ark
air chall *adv phr* lost
air chois *adv phr* in operation **cuir a. ch.** *v* establish, set up, institute
air choreigin *adv phr* or other **fear/tè a. ch.** someone or other
air chùl *adv phr* behind, rejected, lost
air cùl *prep phr* (+ *gen*) behind
air cùlaibh *comp prep* (+ *gen*) behind, at the back of **tha e air do chùlaibh** he/it is behind you
àird(e) *n* **-e, -ean** *f* height, high place, point, headland **sia troighean a dh'àirde** six feet tall
àird *n* **-e, -ean** *f* point of the compass, airt **an àird an iar** the west

air dheireadh *adv phr* behind, last; late **bha am bàta a. dh.** the boat was late
aire *n* heed, attention *f* **thoir an a.** notice; watch! look out! **thoir an a. ort fhèin** take care (of yourself)
air eagal ('s) gu *conj* lest, in case **a. e. gun tuit thu** in case you fall
àireamh *n f* **-eimh, -an** number **à. fòn** phone number
àireamhair *n* **-ean** *m* calculator
air fad *adv* altogether, in total
air falbh *adv* away, in a different place
air feadh *prep phr* (+ *gen*) throughout, all around
airgead *n* **-gid** *m* money, currency; silver **a.-pòcaid** pocket money **a. ullamh** cash
airidh *a* **-e** worthy, deserving **a. air duais** deserving a prize **'s math an a.** it's richly deserved
airidheachd *n f* merit
àirigh *n* **-ean** *f* sheiling, hill pasture; bothy
àirleas *n* **-eis, -an** *m* token **a.-clàir** record token *Also* **eàrlas**
air leth *adv* separate; exceptional, outstanding **cùm an dà rud sin a. l. o chèile** keep these two things separate from each other **duine a. l.** an exceptional man **a. l. math** exceptionally good
air-loidhne *a* online
air muin *prep phr* (+ *gen*) on top of, astride **a. m. eich** on horseback
àirne *n* **-an** *f* kidney
àirneis *n f* furniture **ball a.** an item of furniture
air neo *conj* or, or else
air sàillibh *prep phr* (+ *gen*) because of *Also* **air tàillibh**
air sgàth *prep phr* for the sake of, in the interests of **air mo sgàth-sa** for my sake **a. s. na sìthe** in the interests of peace
airson *prep* (+ *gen*) for, for the sake of; (*before a vn*) desirous of, wanting to **tha iad a. falbh** they want to go
airson gu *conj* because, since
air thoiseach *adv* ahead, in front; (*of a clock*) fast
air thoiseach air *prep phr* ahead of
air thuaiream *adv* at random
airtneal *n* **-eil** *m* weariness, sorrow, dejection *Also* **airsneal**
airtnealach *a* **-aiche** weary, sorrowful, dejected *Also* **airsnealach**
aiseag *n* **-eig/-sig, -an** *m* ferry
aiseal *n* **-eil, -an** *m* axle
aisean *n* **-ein, aisnean** *f* rib *Also* **asna** *f pl* **asnaichean**
aiseirigh *n f* resurrection, resurgence
Àisianach *n* **-aich, -aich** *m* Asian *a* Asian
aisig *v* **aiseag** ferry; restore
aisling *n* **-e, -ean** *f* dream
aiste *prep pron* from/out of her/it
ait *a* **-e** glad, joyful; funny
àite *n* **-an/-achan/-tichean** *m* place **à.-fuirich** dwelling-place, accommodation, habitation **à.-obrach** workplace **à.-suidhe** seat **à. bàn** vacancy **an à.** (+ *gen*) in place of, instead of
àiteigin *n m* somewhere
àiteach *n* **-tich** *m* cultivation, farming **talamh-àitich** *m* arable land
àiteachas *n* **-ais** *m* agriculture
aiteal *n* **-eil, -an** *m* glimpse, ray; breeze; small quantity **a. grèine** a glimpse of sunshine
aiteamh *n* **-eimh** *f m* thaw **tha beagan aiteimh ann** it's thawing a little *Also vn* **ag aiteamh**
aiteann *n* **-tinn** *m* juniper
aitheamh *n* **-eimh, -an** *m* fathom
aithghearr *a* **-a** fast, swift, sudden; short, brief *f* **a dh'a.** *adv phr* soon, shortly **fhuair i bàs a.** she died suddenly
aithghearrachd *n f* shortness, brevity; shortcut **ann an a.** soon, swiftly; in brief
aithisg *n* (**-e**), **-ean** *f* report **a. bhliadhnail** annual report
àithn *v* **-e** command, ordain
aithne *n* knowledge; acquaintance **an a. dhut e?** do you know him? **cuir a. air** *v* get

to know **cuir an a. (a chèile)** *v* introduce (to each other)

àithne *n* **-ntean** *f* order, commandment **na Deich Àithntean** the Ten Commandments

àithneach *a* imperative (*gram*)

aithnich *v* **-neachadh** know, recognize, acknowledge **a bheil thu ga h-aithneachadh?** do you recognize her?

aithreachas *n* **-ais** *m* regret, repentance **ghabh iad (an t-)a.** they regretted it

aithris *n* **-ean** *f* account, report

aithris *v* relate, report, recite

àitich *v* **àiteach/àiteachadh** cultivate; inhabit

aitreabh *n* **-eibh, -an** *m* building, dwelling

àl *n* **àil, àil** *m* brood, young, litter

àlainn *a* **-e/àille** lovely, beautiful, fine

Albàinianach *n* **-aich, -aich** *m* Albanian *a* Albanian

Albais *n f* the Scots language, Scots

Albannach *n* **-aich, -aich** *m* Scot *a* Scottish

alcol *n* **-oil** *m* alcohol

allaban *n* **-ain** *m* wandering **air an a.** wandering; homeless

allail *a* **-e** noble, illustrious

allmharach *n* **-aich, -aich** *m* foreigner, alien

allaidh *a* **-e** wild, fierce

allt *n* **uillt, uillt** *m* stream, burn

alltan *n* **-ain, -ain** *m* little stream, brook

alt *n* **uilt, -an/uilt** *m* joint (*of the body*); aptitude, knack; article (*liter, gram*) **tha alt aice air ceòl** she has an aptitude for music

altachadh *n* **-aidh, -aidhean** *m* grace (*before meals*) **dèan/gabh a.** *v* say grace

altaich *v* **altachadh** relax the joints; salute, thank **tha mi airson mo chasan altachadh** I want to stretch my legs (*See* **altachadh**)

altair *n* **altarach, -ean/altraichean** *f* altar

altraim *v* **-am/-amas** nurse, dandle, foster, nurture

altram *n* **-aim** *m* fosterage, fostering, nursing

am *def art* the (*used before b, f, m, p*) (*See Forms of the article in Grammar*)

am *poss pron* their (*used before b, f, m, p*)

am *int part* **am pòs thu mi?** will you marry me?

am *prep* equivalent to **an** in (*used before b, f, m, p*) **am Peairt** in Perth

àm *n* **ama, amannan** *m* time, period of time **àm nam Fuadaichean** the time of the Clearances **tha an t-àm agad falbh** it's time you went **tha an t-àm agad!** it's high time! (you did) **anns an eadar-àm** in the meantime, at present **san àm ri teachd** in future

a-mach *adv* out, outwards (*implying motion*)

amadan *n* **-ain, -ain** *f* fool

amaideach *a* **-diche** foolish, silly, ridiculous

amaideas *n* **-eis** *m* foolishness, folly, silliness

a-màireach *adv* tomorrow

amais *v* **amas (+ air)** aim at; chance on, chance to be **ag amas air an targaid** aiming at the target **dh'amais dhomh a bhith ann** I happened/chanced to be there

amar *n* **-air, -an** *m* container for liquid, trough, bath **a.-snà(i)mh** swimming pool

amas *n* **-ais, -an** *m* aim, objective; chance **cha robh ann ach a. gun d' fhuair mi e** it was only by chance that I found it

ambaileans *n* **-ean** *f* ambulance

am bàrr *prep phr* (+ *gen*), *adv* on top of, on the surface of **chì sinn dè thig am b.** we'll see what comes to the surface/to light

ambasaid *n* **-ean** *f* embassy

am-bliadhna *adv* this year

am broinn *prep phr* (+ *gen*) inside, within

Ameireaganach *n* **-aich, -aich** *m* American *a* American
amen *exclam* amen, so let it be
am feast *adv phr* forever; (*after neg*) never **cha ruig iad a. f.** they'll never get there
amh *a* **aimhe** raw; (*of a person*) uncouth
amhach *n* **-aich, -aichean** *f* neck *Also* **amhaich**
a-mhàin *adv* only, alone
àmhainn *n* **-ean** *f* oven
amhairc *v* **amharc (+ air)** see, look at, view
amharas *n* **-ais** *m* suspicion **fo a.** under suspicion, suspect **tha a. agam gu bheil** I suspect so
amharasach *a* **-aiche** suspicious, distrustful
amharc *n* **-airc** *m* seeing, looking, view **dè th' agad san a. a-nis?** what have you in view/in mind now?
àmhghar *n* **-air, -an** *f m* affliction, adversity, anguish, severe trouble
àmhghair *n See* **àmhghar**
amhlaidh *adv* as, in the way that
amhran *n* **-ain, -ain** *m* song
am measg *prep phr* (+ *gen*) among
a-muigh *adv* out, outside (*not implying motion*)
an *def art* the (*See Forms of the article in Grammar*)
an *poss pron* their
an *int part* **an tàinig iad?** have they arrived?
an *prep* in **an Èirinn** in Ireland
an-abaich *a* **-e** unripe
anabarr *n* **-a** *m* excess, too much
anabarrach *a* **-aiche** greatly, extremely, remarkably, excessively **a. mòr** extraordinarily large
ana-cainnt *n* **-e** *f* abusive language, verbal abuse
ana-caith *v* **-eamh** waste, misuse
ana-caitheanaich *n f* waste, misuse **a. air biadh math** a waste of good food
ana-ceartas *n* **-ais** *m* injustice
anacladh *n* **-aidh** *m* handling; protecting
anacothrom *n* **-uim** *m* injustice, hardship, handicap
ana-creideas *n* **-eis** *m* disbelief, scepticism
an aghaidh *prep phr* (+ *gen*) against
anail *n* **-e/analach, -ean** *f* breath; rest **a. na beatha** the breath of life **a. a' Ghàidheil am mullach** the Gael's rest is (*when he/she reaches*) the summit **leig d' a.** get your breath back/have a rest
an-àird(e) *adv* up, upwards
analachadh *n* **-aidh** *m* aspiration (*gram*)
a-nall *adv* over (*from the other side*), to this side
anam *n* **-a, anman/anmannan** *m* soul
anann *n* **-ainn** *m* pineapple
anarag *n* **-aig, -an** *f* anorak
anart *n* **anairt** *m* linen **anartan** clothes on a line **a.-leapa** bed linen **a.-bùird** table linen
an asgaidh *adv* free (of charge), for nothing **saor is an a.** free, gratis
an ath- *pref* (*usually lenites*) next **an ath-d(h)oras** *adv* next door **an ath-bhliadhna** *adv* next year, the following year **an ath-oidhch'** *adv* tomorrow night **an ath sheachdain** *adv* next week, the following week
an ceann *prep phr* (+ *gen*) after, at the end of
an ceartuair *adv* at present, just now; shortly **thig iad an c.** they'll come shortly/presently
an cois *prep phr* (+ *gen*) beside; (*met*) in the course of, as part of
an comhair *prep phr* (+ *gen*) in the direction of **an c. a chùil** backwards **an c. a chinn** forwards, head first
an còmhnaidh *adv* always, constantly
an-dè *adv* yesterday
an deaghaidh *prep phr See* **an dèidh**
an dèidh *prep phr* (+ *gen*) after; despite **cairteal an d. uair** quarter past one **is toigh leam e**

an d. sin I like him nevertheless/despite that **an d. sin 's na dhèidh** for all that, after all **an d. làimhc** afterwards, subsequently
an-diugh *adv* today **feasgar a.** this afternoon **san latha a.** these days
an-dràsta *adv* just now, now, at present **a. 's a-rithist** now and again
an ear *adv* east, eastern, eastwards **an àird an ear** the east
an-earar *adv* the day after next/tomorrow
an ear-dheas *adv* south-east, south-eastwards **gaoth an e.** a south-east wind
an ear-thuath *adv* north-east, north-eastwards **a' dol dhan ear-thuath** going north-eastwards
anfhann *a* **-ainne** weak, feeble, infirm
an-fhoiseil *a* **-e** restless, uneasy, ill-at-ease, troubled
an iar *adv* west, western, westwards **na h-Eileanan an Iar** the Western Isles
an iar-dheas *adv* south-west, south-westwards **oiteag on i.** a breeze from the south-west
an iar-thuath *adv* north-west, north-westwards
an impis *adv* about to, on the point of
an-iochdmhor *a* **-oire** unmerciful, unpitying, unfeeling
an làthair *adv* present *prep phr* (+ *gen*) in the presence of
an lùib *prep phr* (+ *gen*) among, involved in, in the course of, attached to
a-nìos *adv* up (*from below*)
a-nis *adv* now *Also* **a-nise, a-nist**
anmoch *a* **-olche** late
ann(san) *rel pron* in him/it; he, it **'s e oileanach a th' ann** he's a student
ann *adv* in existence, there; in it **'s e latha math a th' ann** it's a fine day
ann *prep* in a (*followed by* **an,** *by* **am** *before b, f, m, p, by* **a** *before h*) **ann an taigh** in a house **ann am bùth** in a shop **ann a Hiort** in St Kilda
annad(sa) *prep pron* in you (*sg*); you
annaibh(se) *prep pron* in you (*pl & pol*); you
annainn(e) *prep pron* in us; we
annam(sa) *prep pron* in me; I
annas *n* **-ais, -an** *m* rarity, novelty; unusual object/event **thug iad an t-a. às** the novelty wore off for them
annasach *a* **-aiche** unusual, novel; strange, odd
annlan *n* **-ain** *m* condiment, accompaniment to main food being eaten
anns *prep* (+ *art*) in (the) *Also used before* **gach a. gach taigh** in every house
annsa *a* better/best liked, preferred **an tè a b' a. leam** the woman I liked best
annsachd *n f* love, affection or object of these **m' a.** my beloved
ann(san) *prep pron* in him/it; he/it
annta(san) *prep pron* in them; they
a-nochd *adv* tonight
ànradh *n* **-aidh** *m* misfortune, distress
an seo *adv* here
anshocair *n* **-ean/-ocran** *f* unease; discomfort; illness
anshocrach *a* **-aiche** uneasy; discomforted, distressed, distressing; suffering from illness *Also* **anshocair**
an sin *adv* there
an siud *adv* over there
antaidh *n* **-ean** *f* aunt(ie)
an toiseach *adv* first, to begin with
an uair a *conj* when (*equivalent to* **nuair)**
an uair sin *adv phr* then, after that
a-nuas *adv* down (*from above*) *See also* **a-nìos**
an-uiridh *adv* last year

a-null *adv* over (*to the other side*) **a-null 's a-nall** hither and thither
a-nunn *adv See* **a-null**
aobhar *n See* **adhbhar**
aobrann *n See* **adhbrann**
aocoltach *a* **-aiche** unlike, unalike, dissimilar **glè a. ri chèile** very unlike one another
aodach *n* **-aich/-aichean** *m* clothes, cloth, material *pl* cloths of different kinds, clothes on a line **a.-leapa** bedclothes **a.-oidhche** night-clothes
aodann *n* **-ainn** *m* face (*human or geog*)
aodannan *n* **-ain, -ain** *m* false-face, mask
aodomhainn *a* **-e** shallow
aog *n* **aoig** *m* **an t-aog** death
aogas *n* **-ais** *m* face, appearance, countenance
aoibhinn *a* **-e** joyful, glad; pleasant
aoibhneach *a* **-niche** joyful, happy, glad; pleasant
aoidion *n* **-a, -an** *m* leak
aoidionach *a* **-aiche** leaky, leaking
aoigh *n* **-ean** *m* guest
aoigheachd *n f* hospitality **bha iad air a. againn** we had them as guests/they were our guests
aoigheil *a* **-e** hospitable; genial
aoir *n* **-e, -ean** *f* satire
aois *n* **-e, -ean** *f* age **dè an a. a tha i?** how old is she? **A. an Iarainn** the Iron Age
aol *n* **aoil** *m* lime
aom *v* **-adh** incline, bend **sna lathaichean a dh'aom** in days gone by
aomadh *n* **-aidh** *m* act of inclining or bending; inclination, tendency
aon *n* **aoin** *m* one (*of anything*) *normally written* **a h-aon**; each **not an t-aon** £1 each
aon *num a* one; only; same **sin an (t-)aon dath** that's the same colour *Also* **aona**
aonach *n* **-aich, -aich** *m* high or steep place, ridge **A. Eagach** the Serrated Ridge (in Glencoe)
aonach *n* **-aich** *f m* panting, state of being out of breath **bha a. orm** I was out of breath
aonachd *n f* unity
aonad *n* **-aid, -an** *m* unit
aonadh *n* **-aidh, -aidhean** *m* union, unity, merger **a. ciùird** (trade) union **an t-A. Eòrpach** the European Union
aonaich *v* **-achadh** unite, integrate, combine
aonaichte *a* united, integrated
aonan *n* **-ain** *m* one (*of anything*)
aonar *n* **-air** *m* one person; state of being alone **bha i na h-a.** she was alone *Also* **ònar**
aonaran *n* **-ain, -ain** *m* hermit, loner, recluse *Also* **ònaran**
aonar(an)ach *a* **-aiche** lonely, solitary
aonaranachd *n f* isolation, loneliness, solitude *Also* **aonranas, ònrachd**
aon-deug *n, a* eleven **aon duine deug** eleven men/persons
aon-ghuthach *a* **-aiche** unanimous
aonta *n* **-n** *m* agreement, assent, consent **cuir a. ri** *v* agree to, approve
aontachadh *n* **-aidh** *m* agreement, act of agreeing
aontaich *v* **-achadh** agree, consent
aontaichte *a* agreed
aoradh *n See* **adhradh**
aosta *a* old, elderly, aged *Formerly* **aosda**
aotraman *n* **-ain, -ain** *m* bladder
aotrom *a* **-ruime** light; light-hearted
aotromaich *v* **-achadh** lighten; alleviate
apa *n* **-ichean** *m* ape
aparan *n* **-ain, -ain** *m* apron
ar *poss pron* our **Ar n-Athair a tha air Nèamh** Our Father which art in Heaven
ar *def v* seems *in phr* **ar leam** it seems to me, I think
àr *n* **àir** *m* battle, battlefield, slaughter
ar-a-mach *n* rebellion, rising

A. nan Seumasach the Jacobite Rebellion/Rising
àra *n* **àrann, àirnean** *f* kidney
Arabach *n* **-aich, -aich** *m* Arab *a* Arabian, Arabic
àrachas *n* **-ais** *m* insurance
àrach *n* **-aich** *m* raising, upbringing, rearing
àradh *n* **-aidh, -aidhean** *m* ladder
àraich *v* **àrach** raise, bring up, rear
àraid(h) *a* **-e** certain, particular; odd, peculiar
Arainneach *n* **-nich, -nich** *m* someone from Arran *a* from, or pertaining to, Arran
àrainneachd *n f* environment
aran *n* **arain** *m* bread **a.-coirce** oat bread, oatcake **a.-cridhe** gingerbread
a-raoir *adv* last night
araon *adv* together, both **a. mise is tusa** both you and I
arbhar *n* **-air** *m* corn
àrc *n* **-a/àirce, -an** *f* cork, cork cap (*in bottle*)
Arcach *n* **-aich, -aich** *m* Orcadian *a* Orcadian
arc-eòlaiche *n* **-an** *m* archaeologist
arc-eòlas *n* **-ais** *m* archaeology
àrd *a* **àirde** high, tall; loud (*of sound*) *pref* principal, high, chief
àrd *n See* **àird(e)**
àrdachadh *n* **-aidh** *m* raising, increasing, elevation; promotion **fhuair sinn à. pàighidh** we got a pay rise
àrdaich *v* **-achadh** raise, increase, elevate; promote
àrdaichear *n* **-eir, -an** *m* lift
àrdan *n* **-ain** *m* pride, arrogance, haughtiness
àrdanach *a* **-aiche** proud, arrogant, haughty
àrd-chùirt *n* **-e, -ean** *f* high court
àrd-doras *n* **-ais** *m* lintel
àrd-easbaig *n* **-e, -ean** *m* archbishop
àrd-ghuthach *a* **-aiche** loud-voiced
àrd-ìre *n* **-an** *f* higher, higher grade/level **deuchainnean na h-Àrd Ìre** Higher exams **foghlam a.** *m* higher education
àrd-oifigear *n* **-eir, -an** *m* chief executive, senior officer
àrd-ollamh *n* **-aimh, -an** *m* professor
àrd-sgoil *n* **-e, -tean** *f* secondary school, high school
àrd-sheanadh *n* **-aidh, -aidhean** *m* general assembly (*eg of a Church*)
àrd-urram *n* **-aim, -an** *m* high honour, distinction; renown
àrd-ùrlar *n* **-air, -air** *m* stage, platform
a rèir *prep phr* (+ *gen*) according to **a. r. c(h)oltais** apparently
a-rèist(e) *adv* then, therefore, in that case
argamaid *n* **-e, -ean** *f* argument, dispute
argamaidich *v* **argamaid** argue
(a-)riamh *adv* ever, always
a-rithist *adv* again **an-dràsta 's a.** now and again, occasionally *Also* **a-rìs**
arm *n* **airm, airm** *m* army *Also* **armailt**
armachd *n f* arms, armour, weaponry
armaich *v* **-achadh** arm, equip with weapons
armaichte *a* armed
àrmann *n* **-ainn, -ainn** *m* hero, warrior
armlann *n* **-ainn, -an** *f* armoury, arsenal
ars *def v* said (**arsa** *before consonants*)
àrsaidh *a* **-e** ancient, antiquated
àrsair *n* **-ean** *m* antiquarian
àrsaidheachd *n f* quality of being ancient; antiquarianism; archaeology
artaigil *n* **-ean** *m* article
as *v rel form* of **is** (who/that) is **am fear as motha** the one that is biggest, the biggest one
as *prep* in *contraction of* **anns** *used in phrases* **as t-earrach, as t-samhradh, as t-fhoghar** in spring, in summer, in autumn

às *adv* out **chaidh an teine às** the fire went out **leig às e** let it go **rinn e às** he made off/ran for it/escaped **thàrr e às** he escaped
às *prep* out of
às(-san) *prep pron* from/out of him/it
asad(sa) *prep pron* out of you (*sg*)
asaibh(se) *prep pron* out of you (*pl & pol*)
asainn(e) *prep pron* out of us
asal *n* **-ail, -ail** *f m* ass, donkey **a.-stiallach** zebra *Also* **aiseal**
asam(sa) *prep pron* out of me
às aonais *prep phr* (+ *gen*) without, in the absence of
asbhuain *n f* stubble (*in field*)
às dèidh *prep phr* (+ *gen*) after, following *Also* **às deaghaidh**
às eugmhais *prep phr* (+ *gen*) without, lacking
asgaidh *n* **-ean** *f* gift *normally only used in phr* **an a.** free (*of charge*), for nothing
asgair *n* **-ean** *m* apostrophe
aslaich *v* **-achadh** supplicate, beseech
às leth *prep phr* (+ *gen*) on behalf of **rinn e sin às mo leth-sa** he did that on my behalf
asta(san) *prep pron* from/out of them
a-staigh *adv* in, inside; at home
astar *n* **-air, -air/-an** *m* distance; speed; journey **a. dheich mìle** a distance of ten miles **aig a.** at speed
a-steach *adv* in, into (*implying motion*) **thig a.** come in **chaidh iad a. dhan bhaile** they went into (the) town **cha tàinig e riamh a. orm** it never crossed my mind
Astràilianach *n* **-aich, -aich** *m* Australian *a* Australian
at *n* **-an** *m* swelling
at *v* **at/-adh** swell, puff up
ath *a* (+ *len*) (*preceded by def art*) next **an ath uair** the next time **an ath mhìos** next month
àth *n* **-an** *m* ford
àth *n* **-a, -an** *f* kiln; old barn/outhouse
ath- *pref* (+ *len*) re- **ath-aithris** *v* repeat, reiterate **ath-chruthaich** *v* recreate
athair *n* **athar, athraichean** *m* father **a.-cèile** father-in-law **athraichean** forefathers
athaiseach *a* **-siche** dilatory, tardy
a thaobh *prep phr* (+ *gen*) concerning, regarding, on that account **na biodh dragh ort a th. sin** don't worry on that account
atharrachadh *n* **-aidh, -aidhean/atharraichean** *m* change, alteration **a. nan gràs** religious conversion **thàinig a. air** he changed
atharraich *v* **-achadh** change, alter **tha an t-àite air atharrachadh** the place has changed
atharrais *n f* imitation, mimicry **dèan a. air** *v* imitate
atharrais (+ **air**) *v* mimic, imitate **bha e ag a. orm** he was mimicking me
ath-bheothachadh *n* **-aidh** *m* revival, rejuvenation **Linn an Ath-Bheothachaidh** the Renaissance Period
ath-bheothaich *v* **-achadh** revive, rejuvenate, revitalize
ath-chruthaich *v* **-achadh** re-create
athchuinge *n* **-an** *f* entreaty, petition
ath-dhìol *v* **-adh** repay
ath-leasachadh *n* **-aidh** *m* reform, redevelopment, amendment **an t-A.** the Reformation
ath-leasaich *v* **-achadh** reform, redevelop, amend
ath-nuadhachadh *n* **-aidh** *m* renewal, renovation
ath-nuadhaich *v* **-achadh** renew, renovate, reinvigorate
àth-sgrìobh *v* **-adh** rewrite; transcribe
ath-sgrùdadh *n* **-aidh, -aidhean** *m* revision, review
a thuilleadh *prep phr* (+ **air**) in addition to, as well as
atmhorachd *n f* inflation **ìre na h-a.** inflation rate

B

b' *v part* shortened version of **bu**, was (*used before vowels*)
bà-bà *n* soothing sound made to child indicating sleep
bac *n* **baic/baca, -an** *m* impediment, hindrance, obstruction, restraint; rowlock; bank
bac *v* **-adh** impede, hinder, obstruct, restrain, prevent
bacach *n* **-aich, -aich** *m* lame person, cripple
bacach *a* **-aiche** lame, crippled
bacadh *n* **-aidh, -aidhean** *m* impediment, hindrance, obstruction, restraint, delay, handicap **cuir b. air** *v* obstruct, hinder
bacan *n* **-ain, -ain** *m* stake, tether-stake; crook, crooked staff; hindrance **b.-dorais** hinge of a door
bachall *n* **-aill, -aill/-an** *m* staff, crozier
bachlach *a* **-aiche** curly, curled
bachlag *n* **-aig, -an** *f* curl, ringlet; shoot (*of plant*)
bachlagach *a* **-aiche** curly, curled
bad *n* **baid, -an** *m* spot, place, part, area; tuft, bunch, cluster; clump, thicket **anns a' bhad** at once, immediately
badan *n* **-ain, -anan/-ain** *m* a small cluster or tuft, thicket; nappy
badeigin *adv* somewhere
badhbh *n* **baidhbh, -an** *f* witch, old hag
Badhlach *n* **-aich, -aich** *m* someone from Benbecula *a* from, or pertaining to, Benbecula
baga *n* **-ichean/-nnan** *m* bag, case
bagaid *n* **-e, -ean** *f* cluster, bunch
bagair *v* **-t/bagradh** threaten, menace
bagairt *n* **-e, -ean** *f* threat, threatening
bagarrach *a* **-aiche** threatening, ominous, menacing
bàgh *n* **bàigh, bàigh/-(ann)an** *m* bay
bagradh *n* **-aidh, -aidhean** *m* threat, threatening, menacing
baibheil *a* **-e** marvellous, tremendous, terrific
baic *n* **-ichean** *m* bike, motorbike
bàidh *n* **-e** *f* kindness, affection, tenderness
bàidheil *a* **-e** kind, affectionate, friendly **b. ri** affectionate to, well-disposed to
baidhsagal *n* **-ail, -an** *m* bicycle
baile *n* **bailtean** *m* town, village, township **b. beag** village **b. mòr** city **aig b.** at home
bailiùn *n* **-aichean** *m* balloon
bàillidh *n* **-ean** *m* factor; baillie, magistrate
bainne *n m* milk **b. goirt** sour milk
baintighearna *n* **-n** *f* lady
bàirligeadh *n* **-gidh, -gidhean** *m* summons of removal, eviction order
bàirlinn *f See* **bàirligeadh**
bàirneach *n* **-nich, -nich** *f* barnacle, limpet
baist *v* **-eadh** baptize
Baisteach *n* **-tich, -tich** *m* Baptist *a* Baptist **an Eaglais Bhaisteach** the Baptist Church
baisteadh *n* **-tidh, -tidhean** *m* baptism, christening
bàl *n* **bàil, bàil/bàiltean** *m* ball, dance
balach *n* **-aich, -aich** *m* boy, lad **bu tu am b.!** well done, lad!
balachan *n* **-ain, -ain** *m* young boy, young lad
balaist(e) *n f m* ballast
balbh *a* **-a/bailbhe** dumb, mute, silent, quiet (*of weather*)
balbhachd *n f* dumbness, muteness
balbhan *n* **-ain, -ain** *m* dumb person, mute
balg *n* **builg, builg** *m* blister; abdomen; leather bag **b.-sèididh** bellows **b.-shaighead** quiver
balgair *n* **-e, -ean** *m* rogue, rotter, scoundrel
balgam *n* **-aim, -(ann)an** *m* mouthful (*of drink*), sip **b. tì** a drop of tea

balgan-buachair *n* **balgain-b.**, **balgain-b.** *m* mushroom
ball *n* **buill**, **buill** *m* member, limb **Ball Pàrlamaid, Buill Phàrlamaid** *m* Member of Parliament **B. P. na h-Alba** Member of the Scottish Parliament
ball *n* **buill**, **buill** *m* ball *Also* **bàl(l)a**
balla *n* **-chan/-ichean** *m* wall, rampart
ballach *a* **-aiche** spotted, speckled
ball-basgaid *n* **buill-**, **buill-** *m* basketball
ball-coise *n* **buill-**, **buill-** *m* football
ball-dòbhrain *n* **buill-** *m* mole (*on skin*)
ball-lìn *n* **buill-**, **buill-** *m* netball
ball-maise *n* **buill-**, **buill-** *m* accessory, ornament
ballrachd *n f* membership
ball-seirce *n* **buill-**, **buill-** *m* beauty spot
ball-stèidhe *n* **buill-**, **buill-** *m* baseball
bàn *a* **bàine** fair, fair-haired; white, pale; vacant, fallow, blank **talamh bàn** *m* fallow ground **duilleag bhàn** *f* blank sheet **eaglais bhàn** *f* vacant charge (*relig*)
bàn- *pref* light, pale **bàn-dhearg** light red
ban(a) *pref* used to give female version of one's identity or occupation, female, woman **ban-Albannach** *f* Scotswoman **bana-chlèireach** *f* clerkess
bana-bhuidseach *n* **-sich**, **-sichean** *f* witch
banacharaid *n* **-ean** *f* female friend, girlfriend
banachdach *n* **-aich** *f* **a' bhanachdach** vaccination
bana-chliamhainn *n* **-chleamhna**, **-chleamhnan** *f* daughter-in-law
banachrach *n* **-aich** *f* **a' bhanachrach** smallpox
bànag *n* **-aig**, **-an** *f* grilse, sea trout
bana-ghaisgeach *n* **-gich**, **-gich** *f* heroine, female warrior
bana-ghoistidh *n* **-ean** *f* godmother
banail *a* **-e/-ala** feminine, womanly, modest
banais *n* **bainnse**, **bainnsean** *f* wedding **bean na bainnse** *f* the bride **fear na bainnse** *m* the bridegroom
banaltram *n* **-aim**, **-an** *f* nurse
bana-mhaigh(i)stir-sgoile *n* **-mhaigh(i)stirean-** *f* headmistress
bana-mhaigh(i)stir *n* **-ean** *f* mistress (*figure of authority*)
banana *n* **-than** *m* banana
bana-phrionnsa *n* **-n** *f* princess
banas-taighe *n f* housekeeping; home economics
banca *n* **-ichean** *m* bank (*fin*) **B. na h-Alba** Bank of Scotland **B. Rìoghail na h-Alba** Royal Bank of Scotland **B. Dhail Chluaidh** Clydesdale Bank
bancair *n* **-ean** *m* banker
bancaireachd *n f* banking
ban-diùc *n* **-an** *f* duchess
bangaid *n* **-ean** *f* banquet, feast
ban-iarla *n* **-n** *f* countess
bann *n* **-a**, **-an/-tan** *m* band, belt, bandage; tie, hinge
bannal *n* **-ail**, **-an** *m* band, troupe, group, panel (*of people*)
ban(n)trach *n* **-aich**, **-aichean** *f m* widow, widower
ban-ogha *n* **-oghaichean/ -oghachan** *f* grand-daughter
banrigh *n* **-rean** *f* queen *Also* **ban-righinn**
baobh *n See* **badhbh**
baoghalta *a* foolish, silly, idiotic
baoit *n f* bait
baoth *a* **baoithe** foolish, simple (*of mind*)
bàr *n* **bàir**, **-aichean** *m* bar (*pub*)
bara *n* **-chan/-ichean** *m* barrow, wheelbarrow
barail *n* **-e**, **-ean** *f* opinion **dè do bharail?** what do you think?
baraille *n* **-ean** *m* barrel
barantaich *v* **-achadh** accredit
barantas *n* **-ais**, **-ais/-an** *m* guarantee, authority, surety, commission
bàrd *n* **bàird**, **bàird** *m* poet, bard

bàrdachd *n f* poetry
bargan *n* **-ain, -ain/-an** *f m* bargain
barganaich *v* **-achadh** bargain, make a deal
bàrr *n* **barra, barran** *m* top, surface, crest; cream **a bhàrr air** besides **thig am b.** *v* surface
Barrach *n* **-aich, -aich** *m* someone from Barra *a* from, or pertaining to, Barra
barrachd *n f* more **b. air** more than
barraichte *a* super, supreme, superlative, excellent
barraid *n* **-e, -ean** *f* terrace
barrall *n* **-aill, -aillean** *m* shoelace
bas *n* **boise, -an** *f* palm (*of hand*)
bàs *n* **bàis, bàis** *m* death **a' dol bàs** dying out
bàsaich *v* **-achadh** die
basgaid *n* **-e, -ean** *f* basket **b.-sgudail** waste-basket
bàsmhor *a* **-a** mortal
bàsmhorachd *n f* mortality
bata *n* **-ichean** *m* stick, staff
bàta *n* **-ichean** *m* boat **bàt'-aiseig** ferry **b.-cargu** cargo boat **bàt'-iasgaich** fishing boat **b.- sàbhalaidh** lifeboat **b.-siùil** sailing boat **b.-smùid** steamer, steamboat **b.-teasairginn** lifeboat **b.-tumaidh** submarine
batail *n* **-ean** *m* battle
bataraidh *n* **-ean** *f m* battery
bàth *v* **-adh** drown, extinguish, muffle (*sound*)
bàthach *n* **bàthcha/-aich, bàthchannan/-aichean** *f* byre, cowshed *Also* **bàthaich**
bàthadh *n* **-aidh, -aidhean** *m* drowning
bathais *n* **-ean** *f* forehead, brow
bathar *n* **-air** *m* goods, wares, merchandise **b. bog** software
bàthte *a* drowned
beachd *n* **-a, -an** *m* opinion, view, viewpoint; idea **dè do bheachd?** what do you think? **bha i a' dol às a b.** she was going crazy **gabh b. air** *v* consider
beachdaich *v* **-achadh** consider, think about, speculate, reflect on
beachdail *a* **-e** reflective, meditative, observant
beachd-smaoinich/smuainich *v* **-neachadh** meditate, contemplate
beachd-smaoin/smuain *n* **-tean** *f* idea, theory
beachlann *n* **-ainn, -annan** *f* beehive
beadaidh *a* **-e** disrespectful, impudent, forward
beadradh *n* **-aidh** *m* flirting, fondling, caressing
beag *a* **bige/lugha** small, little, wee **b. air bheag** little by little **is b. orm ...** I dislike ...
beagaich *v* **-achadh** diminish, lessen **b. air** cut down on, reduce
beagan *adv* a little, a trifle, somewhat **b. tràth** a little early
beagan *n* **-ain** *m* a little, a few
beag-chuid *n* **-chodach, -chodaichean** *f* minority
beairt *n* **-e, -ean** *f* machine, equipment, engine **b.-fhighe** loom **b.-iasgaich** fishing tackle *Also* **beart**
beairteach *a* **-tiche** rich, wealthy *Also* **beartach**
beairteas *n* **-eis** *m* riches, wealth *Also* **beartas**
bealach *n* **-aich, -aichean** *m* mountain pass, way, gap
bealaidh *n* **-ean** *m* broom (*plant*)
Bealltainn *n* **-e** *f* May Day, first day of May, Beltane
bean *n* **mnà/mnatha, mnathan** *f* wife, woman *dat* **mnaoi** *gen pl* **bhan a mhnathan- 's a dhaoin' -uaisle!** ladies and gentlemen!
bean *v* **-tainn (+ ri/do)** touch, handle, meddle with
bean-bainnse *n f* bride **bean na bainnse** the bride
bean-ghlùine *n* **mnà-glùine, mnathan-glùine** *f* midwife
beannachadh *n* **-aidh, -aidhean** *m* blessing, benediction
beannachd *n* **-an** *f* blessing **b. leat** goodbye **mo bheannachd ort!** well done!

beannag *n* **-aige, -an** *f* shawl
beannaich *v* **-achadh** bless
beannaichte *a* blessed, religious
bean-phòsta *n* **mnà-pòsta, mnathan-pòsta** *f* wife **a' Bhean-Phòsta (A' Bh) NicLeòid** Mrs MacLeod *Formerly* **bean-phòsda**
bean-sìthe *n* **mnà-, mnathan-** *f* fairy *Also* **bean-shìth**
bean-taighe *n* **mnà-, mnathan-** *f* housewife **b. an taighe** the lady of the house
bean-teagaisg *n* **mnà-, mnathan-** *f* teacher
bean-uasal *n* **mnà-, mnathan-** *f* lady
beàrn *n* **beàirn, -an** *f m* gap, space, hiatus, breach, cleft
beàrnan-brìde *n* **beàrnain-, beàrnain-** *m* dandelion
Beàrnarach *n* **-aich** *m* someone from Bernera(y) *a* from, or pertaining to, Bernera(y)
beàrr *v* **bearradh** cut (*hair*), shave, clip, shear, prune
bearradair *n* **-ean** *m* barber, cutter
bearradaireachd *n f* sharp wit
bearradh *n* **-aidh, -aidhean** *m* precipice, steep rockface; shearing
beatha *n* **-nnan** *f* life **'s e do bheatha** you're welcome
beathach *n* **-aich, -aichean** *m* beast, animal **b.-mara** sea mammal
beathachadh *n* **-aidh, -aidhean** *m* living, sustenance, nourishment
beathadach *n* **-aich** *m* beaver
beathaich *v* **-achadh** feed, nourish, sustain
beath-eachdraiche *n* **-an** *m* biographer
beath-eachdraidh *n* **(-e), -ean** *f* biography
bèibidh *n* **-ean** *m* baby
beic *n* **-ean/-eannan** *f* curtsy **dèan b.** *v* curtsey
bèicear *n* **-eir, -an** *m* baker
bèicearachd *n f* baking
Beilgeach *n* **-gich, -gich** *m* Belgian *a* Belgian
being *n* **-e, -ean** *f* bench
beinn *n* **-e, beanntan** *f* mountain, ben
beinn-theine *n* **-teine, beanntan-teine** *f* volcano
beir *irr v* **breith/beireachdainn** bear, take, hold (*See irr v* **beir** *in Grammar*) **b. air** catch (up with) **b. leanabh** give birth to a child **b. ugh** lay an egg
beirm *n* **-e, -ean** *f* yeast
beirmear *n* **-an** *m* enzyme
beithe *n* **-an** *f* birch, birch wood **craobh b.** *f* birch tree
beithir *n* **beathrach, beathraichean** *f m* thunderbolt
beò *a* **beotha** alive **cha robh duine b. ann** there wasn't a soul there
beò *n m* lifetime **rim bheò** during my life
beò-ghainmheach *n* **-ghainmhich** *f* quicksand
beò-ghlacadh *n* **-aidhean** *m* obsession
beòshlaint *n* **-ean** *f* livelihood, living
beothachadh *n* **-aidh** *m* animation, enlivening, kindling
beothaich *v* **-achadh** enliven, animate, quicken, kindle, stir
beothail *a* **-e/-ala** lively, vital, vivacious, animated
beothalachd *n f* liveliness, vitality, animation
beuc *n* **-an** *m* roar, bellow
beuc *v* **-adh/-ail** roar, bellow
beud *n* **-an** *m* pity, shame; harm, loss, damage **is mòr am b.!** what a pity!
beugaileid *n* **-ean** *f* bayonet *Also* **bèigneid**
beul *n* **beòil, beòil** *m* mouth, opening **dùin do bheul!** be quiet! **b. an latha** daybreak, dawn **b. na h-oidhche** twilight, dusk **droch bheul** verbal abuse **air a b(h)eul fodha** face down
beulach *a* **-aiche** talkative, plausible
beulaibh *n m* front (part) **air b.** (+ *gen*) in front of
beul-aithris *n* **beòil-, -aithrisean** *f* oral tradition, folklore
beum *n* **-a, -an/-annan** *m* blow,

stroke; reproach
beurla *n f* speech, language **Beurla** English **B. Ghallda** Scots (*lang*) **B. Shasannach** English
beus *n* **-a, -an** *f* virtue, conduct
beus *n* **-a, -an** *f* bass, bass (*instrument*)
beus *a* **-a/bèise** bass (*mus*)
beusach *a* **-aiche** virtuous, moral
beusail *a* **-e/-ala** ethical
beusalachd *n f* moral behaviour, ethics
bha *irr v* was, were (*See verb* **to be** *in Grammar*)
bhan *n* **-aichean** *f* van
bhàn *adv See* **a-bhàn**
bhàrr *prep* (+ *gen*) from, from off, down from
bhàsa *n* **-ichean** *f* vase
bhathar/bhathas *irr v* was, were (*passive form*) (*See verb* **to be** *in Grammar*)
bheat *n* **-a, -aichean** *m* veterinary surgeon
bheil *irr v* am? is? are? (*See verb* **to be** *in Grammar*)
bheir *irr v* will give, will bring, will take (*See irr v* **thoir** *in Grammar*)
bhidio *n* **-than** *f* video
bhiodh *irr v* would be (*See verb* **to be** *in Grammar*)
bhith *irr v See* **a bhith**
bhitheadh *irr v* would be (*See verb* **to be** *in Grammar*)
bho *conj* since
bho *prep* from
bho chionn *prep phr* since, ago (*equivalent to* **o chionn**) **b. c. mìos** a month ago **b. c. ghoirid** recently, a short time ago
bhod *aug prep* from your (*sg*)
b(h)olcàno *n* **-than** *m* volcano
bhom *aug prep* from my; from their
bhon *aug prep* from the; from their
bhon (a) *conj* since
bhor *aug prep* from our, from your
bhos *adv See* **a-bhos**
bhòt *n* **-a, -aichean** *f* vote
bhòt *v* **-adh** vote
bhòtadh *n* **-aidh** *m* voting, poll
bhuaibh(se) *prep pron* from you (*pl & pol*)
bhuainn(e) *prep pron* from us
bhuaipe(se) *prep pron* from her; from it
bhuaithe(san) *prep pron*; from him; from it *adv* **chaidh e bhuaithe** he/it deteriorated
bhuam(sa) *prep pron* from me
bhuapa(san) *prep pron* from them
bhuat(sa) *prep pron* from you (*sg*)
bhur *poss pron* your (*pl & pol*)
bi *irr v* be (*See verb* **to be** *in Grammar*)
biadh *n* **bìdh, -an** *m* food, meal
biadhlann *n* **-ainne, -an** *f* canteen, refectory, dining-hall
bian *n* **bèin, bèin** *m* hide, skin (*of animals*), pelt; fur
biast *n* **bèiste, -an** *f* beast; wretch
biastag *n* **-aig, -an** *f* beastie; insect
biast-dhubh *n* **bèiste-duibhe, biastan-dubha** *f* otter *Also* **biast-dubh**
biath *v* **-adh** feed
biathadh *n* **-aidh** *m* feeding; bait
bìd *n* **-e, -ean** *m* bite; cheep
bìd *v* **-eadh** bite
bìdeadh *n* **-didh** *m* biting, bite
bìdeag *n* **-eig, -an** *f* a little bit, morsel
bidean *n* **-ein, -an** *m* pinnacle
bidh *irr v* will be (*See verb* **to be** *in Grammar*)
bidse *n* **-achan** *f* bitch (*person*)
bigein *n* **-ean** *m* rock-pipit, any little bird; (*colloq*) willie (*penis*)
bile *n* **-an** *f* lip, rim, blade (*of grass etc*)
bile *n* **-an** *m* bill (*parliamentary*)
bileag *n* **-eig(e), -an** *f* little blade (*of grass etc*); label; leaflet
bile-bhuidhe *n* **-buidhe, bilean-buidhe** *f* marigold
binid *n* **-e** *f* rennet
binn *n* **-e** *f* judgement, sentence (*of court*), verdict
binn *a* **-e** melodious, harmonious, musical, sweet
binndich *v* **-deachadh** curdle, coagulate

binnean *n* **-ein, -an** *m* pinnacle, highest point, apex, high conical hill
binneas *n* **-eis** *m* melody, sweetness
Bìoball *n* **-aill, -aill** *m* Bible *Also* **Bìobla**
bìodach *a* **-aiche** minute, tiny
biodag *n* **-aig(e), -an** *f* dagger, dirk
biodh *irr v* would be (*See verb* **to be** *in Grammar*)
bìog *n* **-a, -an** *f* chirp, squeak, cheep
bìog *v* **-ail** chirp, squeak
bìogail *n f* chirping, squeaking
biolair *n* **-ean** *f* cress, water-cress
biona *n* **-ichean** *f m* bin
biona-sgudail *n f m* rubbish bin
bior *n* **-a, -an** *m* prickle; knitting needle
biorach *n* **-aich, -aichean** *f* dogfish
biorach *a* **-aiche** sharp, prickly
bioraich *v* **-achadh** sharpen, make pointed
bioran *n* **-ain, -ain/-an** *m* stick, kindler
biorgadh *n* **-aidh, -aidhean** *m* twitch, tingle, sensation of pain
biotais *n m* beet, beetroot
birlinn *n* **-e, -ean** *f* galley (*ship*)
bith *n* **-e, -ean** *f* life, being, existence **nì air b.** anything **às b.** whoever, whatever, wherever **sam b.** any **a' dol à b.** going out of existence
bìth *n* **-e** *f* gum, resin; bitumen, pitch
bith-beò *n f m* livelihood
bith-bhuan *a* **-bhuaine** eternal, everlasting *Also* **biothbhuan**
bith-bhuantachd *n f* eternity *Also* **biothbhuantachd**
bith-cheimigeachd *n f* biochemistry
bith-cheimigear *n* **-eir, -an** *m* biochemist
bitheadh *irr v* would be (*See verb* **to be** *in Grammar*)
bitheag *n* **-eige, -an** *f* microbe, germ
bitheanta *a* often, common, frequent **gu b.** often, regularly
bitheantas *n* **-ais** *m* frequency, generality, normality **am b.** generally, normally
bithear *irr v* am, is, are, will be (*passive form*) (*See verb* **to be** *in Grammar*)
bith-eòlas *n* **-ais** *m* biology
bith-eòlasach *a* biological
bithibh *irr v* be (*pl & pol command*) **b. sàmhach!** be quiet! (*See verb* **to be** *in Grammar*)
biùg *n m* sound; faint light
biùgan *n* **-ain, -ain/-anan** *m* torch, faint light
biùro *n* **-than** *m* bureau
biurocrasaidh *n* **-ean** *m* bureaucracy
blaigeard *n* **-eird, -an** *m* brat, blackguard, scoundrel *Also* **bleigeard**
blais *v* **blasad(h)** taste
blàr *n* **blàir, -an** *m* battle; plain, sward **cuir b.** *v* fight a battle
blas *n* **blais** *m* taste, flavour; accent
blasad *n* **-aid** *m* taste, tasting, bite **b. bìdh** a taste/bite of food
blasaich *v* **-achadh** add flavour to
blasta *a* tasty, savoury, delicious *Formerly* **blasda**
blàth *a* **blàithe** warm
blàth *n* **blàith, -an** *m* blossom, bloom **fo bhlàth** in bloom
blàthach *n* **-aich** *f* buttermilk
blàthaich *v* **-achadh** warm
blàths *n* **blàiths** *m* warmth
bleideag *n* **-eig(e), -an** *f* flake **bleideagan sneachda** snowflakes **bleideagan coirce** cornflakes
bleith *v* grind
bleoghain(n) *v* **-an(n)** milk
bliadhna *n* **-chan/-ichean** *f* year **am-b.** this year **a' Bhliadhn' Ùr** New Year **B. Mhath Ùr!** Happy New Year!
bliadhnail *a* annual, yearly **coinneamh bhliadhnail** *f* annual meeting
blian *a* **-a** insipid

blian *v* **-adh** sunbathe, bask in sun
blobhsa *n* **-ichean** *f m* blouse
bloc *n* **-a, -aichean** *m* block
bloigh *n* **-e, -ean** *f* fragment, scrap (of); incomplete state **dh'fhàg sibh e na bhloigh** you left it half-finished **rinn mi b. èisteachd ris** I half-listened to it
bloinigean-gàrraidh *n* **bloinigein-** *m* spinach
blonag *n* **-aig, -an** *f* lard *Also* **blonaig**
bò *n* **bà, bà** *f* cow *dat* **boin** *gen pl* **bò b. bhainne** milking cow, milch-cow
boban *n* **-ain, -ain/-an** *m* bobbin
bobhla *n* **-ichean** *m* bowl
bobhstair *n* **-ean** *m* bolster, mattress *Also* **babhstair**
boc *n* **buic, buic** *m* buck **boc-earba** roebuck
boc *v* **-adh/-ail** leap, skip
bòc *v* **-adh** swell, bloat, inflate
bocadaich *n* **-e** *f* leaping, skipping
bòcadh *n* **-aidh, -aidhean** *m* swelling, eruption
bòcan *n* **-ain, -ain** *m* hobgoblin, spectre, apparition, ghost
bochd *n* **-a** *m* poor person **na bochda** the poor *a* **-a** poor, wretched, ill
bochdainn *n* **-e** *f* poverty; ill-health
bod *n* **boid/buid, boid/buid** *m* penis
bodach *n* **-aich, -aich** *m* old man **b.-feannaig** scarecrow **b.-ruadh** cod **b.-sneachda** snowman **B. na Nollaig** Santa Claus
bodha *n* **-chan/-ichean** *m* submerged rock, reef
bodhaig *n* **-e, -ean** *f* body
bodhair *v* **bòdhradh** deafen
bodhar *n* **-air, -air** *m* deaf person
bodhar *a* **buidhre** deaf
bòdhradh *n* **-aidh** *m* deafening; boring
bòdhran *n* **-ain, -ain/-an** *m* bodhran (*drum*)
bodraig *v* **-eadh** bother **na b.** don't bother
bog *v* **-adh** dip, immerse, soak, steep
bog *a* **buige** soft, boggy, moist, damp (*of weather*) **b. fliuch** sodden, soaking wet
bogadaich *n* bobbing
bogadh *n* **-aidh** *m* dipping, immersing, steeping; bobbing
bogaich *v* **-achadh** soften, moisten; mellow
bog-chridheach *a* soft-hearted
bogha *n* **-chan** *m* bow; bulge
bogha-frois *n* **-froise, boghachan-** *m* rainbow
bog(l)ach *n* **-aich, -aichean** *f* bog, swamp, quagmire, marsh
bogsa *n* **-ichean** *m* box; accordion **b.-ciùil** acordion **b.-fòn** phone box **b.-litrichean** letter-box **b.-mhaidseachan** matchbox *Also* **bocsa**
bogsadh *n* **-aidh** *m* boxing *Also* **bocsadh**
bogsaig *v* **-eadh** box (*fight*) *Also* **bocsaig**
bogsaigeadh *n* **-gidh** *m* boxing *Also* **bocsaigeadh**
bogsair *n* **-ean** *m* boxer *Also* **bocsair**
bòid *n* **-e, -ean** *f* vow, oath
Bòideach *n* **-dich, -dich** *m* someone from Bute *a* from, or pertaining to, Bute
bòidhchead *n* **-chid** *f* beauty, comeliness
bòidheach *a* **bòidhche** beautiful, pretty, bonny
bòidich *v* **-deachadh** vow, swear
boil(e) *n* **-e** *f* frenzy, rage, madness **air bhoil(e)** in a frenzy
bòilich *n f* bawling, idle talk
boillsg *n* **-e, -ean** *m* gleam, shine, flash
boillsg *v* **-eadh** gleam, shine, flash
boillsgeach *a* **-giche** gleaming, shining
boillsgeadh *n* **-gidh, -gidhean** *m* gleam, shine, flashing
boineid *n See* **bonaid**
boinne *n* **-an/-achan** *f* drop (*of liquid*)
boinneag *n* **-eige, -an** *f* little drop (*of liquid*)

boireann *a* female, feminine (*gram*)
boireannach *n* **-aich, -aich** *m* woman
boireannta *a* effeminate; feminine (*gram*)
bois *n* **-e, -ean** *f* palm (*of hand*)
boiseag *n* **-eige, -an** *f* palmful, handful; slap **cuir b. air d' aodann** *v* wash your face quickly
boiteag *n* **-eig, -an** *f* worm *Also* **baoiteag**
boladh *n* **-aidh, -aidhean** *m* scent, smell
bolt *n* **-a, -aichean** *m* bolt, roll of wallpaper
boltaig *v* **-eadh** wallpaper
boltaigeadh *n* **-gidh** *m* wallpapering
boltrach *n* **-aich, -aich** *m* scent, fragrance
boma *n* **-ichean** *m* bomb
bonaid *n* **-e, -ean** *f m* bonnet
bonn *n* **buinn, buinn** *m* base, bottom, foundation; sole (*of foot*); coin, medal **b. airgid** silver coin, silver medal **b.-cuimhne** medal, medallion **b.-dubh** heel **b. òir** gold medal
bonnach *n* **-aich, -aich** *m* bannock, small cake
borb *a* **buirbe** fierce, barbaric, savage
borbair *n* **-ean** *m* barber, gents' hairdresser
bòrd *n* **bùird, bùird** *m* table, board **air b.** aboard **b. bàta** boat deck **b.-dubh** blackboard **b.-geal** whiteboard **b.-iarnaigidh** ironing table **b. locha** bank of loch **b.-sgeadachaidh** dressing table **b.-sgrìobhaidh** writing table, bureau **b.-stiùiridh** board of directors
bòst *n* **-a, -an** *m* boast *Formerly* **bòsd**
bòst *v* **-adh** boast *Formerly* **bòsd**
bòstail *a* **-e** boastful *Formerly* **bòsdail**
bòstair *n* **-ean** *m* boaster *Formerly* **bòsdair**
botal *n* **-ail, -ail** *m* bottle **b.-teth** hot-water bottle
bòtann *n* **-ainn, -an** *f m* boots, wellington boots
bothag *n* **-aig, -an** *f* bothy, small hut; hovel
brà *n* **-than** *f* quern
bracaist *n* **-e, -ean** *f* breakfast **leabaidh is b.** bed and breakfast
brach *v* **-adh** ferment, malt
brachadh *n* **-aidh** *m* fermenting, malting
bradan *n* **-ain, -ain** *m* salmon
brag *n* **braig, -an** *m* crack (*sound*), bang; report (*of gun*)
bragadaich *n m* crackling (*sound*), banging; gunfire
bragail *n f* crackling (*sound*), banging
bragail *a* **-e** cocky, self-confident
braich *n* **-e** *f* malt, fermented grain
braidhm *n* **brama, bramannan** *m* fart **leig b.** *v* break wind
braidseal *n* **-eil, -an** *m* roaring fire
bràigh *n* **-e/bràghad, -eachan** *m* brae, upper part; chest (*person*)
bràigh *n* **-e, -dean** *f m* hostage, captive
braighdeanas *n* **-ais** *m* captivity, bondage, confinement
bràiste *n* **-an** *f* brooch
bràmair *n* **-ar, -ean** *m* lover, boyfriend, girlfriend
branndaidh *n f* brandy
braoisg *n* **-e, -ean** *f* grin
braoisgeil *n f* grinning; giggling
braon *n* **braoin, braoin** *m* drop (*of liquid*)
bras *a* **braise** rash, impetuous, hasty
bras-shruth *n* **-an** *m* torrent
brat *n* **-a, -an** *m* cover, sheet, mantle **b.-làir/b.-ùrlair** carpet, rug, mat
bratach *n* **-aich, -aichean** *f* flag, banner
bratag *n* **-aig, -an** *f* caterpillar
brath *n* **-a, -an** *m* information, notice, message **b. naidheachd** press statement/release **cò aige tha b.?** who knows?
brath *v* **-adh** betray, inform on
brathadair *n* **-ean** *m* betrayer, informer

brathadh *n* **-aidh** *m* betraying, betrayal, treason
bràthair *n* **-ar, bràithrean** *m* brother **b.-athar** uncle (*father's brother*) **b.-cèile** brother-in-law **b.-màthar** uncle (*mother's brother*)
breab *n* **-a, -an** *f m* kick
breab *v* **-adh** kick, stamp
breabadair *n* **-ean** *m* weaver; daddy-longlegs
breac *n* **brice** *f* **a' bhreac** pox, smallpox
breac *n* **bric, bric** *m* trout; salmon (*in some dialects*)
breac *a* **brice** speckled, spotted, brindled
breacadh-seunain *n* **breacaidh-** *m* freckles *Also* **breac-sheunain** *f*
breacag *n* **-aig, -an** *f* scone, bannock, pancake
breacan *n* **-ain, -ain/an** *m* plaid, tartan
breacan-beithe *n* **breacain-, breacain-** *m* linnet, chaffinch
breac an t-sìl *n* **bric-, bric-** *m* wagtail
breac-bhallach *a* **-bhallaiche** freckled
breac-òtraich *n* **bric-** *f* **a' bhreac-òtraich** chickenpox
brèagha *a* beautiful, fine, lovely
Breatannach *n* **-aich, -aich** *m* Briton *a* British
brèid *n* **-e, -ean** *m* patch, kerchief
brèig *n* **-e, -ean** *f* brake (*as in car*)
breige *n* **-gichean/-geachan** *f* brick
brèige *a* false, deceiving, artificial
breisleach *n* **-lich** *f m* confusion, delirium **ann am breislich** in a state, delirious
breisleachail *a* confused, delirious
breislich *v* **-leachadh** rave, confuse
breith *n f* birth **co-là-b.** birthday
breith *v* bear, catch (*See irr v* **beir** *in Grammar*) **b. air** catch hold of
breith *n f* judgement, sentence, verdict **thoir b.** *v* pass judgement, give a verdict
breitheamh *n See* **britheamh**
breitheanas *n* **-ais, -an** *m* judgement **thig b. ort** *v* you'll suffer for it
breithneachadh *n* **-aidh** *m* judging, consideration
breithnich *v* **-neachadh** judge, consider
breòite *a* infirm, frail, sickly
breòiteachd *n f* infirmity, frailty
breoth *v* **-adh** rot, putrefy
breug *n* **brèige, -an** *f* lie, untruth
breug *v* **-adh** entice, coax, cajole
breugach *a* **-aiche** lying, dishonest, deceitful, false
breugaire *n* **-an** *m* liar
breugnaich *v* **-achadh** falsify; refute, rebut
breun *a* **brèine** putrid, stinking, nasty
briathar *n* **-air, -thran** *m* word, saying, term
briathrach *a* **-aiche** wordy, talkative, loquacious, verbose
briathrachas *n* **-ais** *m* terminology
brìb *n* **-e, -ean/-eachan** *f* bribe
brìb *v* **-eadh** bribe
brìbearachd *n f* bribery
brìgh *n* **-ean** *f* meaning; substance, essence; pith, juice **do bhrìgh** *conj* because (of)
briod *n* **-a, -an/-aichean** *m* breed, type
briod *v* **-achadh/-adh** breed
brìodal *n* **-all** *m* expressions of endearment; flattery, lover's talk
briogais *n* **-ean** *f* trousers, breeches **b.-snàimh** swimsuit
brìoghmhor *a* **-a** meaningful; energetic, substantial, substantive; sappy, pithy
briosgaid *n* **-e, -ean** *f* biscuit
bris(t) *v* **-(t)eadh** break, smash
bris(t)eadh *n* **-(t)idh** *m* breaking, smashing, break, breach **b. an latha** daybreak **b.-cridhe** heartbreak **b.-dùil** disappointment
brisg *a* **-e** brittle, crisp
brisgean *n* **-ein, -an** *m* crisp; silverweed; gristle **brisgein** crisps

briste *past part* broken
britheamh *n* **-eimh, -an** *m* judge, adjudicator, umpire
broc *n* **bruic, bruic** *m* badger
brochan *n* **-ain** *m* gruel, porridge; hotch-potch **dèan b. de** *v* make a mess of
brod *n* **bruid, -an** *m* goad, prickle; the best of anything **brod na sìde** excellent weather
brod *v* **-adh** goad, poke; stimulate, spur
brodaich *v* **-achadh** stimulate, kindle
bròg *n* **bròige, -an** *f* shoe, boot **brògan-cleasachd** sports shoes, trainers **b. na cuthaig** pansy **brògan-spèilidh** skates
broidse *n* **-sichean** *m* brooch
broilleach *n* **-lich, -lichean** *m* breast, bosom, chest
bròinean *n* **-ein** *m* poor soul (*male*)
broinn *n* **-e** *f* belly **am b.** inside, within
bròn *n* **bròin** *m* sorrow, grief, sadness **fo bhròn** sad, sorrowful
brònach *a* **-aiche** sad, sorrowful, mournful
brònag *n* **-aig** *f* poor soul (*female*)
brosgal *n* **-ail** *m* flattery
brosnachadh *n* **-aidh** *m* encouragement, inspiration
brosnachail *a* **-e** encouraging, inspiring
brosnaich *v* **-achadh** encourage, inspire, spur, provoke
brot *n* **-a, -an** *m* broth, soup
broth *n* **-a, -an** *m* rash
brù *n* **broinne/bronn, brùthan** (*dat* **broinn)** *f* belly, womb
bruach *n* **-aich(e), -aichean/-an** *f* bank (*of river*), edge
bruadair *v* **-ar** dream
bruadar *n* **-air, -an** *m* dream
bruaillean *n* **-ein** *m* trouble, confusion
brùchd *v* **-adh** belch **b. a-mach** break out
brùchd *n* **-a, -an** *m* belch
brù-dhearg *n* **brùthan-dearga** *m* robin (redbreast)
bruich *v* boil, cook
bruich *a* **-e** boiled, cooked
bruid *n* **-e, -ean** *f* captivity
brùid *n* **-e, -ean** *f m* brute, beast
brùidealachd *n f* brutality
brùideil *a* **-e** brutal
bruidhinn *n* **bruidhne** *f* talk, conversation
bruidhinn *v* talk, speak, say **b. ri** talk/speak to
bruis *n* **-e, -ean/-eachan** *f* brush **b.-chinn/fuilt** hairbrush **b.-fhiaclan** toothbrush **b.-pheant** paintbrush
bruis(ig) *v* **-eadh** brush, sweep
brùite *a* bruised, oppressed
brùth *v* **-adh** bruise; press, push
bruthach *n* **-aich, -aichean** *f m* hillside, slope, brae **le b.** downhill **ri b.** uphill
bruthainn *n* **-e** *f* sultriness, sultry heat
bruthainneach *a* sultry
bu *v* was, were (*See verb* **to be** *in Grammar*)
buabhall *n* **-aill** *m* buffalo, unicorn
buachaille *n* **-an** *m* herdsman, cowherd, shepherd
buachailleachd *n f* herding
buachaillich *v* **-leachd** herd, tend cattle
buachar *n* **-air** *m* dung
buadh *n* **buaidh, -an/annan** *f* quality, property, attribute, virtue, talent
buadhach *a* **-aiche** victorious; talented; influential
buadhaich *v* **-achadh** win, triumph
buadhair *n* **-ean** *m* adjective
buadhmhor *a* **-oire** victorious; talented; influential
buaic *n* **-e, -ean** *f* wick
buaidh *n* **-e, -ean** *f* success, victory, sway, influence, effect, impact **fo bhuaidh** under the influence of **thoir b. air** *v* affect
buail *v* **bualadh** hit, strike, beat, thresh, crash into
buaile *n* **-ltean** *f* fold (*for animals*); circle, ring
buailteach *a* **-tiche** liable (to), apt

(to), inclined (to), susceptible (to)
buain *n* **buana** *f* harvest, reaping, cutting **b. mhòna** peat cutting
buain *v* reap, cut (*eg hay*), harvest
buair *v* **-eadh** tempt, lure, worry, trouble
buaireadh *n* **-ridh, -ridhean** *m* temptation, trouble
buaireas *n* **-eis, -an** *m* turbulence, trouble
buaireasach *a* **-aiche** turbulent, stormy, troublesome
bualadh *n* **-aidh** *m* hitting, striking, beating, threshing **b. bhasan** clapping, applause
buamastair *n* **-ean** *m* boor, blockhead, oaf
buan *a* **buaine** lasting, enduring
buannachd *n* **-an** *f* profit, gain, advantage
buannachdail *a* **-e** profitable, advantageous
buannaich *v* **-achadh** win, gain
buar *n* **-buair** *m* herd of cattle
buarach *n* **-aich, -aichean** *f* cow-fetter
bucaid *n* **-e, -ean** *f* bucket
bucall *n* **-aill** *m* buckle
bucas *n* **-ais, -ais** *m* box
bugair *n* **-ean** *m* bugger
buideal *n* **-eil** *m* bottle, flask, cask
buidhe *a* yellow **nach b. dhut!** aren't you lucky!
buidhe *pref* yellow-tinted **b.-ruadh** auburn
buidheach *a* **-iche** satisfied, grateful, thankful
buidheach *n* **-dhich** *f* **a' bhuidheach** jaundice
buidheachas *n* **-ais** *m* gratitude, thanks, thanksgiving
buidheag *n* **-eig, -an** *f* goldfinch
buidheagan *n* **-ain, -ain** *m* egg-yolk
buidheann *n* **buidhne/-dhinn, buidhnean** *f m* group, band, organization, agency **b.-ciùil** band **b.-obrach** working party
buidhinn *v* win, gain
buidhre *n f* deafness
buidseach *n* **-sich, -sichean/-seachan** *f m* wizard
bana-bhuidseach *f* witch
buidseachd *n f* witchcraft
bùidsear *n* **-eir, -an** *m* butcher
buidseat *n* **-eit, -an** *m* budget
buidsidh *n* **-ean** *m* budgie
buil *n* **-e, -ean** *f* effect, consequence, outcome, impact **thoir gu b.** *v* bring into effect, carry out, complete **bidh a' bhuil ann!** you'll see what will happen!
buileach *a* complete, absolutely, fully **nas miosa b.** worse still **gu b.** completely, entirely **chan eil e b. deiseil** it is not quite ready
buileann *n* **-linn, -an** *f* loaf
builgean *n* **-ein, -an** *m* bubble, blister
builgeanach *a* bubbly, blistered
builich *v* **-leachadh** bestow, grant
buille *n* **-an** *f* blow, hit, strike; emphasis, stress; beat (*mus*) **b.-cinn** header (*in football*)
buin *v* **buntainn/buntail** belong to **b. do** belong to; concern **b. ri** apply (to)
buinneach *n* **-eich** *f* **a' bhuinneach** diarrhoea
buinneag Bhruisealach *n* **buinneig Bruisealaich, buinneagan Bruisealach** *f* Brussels sprout
buinnig *v* **-eadh** win
buinteanas *n* **-ais** *m* relationship, connection
bùirean *n* **-ein, -ein/-an** *m* roar, bellow
bùirich *n* **-e, -ean** *f* roaring, bellowing *Also* **bùireanaich**
Bulgàirianach *n* **-aich** *m* Bulgarian *a* Bulgarian
bumailear *n* **-eir, -an** *m* boor, oaf, bungler
bumpair *n* **-ean** *m* bumper
bun *n* **-a/buin, -an/buin** *m* base, bottom, stump; root; mouth (*of river*) **b.-craoibhe** stump of tree
bunait *n* **-e, -ean** *f m* foundation, base, basis
bunaiteach *a* **-tiche** fundamental, basic
bunasach *a* **-aiche** original, fundamental

bun-bheachd *n* **-a, -an** *m* concept, notion
bun-os-cionn *adv* upside-down, topsy-turvy **cuir b.** *v* turn upside down
bun-reachd *n* **-a, -an** *m* constitution (*of org*)
bun-sgoil *n* **-e, -tean** *f* primary school
bun-stèidh *n* **buin-, buin-** *m* basis, constitution (*of org*)
buntainneach *a* **-niche** relevant
buntanas *n* *See* **buinteanas**
buntàta *n m* potato, potatoes (*sg & pl*)
bùrach *n* **-aich** *m* mess, guddle, shambles **abair b.!** what a shambles!
bùrn *n* **bùirn** *m* water
burraidh *n* **-ean** *m* boor, oaf; bully
burraidheachd *n f* bullying
burras *n* **-ais, -ais** *m* caterpillar
bùrt *v* mock, scoff, ridicule **bha e gam bhùrt às** he was ridiculing me
bus *n* **-aichean** *m* bus
bus *n* **buis, -an/buis** *m* mouth, lip, snout, cheek **bha b. air** he was sullen
busach *a* **-aiche** sullen, glum
butarrais *n f* hotch-potch **dèan b. de** *v* make a mess of
bùth *n* **-a, -an/bùith(t)ean** *f* shop, booth **b.-èisg** fish shop **b.-leabhraichean** bookshop
buthaid *n* **-e, -ean** *f* puffin

C

cab *n* **caib, -an** *m* mouth (*colloq*) **dùin do chab!** shut your trap!
cabach *a* **-aiche** talkative (*often of a small child*), garrulous; gap-toothed
cabadaich *n f* blethering, chattering
càball *n* **-aill, -aill** *m* cable
cabar *n* **-air, -air/-an** *m* rafter; any large piece of wood, eg caber (*for tossing*); deer's antler **fo mo chabair-sa** under my roof
cabhag *n* **-aig** *f* hurry, haste **a bheil c. ort?** are you in a hurry? **dèan c.!** *v* hurry! *Also* **cabhaig**
cabhagach *a* **-aiche** hurried, hasty; impatient
cabhlach *n* **-aich, -aich/-aichean** *m* fleet **an C. Rìoghail** the Royal Navy
cabhsair *n* **-ean** *m* pavement, sidewalk; causeway
cac *n* **cac(a)** *m* excrement, (*vulg*) crap, shit
cac *v* **cac/-adh** excrete, defecate
caca *a* rotten, nasty
càch *pron* **chàich** (*of people*) the rest, the others
cachaileith *n* **-ean** *f* gate, entrance
cadal *n* **-ail, -ail/an** *m* sleep **tha an c. orm** I'm sleepy **a bheil iad nan c.?** are they asleep? **c.-deilgneach** pins and needles
cadalach *a* **-aiche** sleepy
cafaidh *n* **-ean** *f m* cafe
cagailt(e) *n* **(-e), -(e)an** *f* hearth
cagainn *v* **cagnadh** chew, gnaw
cagair *v* **-arsaich** whisper
cagar *n* **-air, -airean** *m* whisper; secret **a chagair** my darling **cuir c. na chluais** whisper in his ear
caibeal *n* **-eil, -eil/-an** *m* chapel; family burial area
caibideil *n* **-ean** *f m* chapter
caidil *v* **cadal** sleep
caidreachas *n* **-ais, -an** *m* alliance, federation; companionship
càil *n* **-e, -ean** *f* appetite, disposition, desire; appearance; anything **chan eil e a' tighinn rim chàil** it doesn't appeal to me **c. an latha** the first appearance of day **chan eil c. ann** there's nothing there **bheil c. às ùr?** is there anything new/any news?
cailc *n* **-e , -ean** *f* chalk, piece of chalk
caileag *n* **-eig, -an** *f* girl, lass, young woman
càilear *a* **-eire** attractive, pleasing
cailin *n* **-ean** *f* maiden, young woman
caill *v* **call** lose
cailleach *n* **-lich(e), -an** *f* old woman **c.-dhubh** nun

c.-oidhche owl
càin *n* **-e, -tean** *f* fine **chaidh c. air** he was fined
càin *v* **-eadh** scold, criticize, denounce
cainb *n* **-e** *f* hemp, cannabis (*plant*)
càineadh *n* **-nidh** *m* criticism
caineal *n* **-eil** *m* cinnamon
cainnt *n* **-e, -ean** *f* speech, conversation, language **droch c(h)ainnt** bad language, swearing
caiptean *n* **-ein, -an** *m* captain, skipper, ship's master
cairbh *n* **-e, -ean** *f* carcase, corpse
càirdeach *a* **-diche** related (to) **tha i c. dhomh** she is related to me
càirdeas *n* **-eis** *m* kinship, relationship; friendship **tha c. fad' às eadarainn** we are distantly related **cha do mhair an c.** the friendship did not last
càirdeil *a* **-e** friendly
càirean *n* **-ein, -an** *m* palate
càirich *v* **càradh** repair, mend, arrange; place, lay **a' càradh na leapa** making the bed **c. an sin e** put it down there
cairt *n* **-e, -ean** *f* card; chart **c.-creideis** credit card **c.-iùll** chart **c. Nollaig** Christmas card **c.-p(h)uist** postcard
cairt *n* **-e/cartach, -ean** *f* cart
cairteal *n* **-eil, -an/-eil** *m* quarter **c. na h-uarach** quarter of an hour
caisbheart *n* **-eirt** *f* footwear
càis(e) *n* **-an** *f m* cheese
Càisg *n* **-e** *f* **a' Chàisg** Easter
caisg *v* **casg/casgadh** check, stop, proscribe
caismeachd *n* **-an** *f* march (*mus*), martial song; alarm
caisteal *n* **-eil, -an/-eil** *m* castle
càit(e) *int pron, adv* where **c. a bheil thu?** where are you? **chan eil fhios aca c. a bheil i** they don't know where she is
caith *v* **-eamh/caith** spend, use up; wear; throw
caitheamh *n* **-eimh** *f m* spending, using up **a' chaitheamh** consumption, tuberculosis **c.-beatha** way of life, behaviour
caithris *v* watch at night, keep a vigil
caithriseach *a* watchful, vigilant; sleepless
Caitligeach *n* **-gich, -gich** *m* Catholic, Roman Catholic *a* Roman Catholic
càl *n* **càil** *m* cabbage, kail
caladh *n* **-aidh, -aidhean** *m* harbour, port; (*met*) place of rest *Also* **cala**
càl-colaig *n* **càil-colaig** *m* cauliflower
calg-dhìreach *adv* direct, directly **c. an aghaidh** completely against, diametrically opposed to
call *n* **call(a)** *m* loss; defeat **air chall** lost **'s e c. a bh' ann** it was a pity
callaid *n* **-e, -ean** *f* fence, hedge, partition
Callainn *n* **-e** *f* **a' Challainn** New Year's Day **Oidhche Challainn** Hogmanay
calltainn *n* **-ean** *m* hazel
calma *a* brave, strong, hardy
calman *n* **-ain, -ain** *m* dove, pigeon
calpa *n* **-nnan** *m* calf of leg; (*fin*) capital
calpachas *n* **-ais** *m* capitalism
cam *a* **caime** crooked, bent; one-eyed **cama-chasach** bow-legged
camag *n* **-aig(e), -an** *f* curl, ringlet of hair; (*in writing*) bracket
caman *n* **-ain, -ain** *m* stick for shinty, hockey etc.
camanachd *nf* shinty *Also vn* **a' c.** playing shinty
camara *n* **-than** *m* camera
camas *n* **-ais, -ais/-an** *m* wide bay
càmhal *n* **-ail, -ail** *m* camel
camhana(i)ch *n* **-aich, -aich** *f* dawn
campa *n* **-ichean** *m* camp
campaich *v* **-achadh** camp, encamp
can *v* **-tainn/-tail/-ail** say
cana *n* **-ichean** *m* can, tin

canabhas *n* **-ais** *m* canvas
canach *n* **-aich** *m* bog-cotton, cotton-grass
cànain *n See* **cànan**
canàl *n* **-àil, -aichean** *m* canal
cànan *n* **-ain, -an** *f m* language, tongue, speech **mion-chànan** minority language
canastair *n* **-ean** *m* canister, can, tin
Canèidianach *n* **-aich, -aich** *m* Canadian *a* Canadian
cangarù *n* **-than** *m* kangaroo
cànran *n* **-ain** *m* whingeing, grumbling, girning
cànranach *a* **-aiche** whingeing, grumbling, girning; fretful (*of small child*)
caoch *See* **cuthach**
caochail *v* **caochladh** change, alter; die, pass away
caochladh *n* **-aidh** *m* change, variation, different state; death **tha fhios agamsa air a chaochladh** I know different(ly)
caochlaideach *a* **-diche** changeable, variable, fickle
caog *v* **-adh** wink, close one eye (so as) to take aim
caogad *n* **-aid, -an** *m* fifty
caoidh *v* mourn, grieve, lament
caoin *a* **-e** kind, gentle, mild
caoin *v* **-eadh** weep, weep for, cry
caol *n* **caoil, caoil/caoiltean** *m* channel, narrows, kyle; narrow part of anything **Caol Loch Aillse** Kyle of Lochalsh **c.-shràid** lane, alley **c. an dùirn** the wrist
caol *a* **caoile** slender, thin, narrow
caolan *n* **-ain, -ain/-an** *m* gut, intestine
caolas *n* **-ais, -ais** *m* channel, narrows, kyle
caomh *a* **caoimhe** tender, kind, gentle; beloved, dear **is c. leam** I like
caomhain *v* **caomhnadh** save, economize on **ma bhios sinn air ar caomhnadh** if we are spared
caomhnadh *n* **-aidh** *m* saving, economizing
caora *n* **-ch, -ich** *f* sheep
caoran *n* **-ain, -ain** *m* small lump of peat; deeper part of a peat-bank
caorann *n* **-ainn, -ainn/-ainnean** *m* rowan, mountain ash
capall *n* **-aill, -aill** *m* mare; (*less commonly*) horse **c.-coille** capercaillie
car *n* **cuir, -an** *m* turn, twist, bend **cuir car dheth** capsize it/overturn it **a' cur charan** rolling/going round **car a' mhuiltein** somersault **thug e mo char asam** he got round me/tricked me **a' chiad char sa mhadainn** first thing in the morning
car *prep* during, for **car ùine** for some time *adv* about, somewhat **car daor** somewhat dear
càr *n* **càr/càir, -aichean** *m* car
carabhaidh *n* **-ean** *f* boyfriend
carabhan *n* **-aichean** *f m* caravan
carach *a* **-aiche** cunning, wily, sly, crafty, underhand
carachd *n f* wrestling
caractar *n* **-air, -an** *m* character
càradh *n* **-aidh** *m* mending, act of mending, repairing; condition, state
caraich *v* **-achadh** move, stir **cha do charaich e** he didn't budge
càraich *v See* **càirich**
caraid *n* **(-e), -(e)an/càirdean** *m* friend; relative (*especially in plural* **càirdean**) (*in corresp*) **A charaid/bhanacharaid** Dear ...
càraid *n* **-e, -ean** *f* couple, pair, married couple
caran *adv* somewhat, a little **c. anmoch** a bit late
carbad *n* **-aid, -an** *m* vehicle, car, conveyance, chariot, coach **c.-eiridinn** ambulance
Carghas *n* **-ais** *m* **an Carghas** Lent, any period of suffering
càrn *n* **càirn/cùirn, càirn/cùirn** *m* cairn, heap of stones (*often found in hill/mountain names*)
càrn *v* **-adh** heap, pile up; (*met*) accumulate **a' càrnadh airgid** accumulating/piling up money

càrnabhail *n* **-ean** *m* carnival
càrnan *n* **-ain, -ain** *m* small cairn; hill (*often found in place-names*)
carragh *n* **-aigh, -aighean** *m* pillar, erect stone **c.-cuimhne** memorial, monument
carraig *n* **(-e), -ean** *f* rock, pinnacle **C. nan Àl** the Rock of Ages
carraigean *n* **-ein** *m* carrageen (*seaweed used to make milk pudding*)
carson *int pron, adv* why
cartadh *n* **-aidh** *m* mucking out, clearing; clearance; tanning
carthannas *n* **-ais** *m* charity, compassion, tenderness **buidheann carthannais** *f m* a charity
cartùn *n* **-ùin, -aichean** *m* cartoon
cas *n* **coise, casan** *f* foot, leg; handle, shaft (*broom, spade, hammer etc*) **a bheil i air a cois?** is she up and about? **chaidh mi ann dhe mo chois** I went there on foot/I walked there **an cois** (+ *gen*) beside, as a result of, with **an cois na mara** close by the sea **an cois na litreach** enclosed with the letter **cuir air chois** *v* set up **thoir do chasan leat!** be off!/get off!
cas *a* **caise** steep, sudden, headlong; quick-tempered
càs *n* **càis, -an** *m* difficulty, emergency, predicament
casad *n* **-aid, -an** *m* cough **dèan c.** *v* cough
casadaich *n f* coughing *Also vn* **a' c.**
casa-gòbhlach, casa-gòbhlagain *adv* astride
casaid *n* **-e, -ean** *f* complaint, accusation, charge; prosecution **bha droch chasaid na aghaidh** he faced a serious accusation
cas-cheum *n* **-chèim/-a, -an** *m* path, footpath, track
cas-chrom *n* **coise-cruime, casan-croma** *f* foot-plough
casg/casgadh *n* **casg/casgaidh** *m* checking, stopping, preventing **casg/casgadh-gineamhainn** contraception **casg/casgadh-breith** abortion **cuir c. air** *v* stop, restrain, check
casruisgte *a* barefoot
cat *n* **cait, cait** *m* cat
catalog *n* **-oig, -an** *f m* catalogue
cath *n* **(-a), -an/-annan** *m* battle
cathadh *n* **-aidh, -aidhean** *m* snowstorm, snowdrift **c.-mara** sea-spray, spindrift *Also* **cabhadh**
cathag *n* **-aig, -an** *f* jackdaw
cathair *n* **cathrach, cathraichean** *f* chair; city **c.-bhaile** city **c.-chuibhle** wheelchair **c.-eaglais** cathedral
catharra *a* civil, civic
cathraiche *n* **-an** *m* chair (*person*)
ceacharra *a* awkward, perverse, cussed
cead *n* **-a, -an** *m* permission, permit **c.-siubhail** travel permit, passport **tha a chead aige** it serves him right, he well deserves it (*whether good or bad*) **c.-dealbha(cha)idh** planning permission
ceadaich *v* **-achadh** permit, allow
ceadaichte *a* permitted, allowed, permissible **chan eil e c. smocadh** smoking is not permitted
ceàird *n* **-e, -ean** *f* craft, trade, profession **fear-ceàirde** tradesman, craftsman
ceala-deug *n f* fortnight
cealg *n* **ceilge** *f* deceit, wiles, treachery
cealgach *a* **-aiche** deceitful, wily, treacherous, underhand
cealgair(e) *n* **-e, -ean** *m* deceiver, cheat
cealla *n* **cille, -n/cilltean** *f* cell (*biol*); cell, church, churchyard **Calum Cille** Columba
ceanalta *a* gentle, mild; comely, handsome
ceangail *v* **-al** tie, bind, connect, unite
ceangailte *a* tied up, connected, united
ceangal *n* **-ail, -glaichean** *m* tie, bond, connection, link

ceann *n* **cinn, cinn** *m* head; end; top **tha mo cheann goirt** I have a headache **cuir an c. dhan bhotal** put the top back on the bottle **c. an rathaid** the end of the road **o cheann gu c.** from end to end **air a' cheann thall** eventually **an c. mìos** in/after a month **ag obair air a c(h)eann fhèin** self-employed
ceannach *n* **-aich** *m* buy, purchase, buying, purchasing
ceannaich *v* **-ach** buy, purchase
ceannaiche *n* **-an** *m* merchant, dealer, buyer
ceannairceach *n* **-cich** *m* terrorist, rebel
ceannard *n* **-aird, -an** *m* head, chief, leader, commander
ceann-bhaile *n* **cinn-bhaile, -bhailtean** *m* capital city
ceann-bliadhna *n* **cinn-, cinn-** *m* birthday, anniversary
ceann-cinnidh *n* **cinn-, cinn-chinnidh** *m* clan chief
ceann-feadhna *n* **cinn-, cinn-** *m* clan chief
ceann-latha *n* **cinn-, cinn-** *m* deadline, day something is due, date
ceann-pholan *n* **cinn-pholain, -pholain** *m* tadpole
ceannruisgte *a* bare-headed
ceannsaich *v* **-achadh** subdue, conquer, master, control
ceann-suidhe *n* **cinn-, cinn-** *m* president **C. nan Stàitean Aonaichte** the President of the United States
ceann-uidhe *n* **cinn-, cinn-** *m* destination
ceap *n* **cip, -an/cip** *m* sod, piece of turf; block **c.-bròige** shoemaker's last
ceap *n* **-(a), -an** *m* cap
ceapaire *n* **-an** *m* sandwich
cearbach *a* **-aiche** awkward, inept, unfortunate, misguided
cearban *n* **-ain, -ain** *m* shark
cearc *n* **circe, -an** *f* hen **c.-fhraoich** grouse
cearcall *n* **-aill, -aill** *m* circle, hoop, ring **c. mun ghealaich** a ring round the moon
ceàrd *n* **ceàird, -an/-annan** *m* tinker
ceàrdach *n* **-aich, -aichean** *f* smithy, forge
ceàrn *n* **-a, -an/-aidhean** *f* quarter, particular area, zone, district
ceàrnach *a* square
ceàrnag *n* **-aig, -an** square *f* **C. Sheòrais** George Square
ceàrr *a* **-a** wrong, incorrect; left **an làmh cheàrr** the left hand
ceart *a* **-a** right, correct, just; (*before noun + len*) same **an uair cheart** the correct time **an làmh cheart** the right hand **cuir c.** *v* correct **an c. dhuine** the very same man **aig a' cheart àm** at the same time **a cheart cho ... ri ...** just as ... as ...
ceartachadh *n* **-aidh, -aidhean** *m* correction, marking, the act of correction
ceartaich *v* **-achadh** correct, put right, rectify
ceartas *n* **-ais** *m* justice **le c. ...** strictly speaking ...
ceart-cheàrnach *a* right-angled
ceartuair *adv preceded by* **an** at present, these days; shortly
ceas *n* **-a, -aichean** *m* suitcase
ceasnachadh *n* **-aidh, -aidhean** *m* questioning, interrogation; examination (*educ*)
ceasnaich *v* **-achadh** question, interrogate
ceatharnach *n* **-aich, -aich** *m* strongly built man, warrior
ceathrad *n* **-aid, -an** *m* forty
ceathramh *n* **-aimh, -an** *m* quarter; quatrain
ceathramh *a* fourth **an c. fear** the fourth one
ceathramh deug *a* fourteenth (*preceded by art* **an**) **an c. fear deug** the fourteenth one
ceathrar *n m* four (people)
cèic *n* **-e, -ichean** *f m* cake
cèidse *n* **-achan/-sichean** *f* cage
ceil *v* **ceil/-tinn/cleith** conceal, hold back information
cèile *n f m* spouse; fellow, match,

another **athair-c.** father-in-law **màthair-chèile** mother-in-law **bu toigh leotha a chèile** they liked one another/each other **thuit e às a chèile** it fell apart
ceileir *v* **-earadh** chirp, warble (*usually of birds*)
cèilidh *n* **-idhean** *f m* ceilidh, concert; visit **chaidh mi air chèilidh orra** I paid them a visit
ceilp *n* **-e** *f* kelp
Ceilteach *n* **-tich, -tich** *m* Celt *a* **-tiche** Celtic
ceimig *n* **-ean** *f* (a) chemical
ceimigeach *a* **-giche** chemical
ceimigeachd *n f* chemistry
ceimigear *n* **-eir, -an** *m* chemist
cèin *a* **-e** distant, foreign
cèir *n* **-e** *f* wax
ceirsle *n* **-an** *f* clew, ball (*of wool*) *Also* **ceirtle**
cèis *n* **-e, -ean** *f* receptacle, case **c.-litreach** envelope
cèiseag *n* **-eig, -an** *f* cassette
ceist *n* **-e, -ean** *f* question, query; issue, problem; sum in arithmetic **cuir c.** *v* ask a question
ceisteachan *n* **-ain, -ain** *m* questionnaire
ceistear *n* **-eir, -an** *m* questioner, quizmaster; catechist
Cèitean *n* **-ein** *m* **an C.** the month of May
ceithir *n, a* four **c.-chasach** four-legged
ceithir-deug *n, a* fourteen **ceithir taighean deug** fourteen houses
ceò *n* **ceò/ceotha, -than/ ceothannan** *f m* mist, fog; smoke **Eilean a' Cheò** the Misty Isle (the Isle of Skye)
ceòl *n* **ciùil** *m* music **c.-mòr** pibroch **c.-beag** light music for the pipes **c.-gàire** mirth **luchd-ciùil** musicians
ceòlmhor *a* **-oire** musical, tuneful, melodious
ceòthach *a* **-aiche** misty, foggy
ceud *n* **-an** *m* a hundred *a* a hundred **bha c. cabhag orra** they were in a great hurry **... sa cheud ...** per cent **c. taing** thanks a lot
ceudameatair *n* **-ean** *m* centimetre
ceudamh *a* (*preceded by art* **an**) hundredth
ceud-chasach *n* **-chasaich, -chasaich** *m* centipede
ceudna *a* (*preceded by art* **an**) same **air an dòigh cheudna** in the same way **mar an c.** also, likewise
ceum *n* **cèim/-a, -an/-annan** *m* step; footpath; (*university*) degree **c. air cheum** step by step
ceumnaich *v* **-achadh** graduate; take a step
ceus *v* **-adh** crucify **chaidh Crìosd a cheusadh** Christ was crucified
cha *neg part* not (*often lenites*) **cha bheag sin** that is not small, that's quite a lot
chaidh *irr v* went (*See irr v* **rach** *in Grammar*)
chan *neg part* (*used before vowels and fh*) **chan aithne dhomh i** I don't know her **chan fhuirich mi** I won't stay
chaoidh *See* **a-chaoidh**
cheana *See* **a-cheana**
chì *irr v* will see, can see (*See irr v* **faic** *in Grammar*)
cho *adv* as, so **cho dearg ris an fhuil** as red as blood
chon *prep See* **chun**
chuala *irr v* heard (*See irr v* **cluinn** *in Grammar*)
chum *See* **a chum**
chun *prep* (+ *gen*) to, towards, as far as
chunnaic *irr v* saw (*See irr v* **faic** *in Grammar*)
cia *int pron* who, which, what; how *See* **cò**
ciad *a* first **an c. latha** the first day (*often takes feminine form*) **a' chiad latha**
ciad-fhuasgladh *n* **-fhuasglaidh** *m* first aid
ciall *n* **cèille** *f* sense, reason, understanding **dìth na cèille** lack of sense **a' dol às a chiall** going mad, losing his reason **a chiall!** goodness!

ciallach *a* **-aiche** sensible, reasonable
ciallaich *v* **-achadh** mean, intend
ciamar *int pron, adv* how **c. a tha thu?** how are you?
cia mheud *int pron, adv* how many **cia mh. iasg a fhuair thu?** how many fish did you get? **cia mh. aca a bh' ann?** how many of them were there? Also **cò mheud**
cian *a* **cèine** distant, remote
cianail *a* **-e** mournful, melancholy; terrible **c. fuar** terribly cold
cianalas *n* **-ais** *m* nostalgia, homesickness, melancholy **bha an c. orm** I felt homesick/nostalgic
ciar *v* **-adh** darken, grow dark
ciar *a* **-a/cèire** dusky, darkening; swarthy
ciatach *a* **-aiche** *m* pleasant, elegant, graceful, becoming, agreeable **bidh sin c.** that will be fine
cidhe *n* **-achan** *m* quay, pier
cidsin *n* **-ean** *m* kitchen
cileagram *n* **-aim, -an** *m* kilogram
cilemeatair *n* **-ean** *m* kilometre
cill *n* **-e, -tean** *f* church, churchyard (*common in place names*) **Cill Rìmhinn** St Andrews
cinn *v* **-tinn** grow, increase
cinneach *n* **-nich** *m* nation; gentile; a character **'s e c. a th' ann!** he's a hard case!
cinneadh *n* **-nidh, -nidhean** *m* clan, tribe, race; surname
cinnt *n* **-e** *f* sureness, certainty **le c.** definitely, certainly
cinnteach *a* **-tiche** sure, certain, reliable
cìobair *n* **-ean** *m* shepherd
cìoch *n* **cìche, -an** *f* female breast
cion *n m* lack, want, shortage **c. cosnaidh** unemployment
cionnas *adv* how **c. a fhuair e sin?** how did he get that?
ciont(a) *n* **-(a), -(an)** *m* guilt
ciontach *a* **-aiche** guilty
ciopair *n* **-ean** *m* kipper
ciorram *n* **-aim** *m* disability
ciorramach *n* **-aich, -aich** *m* disabled person
ciorramach *a* **-aiche** disabled, handicapped
ciotach *a* **-aiche** left-handed
cìr *n* **-e, -ean** *f* comb; cud **cìr-mheala** honeycomb
cìr *v* **-eadh** comb
cìrean *n* **-ein** *m* comb or crest of a bird
cìs *n* **-e, -ean** *f* tax **Cìs Comhairle** Council Tax **cìs cosnaidh** income tax
ciste *n* **-achan** *f* chest **c.-dhràthraichean** chest of drawers **c.-laighe** coffin
ciùb *n* **-an** *m* cube
ciudha *n* **-ichean** *f m* queue
ciùin *a* **-e** calm, mild, meek **duine c.** an even-tempered man
ciùinich *v* **-neachadh** calm, pacify, appease
ciùrr *v* **-adh** hurt very painfully
ciutha *n* **-chan** *m* cue (*hair*)
ciùthran *n* **-ain, -ain** *m* drizzle
clach *n* **cloiche, -an** *f* stone **c.-ghràin** granite **c.-iùil** magnet **c.-mhuilinn** millstone **c.-sùla** eyeball
clach *v* **-adh** stone
clachair *n* **-ean** *m* stonemason
clachan *n* **-ain, -ain** *m* village, hamlet; stepping-stones
clach-mheallain *n* **cloiche-meallain, clachan-meallain** *f* hailstone
cladach *n* **-aich, -aichean** *m* shore, coast
cladh *n* **-a/claidh, -an/-annan** *m* cemetery
cladhaich *v* **-ach** dig
cladhan *n* **-ain, -ain** *m* channel
clag *n* **cluig, cluig/-an** *m* bell
claidheamh *n* **-eimh, -an/claidhmhnean** *m* sword **c.-mòr** claymore
claigeann *n* **-ginn, -ginn** *m* skull **ag èigheach àird a claiginn** shouting at the top of her voice
clais *n* **-e, -ean** *f* furrow, ditch, trench
claisneachd *n f* hearing **cùm cluas ri c.** keep an ear to the

ground
clamhan *n* **-ain, -ain** *m* buzzard; kite
clann *n* **cloinne** *f* (*sg n*) children (*often lenited in gen*) **triùir chloinne** three children *Used in clan names, eg* **Clann Dòmhnaill** Clan Donald
clann-nighean *n* **-nighinn** *f* (*sg n*) girls, young women
claoidh *v* **-eadh** weary, oppress, vex, harass
claoidhte *a* exhausted, worn out
claon *a* **-oine** slanting, inclining, squint; (*met*) partial **c.-bharail** prejudice **c.-bhreith** prejudice, unjust verdict
claon *v* **-adh** slope, veer; (*met*) incline
clàr *n* **-àir, -àir** *m* board, table, level surface; table (*of figures*), programme (*of events*), form (*for filling*); record **c.-ama** timetable **c.-amais** index **c.-aodainn** brow, forehead **c.-bìdh** menu **c.-dùthcha** map **c.-gnothaich** agenda **c.-iarrtais** application form **c.-innse** contents list **c.-oideachais** curriculum
clàrachadh *n* **-aidh** *m* recording, registration
clàraich *v* **-achadh** record, register, tabulate, arrange into tables
clàrsach *n* **-aich, -aichean** *f* harp
clàrsair *n* **-ean** *m* harper, harpist
clas *n* **-aichean** *m* class (*in schools etc*)
clasaigeach *a* **-giche** classical
cleachd *v* **-adh** use, employ, deploy, practise, be accustomed (to), be used (to) **chleachd mi a bhith a' snàmh** I used to swim
cleachdadh *n* **-aidh, -aidhean** *m* use; custom, habit, practice, convention
cleachdte (ri) *past part* accustomed to, used to
cleamhnas *n* **-ais** *m* relationship by marriage
cleas *n* **-an** *m* play, trick, clever feat; way **rinn esan c. chàich** he did what the others did
cleasachd *n f* play, playing
cleasaich *v* **-achd** play, perform feats
cleasaiche *n* **-an** *m* actor, performer, conjurer
clèir *n* **-e, -ean** *f* **a' chlèir** the clergy; presbytery
clèireach *n* **-rich, -rich** *m* cleric; clerk *a* presbyterian
cleith *See* **ceil**
cleòc(a) *n* **-a, -aichean** *m* cloak
clì *n* **-the** *f* strength, vigour
clì *a* left; wrong **an làmh chlì** the left hand
cliabh *n* **clèibh, clèibh** *m* creel, basket, hamper; person's chest
cliamhainn *n* **cleamhna, cleamhnan** *m* son-in-law **bana-chliamhainn** *f* daughter-in-law
cliath *n* **clèithe, -an** *f* grid; harrow **c.-chruidh** cattle grid
cliath *v* **-adh** harrow
cliatha(i)ch *n* **-aich, -ean** *f* side (*of person or thing*)
cliobach *a* **-aiche** clumsy, awkward
clis *a* **-e** quick, nimble, agile
clisg *v* **-eadh** move suddenly, start (*through fear or alarm*); **bi air do chlisgeadh** be very afraid of something **bha mi air mo chlisgeadh roimhe** I was terrified of it
clisgear *n* **-eir , -an** *m* exclamation (*gram*)
clisg-phuing *n* **-phuing(e), -phuingean** *f* exclamation mark
cliù *n m* fame, reputation; praise **c.-mhilleadh** *m* libel, slander
cliùiteach *a* **-tiche** famous, celebrated
clò *n* **clò/-tha, clòith(n)tean** *m* cloth (*especially tweed woven on looms*), a piece of tweed **an Clò Mòr/Hearach** Harris Tweed
clò *n m* print; press **cuir an c.** *v* print
clobha *n* **-chan** *m* pair of tongs
clòbhar *n* **-air** *m* clover
clobhd(a) *n* **-(a), -an** *m* cloth (*for wiping*), clout **c.-sgùraidh** scouring cloth

clobhsa *n* **-n/-ichean** close *m* (*in tenement*)
clò-bhuail *v* **-bhualadh** print (*a book*) **-bhuailte** (*past part*) printed
clò-bhualadair *n* **-ean** *m* printer, printing firm; publisher
clò-bhualadh *n* **-aidh** *m* printing, the work of printing
cloc *n* **-aichean** *m* clock
clogad *n* **-aid, -an** *m* helmet, headpiece *Also* **clogaid**
clòimh *n* **-e, -ean** *f* wool
closach *n* **-aich, -aichean** *f* carcase
clòsaid *n* **(-e), -ean** *f* closet, small back room
clostar *n* **-air, -air** *m* loud thump or noise of falling (*person or thing*); large specimen of something
cluain *n* **-e, -tean** *f* green plain, meadow, pasture
cluaineas *n* **-eis** *m* retirement **chaidh e air chluaineas** he retired (*from work*)
cluaran *n* **-ain, -ain** *m* thistle
clua(i)s *n* **-e, -asan** *f* ear
cluasag *n* **-aig, -an** *f* pillow
club *n* **-aichean** *m* club (*organization*) **c. òigridh** youth club
cluich *n* **-e, -ean** *m* play, game **c.-bùird** board game
cluich *v* **cluich/-e/-eadh** play (*sport or musical instrument*)
cluicheadair *n* **-ean** *m* player, actor **c.-chlàr** record-player
cluinn *irr v* hear, listen (*See irr v* **cluinn** *in Grammar*)
cnag *n* **cnaig(e), -an** *f* pin, peg, knob, piece of wood **c.-aodaich** clothes peg **c.-dealain** electric plug **sin c. na cùise** that's the nub of the matter
cnàimh *n* **-e/cnàmha, -ean/ cnàmhan** *m* bone **c. an droma** the backbone
cnàimhneach *n* **-nich, -nichean** *m* skeleton
cnàimhseag *n* **-eig, -an** *f* pimple on face, acne
cnàmh *v* chew, digest; wear away, decay **tha a' bhò a' c. a cìre(adh)** the cow is chewing the cud
cnap *n* **cnaip, -an** *m* knob; lump, small hill
cnapach *n* **-aich, -aich** *m* young boy (*not a small child*)
cnapach *a* **-aiche** lumpy
cnap-starra *n* **cnaip-, cnapan-** *m* obstacle, obstruction (*Also met*)
cnatan *n* **-ain, -ain** *m* common cold **bha an c. orm** I had the cold
cnead *n* **-a, -an** *m* groan **cha robh c. air** there was nothing wrong with him
cneasta *a* humane, moderate, decent, modest *Formerly* **cneasda**
cnò *n* **cnò/cnotha, cnothan/cnòithtean** *f* nut **c.-challtainn** hazelnut **c.-còco** coconut **gall-chnò** walnut
cnoc *n* **cnuic, cnuic/-an** *m* hill
cnocach *a* **-aiche** hilly
cnocan *n* **-ain, -ain** *m* hillock, small hill
cnot *n* **-an** *m* knot that is tied; door-bar
cnòthach *a* **-aiche** nutty
cnuasaich *v* **-achadh** reflect, ponder, ruminate; collect, accumulate
cnuimh *n* **-e, -ean** *f* worm, maggot **c.-thalmhainn** earthworm *Also* **cruimh**
cò *int pron, adv* who? which? **cò sibh?** who are you? **cò agaibh a dhèanadh sin?** which of you would do that? **tha fhios aicese cò iad** she knows who they are **cò às a tha thu?** where are you from?
co-aimsireil *a* **-e** contemporary
co-aois *n See* **comhaois**
cobhair *n* **còbhrach** *f* help, aid, succour, relief **rinn iad c. oirnn** they came to our rescue
co-bhann *n* **-bhuinn, -an** *f* bond, league, confederacy **an co-bhoinn/co-bhuinn ri** in co-operation/league with
co-bhanntachd *n* **-an** *f* coalition
cobhar *n* **-air** *m* foam, froth

còc *n* **-an** *m* coke (*drink & fuel*)
còcaire *n* **-an** *m* cook, chef
còcaireachd *n f* cooking, cookery
cochall *n* **-aill, -aill** *m* husk, shell, hood **theab i a dhol à c. a cridhe** she nearly died of fright
co-cheangail *v* **-al** connect, bind together, involve with each other
co-cheangal *n* **-ail, -ail/-glan** *m* connection **an c. ri** in connection with
co-cheangailte *a* (+ **ri**) connected (to), in connection with, related (to)
co-chomann *n* **-ainn, -ainn** *m* society, association, co-operative **C. Nis** Ness Community Co-operative
co-chomhairle *n* **-an** *f* consultation
co-chòrdadh *n* **-aidh, -aidhean** *m* agreement, accord, alliance
co-chruinneachadh *n* **-aidh, -aidhean** *m* assembly, gathering, convention; compilation, collection
còco *n m* cocoa
còd *n* **-aichean** *m* code **còd puist** postcode
co-dheth *adv See* **co-dhiù**
co-dhiù *adv* anyway, whatever happens **c. no co-dheth** anyway
co-dhùin *v* **-dhùnadh** conclude, decide
co-dhùnadh *n* **-aidh, -aidhean** *m* conclusion, decision
co-èignich *v* **-èigneachadh** urge, persuade strongly, force, compel
cofaidh *n f m* coffee
co-fhaireachdainn *n f* sympathy
co-fharpais *n* **(-e), -ean** *f* competition, contest
co-fhlaitheas *n* **-eis** *m* confederation **An C.** The Commonwealth
co-fhreagair *v* **-t** match, correspond
cofhurtachd *n f* comfort
cofhurtaich *v* **-achadh** comfort, console
cofhurtail *a* **-e** comfortable
cogadh *n* **-aidh, -aidhean** *m* war **an Dàrna C.** the Second World War
cogais *n* **(-e), -ean** *f* conscience
cogaiseach *a* **-siche** conscientious, honest
co-ghin *v* **-eadh/-tinn** have sexual intercourse, copulate
co-ghnìomhair *n* **-ean** *m* adverb
coibhneas *n* **-eis, -an** *m* kindness, generosity
coibhneil *a* **-e** kind, kindly, generous
coidse *n* **-achan** *f* coach
còig *n, a* five
còig-cheàrnach *n* **-aich, -aichean** *m* pentagon
còig-deug *n, a* fifteen **còig mìosan deug** fifteen months
còigeamh *n* **-eimh** *m* a fifth *a* fifth **an c. fear** the fifth one
còignear *n m* five (people)
coigreach *n* **-rich, -rich** *m* stranger, foreigner
coileach *n* **-lich, -lich** *m* cockerel **c.-gaoithe** weathercock
coilean *v* **-adh** fulfil, accomplish, complete *Formerly* **coimhlion**
coileanta *a* perfect, accomplished, complete **an tràth c.** the perfect tense
coilear *n* **-eir, -an** *m* collar
coilion *v See* **coilean**
coille *n* **-ltean** *f* wood, forest
coilleag *n* **-eig, -an** *f* cockle; sand-dune
coimeas *n* **-eis** *f* comparison, likeness **an c. ri** compared to, in comparison to **chan eil a c. ann** there's no-one like her **dèan c. eatarra** *v* compare them
coimeas *v* compare
coimeasgaich *v* **-achadh** mix together, mingle
coimheach *a* **-mhiche** foreign, alien; shy, 'strange' (*of a small child*), unfriendly
coimhead *v* look, look at; keep watch over
coimhearsnach *n* **-aich, -aich** *m* neighbour
coimhearsnachd *n f* neighbourhood, vicinity, community

coimisean *n* **-ein, -an** *m* commission **an C. Eòrpach** the European Commission
coimiseanair *n* **-ean** *m* commissioner
coimpiutair *n* **-ean** *m* computer
coimpiutaireachd *n f* computing
coineanach *n* **-aich, -aich** *m* rabbit
còinneach *n* **-nich** *f* moss
coinneachadh *n* **-aidh** *m* meeting, the act of meeting
coinneal *n* **coinnle, coinnlean** *f* candle
coinneamh *n* **-eimh, -an** *f* meeting, appointment; religious service **c. naidheachd** press conference
coinnich *v* **-neachadh** meet **c. ri** meet with
coinnlear *n* **-eir/-an** *m* candlestick *Also* **coinnleir**
co-ionann *a* equal, equivalent to
co-ionannachd *n f* state of being equal, equality **c. chothroman** equal opportunities (*policy*)
còir *n* **-e/còrach, -ean/còraichean** *f* what is right; obligation; right, privilege, claim **tha c. agad sin a dhèanamh** you ought to do that **bu chòir dhut fheuchainn** you should try it **ag agairt do chòraichean** claiming your rights
còir *a* **-e** worthy, decent; just, honest; kind, generous; gentle, docile **cho c. ris an fhaoileig** as kind as kind can be **cù c.** *m* a well-behaved dog
coirbte *a* corrupt
coirce *n m* oats **aran-c.** *m* oatmeal bread
coire *n* **-achan** *m* kettle, cauldron; corrie **C. a' Cheathaich** the Misty Corrie
coire *n* **-achan** *f* fault, wrongdoing; blame **na bi a' cur na c. ormsa** don't lay the blame on me
coireach *a* **-riche** at fault, blameworthy **'s tu fhèin as c.** you're the one who's to blame
coirich *v* **-reachadh** blame
coiridh *n* **-ean** *m* curry (*the food*)
coiseachd *n f* walking
coisich *v* **-seachd** walk
coisiche *n* **-an** *m* walker, pedestrian
coisinn *v* **cosnadh** earn, win, gain; deserve
còisir *n* **-e/còisre, -ean** *f* choir *Also* **c.-chiùil**
coisrig *v* **-eadh** consecrate, dedicate; sanctify
coisrigte *a* consecrated, sanctified **uisge c.** *m* holy water
coitcheann *a* **-chinne** common, public, general, standard
coitcheannas *n* **-ais** *m* generality
coitheanal *n* **-ail, -an** *m* congregation
coitich *v* **-teachadh** press, persuade; campaign, lobby
co-labhairt *n* **-ean** *f* conference, seminar
co-là-breith *n* **-làithean-/-lathaichean-** *m* birthday
cola-deug *n f* fortnight
colag *n* **-aig, -an** *f* cauliflower
colaiste *n* **-an** *f m* college
colann *n* **-ainn, -an/-ainnean** *f* body
colbh *n* **cuilbh, cuilbh/-an** *m* pillar, column; column (*in newspaper*)
Colach *n* **-aich, -aich** *m* someone from Coll *a* from, or pertaining to, Coll
coltach *a* **-aiche** like, apparent, likely; healthy/robust-looking (*pronounced in some areas with the t silent*) **tha i c. riut** she's like you **tha e c. gu bheil i tinn** it seems she's ill **chan eil sin glè choltach** that's not very likely **duine mòr c.** a big robust-looking man
coltaich *v* **-achadh** (+ **ri**) liken (to)
coltas *n* **-ais** *m* appearance, likeness; expression (*on face*) **a rèir c(h)oltais** apparently, seemingly, by the looks of it **bha c. an acrais orra** they looked hungry
com *n* **cuim** *m* chest, upper part

of the body, trunk
coma *a* indifferent, unconcerned, uncaring **tha mi c. cò a thig** I don't care who comes **o. lcat** never mind **tha mi c. dheth** I don't like it **c. co-dhiù/co-aca** couldn't care less, past caring, totally indifferent
comaig *n* **-ean** *f m* comic (*children's paper*)
comaig *a* **-e** comical, funny
comain *n* **-ean** *f* obligation for something done for one **tha mi fada nad chomain** I'm much obliged to you
comain *n* **-ean** *m* communion **a ciad chomain** her first communion
comanachadh *n* **-aidh** *m* communion; season of communion services
comanaich *v* **-achadh** take communion, be a communicant in church
comann *n* **-ainn, -ainn** *m* society, association; company, fellowship
comas *n* **-ais, -an** *m* ability **tha e gun chomas labhairt** he is without the power of speech
comasach *a* **-aiche** able, capable, talented **dèan c.** *v* enable, facilitate
comataidh *n* **-ean** *f* committee
combaist *n* **-e, -ean** *f* compass (*for direction*)
comhair *n f* direction **thuit mi an c. mo chùil** I fell backwards **an c. gach ama** now and then, from time to time **bha e fa chomhair na cùirt** he was before/in front of the court
comhairle *n* **-an** *f* advice, counsel; council **thug i deagh chomhairle orm** she gave me good advice **C. na Gàidhealtachd** the Highland Council
comhairleach *n* **-lich, -lich** *m* adviser, counsellor
comhairlich *v* **-leachadh** advise, guide
comhairliche *n* **-an** *m* councillor, adviser
comhaois(e) *n* **(-e), (e)an** *m* person the same age, peer, contemporary **tha iad nan comhaoisean** they are the same age
comharra(dh) *n* **comharra/-aidh, comharran/-aidhean** *m* mark, sign **c.-ceiste** question mark **c.-stiùiridh** landmark
comharrachadh *n* **-aidh** *m* marking
comharraich *v* **-achadh** mark, indicate, earmark, identify
comharraichte *a* noteworthy, special, exceptional
comhart *n* **-airt, -an** *m* dog's bark
comhartaich *n f* (*continuous*) barking
còmhdach *n* **-aich** *m* covering, cover
còmhdaich *v* **-achadh** cover, clothe
còmhdaichte *a* covered, clothed
còmhdhail *n* **-dhala(ch), -ean** *f* congress, convention; meeting, tryst; transport
cò mheud *See* **cia mheud**
còmhla *n* **-chan/-idhean** *f* door, door-leaf, door of cupboard
còmhla *adv* together **ràinig iad c.** they arrived together **c. ri** *prep phr* along/together with
còmhlan *n* **-ain, -ain** *m* group, band (*usually small*) **c.-ciùil** music group, band
còmhnaidh *n* **-ean** *f* residence, dwelling, house
còmhnaich *v* **-aidh** reside, live, stay; continue
còmhnard *a* **-airde** level, flat, even, smooth
còmhradh *n* **-aidh, -aidhean** *m* conversation, dialogue **dèan c.** *v* converse, chat
còmhrag *n* **-aig, -an** *f* fight, struggle, conflict, combat **c.-dithis** duel
còmhraideach *a* **-diche** talkative, chatty, fond of conversation
còmhstri *n* **-thean** *f* strife, struggle, conflict; rivalry, disagreement
compàirt *n* **(-e)** *f* partnership, share, participation

compàirtich *v* **-teachadh** share, divide, take part, participate; communicate
companach *n* **-aich, -aich** *m* companion, partner; spouse
companaidh *n* **-ean** *f m* company (*org*), firm
companas *n* **-ais** *m* company (*personal*), companionship
comraich *n* **-ean** *f* sanctuary, protection **Comraich Ma-Ruibhe/a' Chomraich** Applecross **c. phoilitigeach** political asylum
còn *n* **-aichean** *m* cone
conair(e) *n* **(-e)** , **-(e)an** *f* rosary; path, way
conaltradh *n* **-aidh** *m* conversation, communication; company (*social*)
conas *n* **-ais** *m* contention, quarrel; teasing **chuir e c. orm** it annoyed me *Also vn* **a' c. bha iad a' c. rithe** they were teasing her
conasg *n* **-aisg** *m* whins, gorse
connadh *n* **-aidh, -aidhean** *m* fuel **c. làmhaich** ammunition, munitions
connlach *n* **-aich** *f* straw
connrag *n* **-aig, -an** *f* consonant
connsachadh *n* **-aidh** *m* quarrel, argument, dispute, feud
connsaich *v* **-achadh** quarrel, argue, dispute, feud, wrangle
connspaid *n* **(e), -ean** *f* quarrel, dispute, strife, contention
connspaideach *a* **-diche** disputatious, quarrelsome, contentious, confrontational
conntraigh *n* **-ean** *f* neap tide
consal *n* **-ail, -an** *m* consul
co-obraich *v* **-obrachadh** work with, co-operate with, collaborate
co-obrachadh *n* **-aidh** *m* co-operation, collaboration
co-ogha *n* **-ichean** *m* cousin
co-òrdanaich *v* **-achadh** co-ordinate
co-òrdanaiche *n* **-an** *m* co-ordinator
cop *n* **coip** *m* foam, froth
còp *v* **-adh** tip up (*a load*); capsize
copag *n* **-aig, -an** *f* dock, docken
copan *n See* **cupan**
copar *n* **-air** *m* copper (*metal*)
cor *n* **coir/cuir** *m* state, condition **cor an t-saoghail** the state the world is in **dè do chor?** how are you?/how are you doing? **air chor sam bith** under any circumstances
còrd *v* **-adh** agree, come to an agreement; (+ **ri**) give enjoyment/pleasure to **chòrd e rium** I enjoyed it
còrdadh *n* **-aidh, -aidhean** *m* agreement, pact
còrn *n* **cùirn, cùirn** *m* horn (*mus*), drinking horn; corn (*on foot*)
Còrnach *n* **-aich, -aich** *m* someone from Cornwall *a* Cornish
còrnair *n* **-ean** *m* corner
corp *n* **cuirp, cuirp** *m* body; corpse **c.-eòlas** anatomy
corporra *a* corporal, bodily; corporate
còrr *n f m* an excess; remainder, (*fin*) balance; more **na ith an c./a' chòrr** don't eat any more **còrr is mìle duine** over a thousand men
corra *a* odd, occasional, irregular **bidh c. dhuine a' dol ann** the odd person goes there **c. uair** occasionally, now and then
corra-biod(a) *n m* state of alertness/readiness; (*preceded by* **air**) on tiptoe **bha e air a chorra-biod(a)** he was on tiptoe
corrach *a* **-aiche** steep; rough; unsteady, unstable (*eg boat*)
corrag *n* **-aig, -an** *f* finger
corra-ghritheach *n* **-g(h)rithich, corrachan-gritheach** *f* heron
corran *n* **-ain, -ain** *m* sickle; point of land running into the sea; crescent
còrr-mhial *n* **-a, -an** *f* gnat, hornet
còs *n* **còis, -an** *m* cave, hollow, recess; any sheltered place
còsach *a* **-aiche** cavernous; porous, hollow; sheltered, snug, cosy

cosamhlachd *n* **-an** *f* parable
cosg *v* **cosg(adh)** cost; spend; run out, be used up **dè a chosg sin?** how much did that cost? **dè a chosg thu air?** what did you spend on it? **tha an t-airgead air c.** the money has run out
cosgail *a* **-e** costly, expensive
cosgais *n* **-e, -ean** *f* cost, expense
co-sheirm *n* **-e, -ean** *f* harmony (*mus*)
co-shìnte *a* parallel
cosmhail *a* **-e** like, resembling
cosnadh *n* **-aidh, -aidhean** *m* earnings, way of earning, work, employment **gun chosnadh** unemployed **ionad cosnaidh** *m* job centre
cost(a) *n* **-taichean** *m* coast, shore
còta *n* **-ichean** *m* coat **c.-bàn** petticoat
cotan *n* **-ain** *m* cotton, cotton-wool
cothaich *v* **-achadh** contend with
cothlamadh *n* **-aidh** *m* mixture, merger, merging
cothrom *a* **-ruime** even
cothrom *n* **cothruim, -an** *m* chance, opportunity; equilibrium, balance; fair play **C. na Fèinne** fair play, a fair opportunity, a sporting chance **chan eil c. air** it can't be helped **a bheil thu air chothrom?** are you fit/able?
cothromach *a* **-aiche** just, equitable, reasonable, fair, balanced
cothromaich *v* **-achadh** weigh; make equal, balance; consider
co-thuiteamas *n* **-ais, -an** *m* coincidence
cràbhach *a* **-aiche** devout, religious, pious
cràbhadh *n* **-aidh** *m* piety, devoutness
crac *n* **craic** *f* chat, crack
cràdh *n* **cràidh** *m* pain, suffering **bha c. air** he was in pain
craiceann *n* **-cinn, -an** *m* skin
cràidh *v* **cràdh(adh)** pain, torment
cràiteach *a* **-tiche** painful
crann *n* **cruinn/croinn, cruinn/croinn/crainn** *m* mast or other long rod; plough (*also* **crann-treabhaidh**); bolt, bar, beam; lot; cran (*measure for herring*); tree **a' cur chrann** casting lots **an C.-ceusaidh** the Cross (*of Christ*) **c.-fìona** vine **c.-ola** oilrig **c.-sneachd(a)** snowplough
crannchur *n* **-uir, -an** *m* casting of lots, lottery **an C. Nàiseanta** the National Lottery **c.-gill** raffle
craobh *n* **-oibhe, -an** *f* tree **c.-challtainn** hazel tree **c.-dharaich** oak tree **c.-ghiuthais** pine tree
craobhag *n* **-aig, -an** *f* plant; bush; small tree
craobh-sgaoil *v* **-eadh** broadcast, transmit; promulgate, propagate
craol *v* **-adh** broadcast, transmit; promulgate, propagate
craoladair *n* **-ean** *m* broadcaster
craoladh *n* **-aidh** *m* broadcasting, broadcast, transmission
craos *n* **-ois, -an** *m* large mouth, maw; gluttony
craosach *a* **-aiche** wide-/large-mouthed; gluttonous
crath *v* **-adh** shake, wave; sprinkle
crathadh-làimhe *n* **crathaidhean-** *m* handshake
creach *n* **creiche, -an** *f* plunder, booty; ruin, destruction **Mo chreach!** Alas! **Mo chreach-sa thàinig!** Goodness gracious me!
creach *v* **-adh** plunder, rob, ruin
creachan(n) *n* **-ain(n), -ain(n)** *m* scallop
crèadh *n* **crèadha/creadha** *f* clay
crèadhadair *n* **-ean** *m* potter
crèadhadaireachd *n* *f* pottery
creag *n* **creige, -an** *f* rock; crag, cliff, precipice
creagach *a* **-aiche** rocky
creamh *n* **-a** *m* garlic **c.-gàrraidh** leek, leeks
crèapailt(e) *n* **-(e)an** *m* garter *Also* **crèibilt(e)**
creathail *n* **(-e), -ean** *f* cradle *Also* **creathall**

creid *v* **-sinn** believe **chan eil mi ga chreidsinn** I don't believe it **cha chreid mi nach coisich mi** I think I shall walk
creideamh *n* **-eimh, -an** *m* faith; religion, religious belief
creideas *n* **-eis** *m* credit (*moral, fin*), credibility; faith, trust **chan eil cus creideis agam ann** I don't have much faith in him
creidhean *n* **-ein, -an** *m* crayon
creim *See* **criom**
creithleag *n* **-eig, -an** *f* cleg
creuchd *n* **-a, -an** *f* wound
creud *n* **(-a), -an** *f* creed; belief
creutair *n* **-ean** *m* creature, animal; (*Lewis*) female **an c.!** the poor thing!
criathar *n* **-air, -an** *m* sieve, riddle
criathraich *v* **-rachadh/-radh** sieve; (*met*) weigh up, assess
cridhe *n* **-achan** *m* heart **na biodh a chridh' agad ...!** don't dare ...!
cridhealas *n* **-ais** *m* heartiness, merriment, conviviality
cridheil *a* **-e** hearty, cheerful
crìoch *n* **crìche, -an** *f* end, conclusion; limit, boundary, border **na Crìochan** the Borders **cuir c. air** *v* finish it **thoir gu crìch** *v* bring to a close/an end **c.-ghrèine** tropic
crìochnaich *v* **-achadh** finish, complete, bring to an end
crìochnaichte *a* finished, completed, concluded
criogaid *n* *f* cricket (*sport*)
criom *v* **-adh** gnaw, nibble, chew; erode
criomag *n* **-aig, -an** *f* small bit, fragment, morsel
crìon *a* **crìne, -a** small, mean, trifling; withered, shrunken, dried up
crìon *v* **-adh** wither, fade, decay
crìonadh *n* **-aidh** *m* withering, decay, decline
crioplach *n* **-aich, -aich** *m* cripple
crios *n* **(-a), -an/-achan** *m* belt, strap **c.-sàbhalaidh** lifebelt
Crìosdachd *n* *f* **a' Chrìosdachd** Christianity; Christendom
Crìosdaidh *n* **-ean** *m* Christian *a* **-e** Christian
Crìosdail *a* **-e** Christian **an creideamh C.** the Christian religion
Crìosdalachd *n* *f* Christianity; Christian disposition
criostal *n* **-ail, -an** *m* crystal *a* crystal
cripleach *See* **crioplach**
crith *n* **(-e), -ean** *f* trembling, shaking, shivering **air chrith leis an eagal** trembling with fear
critheanach *a* **-aiche** shaky, unsteady; causing shaking
critheann *n* **-thinn, -an** *m* aspen tree
crith-thalmhainn *n* **crithe-talmhainn/-thalmhainn, crithean-talmhainn** *f* earthquake
crò *n* **-tha, -than** *m* pen for animals, fold; eye of a needle
croch *v* **-adh** hang (*person or thing*) **chaidh a chrochadh** he was hanged
crochadair *n* **-ean** *m* hangman; hanger
crochadh *n* **-aidh** *m* hanging (*of things or people*) **an c. air** dependent (on) **an c. air an t-sìde** depending on the weather
crochte *a* hung, hanging
crodh *n* **cruidh** *m* (*sg n*) cattle, kine **c.-bainne** dairy cows
crò-dhearg *a* crimson
cròg *n* **cròige, -an** *f* large hand; palm of the hand **làn cròige** a handful, fistful
crogall *n* **-aill, -aill** *m* crocodile
crogan *n* **-ain, -ain** *m* jar, pitcher, tin **c.-silidh** jam-jar
cròic *n* **-e, -ean** *f* antlers; foam on liquids or on the sea
croich *n* **-e, -ean** *f* gallows
cròileagan *n* **-ain, -ain** *m* playgroup
crois *n* **-e, -ean** *f* cross; difficulty, mishap **c.-rathaid** crossroads **bha e ann an c.** he was in a fix **bha e ri c.** he was up to no good
croiseil *a* **-e** awkward, problematic
croit *n* **-e, -ean** *f* croft *Also* **crait,**

cruit
croit *n* **-e** *f* hump, hunch
croitear *n* **-eir, -an** *m* crofter
croitse *n* **-achan** *f* crutch
crom *a* **cruime** bent, crooked, curved **ceann c.** *m* a bowed head
crom *v* **-adh** bend, stoop; descend
cromag *n* **-aig, -an** *f* hook; shepherd's crook; apostrophe
cron *n* **croin, -an** *m* harm, damage, fault, crime **cha dèan e c. ort** it'll not harm you
cronaich *v* **-achadh** rebuke, reprimand, censure
cronail *a* **-e** harmful, damaging, pernicious
crònan *n* **-ain, -ain** *m* croon, low singing, humming, purring, any low murmuring sound **c. nan allt** the murmuring of the streams
crosgag *n* **-aig, -an** *f* starfish
crosta *a* cross, angry, irascible, irritable *Formerly* **crosda**
crotach *a* **-aiche** stooped, humpbacked
crotair(e) *n* **-an** *m* hunchback
crotal *n* **-ail** *m* lichen
cruach *n* **cruaiche, -an** *f* pile, heap, stack **c.-arbhair/fheòir/mhòna(ch)** corn-/hay-/peat-stack *Also found in hill/mountain names*
cruach *v* **-adh** pile or heap up; make into a stack
cruachann *n* **-ainn, -ainn/cruaichnean/-an** *f* hip, haunch *Also* **cruachan**
cruadal *n* **-ail, -an** *m* hardship, adversity, difficulty
cruadhaich *v* **-achadh** harden, solidify
cruaidh *n* **-dhach, -ean** *f* steel; stone (*used as anchor*)
cruaidh *a* **-e** hard; difficult; mean; hardy **c.-chàs** *m* danger, extremity, adversity **c.-cheasnaich** cross-examine **c.-chridheach** hard-hearted
cruas *n* **-ais** *m* hardness, hardihood; meanness
crùb *v* **-adh** crouch, squat
crùbach *a* **-aiche** lame or otherwise crippled
crùbag *n* **-aig, -an** *f* crab
crùbain *n* **-ain** *m* crouch, squat **dèan c.** *v* crouch, squat **na c(h)rùban** crouching, squatting
crudha *n* **cruidhe, cruidhean** *m* horseshoe
cruinn *a* **-e** round, circular; gathered together; compact, neat **c.-leum** *m* standing jump
cruinne *n m* the world (*f in gen* **na cruinne**); roundness
cruinneachadh *n* **-aidh, -aidhean** *m* gathering; function; collection
cruinne-cè *n m* **an C.** the world, the universe
cruinn-eòlas *n* **c.-eòlais** *m* geography (*subject*)
cruinnich *v* **-neachadh** collect, assemble, gather together; come together
crùisgean *n* **-ein, -an** *m* cruisie, oil-lamp
Cruithneach *n* **-nich, -nich** *m* Pict *a* Pictish
cruithneachd *n f m* wheat
crùn *n* **crùin, crùintean** *m* crown
crùn *v* **-adh** crown
crùnadh *n* **-aidh** *m* crowning, coronation
cruth *n* **(-a), -an** *m* form, shape, appearance **c.-atharrachadh** *m* transformation
cruthachail *a* **-e** creative
cruthaich *v* **-achadh** create, make
cruthaigheachd *n f* **a' Chruthaigheachd** Creation, the world **A Chruthaigheachd!** My goodness!
cruthaighear *n* **-eir** *m* **an C.** God, the Creator *Also* **cruthadair, cruithear**
cù *n* **coin, coin** *m* dog **cù-chaorach** sheepdog
cuach *n* **cuaiche, -an** *f* drinking cup, quaich; fold, curl of hair
cuagach *a* **-aiche** lame, limping
cuaille *n* **-an** *m* cudgel, club
cuairt *n* **-e, -ean** *f* circuit, round trip, trip (*generally*), excursion; round (*sport*); individual planks

in a clinker-built boat **chaidh sinn c. dhan Fhraing** we took a trip to France **c. dheireannach** final round **c.-ghaoth** eddying wind, whirlwind **c.-litir** circular, newsletter

cuairtich *v* **-teachadh** circulate

cuan *n* **cuain, cuain/-tan** *m* ocean, sea **an C. Siar** the Atlantic Ocean **an C. Sèimh** the Pacific Ocean

cuaraidh *n* **-ean** *f m* quarry

cuaran *n* **-ain, -an** *m* light shoe, sandal

cuartaich *v* **-achadh** surround, enclose; perform, conduct **a' cuartachadh an adhraidh** conducting worship

cùbaid *n* **(-e), -ean** *f* pulpit *Also* **cùbainn**

cubhaidh *a* **-e** fit, becoming, seemly, appropriate, fitting

cùbhraidh *a* **-e** fragrant

cucair *n* **-ean** *m* cooker

cudromach *a* **-aiche** important, weighty; heavy

cudthrom *See* **cuideam**

cudthromach *See* **cudromach**

cugallach *a* **-aiche** unstable (*also met*), wobbly, shoogly, unsteady; precarious

cuibheall *n* **cuibhle, cuibhleachan, cuibhlichean** *f* wheel **c.-stiùiridh** steering-wheel **c.-shnìomh** spinning-wheel

cuibheasach *a* **-aiche** sufficient; tolerable, middling

cuibhil *v* **cuibhleadh** wheel, roll along

cuibhle *n* **-an/-lichean** *f* wheel *See* **cuibheall**

cuibhlich *v* **-leachadh** *See* **cuibhil**

cuibhreann *n* **-rinn, -an** *f m* portion, part, instalment, allowance; (*met*) portion in life, fate

cuibhrig(e) *n* **-e, -ean/-an** *f m* cover, coverlet, bed-cover

cuid *n* **cuid/codach, -ean/codaichean** *f* share, part; belongings, property, resources; *often used to indicate possession*; some (people) **c. na h-oidhche** board and lodgings, bed and breakfast **mo chuid fhìn** my own/my own property/resources **mo chuid airgid/aodaich/chloinne** my money/clothes/children **canaidh c. nach eil sin ceart** some people say that's not right **chan eil e an dara c. fuar no teth** it is neither hot nor cold **a' mhòr-chuid** the majority

cuideachadh *n* **-aidh** *m* help, assistance, aid

cuideachail *a* **-e** helpful

cuideachd *n f* company, group of people **bha e math a bhith nur c.** it was good to be in your company

cuideachd *adv* also, as well; together

cuideachdail *a* **-e** sociable, companionable

cuideam *n* **-eim, -an** *m* weight

cuideigin *pron* someone, somebody

cuide ri *prep* with, along with, in the company of

cuidhteag *n* **-eig, -an** *f* whiting

cuidhteas *n* receipt; riddance **fhuair mi c. an cnatan mu dheireadh thall** I finally got rid of the cold

cuidich *v* **-deachadh** help, assist, aid

cùil *n* **(-e), -tean** *f* corner, nook, recess, any secluded or private place **c.-chumhang** a tight spot, a fix

cuilbheart *n* **-eirt, -an** *f* wile, stratagem

cuilc *n* **-e, -ean** *f* reed

cuileag *n* **-eig, -an** *f* fly **a bheil a' chuileag ann?** are the midges out?

cuilean *n* **-ein, -an** *m* puppy

cuileann *n* **-linn, -an** *m* holly

cuimhne *n f* memory, remembrance **tha c. mhath aige** he has a good memory **an robh cuimhn' aice ort?** did she remember you? **mas math mo chuimhne** if my memory serves me right **chaidh e glan às mo chuimhne** I completely forgot (about it) **cuir nan c.** *v* remind them

cuimhneachan *n* **-ain, -ain** *m* memorial, remembrance, commemoration, keepsake **mar chuimhneachan ormsa** in remembrance of me

cuimhnich *v* **-neachadh** remember, recall, bear in mind, commemorate

cuimir *a* **-e** brief, concise; (*of person*) shapely, well-proportioned, handsome

Cuimreach *n* **-rich, -rich** *m* someone from Wales *a* Welsh

cuimse *n* **-an** *f* aim, mark; moderation

cuimseach *a* **-siche** moderate, reasonable; (*of person*) sure of aim **c. math** reasonably good

cuimsich *v* **-seachadh** aim; hit a mark or target, target

cuin(e) *int pron, adv* when **c. a thig iad?** when will they come? **chan eil fhios agamsa c. a thig iad** I don't know when they will come

cuing *n* **-e, -ean** *f* yoke, bond, restraint **c./a' chuing** (*pronounced* **a' chaoidh** *but nasally*) asthma

cuingealaich *v* **-achadh** restrict, limit

cuinneag *n* **-eig, -an** *f* pail, bucket

cuinnean *n* **-ein, -an** *m* nostril

cuip *n* **-e, -ean/-eachan** *f* whip

cuip *v* **-eadh** whip

cuir *v* **cur** put, place, lay; send; set; sow, plant; cast **c. buntàta** plant potatoes **c. clèibh/lìn** set creels/nets **c. fios/litir** send word/a letter **c. fios air …** send for … **c. gaoisid** shed coat **c. sneachda** snow *Also featured in many idioms eg* **c. air bhonn** set up **c. air chois** set up, establish **c. a-mach** issue; vomit, be sick **c. an aghaidh** oppose **c. an cèill** express, declare **c. an ìre** pretend **c. às do** abolish **c. às leth** accuse **c. dheth** postpone **c. fàilte air** welcome **c. geall** bet, lay wager **c. ìmpidh air** urge **c. ri** add to **c. romhad** decide (to) **dè tha cur riut?** what's troubling you? **c. troimh-a-chèile** upset, confuse

cuireadh *n* **-ridh, -idhean** *m* invitation

cuirm *n* **-e, -ean** *f* feast, banquet **c.-chiùil** concert **c.-chnuic** picnic

cùirt *n* **-e/cùrtach, -ean** *f* court **c.-lagha** court of law

cùirtean *n* **-ein, -an** *m* curtain *Also* **cùirtear**

cùis *n* **-e, -ean** *f* matter, affair; cause; object, butt **sin mar a tha a' chùis** that's how things are/stand **c.-bhùirt/bhùrta** a laughing-stock **c.-eagail** something to be feared **c.-lagha** a court case **c.-mhaslaidh** a disgrace **an dèan thu a' chùis air?** will you manage it? **rinn iad a' chùis oirnn** they defeated us **nì sin a' chùis** that'll do/that'll suffice

cuisean *n* **-ein, -an** *f m* cushion

cuisle *n* **-an** *f* vein, blood-vessel, artery **c.-chiùil** pipe (*mus*)

cuislean *n* **-ein, -an** *m* flute

cuithe *n* **-achan** *f* pit, trench; fold for animals **c. sneachda** snowdrift

cùl *n* **cùll, cùil/cùiltean** *m* back; (*in poetry*) hair **c. an taighe** the back of the house **cuir c. ris** *v* abandon it/leave it/stop it **c.-chàin** *v* backbite, slander **c.-chàineadh** *n m* backbiting, slander **c.-taic** *n f* support **'s e Gàidheal gu chùl a th' ann** he's a Gael through and through

cùlaibh *n m* back, back part of anything **air do chùlaibh** behind you

culaidh *n* **-e, -ean** *f* garment, apparel; object, butt **c.-choimheach** fancy dress **c.-mhagaidh** object of scorn/mockery

cùlaist *n* **-e, -ean** *f* utility room, scullery

cularan *n* **-ain, -ain** *m* cucumber

cullach *n* **-aich, -aich** *m* male cat, tomcat; boar

cùl-mhùtaireachd *n* **cùil-** *f* smuggling; mutinying, plotting
cultar *n* **-air, -an** *m* culture
cultarach *a* **-aiche** cultural
cum *v* **-adh** shape, form, compose, fashion
cùm *v* **cumail** keep, retain; support; hold **a bheil thu a' cumail gu math?** are you keeping well? **dè na chumas e?** how much will it hold? **c. sin dhomh** hold that for me **c. a-mach** claim, make out **c. coinneamh** hold a meeting **c. grèim air** keep hold of **c. ort** keep going, carry on, keep at it **c. suas** keep up, maintain
cumadh *n* **-aidh, -aidhean** *m* shape, form; the act of shaping or forming
cumanta *a* common, ordinary
cumha *n* **-chan** *m* mourning, lamentation; elegy; condition, stipulation
cumhach *a* conditional (*gram*) **an tràth c.** the conditional tense
cumhachd *n* **-an** *f m* power, strength; authority
cumhachdach *a* **-aiche** powerful, mighty
cumhain *v See* **caomhain**
cumhang *a* **-ainge/cuinge** narrow, tight; narrow-minded
cùmhnant *n* **-aint, -an** *m* contract, agreement, covenant; condition **c.-obrach** contract of employment
cunbhalach *a* **-aiche** regular, constant, steady, consistent
cungaidh *n* **-ean** *f* ingredients; implement **c.-leighis** medicine, cure
cunnart *n* **-airt, -an** *m* danger, risk
cunnartach *a* **-aiche** dangerous, risky
cunnradh *n* **-aidh, -ean** *m* bargain, contract, deal, treaty
cunnt *v* **-adh/-as/-ais** count
cunntas *n* **-ais, -an** *f m* (*fin, general*) account; arithmetic **c.-beatha** CV **c.-bheachd** opinion poll **c.-sluaigh** census
cunntasachd *n f* accountancy, accounting
cunntasair *n* **-ean** *m* accountant
cuntair *n* **-ean** *m* counter (*in shop etc*) *Also* **cunntair**
cupa *n* **-nnan** *m* cup *Also* **cupan**
curaidh *n* **-ean** *m* hero, champion, warrior
cùram *n* **-aim, -an** *m* care, responsibility, charge, trust; anxiety, worry; religious conversion **ghabh mi c. a' ghille** I took care of/took responsibility for the boy **fo chùram** anxious/concerned **na biodh c. ort** don't be anxious/concerned **tha an c. oirre** she's been converted (*relig*)
cùramach *a* **-aiche** careful, responsible; anxious
cur na mara *n m* seasickness
currac *n* **-aic, -aicean** *m* cap, bonnet
curracag *n* **-aig, -an** *f* peewit, lapwing; haycock
curran *n* **-ain, -ain** *m* carrot
cùrsa *n* **-ichean** *f m* course
cur-seachad *n* **-an** *m* pastime, hobby
cus *n m* excess, too much, too many; (*less usual*) many **tha cus airgid aige** he has too much money **tha iad a' cur cus bheannachdan thugad** they send you lots of good wishes
cusbann *n f* customs, excise
cuspair *n* **-ean** *m* subject, topic
cut *v* **-adh** gut (*fish*)
cuthach *n* **-aich** *m* rage, fury; madness **duine-cuthaich** madman, wild man **bha an c. dearg oirre** she was mad with rage
cuthag *n* **-aig, -an** *f* cuckoo

D

dà *a* two (+ *dat sg & len*) **dà chaileig** two girls
da *aug prep* to his, for his
dachaigh *n* **(-e), -ean** *f* home **gun d.** homeless
dà-chànanach *a* bilingual
dà-chànanas *n* **-ais** *m*

bilingualism
dà-chasach *a* **-aiche** two-footed
dad *n f* anything **dad ort!** hang on! wait a minute!
dadaidh *n* **-ean** *m* dad, daddy
dadam *n* **-aim, -an** *m* atom
dadamach *a* atomic
dà-dheug *n, a* twelve (*nouns in their singular form are inserted between* **dà** *and* **dheug** *and are lenited*) **dà dhuine dheug** twelve men/persons
dà-dhualach *a* two-ply
dà fhichead *n, a* forty (*lit* two score)
dà-fhillte *a* two-fold, double, compound
daga *n* **-ichean** *m* pistol
dàibhear *n* **-eir, -an** *m* diver
dàibhig *v* **-eadh** dive
dail *n* **dalach, -ean** *f* dale, meadow
dàil *n* **dàlach, dàlaichean** *f* delay, procrastination; credit **cuir d. ann** *v* delay **air dhàil** on credit
dàimh *n* **-e** *f m* friendship, affinity, relationship
dàimheach *a* **-mhiche** related; relative (*gram*)
dàimhealachd *n f* friendliness
dàimheil *a* **-e** friendly
daingeann *a* **daingne** firm, steadfast, determined, committed
daingneach *n* **-nich, -nichean** *f* stronghold, fortification, fort
daingnich *v* **-neachadh** confirm, ratify; strengthen, consolidate
dàir *n* **dàra/dàrach** *f* breeding, heat, breeding together (*of cattle*) **tha an d. air a' bhoin** the cow is in heat/season
dall *n* **doill, doill** *m* blind person
dall *a* **doille** blind
dall *v* **-adh** blind
dallag an fheòir *n* **dallaige an fh., dallagan an fh.** *f* dormouse
dallag an fhraoich *n* **dallaige an fh., dallagan an fh.** *f* shrew
dalma *a* presumptuous; blatant
dalta *n* **-n** *m* foster-child
daltachd *n f* fosterage
daltag *n* **-aig, -an** *f* bat
dam *n* **-a, -aichean** *m* dam
dàmais *n f* draughts
damaiste *n f* damage; difficulty
damh *n* **daimh, daimh** *m* bullock, ox; stag
Dàmhair *n f* **an D.** October
damhan-allaidh *n* **damhain-, damhain-** *m* spider
dàn *n* **dàin** *m* fate, destiny **bha sin an dàn dhi** that was her destiny
dàn *n* **dàin, dàin** *m* poem
dàna *a* bold, intrepid, daring, presumptuous
dànachd *n f* boldness, daring
dànadas *n* **-ais** *m* boldness, daring
Danmhairgeach *n* **-gich, -gich** *m* Dane *a* Danish
danns *v* **-a(dh)** dance
dannsa *n* **-ichean** *m* dance
dannsa(dh) *n* **(-aidh)** *m* dancing
dannsair *n* **-ean** *m* dancer
daoimean *n* **-ein, -an** *m* diamond
daoine *n m See* **duine**
daolag *n* **-aig(e), -an** *f* beetle **d.-bhreac-dhearg** ladybird
daonna *a* human *Also* **daonda**
daonnachd *n f* humanity *Also* **daondachd**
daonnan *adv* always
daor *a* **daoire** dear, expensive, costly
daorach *n f* **-aich** intoxication, drunkenness **bha an d. air** he was drunk **air an daoraich** on a binge
daorsa *n f* bondage, captivity
dar *aug prep* to our, for our *conj* when
darach *n* **-aich** *m* oak (*tree*)
da-rìribh *adv* indeed, very, in earnest
dàrna *a* second *Also* **dara**
dà-sheaghach *a* **-aiche** ambiguous
dath *n* **-a, -an** *m* colour
dath *v* **-adh** colour; dye
dathadh *n* **-aidh** *m* colouring
dathte *a* coloured
dè *int pron* what? **dè an uair a tha e?** what's the time? **dè an t-ainm a th' ort?** what's your name? **dè cho fad' 's a tha e?** how far is it?

de *prep* of (+ *dat & len*)
deachd *v* **-adh** dictate
deachdadh *n* **-aidh, -aidhean** *m* dictation **inneal-deachdaidh** *m* dictaphone
deadhan *n* **-ain, -ain** *m* dean
deagh *a* (*precedes & lenites n*) good, fine, excellent **d. bhanais** a good wedding
deagh-bheus *n* **-a, -an** *f* virtue
deagh-ghean *n* **-a** *m* goodwill, benevolence
dealachadh *n* **-aidh** *m* parting, separation
dealaich *v* **-achadh** part, separate, differentiate **tha iad air dealachadh** they've separated (*a couple*)
dealaichte *a* separate, separated
dealain *a* electric **teine d.** *m* electric fire **post-d.** *m* e-mail
dealan *n* **-ain** *m* electricity
dealanach *n* **-aich, -aich** *m* lightning
dealanaich *v* **-achadh** electrify
dealanair *n* **-ean** *m* electrician
dealan-dè *n* **dealain-, dealain-** *m* butterfly
dealas *n* **-ais** *m* zeal, eagerness, commitment
dealasach *a* **-aiche** zealous, eager, committed
dealbh *n* **-a/deilbhe, -an/deilbh** *f m* picture, illustration, photograph, form, figure, outline **tog d.** *v* take a picture **d.-chluich(e)** play (*acted*) **d.-èibhinn** cartoon
dealbh *v* **-adh** design, plan
dealbhadair *n* **-ean** *m* photographer, designer
dealbhaiche *n* **-an** *m* draughtsman
dealg *n* **deilg, -an** *f* pin, prickle, skewer
dealgan *n* **-ain, -an** *m* spindle
deàlrach *a* **-aiche** shiny, shining
deàlradh *n* **-aidh, -aidhean** *m* shining, flashing
deàlraich *v* **-adh** shine, flash
dealt *n* **-a** *f m* dew
deamhais *n* **-ean** *f m* shears
deamhan *n* **-ain, -ain** *m* demon, devil **'s e d. a th' annad!** you're a devil!
deamhnaidh *a* **-e** devilish **tha fhios agad d. math** you know damned well
deamocrasaidh *n* **-ean** *m* democracy
deamocratach *n* **-aich, -aich** *m* democrat
deamocratach *a* **-aiche** democratic
dèan *irr v* **-amh** do, make **d. cabhag!** hurry! **d. gàire** laugh **d. air do shocair!** slow down! **d. an gnothach/a' chùis** suffice, manage (+ **air**) beat, overcome
dèanadach *a* **-aiche** industrious, hardworking
deann *n* **-a, -an** *f* force, haste
deannan *n* **-ain, -an** *m* a number, a good few **d. bhliadhnaichean** a good few years
deann-ruith *n* **-e** *f* movement at speed, travel at pace, headlong rush
deanntag *n* **-aige, -an** *f* nettle
dèanta *a* done, complete; stocky (*in build*)
dearbh *v* **-adh** prove, affirm
dearbh *a* (*precedes & lenites n*) certain, sure, identical **gu d. fhèin** indeed **an d. fhear/thè** the very one
dearbhadh *n* **-aidh** *m* proof, identification, trial
dearbhta *a* certain, sure, proven *Also* **dearbhte**
dearc *n* **-an** *f* berry
dearcag *n* **-aig, -an** *f* little berry, currant
dearg *a* **deirge** red, crimson (*also used as an intensive*) **d. amadan/òinseach** an utter fool **d. chuthach** mad rage **d. mhèirleach** a downright thief **d. rùisgte** stark naked
dearg- *pref* reddish **d.-dhonn** reddish brown
deargann *n* **-ainn, -an** *f* flea
dearmad *n* **-aid, -an** *m* omission, oversight (*error*), neglect **dèan d. air** *v* neglect, omit, overlook
dearmadach *a* **-aiche** negligent,

forgetful
dearmaid *v* **-ad** neglect
deàrrs *v* **-adh** shine
deàrrsach *a* **-aiche** shining, gleaming, glistening **d. uisge** *f* downpour
deàrrsadh *n* **-aidh, -aidhean** *m* shining
deas *n, a* **deise** *f* south; right; ready (to) **Uibhist a D.** South Uist **an taobh a d.** the south side **an làmh dheas** the right hand **air an làimh dheis** on the right
deasachadh *n* **-aidh** *m* preparation, editing **neach-deasachaidh** *m* editor
deasaich *v* **-achadh** prepare, edit
deasaichte *a* prepared, edited
deasbad *n* **-aid, -an** *f m* debate **dèan d.** *v* debate
deas-bhriathrach *a* **-aiche** eloquent
deas-chainnt *n* **-e** *f* eloquence
deasg *n* **-a, -an** *m* desk
deas-ghnàth *n* **-ghnàith, -ghnàthan** *m* ceremony, ceremonial
deatach *n* **-aiche, -aichean** *f* smoke, fumes, vapour
deatamach *a* **-aiche** necessary, crucial, essential
ded *aug prep* of your
deic *n* **-e, -ichean** *f m* deck (*of boat*)
deich *n, a* ten
deichead *n* **-eid, -an** *m* decade
deicheamh *n* **-eimh** *m* decimal *num a* tenth
deichnear *n m* ten (people) **d. fhear** ten men
dèideadh *n* **-didh** *m* toothache **a bheil an d. ort?** do you have toothache?
dèideag *n* **-eig, -an** *f* toy; pebble
dèidh *n* **-e, -ean** *f* desire; fondness; aspiration
dèidheil *a* **-e** fond **d. air ...** fond of ...
deifir *n See* **diofar**
deifrichte *See* **diofraichte**
deigh *n* **-e** *f* ice
dèile *n* **-an/-achan** *f* wooden board, plank **d.-bhogadain** see-saw
dèilig *v* **-eadh** (*followed by* **ri**) deal (with), treat
deimhinn(t)e *a* certain, categorical, conclusive
dèine *n f* keenness, commitment; impetus
dèirc *n* **-e, -ean** *f* alms, charity
dèirceach *n* **-cich, -cich** *m* beggar
deireadh *n* **-ridh, -ridhean** *m* end, rear, stern; (*abstr*) finish, conclusion **air d(h).** late ... **mu dheireadh** last **mu dheireadh thall** at (long) last, eventually
deireannach *a* **-aiche** last, latter, final, ultimate; backward
deis *a* **deise** ready, eager, willing
deisciobal *n* **-ail, -ail** *m* disciple
deise *n* **-achan** *f* suit, uniform **d. an Airm** Army uniform **d.-sgoile** school uniform **d.-snàimh** swimsuit
deiseil *a* **-e/eala** ready; finished (with); handy; clockwise
deit *n* **-e, -ichean** *f* date (*fruit*)
dem *aug prep* of my
den *aug prep* of the; of their
deò *n f* breath **thug e suas an d.** he breathed his last **d. gaoithe** a breath of wind
deoc *v* **-adh** suck
deoch *n* **dighe/dibhe, -an/-annan** *f* drink **d. an dorais** stirrup cup **d.-làidir** alcohol **d.-slàinte** toast (*with drink*)
deòin *n* **-e** *f* will, purpose
deònach *a* **-aiche** willing
deònaich *v* **-achadh** grant, vouchsafe, be willing to do
deothail *v* **-al** suck *Formerly* **deoghail**
der *aug prep* of/off our/your
deuchainn *n* **-e, -ean** *f* examination, test, trial; agony
deuchainneach *a* **-niche** trying, agonizing
deucon *n* **-oin, -oin/-an** *m* deacon
deud *n* **-an** *m* denture, tooth
deudach *a* **-aiche** toothy, dental
deug *suff* teen (*in numbers*) **sia-deug** sixteen

deugachadh *n m* a span of 13 to 19 years **d. bhliadhnaichean** a period of between 13 and 19 years
deugaich *v* **-achadh** enter teenage years
deugaire *n* **-an** *m* teenager
deur *n* **deòir, deòir** *m* tear (*drop*)
dha *prep See* **do**
dha *aug prep* to/for his
dha/dhàsan *prep pron* to/for him
dhà *n* two **a dhà** two **na dhà** the two
dhachaigh *adv* home (*ie homewards*)
dhad *aug prep* to/for your
dhà-dheug *n* twelve **a d.** twelve
dhaibh(san) *prep pron* to/for them
dham *aug prep* to/for my; to/for their
dhan *aug prep* to/for the/their
dha-rìribh *adv* indeed, very, in earnest **math d.** excellent, very good
dhe *aug prep* of/off him
dhed *aug prep* of/off your (*sg*)
dhem *aug prep* of/off my
dhen *aug prep* of/off the/their
dher *aug prep* of/off our/your
dheth *adv* off
dheth(san) *prep pron* of/off him
dhi/dhì(se) *prep pron* to/for her
dhibh(se) *prep pron* of/off you
dhinn(e) *prep pron* of/off us
dhìom(sa) *prep pron* of/off me
dhìot(sa) *prep pron* of/off you (*sg*)
dhith(se) *prep pron* of/off her
dhiubh(san) *prep pron* of/off them
dhòmh(sa) *prep pron* to/for me
dhuibh(se) *prep pron* to/for you
dhuinn(e) *prep pron* to/for us
dhuit *See* **dhut**
dhur *aug prep* to/for your
dhut(sa) *prep pron* to/for you (*sg*)
di/dì(se) *prep pron* to/for her
dia *n* **dè, -than** *m* god **Dia** God
diabhal *n* **-ail, -ail/-bhlan** *m* devil **an D.** the Devil
diabhlaidh *a* devilish, diabolical
diadhachd *n f* divinity, godhead; theology, study of divinity; godliness
diadhaidh *a* **-e** godly, devout; divine
diadhaire *n* **-an** *m* theologian, divine
diallaid *n See* **dìollaid**
dian *a* **dèine** keen, vehement, impetuous; intensive, intense
Diardaoin *n m* Thursday
dias *n* **dèise, -an** *f* ear of corn
diathad *n* **-aid, -an** *f* dinner, lunch
dibhearsain *n m* fun, entertainment, diversion
dìblidh *a* **-e** abject, wretched; in difficulty
dìcheall *n* **dìchill** *m* diligence, utmost **rinn iad an d.** they did their best/utmost
dìcheallach *a* **-aiche** diligent, conscientious
dì-chuimhnich *v See* **dìochuimhnich**
Diciadain *n m* Wednesday
Didòmhnaich *n m* Sunday
dìg *n* **-e, -ean** *f* ditch
digear *n* **-eir, -an** *m* digger
Dihaoine *n m* Friday
dìle *n* **-ann, -an** *f* deluge, flood **d. bhàthte** torrential rain
dìleab *n* **-eib(e), -an** *f* legacy, bequest
dìleas *a* **dìlse** faithful, loyal
dilleachdan *n* **-ain, -an** *m* orphan
dìlseachd *n f* faithfulness, loyalty
Diluain *n m* Monday
Dimàirt *n m* Tuesday
dìmeas *n* **-a** *m* disregard, disrespect **dèan d. air** *v* disregard, look down on
dìneasair *n* **-ean** *m* dinosaur
dinn *v* **-eadh** stuff, cram, squeeze in
dìnnear *n* **-eir/-ach, -an** *f* dinner
dinnsear *n* **-eir** *m* ginger
dìobair *v* **-bradh** desert, abandon; fail, come to nothing
dìobhair *v* **(-t)** vomit
dìochuimhne *n f* forgetfulness
dìochuimhneach *a* **-niche** forgetful
dìochuimhnich *v* **-neachadh** forget

diofar *n* **-air** *m* difference; variety **chan eil e gu d.** it doesn't matter
diofraichte *a* different
diog *n* **-an** *m* second (*unit of time*)
diogail *v* **-gladh** tickle
diogalach *a* **-aiche** tickly, ticklish
dìoghail *v* **-ghladh** avenge; pay back, compensate *Also* **dìol**
dìoghaltas *n* **-ais** *m* revenge, vengeance
dìoghras *n* **-ais** *m* enthusiasm
diogladh *n* **-aidh** *m* tickling
dìol *n m* abuse **dèan droch dhìol air** *v* badly abuse
dìolain *a* illegitimate (*as of child*)
dìol-dèirce *n* **diolacha/-an** *m* beggar, wretch, poor soul
dìollaid *n* **-e**, **-ean** *f* saddle
diomb *n m* displeasure, indignation, resentment
diombach *a* **-aiche** displeased, indignant, resentful
diombuan *a* **-uaine** transient, fleeting
dìomhain *a* **-e** vain; idle
dìomhair *a* **-e** mysterious; secret, confidential
dìomhaireachd *n f* mystery; secrecy, confidentiality
dìomhanas *n* **-ais** vanity; idleness
dìon *n* **-a** *m* protection, defence, security
dìon *v* protect, defend, guard
dìonach *a* **-aiche** watertight
dìosgan *n* **-ain**, **-ain** *m* creak
dìosganaich *n* **-e** *f* creaking
dìreach *a* **dìriche** straight, direct; upright
dìreach *adv* just **tha e d. air falbh** he has just gone **seadh d.** just so
dìreadh *n* **-ridh**, **-ridhean** *m* climb, ascent
dìrich *v* **dìreadh/dìreachadh** climb, ascend; straighten, make straight
Disathairne *n m* Saturday
dìsinn/dìsne *n* **dìsne**, **dìsnean** *m* dice, die
dìt *v* **-eadh** condemn, sentence
dìth *n* **-e** *f m* want, lack, deficiency **dè tha dhìth ort?** what do you want? **bha feadhainn a dhìth** there were some missing **a' dol a dhìth** perishing, dying
dìthean *n* **-ein**, **-ein/-an** *m* flower
dithis *n f* two (people); both; pair, couple **an d. aca** the two of them
diù *n m* worth, heed, attention **cha do chuir e d. ann** he paid no attention to it
diùc *n* **-an** *m* duke **ban-d.** *f* duchess
diùid *a* **-e** shy, bashful, reticent
diùlt *v* **-adh** refuse, reject
diùltadh *n* **-aidh**, **-aidhean** *m* refusal, rejection
Diùrach *n* **-aich**, **-aich** *m* someone from Jura *a* from, or pertaining to, Jura
dleastanas *n* **-ais**, **-an** *m* duty, obligation **mar dhleastanas** obligatory
dligheach *a* **-ghiche** due, legitimate
dlùth *n* **-a**, **dlùithe** *m* warp (*weaving*)
dlùth *a* **dlùithe** close (to), near
dlùthaich *v* **-achadh** approach, near; warp (*weaving*)
do *poss pron* your **d'** *before vowels* **d' athair** your father
do *prep* to, for (+ *dat*)
do *v part* (*indicates past tense*) **an do dh'èirich iad?** did they get up?
do *neg pref* in-, im-, un-
do-àireamh *a* innumerable, countless
dòbhran *n* **-ain**, **-ain** *m* otter
doca *n* **-n/-ichean** *m* dock; hollow, hole
docair *n* **-ean** *m* docker
dòcha *a* likely, probable **'s e sin as d.** that's most likely **'s d.** perhaps, maybe **is d. gun tig iad** perhaps they will come
dochainn *v* beat up, hurt, injure
dochann *n* **-ainn** *m* hurt, injury
dòchas *n* **-ais**, **-an** *m* hope **tha mi an d. gum faic mi iad** I hope I'll see them
dòchasach *a* **-aiche** hopeful
dod *aug prep* to your

do-dhèanta *a* impossible, impractical, impracticable
do-fhaicsinneach *a* **-niche** invisible
dòigh *n* **-e, -ean** *f* way, method, manner **d.-beatha** way of life, lifestyle **cuir air d.** *v* repair; arrange, organize **tha i air a d.** she is happy
dòigheil *a* **-e** well-arranged, contented, sensible, reasonable **tha e gu d.** he is well
doile *n* **-lichean** *f* doll
doileag *n* **-eig, -an** *f* (small) doll
doilgheas *n* **-eis** *m* affliction, vexation, sorrow
doille *n f* blindness
doilleir *a* **-e** dark, gloomy
doimhne *n f* depth **an d.** the sea
doimhneachd *n f* depth
doineann *n* **-ninn, -an** *f* tempest
doirbh *a* **-e/dorra** difficult
doire *n* **-an/-achan** *f m* grove, thicket
dòirt *v* **dòrtadh** pour; spill
dol *n m* going (*See irr v* **rach** *in Grammar*)
dol-a-mach *n m* exit; behaviour **anns a' chiad d.** initially **dè an d. a th' ort?** what are you up to?
dol-a-steach *n m* entrance
dolaidh *n f* harm, detriment **chaidh e a dholaidh** it perished/rotted
dolair *n* **-ean** *m* dollar
dol air adhart *n m* carry-on
dol-às *n m* escape **cha robh d. againn** we had no way out, we found it unavoidable
dom *aug prep* to/for my/their
domhainn *a* **doimhne/-e** deep; profound
domhan *n* **-ain** *m* universe
don *prep pron* to/for the/their
dona *a* **miosa** bad
donas *n* **-ais** *m* devil **an D.** the Devil **an D. ort!** Drat you!
donn *a* **duinne** brown, brown-haired
donnalaich *n f* howling
dor *aug prep* to/for you (*pl & pol*)
dòrainn *n* **-e, -ean** *f* anguish, agony
dòrainneach *a* **-niche** anguished, excruciating
doras *n* **-ais, dorsan** *m* door **d.-aghaidh** front door **d.-cùil** back door **d.-èiginn** emergency exit
dorch(a) *a* **duirch(e)** dark, dark-haired, dusky
dorchadas *n* **-ais** *m* darkness
dòrlach *n* **-aich, -aich** *m* handful
dòrn *n* **dùirn, dùirn** *m* fist
dorsair *n* **-ean** *m* doorman, janitor
dòrtadh *n* **-aidh, -aidhean** *m* pouring **bha d. uisge ann** it was pouring (with) rain
dos *n* **dois/duis, duis, -an** *m* bush, tuft; drone (*of bagpipe*)
dòs *v* **-adh** dose
do-sheachanta *a* unavoidable, inevitable
dotair *n* **-ean** *m* doctor
dòtaman *n* **-ain, -an** *m* spinning top
drabasta *a* lewd, obscene
dragh *n* **-a, -annan** *m* bother, trouble; worry **bha d. oirre** she was worried **na gabh d.** *v* don't worry/go to any trouble
dragh *v* **-adh** tug
draghadh *n* **-aidh, -aidhean** *m* a tug **thug i d. air** *v* she gave it a tug
draghail *a* **-e/-ala** worried, worrying, troublesome
dràibh *v* **-eadh** drive
dràibhear *n* **-eir, -an** *m* driver
dràibh(ig) *v* **-eadh** drive
drama *n* **-ichean** *m* dram (*of whisky*)
dràma *n f* drama
dranndan *n* **-ain** *m* murmur, drone; snarl
draoidh *n* **-ean** *m* wizard, sorcerer, druid
draoidheachd *n f* wizardry, sorcery; magic; druidism
drathair *n* **dràthraichean** *m* drawer (*in furniture*)
drathais *n* **-e, -ean** *f* drawers, pants, knickers *Also* **drathars**
dreach *n* **-a, -an** *m* appearance
dreachd *n* **-an** *f* draft
dreag *n* **dreige, -an** *f* meteor
dreagaire *n* **-an** *m* satellite

dreallag *n* **-aige, -an** *f* swing (*for play*)
dream *n* **-a, -annan** *m* people, tribe
drèana *n* **-ichean** *f* drain, ditch
dreas(a) *n* **-(a)ichean** *f m* dress
dreasair *n* **-ean** *m* dresser (*furniture*)
dreathan-donn *n* **dreathain-duinn, dreathain-donna** *m* wren
drèin *n* **-e, -ean** *f* scowl **chuir i d. oirre** *v* she pulled a face
dreuchd *n* **-an** *f* profession, occupation, office (*position*) **leig i dhith a d.** *v* she retired
driamlach *n* **-aich, -aich/-aichean** *f m* fishing line
drile *n* **-lichean** *f* drill (*mech*)
drilig *v* **-eadh** drill (*mech*)
drioftair *n* **-ean** *m* drifter (*fishing boat*)
drip *n* **-e** *f* bustle
dripeil *a* **-e** very busy, bustling
dris *n* **-e, -ean** *f* bramble
drithlinn *n m* malfunction **chaidh e d.** it malfunctioned
driùchd *n* **-an** *m* dew
dròbh *n* **dròibh, -an** *f m* drove
dròbhair *n* **-ean** *m* drover
droch *a* bad (*precedes & lenites n*) **d. shìde** bad weather **d. c(h)ainnt** bad language
drochaid *n* **-e, -ean** *f* bridge
droch-bheus *n* **-a, -an** *f* bad behaviour, immorality
droch-nàdarrach *a* **-aiche** bad-natured, ill-tempered
droga *n* **-ichean** *f* drug
droigheann *n* **-ghinn** *m* thorn
droman *n* **-ain** *m* elder tree
drudhag *n* **-aig, -an** *f* drop (*of liquid*); sip *Also* **drùdhag**
druid *n* **-e, -ean** *f* starling
druid *v* **-eadh** shut
drùidh *v* **drùdhadh** soak, penetrate; impress, influence **dhrùidh e orm** it impressed me
drùidhteach *a* **-tiche** penetrating; impressive
druim *n* **droma, dromannan** *m* back; ridge (*topog*)
druma *n* **-chan/-ichean** *f m* drum
duais *n* **-e, -ean** *f* prize, reward; wages
dual *n* **duail, -an** *m* lock (*of hair*), plait; strand
dual *n* **duail** *m* hereditary right, inherited character or quality **mar bu d. dha** as was his custom
dualach *a* **-aiche** curled, plaited
dualag *n* **-aig, -an** *f* curl (*of hair*), ringlet
dualchainnt *n* **-e, -ean** *f* speech of a particular area, dialect
dualchas *n* **-ais** *m* heritage, tradition
dualchasach *a* **-aiche** traditional
dual(t)ach *a* **-aiche** liable (to), inclined (to)
duan *n* **duain, duain** *m* poem
duanag *n* **-aig, -an** *f* ditty
duanaire *n* **-an** *m* anthology
dùbailte *a* double
dubh *n* **duibh** *m* black (*colour*); ink; pupil (*of eye*)
dubh *a* **duibhe** black **d. dorcha** pitch-dark/-black
dubh *v* **-adh** blacken **d. às** erase, excise
dubh- *pref* dark **d.-ghorm** dark blue
dubhach *a* **-aiche** sad, melancholy
dubhadh *n* **-aidh** *m* blackening, darkening, eclipse **d. na grèine/gealaich** eclipse of the sun/moon
dubhag *n* **-aig, -an** *f* kidney
dubhan *n* **-ain, -ain** *m* hook
dubhar *n* **-air** *m* shade
dubh-cheist *n* **-cheistean** *f* puzzle
dubh-fhacal *n* **-ail, -ail/-fhaclan** *m* riddle, enigma
Dùbhlachd *n f* **an D.** December
dùbhlan *n* **-ain, -ain** *m* challenge, defiance **thug i d. dha** she defied/challenged him
dùblaich *v* **-achadh** double, duplicate
dùdach *n* **-aiche, -aichean** *f m* horn (*in car*), hooter
dùil *n* **-e, -ean** *f* expectation **tha d. aice ri leanabh** she's expecting (a baby) **ma-tha, tha mi 'n d.** I should think so (too)

dùil *n* **-e, -ean** *f* element
duileasg *n* **-lisg** *m* dulse
duilgheadas *n* **-ais, -an** *m* difficulty, problem
duilich *a* **duilghe** sad, regrettable; difficult **tha mi d.** I'm sorry
duilleach *n* **-lich,** *m* foliage
duilleachan *n* **-ain, -ain** *m* leaflet
duilleag *n* **-eige, -an** *f* leaf; sheet (*of paper*); page **taobh-duilleig(e) 6** page 6
duilleagach *a* **-aiche** leafy
dùin *v* **dùnadh** close, shut
duine *n* **daoine** *m* man, person, anyone; husband **a bheil d. a-staigh?** is there anyone in? **a h-uile d.** everyone, everybody **d.-uasal** gentleman, nobleman **d. sam bith** anyone
duinealas *n* **-ais** *m* manliness
duineil *a* **-e** manly
dùinte *a* closed, shut; reserved, withdrawn
duiseal *n* **-eil, -an** *f* flute
dùisg *v* **dùsgadh** wake, awaken, rouse
Dùitseach *n* **-ich** *m* Dutch person *a* Dutch
dùmhail *a* **-e** dense; crowded, congested
dùn *n* **dùin, dùin** *m* fort; heap
dùnadh *n* **-aidh, -aidhean** *m* closure, closing, ending
dùnan *n* **-ain, -ain** *m* small fort; small heap; dunghill
dùr *a* **dùire** dour; stubborn
dur *aug prep* to your (*pl & pol*)
dùrachd *n* **-an** *f* sincerity, earnestness, wish **le deagh dhùrachd** with best wishes/yours sincerely
dùrachdach *a* **-aiche** sincere, fervent, impassioned
dùraig *v* **-eadh** dare, venture; desire **dhùraiginn falbh** I'd like to go
durcan *n* **-ain, -ain** *m* cone (*on tree*)
dùrdail *n* **-e** *f* crooning, cooing
dusan *n* **-ain** *m* dozen (+ *sg*) **d. ugh** a dozen eggs **leth-d.** half a dozen
dùsgadh *n* **-aidh, -aidhean** *m* waking, awakening, rousing **d. spioradail** religious revival
duslach *n* **-aich** *m* dust; mortal remains
dust *n m* dust
dust/dustaig *v* **-adh/-eadh** dust
dustair *n* **-ean** *m* duster
dùthaich *n* **dùthcha, dùthchannan** *f* country **air an d.** in the countryside
dùthchail *a* **-e** rural
dùthchas *n* **-ais** *m* place of origin, homeland; heredity, heritage
dùthchasach *a* **-aiche** native, indigenous, hereditary

E

e *pron* he, him, it
eabar *n* **-air** *m* mud, mire
Eabhra *n f* Hebrew (*language*)
Eabhra(idhea)ch *n* **-aich, -aich** *m* Hebrew *a* Hebrew
eacarsaich *n* **-e, -ean** *f* exercise; capering about
each *n* **eich, eich** *m* horse **e.-aibhne** hippopotamus **e.-uisge** water-horse, kelpie
eachdraiche *n* **-an** *m* historian
eachdraidh *n* **-e, -ean** *f* history, chronicle
eachdraidheil *a* **-e** historic, historical
eaconamach *a* economic, economical
eaconamachd *n f* economics
eaconamaidh *n* **-ean** *m* economy
eaconamair *n* **-ean** *m* economist
eaconamas *n* **-ais** *m* economics **e. dachaigh** home economics
Eadailteach *n* **-tich, -tich** *m* Italian *a* Italian
Eadailtis *n f* Italian (*language*)
eadar *prep* (+ *len*) between **e. ... agus ...** both ... and ... **e. bheag is mhòr** both large and small **e. dhà bharail** in two minds *Does not always lenite*
eadaraibh(se) *prep pron* between you (*pl & pol*)
eadarainn(e) *prep pron* between us

eadar-àm *n* **-ama** *m* **-amannan** *m* interim period, interval **anns an e.** in the interim, meantime
eadar-bhreith *n* **-e, -ean** *f* arbitration
eadar-bhreithnich *v* **-neachadh** arbitrate
eadar-dhà-lionn *adv* floundering; hesitating, undecided
eadar-dhà-shian *n f* a break in a spell of adverse weather
eadar-dhealachadh *n* **-aidh, -aidhean** *m* difference, distinction, differentiation
eadar-dhealaich *v* **-achadh** distinguish, differentiate, discriminate
eadar-dhealaichte *a* different, distinctive **e. bho** distinct from
eadar-ghuidhe *n* **-achan** *m* intercession, mediation
eadar-lìon *n* **-lìn** *m* **an t-Eadar-lìon** the Internet
eadar-mheadhanach *a* intermediate
eadar-mheadhanair *n* **-ean** *m* intermediary; Redeemer (*relig*)
eadar-nàiseanta *a* international
eadar-roinneil *a* inter-departmental, inter-regional
eadar-sholas *n* **-ais** *m* twilight
eadar-theangachadh *n* **-aidh, -aidhean** *m* translation (*of languages*) **e. mar-aon** simultaneous translation
eadar-theangaich *v* **-achadh** translate
eadar-theangaiche *n* **-an** *m* translator
eadar-ùine *n f* interval, intermission
eadhon *adv* even
eadradh *n* **-aidh, -aidhean** *m* milking time
eadraiginn *n* **-e, -ean** *f* intervention, mediation **rach san e.** *v* intervene, mediate
eag *n* **eige, -an** *f* nick, notch, jag
eagach *a* **-aiche** jagged, serrated, notched
eagal *n* **-ail** *m* fear, fright **an robh an t-eagal ort?** were you afraid? **bha e. mo bheatha orm** I was scared stiff **air e. 's gum faic iad sinn** in case/lest they see us
eagalach *a* **-aiche** fearful, afraid; frightful, dreadful **e. fuar** fearfully cold
eag-eòlas *n* **-ais** *m* ecology
eaglais *n* **-e, -ean** *f* church **E. na h-Alba** the Church of Scotland **an E. Bhaisteach** the Baptist Church **an E. Chaitligeach** the Catholic Church **an E. Easbaigeach** the Episcopal Church **an E. Shaor** the Free Church **an E. Shaor Chlèireach** the Free Presbyterian Church **an E. Stèidhichte** the Established Church
eagnaidh *a* **-e** exact, precise
eagranaich *v* **-achadh** arrange, organize, place in order
eala *n* **-chan** *f* swan
èalaidh *v* **-adh** creep, move stealthily, steal away
ealain *n* **-e, -ean** *f* art **Comhairle nan E.** the Arts Council
ealamh *a* **-aimhe** quick, swift, ready
ealanta *a* skilful, skilled, ingenious, expert, artistic
ealantas *n* **-ais** *m* skill, ingenuity
ealla *n f* watching **gabh e. ris** take stock of it, watch him
eallach *n* **-aich, -aich** *m* burden, load
ealt *n* **-a, -an** *f* flock of birds; bird life
ealtainn *n* **-e, -ean** *f* razor
eanchainn *n* **-e, -ean** *f* brain **tha deagh e. aice** she has a good brain
eangarra *a* irritable, cross
eanraich *n* **-e** *f* soup
ear *n f* east **an ear** the east **Cille Bhrìghde an Ear** East Kilbride **chaidh iad an ear 's an iar** they scattered **an ear-dheas** the south-east **an ear-thuath** the north-east **an Ear Mheadhanach** the Middle East
earail *n* **-alach -alaichean** *f* exhortation; warning
earalaich *v* **-achadh** exhort, caution; warn

earalas *n* **-ais** *m* foresight, precaution
earb *n* **-a, -aichean** *f* roe-deer
earb *v* **earbsa** trust, rely, confide
earball *n* **-aill, -aill** *m* tail
earbsa *n f* reliance, confidence, trust **cha chuirinn e. ann** I wouldn't trust him/it
earbsach *a* **-aiche** reliable, trustworthy
eàrlas *n* **-ais, -ais** *m* pledge, token **e. clàir** record token
eàrr *n* **-a, -an** *m* tail, end, conclusion **e.-ràdh** *m* tailpiece
earrach *n* **-aich, -aich** *m* spring **as t-e.** in spring
earrann *n* **-ainn, -an** *f* section, portion, sector; (*fin*) share; (*liter*) passage, verse *Also* **earrainn**
earranta *a* limited (*as of company*)
eas *n* **-a, -an** *m* waterfall, cascade, cataract
easag *n* **-aig, -an** *f* pheasant
eas-aonta *n* **-n** *f* disagreement, dissent, discord, disunity
eas-aontach *a* **-aiche** dissenting, dissident, discordant
eas-aontachd *n* **-an** *f* disagreement, dissent, discord, disunity
eas-aontaich *v* **-achadh** disagree, dissent
easaontas *n* **-ais** *m* disobedience, transgression
easbaig *n* **-e, -ean** *m* bishop **àrd-e.** archbishop
Easbaigeach *n* **-gich, -gich** *m* Episcopalian *a* Episcopalian, episcopal
easbhaidh *n* **-e, -ean** *f* want, lack, defect **chan eil càil a dh'e. oirnn** we lack for nothing
easbhaidheach *a* **-dhiche** deficient, defective
eascaraid *n* **-cairdean** *m* enemy, foe
èasgaidh *a* **-e** willing, ready (to), keen, obliging; active
easgann *n* **-ainn, -an** *f* eel
eas-onair *n* **-e** *f* dishonour
eas-onarach *a* **-aiche** dishonest, dishonourable
eas-umhail *a* **-e** disobedient, insubordinate
eas-ùmhlachd *n f* disobedience, insubordination
eas-urram *n* **-aim** *m* dishonour, disrespect
eas-urramach *a* **-aiche** dishonourable, disrespectful
eathar *n* **-air, eathraichean** *f m* boat
eatarra(san) *prep pron* between them
èibh *n* **-e, -ean** *f* shout, call, cry
èibh *v* **-each** shout, call, cry
èibhinn *a* **-e** funny, amusing, humorous
èibhleag *n* **-eige, -an** *f* live coal, cinder
èideadh *n* **-didh, -didhean** *m* dress, clothing, garb, uniform
eidheann *n* **eidhne** *f* ivy
èifeachd *n f* effectiveness, efficacy
èifeachdach *a* **-aiche** effective, effectual, efficient
èifeachdail *a* **-e** effectual, effective
Eigeach *n* **Eigich, Eigich** *m* someone from Eigg *a* from, or pertaining to, Eigg
eigh *n* **-e** *f* ice
èigh *n* **-e, -ean** *f* shout, call, cry
èigh *v* **-each** shout, call, cry
eighe *n* **-achan** *f* file (*impl*)
èigheach *n* **-ghich** *f* shouting, calling, proclamation *Also* **èigheachd**
eighre *n f* ice
-eigin *suff* some **cuideigin** someone **rudeigin** something
èiginn *n f* necessity, emergency, straits **air è.** only just, with difficulty **ann an è.** as a last resort
èiginneach *a* **-niche** desperate, essential *Also* **èigeannach**
èignich *v* **èigneachadh** compel, force; rape
eil *irr v* was, were (*never used on its own*) (*See verb* **to be** *in Grammar*)
Eilbheiseach *n* **-sich, -sich** *m* someone from Switzerland *a*

Swiss
èildear *n* **-eir, -an** *m* (church) elder
eile *a* other, another, else **fear e.** another one (*m*) **tè e.** another one (*f*) **cò e.?** who else?
èileadh *n See* **fèileadh**
eileamaid *n* **-e, -ean** *f* element
eilean *n* **-ein, -an** *m* island, isle
eileanach *n* **-aich, -aich** *m* islander
eileatrom *n* **-oim, -an** *m* hearse, bier
eilid *n* **èilde, èildean** *f* hind
eilthireach *n* **-rich, -rich** *m* exile, alien
eilthireachd *n f* exile
einnsean *n* **-ein, -an** *m* engine **e.-smàlaidh** fire engine
einnseanair *n* **-ean** *m* engineer
Èipheiteach *n* **-tich, -tich** *m* Egyptian *a* Egyptian
eireachdail *a* **-e** handsome, comely
eireag *n* **-eige, -an** *f* pullet, young hen
Èireannach *n* **-aich, -aich** *m* Irish person *a* Irish
èirich *v* **èirigh** rise, arise, get up; happen to, befall **dè dh'èirich dhaibh?** what happened to them? **chan eil càil ag èirigh dhaibh** they are all right, they are coming to no harm
èirig *n* **-e, -ean** *f* ransom, forfeit, reparation
èirigh *n f* rising, arising, getting up, uprising
Èirisgeach *n* **-gich, -gich** *m* someone from Eriskay *a* from, or pertaining to, Eriskay
eirmseach *a* **-siche** witty, sharp-witted
èis *n* **-e, -ean** *f* need, want; delay, impediment **Clann ann an Èis** Children in Need
èiseil *a* **-e** needy, urgently required
eisimeil *n* **-e** *f* dependence **an e. air** dependent on **an e. Dhòmhnaill** dependent on Donald
eisimeileach *a* **-liche** dependent
eisimpleir *n* **-ean** *f m* example **mar e.** for example
eisir *n* **-ean** *m* oyster
eisirean *n* **-ein, -an** *m* scallop, clam
èislean *n* **-ein** *m* grief, sorrow **fo è.** sorrowing, dejected
èist *v* **-eachd** (**+ ri**) listen (to) *Formerly* **èisd**
èisteachd *n f* listening, audition; confession (*relig*) **luchd-e.** *m* audience *Formerly* **èisdeachd**
eòlach *a* **-aiche** knowledgeable, acquainted (with) **a bheil thu e. air?** do you know him/it?
eòlaiche *n* **-an** *m* expert **e.-inntinn** psychologist
eòlas *n* **-ais, -an** *m* knowledge, acquaintance **e.-bodhaig** anatomy **e.-inntinn** psychology **cuir e. air** *v* get to know
eòrna *n m* barley **Tìr an E.** *lit* the Land of the Barley (*a poetic name for the island of Tiree*)
Eòrpach *n* **-aich, -aich** *m* European *a* **-aiche** European
esan *emph pron* he, him, it
eu- *neg pref* dis-, in-, mis-, un- *etc*
euchd *n* **-an** *m* feat, exploit, achievement
eucoir *n* **eucorach, -ean** *f* crime, misdemeanour, misdeed
eu-còir *a* **-e** unkind, stingy
eu-coltach *a* **-aiche** unlike, dissimilar, unlikely
eu-coltas *n* **-ais** *m* unlikelihood, dissimilarity
eu-comas *n* **-ais, -an** *m* inability
eu-comasach *a* **-aiche** (**+ do**) unable (to)
eucorach *n* **-aich, -aich** *m* criminal, miscreant, rascal **'s e e. a th' ann** he's a rascal
eud *n m* zeal, jealousy
eudach *n* **-aich** *m* jealousy **bha e ag e. rithe** he was jealous of her *a* **-aiche** jealous
eudail *n* **-ean** *f* dear, darling, treasure **m' eudail** my dear
eudar *n See* **feudar**
eudmhor *a* **-oire** zealous; jealous
eu-dòchas *n* **-ais** *m* hopelessness, despair

eu-dòchasach *a* **-aiche** hopeless, despairing
eu-domhainn *a* **-e** shallow
eug *n* **èig** *m* death
eug *def v* die, decease **dh'eug e** he died
eugsamhail *a* **-e/-mhla** various, manifold, miscellaneous, incomparable
eun *n* **eòin, eòin** *m* bird, fowl **e. dubh an sgadain** guillemot **e.-eòlas** *m* ornithology **e.-Frangach** turkey **e.-fraoich** grouse, moorhen **e.-mara** seabird **e.-tràghad** wader **e.-tumaidh** diver **eunlann** *f m* cage, aviary
eunach *n* **-aich** *m* fowling
eunadair *n* **-ean** *m* fowler
eunlaith *n* **-e** *f* birds, fowls, bird life
euslaint *n* **-e, -ean** *f* ill-health, sickness
euslainteach *n* **-tich, -tich** *m* invalid, patient
euslainteach *a* **-tiche** ill, sickly, unhealthy

F

fàbhar *n* **-air, -an** *m* favour
fàbharach *a* **-aiche** favourable; providential
fabhra *n* **-n** *m* eyelid
facal *n* **-ail, -ail/faclan** *m* word **f. air an fhacal** word for word
fa chomhair *prep phr* (+ *gen*) opposite
faclair *n* **-ean** *m* dictionary
facs *n* **-aichean** *m* fax
factaraidh *n* **-ean** *f m* factory
fad *n* **faid** *m* length, distance **air f.** all, altogether **air fhad** lengthways **f. an latha** all day **f. an t-siubhail** all the time **fhad 's** while
fàd *n* **fàid/fòid, -an** *m* a peat
fada *a* **faide** long **dè cho f.?** how long? **fad' às** distant, remote **f. nas fheàrr** much better **gun èirigh** late getting up **fad-ùine** long term **'s fhada bhon uair sin** long time no see
fadachd *n f* longing, yearning **bha f. oirnn ...** we were longing for ... **a' gabhail f.** longing, wearying
fadalach *a* **-aiche** late, slow
fadhail *n* **-ail/fadhlach, fadhlaichean** *f* ford
fad-fhulangach *a* **-fhulangaiche** long-suffering
fa-dheòidh *adv* at last
fàg *v* **-ail** leave; depart, go **f. air** accuse, allege
fagas *a* **faisge** near **am f.** near
faghaid *n* **-e, -ean** *f* hunt
faic *v* **-inn** see (*See irr v* **faic** *in Grammar*)
faiceall *n* **-cill** *f* care, caution *Also* **faicill**
faiceallach *a* **-aiche** careful, cautious, wary **bi f.!** be careful! *Also* **faicilleach**
faiche *n* **-an** *f* lawn, plain, meadow
faicsinneach *a* **-niche** visible, conspicuous
fàidh *n* **-e, -ean** *m* prophet
faidhbhile *n* **-an** *f m* beech
fàidheadaireachd *n* **-an** *f* prophecy
faidhle *n* **-achan** *m* file
faigh *v* **-inn** get, obtain, acquire, receive **f. a-mach** find out, ascertain
faighean *n* **-ein, -an** *m* vagina
faighnich *v* **-neachd** question, ask, enquire **f. dhith** ask her
failbheachan *n* **-ain** *m* earring
failc *n* **-e, -ean** *f* guillemot
fàileadh *n* **-(e)idh, -(e)idhean** *m* smell
faileas *n* **-eis, -an** *m* shadow
faileasach *a* **-aiche** shadowy
fàil(l)idh *a* **-e** stealthy **gu f.** quietly
faillich *v* **-leachadh** (+ **air**) defeat **dh'fhaillich e orm** I failed to do it/I couldn't manage it/he got the better of me *Also* **fairtlich**
fàillig *v* **-eadh** fail
fàilligeadh *n* **-gidh, -gidhean** *m* failure; flaw, defect
failmean *n* **-ein, -an** *m* kneecap
fail-mhuc *n* **failean-** *f* pigsty
fàilneachadh *n* **-aidh, -aidhean** *m*

failing
fàilt(e) *n* **-(e)an** *f* welcome **cuir f. air ...** *v* welcome ... **ceud mìle f.** a hundred thousand welcomes, the warmest of welcomes
fàilteachadh *n* **-aidh** *m* welcoming, reception
fàiltich *v* **-teachadh** welcome, greet
fàiltiche *n* **-an** *m* receptionist
faing *n* **-e, -ean** *f* fank, sheep-pen
fàinne *n* **-achan** *f m* ring **f.-cluaise** earring **f.-gealladh-pòsaidh** engagement ring **f.-pòsaidh** wedding ring
faire *n* **-an** *f* watch, watching, guard **neach-f.** guard
fàire *n* **-an** *f* horizon **air f.** on the horizon
faireachadh *n* **-aidh** *m* feeling, sensation, sense
faireachdainn *n* **-ean** *f* feeling, sensation, sense
fàireag *n* **-eig, -an** *f* gland
fairge *n* **-achan/-annan** *f* sea, ocean
fairich *v* **-reachdainn/-reachadh** feel, sense
fairtleachadh *n* **-aidh** *m* failing
faisg *a* **-e** near **nas fhaisge** nearer **f. air** near/close (to)
fàisg *v* **fàsgadh** squeeze, press
fàisneachd *n* **-an** *f* prophecy
fàisnich *v* **-neachadh** prophesy
fàitheam *n* **-eim, -an** *m* hem
fàl *n* **fàil, fàil** *m* hedge, dyke **fàl an rathaid** (*of road*) verge
falach *n* **-aich** *m* hiding-place, concealment **cuir am f. e** *v* hide it **chaidh iad am f.** they hid **f.-fead** hide and seek
falaich *v* **-ach**, hide, conceal
falaichte *a* hidden, concealed, secret
falamh *a* **-aimhe** empty, void
falamhachd *n* *f* emptiness, vacuum
falbh *v* go **air f.** gone away
falbhanach *a* **-aiche** wandering, unsettled
fallain *a* **-e** healthy, wholesome, sound **slàn f.** safe and sound
fallaineachd *n* *f* health
fallas *n* **-ais** *m* sweat, perspiration **bha (am) f. orm** I was sweating
fallasach *a* **-aiche** sweaty
falmadair *n* **-ean** *m* helm
falmhaich *v* **-achadh** empty
falt *n* **fuilt, fuilt** *m* hair
famh *n* **faimh, faimh/-an** *f m* mole (*animal*)
famhair *n* **-ean** *m* giant
fan *v* **-tainn** wait, stay, remain
fanaid *n* **-e** *f* mockery, mocking, derision **a' dèanamh f. air** *v* mocking him, deriding it
fànas *n* **-ais** *m* outer space **f.-long** *f* spaceship
fa-near *adv* under consideration **thoir f.** notice, observe, be aware of
fang *n* **faing, faing/-an** *m* fank, sheep-pen
fann *a* **-a/fainne** faint, feeble, weak
fannaich *v* **-achadh** grow faint, faint, weaken
fanntaig *v* **-eadh** faint
faobhar *n* **-air, -an** *m* edge (*as of knife*) **cuir f. air** *v* sharpen it
faobharaich *v* **-achadh** sharpen
faochag *n* **-aig, -an** *f* whelk, winkle
faod *def v* may, can **am f. mi smocadh?** may I smoke? **faodaidh tu fuireach** you may/can wait/stay
faoileag *n* **-eig, -an** *f* seagull
faoilidh *a* **-e** generous, liberal, hospitable
Faoilleach/Faoilteach *n* **-lich/-tich** *m* **am F.** January
faoin *a* **-e** vain, silly, pointless, futile
faoineas *n* **-eis** *m* vanity, futility **'s e f. a th' ann** it's pointless
faoinsgeul *n* **-eil/-a, -an** *m* idle talk, fiction, myth
faoisid *n* **-e, -ean** *f* confession (*relig*)
faoisidich *v* **-deachadh** confess (*relig*)
fao(tha)chadh *n* **-aidh** *m* relief, respite
far *prep See* **bhàrr**

far *conj* where **sin far a bheil iad** that's where they are
faradh *n* **-aidh, -aidhean** *m* fare (*price*)
fàradh *n* **-aidh, -aidhean** *m* ladder
far-ainm *n* **-e, -ean** *m* nickname
faram *n* **-aim** *m* loud noise; percussion
faramach *a* **-aiche** noisy, resounding
farasta *See* **furasta**
farchluais *n* **-e** *f* eavesdropping *Also vn* **a' f.**
fàrdach *n* **-aich, -aichean** *f* house, dwelling, lodging
farmad *n* **-aid** *m* envy
farmadach *a* **-aiche** envious
farpais *n* **-e, -ean** *f* competition
farpaiseach *n* **-sich, -sich** *m* competitor
farsaing *a* **-e** wide, wide-ranging, extensive **fad' is f.** far and wide
farsaingeachd *n f* width, extent, area **san fharsaingeachd** in general, on the whole
farsainn *a* **-e** *See* **farsaing**
farspag *n* **-aig, -an** *f* great black-backed gull
fàs *n* **fàis** *m* growth
fàs *a* **-a** empty, waste, desolate, fallow
fàs *v* grow, become **a' fàs sean** getting/growing old
fàsach *n* **-aich, -an** *f m* wilderness, desert
fàsachadh *n* **-aidh, -aidhean** *m* depopulation
fàsaich *v* **-achadh** depopulate, clear (*of people*), lay waste
fàsail *a* **-e/-ala** desolate (*of places*)
fasan *n* **-ain, -ain/-an** *m* fashion
fasanta *a* fashionable
fasgach *a* **-aiche** sheltered
fasgadh *n* **-aidh, -aidhean** *m* shelter
fa sgaoil *adv* loose
fasgnadh *n* **-aidh** *m* winnowing
fastadh *n* **-aidh, -aidhean** *m* hiring, employing, employment *Formerly* **fasdadh**
fastaidh *v* **-adh** hire, employ *Formerly* **fasdaidh**
fastaidhear *n* **-an** *m* employer *Formerly* **fasdaidhear**
fàth *n m* reason, cause, opportunity
fathann *n* **-ainn, -an** *m* rumour, hearsay
feabhas *n* **-ais** *m* improvement **a' dol am f.** getting better, improving, healing
feachd *n* **-an** *f* army, host **F. an Adhair** the (Royal) Air Force
fead *n* **-an** *f* whistle (*by person*) **dèan/geàrr f.** *v* whistle
fead *v* **-ail/-alaich/-arsaich/ -aireachd** whistle
feadag *n* **-aige, -an** *f* whistle, flute; plover
feadaireachd *n f* whistling
feadan *n* **-ain, -ain** *m* chanter (*of bagpipes*); water pipe, water duct
feadh *n m* length **air f.** throughout, during (+ *gen*) **am f.** while, whilst
feadhainn *n* **feadhna/feadhnach** *f* people, some **f. aca** some of them **an fheadhainn sin** those **an fheadhainn dhearg** the red ones
feagal *n See* **eagal**
feàirrde *a* better **'s fheàirrd' thu sin** you are the better of that **b' fheàirrde mi norrag** I'd be the better of a nap
fealla-dhà *n f* fun, jest **ri f.** in fun/jest
feall-fhalach *n* **-aich, -aichean** *m* ambush
feallsanach *n* **-aich, -aich** *m* philosopher
feallsanachd *n* **-an** *f* philosophy
feamainn *n* **-ann/-mnach/ feamad** *f* seaweed
feann *v* **-adh** skin, flay
feannag *n* **-aige, -an** *f* crow; lazybed (*for planting*), rig
feanntag *n* **-aige, -an** *f m* nettle
feansa *n* **-ichean** *f m* fence
fear *n* **fir, fir** *m* man, male, one (*referring to masculine subject*) **am f. sin** that one **f. sam bith** anyone **f. an taighe** chairman (*of concert*)

fearail *a* **-e/-ala** manly, manful, brave
fearalachd *n f* manliness, manfulness
fearann *n* **-ainn** *m* land, ground **am mòr-fhearann** the common grazing
fearas-chuideachd *n* **fearais-** *f* diversion, pastime
fearas-feise *n* **fearais-** *f* homosexuality
fear-bainnse *n* **fir-, fir-** *m* bridegroom *Also* **fear na bainnse**
fear-brèige *n* **fir-bhrèige, fir-** *m* puppet **na Fir Bhrèige** the Callanish Stones
fear-bùtha *n* **fir-, fir-** *m* shopkeeper *Also* **fear na bùtha**
fear-cathrach *n* **fir-, fir-** *m* chairman *Also* **fear na cathrach**
fear-ceàird *n* **fir-, fir-** *m* tradesman
fear-ciùil *n* **fir-, fir-** *m* musician
fear-deasachaidh *n* **fir-, fir-** *m* editor
fear-ealain *n* **fir-, fir-** *m* artist
feareigin *pron* someone (*male*)
fearg *n* **feirge** *f* anger, ire, wrath **cuir f. air** *v* anger, annoy **bha an fhearg air** he was angry/annoyed
feargach *a* **-aiche** angry
fear-gnothaich *n* **fir-, fir-** *m* businessman
fear-labhairt *n* **fir-, fir-** *m* spokesman
fear-lagha *n* **fir-, fir-** *m* lawyer (*male*)
feàrna *n f* alder
fear-pòsta *n* **fir-phòsta, fir-phòsta** *m* married man
feàrr *a* better **nas fheàrr** better **is fheàrr leis ...** he prefers ... **is fheàrr dhi ...** she had better ...
fearsaid *n* **-e, -ean** *f* spindle
fear-smàlaidh *n* **fir-, fir-** *m* fireman
fear-stiùiridh *n* **fir-, fir-** *m* director (*male*)
feart *n* **feirt, -an** *f* notice, attention **na toir f. air** pay no heed to him/it
feart *n* **-a, -an** *m* quality, virtue, characteristic
fear-teagaisg *n* **fir-, fir-** *m* teacher (*male*)
fear-togail *n* **fir-, fir-** *m* builder
feasgar *n* **-air, -air/-an** *m* afternoon, evening *adv* in the afternoon/evening **F. math** Good afternoon/evening **f. Diluain** Monday afternoon/evening
fèath *n* **-a, -an** *f m* calm (*weather*) **bha f. ann** it was calm
fèathach *a* calm (*weather*)
fèileadh *n* **-lidh, -lidhean** *m* kilt
fèill *n* **-e, -(t)ean** *f* festival; fair, market, sale **bha f. mhòr air** it/he was in great demand
fèin *pron* self, selves
fèin-àicheadh *n* **-eidh** *m* self-denial
fèin-dhìon *n* **-a** *m* self-defence
fèin-eachdraidh *n* **-e, -ean** *f* autobiography
fèineil *a* **-e, -eala** selfish
fèin-ìobairt *n* **-e, -ean** *f* self-sacrifice
fèin-mheas *n m* self-respect
fèin-mhurt *n* **-mhuirt** *m* suicide
fèin-riaghladh *n* **-aidh** *m* self-government
fèin-spèis *n* **-e** *f* self-regard, conceit, egotism
fèis *n* **-e, -ean** *f* festival **f. ciùil** music festival **Fèisean nan Gàidheal** the Festivals of the Gaels
feis(e) *n* **-e** *f* sexual intercourse, copulation
fèist *n* **-e, -ean** *f* feast, banquet *Formerly* **fèisd**
fèith *n* **-e, -ean** *f* vein, sinew, muscle
fèith *n* **-e, -ichean** *f* bog, marsh; channel
feith *v* **-eamh** await, wait (for)
fèitheach *a* **-thiche** sinewy, muscular
feòil *n* **feòla** *f* meat **f.-caorach** *n* mutton **f.-muice** pork **f.-uan** lamb **mairt-fheòil** beef
feòirling *n* **-ean** *f* farthing
feòladair *n* **-ean** *m* butcher
feòlmhor *a* **-a/-oire** carnal, sensual
feòrag *n* **-aig, -an** *f* squirrel
feòraich *v* **-ach/-achadh** ask, inquire

feuch *v* **-ainn** try, test; see **f. ri ...** try to ... **f. gun tadhail thu** see and call/be sure to call **f. nach tuit thu** watch/see that you don't fall
feudar *def v* must **'s fheudar gu bheil ...** it would seem that ... **b' fheudar dhaibh** they had to
feum *n* **-a, -annan** *f m* use, need **a bheil f. agad air?** do you need it/him?
feum *def v* have to, need to, must **feumaidh mi falbh** I'll have to go **am f. thu sin a dhèanamh?** must you do that?
feumach *a* **-aiche** needy **bha sinn f. air** we needed it
feumail *a* **-e/-ala** useful
feumalachd *n f* use, utility, expediency
feur *n* **feòir** *m* grass, hay
feurach *n* **-aich** *m* pasture, grazing
feurach *a* **-aiche** grassy
feuraich *v* **-achadh** graze
feusag *n* **-aig, -an** *f* beard
feusagach *a* **-aiche** bearded
feusgan *n* **-ain, -ain** *m* mussel
fhad is a *conj* while, whilst
fhathast *adv* yet, still
fhèin *pron* self, selves (*often used with* **tha** *when returning question*) **leatha f.** by herself, alone
fhìn *pron Variation on* **fhèin** (*in first person only*)
fhuair *irr v* got (*See irr v* **faigh** *in Grammar*)
fiabhras *n* **-ais, -an** *m* fever
fiabhrasach *a* **-aiche** feverish
fiacail *n* **fiacla, fiaclan** *f* tooth **fiaclan fuadain** false teeth
fiach *n* **feich, -an** *m* worth, value; debt **fo fhiachaibh** indebted to, owing to **cuir mar fhiachaibh air** *v* oblige, compel **mar fhiachaibh oirnn(e)** incumbent upon us
fiach *a* **-a** worthwhile, worth **cha d' fhiach e** it's useless **is fhiach dhut seo fhaicinn** you should see this **'s fhiach e an t-saothair** it's worth the effort
fiach *v See* **feuch**
fiaclair *n* **-ean** *m* dentist
fiadh *n* **fèidh, fèidh** *m* deer
fiadhaich *a* **-aiche** wild, fierce; angry, furious
fialaidh *a* **-e** generous, liberal
fialaidheachd *n f* generosity, liberality
fiamh *n* **-a** tinge, hue; fear; expression **f. a' ghàire** a hint of a smile
fianais *n* **-ean** *f* witness, evidence, testimony **tog f.** *v* give evidence; profess faith publicly **thoir f.** *v* witness, testify **am f.** in sight/view
fiar *a* **-a** crooked, bent, squint, slanted **f.-shùileach** squint-eyed
fiaradh *n* **-aidh** *m* bend, squint, slant **air f.** slanting, askew
fiathachadh *n* **-aidh, -aidhean** *m* invitation
fiathaich *v* **-achadh** invite
fichead *n* **fichid, -an** *m* twenty (+ *sg*) **trì f.** sixty
ficheadamh *a* twentieth
fideag *n* **-eig, -an** *f* whistle
fidheall *n* **fìdhle, fìdhlean** *f* fiddle, violin
fìdhlear *n* **-eir, -an** *m* fiddler, violinist
fìdhlearachd *n f* fiddling
fìge *n* **-an** *f* fig
figear *n* **-eir, -an** *m* figure (*arithmetic*)
figh *v* **-e** knit, weave
fighe *n f* knitting, weaving
figheadair *n* **-ean** *m* knitter, weaver
fighte *a* knitted, woven
fileanta *a* fluent
fileantach *n* **-aich, -aich** *m* fluent speaker
fileantachd *n f* fluency
filidh *n* **-ean** *m* poet
fill *v* **-eadh** fold; wrap
filleadh *n* **-lidh, -lidhean** *m* fold, plait
fillte *a* folded, plaited, compound
fine *n* **-achan** *f* clan, tribe, kindred
fìnealta *a* fine, elegant
finn-fuainneach *a* all, entire **fad f. an latha** the livelong day, all day long
fiodh *n* **-a** *m* wood, timber

fìogais *n* **-ean** *f* fig
fiolan *n* **-ain, -an** *m* beetle, earwig **f.-gòbhlach** earwig
fìon *n* **-a** *m* wine **f. dearg** red wine **f. geal** white wine **f.-dhearc** *f* grape **f.-geur** vinegar **f.-lios** *m* vineyard
fìonan *n* **-ain, -ain/-an** *m* vine
fionn *a* **-a** white, fair
fionnach *a* **-aiche** hairy
fionnadh *n* **-aidh** *m* hair (*of animals*)
fionnairidh *n* **-ean** *f* evening **air an fhionnairidh** in the evening
fionnan-feòir *n* **fionnain-, fionnain-** *m* grasshopper
fionnar *a* **-aire/-a** cool (*temp*)
fionnarachadh *n* **-aidh** *m* refrigeration
fionnarachd *n f* coolness (*temp*)
fionnaradair *n* **-ean** *m* refrigerator
fionnaraich *v* **-achadh** cool, refrigerate
fionnsgeul *n* **-eil/-eòil, -an** *m* legend
fìor *a* **-a/fìre** (*precedes & lenites n*) true, real, genuine, actual; very/really **f. mhath** very good **f. amadan** a real fool
fios *n* **-a** *m* knowledge, information **tha f. aice** she knows **cò aige tha f.?** who knows? **fhuair sinn f.** we got word **gun fhios nach ...** in case, lest ... **cuir f. thuca** *v* send them word **tha f. gun tadhail iad** surely they'll call
fiosaiche *n* **-an** *m* fortune-teller, seer
fios-naidheachd *n* **fiosan-** *m* press release
fiosrach *a* **-aiche** knowledgeable, well-informed
fiosrachadh *n* **-aidh, -aidhean** *m* information; experience
fiosraich *v* **-achadh** experience
fiosraichte *a* knowledgeable, informed
fir chlis *n m pl* **na F.** the Aurora Borealis, Northern Lights
fìreanachadh *n* **-aidh** *m* justification
fìreanaich *v* **-achadh** justify
fìreann *a* male, masculine
fìreannach *n* **-aich, -aich** *m* man, male
fìreantachd *n f* righteousness
fìr-eun *n* **-eòin, -eòin** *m* eagle
fìrinn *n* **-e, -ean** *f* truth, fact **an fhìrinn a th' agam** I'm telling the truth, it's true **a dh'innse na f.** to tell the truth **an Fhìrinn** the Bible
fìrinneach *a* **-niche** truthful, factual
fitheach *n* **fithich, fithich** *m* raven
fiù *n m* worth, value **gun fhiù** worthless, useless
fiù *a* worth **fiù is/'s** even **cha robh fiù 's sèithear ann** there wasn't even a chair there
fiùdalach *a* **-aiche** feudal
fiùdalachd *n f* feudalism
flaitheanas *n* **-ais** *m* heaven, paradise
flaitheas *n* **-eis** *m* heaven, paradise
flat *n* **-aichean** *f m* flat; saucer (*Lewis*)
flath *n* **flaith, -an/flaithean** *m* prince, chief
flathail *a* **-e** princely, noble
fleadh *n* **-a, -an** *m* feast, banquet
fleasgach *n* **-aich, -aich** *m* bachelor, youth; best man (*at wedding*)
fleòdradh *n* **-aidh** *m* floating, buoyancy **air f.** afloat
fleòdraich *v* **-radh** float
flin(ne) *n* **-(e)** *m* sleet
fliuch *a* **fliche/fliuiche** wet
fliuch *v* **-adh** wet, moisten
flod *n* **-a** *m* floating, flotation **air f.** floating, afloat
flodach *a* **-aiche** lukewarm (*liquid*)
flùr *n* **flùir, -aichean** *m* flower
flùr *n* **flùir** *m* flour
flùranach *a* **-aiche** flowery
fo *prep* (+ *dat*) under, below, beneath; under the influence of **fon bhòrd** under the table **fo mhulad** sad
fo-aodach *n* **-aich** *m* underclothes, underwear
fochann *n* **-ainn** *m* corn in blade
fo-cheumnaiche *n* **-an** *m* undergraduate

fo-chomataidh *n* **-ean** *f* sub-committee
fod *aug prep* under your (*sg*)
fòd/fòid *n* **fòide, -ean** *f* turf, peat, clod **fon fhòid** underground, buried
fodar *n* **-air** *m* fodder, straw
fodha *adv* underneath, sunken **chaidh am bàta f.** the boat went down/sank
fodha(san) *prep pron* under him/it; below him/it
fodhad(sa) *prep pron* under/ below you (*sg*)
fodhaibh(se) *prep pron* under/ below you (*pl & pol*)
fodhainn(e) *prep pron* under/ below us
fodham(sa) *prep pron* under/ below me
fodhpa(san) *prep pron* under/ below them
fògair *v* **fògradh/-t** expel, banish
fògairt *n f* expelling, expulsion, banishing, banishment
fògarrach *n* **-aich** *m* exile, refugee
foghain *v* **fòghnadh** suffice **fòghnaidh sin** that will suffice **fòghnaidh na dh'fhòghnas!** enough is enough!
foghar *n* **-air** *m* autumn, harvest **am f.** autumn **as t-fhoghar** in autumn
foghlaim *v* **-am** educate, learn
foghlaim(ich)te *a* educated, learned
foghlam *n* **-aim** *m* education **f. tron Ghàidhlig** Gaelic-medium education
fòghnan *n* **-ain** *m* thistle **F. na h-Alba** the Thistle of Scotland
fògradh *n* **-aidh** *m* expelling, expulsion, banishing, banishment
foidhpe(se) *prep pron* under/ below her
foighidinn *n* **-e** *f* patience
foighidneach *a* **-niche** patient
foileag *n* **-eig, -an** *f* pancake
foill *n* **-e** *f* deceit, fraud, treachery
foillseachadh *n* **-aidh, -aidhean** *m* publishing, publication; revealing
foillsich *v* **-seachadh** publish; reveal
foillsichear *n* **-eir, -an** *m* publisher
foinne *n* **-an** *f m* wart
foirfe *a* perfect **dèan f.** *v* perfect
foirfeach *n* **-fich, -fich** *m* church elder
foirfeachd *n f* perfection
foirm *n* **-ean** *m* form (*document*)
foirmeil *a* **-e/-eala** formal
fòirneart *n* **-eirt** *m* violence, oppression
fois *n* **-e** *f* rest, leisure
follais *n f* openness, display, view, publicity **am f.** visible, displayed **thàinig e am f.** it became evident/public, it came to light
follaiseach *a* **-siche** obvious, evident, public
fom *aug prep* under my/their, below my/their
fòn *n* **-aichean** *f m* telephone
fòn/fònaig *v* **-adh/-eadh** telephone
fon *aug prep* under their, under the, below their, below the
fonn *n* **fuinn, fuinn** *m* tune, air; mood **dè 'm fonn a bh' air?** what form was he in?
fonnmhor *a* **-oire** *a* tuneful, melodious
for *aug prep* under our, below our; under your, below your
for *n* **foir** *m* awareness, alertness, attention **cha robh for aca gu ...** they had no idea that ...
forail *a* **-e** aware, alert
fo-rathad *n* **-aid/-rothaid, -an/-ròidean** *m* subway, underground route
forc(a) *n* **-a, -an/-aichean** *f* fork
fòr-chàin *n* **-e, -ean** *f* surtax
fòr-chìs *n* **-e, -ean** *f* surcharge
fòrladh *n* **-aidh** *m* leave, furlough
fo-roinn *n* **-e, -ean** *f* sub-division
forsair *n* **-ean** *m* forester
forsaireachd *n f* forestry
fortan *n* **-ain** *m* fortune, luck
fortanach *a* **-aiche** fortunate, lucky
fosgail *v* **-gladh** open
fosgailte *a* open, frank
fosgailteachd *n f* openness, frankness

fosgarra *a* open, frank, forthcoming, candid
fosgarrachd *n f* candour, openness
fo-sgiorta *n* **-ichean** *f* underskirt
fosgladh *n* **-aidh, -aidhean** *m* opening, aperture; opportunity
fosglair *n* **-ean** *m* opener (*implement*)
fo-thaghadh *n* **-aidh, -aidhean** *m* by-election
fo-thiotal *n* **-ail, -alan** *m* subtitle
fo-thìreach *a* subterranean
fradharc *n* **-airc** *m* eyesight, vision
Fraingis *n f* French (*language*)
Frangach *n* **-aich, -aich** *m* French person *a* French
fraoch *n* **-oich** *m* heather
fras *n* **froise, -an** *f* shower (*of rain*)
fras *v* **-adh** shower
frasach *a* **-aiche** showery
frasair *n* **-ean** *m* shower (*in bathroom*)
freagair *v* **-t/-gradh** answer, reply, respond; suit
freagairt *n* **-ean** *f* answer, reply, response
freagarrach *a* **-aiche** suitable, appropriate
frèam *n* **-a, -aichean** *m* frame, framework **f. streap** climbing frame
freastal *n* **-ail** *m* providence; service *Formerly* **freasdal**
freiceadan *n* **-ain, -ain/-an** *m* guard, watch
freumh *n* **-a, -an/-aichean** *m* root, source
freumhaich *v* **-achadh** root
frìde *n* **-an** *f* insect
frids *n* **-ichean** *m* fridge, refrigerator
frioghan *n* **-ain, -ain** *m* bristle, barb
frionas *n* **-ais** *m* fretfulness, vexation, over-sensitivity
frionasach *a* **-aiche** fretful, vexed, over-sensitive
frìth *n* **-e, -ean** *f* deer forest
frith-ainm *n* **-e, -ean** *m* nickname
frith-bhaile *n* **-ltean** *m* suburb
frithealadh *n* **-aidh** *m* service, attendance
fritheil *v* **-ealadh** attend, serve, wait on, minister (to)
frith-rathad *n* **-aid, -ròidean/-an** *m* lane, path
fròg *n* **fròige, -an** *f* hole, chink, niche, nook, den
froga *n* **-ichean** *m* frock
frogail *a* **-e** lively, cheerful
frois *v* **-eadh** scatter seed, thresh
fuachd *n* **-an** *m* cold (*atmos, med*) **bha am f. orm** I had the cold
fuadach *n* **-aich, -aichean** *m* banishment, expulsion **na Fuadaichean** the (Highland) Clearances
fuadaich *v* **-ach(adh)** expel, banish, chase away
fuadain *a* **-e** false, artificial
fuaigheal *n* **-eil** *m* seam, sewing
fuaigheil *v* **-eal** sew, stitch
fuaim *n* **-e, -ean** *f m* sound, noise
fuaimneach *a* **-niche** noisy
fuaimneachadh *n* **-aidh, -aidhean** *m* pronunciation
fuaimreag *n* **-eig, -an** *f* vowel
fuamhaire *n* **-an** *m* giant
fuar *a* **fuaire** cold
fuarachd *n f* dampness, mouldiness
fuaradair *n* **-ean** *m* refrigerator, fridge
fuaraich *v* **-achadh** cool, chill
fuaraidh *a* **-e** damp, chilly, mouldy
fuaralachd *n f* frigidity
fuaran *n* **-ain, -ain/-an** *m* spring (*water*), fountain
fuasgail *v* **-gladh** loosen, untie, release; solve, resolve
fuasgladh *n* **-aidh, -aidhean** *m* solution; release
fuath *n* **-a, -an** *m* hate, hatred, antipathy
fuathaich *v* **-achadh** hate, loathe, detest
fùc *v* **-adh** full (cloth), press, squeeze
fùdar *n* **-air, -an** *m* powder
fùdaraich *v* **-achadh** powder
fuidheall *n* **-dhill** *m* remainder, financial balance

fuigheall *n See* **fuidheall**
fuil *n* **fala** *f* blood, gore **f.-mìos** period (*menstrual*)
fuilear *n* necessity **chan fhuilear dhuinn** we need to **cha b' fhuilear dhaibh uile e** they would need it all
fuiling *v* **fulang** suffer, bear, endure
fuilteach *a* **-tiche** bloody
fuiltean *n* **-ein, -an** *m* single hair
fuin *v* **-e(adh)** bake
fuineadair *n* **-ean** *m* baker
fuireach *n* **-rich** *m* waiting, staying, dwelling
fuirich *v* **-reach** wait; stay, live **f. rium** wait for me **tha iad a' f. ann an Dùn Èideann** they live in Edinburgh
fùirneis *n* **-ean** *f* furnace
fulang *n* **-aing** *m* endurance, suffering
fulangach *a* **-aiche** suffering, patient; passive (*gram*) **fad-fhulangach** long-suffering
fulangas *n* **-ais** *m* suffering, passion (*of Christ*)
fulmair *n* **-e, -ean** *m* fulmar
furachail *a* **-e** watchful, vigilant, alert, attentive
furan *n* **-ain** *m* welcome, hospitality **fàilte is f.** a warm welcome
furasta *a* **fasa** easy **nas fhasa** easier *Formerly* **furasda**
furm *n* **fuirm, fuirm/furman** *m* form, bench; stool
furtachd *n f* relief, help, deliverance, solace
furtaich *v* **-achadh** relieve, aid, console

G

ga *aug prep* at his/its (+ *len*), at her/its **a bheil thu ga fhaicinn?** do you see him/it? **chan eil mi ga tuigsinn** I don't understand her
gabh *v* **-ail** take, hold; be possible **an do ghabh sibh biadh?** have you eaten? **g. brath air** take advantage of, exploit **g. os làimh** undertake **g. mo leisgeul** excuse me **g. ri** accept, adopt, approve **g. a-steach** include, encompass **g. òran** sing a song **cha ghabh e (a) chreidsinn** it's incredible **cho luath 's a ghabhas** as soon as possible **gabhaidh e ceud** it will hold a hundred
gàbhadh *n* **-aidh, -aidhean** *m* peril, danger
gàbhaidh *a* **-e** perilous, dangerous
gabhail *n* **-alach, -alaichean** *m* lease, tenure
gabhaltach *a* **-aiche** infectious, contagious
gabhaltas *n* **-ais** *m* tenancy, tenure
gach *a* each, every
gad *n* **goid, goid/-an** *m* withe; goad **gad èisg** a number of fish carried by a withe, wire or string
gad *aug prep* at your **chan eil mi gad chreidsinn** I don't believe you
gadaiche *n* **-an** *m* thief
gadhar *n* **-air, -air** *m* hound
gàg *n* **gàige, -an** *f* chink, fissure, chap in skin
gagach *a* **-aiche** stuttering, stammering
gàgail *n* **-e** *f* cackling
Gàidheal *n* **-eil, -eil** *m* Gael, Highlander
Gàidhealach *a* **-aiche** Highland **crodh G.** *m* Highland cattle
Gàidhealtachd *n f* **a' Ghàidhealtachd** the Highlands
Gàidhlig *n* **-e** *f* Gaelic **a bheil G. agad?** do you speak Gaelic? *a* Gaelic
gailbheach *a* **-bhiche** stormy
gailearaidh *n* **-ean** *m* gallery
gaileis *n f* braces *pl* **-ean** *Also* **galais**
gailleann *n* **-linn, -an** *f* storm, tempest
gainmheach *n* **-mhich/ gainmhche(adh)** *f* sand
gainne *n f* scarcity, shortage, want

gainnead *n* **-nid** *m* scarcity, shortage, want
gain(n)eamh *n* **-eimh** *f* sand
gàir *n* **-e, -ean** *m* shout, roar
gàir *v* **-eachdainn/-eachdaich** laugh
gairbhe *n f* thickness; roughness
gàirdeachas *n* **-ais** *m* rejoicing, joy **dèan g.** *v* rejoice
gàirdean *n* **-ein, -an** *m* arm
gàire *n f m* laugh **dèan g.** *v* laugh
gàireachdainn *n f* laughter, laughing *Also* **gàireachdaich**
gairm *n* **-e, -ean/-eannan** *f* call, cry, proclamation **g. coilich** cockcrow
gairm *v* call (out), cry (out), crow (*as cockerel*); summon **g. coinneamh** convene meeting
gairmeach *a* vocative **an tuiseal g.** the vocative case
gàirnealair *n* **-ean** *m* gardener
gàirnealaireachd *n f* gardening
gaiseadh *n* **-sidh, -sidhean** *m* defect in crops, blight **g. a' bhuntàta** potato blight
gaisgeach *n* **-gich, -gich** *m* hero, warrior, champion
gaisge(achd) *n f* heroism, bravery, valour
gaisgeil *a* **-e** heroic, brave, valorous
galan *n* **-ain, -an** *m* gallon
galar *n* **-air, -an** *m* disease **an g. roilleach/ronnach** foot and mouth disease *Also* **galair**
Gall *n* **Goill, Goill** *m* Lowlander, stranger **Innse G.** the Hebrides
galla *n* **-chan** *f* bitch
gallan *n* **-ain, -ain/-an** *m* stalk; (*met*) lad, hero
gallda *a* foreign, strange **G.** Lowland **a' Mhachair Ghallda** the Lowlands *f*
Galldachd *n f* **a' Ghalldachd** the Lowlands
gam *aug prep* at my **a bheil thu gam chluinntinn?** do you hear me?
gamhainn *n* **gamhna/gaimhne, gamhna/gaimhne/gamhnaichean** *m* stirk, year-old calf
gamhlas *n* **-ais** *m* malice, hatred, revenge
gamhlasach *a* **-aiche** malicious, malevolent, vindictive
gan *aug prep* at their **cuin a tha thu gan coinneachadh?** when are you meeting them?
gann *a* **gainne** scarce, limited
gànraich *v* **-achadh** dirty, soil, besmirch
gaoid *n* **-e, -ean** *f* blemish, defect, flaw
gaoir *n* **-e, -ean** *f* noise, cry (*of pain*); thrill **chuir e g. nam fheòil** it made my flesh creep
gaoisid *n* **-e, -ean** *f* a hair
gaoisnean *n* **-ein, -einean** *m* a hair *Also* **gaoistean**
gaol *n* **gaoil** *m* love **tha g. agam ort** I love you **A ghaoil!** Love!
gaolach *a* **-aiche** loving, dear
gaoth *n* **gaoithe, -an** *f* wind **g. an iar** a westerly wind
gaothach *a* **-aiche** windy
gar *v* **-adh** warm, heat (*especially self*)
gar *aug prep* at our **chan eil e gar faicinn** he's not seeing us
gàradh *See* **gàrradh**
garaids *n* **-ean** *f* garage
garbh *a* **gairbhe** rough, rugged, coarse; thick; wild (*of weather*) *adv* extremely **g. trang** very busy
garbhlach *n* **-aich, -aichean** *m* rugged terrain
garg *a* **gairge** fierce, ferocious
ga-rìribh *adv See* **dha-rìribh**
gàrlach *n* **-aich** *m* nyaff, impudent fellow
gàrradair *n* **-ean** *m* gardener
gàrradaireachd *n f* horticulture
gàrradh *n* **-aidh, -aidhean** *m* garden, wall, dyke **g. margaidh** market garden
gartan *n* **-ain, -ain/-an** *m* tick (*insect*); garter
gas *n* **-an** *m* gas
gas *n* **gaise, -an/gaisean** *f* stalk, stem
gasta *a* fine, splendid *Formerly* **gasda**
gath *n* **-a, -an/annan** *m* sting, dart; ray, beam (*of light*) **g. grèine** sunbeam

ge *conj* although **ge b' e** whoever, whatever
gèadh *n* **geòidh, geòidh** *f m* goose
geal *a* **gile** white
gealach *n* **-aich, -aichean** *f* moon **g. ùr** new moon
gealag *n* **-aig, -an** *f* sea trout
gealagan *n* **-ain, -ain** *m* white of egg
gealbhonn *n* **-bhuinn, -an** *m* sparrow
geall *n* **gill, gill** *m* promise, pledge, bet, wager **cuir g.** *v* bet, wager
geall *v* **-tainn** promise, pledge; wager
gealladh *n* **-aidh, -aidhean** *m* promise, pledge **g.-pòsaidh** engagement (*to marry*), betrothal
gealltanach *a* **-aiche** promising, hopeful
gealltanas *n* **-ais, -ais** *m* promise, pledge
gealtach *a* **-aiche** cowardly, timorous, timid
gealtaire *n* **-an** *m* coward
gèam *n* **geama, geamannan/ geamachan/geamaichean** *m* game, match
geamair *n* **-ean** *m* gamekeeper
geamhrachail *a* **-e** wintry
geamhradh *n* **-aidh, -aidhean** *m* winter
geamhraich *v* **-achadh** winter, feed during winter
gean *n* **-a** *m* mood, humour **g. math/deagh ghean** goodwill
geanail *a* **-e** cheerful, pleasant
geanm-chnò *n* **-chnòtha, -chnòthan** *f* chestnut
geansaidh *n* **-ean** *m* jersey, sweater, jumper
gearain *v* **-an** complain, grumble, moan
gearan *n* **-ain, -an** *m* complaint, moan, objection **dèan g.** *v* complain *Also* **gearain**
gearanach *a* **-aiche** complaining, grumbling, moaning *Also* **gearaineach**
gearastan *n* **-ain, -ain** *m* garrison *Formerly* **gearasdan**
geàrd *n* **geàird, -an** *m* guard
Gearmailteach *n* **-tich, -tich** *m* German *a* German
Gearmailtis *n f* German (*lang*)
geàrr *n* **-a, -an** *f* hare
geàrr *a* **giorra** short
geàrr *v* **gearradh** cut
gearradh *n* **-aidh** *m* cut, cutting **g. cainnte** sharp wit
geàrraidh *n* **-ean** *m* common grazing, pasture land
Gearran *n* **-ain** *m* **an G.** February
geàrr-chunntas *n* **-ais, -an** *m* minute (*of meeting*), summary
geas *n* **-a/geis, -an** *f* charm, spell **fo gheasaibh** under a spell, spellbound
geasachd *n* **-an** *f* enchantment, charm
geata *n* **-ichean/-chan** *m* gate
ged *conj* though, although
ged-thà *adv* though
gèile *n* **-achan/-an** *m* gale
gèill *v* **-eadh** submit, yield, give in/way
geilt *n* **-e** *f* terror, fear
geimheal *n* **-eil, -mhlean** *m* fetter
geimhleag *n* **-eig, -an** *f* crowbar, lever
geir *n* **-e** *f* tallow, suet; fat
gèire *n f* sharpness, acuteness; bitterness
geòcach *a* **-aiche** gluttonous, voracious
geòcaire *n* **-an** *m* glutton
geòcaireachd *n f* gluttony
geodal *n* **-ail** *m* flattery
geodha *n* **-chan/-ichean** *f m* creek, cove *Also* **geò**
geòla *n* **(-dh), -chan** *f* yawl, small boat
ge-tà *adv* though
geug *n* **gèige, -an** *f* branch (*of tree*)
geum *n* **-a/gèime, -an** *m* low, lowing, bellow
geum *v* **-naich** low, bellow
geur *a* **gèire** sharp. sharp-witted, discerning; bitter
geuradair *n* **-ean** *m* sharpener
geuraich *v* **-achadh** sharpen
geur-amhairc *v* **-amharc**

scrutinize, study closely
geurchuiseach *a* **-siche** perceptive, discerning, shrewd
geur-leanmhainn *n* **-ean** *m* persecution **dèan g.** *v* persecute
gheat *n* **-aichean** *f* yacht *Also* **geat**
gheibh *irr v* will get (*See irr v* **faigh** *in Grammar*)
ghia *exclam* Yuch!
giall *n* **-a/gèille, -an** *f* jaw, jowl
gibht *n* **-ean** *f* gift
Giblean *n* **-ein** *m* **an G.** April
gidheadh *adv* nevertheless, yet
gilb *n* **-e, -ean** *f* chisel *Also* **geilb**
gilead *n* **gilid** *m* whiteness
gille *n* **-an** lad, boy; servant **g.-cruidh** cowboy **g.-frithealaidh** waiter, servant **g.-Caluim** sword dance
gille-brìghde *n* **-bhrìghde, gillean-** *m* oystercatcher
gille-mirein *n* **gillean-** *m* whirlygig
gin *v* **-eadh/-eamhainn** beget, generate, reproduce
gin *pron* any, anyone, anything **a bheil g. agad?** do you have any?
gine *n* **-achan** *f* gene
gineachas *n* **-ais** *m* genesis, beginning
gineadh *n* **ginidh** *m* conception
ginealach *n* **-aich, -aich** *m* generation
gineamhainn *n m* conception, begetting
ginideach *a* genitive **an tuiseal g.** the genitive case
ginidh *n* **-ean** *m* guinea
gintinn *n m* reproduction
gintinneachd *n f* genetics
giobach *a* **-aiche** hairy, shaggy
gìodhar *n* **-air, -dhraichean** *m* gear (*in engine*)
gìogan *n* **-ain, -ain/-an** *m* thistle
giomach *n* **-aich, -aich** *m* lobster
gionach *a* **-aiche** greedy
giorna-giùirne *n* **-giùrnean** *f* helter-skelter (*slide*)
giorra *a See* **goirid, geàrr**
giorrachadh *n* **-aidh** *m* shortening, abbreviation; synopsis
giorrad *n* **-aid** *m* shortness, brevity
giorraich *v* **-achadh** shorten, abbreviate
gìosg *n* **-an** *m* creaking, gnashing
gìosg *v* **-ail** creak, gnash
giotàr *n* **-àir, -an** *m* guitar
giùlain *v* **-an** carry, bear; comport, conduct (*oneself*)
giùlan *n* **-ain, -an** *m* carrying, carriage; conduct, behaviour; bier
giullachd *n f* handling, treatment **droch ghiullachd** maltreatment, being treated badly
giuthas *n* **-ais** *m* fir, pine
glac *n* **glaice, -an** *f* hollow (*in land or hand*); narrow valley, defile
glac *v* **-adh** catch, seize, grasp
glag *n* **glaig** *m* thud, noise of something falling
glag *n See* **clag**
glagadaich *n* **-e** *f* rattling; prattling, loud talk
glaine *n f* cleanliness, purity
glainne *n* **-achan/-nichean** *f* glass **g.-sìde** barometer
glainnichean *n f pl* spectacles, glasses *Also* **glainneachan**
glaisean *n* **-ein, -an** *m* sparrow
glaiste *a* locked
glamh *v* **-adh** gobble, devour
glan *a* **glaine** clean, pure; splendid, fine
glan *adv* completely, totally **g. às a chiall** absolutely crazy
glan *v* **-adh** clean, wash
glaodh *n* **-oidh, -an** *m* cry, call, shout
glaodh *v* **-ach/-aich** call, shout
glaodh *n* **-oidh** *m* glue
glaodh *v* **-adh** glue
glaodhaich *n m* shouting, calling, bawling
glaodhan *n* **-ain** *m* pith, pulp
glaoic *n See* **gloidhc**
glas *n* **glaise, -an** *f* lock **g.-làmh** handcuff
glas *a* **glaise** grey; (*of land*) green
glas *v* **-adh** lock
glas- *pref* grey-coloured
glasach *n* **-aich, -aichean** *m* green field
glasraich *n f* greens, vegetables

glè *adv* very, fairly (+ *len*) **g. mhath** very good/well, fairly good/well
gleac *v* **-adh** struggle, wrestle
gleadhraich *n f* din, excessive noise
gleann *n* **glinne, glinn/-tan** *m* glen
gleans *n* **-a, -an** *m* shine **bha g. às** it shone
glèidh *v* **gleidheadh** keep, retain, preserve, observe
glèidhte *a* preserved, reserved, kept
glèidhteachas *n* **-ais** *m* conservation, preservation **neach-glèidhteachais** *m* conservationist
gleoc *n* **-a, -aichean** *m* clock
gleus *n* **-a, -an** *f m* order, trim; tune, key **air ghleus** in tune
gleus *v* **-adh** prepare; adjust; tune
gleusta *a* prepared; tuned; skilled; shrewd *Formerly* **gleusda**
glic *a* **-e** wise, prudent, sensible
gliocas *n* **-ais** *m* wisdom, prudence
gliog *n* **-a, -an** *m* click, tick, tinkle
gliong *n* **-a, -an** *m* clink, clang, jingle
gliongarsaich *n f* clinking, clanging
gloc *v* **-ail** cluck (*as of hen*), cackle
gloidhc *n* **-e, -ean** *f* fool, idiot **chan eil ann ach g.** he's just a fool
gloine *n See* **glainne**
glòir *n* **-e/glòrach** *f* glory; speech **droch ghlòir** bad language
glòir-mhiann *n* **-a** *f m* ambition
glòir-mhiannach *a* **-aiche** ambitious
glòraich *v* **-achadh** glorify
glòrmhor *a* **-oire** glorious
gluais *v* **gluasad** move
gluasad *n* **-aid, -an** *m* movement, motion; gait, carriage
gluasadach *a* **-aiche** moving, mobile
glug *n* **gluig, -an** *m* glug, gurgle; gulp
glugan *n* **-ain** *m* bubbling, gurgling
glumag *n* **-aig, -an** *f* small pool, puddle; mouthful of bile
glùn *n* **glùine, glùinean/glùintean** *f* knee **bean-ghlùine** *f* midwife *Also* **glùin**
glutach *a* **-aiche** gluttonous
glutaire *n* **-an** *m* glutton
gnàth *n* **-a, -an/-annan** *m* habit, custom, practice **a-ghnàth** always
gnàth *a* usual, habitual, common
gnàthach *a* **-aiche** customary, habitual, usual
gnàthasach *a* **-aiche** idiomatic
gnàthas-cainnt *n* **-e, gnàthasan-** *m* idiom
gnàth-fhacal *n* **-ail, -clan** *m* proverb
gnàths *n m* usage
gnè *n f* kind, type, nature; sex, gender
gnìomh *n* **-an/-aran** *m* action, act, deed **cuir an g.** *v* put into practice, carry out
gnìomhach *a* **-aiche** active, industrious; executive
gnìomhachas *n* **-ais** *m* industry
gnìomhair *n* **-ean** *m* verb
gnoban *n* **-ein, -an** *m* little hill or knoll
gnog *n* **gnoig, -an** *m* knock
gnog *v* **-adh** knock
gnogadh *n* **-aidh, -aidhean** *m* knock, knocking
gnòsadaich *n f* grunting *Also vn*
gnothach *n* **-aich, -aichean** *m* business, matter **a dh'aon ghnothach** on purpose, deliberately **an dèan siud an g.?** *v* will that do? **na gabh g. ris** *v* don't have anything to do with it **rinn iad an g.** *v* they managed; they won *Also* **gnothaich**
gnù *a* surly, sullen
gnùis *n* **-e, -ean** *f* countenance, face
gò *n m* blemish, defect, fault **gun ghò** faultless, without guile
gob *n* **guib, guib/-an** *m* beak, bill (*of bird*); sharp point (*of object*); (*colloq*) gob, mouth
gobach *a* **-aiche** nebby, brash;

beaked
gobag *n* **-aig, -an** *f* nebby/brash female
gobha *n* **-nn/-inn, goibhnean** *m* smith, blacksmith
gobhal *n* **-ail/goibhle, goibhlean** *m* fork; crotch
gobhar *n* **-air/goibhre, -air/goibhrean** *f m* goat
gòbhlach *a* forked; astride
gòbhlag *n* **-aig, -an** *f* fork; earwig
gòbhlan-gainmhich *n* **gòbhlain-, gòbhlanan/gòbhlain-** *m* sand martin
gòbhlan-gaoithe *n* **gòbhlain-, gòbhlanan-/gòbhlain-** *m* swallow
goc *n* **-a, -an/-aichean** *m* tap, faucet, stopcock
gocan *n* **-ain, -an** *m* acolyte, pert little person; whinchat **g. cuthaige** cuckoo's follower, titlark
gog *n m* cluck, cackle
gogaid *n* **-e, -ean** *f* coquette, flirt
gogail *n f* clucking, cackling
goid *n* **-e** *f* theft, stealing
goid *v* steal
goil *v* boil **air ghoil** boiling
goile *n* **-an/-achan** *f* stomach; appetite
goileach *a* **-liche** boiling **uisge g.** *m* boiling water
goir *v* **-sinn** call
goireas *n* **-eis, -an** *m* facility, amenity, resource, convenience
goireasach *a* **-aiche** convenient
goirid *a* **giorra** short, brief *adv* shortly **o chionn ghoirid** recently *prep* near **g. dhan bhaile** near the town
goirt *a* **-e** sore, painful; sour
goirtean *n* **-ein, -an** *m* small field, enclosure
goirtich *v* **-teachadh** hurt *Also* **gortaich**
goistidh *n* **-ean** *m* sponsor, godfather; gossip (*person*)
gonadh *n* **-aidh** *m* wounding, stinging **g. ort!** blast you!
gòrach *a* **-aiche** foolish, silly, daft, stupid
gòraiche *n f* folly, silliness, stupidity
gorm *a* **guirme** blue; green (*of grass*); (*met*) green, naive
gort *n* **-a** *f* famine, starvation
gràbhail *v* **-al/-aladh** engrave
gràbhalaiche *n* **-an** *m* engraver
grad *a* **graide** sudden, quick, swift, immediate **gu g.** suddenly, quickly
gràdh *n* **gràidh** *m* love **thugainn, a ghràidh** come on, love/dear
gràdhach *a* **-aiche** loving, dear, beloved
gràdhaich *v* **-achadh** love
gràdhag *n* **-aig** *f* love (*term of endearment applied to a woman*)
gràdhmhor *a* **-oire** loving
graf *n* **-a, -aichean** *m* graph
gràin *n* **-e** *f* loathing, abhorrence **bha g. aice air** she hated him/it
gràin-cinnidh *n* **gràine-cinnidh** *f* racism
gràineag *n* **-eig, -an** *f* hedgehog
gràineil *a* **-e** loathsome, abhorrent, disgusting, heinous
gràinich *v* **-neachadh** scunner, put one off, cause to hate/loathe
gràinne *n* **-an** *f* grain
gràinnean *n* **-ein, -an** *m* granule
gràisg *n* **-e, -ean** *f* rabble, mob
gram *n* **-a, -an/-aichean** *m* gram
gràmar *n* **-air** *m* grammar
gràn *n* **gràin, gràin** *m* grain, cereal
grànda *a* **gràinde** ugly
grannda *a See* **grànda**
gràpa *n* **-n** *m* graip, fork (*agric*)
gràs *n* **gràis, -an** *m* grace
gràsmhor *a* **-oire** gracious
greabhal *n* **-ail** *m* gravel
greadhnach *a* **-aiche** joyful, convivial; majestic
greadhnachas *n* **-ais** *m* joy, conviviality; pomp, majesty
greallach *n* **-aiche** *f* entrails, intestines
greann *n* **greinn** *m* scowl, irritation **bha g. air** he was scowling
greannach *a* **-aiche** wild, rough (*weather*); surly, crabbit, ill-tempered

greannmhor *a* **-oire** amusing, agreeable; comely
greas *v* **-ad** hasten, hurry **g. ort!** hurry up!
grèata *n* **-ichean** *m* grate
greideal *n* **-eil/-ach, -an** *f* griddle, girdle (*baking*)
grèidh *v* **-eadh** grill; groom (*eg horses*) **droch ghrèidheadh** bad treatment
greigh *n* **-e, -ean** *f* herd, stud
grèim *n* **-e, -ean/ -eannan** *m* hold, grip, grasp; custody; morsel; stitch (*of clothing*) **g. làimhe** handshake **g. bìdh** bite of food **an g. aig a' phoileas** in police custody
greimeil *a* **-e** resolute, firm, persistent
greimich *v* **-meachadh** grip, grapple, grasp
greis *n* **-e, -ean** *f* a while, spell (*of time*)
grèis *n* **-e** *f* embroidery **obair-ghrèis** *f* embroidery
greiseag *n* **-eig** *f* a short while
Greugach *n* **-aich, -aich** *m* Greek *a* Greek, Grecian
Greugais *n f* Greek (*lang*)
greusaiche *n* **-an** *m* shoemaker, cobbler
grian *n* **grèine** *f* sun **èirigh na grèine** sunrise *f* **dol fodha na grèine** *m* sunset
grianach *a* **-aiche** sunny
grinn *a* **-e** fine, elegant; neat; pretty
grinneal *n* **-eil** *m* gravel
grinneas *n* **-eis** *m* elegance
grìob *n* **-a, -an** *m* coastal precipice
grìogag *n* **-aig, -an** *f* bead
Grioglachan *n* **-ain** *m* **an G.** Pleiades, constellation
Griomasach *n* **-aich, -aich** *m* someone from Grimsay *a* from, or pertaining to, Grimsay
grìos *n* **-a, -achan** *m* grill
grìos *v* **-ad/-adh** blaspheme, swear
grìosad *n* **-aid** *m* blasphemy, swearing
grìosaich *v* **-achadh** grill
griùthrach *n* **-aich** *f* **a' ghriùthrach** measles *Also* **griùthlach**
grod *a* **-a/groide** rotten, putrid
grod *v* **-adh** rot, putrefy
gròiseid *n* **-e, -ean** *f* gooseberry
gruag *n* **gruaig, -an** *f* hair; wig
gruagach *n* **-aiche, -aichean** *f* young woman, maiden
gruagaire *n* **-an** *m* hairdresser
gruaidh *n* **-e, -ean** *f* cheek (*of face*)
gruaim *n* **-e** *f* gloom, sullenness
gruamach *a* **-aiche** gloomy, sullen, stern
grùdadh *n* **-aidh** *m* brewing; distilling **taigh-grùdaidh** *m* brewery; distillery
grùdaire *n* **-an** *m* brewer; distiller
grùdaireachd *n* **-an** *f* brewing; distilling
grùid *n* **-e** *f* dregs
grunn *n* **gruinn** *m* several, a good number
grunnaich *v* **-achadh** wade, paddle (*in water*)
grunnan *n* **-ain, -annan** *m* a few, small group
grunnd *n* **gruinnd/-a, -an** *m* ground; bottom (*of sea*)
gruth *n* **-a** *m* crowdie, curds
grùthan *n* **-ain, -an** *m* liver
gu *adv pref* (*equivalent to -(i)ly in English adverbs*) *eg* **gu snog** nicely
gu *conj* that (*used to introduce positive subordinate clauses*) **chì mi gu bheil thu trang** I see that you're busy
gu *conj* so that; until **fuirich gu sia uairean** wait till six o'clock
gu *prep* to, towards
gual *n* **guail** *m* coal
gualaisg *n* **-e, -ean** *m* carbohydrate
gualan *n* **-ain, -an** *m* carbon
gualann *n* **-ainn/guailne, guailnean/guaillean** *f* shoulder *Also* **guala, gualainn**
guàna *n m* fertilizer
guanach *a* **-aiche** light, giddy
gu bràth *adv* forever
gucag *n* **-aig, -an** *f* bud, bubble
gucag-uighe *n* **gucaig-, gucagan-** *f* egg-cup

gud *aug prep* to your
gu dè? *interr pron* what?
gu dearbh *adv* indeed
gu deimhinn(e) *adv* certainly
guga *n* **-ichean** *m* young solan goose or gannet
guidh *v* **-e** wish; entreat, pray, implore
guidhe *n* **-achan** *f m* wish; entreaty; swear-word
guil *v* **gul** cry, weep *Also* **a' gal**
guilbneach *n* **-nich, -nich** *f m* curlew
guin *n* **-ean** *m* sting, pang, dart
guin *v* **-eadh** sting, wound
guineach *a* **-niche** stinging, venomous, wounding
guir *v* **gur** hatch, breed
guirean *n* **-ein, -an** *m* pimple, pustule
guirmean *n* **-ein** *m* indigo **g. an fhraoich** bluebell
guiseid *n* **-e, -ean** *f* gusset
gul *n* **guil** *m* crying, weeping
gu lèir *adv* altogether, completely, entirely
gu leòr *adv* enough, plenty, galore
gu leth *adj phr* and a half **uair gu l.** an hour and a half
gum *conj* that (*used to introduce positive subordinate clauses where verb begins in b, f, m, p*)
gum *aug prep* to my, to their
gùn *n* **gùin, gùintean** *m* gown **gùn-oidhche** nightgown, nightie
gun *conj* that (*used to introduce positive subordinate clauses*)
gun *prep* (+ *len*) without
gun *aug prep* to the; to their
gun fhios nach *conj* in case, lest
gun fhiosta *adv* unawares, inadvertently
gunna *n* **-ichean/-chan** *m* gun
gur *n* **guir** *m* brood, hatch
gur *aug conj* that (*used to introduce positive subordinate clauses before nouns and adjectives*)
gur *aug prep* to you (*pl & pol*)
gur *aug prep* at your (*pl & pol*)
gur *aug prep* to our, to your (*pl & pol*)
gurraban *n* **-ain** *m* crouching, hunkering **bha e na ghurraban** he was crouching
gu ruig(e) *prep* up to, as far as, until
gus *prep* so that, in order to
gus *prep* to, until
gus *conj* so that, until
guth *n* **-a, -an** *m* voice; word, mention **cha chuala mi g.** I didn't hear anything **gun ghuth air ...** not to mention ..., to say nothing of ...
gu tur *adv* entirely, completely, totally, altogether

H

h- *part* (*used before words beginning in a vowel when preceded by* **a**)
hàidridean *n, a* **-ein** *m* hydrogen
hallò *exclam* hello
ham(a) *n m* bacon
hamstair *n* **-ean** *m* hamster
hangair *n* **-ean** *m* hangar; hanger
heactair *n* **-ean** *m* hectare
Hearach *n* **-aich, -aich** *m* someone from Harris *a* from, or pertaining to, Harris *Also* **Tearach**
heileacoptair *n* **-ean** *m* helicopter
Hiortach *n* **-aich, -aich** *m* someone from St Kilda *a* from, or pertaining to, St Kilda *Also* **Tiortach, Hirteach, Tirteach**
hocaidh *n m* hockey
hòro-ghealladh *n f m* celebration, fling, rave
hù-bhitheil *n f m* stramash

I

i *pron* she, her, it
iad *pron* they, them **iad seo** these **iad sin** those
iadh-shlat *n* **-shlait** *f* honeysuckle
iadsan *emph pron* they, them
iall *n* **èill, -an** *f* thong, leash, strap; shoelace
ialtag *n* **-aig, -an** *f* bat (*mammal*)
Iapanach *n, a* **-aich, -aich** *m* Japanese

iar *n f* west **an taobh an i.** the west side **i.-dheas** south-west **i.-thuath** north-west
iar- *pref* deputy, vice-, assistant **i.-cheann-suidhe** *m* vice-president
iarainn *a* iron
iarann *n* **-ainn, -an** *m* iron (*metal, impl*) **a bheil an t-i. air?** is the iron on?
iar-cheumnach *a* postgraduate
iar-cheumnaiche *n* **-an** *m* postgraduate
iargain *n f* sorrow, grief, pain
iargalt(a) *a* **-ailte/-alta** surly, forbidding
iarla *n* **-n/-chan** *m* earl
iarlachd *n f* earldom
iar-leasachan *n* **-ain** *m* suffix
iarmad *n* **-aid, -an** *m* remnant; offspring, race
iarmailt *n* **-e, -ean** *f* sky, firmament
iarnaig *v* **-eadh** iron
iar-ogha *n* **-chan/-ichean** *m* great-grandchild **tha iad anns na h-iar-oghachan** they are second cousins
iarr *v* **-aidh** ask (for), request, seek, want **i. orra tadhal** ask them to call (in)
iarrtach *a* demanding
iarrtas *n* **-ais, -an** *m* request, demand, application
iasad *n* **-aid, -an** *m* loan **air i.** on loan **am faigh mi i. dhen pheann agad?** may I borrow your pen?
iasg *n* **èisg, èisg** *m* fish **i. locha** freshwater fish **i. mara** seafish **i. òir** goldfish
iasgach *n* **-aich** *m* fishing, angling **bha e ris an i. fad a bheatha** he was a fisherman all his life
iasgaich *v* **-ach** fish, angle
iasgair *n* **-ean** *m* fisherman, angler
iath *v* **-adh** surround, envelop, encircle
iathaire *n* **-an** *m* aerial
'ic *contr* short for **mhic** of the son **mac Iain 'ic Sheumais** the son of John son of James
idir *adv* at all
ifrinn *n* **-e, -ean** *f* hell
Ìleach *n* **Ìlich, Ìlich** *m* someone from Islay *a* from, or pertaining to, Islay
ìm *n* **ime** *m* butter **ì. ùr** fresh butter **ì. saillte** salted butter
imcheist *n* **-ean** *f* anxiety, perplexity, doubt **fo i.** anxious **bha i. oirre mu dheidhinn** she was worried about it
imich *v* **imeachd** go, depart, leave
imleag *n* **-eige, -an** *f* navel
imlich *v* lick
ìmpidh *n* **-e, -ean** *f* entreaty, petition, persuasion **chuir e i. oirnn fuireach** he implored us to stay/wait
ìmpire *n* **-ean** *m* emperor *Also* **ìompaire**
ìmpireachd *n* **-an** *f* empire *Also* **ìompaireachd**
impis *n f* imminence **an i.** on the point of, about to
imprig *n* **-ean** *f* removal (*house*), flitting **rinn iad i.** they flitted
imrich *n* **-e, -ean** *f* removal (*house*), flitting
inbhe *n* **-an** *f* rank, status, prestige
inbheach *n* **-bhich, -bhich** *m* adult
inbheach *a* **-bhiche** adult, mature
inbhir *n* **-e, -ean** *m* confluence, inver
inc *n f m* ink
ìne *n* **-an** *f* nail (*on finger*); claw, talon
in-imrich *n* **-e** *f* immigration
in-imriche *n* **-ean** *m* immigrant
inneal *n* **-eil, -an** *m* machine, instrument, engine **i.-ciùil** musical instrument **i.-fighe** knitting machine **i.-measgachaidh** mixer **i.-nigheadaireachd** washing machine
innean *n* **-ein, -an** *m* anvil
innear *n* **-arach** *f* dung, manure *Also* **inneir**
innidh *n f* bowel
innis *n* **innse, innsean** *f* island; meadow, pasture
innis *v* *See* **inns**
Innis-Tìleach *n* **-Tìlich, -Tìlich** *m*

Icelander *a* Icelandic
innleachd *n* **-an** *f* invention, device, mechanism, scheme; ingenuity; wile, tactic
innleachdach *a* **-aiche** ingenious, inventive; cunning, tactical
innleadair *n* **-ean** *m* engineer, inventor **i. dealain** electrical engineer
innleadaireachd *n f* engineering
innlich *v* **-leachadh** invent, devise, engineer
inns *v* **-e(adh)** (+ **do**) tell, relate **i. dhi** tell her
Innseanach *n* **-aich**, **-aich** *m* Indian *a* Indian
innte(se) *prep pron* in her(self), in it(self) **'s e cleasaiche a th' i.** she's an actress
inntinn *n* **-e**, **-ean** *f* mind, intellect
inntinneach *a* **-niche** interesting; encouraging, positive-minded
inntleachd *n* **(-a)** *f* intelligence, intellect
inntleachdail *a* **-e** intellectual
inntrig *v* **-eadh** enter
ìobair *v* **ìobradh/-t** sacrifice
ìobairt *n* **-e**, **-ean** *f* sacrifice, offering
ìoc *v* **-adh** pay, render
iochd *n f* mercy, clemency, compassion
ìochdar *n* **-air**, **-an** *m* bottom, lower part
ìochdaran *n* **-ain**, **-an** *m* subject, inferior, subordinate
iochdmhor *a* **-oire** merciful, clement, compassionate
ìocshlaint *n* **-e**, **-ean** *f* medicine, balm
iodhal *n* **-ail**, **-an** *m* idol **i.-adhradh** idolatry
iodhlann *n* **-ainn**, **-an** *f* stackyard, cornyard
iogart *n* **-airt**, **-an** *f m* yoghurt
ioghnadh *n See* **iongnadh**
iolach *n* **-aich**, **-aich** *m* shout, roar (*of triumph*)
iolair(e) *n* **-(e)an** *f* eagle **i.-uisge** osprey, sea eagle
iolra *n* **-n** *m* plural *a* plural
iomadach *a* (*precedes n*) many, many a, numerous
iomadh *a* (*precedes n*) many, many a, numerous
ioma-dhathach *a* **-aiche** multi-coloured
iomadh-fhillte *a* complex, compound, manifold
iomagain *n* **(-e)**, **-ean** *f* worry, concern, anxiety **fo i.** worried, concerned
iomagaineach *a* **-niche** worried, concerned, anxious
ioma-ghaoth *n* **-ghaoith**, **-an** *f* whirlwind
iomain *n* **-e** *f* shinty; driving (*as of cattle*)
iomain *v* play shinty; drive (*as of cattle*)
iomair *n* **-e**, **-ean** *m* ridge (*ploughed*), piece of land
iomair *v* **iomradh** row (*boat*)
iomairt *n* **-e**, **-ean** *f* enterprise, initiative; campaign, venture **dèan i.** *v* campaign
iomall *n* **-aill**, **-aill** *m* border, limit, edge, margin, periphery **i. a' bhaile** the suburbs
iomallach *a* **-aiche** remote, isolated, peripheral
iomarra *a* plural
ioma-shruth *n* **-a**, **-an** *m* cross-current, eddying stream or tide
iomchaidh *a* **-e** suitable, appropriate, proper, fitting
iomchair *v* **-ar** carry, bear
ìomhaigh *n* **-ean** *f* image, statue; countenance
iomlaid *n* **-e**, **-ean** *f* change, exchange
iomlan *a* **-aine** complete, whole, total **gu h-i.** altogether, entirely
iomnaidh *n f* concern, anxiety **chuir e i. oirnn** it worried us
iompachadh *n* **-aidh**, **-aidhean** *m* religious conversion
iompachan *n* **-ain**, **-an** *m* convert (*relig*)
iompaich *v* **-achadh** convert (*relig*) **chaidh a h-iompachadh** she was converted
iomradh *n* **-aidh**, **-aidhean** *m* mention, report, reference; rowing (*boat*) **dèan i. air** *v* mention

iomraiteach *a* **-tiche** famous, renowned, celebrated
iomrall *n* **-aill, -an** *m* wandering, straying; error **chaidh sinn (air) i.** *v* we got lost
iomrallach *v* wandered, confused, mistaken
ionad *n* **-aid, -an** *m* place **i. fàilte** reception (*area*) **i. fiosrachaidh turasachd** tourist information centre **i. slàinte** health centre
ionadail *a* **-e** local **riaghaltas i.** *m* local government
ionaghailt *n* **-e, -ean** *f* pasture, grazing
ionaltair *v* **-tradh** pasture, graze
ionaltradh *n* **-aidh, -aidhean** *m* pasture, grazing
ionann *a* same, equal, alike, identical **chan i. iad idir** they are not at all alike
iongantach *a* **-aiche** surprising; wonderful
iongantas *n* **-ais, -an** *m* surprise; wonder
iongnadh *n* **-aidh, -aidhean** *m* surprise, wonder **chuir e i. orm** it surprised me **is beag an t-i.** little wonder
ionmhainn *a* **-e/annsa** beloved, dear
ionmhas *n* **-ais, -an** *m* finance, riches, treasure **Roinn an Ionmhais** the Finance Dept
ionmhasail *a* **-e** financial
ionmhasair *n* **-ean** *m* treasurer
ion-mhiannaichte *a* highly desirable
ionmholta *a* praiseworthy, laudable, commendable
ionnan *See* **ionann**
ionndrainn *n f m* missing, longing (for)
ionndrainn *v* miss, long (for)
ionnlaid *v* **-ad** wash, bathe **seòmar/rùm i.** *m* bathroom
ionnsachadh *n* **-aidh** *m* learning; instruction
ionnsaich *v* **-achadh** learn; (+ **do**) teach
ionnsaichte *a* learned, educated
ionnsaigh *n* **-ean** *f m* attack, assault, onslaught, invasion **thug iad i. oirnn** *v* they attacked us **a dh'i.** (+ *gen*) to, towards
ionnsramaid *n* **-e, -ean** *f* instrument
ionracas *a* **-ais** *m* righteousness, integrity, probity
ionraic *a* **-e** righteous, honest, just
iorghail *n* **-ean** *f* tumult, uproar
iorram *n* **-aim, -aim** *m* rowing song; repetitive song or remarks
ìosal *a* **ìsle** low, lowly **gu h-ì.** down below
ìre *n* **-an** *f* level, stage, grade, rate; maturity **an Ì. Choitcheann** Standard Grade (*exam*) **an Ard Ì.** Higher Grade (*exam*) **an ì. mhath** quite; almost **gu ì. mhòir** to a large extent **air tighinn gu ì.** having reached maturity
iriosal *a* **-aile** humble, lowly
irioslachd *n f* humility, lowliness
irioslaich *v* **-achadh** humble, humiliate
iris *n* **-e, -ean** *f* magazine, periodical
is *irr v* (*copula of verb* **to be**) am, is, are (*often abbreviated* to **'s**) **'s e oileanach a th' ann** he's a student
is *conj* and (*contr of* **agus**)
isbean *n* **-ein, -an** *m* sausage
ise *emph pron* she, her, it
ìseal *a See* **ìosal**
isean *n* **isein, -an** *m* chick, chicken; bird; young **droch i.** a bad egg (*colloq*), brat **i. deireadh linn** a tail-end baby
ìslich *v* **ìsleachadh** lower; humble
is mathaid *adv* perhaps, maybe
Israelach *n* **-lich, -lich** *m* Israeli *a* Israeli *Also* **Iosaraileach**
ist *interj* wheest, hist!, hush!, quiet!
ite *n* **-an** *f* feather; fin
iteach *n* **itich** *m* plumage
iteach *a* **itiche** feathered, feathery
iteachan *n* **-ain, -ain/-an** *m* weaver's bobbin
iteag *n* **-eig, -an** *f* small feather; flight **air (an) iteig** flying
iteagach *a* **-aiche** feathered, feathery

itealaich *v* **-achadh** fly
itealan *n* **-ain, -ain** *m* aeroplane
iteileag *n* **-eig, -an** *f* kite (*sport*)
ith *v* **-e** eat
iubailidh *n* **-ean** *f* jubilee
iubhar *n* **-air, -an** *m* yew
iuchair *n* **iuchrach, iuchraichean** *f* key; roe of fish
Iuchar *n* **-air** *m* **an t-I.** July
Iùdhach *n* **-aich, -aich** *m* Jew *a* Jewish
iùil-tharraing *n* **-e, -ean** *f* magnetism
iùil-tharraingeach *a* **-giche** magnetic
iùl *n* **iùil, iùilean** *m* guidance, direction **neach-iùil** *m* guide
Iupatar *n* **-air** *m* Jupiter
iutharn(a) *n f* hell

L

là *n* **làithean/lathaichean** *m* day
làbha *n f* lava
labhair *v* **-t** speak, talk
labhairt *n f* speaking, talking **neach-l.** *m* spokesperson
lach *n* **-a, -an/-ain** *f* wild duck
lachan *n* **-ain, -ain** *m* guffaw **l.-gàire** hearty laugh
lachanaich *n f* laughing heartily
lachdann *a* **-ainne** dun, tawny, swarthy
ladar *n* **-air, -an** *m* ladle
ladarna *a* bold, shameless, blatant, presumptuous
ladarnas *n* **-ais** *m* boldness, shamelessness, presumptuousness
ladhar *n* **-air/-dhra, -dhran** *m* hoof
lag *n* **laig/luig, -an** *f m* hollow
lag *a* **laige** weak, feeble, faint
lagaich *v* **-achadh** weaken, undermine *Also intrans*
lagais *n* **-ean** *f* slag heap, rubbish dump
lagan *n* **-ain, -an** *m* small hollow
lagchuiseach *a* **-siche** faint-hearted, unenterprising, weak-willed
lagh *n* **-a, -annan** *m* law **dèan l.** *v* legislate **l. baile** bye-law
laghach *a* **-aiche** nice, pleasant, fine
laghail *a* **-e** lawful, legal
laghairt *n* **-ean** *f m* lizard
Laideann *n* **-dinn(e)** *f* Latin
làidir *a* **-e** strong, robust
laige *n f* weakness, faintness
laigh *v* **-e** lie (down) **a' dol a laighe** going to bed
laigse *n* **-an/-achan** *f* weakness, defect **chaidh e ann an l.** he fainted
làimh ri *adv* near, close to
làimhsich *v* **-seachadh** handle, treat
laimrig *n* **-e, -ean** *f* landing-place, small harbour *Also* **laimhrig**
lainnir *n* **-e** *f* radiance, glitter
lainnireach *a* **-riche** radiant, glittering, gleaming
làir *n* **-e/làrach, -ean/-idhean/-ichean** *f* mare **l.-bhreabaidh** rocking-horse **l.-mhaide** see-saw
la(i)ste *a* lit
làitheil *a* daily
làmh *n* **làimhe, -an** *f* hand **l. ri làimh** hand in hand **an l. dheas/cheart** the right hand **an l. chlì/ cheàrr** the left hand **l.-an-uachdair** the upper hand **gabh os làimh** *v* undertake **ri làimh** at hand **obair-làimhe** *f* manual work **rug e air làimh oirre** he shook hands with her
làmhachas-làidir *n* **làmhachais-** *m* force
làmhagh *n* **-aigh, -aighean** *f* hand-axe *Also* **làmhag**
làmhchair *a* **-e** handy, dexterous
làmh-sgrìobhadh *n* **-aidh** *m* handwriting
làmh-sgrìobhainn *n* **-e, -ean** *f* manuscript
lampa *n* **-ichean** *f m* lamp
làn *a* **làine** full, complete **tha mi l.-chinnteach** I'm quite sure/certain **tha l.-earbs' agam ann** I have complete confidence in him **tha a l.-thìd' agad ...** it is high time you ... **làn-ùine** full-time
làn *n* **làin, làin** *m* tide **l. àrd** a high tide **l.-mara** (high) tide

langa *n* **-an/-annan** *f* ling (*fish*)
langan *n* **-ain**, **-an** *m* bellowing (*of deer*), bellow
langanaich *n* **-e** *f* lowing, bellowing (*of deer*)
langasaid *n* **-e**, **-ean** *f* sofa, couch, settee
lann *n* **lainn, -an** *f* enclosure, repository
lann *n* **-a/lainne**, **-an** *f* blade, sword; scale (*on fish*)
lannsa *a* **-ichean** *f* lance, lancet
lannsair *n* **-ean** *m* surgeon
lanntair *n* **-ean** *m* lantern *Also* **lainntear** *f*
laoch *n* **laoich, laoich** *m* hero, warrior, champion
laochan *n* **-ain**, **-ain** *m* little hero (*term of endearment*) **sin thu fhèin, a laochain** well done, my lad/little pal
laogh *n* **laoigh**, **laoigh** *m* calf
laoidh *n* **-e**, **-ean** *f m* hymn, anthem, lay
laoidheadair *n* **-ean** *m* hymnbook
lapach *a* **-aiche** weak, feeble, frail
làr *n* **làir**, **làir/-an** *m* floor, ground
làrach *n* **-aich**, **-aichean** *f m* site; ruin **l.-lìn** website **an l. nam bonn** on the spot, immediately
làraidh *n* **-ean** *f* lorry **l. an sgudail** the bin/refuse lorry
làrna-mhàireach *adv* the next day
las *v* **-adh** light
lasachadh *n* **-aidh**, **-aidhean** *m* slackening; discount, rebate
lasadair *n* **-ean** *m* match (*to light*)
lasadh *n* **-aidh**, **-aidhean** *m* lighting; flash
lasaich *v* **-achadh** slacken, ease off
lasair *n* **lasrach**, **lasraichean** *f* flame
lasgan *n* **-ain**, **-ain** *m* outburst **l. gàire** hearty laugh, peal of laughter
lasganaich *n* **-e** *f* hearty laughter
lasrach *a* **-aiche** flaming
lastaig *n, a* **(-e)** *f* elastic
lath *v* **-adh** numb **theabadh mo lathadh** I was nearly frozen
latha *n* **làithean/-lchean** *m* day **Latha na Sàbaid** the Sabbath, Sunday **l.-breith** birthday
latheigin *adv* some day **l.-fèille** public holiday, fair day **L. Luain** Doomsday **làithean-saora/ saor-làithean** holidays **l. brèagha air choreigin** some fine day **nach ann oirnn a thàinig an dà l.!** how our circumstances have changed!
làthach *n* **-aich/làthcha** *f* mire, clay
làthair *n* **-e** *f* presence **an l.** present
le *prep* (+ *dat*) with, by **'s ann le Iain a tha e** it belongs to John **le chèile** both, together
lèabag *n* **-aig**, **-an** *f* flounder
leabaidh *n* **leapa**, **leapannan** *f* bed *Also* **leaba**
leabhar *n* **-air**, **leabhraichean** *m* book **L. Aithghearr nan Ceist** the Shorter Catechism **l.-iùil** guidebook **l.-latha** diary **l.-seòlaidh** address book **l.-sgrìobhaidh** notebook
leabharlann *n* **-ainn**, **-an** *f m* library
leabharlannaiche *n* **-an** *m* librarian
leabhrachan *n* **-ain**, **-ain** *m* pamphlet, brochure
leabhran *n* **-ain**, **-ain/-an** *m* booklet
leac *n* **lic/lice**, **-an** *f* flagstone, slab, flat stone; tombstone
leag *v* **-ail** knock down, fell, demolish **l. boma** drop a bomb
leagh *v* **-adh** melt, dissolve, smelt; liquidate
leaghadair *n* **-ean** *m* smelter
leam(sa) *prep pron* with me; by me **leam fhìn** alone **'s ann leamsa a tha e** it's mine **leam-leat** fickle, non-committal
leamh *a* **-a** vexing, sarcastic; importunate
leamhaich *v* **-achadh** vex, irk, irritate; importune
leamhan *n* **-ain** *m* elm
leamhnagan *n* **-ain**, **-an** *m* stye (*in eye*)
lean v **-tainn/-tail** follow,

continue, pursue **l. ort!** continue!, keep going! **ri leantainn** to follow/be continued
leanabachd *n f* childhood, infancy, childishness
leanabail *a* **-e** childish, juvenile
leanaban *n* **-ain, -an** *m* infant, small child
leanabh *n* **-aibh, -an/leanaban** *m* child, infant
lèanag *n* **-aig, -an** *f* little meadow, lawn
leanailteach *a* **-tiche** continuous, lingering
leann *n* **-a, -tan** *m* beer, ale; (*any*) liquid
leannan *n* **-ain, -an** *m* lover, sweetheart
leannanachd *n f* courtship
leann-dubh *n* **-duibh** *m* melancholy
leantail/leantainn *n m* following, continuing
leantainneach *a* **-niche** continuous, lingering; sticky
leantainneachd *n f* continuity *Also* **leantalachd**
learag *n* **-aige, -an** *f* larch
learg *n* **-a** *f* black-throated diver
leas *n m* benefit, advantage **cha leig/ruig thu l.** *v* you needn't (bother)
leas- *pref* depute, deputy **l.-stiùiriche** *m* deputy director
leasachadh *n* **-aidh, -aidhean** *m* development, improvement, reformation, supplement **an t-Ath-L.** the Reformation **l.-fala** blood transfusion
leasaich *v* **-achadh** develop, improve, rectify; fertilize
leasaichte *a* developed, improved, rectified; fertilized
leasan *n* **-ain, -ain/-an** *m* lesson
leat(sa) *prep pron* with you; by you
leatas *n* **-ais, -an** *m* lettuce
leatha(se) *prep pron* with her, by her
leathad *n* **-aid/leothaid, -an/leòidean** *m* slope, brae
leathan(n) *a* **leatha/leithne** broad, wide *Also* **leathainn**
leathar *n* **-air** *m* leather
led *aug prep* with your, by your
leibh(se) *prep pron* with you; by you (*pl & pol*)
leibideach *a* **-diche** inept, defective; accidental, unfortunate
leig *v* **-eil** let, allow, permit **l. anail** draw breath, take a breather **l. leatha** leave her alone **na l. dad ort** don't let on **l. ort nach eil fhios agad** pretend you don't know **l. mu sgaoil** release **l. ris** reveal, show
leigeadh *n* **-gidh** *m* letting, allowing; discharge (*from boil etc*)
leigeil *n* **-ealach** *m* letting, allowing **l. fala** blood-letting
lèigh *n* **-e, -ean** *m* surgeon, physician **l.-lann** *f m* surgery
leigheas *n* **-eis, -an** *m* cure, remedy, healing **l.-inntinn** psychiatry
lèigh-eòlas *n* **-ais** *m* medicine (*science*)
leighis *v* **-gheas** cure, heal
lèine *n* **lèintean** *f* shirt **l.-mharbh** shroud
leinn(e) *prep pron* with us; by us
lèir *a* visible, clear
lèir *a* altogether **gu l.** altogether, in total
lèir *v* **-eadh** torment, pain
lèirmheas *n* **-eis, -an** *m* review (*liter*), overview
lèirsgrios *n* **-an** *m* total destruction, utter ruin
lèirsinn *n* **-e** *f* vision, sight; insight, perception
lèirsinneach *a* **-niche** discerning, perceptive, enlightened, visionary; visible
leis *prep* with, by (+ *def art*); his; downwards **l. an droch shìde** because of the bad weather **l. a' bhrutha(i)ch** down the brae/hill
leis(-san) *prep pron* with him; by him; his **an ann leis-san a tha e?** is it his?
leisg *a* **-e** lazy, slothful; reluctant
leisg(e) *n f* laziness, sloth, reluctance **bha l. air faighneachd** he was reluctant to ask

leisgeadair *n* **-ean** *m* lazy person, lazybones
leisgeul *n* **-eil, -an** *m* excuse, apology (*for absence*) **gabh mo l.!** excuse me!, pardon me!
leiteachas *n* **-ais** *m* partiality, bias
leithid *n* **-e, -ean** *f* such, the like **chan fhaca duine riamh a l.** no one has ever seen the like
leitir *n* **-e/leitreach, -ean/ leitrichean** *f* hillside, slope
lem *aug prep* with my, by my
len *aug prep* with their, by their
leòbag *n f See* **lèabag**
Leòdhasach *n* **-aich, -aich** *m* someone from Lewis *a* from, or pertaining to, Lewis
leòinteach *n* **-tich, -tich** *m* wounded person, casualty
leòm *n* **leòim(e)** *f* pride, conceit
leòmach *a* **-aiche** well-dressed, smart (*dress*); conceited
leòman *n* **-ain, -ain** *m* moth
leòmhann *n* **-ainn, -ainn** *m* lion **l.-mara** sea lion
leòn *n* **leòin, -tan** *m* wound
leòn *v* **leòn/-adh** wound
leònte *a* wounded, afflicted
leòr *n f* enough, sufficiency **an d' fhuair thu do l.?** did you get enough/your fill? **gu l.** plenty, enough **ceart gu l.** OK
l(e)òsan *n* **-ain, -ain** *m* window pane
leotha(san) *prep pron* with them; by them
ler *aug prep* with our, by our; with your, by your
leth *n m* half *a* separate **air l.** exceptional **às l.** on behalf of **fa l.** each one, individually **gu l.** and a half **l. mar l.** half and half, share and share alike
leth- *pref* half-, semi-
leth-aon *n* **-aoin, -an** *m* twin
lethbhreac *n* **-ric, -ric** *m* copy, photocopy, duplicate **dèan l.** *v* duplicate
leth-bhreith *n* **-e** *f* partiality, discrimination **dèan l.** *v* discriminate
leth-bhruich *v* **(-eadh)** parboil, half-boil
lethchar *adv* somewhat
leth-chas *n* **-choise, -an** *f* (only) one foot **air leth-chois** on one foot
lethcheann *n* **-chinn, -chinn** *n* temple, side of head, cheek (*phys*)
leth-chearcall *n* **-aill, -aill/-an** *m* semi-circle
leth-cheud *n* **-an** *m* fifty (+ *sg*) **l. bliadhna** fifty years
lethchiallach *n* **-aich, -aich** *m* half-witted person
leth-chruinne *n* **-an** *m* hemisphere
leth-chrùn *n* **-chrùin, -chrùin/ -chrùintean** *m* half-crown
leth-chuairt *n* **-e, -ean** *f* semi-circle
letheach *a* half **l. slighe** half-way
leth-fhacal *n* **-ail, -ail/-fhaclan** *m* byword
leth-làmh *n* **-làimhe, -an** *f* (only) one hand
leth-mhìle *n* **-mhìltean** *m* half-mile; five hundred
lethoireach *a* isolated, remote
leth-phinnt *n* **-ean** *m* half pint
leth-phunnd *n* **-phuinnd, -phuinnd** *m* half pound
leth-shùil *n* **-shùla, -ean** *f* (only) one eye
leth-uair *n* **-uarach, -ean** *f* half-hour **l. an dèidh uair** half past one
leud *n* **leòid, -an** *m* breadth, width
leudaich *v* **-achadh** broaden, widen, expand, enlarge
leug *n* **lèig, -an** *f* jewel, precious stone
leugh *v* **-adh** read
leughadair *n* **-ean** *m* reader
leughadh *n* **-aidh** *m* reading
leum *n* **lèim/-a, -annan** *f m* leap, jump, spring **l. àrd** high jump **l. droma** lumbago **l. fhada** long jump
leum *v* **leum/-adaich** leap, jump, spring **l. a sròn** she had a nosebleed
leumadair *n* **-ean** *m* jumper (*sport*); dolphin

leus *n* **leòis, leòis** *m* ray, light; blister
liac *v* **-radh** smear, spread
liagh *n* **lèigh, -an** *f* ladle; blade of oar
liath *a* **lèithe** grey, blue-grey, blue; grey-haired
liath *v* **-adh** make grey, become grey **tha fhalt air liathadh** his hair has gone grey
liath- *pref* grey-tinted
liath-reothadh *n* **-reothaidh** *m* hoar-frost
lìbhrig *v* **-eadh** deliver
lìbhrigeadh *n* **-gidh, -gidhean** *m* delivery (*not phys*)
lideadh *n* **lididh, lididhean** *m* syllable *Also* **lide**
lighiche *n* **-an** *m* doctor, physician **l.-inntinn** psychiatrist
lilidh *n* **-ean** *f* lily
lìnig *v* **-eadh** line (*clothes etc*)
lìnigeadh *n* **-gidh, -gidhean** *m* lining (*in clothes*) *Also* **lìnig**
linn *n* **-e, -tean** *f m* century, age, generation, era **ri l.** because of (+ *gen*)
linne *n* **-achan/linntean** *f* pool, pond
liodraig *v* **-eadh** beat up, leather
lìogach *a* **-giche** sly, cunning
liomaid *n* **-e, -ean** *f* lemon *Also* **liomain**
lìomh *n* **-a** *f* polish, gloss
lìomh *v* **-adh** polish
lìomharra *a* polished, glossy
lìon *n* **lìn, lìn, -tan** *m* net, web **l. iasgaich** fishing net **lìn-mhòra** long-lines
lìon *n* **lìn** *m* flax, lint
lìon *v* **-adh** fill, replenish
lìonadh *n* **-aidh** *m* filling, replenishing; incoming tide
lìonmhor *a* **-a** numerous, plentiful
lionn *n* **-a, -tan** *m* (*any*) liquid
lios *n* **-a/lise, -an** *f m* garden
Liosach *n* **-aich, -aich** *m* someone from Lismore *a* from, or pertaining to, Lismore
liosta *n* **-ichean** *f* list (*written*)
liotach *a* **-aiche** lisping, slurring
liotair *n* **-ean** *m* litre
lip *n* **-e, -ean** *f* lip
lite *n* *f* porridge
litir *n* **litreach, litrichean** *f* letter
litreachadh *n* **-aidh** *m* spelling, orthography
litreachas *n* **-ais** *m* literature
litrich *v* **-reachadh** spell
liubhair *v* **-t** (*not phys*) deliver
liùdhag *n* **-aig, -an** *f* doll
liùg *v* **-adh** creep, steal, sneak a look at
liùgach *a* **-aiche** creeping, sneaking
liùgh *n* **-a, -achan** *f* lythe *Also* **liugha**
liut *n* **liuit** *f* knack, aptitude **l. air ...** aptitude for ...
liuthad *a* so many (*precedes n*)
lobh *v* **-adh** rot, putrefy
lobhadh *n* **-aidh** *m* rot
lobhar *n* **-air, -air** *m* leper
lobhta *n* **-ichean** *m* loft *Also* **lobht**
lobhte *a* rotten, putrid *Also* **loibh(t)**
locair *n* **-ean/locraichean** *f* carpenter's plane
locair *v* **locradh** plane
loch *n* **-a, -an** *f m* loch, lake **l. mara** sea loch
lochan *n* **-ain, -ain** *m* small loch
lochd *n* **-a, -an** *m* fault, defect, malice
lochdach *a* **-aiche** faulty, harmful, malicious
Lochlannach *n* **-aich, -aich** *m* Scandinavian, Viking *a* Scandinavian, Viking
lòchran *n* **-ain, -ain** *m* lantern, lamp
lod *n* **-a, -an** *m* load
lof *n* **-a, -aichean** *f m* loaf
logaidh *n* **-ean** *m* forelock, fringe (*of hair*), mane
loidhne *n* **-nichean** *f* line **l.-taice** helpline
loidseadh *n* **-sidh, -sidhean** *m* lodging
loidsear *n* **-eir, -an** *m* lodger
lòineag *n* **-eige, -an** *f* flake, snowflake; small tuft of wool
loingeas *n* **-eis** *m* ship; fleet, navy **l.-cogaidh** warship *Also* **luingeas**
loinid *n* **-e, -ean** *f* churn, whisk

lòinidh *n f m* **an l.** rheumatism, sciatica
loinn *n* **-e** *f* elegance, comeliness, fine finish **tha l. air** it is elegant
loinneil *a* **-e** elegant, comely
loireach *a* **-riche** soiled, bedraggled, messy
loireag *n* **-eig, -an** *f* untidy or messy female
loisg *v* **losgadh** burn, inflame, fire
loisgte *a* burnt
lom *a* **luime** bare, naked; thin, threadbare
lom *v* **-adh** make bare, shear, shave
lomadair *n* **-ean** *m* shears; shearer, shaver, mower
lomadh *n* **-aidh** *m* making bare, shearing, fleecing, shaving, mowing
lomair *v* **lomradh** mow, shear, fleece
lomaire *n* **-an** *m* mower, shearer
loma-làn *a* brimful, completely full
lomnochd *a* naked, bare, undressed *n f* nakedness, nudity
lon *n* **loin, loin** *m* elk
lòn *n* **lòin, lòintean** *m* pool; meadow
lòn *n* **lòin** *m* food, provisions, lunch; livelihood
lon-dubh *n* **loin-duibh, loin-dubha** *m* blackbird
long *n* **luinge, -an** *f* ship **l.-bhriseadh** *m* shipwreck **l.-chogaidh** warship **l.-fànais** spaceship **l.-fo-mhuir** submarine
lorg *n* **luirge, -an** *f* track, trace; staff, stick **a bheil l. agad air?** do you know where it/he is?
lorg *v* find, discover, trace, search for
los *conj* so that, because **air l.** for, on account of
losgadh *n* **-aidh, -aidhean** *m* burn, burning, combustion, firing **l.-bràghad** heartburn
losgann *n* **-ainn, -an** *m* toad; frog
lot *n* **-a, -aichean** *f* allotment, croft
lot *n* **-a, -an** *m* wound
lot *v* **-adh** wound
loth *n* **-a, -an** *f m* filly, colt
luach *n m* value, worth
luachair *n* **luachrach** *f* rushes
luachmhor *a* **-oire** valuable, precious
luadh *n* **luaidh, luaidh(ean)** *m* waulking (*of tweed*), fulling (*cloth*) **òran luaidh** waulking song *Also* **luadhadh**
luaidh *v* **luadh** waulk, full (*tweed*)
luaidh *n m* mention, praise; beloved person **dèan l. air** *v* make mention of **mo l.** my dear
luaidh *v* mention, praise
luaidh(e) *n* **-e** *f m* lead
luaineach *a* **-niche** restless, fickle
luaireag *n* **-eig, -an** *f* storm petrel
luaisg *v* **luasgadh** shake, toss, rock, wave, swing
luaisgeanach *a* **-aiche** shaking, tossing, swaying, unsettled
luamhan *n* **-ain, -an** *m* lever
luasgan *n* **-ain, -an** *m* shaking, tossing, swaying
luath *n* **luaith/-a** *f* ash, ashes *Also* **luaithre**
luath *a* **luaithe** fast, swift, speedy
luaths *n* **luaiths** *m* speed, swiftness, velocity
lùb *n* **lùib, -an** *f* bend, curve
lùb *v* **-adh** bend
lùbach *a* **-aiche** bending, winding; pliant
lùbte *a* bent
luch *n* **-a/-ainn, -an** *f* mouse **l.-fheòir** fieldmouse
luchag *n* **-aig, -an** *f* little mouse
lùchairt *n* **-e, -ean** *f* palace
lucharan *n* **-ain, -ain** *f* dwarf
luchd *n m* people *used to form collective nouns for groups of people eg* **neach-cunntais** accountant **l.-cunntais** accountants
luchd *n* **-a, -an** *m* load, cargo
luchdaich *v* **-achadh** load
luchd-aideachaidh *n m* professing Christians
luchd-amhairc *n m* spectators
luchd-casaid *n m* accusers, prosecution **l.-c. a' Chrùin** the

Crown prosecutors
luchd-ceanna(i)ch *n m* buyers
luchd-ciùil *n m* musicians
luchd-coimhid *n m* spectators, observers
luchd-dàimh *n m* kindred
luchd-ealain *n m* artist(e)s
luchd-èisteachd *n m* audience, listeners
luchd-eòlais *n m* acquaintances
luchd-foillseachaidh *n m* publishers
luchd-fòirneirt *n m* terrorists, oppressors
luchd-frithealaidh *n m* attendants; waiters, waitresses
luchd-leughaidh *n m* readers, readership
luchd-naidheachd *n m* journalists, reporters
luchd-obrach *n m* workers, staff
luchd-riaghlaidh *n m* rulers
luchd-sàbhalaidh *n m* rescuers
luchd-seinn *n m* singers
luchd-sgrùdaidh *n m* inspectors **l.-s. nan sgoiltean** school inspectors
luchd-siubhail *n m* travellers
luchd-smàlaidh *n m* firefighters
luchd-stiùiridh *n m* directors
luchd-tagraidh *n m* pleaders, advocates
luchd-trusaidh *n m* collectors **l.-t. nam fiach** debt collectors
luchd-turais *n m* tourists
lùdag *n* **-aig, -an** *f* (the) little finger, pinkie; hinge
luga *n* **-n/-ichean** *f* lugworm, sandworm
lugha *a* less, least **is l. orm e** I hate it/him
lùghdachadh *n* **-aidh** *m* decrease, reduction, lessening, diminution, downturn
lùghdaich *v* **-achadh** decrease, reduce, lessen, diminish
luibh *n* **-e, -ean** *f m* plant, herb; weed **l.-eòlaiche** *m* botanist **l.-eòlas** *m* botany
Lugsamburgach *n* **-aich, -aich** *m* someone from Luxemburg *a* from, or pertaining to, Luxemburg
luibhre *n f* **an l.** leprosy
luideach *a* **-diche** silly, daft; shabby, untidy
luideag *n* **-eig, -an** *f* rag
luidhear *n* **-eir, -eirean** *f* vent, chimney; ship's funnel
Luinneach *n* **-nich, -nich** *m* someone from Luing *a* from, or pertaining to, Luing
luinneag *n* **-eig, -an** *f* ditty, song
Lùnastal *n* **-ail** *m* **an L.** August *Formerly* **an Lùnasdal**
lurach *a* **-aiche** lovely, beautiful, pretty, attractive
lurgann *n* **-ainn, -an** *f* shin
lurmachd *a See* **lomnochd**
lus *n* **-a/luis, -an** *m* plant, herb **l. a' chrom-chinn** daffodil **l. nam ban-sìth** foxglove **l. nan cluas** saxifrage
luthaig *v* **-eadh** wish, desire *Also* **lùig**
lùth-chleas *n* **-a, -an** *m* athletics, sport
lùth-chleasachd *n f* athletics, sport
lùth-chleasaiche *n* **-an** *m* athlete, sportsman, sportswoman
lùthmhor *a* **-oire** strong, powerful, athletic, vigorous
lùth(s) *n* **lùith(s)** *m* strength, power, vigour, energy **cion lùith(s)** lack of power/energy **gun l.** unable to move

M

m' *poss pron* my (*used before words beginning in vowels or* **fh**)
ma *conj* if
ma *aug prep* about his/her/its
màb *v* **-adh** abuse, vilify
mabach *a* **-aiche** stammering, stuttering, lisping
mac *n* **mic, mic** *m* son **m. bràthar/peathar** nephew
mac-an-aba *n m* ring finger
macanta *a* meek, gentle, mild
macantas *n* **-ais** *m* meekness, mildness
mach *adv* out (*used of motion*) **m. à seo!** let's be off!; out you go! **m. air a chèile** at odds

machair *n* **e-/machrach, machraichean** *f m* machair, sandy arable land near coast
machlag *n* **-aig, -an** *f* uterus, womb, matrix
mac-meanmna *n* **mic-** *m* imagination *Also* **mac-meanmainn**
mac-samhail *n* **mic-** *m* replica, facsimile, duplicate; likeness
mac-talla *n* **mic-** *m* echo
madadh *n* **-aidh, -aidhean** *m* hound, dog **m.-allaidh** wolf **m.-ruadh** fox
madainn *n* **maidne, maidnean** *f* morning **M. mhath!** Good morning!
mag *v* **-adh** mock, scoff, laugh at, jeer
magadh *n* **-aidh** *m* mocking, scoffing, jeer **cùis-mhagaidh** *f* object of ridicule
magail *a* **-e** scoffing, mocking; apt to mock
magairle *n* **-an** *f m* testicle
màgaran *n* **-ain** *m* crawling on all fours **air mhàgaran** on all fours
maghar *n* **-air, -airean** *m* bait (*fishing*), artificial fly *vn* **a' m.** fishing while moving
maide *n* **-an** *m* stick, wood **m.-tarsainn** beam, cross-beam
maids *v* **-eadh/-igeadh** match
maids(e) *n* **-sichean** *m* match (*light*); match (*game*)
màidsear *n* **-eir, -an** *m* major **M. na Pìoba** Pipe Major
Màigh *n* **-e** *f* **a' Mhàigh** May
maighdeann *n* **-dinn, -an/-dinnean** *f* maiden **m.-phòsaidh** bridesmaid **m.-mhara** mermaid
maigheach *n* **-ghiche, -ghichean** *f* hare
maigh(i)stir *n* **-ean** *m* master **Mgr MacÌomhair** Mr MacIver **m.-sgoile** schoolmaster, headmaster
màileid *n* **-e, -ean** *f* bag, suitcase
maill(e) *n* *f* slowness, tardiness, delay **chuireadh maill oirnn** we were delayed
maille ri *prep* (along) with
mair *v* **-sinn/-eachdainn** last, endure
maireann *a* living, extant **... nach m.** the late ... **ri do mhaireann** during your lifetime, as long as you live
maireannach *a* **-aiche** lasting, enduring, everlasting, permanent
mairg *a* woeful, pitiable
màirnealach *a* **-aiche** dilatory, slow
màirnealachd *n* *f* slowness, delay
mairsinneach *a* **-niche** lasting, long-lasting
mairtfheòil *n* **-òla** *f* beef
maise *n* *f* beauty, loveliness, comeliness **ball-m.** beauty spot (*on face*); ornament
maiseach *a* **-siche** beautiful, lovely, comely
maistreadh *n* **-ridh** *m* churning (*making butter*)
maith *v* *See* **math**
màl *n* **màil, màil** *m* rent **air mhàl** rented
mala *n* **-idhean/-ichean/mailghean** *f* eyebrow; brow
malairt *n* **-ean** *f* trade, exchange, commerce, business
màlda *a* modest, coy; gentle, mild
mall *a* **maille** slow, tardy
mallachd *n* **-an** *f* curse
mallaich *v* **-achadh** curse
mallaichte *a* cursed, accursed
màm *n* **màim, -an** *m* large round hill
mamaidh *n* **-ean** *f* mammy, mummy
màm-slèibhe *n* **màim-, màman-** *m* avalanche
manach *n* **-aich, -aich** *m* monk
manachainn *n* **-e, -ean** *f* monastery
manadh *n* **-aidh, -aidhean** *m* omen, warning (*supernatural*), apparition; prophecy **cuir air mhanadh** *v* prophesy
manaidsear *n* **-eir, -an** *m* manager
Manainneach *n* **-nich, -nich** *m* Manx person *a* Manx
mang *n* **mainge, -an** *f* fawn
mànran *n* **-ain, -an** *m* tuneful sound, melody, crooning

mànranach *a* **-aiche** tuneful, melodious, crooning
maodal *n* **-ail, -an** *f* stomach, paunch
maoidh *v* **-eadh** threaten, reproach
maoidheadh *n* **-dhidh, -dhidhean** *m* threat, threatening
maoil *n* **-ean** *f* forehead, brow
maoin *n* **-e, -ean** *f* wealth, riches, fund
maoineachas *n* **-ais** *m* finance
maoinich *v* **-neachadh** finance, fund
maoiseach *n* **-sich, -sichean** *f* doe
maol *n* **maoil, maoil** *f m* rounded headland, mull; promontory **M. Chinn Tìre** Mull of Kintyre
maol *a* **maoile** blunt; bald; hornless; stupid
maor *n* **maoir, maoir** *m* bailiff, steward, constable **m.-cladaich** coastguard
maorach *n* **-aich** *m* shellfish
maoth *a* **maoithe** soft, tender
maothaich *v* **-achadh** soften; mitigate
mapa *n* **-ichean** *m* map
mar *a, adv, prep* (+ *len*), *conj* as, like **mar seo** *adv* like this, thus **mar sin** *adv* like that, therefore **mar sin leat/leibh** *adv* goodbye **mar a** *conj* as
mar *aug prep* about our
marag *n* **-aig, -an** *f* blood-pudding **m. dhubh** black pudding **m. gheal** white pudding
maraiche *n* **-an** *m* seaman, mariner
mar an ceudna *adv* also, likewise, too
mar-aon *adv* together, as one, in concert
marbh *n* **mairbh, mairbh** *m* dead person **na mairbh** the dead **m. na h-oidhche** the dead of night
marbh *a* **mairbhe** dead
marbh *v* **-adh** kill
mar-bhith *n f* fault **gun m.** without fault
marbhrann *n* **-ainn, -an** *m* elegy
marbhtach *a* **-aiche** deadly; mortal
marcachd *n f* riding, horsemanship
marcaich *v* **-achd** ride
marcaiche *n* **-an** *m* rider, horseman
marc-shluagh *n* **-aigh** *m* cavalry, horsemen
mar eisimpleir *adv* for example
margadh *n* **-aidh, -aidhean** *f* market **m. nan earrannan** stock exchange
margaid *n* **-e, -ean** *f* market
màrmor *n* **-oir** *m* marble
màrsail *n* **-e** *f* marching, march
marsanta *n* **-n** *m* merchant
mart *n* **mairt, mairt** *m* cow, steer
Màrt *n* **Màirt** *m* **am M.** March
mar-thà *adv* already
màs *n* **màis, -an** *m* buttock, bottom, posterior
mas *conj See* **mus**
maslach *a* **-aiche** disgraceful, shameful
masladh *n* **-aidh, -aidhean** *m* disgrace, reproach
maslaich *v* **-achadh** disgrace, put to shame
ma-tà *adv* then, in that case
matamataig *n m* mathematics
math *n* **maith** *m* good, benefit **m. a' phobaill** the public interest/good **dè (am) m. a bhith a' bruidhinn?** what's the use of talking?
math *a* **feàrr** good **gu m.** well **m. air ...** good at ... **gu m. fuar** quite cold **chan eil m. dhut ...** you must not ... **mas m. mo chuimhne** if I remember correctly **'s m. sin** that's good **m. dha-rìribh** very good indeed, excellent
math *adv* well
math *v* **-adh** forgive, pardon **m. dhuinn ar peacaidhean** forgive us our sins
ma-thà *adv* then, in that case
mathachadh *n* **-aidh** *m* manure, manuring
mathaich *v* **-achadh** manure
màthair *n* **-ar, màthraichean** *f* mother **m.-chèile** mother-in-law

mathan *n* **-ain, -an** *m* bear **m.-bàn** polar bear
mathanas *n* **-ais** *m* forgiveness, pardon *Also* **maitheanas**
mathas *n* **-ais** *m* goodness, virtue *Also* **maitheas**
math dh'fhaodte *conj* perhaps, maybe
meaban *n* **-ain, -ain** *m* upstart; something damaged
meacan-ruadh *n* **meacain-ruaidh, meacanan-ruadha** *m* radish
meadhan *n* **-ain, -an** *m* middle, centre; medium, means **na meadhanan** the media **teis-m.** the very centre **m.-aois** middle age **na M.-Aoisean** the Middle Ages **m.-chearcall** equator
meadhanach *a* **-aiche** middling, so-so, mediocre; intermediate, central
meadhan-là/latha *n* **meadhain-** *m* midday
meadhan-oidhche *n* **meadhain-** *m* midnight
meadh-bhlàth *a* lukewarm
meadhrach *a* **-aiche** glad, joyous, merry
meal *v* **-tainn/-adh** enjoy, relish **M. do naidheachd!** Congratulations! **m. is caith e** enjoy it and make good use of it
meal-bhuc *n* **-bhuic, -an** *f* melon
meall *n* **mill, mill** *m* lump; round hill; large number; shower (*of rain*) **m.-sgòrnain** Adam's apple
meall *v* **-adh** deceive **... mura h-eil mi air mo mhealladh** ... if I'm not mistaken
mealladh *n* **-aidh** *m* deception, deceiving
meallta *a* deceptive, deceitful, misleading
meamhran *n* **-ain** *m* membrane
mean *a* little **m. air mhean** little by little, gradually
mèanan, mèananaich *n See* **mèaran, mèaranaich**
meanbh *a* **-a** minute, diminutive
meanbhchuileag *n* **-eig, -an** *f* midge
meang *n* **-a/ming, -an** *f* blemish, flaw, abnormality **gun mheang** faultless
meang(l)an *n* **-ain, -an** *m* branch (*of tree*), bough
meanmnach *a* **-aiche** spirited, lively
meann *n* **minn, minn** *m* kid (*animal*)
meannt *n* **-a** *m* mint
meantraig *v* **-eadh** venture, dare
mear *a* **-a** merry, playful
mearachd *n* **-an** *f* mistake, error
mearachdach *a* **-aiche** mistaken, erroneous, inaccurate
mèaran *n* **-ain, -an** *m* yawn
mèaranaich *n* **-e** *f* yawning *Also vn* **a' m.**
mèarrs *v* **-adh/-ail** march
mèarrsadh *n* **-aidh** *m* march, marching
meas *n m* esteem, respect; evaluation, assessment **le m.** yours sincerely (*in letter*)
meas *n* **-a, -an** *m* fruit
meas *v* **meas/-adh** consider, esteem; reckon, estimate, value
measadh *n* **-aidh, -aidhean** *m* assessment, evaluation, appraisal, reckoning
measail *a* **-e** fond; respected, esteemed **m. air ...** fond of ...
measarra *a* temperate, moderate, sober
measarrachd *n f* temperance, restraint
measg *n* **am m.** (+ *gen*) among, amongst
measgachadh *n* **-aidh, -aidhean** *m* mixture, combination
measgaich *v* **-achadh** mix, mingle
meata *a* timid, faint-hearted, feeble
meatailt *n, a* **-e, -ean** *f* metal
meatair *n* **-ean** *m* metre (*length*)
meidh *n* **-e, -ean** *f* balance, scales **air mheidh** in the balance
meigeadaich *n f* bleating (*of goat or kid*)
meil *v* **-ich/-eadh** grind
mèil *v* **-ich** bleat
meileabhaid *n f* velvet
mèilich *n f* bleating
meilich *v* **-leachadh** chill, benumb

mèinn *n* **-e, -ean** *f* mine (*mil, ind*)
mèinn *n* **-e** *f* disposition, temperament
mèinneadair *n* **-ean** *m* miner
mèinnear *n* **-eir, -an** *m* mineral; miner
mèinnearachd *n f* mining, mineralogy
mèinnearach *a* **-aiche** mineral, mineralogical
mèinneil *a* **-e** placid, gentle, refined
meirg *n* **-e** *f* rust
meirg *v* **-eadh** rust, corrode
meirgeach *a* **-giche** rusty
mèirle *n f* theft, thieving **ri m.** thieving **dèan m.** *v* thieve, steal
mèirleach *n* **-lich, -lich** *m* thief
meòrachadh *n* **-aidh, -aidhean** *m* meditation, deliberation
meòraich *v* **-achadh** meditate, deliberate, reflect *Also* **meòmhraich**
meòrachan *n* **-ain, -ain** *m* memorandum
meud *n* **-an** *m* size, extent, amount
meudachd *n f* size, bulk
meudaich *v* **-achadh** increase, enlarge
meug *n* **meòig** *m* whey
meur *n* **meòir, meòir/-an** *f* finger, digit; branch (*org*); knot (*in wood*) **m.-lorg** fingerprint **m.-chlàr** keyboard
meuran *n* **-ain, -ain/-an** *m* thimble; knot (*in wood*)
mì- *neg pref* not, dis-, ill-, in-, mis-, -less
mi(se) *pron* I, me
miadhail *a* **-e** respected, esteemed; fond **m. air ...** fond of ...
miag *v* **-ail** mew
mial *n* **-a, -an** *f* louse; tick
mial-chù *n* **-choin, -choin** *m* greyhound
mia(tha)laich *n f* mewing *Also vn* **a' m.**
miann *n* **-an** *f m* desire, wish **bu mhiann leam** I would like
miannaich *v* **-achadh** desire
mias *n* **mias/mèise, -an** *f* basin
miast(r)adh *n* **-aidh** *m* havoc, vandalism
mì-bheusachd *n f* indecency, impropriety
mì-chàilear *a* unpleasant, disagreeable, distasteful
mì-chiatach *a* **-aiche** unseemly, improper; outrageous
mì-chinnt *n f* uncertainty
mì-chinnteach *a* **-tiche** uncertain
mì-chliù *n* disrepute, dishonour
mì-chofhurtail *a* **-e** uncomfortable
mì-chùramach *a* **-aiche** careless
mì-dhòigh *n f* lack of method, lack of care; deprivation
mì-dhòigheil *a* **-e** unmethodical, disorganized
mì-fhaiceallach *a* **-aiche** careless
mì-fhallain *a* **-e** unhealthy, unwholesome
mì-fhoighidneach *a* **-niche** impatient
mì-fhortanach *a* **-aiche** unfortunate, unlucky
mì-fhreagarrach *a* **-aiche** unsuitable
mì-ghean *n* **-a** *m* discontent, melancholy
mì-ghnàthaich *v* **-achadh** abuse
mì-ghoireasach *a* **-aiche** inconvenient
mì-iomchaidh *a* **-e** improper
mì-laghail *a* **-e** unlawful, illegal
mil *n* **meala/mealach, mealan** *f* honey
mìle *n* **mìltean** *f m* thousand; mile
milis *a* **mìlse** sweet; harmonious (*mus*)
mill *v* **-eadh** spoil, mar, ruin
milleadh *n* **-lidh** *m* spoiling, marring, ruining
millean *n* **-ein/-an** *m* million
millteach *a* **-tiche** destructive, ruinous, prodigal, detrimental
mìlseachd *n f* sweetness
mìlsean *n* **-ein, -ein/-an** *m* sweet, dessert
mì-mhisneachadh *n* **-aidh** *m* discouragement
mì-mhisneachail *a* **-e** discouraging, disheartening
mì-mhisnich *v* **-neachadh** discourage, dishearten

mì-mhodh *n* **-mhoidh, -a** *m* impoliteness, misbehaviour, impertinence **na bi ri m.!** don't misbehave
mì-mhodhail *a* **-e** impolite, misbehaved, rude, discourteous
min *n* **-e** meal *f* **m.-choirce** oatmeal **m.-fhlùir** white flour **m.-sàibh** sawdust
mìn *a* **-e** smooth, soft, delicate
mì-nàdarrach *a* **-aiche** unnatural
mìneachadh *n* **-aidh, -aidhean** *m* interpretation, explanation
mìnich *v* **mìneachadh** interpret, explain
minig *a* often, frequent
minig *v* **-eadh** mean
ministear *n* **-eir, -an** *m* minister **M. na Còmhdhail** the Transport Minister
ministrealachd *n f* ministry (*relig, polit*) **M. an Dìon** the Ministry of Defence
miogadaich *n See* **meigeadaich**
mion *a* **-a** minute, small, on a small scale **m.-chunntas** *f m* detailed account **m.-eòlach (+ air)** fully conversant with, expert in **m.-sgrùd** *v* scrutinize, analyze
mionach *n* **-aich, -aichean** *m* stomach, intestines, entrails
mionaid *n* **-e, -ean** *f* minute **fuirich m. bheag** wait a second
mionaideach *a* **-diche** precise, detailed, exact **gu m.** minutely, in detail
mì-onarach *a* **-aiche** dishonest, dishonourable
mion-chànan *n* **-ain, -an** *f m* minority language
mionnachadh *n* **-aidh** *m* swearing
mionnaich *v* **-achadh** swear; curse
mionnaichte *a* convinced, certain
mionnan *n* **-ain, -ain/-an** *m* oath **mo mhionnan!** I swear!
mions *n* **-a** *m* mince
mìorbhail *n* **-e, -ean** *f* marvel, miracle
mìorbhaileach *a* **-liche** marvellous, miraculous
mìos *n* **-a, -an** *f m* month **m. nam pòg** honeymoon
miosa *a See* **dona**
mìosachan *n* **-ain, -ain** *m* calendar
mìosail *a* monthly
miotag *n* **-aig, -an** *f* glove, mitten
mìr *n* **-e, -ean** *m* bit, piece, fragment
mire *n f* merriment, mirth, frolic
mìrean *n* **-ein, -ein/-an** *m* particle, small piece
mì-reusanta *a* unreasonable
mì-riaghailt *n* **-e, -ean** *f* disorder, irregularity
mì-riaghailteach *a* **-tiche** disorderly, unruly, irregular
mì-rian *n f* disorder, disorganization
mì-rianail *a* **-e** disordered, disorderly
mì-riaraichte *a* dissatisfied
mì-rùn *n* **-rùin** *m* malice, ill will
miseanaraidh *n* **-ean** *m* missionary
misg *n* **-e** *f* drunkenness, intoxication **air mhisg** drunk
misgear *n* **-eir, -an** *m* drunkard, boozer
mì-sgiobalta *a* untidy
mì-shealbh *n* **-sheilbh** *m* misfortune, ill-luck **gheibh thu do mhì-shealbh** you'll catch it (*met*)
mì-shealbhach *a* **-aiche** unfortunate, unlucky
mì-shona *a* unhappy, discontent
misneachail *a* **-e** courageous, encouraging; confident
misneachd *n f* courage, encouragement, boldness; confidence *Also* **misneach**
misnich *v* **-neachadh** encourage, embolden
miste *a* worse **cha bu mhiste tu sin** you would be none the worse of that
mì-thaingealachd *n f* ingratitude
mì-thaingeil *a* **-e** ungrateful
mì-thaitneach *a* **-niche** unpleasant, disagreeable
mì-thlachdmhor *a* **-oire** unpleasant, disagreeable
mì-thoileachas *a* **-ais** *m* displeasure, unhappiness,

discontent
mì-thoilichte *a* unhappy, displeased, discontent
mì-thuarail *a* **-e** ill-looking, looking off-colour
mo *poss pron* my, mine (+ *len*) **mo chreach!** Alas! **mo thogair!** who cares? (**m'** *before vowels or* **fh**)
moch *a* **moich(e)** early **o mhoch gu dubh** from dawn till dusk
mocheirigh *n f* rising early
mòd *n* **mòid, -an** *m* mod, assembly, court **am Mòd Nàiseanta** the National Mod
modail *n* **-e, -ean** *f* model
modal *n* **-ail, -an** *m* module
modh *n* **-a, -an/-annan** *f m* manner, mode, behaviour; procedure, process; mood (*gram*)
modhail *a* **-e** polite, mannerly, courteous
mogal *n* **-ail, -ail** *m* mesh (*of net*)
mogan *n* **-ain, -an** *m* stash (*of money*); slipper
mòine *n* **mòine/mòna(dh)/mònach** *f* peat, moss **buain na mòna** cutting peat
mòinteach *n* **-tich, -tichean** *f* moor, moorland
moit *n* **-e** *f* pride
moiteil *a* **-e** proud
mol *n* **moil/-a, -an** *m* shingle, shingle beach
mol *v* **-adh** praise; recommend, propose
molach *a* **-aiche** hairy, shaggy, rough
moladh *n* **-aidh** *m* praise; recommendation
molag *n* **-aig, -an** *f* pebble
moll *n* **muill** *m* chaff
molldair *n* **-ean** *m* mould
molt *n* **muilt, muilt** *m* wedder (*sheep*)
moltach *a* **-aiche (+ air)** praising, laudatory
mòmaid *n* **-e, -ean** *f* moment
monadail *a* **-e** hilly, mountainous
monadh *n* **-aidh, -aidhean** *m* moor, hill, mountain **am M. Ruadh** the Cairngorms
monaiseach *n* **-siche** slow, dull; self-effacing
monmhar *n* **-air, -an** *m* murmur
mòr *a* **motha/mò** big, great, large **tha iad mòr aig a chèile** they are great friends **cha mhòr gum faca sinn iad** we hardly saw them **cha mhòr nach do thuit mi** I almost fell **bha e mòr leam faighneachd** I was reluctant to ask **mòr às fhèin** haughty
mòrachd *n f* greatness, majesty
morair *n* **-ean** *m* lord, peer **Taigh nam Morairean** the House of Lords
moralta *a* moral
moraltachd *n f* morality
mòran *n* **-ain** *m* many, much, a lot *adv* much
mòr-bhùth *n* **-a, -an/-bhùithtean** *f* supermarket
mòr-chuid *n f* majority
mòrchuis *n* **-e** *f* pride, haughtiness, conceit
mòrchuiseach *a* **-siche** haughty, conceited, pompous
mòr-chuisle *n* **-an** *f* artery
mòr-dhail *n* **-ean** *m* convention, assembly, congress
morgaidse *n* **-an** *m* mortgage
morghan *n* **-ain** *m* gravel, shingle
mòr-ghath *n* **-a, -an** *m* harpoon, trident
mòr-roinn *n* **-e, -ean** *f* continent
mòr-shluagh *n* **-aigh, -an** *m* populace, host, multitude
mòr-thìr *n* **-e, -ean** *m* mainland, continent
mosach *a* **-aiche** miserable, nasty, inclement (*weather*); mean (*person*)
mosgaideach *a* **-diche** dilatory, slow, unreliable
mosgail *v* **-gladh** arouse, waken
motair *n* **-ean** *m* motor **m.-baic** motorbike **m.-baidhsagal** motorbicycle
motha *a See* **mòr**
mothachadh *n* **-aidh, -aidhean** *m* consciousness, awareness; sensation **gun mhothachadh** unconscious

mothachail *a* **-e** conscious, aware
mothaich *v* **-achadh** notice, perceive
mothar *n* **-air, -air** *m* loud shout *Also* **mòthar**
mu *prep* about, around
muc *n* **muice, -an** *f* pig, sow
mùch *v* **-adh** stifle, suppress, smother, extinguish
mu choinneamh *prep phr* (+ *gen*) opposite **mu ch. na bùtha** opposite the shop
mu chuairt *adv*, *prep phr* (+ *gen*) around **mu ch. an t-saoghail** around the world
muc-mhara *n* **muic-mhara/muice-mara, mucan-mara** *f* whale
mud *aug prep* about your (*sg*)
mu dheidhinn *prep phr* (+ *gen*) about, concerning **mu dh. na coinneimh** about the meeting
mu dheireadh *adv* eventually, finally, at last **mu dh. thall** at long last
muga *n* **-nnan** *f m* mug
mùgach *a* **-aiche** sullen, surly; gloomy
muicfheòil *n* **-òla** *f* pork
muigh *adv* **a-muigh** out, outside
Muileach *n* **-lich, -lich** *m* someone from Mull *a* from, or pertaining to, Mull
muileann *n* **-linn/muilne, -an/muilnean** *f m* mill **m.-gaoithe** windmill
muile-mhàg *n* **muileacha-màg** *f* toad
muilicheann *n* **-chinn, -chinnean** *m* sleeve (*clothing*) *Also* **muinichill**
muillear *n* **-eir, -an** *m* miller
muiltfheòil *n* **-òla** *f* mutton
muime *n* **-achan** *f* step-mother, foster mother
muin *n f* back **air m.** (+ *gen*) on top of **dèan m.** *v* have sexual intercourse
mùin *v* **mùn** urinate
muineal *n* **-eil, -an** *m* neck
muing *n* **-e, -ean** *f* mane
muinighin *n* **-e** *f* trust, confidence
muinntir *n* **-e** *f* people, folk
muinntireas *n* **-eis** *m* domestic service **air mhuinntireas** in service
muir *n* **mara, marannan** *f m* sea, ocean **m.-làn** high tide **m.-tràigh** low water
mùirn *n* **-e** *f* cheerfulness, joy; affection
mùirneach *a* **-niche** cheerful, joyful; beloved, precious
muirsgian *n* **-sgein, -an** *f m* razorfish
mulad *n* **-aid** *m* sadness, sorrow **fo mhulad** sad, sorrowful
muladach *a* **-aiche** sad, sorrowful; pitiful
mullach *n* **-aich, -aich/-aichean** *m* top, summit
mum *aug prep* about my; about their
mùn *n* **mùin** *m* urine
mun *aug prep* about the; about their
muncaidh *n* **-ean** *m* monkey
mun cuairt *adv* around
mur(a) *conj* unless, if not
mur *aug prep* about our; about your (*pl & pol*)
muran *n* **-ain** *m* marram grass, sea-bent, bent-grass
murt *n* **muirt, muirt** *m* murder
murt *v* **murt/-adh** murder
murtaidh *a* **-e** sultry
murtair *n* **-ean** *m* murderer
mus *conj* before
mu seach *adv* alternately; aside **tè mu s.** one after the other
mu sgaoil *adv* loose, at large **leig mu s.** *v* set free, release
mùth *v* **-adh** change, alter, mutate
mu thimcheall *prep phr* (+ *gen*) about, around, concerning
mu thràth *adv* already, before

N

na *def art* the (*used before pl forms not in gen case*), of the (*used before sg forms of feminine nouns in gen case*) **na h-ùbhlan** the apples **na h-uinneige** of the window
na *neg part* do not (*used in negative commands*) **na bi (cho)**

gòrach! don't be (so) silly! **na can an còrr!** don't say any more, say no more!
na *conj* than (*used in comparison of two items*) **tha an tè seo nas motha na an tè sin** this one is bigger than that one
na *rel pron* what, that (which), as much **sin na ghabhas e** that is as much as/all (that) it will take
na *aug prep* in her, in his (+ *len*), in it **na baga** in her bag **na bhaga** in his bag **tha i na dotair** she's a doctor **tha e na shaor** he's a joiner **bha i na cadal** she was asleep **bha e na chadal** he was asleep
na *contr of* **an do seo far na thachair e** this is where it happened
nàbachd *n f* neighbourhood
nàbaidh *n* **-ean** *m* neighbour; (*colloq*) mate
nach *neg conj* whom, that/those … not **an fheadhainn n. robh an làthair** those who were not present
nad *aug prep* in your (+ *len*) **nad phòcaid** in your pocket **a bheil thu nad dhùisg?** are you awake?
nàdar *n* **-air** *m* nature; type **bha n. de dh'eagal orm ...** I was somewhat afraid to ...
nàdarrach *a* **-aiche** natural
naidheachd *n* **-an** *f* news; story, anecdote **Dè do n.?** What's your news?
naidhlean *n* **-ein** *m* nylon
nàimhdeas *n* **-eis** *m* enmity, hostility
nàimhdeil *a* **-e** hostile
nàire *n f* shame, embarrassment **an robh nàir' ort idir?** were you not ashamed? **duine gun n.** a brazen man **mo nàir' ort!** shame on you!
nàisean *n* **-ein, -an** *m* nation
nàiseanta *a* national **Partaidh N. na h-Alba** the Scottish National Party **Dualchas N. na h-Alba** Scottish National Heritage
nàlseantach *n* **-aich, -aich** *m* nationalist
nàiseantachd *n f* nationalism, nationality
naisgear *n* **-eir, -an** *m* conjunction (*gram*)
nall *adv See* **a-nall**
nam *def art* of the (*used before words beginning in b, f, m, p in gen pl*)
nam *conj* if (*followed by the conditional form of verbs beginning in b, f, m, p*) **nam bruthadh tu am putan** if you pressed the button
nam *aug prep* in my (+ *len*) **nam thaigh fhèin** in my own house **bha mi nam chadal** I was asleep
nàmhaid *n* **-ad, -ean** *m* enemy, foe
nan *def art* of the (*used before words other than those beginning in b, f, m, p in gen pl*)
nan *conj* if (*followed by the conditional form of the verb*) **nan innseadh tu dhomh dè tha dhìth ort** if you'd tell me what you want
nan *aug prep* in their **nan obraichean** in their jobs **bha iad nan seasamh** they were standing
naochad *n* **-aid, -an** *m* ninety
naoi *n, a* nine *Also* **naodh**
naoi-deug *n, a* nineteen **naoi nota deug** nineteen pounds *Also* **naodh-deug**
naoidheamh *a* ninth *Also* **naodhamh**
naoidheamh-deug *a* nineteenth **an naoidheamh latha deug** the nineteenth day *Also* **naodhamh-d.**
naoidhean *n* **-ein, -an** *m* infant, baby
naoinear *n f m* nine (people) *Also* **naodhnar**
naomh *a* **naoimhe** holy, sacred, saintly
naomh *n* **naoimh, naoimh** *m* saint
naomhachadh *n* **-aidh** *m* sanctification
naomhachd *n f* holiness, saintliness, sanctity

naomhaich *v* **-achadh** sanctify
naosg *n* **naoisg, naoisg** *m* snipe
nar *aug prep* in our **nar cùram** in our care **bha sinn nar sìneadh** we were having a lie-down
nàr *a* **nàire** shameful, disgraceful
nàrach *a* **-aiche** ashamed, shamefaced; bashful
nàraich *v* **-achadh** shame, embarrass, disgrace **bha sinn air ar nàrachadh** we were ashamed
nas *aug pron (used with comparative forms of adjectives)* **nas motha na** bigger than
nathair *n* **nathrach, nathraichean** *f* snake, serpent
neach *n m* person, individual (**luchd** *is used as the pl of* **neach) n. sam bith** anyone
neach-casaid *n m* procurator **N.-c. a' Chrùin** Procurator Fiscal *pl* **Luchd-casaid**
neach-cathrach *n m* chairperson, chair
neach-ceàirde *n m* tradesperson
neach-ceasnachaidh *n m* questioner, interviewer, quizmaster, inquisitor
neach-ciùil *n m* musician
neach-comhairleachaidh *n m* adviser
neach-cuideachaidh *n m* helper, assistant, aide
neach-deasachaidh *n m* editor
neach-deilbh *n m* designer
neach-ealain *n m* artist(e)
neach-frithealaidh *n m* waiter, attendant
neach-gairm *n m* convener
neach-gnothaich *n m* business person
neach-ionaid *n m* proxy, agent, substitute
neach-iùil *n m* guide
neach-labhairt *n m* spokesperson, speaker
neach-lagha *n* **-a** *m* lawyer, solicitor
neach-obrach *n m* worker, employee
neach-riaghlaidh *n m* ruler, governor
neach-sàbhalaidh *n m* rescuer
neach-sgrùdaidh *n m* examiner, inspector
neach-stiùiridh *n m* director
neach-teagaisg *n m* teacher
neach-togail *n m* builder
neach-treòrachaidh *n m* guide
nead *n* **nid, nid/-an** *f m* nest
neadaich *v* **-achadh** nest, nestle
nèamh *n* **nèimh, -an** *m* heaven
nèamhaidh *a* heavenly
neamhnaid *n* **-e, -ean** *f* pearl, jewel
nèapaigin *n* **(-e), -ean** *f* napkin; handkerchief
nèapraigear *n* **-eir, -an** *m* handkerchief *Also* **nèapraige**
nearbha(sa)ch *a* **-a(sa)iche** nervous
neart *n* **neirt, -an** *m* strength, might, force
neartaich *v* **-achadh** strengthen
neartmhor *a* **-oire** strong, powerful
neas *n* **-a, -an** *m* weasel, stoat
neasgaid *n* **-e, -ean** *f* boil, ulcer
nèibhidh *n* **-ean** *m* navy
neo *conj* or
neo- *neg pref* in-, un-, -less
neo-abaich *a* **-e** unripe
neo-àbhaisteach *a* **-tiche** unusual, exceptional
neo-airidh *a* **-e** unworthy, undeserving
neo-ar-thaing *a* independent **air do n.** whether you like it or not **n. bruidhinn, ach cha dèan e dad** plenty talk but no action
neo-ar-thaingeil *a* independent-minded; ungrateful
neo-bhàsmhor *a* immortal
neo-chaochlaideach *a* unchangeable
neochoireach *a* **-riche** innocent, blameless
neo-chumanta *a* uncommon, unusual
neo-chùramach *a* **-aiche** negligent, careless, inattentive
neo-dhiadhachd *n f* atheism
neo-dhiadhaire *n* **-an** *m* atheist
neo-dhìlseachd *n f* infidelity, disloyalty
neo-eisimeileach *a* **-liche**

independent
neo-eisimeileachd *n f* independence
neo-fhoirmeil *a* **-e** informal
neo-fhoirmeileachd *n f* informality
neòghlan *a* **-aine** unclean
neoghlaine *n f* uncleanness, uncleanliness
neo(i)chiontach *a* **-aiche** innocent
neo(i)chiontachd *n f* innocence
neòinean *n* **-ein, -ein/-an** *m* daisy **n.-grèine** sunflower
neo-làthaireachd *n f m* absence
neo-mhearachdach *a* **-aiche** unerring, infallible, correct
neònach *a* **-aiche** strange, unusual, curious
neoni *n m* nothing, zero
neo-oifigeil *a* **-e** unofficial
neo-riaghailteach *a* **-tiche** irregular
neo-thruacanta *a* pitiless, unmerciful, implacable
neul *n* **neòil, neòil** *m* cloud; hue; faint **chaidh e ann an n.** he fainted
neulach *a* **-aiche** cloudy
nì *n* **nithean** *m* thing **nì sam bith** anything **air sgàth Nì Math!** for goodness's sake!
nì *irr v* will do, will make (*See irr v* **dèan** *in Grammar*)
nic *n* daughter (of) (*used only in surnames of women*) **Sìne NicDhùghaill** Jean MacDougall
nigh *v* **-e** wash, clean
nigheadair *n* **-ean** *m* washing machine
nigheadaireachd *n f* washing **an do rinn thu an n.?** have you done the washing?
nigheadair-shoithichean *n* **nigheadairean-** *m* dishwasher
nighean *n* **nighinne/ighne, -an/ighnean** *f* girl, daughter **n. bràthar/n. peathar** niece
nìghneag *n* **-eig, -an** *f* young girl, little girl *Also* **nìonag**
nimh *n* **-e** *m* poison, venom
nimheil *a* **-e** poisonous, venomous, virulent
Nirribheach *n* **-bhich, -bhich** *m* Norwegian *a* Norwegian
nis *adv* now *See* **a-nis**
nithear *irr v* will be done, will be made (*See irr v* **dèan** *in Grammar*)
nitheigin *pron* something
niùclas *n* **-ais, -an** *m* nucleus
niùclasach *a* nuclear
no *conj* or
nobhail *n* **-e, -ean** *f* novel
nochd *v* **-adh** appear; reveal, show
nodha *a* new **ùr n.** brand new
nòisean *n* **-ein, -ein** *m* notion; attraction **bha n. mòr aige dhi** he was greatly attracted to her
Nollaig *n* **-e, -ean** *f* **an N.** Christmas **N. Chridheil!** Merry Christmas!
norra(dh) *n m* wink of sleep, nap **cha d' fhuair sinn n. cadail** we didn't get a wink of sleep
norradaich *n* **-e** *f* nodding off, dozing *Also vn* **a' n.**
norrag *n* **-aig, -an** *f* nap, snooze, forty winks
nòs *n* **nòis, -an** *m* habit, custom; style **seinn san t-seann n.** traditional style singing *f*
nota *n* **-ichean** *f* note; pound sterling
nuadh *a* **nuaidhe** new **nuadh-bhàrdachd** modern poetry **an Tiomnadh N.** the New Testament
nuair a *conj* when
nuairsin *adv See* **an uair sin**
nuallanaich *n* lowing, bellowing (*of animals*)
nuas *adv* up, upwards *See* **a-nuas**
null *adv* over (*to the other side*) *See* **a-null**
nur *aug prep* in your (*pl & pol*) **a bheil sibh nur dùisg?** Are you awake?
nurs *n* **-aichean** *f* nurse

O

ò *exclam* O! Oh!
o *prep* from **o cheann gu ceann** from end to end *Also* **bho**

o (a) *conj* since **tha greis o thachair e** there's a while since it happened *Also* **bho**
òb *n* **-a/òib, -an** *m* bay, creek
obair *n* **obrach/oibre, obraichean/oibrichean** *f* work, job, employment, labour **o.-làimhe** handiwork **o.-taighe** housework **a dh'aon o./mar aon o.** intentionally, deliberately **gun o.** unemployed
òban *n* **-ain, -ain** *m* small bay, little creek
obann *a* **obainne** sudden **gu h-o.** suddenly
obh *exclam* **obh, obh!** Oh dear!
obraich *v* **-achadh/obair** work
obraiche *n* **-an** *m* worker *Also* **oibriche**
och *exclam* Alas! Ah!
ochanaich *n* **(-e)** *f* sighing
ochd *a* eight *n* **a h-ochd**
ochdad *n* **-aid, -an** *m* eighty
ochdamh *a* eighth
ochd-cheàrnach *n* **-aich** *m* octagon
ochd-deug *n, a* eighteen **ochd troighean deug** eighteen feet
ochdnar *n f m* eight (people)
o chionn *prep* since, ago **o ch. f(h)ada** a long time ago
od *aug prep* from your (*sg*)
odhar *a* **-air/uidhre** dun-coloured
ofrail *n* **-e, -ean** *f* offering, sacrifice
òg *a* **òige** young, youthful
ògail *a* **-e** youthful, young
òganach *n* **-aich, -aich** *m* youth, youngster
ogha *n* **-ichean/-chan** *m* grandchild **tha iad anns na h-oghaichean** they are cousins
Ògmhios *n* **-ios(a)** *m* **an t-Ò.** June
ogsaidean *n* **-ein** *m* oxygen
oide *n* **-an** *m* step-father; tutor
oideachas *n* **-ais** *m* education, tuition
oidhche *n* **-annan** *f* night **O. mhath** Good night **o. h-Aoine** Friday night **O. Challainn** Hogmanay **O. Shamhna** Halloween **air an o.** at night
oidhirp *n* **-e, -ean** *f* attempt, effort **dèan o.** *v* try
oifig *n See* **oifis**
oifigeach *n* **-gich, -gich** *m* official, officer
oifigear *n* **-eir, -an** *m* officer, official **àrd-o.** chief executive
oifigeil *a* **-e** official
oifis *n* **-e, -ean** *f* office **o. a' phuist** post office
òigear *n* **-eir, -an** *m* youth, youngster
òigh *n* **-e, -ean** *f* virgin, maiden
oighre *n* **-achan** *m* heir
oighreachd *n* **-an** *f* estate, inheritance
òigridh *n f* (*coll*) youth, youngsters
oilbheum *n* **-eim, -an** *m* offence
oilbheumach *a* **-aiche** offensive
oileanach *n* **-aich, -aich** *m* student
oilisgin *n* **-ean** *f m* oilskin
oillt *n* **-e, -ean** *f* horror, dread, terror
oillteil *a* **-e** horrific, horrid, dreadful, terrifying
oilltich *v* **-teachadh** horrify, terrify
oilthigh *n* **-ean** *m* university
òinseach *n* **-siche, -sichean** *f* fool (*female*), foolish woman
oir *n* **-e, -ean** *f m* edge, border, margin, fringe **air an o.** at the edge
oir *conj* for, because
oirbh(se) *prep pron* on you (*pl & pol*)
òirdheirc *a* **-e** glorious; illustrious
òirleach *n* **-lich, -lich** *f* inch
oirnn(e) *prep pron* on us
oirre(se) *prep pron* on her
oirthir *n* **-e, -ean** *f* coast, seaboard
oisean *n* **-ein, -an** *m* corner *Also* **oisinn**
oiteag *n* **-eig, -an** *f* breeze, gust of wind
oitir *n* **-e/oitreach, -ean** *f* bank in sea **o. gainmhich** sandbank
òl *v* drink
ola *n* **-ichean** *f* oil **clàr o.** oil production platform
olc *n* **uilc** *m* evil, wickedness

olc *a* evil, wicked, bad
ollamh *n* **-aimh, -an** *m* doctor (*acad*), professor **An t-Oll. MacLeòid** Dr MacLeod **àrd-o.** professor
om *aug prep* from my; from their
òmar *n* **òmair** *m* amber
on *aug prep* from their; from the
on a *conj* since
onair *n* **-e, -ean** *f* honour **air m' onair!** honestly!
onarach *a* **-aiche** honest, honourable
onfhadh *n* **-aidh, -aidhean** *m* blast, storm, raging sea
onghail *n* **-e** *f* uproar, tumult
ònrachd *n f* solitude **bha i na h-ò.** she was alone
òr *n* **òir** *m* gold
or *aug prep* from our, from your
òrach *a* **-aiche** golden
òraid *n* **-e, -ean** *f* speech, lecture, oration, talk **thoir seachad ò./dèan ò.** *v* give a talk/lecture
òraidiche *n* **-an** *m* speaker, lecturer
orainds *a See* **orains**
oraindsear *n See* **orainsear**
orains *a* **-e** orange
orainsear *n* **-eir, -an** *m* orange
òran *n* **òrain, òrain** *m* song **gabh ò.** *v* sing a song **ò. càraid** duet **ò. luaidh** waulking song *Also* **amhran**
òr-bhuidhe *a* golden yellow, auburn
òr-cheàrd *n* **-chèird, -an** *m* goldsmith, jeweller
òrd *n* **ùird, ùird/-an** *m* hammer
òrdag *n* **-aig, -an** *f* thumb, toe **an ò. mhòr** the big toe
òrdaich *v* **-achadh** order, ordain, decree
òrdail *a* **-e** orderly, methodical; ordinal
òrdan *n* **-ain, -ain** *m* order
òrdugh *n* **-uigh, -uighean** *m* order, command, decree; order (*arrangement*) **o. cùirte** court order, injunction **cuir an ò.** arrange *v* **na h-òrduighean** the communion services
òr-iasg *n* **-èisg, -èisg** *m* goldfish
orm(sa) *prep pron* on me
orra(san) *prep pron* on them
ort(sa) *prep pron* on you (*sg*)
osag *n* **osaig, -an** *f* breeze, gust
osan *n* **osain/-an** *m* hose, stocking
os cionn *prep phr* (+ *gen*) above, over **os ar cionn** above us
osgarra *a* audible
os ìosal *adv* secretly, covertly, quietly
os-nàdarra(ch) *a* supernatural
osna(dh) *n* **osna(idh), -aidhean** *f m* sigh **dèan/leig o.** *v* sigh
osnaich *n* **-e, -ean** *f* sighing *Also vn* **ag o.**
ospadal *n* **-ail, -an** *m* hospital
ostail *n* **-ean** *f* hostel **o.-òigridh** youth hostel
òstair *n* **-ean** *m* hotelier, innkeeper
Ostaireach *n* **-rich, -rich** *m* Austrian *a* Austrian
othail *n* **-e, -ean** *f* hubbub, tumult, uproar; rejoicing
othaisg *n* **-e, -ean/ òisgean** *f* year-old ewe, hog
òtrach *n* **-aich, -aichean** *m* dunghill, rubbish dump, midden *Also* **òcrach**

P

paca *n* **-nnan** *m* pack *Also* **pac**
pacaid *n* **-e, -ean** *f* packet
pacaig *v* **-eadh** pack
pacaigeadh *n* **-gidh** *m* packing *Also* **pacadh**
pàganach *n* **-aich, -aich** *m* pagan, heathen *a* pagan
pàganachd *n f* paganism, heathenism
paidh *n* **-ean/-ichean** *m* pie **p. ubhail** apple pie
paidhir *n* **pàidhrichean** *f m* pair **p. bhrògan** pair of shoes
paidirean *n* **-rin, -rinean** *m* rosary; string of beads
paidse *n* **-sichean** *f* patch
pàigh *v* **-eadh** pay
pàigheadh *n* **-ghidh** *m* pay, payment, wages
pàillean *n* **-ein, -an** *m* pavilion, marquee, tent

pailm *n* **-e** *f* palm (*tree*)
pailt *a* **-e** plentiful, abundant
pailteas *n* **-eis** *m* plenty, abundance **tha (am) p. againn** we have plenty
pàipear *n* **-eir, -an** *m* paper; newspaper **p.-balla** wallpaper **p.-gainmhich** sandpaper **p.-naidheachd** newspaper **am P. Beag** the West Highland Free Press
pàipearaich *v* **-achadh** paper, wallpaper
pàipeir *a* paper
pàirc(e) *n* **-(e), -(e)an** *f* park **p. chàraichean** car park
paireafain *n m* paraffin *Also* **parafan**
pairilis *n f m* paralysis, palsy
pàirt *n* **-ean** *m* part, portion **gabh p. an** *v* take part in, participate
paisean *n* **-ein, -an** *m* faint **chaidh e ann am p.** *v* he fainted *Also* **paiseanadh**
paisg *v* **pasgadh** fold, wrap
paisgte *a* folded, wrapped
pàiste *n* **-an** *m* infant, child *Formerly* **pàisde**
pait *n* **-e, -ean** *f* lump, swelling (*on body*)
pàiteach *a* **-tiche** thirsty, parched
pana *n* **-ichean** *m* pan
pannal *n* **-ail, -an** *m* panel **P. na Cloinne** the Children's Panel
Pàp(a) *n* **-(a)n/-(a)chan** *m* Pope **am Pàp(a)** the Pope
Pàpanach *n* **-aich, -aich** *m* Roman Catholic *a* Roman Catholic
paraist(e) *n* **-an** *m* parish *Formerly* **paraisd(e)**
pàrant *n* **-an** *m* parent
pàrlamaid *n* **-e, -ean** *f* parliament **P. na h-Alba** the Scottish Parliament **P. na h-Eòrpa** the European Parliament
Pàrras *n* **-ais** *m* Paradise
parsail *n* **-ean** *m* parcel
partaidh *n* **-ean** *f m* party **p. poilitigeach** political party
partan *n* **-ain, -an** *m* small crab
pasgan *n* **-ain, -ain/-an** *m* package, bundle
pathadh *n* **-aidh** *m* thirst **a bheil am p. ort?** are you thirsty?
pàtran *n* **-ain, -an** *m* pattern
peacach *n* **-aich, -aich** *m* sinner
peacach *a* **-aiche** sinful
peacadh *n* **-aidh, -aidhean** *m* sin
peacaich *v* **-achadh** sin
peall *n* **pill, pillean** *m* pelt, hide
peallach *a* **-aiche** hairy, shaggy
peanas *n* **-ais, -an** *m* punishment, penalty
peanasaich *v* **-achadh** punish, penalize
peann *n* **pinn, pinn/-tan** *m* pen
peansail *n* **-ean** *m* pencil
peant *n* **-aichean/-an** *m* paint
peant *v* **-adh** paint
peantair *n* **-ean** *m* painter, decorator
pearsa *n* **-chan** *m* person
pearsanta *a* personal, subjective
pearsantachd *n* **-an** *f* personality
pears-eaglais *n* **pearsan-/pearsachan-** *m* cleric, clergyman
peasair *n* **-srach, -sraichean** *f* pea, peas
peasan *n* **-ain, -an** *m* brat, imp
peata *n* **-n/-aichean/-chan** *m* pet **p.-ruadh** puffin
peatrail *n m* petrol *Also* **peatroil**
peighinn *n* **-e, -ean** *f* old penny; pennyland (*topog*)
peile *n* **-lichean** *m* pail *Also* **peidhil**
pèileag *n* **-eig, -an** *f* porpoise
peilear *n* **-eir, -an** *m* bullet **dh'fhalbh iad aig p. am beatha** they went off at high speed
pèin *See* **fhèin**
peinnsean *n* **-ein** *m* pension **p. na Stàite** the State pension
peirceall *n* **-cill/-cle, -an/-clean** *m* jaw, jawbone
peitean *n* **-ein, -an** *m* waistcoat, sweater
peitseag *n* **-eig, -an** *f* peach
peucag *n* **-aig, -an** *f* peacock
peur *n* **-a, -an** *f* pear
Pharasach *n* **-aich, -aich** *m* Pharisee
pian *n* **pèin, -tan** *f* pain, torment
pian *v* **-adh** pain, torment, annoy

plàna *n* **-than** *m* piano
piantach *a* **-aiche** painful *Also* **piantail**
pic *n* **-e, -ean** *m* pickaxe, pick
picil *n* **-e** *f* pickle
pige *n* **-achan** *m* pitcher, earthen jar *Also* **pigidh**
pile *n* **pilichean/-achan** *f m* pill
pillean *n* **-ein, -an** *m* pillion, cushion, saddle
pinc *a* **-e** pink
pinnt *n* **-ean** *m* pint **p. leann(a)** a pint of beer **leth-phinnt** half a pint
pìob *n* **-a, -an** *f* pipe; bagpipe **p.-analach** windpipe **p.-chiùil** bagpipe **p.-mhòr** Highland bagpipe **p.-uisge** water pipe
pìobair(e) *n* **-(e)an** *m* piper
pìobaireachd *n f* piping; pibroch
pìoban *n* **-ain, -ain/, -an** *m* tube, small pipe
piobar *n* **-air** *m* pepper
piobraich *v* **-achadh** incite, pep up, urge; pepper
pioc *v* **-adh** pick at, nibble
Piocach *n* **-aich, -aich** *m* Pict
piocach *n* **-aich** *m* saithe, coalfish
piorbhaig *n* **-e, -ean** *f* wig
piorna *n* **-chan** *f* pirn, bobbin, reel
pìos *n* **-an** *m* piece, section; sandwich; (*colloq*) talent **'s e pìos a th' innte** she's a bit of all right, she's a smasher
piseach *n* **pisich** *f* improvement, prosperity **thàinig p. mhòr air** he/it has improved greatly
piseag *n* **-eig, -an** *f* kitten
pit *n* **-e, -ean** *f* female genitalia, vulva
pitheid *n* **-e, -ean** *f* parrot; magpie *Also* **pioghaid**
piullach *a* **-aiche** untidy, unkempt, shabby; wan *Also* **piollach**
piuthar *n* **peathar, peathraichean** *f* sister **p.-athar** aunt (*on father's side*) **p.-chèile** sister-in-law **p.-màthar** aunt (*on mother's side*)
plaide *n* **-an/-achan** *f* blanket
plàigh *n* **-e, -ean** *f* plague **'s e p. a th' ann** he's/it's a pest
plana *n* **-ichean** *m* plan
planaid *n* **-e, -ean** *f* planet
planaig *v* **-eadh** plan
plangaid *n* **-e, -ean** *f* blanket
plannt *n* **-a, -aichean** *m* plant
plaosg *n* **-oisg, -an** *m* husk, peel, shell, pod
plàst *n* **-a, -an/-aidhean** *m* plaster
plastaig *n* **-e, -ean** *f m* plastic *a* plastic
pleadhag *n* **-aig, -an** *f* paddle; dibble *Also* **pleadhan** *m*
pleadhagaich *v* paddle
plèan(a) *n* **-(a)ichean** *f m* aeroplane
plèastar *n* **-an** *m* plaster (*eg wall*)
plèastraig *v* **-eadh** plaster
pleata *n* **-ichean** *m* plait
ploc *n* **pluic, -an** *m* clod; block
plocan *n* **-ain, -an** *m* small clod; small block
plosg *v* **-artaich/-adh** palpitate, throb, gasp, pant
plub *n* **-a, -an** *m* plop (*sound*), splash
plubadaich *n* **-e** *f* plopping, splashing
plubarsaich *n* **-e** *f* plopping, splashing
plubraich *v* plop, splash, slosh, gurgle
plucan *n* **-ain, -an** *m* stopper (*as in bottle*), bung; pimple
pluga *n* **-ichean** *m* plug
pluic *n* **-e, -ean** *f* cheek
pluiceach *a* **-ciche** chubby-cheeked, having large cheeks
plumadaich *n* **-e** *f* plunging, plummeting
plumair *n* **-ean** *m* plumber
plumais *n* **-e, -ean** *f* plum
poball *n* **-aill** *m* people, public
poblach *a* **-aiche** public **gu p.** in public
poblachail *a* republican
poblachd *n f* republic **P. na h-Èireann** the Irish Republic
poca *n* **-nnan** *m* bag, sack **p.-cadail** sleeping bag **p.-droma** haversack
pòcaid *n* **-e, -ean** *f* pocket *Also* **pòca**
pòcair *n* **-ean** *m* poker

pòg *n* **pòige, -an** *f* kiss
pòg *v* **-adh** kiss
poidhleat *n* **-eit, -an** *m* pilot *Also* **pìleat**
poidsear *n* **-eir, -an** *m* poacher
poileas *n* **-lis, -lis** *m* police officer, police **ban-phoileas** *f* policewoman
poileasaidh *n* **-ean** *m* policy **p. àrachais** insurance policy
poileasman *n* **-ain, -ain** *m* policeman
poilitigs *n f* politics *Also* **poileataigs**
poilitigeach *a* **-giche** political
poirdse *n* **-an/-achan** *f m* porch
poit *n* **-e, -ean** *f* pot **p. tì/teatha** teapot **p.-dhubh** small whisky still
pòitear *n* **-eir, -an** *m* tippler, drinker, boozer
pòla *n* **-ichean** *m* pole; Pole **am P. a Deas** the South Pole **am P. a Tuath** the North Pole **p. aodaich** clothes-pole *Also* **pòile**
Pòlainneach *n* **-nich, -nich** *m* Pole *a* Polish
poll *n* **puill, puill** *m* mud, mire, bog; pool
pollag *n* **-aig, -an** *f* small peatbank; small pool; pollock, lythe
poll-mònach *n* **puill-mhònach, puill-mhònach** *m* peatbank *Also* **poll-mòna(dh)**
pònaidh *n* **-ean** *m* pony
pònair *n* **-arach** *f* bean, beans
pong *n* **puing, -an** *m* music note
pongail *a* **-e** methodical, punctilious; punctual; sensible
pòr *n* **pòir, -an** *m* seed; progeny; spore; pore (*in skin*)
pòrach *a* **-aiche** porous
port *n* **puirt, puirt** *m* port, harbour **p.-adhair** airport **p.-iasgaich** fishing port
port *n* **puirt, puirt** *m* tune **port-à-beul** mouth music
Portagaileach *n* **-lich, -lich** *m* Portuguese *a* Portuguese
portair *n* **-ean** *m* porter, janitor; porter (*drink*)
pòs *v* **-adh** marry
pòsadh *n* **-aidh, -aidhean** *m* marriage
post(a) *n* **(-a), puist** *m* postman, postwoman
post *n* **puist, puist** *m* post, stake, stob; post, mail **p.-adhair** airmail **p.-dealain** e-mail
pòsta *a* married **p. aig Eilidh** married to Helen **càraid phòsta** married couple *Formerly* **pòsda**
postachd *n f* postage; postal work
post-oifis *n* **puist-, puist-** *m* post office
prab *n* **praib, -an** *m* rheum (*in eye*)
praban *n* **-ain, -an** *m* shebeen
prab-shùileach *a* **-liche** bleary-eyed
prais *n* **-e, -ean** *f* pot, pan
pràis *n* **-e** *f* brass
pràiseach *a* brass
pram *n* **-a, -aichean** *m* pram
pràmh *n* **pràimh** *m* sorrow, sadness, dejection; slumber **fo phràmh** dejected, sorrowing
prann *See* **pronn**
preantas *n* **-ais, -an** *m* apprentice
preas *n* **pris, pris/-an** *m* bush, shrub
preas *n* **-a, -an** *m* wrinkle, crease, fold
preas *v* **-adh** fold, crease; furrow, wrinkle (*of humans*)
preas(a) *n* **-(a)ichean** *m* press, cupboard **p.-aodaich** wardrobe, clothes cupboard **p.-leabhraichean** bookcase
preasach *a* **-aiche** wrinkled, furrowed
preusant *n* **-an** *m* present, gift
prìne *n* **-nichean/-achan** *m* pin
priob *v* **-adh** wink, blink, twinkle
priobadh *n* **-aidh, -aidhean** *m* wink, winking, blinking **ann am p. na sùla** in the twinkling of an eye
prìobhaideach *a* **-diche** private **an roinn phrìobhaideach** *f* the private sector
prìomh *a* prime, primary, first, chief, principal **p. bhaile** capital city **am P. Mhinistear** the First Minister **p. oifis** head office, headquarters
prìomhaire *n* **-an** *m* prime minister, premier

prionnsa *n* **-n/-ichean** *m* prince **Am. P. Teàrlach** Prince Charles
prionnsapal *n* **-ail, -ail/-an** *m* principle **ann am p.** in principle *Also* **prionnsabal**
prìosan *n* **-ain, -ain/-an** *m* prison
prìosanach *n* **-aich, -aich** *m* prisoner, captive **p. cogaidh** prisoner of war
prìs *n* **-e, -ean** *f* price **dè (a') phrìs a tha e?** how much does it cost?
prìseil *a* **-e** precious, valuable, priceless
pròbhaist *n* **-e, -ean** *m* provost
prògram *n* **-aim, -an** *m* programme
proifeasair *n* **-ean** *m* professor
proifeiseanta *a* professional
pròis *n* **-e** *f* pride, haughtiness
pròiseact *n* **-eict, -an** *f m* project *Also* **pròiseict**
pròiseil *a* **-e** proud, haughty
pronn *a* **pruinne** pounded, mashed, ground, pulverized **buntàta p.** *m* mashed potatoes **airgead p.** *m* loose change
pronn *v* **-adh** pound, mash, grind, pulverize **chaidh a phronnadh** he was beaten up
pronnasg *n* **-aisg** *m* sulphur, brimstone
pronnfheòil *n* **-òla** *f* mince
prosbaig *n* **-ean** *f* binoculars, telescope
Pròstanach *n* **-aich, -aich** *m* Protestant *a* Protestant *Formerly* **Pròsdanach**
prothaid *n* **-e, -ean** *f* profit
puball *n* **-aill, -an** *m* marquee, pavilion
pucaid *n* **-e, -ean** *f* bucket
pùdar *n* **-air, -an** *m* powder
pùdaraich *v* **-achadh** powder
pudhar *n m* harm, injury **cha do chuir e p. orm** it didn't put me up or down
puicean *n* **-ein, -an** *m* poke, small bag; (*met*) small man
puing *n* **-e, -ean** *f* point; degree (*of temperature*)
puinnsean *n* **-ein, -an** *m* poison, venom
puinnseanaich *v* **-achadh** poison
puinnseanta *a* poisonous, venomous **p. fuar** bitterly cold
pump(a) *n* **-(a)ichean** *m* pump
punnd *n* **puinnd, puinnd** *m* pound (*weight*); pound (*money*) **p. Sasannach** pound sterling
pupaid *n* **-ean** *m* puppet
purgadair *n* **-e** *m* purgatory; purifier
purgaid *n* **-e, -ean** *f* purge, purgative
purgaideach *a* **-diche** purgative
purpaidh *a* **-e** purple
put(a) *n* **-a/-(a)ichean** *m* buoy
put *v* **-adh** push, shove, jostle
putan *n* **-ain, -an** *m* button

R

rabaid *n* **-e, -ean** *f* rabbit
rabhadh *n* **-aidh, -aidhean** *m* warning, alarm
rabhd *n* **-a, -an** *m* idle or far-fetched talk, spiel
ràc *n* **ràic, -an** *m* rake (garden); drake
ràc *v* **-adh** rake
racaid *n* **-e, -ean** *f* racket, noise; racquet; skelp
ràcan *n* **-ain, -ain/-an** *m* rake (*garden*); drake
ràc an t-sìl *n* **ràic-, ràcain-** *m* corncrake
rach *irr v* **dol** go (*See irr v* **rach** *in Grammar*) **r. an sàs an** tackle, get involved in **r. an urras do** assure **r. às àicheadh** deny **an rachadh agad air?** could/would you be able to do it?
radan *n* **-ain, -ain** *m* rat
ràdh *n* **-an** *m* saying, adage
rag *a* **raige** stiff, rigid; stubborn, obstinate, inflexible **r.-mharbh** stone dead
rag *v* **-adh** stiffen, benumb **bha sinn air ar ragadh leis an fhuachd** we were numb with the cold
rag-mhuinealach *a* **-aiche** obstinate, stubborn
raidhfil *n* **-ean** *f m* rifle
raige *n f* stiffness, rigidity; obstinacy, stubbornness

raighd *v* **-eadh** ride
raighdeadh *n* **-didh** *m* riding **sgoil raighdidh** *f* riding school
raineach *n* **-nich** *f* fern, bracken *Also* **fraineach**
ràinig *irr v* came, reached, arrived (*See irr v* **ruig** *in Grammar*)
raip *n* **-e** *f* dribble, traces of food round mouth; refuse
ràith(e) *n* **-(e)an/-(e)achan** *f* quarter (*of year*), season
ràitheachan *n* **-ain, -ain** *m* quarterly (*magazine*)
ràmh *n* **ràimh, ràimh** *m* oar
ràn *n* **ràin, ràin** *m* cry; roar, yell
ràn *v* **-aich/-ail** cry; roar, yell
rann *n* **rainn, -an/rainn** *f* verse, stanza
rannsachadh *n* **-aidh, -aidhean** *m* research, investigation, survey
rannsaich *v* **-achadh** research, search, scrutinize, investigate, explore
raon *n* **raoin, -tan/raointean** *m* plain, field; area **r.-cluiche** playing field **r.-laighe** runway **r. ola** oilfield
rapach *a* **-aiche** slovenly, scruffy; inclement, dirty (*weather*)
ràsair *n* **-ean** *m* razor
ràsanach *a* **-aiche** tedious
ràth *n* **-a, -an** *m* raft
rath *n* **-a** *m* prosperity, fortune, luck
rathad *n* **-aid/rothaid, -aidean/ròidean** *m* road, route, way **r.-mòr** main road, trunk road, highway **r.-iarainn** railway, railroad **an r. sin** that way **tog às mo r.!** get out of my way! **chan eil e às an r.** it's not too bad **chaidh e às an r.** he perished
Ratharsach *n* **-aich, -aich** *m* someone from Raasay *a* from, or pertaining to, Raasay
rè *prep* (+ *gen*) during, throughout **rè na h-oidhche** during the night
rèaban *n* **-ain, -an** *m* beard, whiskers
reachd *n* **-an** *m* statute, law, ordinance
reamhar *a* **reamhra/reaimhre** fat, plump
reamhraich *v* **-achadh** fatten
reic *n m* sale **fèill-reic** *f* sale of work
reic *v* sell
reiceadair *n* **-ean** *m* seller, salesman, vendor, auctioneer
rèidh *a* **-e** level, even, smooth; ready
rèidhleach *n* **-lich** *m* space, expanse
rèidhlean *n* **-ein, -an** *m* lawn, sward, green
rèidio *n* **-than** *m* radio
rèile *n* **-lichean** *f m* rail
rèilig *n* **-e, -ean** *f* grave, lair, graveyard, crypt *Also* **roilig**
reimhid *adv See* **roimhe**
rèis *n* **-e, -ean** *f* race (*sport*); span, lifetime
rèis *v* **-eadh** race
rèisimeid *n* **-e, -ean** *f* regiment
rèite *n* **-an** *f* accord, agreement, reconciliation
rèiteach *n* **-tich, -tichean** *m* betrothal; agreement, settlement
reithe *n* **-achan** *m* ram (*male sheep*)
rèitich *v* **-teachadh** reconcile, conciliate, arbitrate; settle, sort out
rèitire *n* **-an** *m* referee
reodh *v See* **reoth**
reòiteag *n* **-eig, -an** *f* ice cream
reoth *v* **-adh** freeze, become frozen
reothadair *n* **-ean** *m* freezer
reothadh *n* **-aidh** *m* frost, freezing
reothart *n* **-airt, -an** *f m* spring tide
reòthte *a* frozen *Also* **reòthta**
reub *v* **-adh** tear, rend, rip
reubal(t)ach *n* **-aich, -aich** *m* rebel
reubaire *n* **-an** *m* pirate, plunderer *Also* **reubadair**
reubte *a* riven, rent
reudan *n* **-ain, -an** *m* timber moth, woodlouse; dry rot
reul *n* **rèil, -tan** *f* star **r.-bhad** *m* constellation **r.-chearbach** *f* comet **r.-eòlas** *m* astronomy **r.-iùil** guiding star, Pole Star
reuladair *n* **-ean** *m* astronomer
reultag *n* **-aig, -an** *f* asterisk
reusan *n* **-ain** *m* reason, cause;

sanity
reusanaich *v* **-achadh** reason
reusanta *a* reasonable, rational **r. math** reasonably good
ri *prep* to; engaged in **tha i ri bàrdachd** she composes poetry **bheil cus agad ri dhèanamh?** do you have a lot to do?
riabhach *a* **-aiche** brindled
riadh *n* **rèidh** *m* interest (*fin*) **chuir e r. mòr dheth** it returned high interest
riaghail *v* **-ghladh** rule, govern, regulate
riaghailt *n* **-e, -ean** *f* rule, regulation
riaghailteach *a* regular, orderly **r. bitheanta** fairly common
riaghaltas *n* **-ais, -an** *m* government **r. ionadail** local government **R. na h-Alba** Scottish Executive
riaghladair *n* **-ean** *m* ruler, governor, regulator
riaghladh *n* **-aidh** *m* ruling, governing
riamh *adv* ever, before *Also* **a-riamh**
rian *n* **-an** *m* order, method, organization; arrangement (*mus*) **tha e às a r.** he is mad, crazy **cuir r. air** *v* organize
rianachd *n f* administration
rianail *a* **-e** methodical, orderly; reasonable
riaraich *v* **-achadh** satisfy, please; share (out), distribute, allocate **doirbh a riarachadh** hard to please
riaraichte *a* satisfied
riasg *n* **rèisg** *m* sedge, dirk-grass, coarse grass, peat moss
riaslach *a* **-aiche** hectic, extremely busy
riasladh *n* **-aidh** *m* struggle, busy toing and froing **bha r. air a' bhoin** the cow was in heat
riatanach *a* **-aiche** necessary, essential; appropriate
ribe *n* **-achan** *f m* snare, trap
ribh(se) *prep pron* to you (*pl & pol*)
ribheid *n* **-e, -ean** *f* reed (*mus*)
rìbhinn *n* **-e, -ean** *f* maiden
rid *aug prep* to your (*sg*)
ridire *n* **-an** *m* knight, sir **An R.** Sir
rìgh *n* **-rean** *m* king **r.-chathair** *f* throne
righinn *a* **rìghne** tough, tenacious, durable
rim *aug prep* to my
rin *aug prep* to their
rinn *irr v* did, made (*See irr v* **dèan** *in Grammar*)
rinn(e) *prep pron* to us
rioban *n* **-ain, -an** *m* ribbon **r.-tomhais** measuring tape *Also* **ribinn** *f*
riochd *n* **-a, -an** *m* appearance, form
riochdaich *v* **-achadh** represent; produce (*eg programme*)
riochdail *a* **-e** beautiful, handsome
riochdair *n* **-ean** *m* pronoun
riochdaire *n* **-an** *m* representative, delegate; producer (*artistic*)
rìoghachd *n* **-an** *f* kingdom, country **an R. Aonaichte** the United Kingdom
rìoghaich *v* **-achadh** reign
rìoghail *a* **-e** royal, regal
rìomhach *a* **-aiche** beautiful, lovely, fine
rìomhachas *n* **-ais** *m* finery, beauty
rionnach *n* **-aich, -aich** *m* mackerel
rionnag *n* **-aige, -an** *f* star **r. (an) earbaill** shooting star
rionnagach *a* **-aiche** starry
rir *aug prep* to our; to your
ris *prep* to **dè tha thu ris?** what are you doing/up to?
ris *adv* exposed (*to view*) **bha a còta-bàn ris** her slip was showing
ris(-san) *prep pron* to him/it
ri taobh *prep phr* (+ *gen*) beside
rithe(se) *prep pron* to her/it
rium(sa) *prep pron* to me
riut(sa) *prep pron* to you
riutha(san) *prep pron* to them
ro *adv* too; very (+ *len*) **ro bheag** too small
ro *prep, adv* before **ro-làimh**

beforehand **ro-ainmichte** *a* aforementioned, aforesaid *Formerly* **roimh**
ro-aithris *a* **-ean** *f* forecast (*weather*); prediction
robach *a* **-aiche** slovenly, untidy, unkempt, squalid
robair(e) *n* **-(e)an** *m* robber
robh *irr v* was, were (*never used on its own*) (*See verb* **to be** *in Grammar*)
roc *n* **ruic/-a, -an** *f* wrinkle, crease; entanglement
roc *v* **-adh** wrinkle, crease
rocach *a* **-aiche** wrinkled, creased
rocaid *n* **-e, -ean** *f* rocket
ròcail *n* **-e** *f* croaking, croak
rocail *v* **rocladh** tangle, entangle
ròcais *n* **-ean** *f* rook **bodach-r.** scarecrow
rod *aug prep* before your (*sg*)
roghainn *n* **-ean** *f m* choice, selection, option **chan eil r. eile ann** there is no alternative **gheibh thu do r.** you can have your pick
roghnaich *v* **-achadh** choose, select
roid *n* **-e, -ean** *f* run before a leap **dh'fhalbh e aig r.** he went off at speed **thug iad r. a-steach dhan bhaile** they nipped into town
roile *n* **-lichean** *f* roll (*bread*)
roilear *n* **-eir, -an** *m* roller **roilearan-spèilidh** roller blades
roilig *v* **-eadh** roll
roimh *prep See* **ro**
roimhe *adv* before, formerly
roimhe(san) *prep pron* before him/it
roimhear *n* **-eir, -an** *m* preposition
roimhpe(se) *prep pron* before her/it
roimh-ràdh *n See* **ro-ràdh**
ròineag *n* **-eig, -an** *f* a single hair
roinn *n* **-e, -ean** *f* share, portion, division, department; region **an R. Eòrpa** Europe
roinn *v* divide, share (out)
roinneil *a* departmental, regional
ro-innleachd *n* **-an** *f* strategy
ròiseid *n* **-e, -ean** *f* resin
ròist *v* **ròstadh** roast
ro-leasachan *n* **-ain, -ain** *m* prefix
rola *n See* **roile**
ròlaist *n* **-e, -ean** *m* exaggeration, fanciful tale
ròlaisteach *a* **-tiche** prone to exaggeration or invention
rom *aug prep* before my
ròmach *a* **-aiche** hairy, shaggy, rough
Romàinianach *n* **-aich, -aich** *m* Romanian *a* Romanian
romhad(sa) *prep pron* before you
romhaibh(se) *prep pron* before you (*pl & pol*)
romhainn(e) *prep pron* before us
romham(sa) *prep pron* before me
romhpa(san) *prep pron* before them
ròn *n* **ròin, ròin** *m* seal
ron *aug prep* before the, before their
rong *n* **-a/roinge, -an** *f* rung, spar; boat-rib
rongach *a* **-aiche** dilatory
ronn *n* **roinn** *m* mucus, slaver, spittle
ròp(a) *n* **-(a), -(a)n/-(a)ichean** *m* rope **r.-anairt/-aodaich** clothes-line
ror *aug prep* before our, before your
ro-ràdh *n* **-ràidh, -an** *m* preface, preamble, prologue, introduction
ros *n* **rois, -an** *m* headland, promontory, peninsula
ròs *n* **ròis, -an** *m* rose
ròs *n* **ròis** knowledge **cha d'fhuair mi ròs air riamh** I never found any trace of him/it
ro-shealladh *n* **-aidh, -aidhean** *m* preview
rosg *n* **ruisg, -an** *m* prose
rosg *n* **ruisg, -an** *m* eyelash, eyelid
rosgrann *n* **-ainn, -an** *m* sentence
ròsta *n* **-ichean** *f m* roast, roast meat
ròsta *a* roasted, roast
roth *n* **-a, -an** *f m* wheel **r. mun ghealaich** a halo round the

moon
rothaig *v* **-eadh** wind (*as clock*)
rothar *n* **-air, -an** *m* bicycle, cycle
ruadh *a* **ruaidhe** reddish-brown, ruddy, ginger **falt r.** red hair
ruaig *n* **-e, -ean** *f* chase, pursuit, flight, rout **chuireadh r. orra** *v* they were routed/put to flight
rua(i)g *v* **ruagadh/ruagail** chase, pursue, rout
ruamhair *v* **-ar** dig, delve; rummage
rubair *n* **-ean** *m* rubber
rùbarab *n* **-aib** *m* rhubarb
rubha *n* **-ichean** *m* point (*of land*), promontory, headland
rùchd *n* **-a, -an** *m* stomach rumble, belch **dèan r.** *v* belch *Also* **rùchdail**
rùchd *v* **-ail** rumble (*in stomach*)
rud *n* **-an** *m* thing **rud sam bith** anything
rùda *n* **-aichean/-n** *m* ram
rùdan *n* **-ain, -an** *m* knuckle
rudeigin *pron, adv* something, somewhat **tha i r. fuar** it's somewhat cold
rudhadh *n* **-aidh** *m* blush, blushing, flush **bha r. na gruaidh** she was flushed, she was blushing
rùdhan *n* **-ain, -ain** *m* small stack of peat, hay or corn
rug *irr v* caught, seized (*See irr v* **beir** *in Grammar*)
ruga *n* **-ichean** *m* rug
rugadh *irr v* was born (*See irr v* **beir** *in Grammar*) **r. is thogadh i ann am Barraigh** she was born and brought up in Barra
ruibh *prep pron See* **ribh**
r(u)idhil *v* **r(u)idhleadh** reel (*dance*)
r(u)idhle *n* **-an/-achan** *m* reel
ruig *irr v* **-hinn/-sinn/-heachd** reach, arrive at (*See irr v* **ruig** *in Grammar*)
ruighe *n* **-an** *f m* forearm; slope (*of hill*), plain
rùilear *n* **-eir, -an** *m* ruler (*measuring*)
ruinn *prep pron See* **rinn**
ruis *n* **-e** *f* elder (*tree*)
Ruiseanach *n* **-aich, -aich** *m* Russian *a* Russian
rùisg *v* **rùsgadh** strip, peel; shear, fleece
rùisgte *a* naked, bare; shorn
ruiteach *a* **-tiche** ruddy
ruith *n* **-e, -ean** *f* running, run; rhythm
ruith *v* run, flow **tha 'n ùine air r. oirnn** we've run out of time
rùm *n* **rùim, rumannan** *m* room; space **rùm-cadail** bedroom **rùm-ionnlaid** bathroom **rùm-suidhe** sitting room **rùm-teagaisg** classroom
Rumach *n* **-aich, -aich** *m* someone from Rum *a* from, or pertaining to, Rum
rùmail *a* **-e** roomy, spacious
rùn *n* **rùin, rùintean** *m* desire, wish, intention, resolution; secret, love
rùnaich *v* **-achadh** desire, wish, intend, resolve
rùnaire *n* **-an** *m* secretary **R. na Stàite** the Secretary of State
rù-rà *a* untidy, topsy-turvy
rùraich *v* **-achadh** search (for); grope
rus *n* **ruis** *m* rice
rùsg *n* **rùisg, -an** peel, rind; bark; fleece
rùsgadh *n* **-aidh** *m* peeling; shearing

S

's *irr v* is (*See verb* **to be** *in Grammar*)
's *conj* and (*contraction of* **agus/is**)
sa *aug prep* in the
-sa *suff* (*used with* **mo, do** my, your *to give emphasis*)
sa *suff* this (*equivalent to* **seo**)
Sàbaid *n* **-ean** *f* Sabbath **Latha/Là na S.** Sunday *Also* **Sàboinn(t)**
sabaid *n* **(-e), -ean** *f* fight, fighting
sabaidich *v* **sabaid** fight
sàbh *n* **sàibh, sàibh/-an** *m* saw
sàbh *v* **-adh** saw
sàbhail *v* **-aladh** save, rescue
sàbhailte *a* safe
sàbhailteachd *n f* safety

sabhal *n* **-ail, -an/saibhlean** *m* barn
sàbhaladh *n* **-aidh** *m* saving, rescuing
sabhs *n* **-a, -an** *m* sauce
sac *n* **saic, saic/-an** *m* burden, load **an sac** asthma
sàcramaid *n* **-e, -ean** *f* sacrament
sad *v* **-ail/-adh** throw
sagart *n* **-airt, -an** *m* priest
sàibhear *n* **-eir, -an** *m* culvert
saideal *n* **-eil, -an** *m* satellite
saidhbhir *a* **-e** rich, wealthy
saidhbhreas *n* **-eis** *m* riches, wealth
saidheans *n* **-an** *m* science
saidhleafòn *n* **-òin, -an** *m* xylophone
saighdear *n* **-eir, -an** *m* soldier
saighead *n* **saighde/saighid, saighdean** *f* arrow
sail *n* **-e, -thean** *f* beam (*as in roof*), joist, large sawn piece of wood
sàil *n* **sàlach/sàla, -ean** *f* heel
sailead *n* **-eid, -an** *m* salad
saill *n f* **-e** fat; pickle, brine
saill *v* **-eadh** salt
saillear *n* **-eir, -an** *f* salt cellar
saillte *a* salty, salted
saimeant *n m* cement
sàirdseant *n* **-an** *m* sergeant
sàl *n* **sàil(e)** *m* salt water **an sàl** the sea
salach *a* **-aiche/sailche** dirty, filthy, foul
salaich *v* **-ach/-achadh** dirty, soil
salann *n* **-ainn** *m* salt
salchar *n* **-air** *m* dirt, filth
salm *n* **sailm, sailm** *f m* psalm **Leabhar nan S.** the Book of Psalms
salmadair *n* **-ean** *m* psalter; psalmist
salmaidh *n* **-ean** *m* psalmist
saltair *v* **-t** trample, tread
sam bith *adv phr* any **duine s. b.** anyone **rud s. b.** anything
samh *n* **saimh, -an** *m* odour, smell
sàmhach *a* **-aiche** silent, quiet **bi s.!** be quiet! **fan s.!** be quiet!, never! (*in surprise*)
samhail *n* **samhla, -ean** *m* likeness, like, equivalent **chan fhaca mi a shamhail** I've not seen his like
Samhain *n* **Samhna** *f* **an t-Samhain** November **Oidhche Shamhna** *f* Halloween
sàmhchair *n* **-e** *f* silence, quietness, quiet
samhla(dh) *n* **-aidh, -aidhean** *m* resemblance, likeness, allegory, figure; apparition
samhlachail *a* figurative; symbolic
samhlaich *v* **-achadh** liken, compare
samhradh *n* **-aidh, -aidhean** *m* summer **as t-s.** in summer
san *aug prep* in their
-san *suff used with* **a** his and **an** their *to give emphasis* **an coire-san** their fault
sanas *n* **-ais, -an** *m* notice, advertisement; whisper **s.-reic** advertisement
sannt *n* **-a** *m* greed, avarice, covetousness
sanntach *a* **-aiche** greedy, avaricious, covetous
sanntaich *v* **-tachadh** covet
saobh *a* **-a/saoibhe** erroneous, false, misguided
saobhaidh *n* **-ean** *m* den, fox's den, lair
saobh-chràbhadh *n* **-aidh, -aidhean** *m* superstition
saobh-chreideamh *n* **-eimh, -an** *m* heresy
saoghal *n* **-ail, -ail/-an** *m* world; lifetime **càit air an t-s. an robh sibh?** where on earth were you?
saoghalta *a* worldly, materialistic
saoibhir *a See* **saidhbhir**
saoil *v* **-sinn/-tinn** think, suppose **s. an tig iad** I wonder if they'll come **saoilibh?** do you think?
saoithean *n* **-ein, -an/-ein** *m* saithe
saor *n* **saoir, saoir** *m* joiner, carpenter
saor *a* **saoire** free; cheap **s. 's an asgaidh** free gratis, free of charge

saor *v* **-adh** free, liberate, exempt
saoradh *n* **-aidh** *m* liberation
saor-chlachair *n* **-ean** *m* freemason
saor-latha *n* **-làithean/ -lathaichean** *m* holiday
saorsa *n f* freedom, liberty **s. chatharra** civil liberty
saorsainn *n* **-e** *f* freedom, liberty
saorsainneachd *n f* joinery, carpentry
saorsainneil *a* **-e** relaxed, at ease
saor-thoil *n* **-e** *f* free-will
saor-thoileach *a* voluntary
saothair *n* **saothrach** *f* labour, toil
saothraich *v* **-achadh** labour, toil
sàr *n* **sàir, sàir** *m* hero, excellent person
sàr *a* (*precedes & lenites n*) very, extremely, true **sàr sheinneadair** a truly great singer
sàrachadh *n* **-aidh** *m* exhaustion, annoyance, bother, harassment
sàraich *v* **-achadh** exhaust, annoy, bother, harass
sàraichte *a* exhausted, exhausting
sàs *n* **sàis** *m* straits, restraint, hold, grasp **an sàs an** involved in, engaged in **chaidh an cur an sàs** they were arrested
sàsachadh *n* **-aidh** *m* satisfaction
sàsaich *v* **-achadh** satisfy
sàsaichte *a* satisfied
Sasannach *n* **-aich, -aich** *m* English person *a* English
sàsar *n* **-air, -an** *m* saucer
sàth *v* **-adh** thrust
sàth *n* **sàith** *m* plenty, surfeit, satiety, abundance
's e *v* it is, he is (*See verb* **bi** *in Grammar*)
seabhag *n* **-aig, -an** *f m* hawk
seac *v* **-adh** wither
seacaid *n* **(-e), -ean** *f* jacket
seach *conj* since, because **s. gu** (+ *v*) since, because
seach *prep* instead of, rather than; compared to
seachad *adv* past **san dol s.** in passing **thoir s.** *v* give (away)
seachad air *prep phr* past, by
seachain *v* **seachnadh** avoid, shun, abstain from
seachd *n, a* seven; (*also used as intensive*) **tha mi s. sgìth dheth** I'm absolutely fed up of it/him
seachdad *n* **-aid, -an** *m* seventy
seachdain *n* **-e/-donach, -ean** *f* week
seachdamh *a* seventh
seachd-deug *n, a* seventeen **seachd latha deug** seventeen days
seachdnar *n f m* seven (people)
seachnadh *n* **-aidh** *m* avoiding, avoidance, shunning
seachran *n* **-ain** *m* wandering **a' dol air s.** wandering, going astray
seach-rathad *n* **-aid, -aidean** *m* bypass
seada *n* **-n/-ichean** *f m* shed
seadag *n* **-aig, -an** *f* grapefruit
seadh *adv* yes, indeed (*used to confirm or lend emphasis*) **s. dìreach** just so
seagal *n* **-ail** *m* rye
seagh *n* **-a, -an** *m* sense, meaning
seàla *n* **-ichean** *f* shawl
sealastair *n* **-ean** *f m* iris (*plant*) *Also* **seileastair**
sealbh *n* **seilbh, -an** *m* fortune; possession, ownership **Aig an t-S. tha brath** Goodness knows **Gu sealladh S. orm** For goodness's sake
sealbhach *a* **-aiche** fortunate, lucky
sealbhadair *n* **-ean** *m* possessor, owner
sealbhaich *v* **-achadh** possess, own
sealg *n* **seilge, -an** *f* hunt
sealg *v* hunt
sealgair *n* **-ean** *m* hunter
sealgaireachd *n f* hunting
seall *v* **-tainn** look, see; show **s. seo!** look at this! **s. dhomh sin** show me that
sealladh *n* **-aidh, -aidhean** *m* view, sight, vision, show, spectacle **às an t-s.** out of sight **an dà shealladh** second sight
Sealtainneach *n* **-nich, -nich** *m* Shetlander *a* Shetland

seamrag *n* **-aig, -an** *f* shamrock
sean *a* **sine** old
seanadair *n* **-ean** *m* senator
seanadh *n* **-aidh, -aidhean** *m* senate, synod, assembly
seanailear *n* **-eir, -an** *m* general
seanair *n* **-ar, -ean** *m* grandfather; ancestor
seanchaidh *n* **-ean** *m* storyteller *Also* **seanachaidh**
seancharra *a* old-looking, old-fashioned *Also* **seangarra**
seanchas *n* **-ais, -an** *m* conversation, chat; lore *Also* **seanachas**
seanfhacal *n* **-ail, -ail/-aclan** *m* proverb
seang *a* **-a** slim, slender
seangan *n* **-ain, -ain/-an** *m* ant
seanmhair *n* **-ar, -ean** *f* grandmother
seann *a* old (*precedes & lenites n*) **s. chàr** an old car **s. fhear** an old one **s. nòs** traditional style **s. taigh** an old house **seann-fhasanta** old-fashioned
seantans *n* **-an** *m* sentence (*gram*)
sear *adv* east, eastern
searbh *a* **-a/seirbhe** bitter, sour, tart
searbhachd *n f* bitterness
searbhadair *n* **-ean** *m* towel
searbhag *n* **-aig, -an** *f* acid
searbhant(a) *n* **-(a)n** *f* servant
searg *v* wither, shrivel, decay
seargach *a* withered, shrivelled, deciduous
seargadh *n* **-aidh** *m* decay
searmon *n* **-oin, -an** *m* sermon
searmonaich *v* **-achadh** preach
searmonaiche *n* **-an** *m* preacher
searrach *n* **-aich, -aich** *m* foal, colt
searrag *n* **-aig, -an** *f* bottle, flask
seas *v* **-amh** stand
seasamh *n* **-aimh, -an** *m* standing, stand, stance
seasg *a* **-a/seisge** barren, sterile
seasgachd *n f* sterility
seasgad *n* **-aid, -an** *m* sixty
seasgaich *v* **-achadh** sterilize
seasgair *a* **-e** snug, comfortable, sheltered, protected
seasmhach *a* **-aiche** steadfast, firm, stable; durable
seat *v* **-adh** set (*except of sun*)
seic *n* **-ean** *f* cheque **leabhar-sheicichean** *m* chequebook
Seiceach *n* **-cich, -cich** *m* Czech *a* Czech
seiche *n f* hide, skin, pelt
sèid *v* **-eadh** blow
seilbh *n* **-e, -ean** *f* possession **gabh s. air** *v* take possession of
seilbheach *a* **-bhiche** possessive; genitive (*gram*)
seilbhich *v* **-bheachadh** possess, own
seilcheag *n* **-eig, -an** *f* snail, slug
seile *n* **-an** *m* spittle, saliva
seileach *n* **-lich, -lich** *m* willow
seillean *n* **-ein, -an** *m* bee
sèimh *a* **-e** gentle, mild, calm **an Cuan S.** the Pacific Ocean
sèimheachadh *n* **-aidh** *m* lenition, aspiration (*gram*)
sèine *n* **-nichean** *f* chain
seinn *n f* singing **s.-phàirteach** harmony
seinn *v* sing
seinneadair *n* **-ean** *m* singer
seirbheis *n* **-ean** *f* service **an t-S. Chatharra** the Civil Service
seirbheiseach *n* **-sich, -sich** *m* servant
seirc *n* **-e** *f* love, charity
seirm *n* **-e** *f* ring, chime, musical sound
seirm *v* ring, chime
seise *n* **-an** *m* one's match, one's equal **thachair a sheise ris** he met his match
seisean *n* **-ein** *m* session
sèist *n* **-e, -ean** *f m* chorus, refrain
sèist *n* **-e, -ean** *f m* siege
sèithear *n* **-thir, sèithrichean** *m* chair **s.-cuibhle** wheelchair **s.-putaidh** pushchair
seo *a* this
seo *pron* this (is); these (are)
seoclaid *n* **-ean** *f* chocolate
seòl *n* **siùil, siùil** *m* sail
seòl *n* **siùil, siùil** *m* method, way **s.-beatha** way of life, lifestyle
seòl *v* **-adh** sail, navigate; direct,

guide
seòladair *n* **-ean** *m* sailor
seòladh *n* **-aidh, -aidhean** *m* sailing; address, direction
seòl-mara *n* **siùil-mara, siùil-mhara** *m* tide
seòlta *a* cunning, crafty
seòltachd *n f* cunning, craftiness, guile
seòmar *n* **-air, seòmraichean** *m* room, chamber **s.-bìdh** dining-room **s.-cadail** bedroom **s.-còmhnaidh** living-room **s.-fuirich** waiting-room **s.-ionnlaid** bathroom **s.-leughaidh** reading-room, study **s.-sgeadachaidh** dressing-room **s.-suidhe** sitting-room **s.-teagaisg** classroom, lecture room
seòrsa *n* **-chan/-ichean** *m* sort, kind, type, species, brand
seòrsaich *v* **-achadh** sort, classify
seotaire *n* **-an** *m* idler, lazybones
seud *n* **seòid, seòid/-an** jewel, gem; (*met*) hero
seudar *n* **-air** *m* cedar
seula *n* **-chan** *m* seal
seulaich *v* **-achadh** seal
seumarlan *n* **-ain, -ain** *m* chamberlain, factor
seun *n* **-a, -an/-tan** *m* charm (*magical*)
seunta *a* charmed, enchanted
sgadan *n* **-ain, -ain** *m* herring
sgàil *n* **-e, -ean** *f* shade, shadow, veil, cover **s.-sùla** eyelid
sgàil *v* **-eadh** shade, screen, mask
sgailc *n* **-e, -ean** *f* slap, sharp blow, skelp, smack **s.-creige** echo
sgailc *v* slap, smack, skelp
sgàilean *n* **-ein, -an** *m* umbrella, screen **s.-grèine** parasol
sgàin *v* **-eadh** split, burst **tha mi gu s.** I've eaten too much/I'm over-full (*lit* I'm about to burst)
sgàineadh *n* **-nidh** *m* split, crack, bursting
sgainneal *n* **-eil, -an** *m* scandal
sgainnealaich *v* **-achadh** scandalize
sgàird *n* **-e** *f* **an s.** diarrhoea
sgairt *n* **-e, -ean** *f* yell, loud cry
sgairt *n* **-e, -ean** *f* **an s.** diaphragm, midriff **bhris(t) e a s.** he ruptured himself
sgairteil *a* **-e** vigorous, brisk, energetic
sgait *n* **-e, -ean** *f* skate (*fish*)
sgaiteach *a* **-tiche** sharp, cutting (*as in remark*); well-expressed, able
sgal *n* **-a, -an** *m* yell; blow
sgàl *n* **sgàil, sgàil** *m* tray
sgal *v* **-thart(aich)** howl, yell
sgalag *n* **-aig, -an** *f* servant, skivvy
sgall *n* **sgaill** *m* bald patch, baldness
sgallach *a* **-aiche** bald
Sgalpach *n* **-aich, -aich** *m* someone from Scalpay *a* from, or pertaining to, Scalpay
sgamhan *n* **-ain, -an** *m* lung
sgannan *n* **-ain, -an** *m* film, membrane
sgaoil *v* **-eadh** spread, scatter, disperse, disseminate; become undone **leig mu s.** *v* free, liberate, loosen
sgaoth *n* **-oith/-otha, -an** *m* swarm; multitude
sgap *v* **-adh** scatter
sgar *v* **-adh/-achdainn** separate, sever
sgaradh *n* **-aidh, -aidhean** *m* separation **s.-pòsaidh** divorce
sgarbh *n* **sgairbh, sgairbh** *m* cormorant
sgarfa *n* **-ichean** *f m* scarf
sgàrlaid *a* **-e** scarlet
Sgarpach *n* **-aich, -aich** *m* someone from Scarp *a* from, or pertaining to, Scarp
sgath *n m* anything; part **cha robh s. airgid aice** she hadn't any money **a h-uile s. dheth** every bit of it
sgàth *n* **-a, -an** *m* sake; shade, protection **air s.** on account of, because of (+ *gen*)
sgath *v* **-adh** lop, cut, prune, slash
sgàthan *n* **-ain, -an** *m* mirror

sgeadaich *v* **-achadh** decorate, adorn, embellish; dress
sgeadaichte *a* decorated; dressed
sgealb *n* **sgeilb, -an** *f* splinter
sgealbag *n* **-aig, -an** *f* forefinger, index finger
sgeama *n* **-ichean** *f m* scheme
sgeap *n* **sgeip, -an/-aichean** *f* beehive
sgeig *n* **-e** *f* derision, ridicule
sgeigeil *a* **-e** derisive
sgeilb *n* **-e, -ean** *f* wood chisel
sgeileid *n* **-e, -ean** *f* saucepan, skillet
sgeilp *n* **-ichean** *f* shelf
sgèimhich *v* **-mheachadh** beautify, adorn
sgeir *n* **-e, -ean** *f* skerry, reef
sgeith *n* **-e** *m* vomit, vomiting
sgeith *v* **sgeith/-eadh** vomit, spew
sgèith *n* flying **air s.** flying
sgèith *v* fly
sgeith-rionnaig *n m* meteor
sgeul *n* **sgeòil, sgeòil** *m* story, tale; trace **a bheil s. orra?** is there any sign of them? *Also* **sgeula** *f*
sgeulachd *n* **-an** *f* story, tale
sgeulaiche *n* **-an** *m* storyteller
sgeunach *a* **-aiche** shy, timid, easily frightened
sgì *n* **sgithe, sgithean** *f* ski
sgì *v* **-theadh** ski
sgialachd *n See* **sgeulachd**
sgiamh *n* **-a, -an** *m* scream, squeal, shriek **dèan s.** *v* scream
sgiamh *v* **-ail** scream, squeal
sgiamhach *a* **-aiche** beautiful
sgiamhaich *v* **-achadh** beautify
sgiamhail *n f* screaming
sgian *n* **sgeine, sgeinean** *f* knife
sgiath *n* **sgèithe, -an** *f* wing; shield
sgiathach *a* winged
sgiathaich *v* **-thadh** fly
sgiathalaich *n f* flying about, fluttering *Also* **sgiathadaich**
Sgiathanach *n*, *a See* **Sgitheanach**
sgil *n* **-ean** *f m* skill
sgileil *a* **-e** skilful
sgillinn *n* **-e, -ean** *f* penny **deich sg.** 10 pence **chan eil s. ruadh agam** I don't have a single penny
sgioba *n* **-n/-idhean** *f m* crew, team
sgiobachd *n f* personnel, manpower
sgiobair *n* **-ean** *m* skipper, captain
sgiobalta *a* tidy, neat; quick
sgioblachadh *n* **-aidh** *m* tidying, tidying-up
sgioblaich *v* **-achadh** tidy, streamline
sgiorradh *n* **-aidh, -aidhean** *m* accident
sgiorrghail *n f* screaming, shrill crying
sgiort(a) *n* **(-a), -(a)n/-(a)ichean** *f* skirt
sgìos *n See* **sgìths**
sgìre *n* **-an** *f* district, parish **sgìr-easbaig** diocese
sgìreachd *n* **-an** *f* district, parish
sgìreil *a* **-e** district, parochial
sgìth *a* **-e** tired
sgitheach *n* **-thich** *m* hawthorn
sgitheadair *n* **-ean** *m* skier
sgitheadh *n* **-thidh** *m* skiing
Sgitheanach *n* **-aich, -aich** *m* someone from Skye *a* from, or pertaining to, Skye
sgìtheil *a* **-e** tiring, wearisome
sgìthich *v* **-theachadh** tire, make or become weary
sgìths *n f* tiredness, weariness, fatigue
sgiùrs *v* **-adh** scourge, lash
sgiùrsair *n* **-ean** *m* scourge
sglàib *n f* plaster
sglàibeadair *n* **-ean** *m* plasterer
sglàibrich *v* plaster
sglèat *n* **-a, -an/-aichean** *f m* slate
sglèat *v* **-adh** slate
sglèatair *n* **-ean** *m* slater
sgleog *n* **-oig, -an** *f* blow, slap
sgoch *v* **-adh** sprain, strain
sgòd *n* **sgòid, -an** *m* (*of sail*) sheet; piece of cloth or garment **cha robh s. aodaich orra** they were completely naked
sgoil *n* **-e, -tean/-ean** *f* school **àrd-s.** high school **bun-s.** primary school **s.-àraich** nursery school **s.-fhonn**

psalmody class
sgoilear *n* **-eir, -an** *m* pupil, scholar
sgoilearach *a* scholastic
sgoilearachd *n f* scholarship
sgoilt *v* **sgoltadh** split, cleave, slit
sgoinneil *a* **-e** terrific, super, superb, smashing, great; strapping (*of person*)
sgol *v* **-adh** rinse
sgoladh *n* **-aidh, -aidhean** *m* rinse, rinsing; (*met*) telling-off
sgolt *v* **-adh** split, cleave, slit
sgoltadh *n* **-aidh** *m* cleft, slit, split
sgona *n* **-ichean** *f m* scone
sgonn *n* **sgoinn/sguinn, -an** *m* block, lump **s. mòr de ghille** a big strapping lad
sgor *n* **sgoir, -an** *m* notch, cut, mark
sgòr *n* **sgòir, -an/-aichean** *m* score (*sport*)
sgorach *a* **-aiche** notched
sgòrnan *n* **-ain, -an** *m* gullet, throat
sgòrnanach *a* **-aiche** bronchial
sgot *n* **sgoit** *m* spot, plot of ground; fragment **cha robh s. aca** they hadn't a clue
sgoth *n* **-a, -an** *f* skiff, small boat
sgòth *n* **-a, -an** *f* cloud
sgòthach *a* **-aiche** cloudy
sgraing *n* **-e, -ean** *f* frown **chuir e s. air** *v* he frowned
sgreab *n* **-a, -an** *f* scab
sgread *n* **-a, -an** *m* shriek, screech
sgread *v* **-ail** shriek, screech **rinn i s.** *v* she shrieked
sgreadhail *n* **-e, -ean** *f* trowel
sgreamh *n* **-a/-eimhe** *m* disgust, loathing
sgreamhaich *v* **-achadh** disgust, nauseate
sgreamhail *a* **-e** disgusting, nauseating, horrible, loathsome
sgreataidh *a* **-e** ugly, horrible
sgreuch *n* **-a, -an** *m* scream, screech **dèan s.** *v* scream, screech
sgreuch *v* **-ail/-adh** scream, screech
sgriach *v* *See* **sgreuch**
sgrìob *n* **-a, -an** *n f* scrape, scratch; stripe; trip **chaidh sinn s. dhan bhaile** we went on a trip to town
sgrìob *v* **-adh** scrape, scratch
sgrìobach *a* **-aiche** striped
sgrìobag *n* **-aig, -an** *f* note (*written*)
sgrìoban *n* **-ain, -an** *m* hoe, rake
sgrìob-cheangail *n* **sgrìoban-ceangail** *f* hyphen
sgrìobh *v* **-adh** write
sgrìobhadair *n* **-ean** *m* writer *Also* **sgrìobhaiche**
sgrìobhadh *n* **-aidh, -aidhean** *m* writing, inscription
sgrìobhte *a* written
sgriobtar *n* **-air, -an** *m* scripture
sgriobtarail *a* **-e** scriptural
sgrios *n* **-a, -an** *m* destruction, ruin
sgrios *v* **sgrios/-adh** destroy, ruin
sgriosail *a* **-e** destructive, ruinous; terrible, awful, dreadful **s. daor** terribly expensive
sgriubha *n* **-ichean** *f m* screw
sgriubhaire *n* **-an** *m* screwdriver
sgròb *v* **-adh** scratch
sgròbadh *n* **-aidh, -aidhean** *m* scratch, scratching
sgrùd *v* **-adh** scrutinize, examine, inspect, audit
sgrùdadh *n* **-aidh, -aidhean** *m* examination, scrutiny, inspection, audit **dèan s. air** *v* scrutinize, examine **neach-sgrùdaidh** *m* examiner, inspector
sguab *n* **-aibe, -an** *f* broom, brush, sweep; sheaf **s. arbhair** a sheaf of corn **s.-fhliuch** mop
sguab *v* **-adh** sweep, brush
sguabadair *n* **-ean** *m* sweeper
sgud *v* **-adh** lop, chop, cut; (+ **leis** *etc*) snatch
sgudal *n* **-ail** *m* rubbish, trash, garbage **làraidh an sgudail** *f* the refuse lorry
sguir *v* **sgur** cease, stop **s. dheth** stop it **s. i a smocadh** she stopped smoking
sgùirt *n* **-e, -ean** *f* lap
sgur *n* **sguir** *m* ceasing, stopping **gun s.** endlessly, constantly, non-stop

sgùr *v* **-adh** scour, cleanse
sgùrr *n* **sgurra, sgurran** *m* steep hill, peak, pinnacle
shìos *adv* down (*stationary*)
shuas *adv* up (*stationary*)
sia *n, a* six
siab *v* **-adh** blow (away), drift
siaban *n* **-ain** *m* sand-drift, sea-spray
siabann *n* **-ainn, -ainn** *m* soap
sia-cheàrnach *n* **-aich, -an** *m* hexagon *a* hexagonal
sia-deug *n, a* sixteen **sia bliadhna deug** sixteen years
sian *n* **sìne, -tan** *f* weather, storm **na siantan** the elements
sian *n See* **sìon**
sianar *n f m* six (people)
siar *a* west, western **an Cuan S.** the Atlantic Ocean
siathamh *a* sixth
sibh(se) *pron* you (*pl & pol*)
sìde *n f* weather **deagh shìde** good weather **droch shìde** bad weather
sil *v* **-eadh** drip, drop, rain **a bheil i a' sileadh?** is it raining?
sileadh *n* **-lidh, -lidhean** *m* dripping; rainfall, precipitation
sileagan *n* **-ain, -an** *m* jar
silidh *n m* jam **crogan s.** jam-jar
similear *n* **-eir, -an** *m* chimney
sìmplich *v* **-leachadh** simplify
sìmplidh *a* **-e** simple, easy
sin *a* that, those
sin *pron* that **an sin** there; then
sìn *v* **-eadh** stretch; pass **sìn a-mach** extend, prolong **sìn dhomh an salann** pass me the salt
sinc *n m* zinc
sinc(e) *n* **-(e)achan/-(e)an** *f m* sink
sine *n* **-an** *f* teat, nipple
sineach *n* **sinich, sinich** *m* mammal
sìneadh *n* **sìnidh** *m* stretch, stretching
singilte *a* single, singular
sinn(e) *pron* we, us
sinn-seanair *n* **-ar, -ean** *m* great-grandfather
sinn-seanmhair *n* **-ar, -ean** *f* great-grandmother
sinnsear *n* **-sir, -sirean** *m* ancestor, forefather
sinnsearachd *n f* ancestry
sìnteag *n* **-eig, -an** *f* hop, bound, stride; stepping-stone
siobhag *n* **-aig, -an** *f* wick
sìobhalta *a* civil, courteous, polite
sìobhaltachd *n f* civility; civilization
sìobra *n* **-than** *m* zebra
sìochail *a* **-e** peaceful, peaceable
sìoda *n* **-chan** *m* silk
siogàr *n* **-air, -an** *m* cigar
sìol *n* **sìl** *m* seed; sperm; progeny
sìolag *n* **-aig, -an** *f* sand-eel
sìolaich *v* **-achadh** seed; beget, propagate; (*intrans*) multiply
sìolaidh *v* subside, settle; filter, strain **s. às** peter out
siolandair *n* **-ean** *m* cylinder
sìol-chuir *v* **-chur** sow
siolp *v* **-adh** slip away, slink off, skulk
sìol(t)achan *n* **-ain, -ain** *m* filter, strainer
sìoman *n* **-ain, -an** *m* rope of straw or hay; line for clothes
sìon *n* anything, something **a h-uile s.** everything
Sìonach *n* **-aich, -aich** *m* Chinese *a* Chinese
sionnach *n* **-aich, -aich** *m* fox
sionnsar *n* **-air, -an** *m* bagpipe chanter
sìor *a* ever, always, continual **s.-mhaireannach** perpetual, everlasting **s.-uaine** evergreen
sioraf *n* **-aif, -an** *m* giraffe
siorc *n* **-a, -an** *m* shark
siorrachd *n* **-an** *f* shire, county *Also* **siorramachd**
sìorraidh *a* ever **gu s.** forever
sìorraidheachd *n f* eternity *Also* **sìorrachd**
siorram *n* **-aim, -an** *m* sheriff *Also* **siorraidh**
sìos *adv* down, downwards
siosar *n* **-air, -an** *f m* scissors
siosarnaich *n f* hissing, hiss
siostam *n* **-aim, -an** *m* system
siota *n* **-ichean** *f* sheet
sir *v* **-eadh** seek, search for
siris(t) *n* **-ean** *f* cherry

sìth *n* **-e** *f* peace, reconciliation
sitheadh *n* **-thidh, -thidhean** *m* speed, onrush, impetuosity
sìthean *n* **-ein, -ein/-an** *m* hillock, knoll, fairy knoll; flower
sitheann *n* **sithinn/sìthne** *f* venison, game; flesh of fowls
sìtheil *a* **-e** peaceful, tranquil, peaceable
sìthich *v* **sìtheachadh** pacify
sìthiche *n* **-an** *m* fairy
sitig *n* **-e, -ean** *f* dunghill, midden; outdoors
sitir *n* **-e** *f* neighing, braying
sitrich *n* **-e** *f* neighing, braying *Also vn* **a' s.**
siubhail *v* **-al** travel, journey; die, pass away
siubhal *n* **-ail, siùbhlaichean** *m* travel **cosgaisean siubhail** *f pl* travel expenses **fad an t-siubhail** all the time
siùbhlach *n* **-aiche, -aichean** *m* traveller; nomad
siùbhlach *a* **-aiche** swift, speedy; wandering; fluent (*speech*)
siùcar *n* **-air, -an** *m* sugar; sweet
siud *pron* that **an siud** there, over there
siùdan *n* **-ain, -an** *m* swing
siuga *n* **-nnan** *f m* jug
siùrsach *n* **-aich, -an** *f* prostitute
siuthad *def v* go on! *pl* **siuthadaibh/siùdaibh**
slabhraidh *n* **-ean** *f* chain
slalc *n* **-ean** *f* blow **thug iad s. air an Riaghaltas** they hit out at the Government
slaic *v* **-eadh** thrash, beat, strike
slaighd *v* **-eadh** slide
slaightear *m* **-eir, -an** *m* rogue *Also* **slaoightear, slaightire**
slàinte *n f* health **bòrd s.** *m* health board **Seirbheis na S.** the Health Service **Slàinte!** Cheers! **S. Mhath!** Good Health! Cheers!
slàinteachail *a* **-e** hygienic
slàinteachas *n* **-ais** *m* hygiene
slàintealachd *n f* sanitation
slaman *n* **-ain** *m* curds, curdled milk **s.-milis** jelly
slàn *a* **slàine** whole, complete, wholesome **s. leat** goodbye, farewell
slànaich *v* **-achadh** heal, cure
slànaighear *n* **-air** *m* saviour **an S.** the Saviour
slaod *n* **slaoid, -an** *m* sledge, raft
slaod *v* **-adh** pull, drag, haul
slaodach *a* **-aiche** slow, tardy, sluggish
slaodair *n* **-ean** *m* sluggard
slapag *n* **-aig, -an** *f* slipper
slat *n* **slait, -an** *f* rod; yard (length) **s.-iasgaich** fishing rod **s.-t(h)omhais** measuring rod; criterion, yardstick
sleagh *n* **-a, -an** *f* spear, javelin
sleamhainn *a* **-e/-mhna** slippery
sleamhnag *n* **-aig, -an** *f* slide
sleamhnaich *v* **-achadh** slip, slide
sleids *n* **-ichean** *m* sledge
sleuchd *v* **-adh** kneel, prostrate self; submit
sliabh *n* **slèibh(e), slèibhtean** *m* mountain, hillside, moor
sliasaid *n* **-e, -ean** *f* thigh
slige *n* **-an/-achan** *f* shell
sligeach *a* **-giche** shelled, having a shell, shelly
sligeanach *n* **-aich** *m* tortoise
slighe *n* **-an** *f* way, path, direction, track, route
slinnean *n* **-ein, -an** *m* shoulder, shoulder-blade
slìob *v* **-adh** stroke; (*met*) flatter
sliochd *n* **-a, -an** *m* offspring, progeny, descendants
slìogach *a* **-aiche** sly, sleekit
slios *n* **-a, -an** *m* side, slope, flank
slis *n* **-e, -ean** *f* slice, rasher
sliseag *n* **-eig, -an** *f* slice, small slice
slisnich *v* **-neadh** slice
sloc *n* **sluic, sluic/-an** *m* pit, cavity, hollow
sloinn *v* **-eadh** give/trace genealogy/family tree
sloinneadh *n* **-nidh, -nidhean** *m* surname; genealogy
sloinntearachd *n f* (*act of giving a*) genealogy
sluagh *n* **sluaigh, slòigh** *m* people, host, crowd
sluagh-ghairm *n* **-e, -ean** *f* war-cry, slogan

sluasaid *n* **-e, -ean** *f* shovel
slugadh *n* **-aidh** *m* swallowing, gulping, devouring; capacity **tha s. mòr aig an talla** the hall has a large capacity
slugan *n* **-ain, -an** *m* gullet
sluig *v* **-eadh/slugadh** swallow
slupraich *n* **-e** *f* slurping; splashing through water
smachd *n f* discipline, authority, control **fo s.** under control **cùm s. air** *v* keep control of
smachdaich *v* **-achadh** discipline
smachdail *a* **-e** authoritative, commanding, disciplinary
smal *n* **smail** *m* spot, stain **gun s.** without blemish **màireach gun s. dhut** have a good day tomorrow
smàl *v* **-adh** extinguish, quench
smàladair *n* **-ean** *m* firefighter
smalan *n* **-ain** *m* grief, sorrow, melancholy
smaoin *n* **-e, -tean** *f* thought, idea
smaoineachadh *n* **-aidh** *m* thinking
smaoin(t)ich *v* **smaoin(t)eachadh/ smaointinn** think
smàrag *n* **-aig, -an** *f* emerald
smèid *v* **-eadh** wave, beckon
smeòrach *n* **-aich, -aichean** *f* thrush
smeur *n* **-a, -an** *f* bramble
smeur *v* **-adh** smear, daub
smid *n* **-e, -ean** *f* syllable, word **cha tuirt e s.** he didn't utter a word
smig *n* **-ean** *f m* chin
smiogaid *n* **-ean** *f m* chin
smior *n* **smir/-a** *m* marrow, pith; strength, pluck, vigour; best part **'s e s. an duin'-uasail a th' ann** he's a real/true gentleman **s.-caillich** spinal marrow
smiorail *a* **-e/-ala** strong, vigorous, doughty, plucky *Also* **smearail**
smiùr *v* **-adh** *See* **smeur**
smoc *v* **-adh** smoke *Also* **smocaig**
smocadh *n* **-aidh** *m* smoking
smodal *n* **-ail** *m* fragments, crumbs; smattering **s. airgid** loose change
smuain *n* **-e, -tean** *f* thought, idea
smuainich *v* **-neachadh** think
smug *n* **smuig, -an** *m* phlegm
smugadaich *n f* spitting
smugaid *n* **-e, -ean** *f* spit, spittle **tilg s.** *v* spit
smùid *n* **-e, -ean** *f* smoke, vapour; intoxication **ghabh e droch s.** *v* he got very drunk
smùirnean *n* **-ein, -ein** *m* mote, atom
smùirneanach *a* atomic
smùr *n* **smùir** *m* dross, dust
sna *aug prep* in the (*before pl nouns*)
snag *n* **snaig, -an** *m* knock, crack
snagadaich *n* **-e** *f* gnashing, grating, chattering (*of teeth*)
snàgail *n* **-e** *f* crawl, crawling
snàgair *n* **-ean** *m* crawler; reptile
snagan-daraich *n* **snagain-, snagain-/snaganan-** *m* woodpecker
snaidhm *n* **-ean, -eannan** *m* knot **cuir s. air** *v* tie a knot in it *Also* **snaoim**
snàig *v* **snàgadh/snàgail** creep, crawl
snàigeach *a* **-giche** creeping, crawling
snàigeadh *n* **-gidh** *m* creeping, crawling
snaigh *v* **-eadh** sculpt, carve, hew
snaigheadair *n* **-ean** *m* sculptor
snaigheadh *n* **-ghidh, -ghidhean** *m* sculpture, carving **bha iad a' s. ris an uair** they were cutting it fine
snàithlean *n* **-ein, -an** *m* thread
snàmh *v* swim
snaoisean *n* **-ein** *m* snuff
snas *n* **snais** *m* accomplishment, elegance, finesse
snasail *a* **-e** accomplished, elegant, well-finished
snasmhor *a* **-oire** accomplished, elegant, well-finished
snàth *n* **-a/snàith, snàithean** *m* thread
snàthad *n* **-aid, -an** *f* needle
snàthainn *n* **-e/snàithe, -ean/ snàithean** *m* thread, single

thread
snàthlainn *n See* **snàithlean**
sneachd(a) *n m* snow **a' cur an t-s.** *v* snowing **bodach-s.** snowman
snèap *n* **snèip, -an** *f* turnip, neep *Also* **snèip**
snigh *v* **-e** leak, drip, seep
snighe *n m* rain penetration from roof, seeping, seepage, drip
snìomh *n* **-a, -an** *m* spinning, twist
snìomh *v* **snìomh/-adh** spin, twist **shnìomh i a h-adhbrann** she twisted/sprained her ankle
snìomhaire *n* **-an** *m* wimble, drill
snìomhan *n* **-ain, -an** *m* spiral
snodhach *n* **-aich** *m* sap
snodha-gàire *n* **snodhan-** *m* smile, quick smile
snog *a* **snoige** nice, lovely, attractive; likeable
snot *v* **-adh** smell, sniff
snuadh *n* **-aidh** hue, complexion, appearance, aspect
so *a See* **seo**
sòbarra *a* sober
sòbhrach *n* **-aich, -aichean** *f* primrose *Also* **seòbhrach**
socair *n* **-e/socrach** *f* ease, rest **gabh air do shocair** take it easy
socair *a* **socraiche, -e** at ease, quiet, tranquil, mild; comfortable
sochair *n* **-(e), -ean** *f* benefit, privilege **s. chloinne** child benefit **s. cion-cosnaidh** unemployment benefit
socharach *a* **-aiche** laid back, easy-going, bashful
socrach *a* **-aiche** at ease, comfortable, sedate
socraich *v* **-achadh** settle; determine, fix
sodal *n* **-ail** *f m* flattery, fawning
sòfa *n* **-than** *f* sofa
soidhne *n* **-achan** *m* sign *Also* **soighne**
soilire *n m* celery
soilleir *a* **-e** clear, bright
soilleireachd *n f* clearness, clarity, clarification, brightness
soilleirich *v* **-reachadh** clear, clarify, illuminate, brighten
soillse *n* **-an** *m* light
soillseach *a* **-siche** bright, clear, shining
soillsich *v* **-seachadh** light, enlighten
soirbh *a* **-e** easy
soirbheachadh *n* **-aidh, -aidhean** *m* success, prosperity
soirbheachail *a* **-e** successful, prosperous
soirbheas *n* **-eis, -eis** *m* success, prosperity; favourable breeze
soirbhich *v* **-bheachadh** succeed, prosper
soircas *n* **-ais, -an** *m* circus
sòisealach *n* **-aich, -aich** *m* socialist
sòisealach *a* **-aiche** socialist
sòisealachd *n f* socialism, social work
sòisealta *a* social **na seirbheisean s.** the social services
sòisealtas *n* **-ais** *m* society
soisgeul *n* **-eil, -an** *m* gospel
soisgeulach *a* **-aiche** evangelical
soisgeulaiche *n* **-an** *m* evangelist
soitheach *n* **-thich, -thichean** *f m* dish; vessel, ship **nigh na soithichean** wash the dishes **s.-sgudail** rubbish bin
soitheamh *a* **-eimhe** tame, docile, tractable, gentle
sòlaimte *a* solemn, dignified
solair *v* **-ar/-aradh** provide, supply, cater for, procure
solarachadh *n* **-aidh** *m* provision, supply, catering, procurement
solaraich *v* **-achadh** provide, supply, cater for, procure
solas *n* **-ais, -ais** *m* light; traffic lights
sòlas *n* **-ais** *m* happiness, joy, solace
sòlasach *a* **-aiche** happy, joyful
so-leaghadh *a* dissoluble
so-leughadh *a* legible
so-loisgeach *a* combustible
solt(a) *a* mild, gentle, placid
so-lùbadh *a* flexible
somalta *a* placid, docile; inactive
son *n m* cause, account **air mo shon-sa** on my behalf

son *prep See* **airson**
sona *a* happy, content
sonas *n* **-ais** *m* happiness, contentment
sònraich *v* **-achadh** specify, stipulate
sònraichte *a* special, particular, specific; remarkable **gu s.** particularly, especially
sop *n* **suip, suip/-an** *m* wisp
soraidh *n f* farewell **s. leibh** farewell (*to you*) (*pl & pol*)
sòrn *n* **sùirn** *m* flue, vent
so-ruighinn *a* accessible *Also* **so-ruigsinn**
so-thuigsinn *a* intelligible, clear
spàgach *a* **-aiche** splay-footed
spàgail *n f* walking awkwardly
spaid *n* **-e, -ean** *f* spade
spaideil *a* **-e** well-dressed, smart
spaidsirich *v* **-searachd** parade, saunter
spàin *n* **-e, -ean/-tean/-eachan** *f* spoon **s.-tì/teatha** teaspoon
Spàinn(t)each *n* Spaniard *a* Spanish
Spàinn(t)is *n f* Spanish (*lang*)
spàirn *n* **-e** *f* effort, exertion, struggle, stress **rinn e s. mhòr** he made a great effort
spàl *n* **spàil, -an** *m* shuttle **s.-fànais** space shuttle **s.-ite** shuttlecock
spanair *n* **-ean** *m* spanner
spàrdan *n* **-ain, -ain/-an** *m* roost
spàrr *n* **sparra, sparran** *m* joist, beam; roost
spàrr *v* **sparradh** thrust, force
spastach *n* **-aich, -aich** *m* spastic
spastach *a* **-aiche** spastic
speach *n* **-a, -an** *f* wasp
speal *n* **-a, -an** *f* scythe
spealg *n* **speilg, -an** *f* splinter, fragment
spealg *v* **-adh** splinter, smash
spèil *n* **-e, -ean** *f* skate
spèil *v* **-eadh** skate
spèileabord *n* **-buird, -buird** *m* skateboard, skateboarding
spèile-deighe *n f* ice skating
spèiliche *n* **-an** *m* skater
speireag *n* **-eig, -an** *f* sparrow-hawk; spitfire, nippy sweetie
spèis *n* **-e** *f* esteem, affection, regard, fondness, attachment **bha s. mhòr aige dhi** he held her in great esteem, he was very fond of her
spèisealta *a* specialist
speuclairean *n m pl* spectacles, glasses **s.-grèine** sunglasses *Also* **speuclair** (*sg*)
speur *n* **-a, -an** *m* sky **na speuran** the heavens, the firmament **s.-sheòladair** spaceman, astronaut **s.-shiubhal** *m* space travel
speur(ad)air *n* **-ean** *m* astronaut, spaceman
speuradaireachd *n f* space exploration
spìc *n* **-e, -ean** *f* spike
spideag *n* **-eig, -an** *f* nightingale; nippy female
spìocach *a* **-aiche** mean, miserly, stingy
spìocaire *n* **-an** *m* miser
spìocaireachd *n f* meanness, miserliness
spìon *v* **-adh** pluck, tug, snatch, wrench
spionnadh *n* **-aidh** *m* strength, vigour
spiorad *n* **-aid, -an** *m* spirit **an S. Naomh** the Holy Spirit
spioradail *a* **-e** spiritual
spioradalachd *n f* spirituality
spìosrach *a* **-aiche** spicy
spìosradh *n* **-aidh, -aidhean** *m* spice
spìosraich *v* **-achadh** spice; embalm
spìosraidh *n f* spices
spiris *n* **-e, -ean** *f* roost, perch
spitheag *n* **-eig, -an** *f* chuckie (*small flat pebble*), skimmer
splais *n* **-ean** *f* splash
splais *v* **-eadh** splash
spleadhach *a* **-aiche** splay-footed *Also* **spliathach**
spleuchd *n* **-a, -an** *m* smarm; stare, gaze
spleuchd *v* spread out, plaster all over; stare, gaze
spliùchan *n* **-ain, -an** *m* tobacco pouch *Also* **spliuchan**
spòg *n* **spòig, -an** *f* paw; claw,

spoke; hand (*of watch/clock*)
spong *n* **spuing, -an** *m* sponge
spor *n* **spuir, -an** *m* spur; claw, talon; flint
sporan *n* **-ain, -ain** *m* purse
sporghail *n f* noisy scramble/scrabble, rustling
spòrs *n* **-a** *f* sport, fun
spòrsail *a* **-e** sporting, sporty; funny, in fun
spot *n* **-an** *f m* spot
spoth *v* **spoth, -adh** castrate, geld
spreadh *v* **-adh** explode, burst
spreadhadh *n* **-aidh, -aidhean** *m* explosion, burst
sprèidh *n* **-e** *f* cattle, livestock
spreig *v* **-eadh** incite
sprochd *n f* dejection, sadness **fo s.** dejected
sprùilleach *n* **-lich** *m* crumbs, fragments, debris
spùill *v* **-eadh** plunder
spùinn *v* **-eadh** plunder
spùinneadair *n* **-ean** *m* plunderer **s.-mara** pirate
spuir *n* **-ean** *m* claw, talon
spùt *n* **-a, -an** *m* spout; very small particle **chan eil s. aige** he has no idea
spùt *v* **-adh** spout, squirt
sràbh *n* **sràibh, -an** *m* straw
srac *v* **-adh** tear, rend
sracadh *n* **-aidh, -aidhean** *m* tear, tearing
sradag *n* **-aig, -an** *f* spark **tha s. innte** she has a quick temper
sràid *n* **-e, -ean** *f* street
srainnsear *n* **-eir, -an** *m* stranger
srann *n* **srainn, -an** *f* snore, hum **dèan s.** *v* snore
srath *n* **-a, -an** *m* wide valley (*usually with river*)
sreang *n* **-a/sreinge, -an** *f* string
sreap *v See* **streap**
sreath *n* **-a, -an** *f m* row, series **an s. a chèile** in a row, in succession
sreothart *n* **-airt, -an** *m* sneeze **dèan s.** *v* sneeze *Also* **sreathart**
sreothartaich *n f* sneezing *Also* **sreathartaich**
srian *n* **srèine, -tan/srèinean** *f* stripe; bridle **cùm s. air do theanga** *v* watch what you say
srianach *a* **-aiche** striped
sròl *n* **sròil, -an** *m* satin
sròn *n* **sròine, -an/sròinean** *f* nose; promontory **ghabh iad san t-sròin e** they took offence at it
sròin-adharcach *n* **-aich** *m* rhinoceros
srùb *n* **srùib, -an** *m* spout
srùbag *n* **-aig, -an** *f* a small drink, a cuppa
srùban *n* **-ain, -ain** *m* cockle
sruth *n* **-a/sruithe, -an** *m* stream, burn; current **leis an t-s.** with the current; (*met*) downhill
sruth *v* **-adh** stream, flow
sruthail *v* **-thladh/srùthladh** wash, rinse
sruthan *n* **-ain, -ain** *m* streamlet, small stream
stàball *n* **-aill, -aill/-an** *m* stable
staca *n* **-nnan** *m* stack
stad *n m* stop, halt, pause **na s.** stationary **chuireadh s. oirnn** *v* we were stopped
stad *v* stop, halt, pause
stad-phuing *n* **-e, -ean** *f* full stop
staid *n* **(-e), -ean** *f* state, condition
staidhre *n* **-richean** *f* stair **shuas an s.** upstairs **shìos an s.** downstairs *Also* **staidhir**
staigh *adv See* **a-staigh**
stail *n* **-e, -ean** *f* still (*for whisky*)
stailc *n* **-ean** *f* strike (*labour*)
stàile *n* **-lichean** *f* stall
stàilinn *n* **-e** *f* steel
staing *n* **-e, -ean** *f* difficulty, predicament **ann an s.** in a quandary/fix
stàirn *n* **-e** *f* loud noise, clamour
stairs(n)each *n* **-s(n)ich, -s(n)ichean** *f* threshold; stone steps/stone path
stais *n* **-e, -ean** *f* moustache
stàit *n* **-e, -ean** *f* state **na Stàitean Aonaichte** the United States
stàiteil *a* **-e/-eala** stately
stàitire *n* **-an** *m* statesman
stàitireachd *n f* statesmanship
stalc *n* **stailc** *m* starch
stalla *n* **-chan** *m* overhanging rock, precipice

stamag *n* **-aig, -an** *f* stomach
stamh *n* **staimh** *m* tangle (*on shore*)
stamp *v* **-adh** stamp, trample
stamp(a) *n* **-(a)ichean** *f* (*postage*) stamp
staoig *n* **-ean** *f* steak
staoin *n* **-e** *f* tin, pewter
stapag *n* **-aig, -an** *f* mixture of meal and cold water
staran *n* **-ain, -an** *m* path (*to house*)
starrag *n* **-aig, -an** *f* hoodie crow
steach *adv See* **a-steach**
steall *n* **still, -an** *f* spout, squirt
steall *v* **-adh** spout, squirt
steallair *n* **-e, -ean** *m* syringe
steapa *n* **-ichean** *f m* step
steatasgop *n* **-oip, -an** *f m* stethoscope
stèidh *n* **-e, -ean** *f* foundation, base, basis
stèidheachadh *n* **-aidh, -aidhean** *m* foundation, establishment
stèidheachd *n f* foundation, institute
stèidhich *v* **-dheachadh** found, establish, set up
steigeach *a* **-giche** sticky
stèisean *n* **-ein, -an** *m* station **s. peatrail** petrol station **s. rèidio** radio station **s. thrèanaichean** train station
stiall *n* **stèill, -an** *f* strip, stripe, streak **cha robh s. orra** they hadn't a stitch on
stiall *v* **-adh** thrash, lash; tear into strips; stripe
stiallach *a* **-aiche** streaky
stìopall *n* **-aill, -aill** *m* steeple
stiorap *n* **-aip, -an** *m* stirrup
stiùbhard *n* **-aird, -an** *m* steward
stiùir *n* **-e/stiùrach, -ean/-ichean** *f* rudder, helm
stiùir *v* **-eadh** steer, direct, guide
stiùireadair *n* **-ean** *m* steersman, helmsman
stiùireadh *n* **-ridh, -ridhean** *m* steering; direction, guidance, management, supervision
stiùiriche *n* **-an** *m* director **S. an Fhoghlaim** the Director of Education
stob *n* **stuib, -an** *m* stump; protrusion **bha mi nam s. a' feitheamh riutha** I was left standing around waiting for them
stob *v* **-adh** stab, thrust
stobach *a* **-aiche** prickly, barbed
stòbha *n* **-ichean** *f m* stove
stoc *n* **stuic, stuic** *m* trunk, stump (*of tree*); stock, livestock
stoc *n* **stuic, stuic** *m* scarf
stoc *v* **-adh** stock
stocainn *n* **(-e), -ean** *f* stocking
stoc-mhargaid *n* **-ean** *f* stock-exchange
stoidhle *n* **-lichean** *f* style
stoighle *n See* **stoidhle**
stò(i)r *v* **stòradh** store
stòiridh *n* **-ean** *f m* story *Also* **stòraidh**
stoirm *n* **-e, -ean** *f m* storm
stoirmeil *a* **-e** stormy
stòl *a* **-a/stòil, -an** *m* stool
stòlda *a* steady, sedate, settled, staid
stòr *n* **stòir, -an/-aichean** *m* store **s.-dàta** database
stòradh *n* **-aidh** *m* storage, storing
stòras *n* **-ais, -ais** *m* riches, wealth, resources
stràc *n* **-àic, -an** *f m* stroke; accent (*in writing*)
strèan *n* **-èin** *m* strain, stress
streap *v* **streap/-adh** climb
streapadair *n* **-ean** *m* climber
strì *n f* strife, struggle, conflict, contention **dèan s.** *v* strive
strì *v* strive, struggle, compete, contest
strìoch *n* **-a, -an** *f* streak; line; hyphen
strìochd *v* **-adh** submit, yield, give in, surrender
strìopach *n* **-aich(e), -aichean** *f* prostitute, whore
strìopachas *n* **-ais** *m* prostitution
stròdhail *a* **-e** prodigal, extravagant, lavish *Also* **strùidheil**
stròdhalachd *n f* prodigality *Also* **strùidhealachd**
structair *n* **-ean** *m* structure
structarail *a* **-e** structural

strùidhear *n* **-eir, -an** *m* spendthrift
strùpag *n See* **srùbag**
struth *n* **-a, -an** *f m* ostrich
stuadh *n See* **stuagh**
stuagh *n* **stuaigh, -an/-annan** *f* wave; gable
stuaim *n* **-e** *f* moderation, temperance, abstemiousness
stuama *a* **stuaime** moderate, temperate, sober, abstemious
stuamachd *n f* temperance, abstemiousness
stùirceach *n* **-ciche** surly, scowling
stuig *v* **-eadh** incite, prompt
stùr *n* **stùir** *m* stour, dust
stuth *n* **-a, -an** *m* stuff, matter; material **s.-fhiaclan** toothpaste
stuthaigeadh *n* **-gidh** *m* starch
sù *n* **-than** *m* zoo *Also* **sutha**
suaicheanta *a* remarkable, notable, prominent
suaicheantas *n* **-ais, -ais** *m* badge, emblem
suaimhneach *a* **-niche** tranquil, quiet
suaimhneas *n* **-eis** *m* rest, tranquillity, quiet
suain *n* **-e** *f* deep sleep, slumber
suain *v* **-eadh** wrap
suainealachadh *n* **-aidh** *m* hypnotism
suainealaiche *n* **-an** *m* hypnotist
suainealas *n* **-ais** *m* hypnosis
Suaineach *n* **-nich, -nich** *m* Swede *a* Swedish
suaip *n* **-e, -ean** *f* slight resemblance
suairce *a* affable; gentle, courteous
suairceas *n* **-eis** *m* affability; gentility, courteousness
suarach *a* **-aiche** insignificant, trifling; mean, contemptible, despicable
suarachas *n* **-ais** *m* insignificance; meanness, contemptibility
suas *adv* up, upwards
suath *v* **-adh** rub, wipe; massage
suathadh *n* **-aidh, -aidhean** *m* rub, rubbing, massage, friction
sùbailte *a* supple, flexible, elastic *Also* **subailte**
sùbailteachd *n f* suppleness, flexibility *Also* **subailteachd**
sùbh *n* **sùibh, -an** *m* berry **s.-craoibh** raspberry **s.-làir** strawberry *Also* **subh**
subhach *a* **-aiche** merry
subhailc *n* **-e, -ean** *f* virtue
subhailceach *a* **-ciche** virtuous
subsadaidh *n* **-ean** *m* subsidy
sùgach *a* **-aiche** joyous
sùgh *n* **-a/sùigh, -an** *m* juice, sap
sùgh *v* **-adh** suck, absorb, soak up *Also* **sùigh**
sùghach *a* **-aiche** absorbent
sùghadh *n* **-aidh** *m* absorption, suction
sùghmhor *a* **-oire** juicy
sùgradh *n* **-aidh** *m* mirth **dèan s.** *v* make merry
suidh *v* **-e** sit **dèan suidhe** *v* take a seat
suidhe *n* **-an/-achan** *m* sitting **àite-s.** *nm* seat
suidheachadh *n* **-aidh, -aidhean** *m* situation, site; state, condition, circumstances
suidheachan *n* **-ain, -ain** *m* seat
suidhich *v* **-dheachadh** settle, place, situate, set, appoint
suidhichte *a* situated, settled, set
suidse *n* **-sichean** *f* switch **cuir s. ri** *v* set on fire
suids-chlàr *n* **-chlàir** *m* switchboard
suigeart *n* **-eirt** *m* jollity, cheerfulness, chirpiness
suigeartach *a* **-aiche** jolly, cheerful, chirpy
sùil *n* **sùla, -ean** *f* eye **s.-bheag** wink **s.-dhubh** black eye **thug e s. air** he had a look at it **s.-chritheach** quagmire
suilbhir *a* **-e** cheerful
sùilich *v* **-leachadh** expect, anticipate
sùim *n* **-e, -eannan** *f* sum, amount; regard, esteem, interest **cha do ghabh e mòran s. dheth** he didn't pay much regard to it
suipear *n* **-eir/-ach, -an** *f* supper
suirghe *n f* courtship, wooing, love-making

suirghiche *n* **-an** *m* wooer, lover
sùist *n* **-e, -ean** *f* flail
sùist *v* **-eadh** flail
suiteas *n* **-eis, -eis** *m* sweet *Also* **suitidh**
sùith *n* **-e** *f m* soot
sùlaire *n* **-an** *m* gannet
sult *n* **suilt** *m* fat; joy
Sultain *n* **-e** *f* **an t-S.** September
sultmhor *a* **-oire** fat, plump; joyful, jolly
sumainn *n* **-e, -ean** *f* surge (*of sea*), billow
sumanadh *n* **-aidh** *m* summons
sunnd *n m* mood, humour **bha iad ann an deagh shunnd** they were in good spirits
sunndach *a* **-aiche** lively, contented, hearty, in good spirits
sùrd *n* **sùird** *m* cheerfulness; eagerness
sùrdag *n* **-aig, -an** *f* leap, bound, skip
sùrdail *a* **-e** energetic
susbaint *n* **-e** *f* substance, content
susbainteach *a* **-tiche** substantial
suth *n* **-a, -an** *m* embryo
suthainn *a* eternal **gu s. sìor** forever and ever, eternally

T

tà *conj* though, although
tàbh *n* **tàibh, -an** *m* spoon net, fishing net
tàbhachd *n f* efficacy, effectiveness; substance; benefit
tàbhachdach *a* **-aiche** effectual, effective; substantial; beneficial
tabhainn *v* **-ann** offer, tender *Also* **tathainn**
tabhair *irr v* give, bestow (*See irr v* **tabhair** *in Grammar*)
tabhairtiche *n* **-an** *m* donor, giver
tabhann *n* **-ainn** *m* offer, offering *Also* **tathann**
tabhannaich *v* bark, yelp
tabhartach *a* liberal; dative **an tuiseal t.** the dative case
tabhartas *n* **-ais** *m* donation, grant, offering, presentation
tac *n* **-a/taic, -annan/-aichean** *f* tack (*of land*)
tac(a) *n f* time, season **mun t. seo an-uiridh** about this time last year **an t. ri** in comparison with
tacaid *n* **-e, -ean** *f* tack
tacan *n* **-ain, -an** *m* a while, a short time
tachair *v* **-t** happen; meet **t. do** happen to (*someone*) **t. ri** meet (with)
tachas *n* **-ais** *m* itch, itchiness *Also* **tachais**
tachais *v* **-as/-ais** scratch
tàcharan *n* **-ain, -an** *m* sprite, ghost; changeling
tachartas *n* **-ais, -an** *m* event, incident, occurrence
tachasach *a* **-aiche** itchy
tachd *v* **-adh** choke, smother, strangle
tacsa *n m* support **an t. ri balla** leaning against a wall
tadhail *v* **-al** call (on), visit
tadhal *n* **-ail, -aichean** *m* visit, call; goal, hail (*in sport*)
tagach *a* **-aiche** stocky
tagair *v* **-t/tagradh** plead, claim, advocate
tagairt *n* **-e** *f* claim
tagh *v* **-adh** choose, select, elect
taghadh *n* **-aidh, -aidhean** *m* choice, selection, election **T. Pàrlamaid** General Election
taghta *a* splendid, fine, chosen, choice
tagradh *n* **-aidh, -aidhean** *m* plea, pleading, claim, submission
tagraiche *n* **-an** *m* advocate, applicant, candidate (*polit*)
tagsaidh *n* **-ean** *f m* taxi
taibhs(e) *n* **-(e)an** *f m* ghost, apparition
taic *n* **-e** *f* support; proximity **t. airgid** financial support **cuir t. ri/thoir t. do** *v* support
taiceil *a* **-e** supportive
taidh *n* **-ean** *f* tie (*necktie*)
taidhr *n* **-ichean** *f* tyre *Also* **taidhear**
taigeis *n* **-e, -ean** *f* haggis
taigh *n* **-e, -ean** *m* house **aig an t.** at home **T. nan Cumantan** the House of Commons **T. nam**

Morairean the House of Lords **t.-beag** toilet **t.-bìdh** restaurant **t.-ceàirde** factory **t.-chearc** henhouse **t.-chon** kennel **t.-cluiche** theatre **t.-cuibhle** wheelhouse **t.-cùirte** courthouse **t.-dhealbh** cinema **t.-dubh** black house, thatched cottage **t.-eiridinn** hospital, infirmary **t.-faire** watch-house, vigil; mortuary **t.-fuine** bakery **t.-glainne** glasshouse **t.-grùide** brewery **t.-òsta** hotel **t.-seinnse** bar, inn, hotel **t.-solais** lighthouse **t.-spadaidh** slaughterhouse **t.-staile** distillery **t.-tasgaidh** museum **t.-tughaidh** thatched cottage

taigheadas *n* **-ais** *m* housing

tàileasg *n* **-eisg** *m* chess; backgammon

tàillear *n* **-eir, -an** *m* tailor

taing *n* **-e** *f* thanks, gratitude **mòran t.** many thanks, thanks very much

taingealachd *n f* gratitude, thankfulness

taingeil *a* **-e** thankful, grateful

tàinig *irr v* came (*See irr v* **thig** *in Grammar*)

tàir *n* **-e, -ean** *f* contempt; difficulty **dèan t. air** *v* deride, scoff at, disparage

tairbeart *n* **-eirt, -an** *f* isthmus

tairbhe *n f* profit, advantage, benefit

tàireil *a* **-e** insulting, disparaging; contemptible, mean

tairg *v* **-sinn/-se(adh)** offer, tender

tairgse *n* **-an** *f* offer, tender

tàirneanach *n* **-aich, -aich** *m* thunder

tàirnge *n See* **tarrang**

tais *a* **-e** moist, damp

taisbean *v* **-adh** reveal, show, exhibit, demonstrate, manifest

taisbeanadh *n* **-aidh, -aidhean** *m* exhibition, display, show

taisbein *v See* **taisbean**

taiseachd *n f* moisture, dampness, humidity

taisg *v* **tasgadh** deposit, store, hoard

taisich *v* **-seachadh** moisten, dampen

taitinn *v* **taitneadh** please, delight (+ **ri**)

taitneach *a* **-niche** pleasant, pleasing, agreeable

taitneas *n* **-eis, -an** *m* pleasure

tàl *n* **tàil, -an** *m* adze

tàladh *n* **-aidh, -aidhean** *m* lullaby; enticing, attracting; soothing

tàlaidh *v* **-adh** entice, attract; soothe; lull

talamh *n* **-aimh/talmhainn, -an** *m* (*the gen sg* **talmhainn** *f is more common*) earth, land, soil **t. àitich** arable land **t. bàn** fallow ground

tàlant *n* **-tan** *m* talent *Also* **tàlann**

tàlantach *a* **-aiche** talented

talla *n* **-chan/-ichean** *f m* hall **t. a' bhaile** the town/village hall **t. ciùil** music hall

tallan *n* **-ain, -an** *m* partition (*phys*)

talmhaidh *a* **-e** earthly, terrestrial; worldly (*of person*)

tàmailt *n* **-e, -ean** *f* chagrin, humiliation, shame, embarrassment; offence, insult

tàmailteach *a* **-tiche** humiliating, embarrassing; humiliated, embarrassed; indignant, insulted

tamall *n* **-aill, -aill** *m* a while, length of time

tàmh *n* **tàimh** *m* rest, repose **a bheil i na t. an-dràsta?** is she idle/out of work at present?

tàmh *v* rest; stay, dwell

tamhasg *n* **-aisg, -an** *m* blockhead, fool; ghost

tana *a* **taine** thin, slender, slim; shallow

tanaich *v* **-achadh** thin

tànaiste *n* **-an** *m* regent

tanalach *n* **-aich** *m* shallow water

tanca *n* **-ichean** *f m* tank

tancair *n* **-ean** *m* tanker

tannasg *n* **-aisg, -aisg** *m* apparition, ghost, spectre

taobh *n* **taoibh, -an** *m* side; way **ri t.** (+ *gen*) beside **t. an fhasgaidh**

the lee side **t. an fhuaraidh** the windward side **t.-duilleig(e)** page (*in book*) **a thaobh** (+ *gen*) concerning, regarding **tha t. aice ri Ìle** she is fond of Islay
taobh *v* **-adh** (+ **ri**) side with, favour
taod *n* **taoid, taoid** *m* halter
taois *n* **-e, -ean** *f* dough
taoisnich *v* **-neachadh** knead
taom *v* **-adh** pour out; bale
tap *n* **-a, -aichean** *f m* tap
tapachd *n f* boldness, sturdiness
tapadh *n* **-aidh** *m* courage **tapadh leat/leibh** thank you
tapaidh *a* **-e** bold, active; well-built
tapais *n* **-ean** *f* carpet
Tarasach *n* **-aich, -aich** *m* native of Taransay *a* from, or pertaining to, Taransay
tarbh *n* **tairbh, tairbh** *m* bull
tarbhach *a* **-aiche** beneficial, advantageous
tarbh-nathrach *n* **tairbh-, tairbh-** *m* dragonfly
tarcais *n* **-e, -ean** *f* contempt, scorn **dèan t. air** *v* scorn, despise *Also* **tarchais**
tarchaiseach *a* **-siche** contemptuous, scornful
targaid *n* **-e, -ean** *f* target
tàrmachan *n* **-ain, -ain** *m* ptarmigan
tàrmaich *v* originate, derive; breed, propagate
tàrmasach *a* **-aiche** fussy, hard to please
tàrr *v* **-sainn/-adh** flee, take off; be in time for **tàrr às** flee, escape **cha do thàrr sinn an t-aiseag** we didn't make the ferry
tarrag *n* **-aig, -an** *f* nail *Also* **tar(r)aig**
tarraing *v* draw, pull, attract **t. anail** draw breath, breathe **t. dealbh** draw a picture **t. à/às** tease **t. air ais** withdraw **a bheil an tì air t.?** has the tea infused?
tarraing *n* **-ean** *f m* attraction; drawing, drag; mention **thoir t. air** mention, refer to
tarraingeach *a* **-giche** attractive
tarrainn *v See* **tarraing**
tarrang *n* **tàirn(g)e, tàirn(g)ean** *f* nail
tarsaing *adv See* **tarsainn**
tarsainn *adv* across, transversely **t. air** *prep* across, over
tarsannan *n* **-ain, -an** *m* cross-beam, transom
tart *n* **tairt** *m* extreme thirst, parchedness; drought
tartmhor *a* **-oire** *m* thirsty, parched
tasgadh *n* **-aidh** *m* deposit, reserve, hoard
tastan *n* **-ain, -an** *m* shilling *Formerly* **tasdan**
tataidh *v* **-adh** attract
tàth *v* **-adh** join together, cement, weld
tàthag *n* **-aig, -an** *f* pointed remark, dig
tathaich *v* frequent, visit
tàthan *n* **-ain, -an** *m* hyphen
tè *n f* one (*f/female*), woman **tè bheag** a whisky (*'a small one'*)
teachd *n m* coming, arrival **t.-a-steach** income, revenue **t.-an-tìr** livelihood, subsistence
teachdaire *n* **-an** *m* messenger, courier
teachdaireachd *n f* message, tidings
teacsa *n* **-ichean** *f m* text
teadaidh *n* **-ean** *m* teddy
teadhair *n* **-dhrach, -dhraichean** *f* tether
teagaisg *v* **-asg** teach, instruct; preach
teagamh *n* **-aimh, -an** *m* doubt **gun t.** without a doubt, undoubtedly, indeed
teagasg *n* **-aisg** *m* teaching, instruction, pedagogy; preaching
teaghlach *n* **-aich, -aichean** *m* family
teagmhach *a* **-aiche** doubtful, dubious
teallach *n* **-aich, -aichean** *m* hearth, fireplace, forge
teampall *n* **-aill, -aill** *m* temple
teanas *n* **-ais** *m* tennis

teanchair *n* **-ean** *m* pincers, tongs; vice
teanga *n* **teanga/-dh, -n/-nnan** *f* tongue
teann *a* **teinne** tight, tense **t. air** near to
teann *v* **-adh** move; commence, begin **t. às an rathad** get out of the way **theann iad ri seinn** they began to sing **t. a-nall** come over here
teannaich *v* **-achadh** tighten
teanntachd *n* **-an** *f* strait, difficulty, austerity
teanta *n* **-ichean** *f m* tent
tèarainte *a* safe, secure
tèarainteachd *n f* safety, security
tearb *v* **-adh** separate (*eg sheep*), part
tearc *a* **teirce** rare, scarce, few
tèarmann *n* **-ainn, -ainn** *m* protection, refuge, sanctuary **t. nàdair** nature reserve
teàrn *v* **-adh** deliver (from), save, rescue *Also* **tèarainn**
teàrr *n* **tearra(dh)** *f* tar
teàrr *v* **tearradh** tar
teas *n m* heat **t.-mheidh** *f* thermometer
teasach *n* **-aich, -aichean** *f* fever
teasadair *n* **-air, -ean** *m* heater
teasaich *v* **-achadh** heat
teasairg *v* **-inn** save, rescue, deliver (from) *Also* **teasraig**
teatha *n f* tea **copan t.** *m* cup of tea
teich *v* **-eadh** flee, escape, retreat
teicneòlach *a* **-aiche** technological
teicneòlas *n* **-ais** *m* technology **t. fiosrachaidh agus conaltraidh** information and communication technology
teicnigeach *a* **-igiche** technical
tèid *irr v* go (*See irr v* **rach** *in Grammar*)
tèile *pron* another one (*f/female*)
teileagram *n* **-aim, -an** *m* telegram
teileasgop *n* **-oip, -an** *f m* telescope
teine *n* **teintean** *m* fire **na theine** on fire **cuir t. ri** *v* set fire to **t.-aighir/t.-èibhinn** bonfire
teinn *n* **-e** *f* strait, predicament
teinntean *n* **-ein, -ein** *m* hearth, fireplace
teip *n* **-ichean** *f* tape, cassette **t.-chlàradair** *m* tape recorder
teirig *v* **-eachdainn/teireachdainn** expire, run out
teirinn *v* **teàrnadh** descend
teirm *n* **-ichean** *f* term *Also* **tearm**
teis-meadhan *n* **-ain** *m* very centre, epicentre
teist *n* **-e, -ean** *f* testimony
teisteanas *n* **-ais, -an** *m* testimony, testimonial, certificate
telebhisean *n* **-ein, -an** *m* television
teò-chridheach *a* **-dhiche** affectionate, warm-hearted
teòclaid *n* **-ean** *f* chocolate
teòma *a* skilful, expert
teòmachd *n f* skill, expertise
teòth *v* **-adh** warm, heat *Also* **teò**
teòthachd *n f* temperature
teothaich *v* **-achadh** warm, heat
teth *a* **teotha** hot
teud *n* **-a/tèid, -an** *m* string (*mus*), chord
tha *irr v* am, is, are; yes (*See verb* **to be** *in Grammar*)
thàinig *irr v* came (*See irr v* **thig** *in Grammar*)
thairis *adv* across, over **a' cur t.** overflowing **a' toirt t.** becoming exhausted
thairis (air) *prep pron* over him
thairis air *prep phr* across, over
thairte *prep pron* over her
thall *adv* over, yonder, on the other side **air a' cheann t.** in the end, ultimately **t. 's a-bhos** here and there **t. thairis** abroad
thalla *v* go!, away!, be off! **t. seo** come here (*Islay*)
thar *prep* (+ *gen*) across, over
tharad(sa) *prep pron* over you (*sg*)
tharaibh(se) *prep pron* over you (*pl & pol*)
tharainn(e) *prep pron* over us
tharam(sa) *prep pron* over me

tharta(san) *prep pron* over them
theab *def v* nearly (did) **t. mi tuiteam** I almost fell **theabadh a bhàthadh** he was almost drowned
theagamh *adv* perhaps
thèid *irr v* (will) go (*See irr v* **rach** *in Grammar*)
their *irr v* (will) say (*See irr v* **abair** *in Grammar*)
theirig *irr v* go! (*See irr v* **rach** *in Grammar*)
thig *irr v* (will) come **t. a-steach** come in **t. orra falbh** they will have to go
thoir *irr v* give, bestow, take **t. leat** take away (with you) **t. air** force, compel **t. an aire** take care **t. gu buil** effect, implement **t. seachad duais** present a prize **t. do chasan leat!** clear off! **t. a thaobh** persuade, beguile **t. am follais** reveal, make public **t. breith** judge **t. sùil (air)** look (at)
thu(sa) *pron* you (*sg*)
thubhairt *irr v* said (*See irr v* **abair** *in Grammar*)
thuca(san) *prep pron* to them
thug *irr v* gave; brought (*See irr v* **beir** *in Grammar*)
thugad(sa) *prep pron* to you (*sg*)
thugaibh(se) *prep pron* to you (*pl & pol*)
thugainn *def v* come on! let's go! *pl* **thugnaibh, thugainnibh**
thugainn(e) *prep pron* to us
thugam(sa) *prep pron* to me
thuice(se) *prep pron* to her
thuige(san) *prep pron* to him **thuige seo** to date, until now
thuirt *irr v* said (*See irr v* **abair** *in Grammar*)
tì *n f* tea **cupa tì** a cup of tea
tiamhaidh *a* **-e** plaintive, poignant, melancholy
ticead *n See* **tiogaid**
tìde *n* **-ean** *f* time **fad na t.** all the time **ri t./tro thìde** through time, eventually **uair a thìde** an hour **tha a thìd' agad sgur** it's time you stopped
tìde-mhara *n* **-mara, tìdean-mara** *f* tide
tidsear *n* **-eir, -an** *m* teacher
tig *irr v* come (*See irr v* **thig** *in Grammar*)
tìgear *n* **-eir, -an** *m* tiger
tigh *n See* **taigh**
tighead *n* **-eid** *m* thickness
tighearna *n* **-n** *m* lord **an T.** the Lord (*God*)
tighearnas *n* **-ais** *m* lordship **T. nan Eilean** the Lordship of the Isles
tighinn *irr v* coming (*See irr v* **thig** *in Grammar*) **Dihaoine seo t.** this coming Friday
tilg *v* **-eil/-eadh** throw, cast **thilg iad air ...** they accused him ...
till *v* **-eadh** return
tìm *n* **-e, -ean** *f* time
timcheall *adv* around
timcheall *prep* (+ *gen*) round, around, about **t. an taighe** around the house **t. air** around, about
timcheallan *n* **-ain, -ain** *m* roundabout
timcheall-ghearradh *n* **-aidh** *m* circumcision
tinn *a* **-e** sick, ill
tinneas *n* **-eis, -an** *m* illness, sickness, disease **an t.-busach** mumps **an t.-mara** seasickness **an t. tuiteamach** epilepsy, dropsy **t. inntinn** mental illness **t. an t-siùcair** diabetes
tiodhlac *n* **-aic, -an** *m* gift, present, donation **t. Nollaig** Christmas present
tiodhlacadh *n* **-aidh, -aidhean** *m* burial, funeral
tiodhlaic *v* **-acadh** inter, bury
tiogaid *n* **-e, -ean** *f* ticket *Also* **tigead, tigeard**
tiomnadh *n* **-aidh** *m* will, bequest, testament **an Seann T.** the Old Testament **an T. Nuadh** the New Testament
tiompan *n* **-ain, -ain/-an** *m* cymbal
tiona *n* **-ichean** *m* tin, can
tionail *v* **-al** gather, collect, assemble
tional *n* **-ail, -an** *m* collection, assembly

tionndaidh *v* **-adh** turn
tionnsgal *n* **-ail/-an** *m* industry; ingenuity, invention
tionnsgalach *a* **-aiche** industrial; inventive
tìoraidh *exclam* cheerio!
tìorail *a* **-e** cosy, sheltered, comfortable
tioram *a* **-a/tiorma** dry
tiormachadh *n* **-aidh** *m* drying **tha t. math ann** there are good drying conditions
tiormachd *n f* dryness, drought
tiormadair *n* **-ean** *m* dryer
tiormaich *v* **-achadh** dry
tiota *n* **-n/-idhean** *m* a moment, a short while
tiotal *n* **-ail, -an** *m* title
tiotan *n* **-ain, -ain** *m* a moment, a short while
tìr *n* **-e, -ean** *f* land **Tìr nan Òg** the Land of (Eternal) Youth
Tiristeach *n* **-tich, -tich** *m* someone from Tiree *a* from, or pertaining to, Tiree *Formerly* **Tirisdeach** *Also* **Tiridheach**
tìr-mòr *n m* mainland **air t.** on the mainland
titheach *a* **tithiche** fond (of) **t. air** keen (on)
tiugainn *def v* come on!, let's go! *pl* **tiugnaibh, tiugainnibh**
tiugh *a* **tighe** thick, fat, dense
tiùrr(a) *n m* seaware left by tide, mark of sea on shore; confused heap **bha t. phàipearan air a' bhòrd** there was a heap of papers on the table
tlachd *n f* pleasure
tlachdmhor *a* **-oire** pleasant, pleasing
tlàth *a* **tlàithe** mild, mellow, soft
toban *n* **-ain, -an** *m* tuft (*of hair, wool etc*)
tobar *n* **-air/tobrach, tobraichean** *f m* well, source (*gen sg* **tobrach** *is f*)
tobhaig *v* **-eadh** tow *Also* **tobh**
tobhta *n* **-ichean** *f* roofless walls, ruin; thwart (*in boat*)
todha *n* **-ichean** *m* hoe *Also* **tobha**
todhaig *v* **-eadh** hoe
todhar *n* **-air** *m* fertilizer, manure, dung **cuir t. air** *v* fertilize, manure
tofaidh *n* **-ean** *m* toffee
tog *v* **-ail** lift, raise, build, construct **thog iad taigh ùr** they built a new house **thogadh i ann an Lios Mòr** she was brought up in Lismore **thog iad orra** they set off **tog às an rathad!** get out of the way! **thog e a' Ghàidhlig ann am Barraigh** he acquired Gaelic in Barra **thog mi ceàrr e** I misunderstood him/it
togair *v* **togradh/-t** wish, desire **a' dèanamh mar a thogras e** doing as he pleases
togalach *n* **-aich, -aichean** *m* building
togarrach *a* **-aiche** keen, willing, enthusiastic
togsaid *n* **-ean** *f* cask, drum *Also* **tocasaid**
toibheum *n* **-eim, -an** *m* blasphemy
toidh *n* **-ean** *m* toy
toigh *a* agreeable, pleasing **is t. leam ...** I like ...
toil *n* **-e, -ean** *f* will, wish **mas e do thoil e** please, if it is your will
toileach *a* **-liche** willing, voluntary
toileachadh *n* **-aidh** *m* pleasure, satisfaction
toileachas *n* **-ais** *m* pleasure, contentment **t.-inntinn** pleasure, contentment
toilich *v* **-leachadh** please
toilichte *a* pleased, happy, glad
toil-inntinn *n* **-(e), -ean** *f* pleasure, contentment, satisfaction
toill *v* **-sinn/-tinn** deserve, merit; be contained in **cha toill e sa bhaga** it's too big for the bag
toillteanas *n* **-ais, -an** *m* deserts, merit
tòimhseachan *n* **-ain, -ain** *m* riddle, puzzle **t.-tarsainn** crossword puzzle
toimhsean *n pl* scales, balances, measures
toinisg *n* **-e** *f* sense, common sense, wit

toinisgeil *a* **-e** sensible
toinn *v* **-eadh/-eamh** twist, twine
toinneamh *n* **-eimh** *m* twist, twisting
toinnte *a* twisted, complex
tòir *n* **-e/tòrach, -ean/-ichean** *f* pursuit **an t. air** (+ *gen*) in pursuit of
toir *irr v* give (*See irr v* **thoir** *in Grammar*)
toirm *n* **-e, -ean** *f* loud murmuring sound, hubbub; hum
toirmeasg *n* **-misg** *m* prohibition, ban; harum-scarum **'s e t. cianail a th' ann** he's a terrible harum-scarum
toirmisg *v* **-measg** forbid, prohibit, ban, proscribe
toirmisgte *a* forbidden, prohibited, banned, proscribed
toirsgeir *n* **-ean** *f* peat iron, peatcutter *Also* **troidhsgeir**
toirt *irr v* giving, bestowing, taking (*See irr v* **thoir** *in Grammar*)
toiseach *n* **-sich, -sichean** *m* beginning, start, front **an t.** at first **air thoiseach** in front **t. tòiseachaidh** at the very beginning
tòiseachadh *n* **-aidh** *m* beginning, starting, start
tòisich *v* **-seachadh** begin, start, commence, initiate **t. air** begin to
toit *n* **-e, -ean** *f* smoke, vapour
toitean *n* **-ein, -ein/-an** *m* cigarette
toll *n* **tuill, tuill** *m* hole, perforation, cavity
toll *v* **-adh** hole, bore, pierce, perforate
tom *n* **tuim, -annan** *m* round hillock/knoll
tomadach *a* **-aiche** bulky, large
tomàto *n* **-than** *m* tomato
tombaca *n* *m* tobacco
tomhais *v* **-as/-ais** measure; guess
tomhas *n* **-ais, -an/toimhsean** *m* measure, measurement, gauge **t.-teas** thermometer
tòn *n* **tòine, -an/tòinean** *f* buttocks, bottom
tonn *n* **tuinn/tuinne, tuinn/-an** *f m* wave (*in sea*)
topag *n* **-aig, -an** *f* skylark
toradh *n* **-aidh, -aidhean** *m* produce, fruit(s); result, outcome, consequence **a thoradh sin** because of that
torc *n* **tuirce, tuirc** *m* boar
torman *n* **-ain, -an** *m* murmur, hum, rumbling
tòrr *n* **torra, torran** *m* mound, heap, conical hill; large quantity or number
torrach *a* **-aiche** fertile, fruitful; pregnant
tòrradh *n* **-aidh, -aidhean** *m* burial, funeral
tosgaire *n* **-an** *m* ambassador, envoy
tosgaireachd *n f* embassy
tost *n* **-a** *m* toast (*bread*)
tost *n m* silence **bha i na t.** she was silent *Formerly* **tosd**
tostair *n* **-ean** *m* toaster
tràchdas *n* **-ais, -ais** *m* thesis, treatise
tractar *n* **-air, -an** *m* tractor
trafaig *n* **-e** *f* traffic
traidhsagal *n* **-ail, -an** *m* tricycle
traidiseanta *a* traditional
tràigh *n* **-e/tràghad, -ean/tràghannan** *f* beach, strand **bha t. mhòr ann an-dè** there was a very low tide yesterday
tràigh *v* **tràghadh** ebb
tràill *n* **-ean** *f m* slave; addict; scoundrel **'s e t. a th' ann** he's a rotter/nasty piece of work
tràillealachd *n f* slavery, servitude, servility
tràilleil *a* slavish, servile
traisg *v* **trasgadh** fast
tràlair *n* **-ean** *m* trawler
tramasgal *n* **-ail** *m* trash; (*met*) confused mess
trang *a* **trainge** busy
trannsa *n* **-ichean** *f* corridor, passage, lobby, aisle
traogh *v* **-adh** subside, abate; drain
traon *n* **traoin, traoin** *m* corncrake
trasg *n* **traisg, -an** *f* fast **latha traisg** *m* fast day

trasgadh *n* **-aidh** *m* fasting
trasta *a* diagonal
trastan *n* **-ain, -ain** *m* cross-beam, diagonal
tràth *a, adv* **tràithe** early
tràth *n* **-a/tràith, -an** *m* time, season; tense **mu thràth** already **an t. caithte** the past tense **an t. làthaireach** the present tense **an t. teachdail** the future tense
tre *prep* through
treabh *v* **-adh** plough
treabhaiche *n* **-an** *m* ploughman
treal(l)aich *n* **-ean** *f* trash; lumber, bits and pieces **bha t. aig a' choinneimh** there were quite a few at the meeting
trèan(a) *n* **-(a)ichean** *f* train
trèanadh *n* **-aidh** *m* training
trèanaig *v* **-eadh** train
treas *a* third
treibhdhireach *a* **-riche** sincere, upright, honest
treibhdhireas *n* **-eis** *m* sincerity, uprightness, honesty
trèiceil *n m* treacle
treidhe *n* **-achan** *f* tray
trèig *v* **-sinn** forsake, quit, desert
trèilear *n* **-eir, -an** *m* trailer
treis *n* **-ean** *f* a while
treiseag *n* **-an** *f* a short while
treòrachadh *n* **-aidh** *m* guidance, direction, leading
treòraich *v* **-achadh** guide, direct, lead
treubh *n* **-a/trèibh, -an** *f* tribe
treud *n* **-a/trèid, -an** *m* flock, herd
treun *a* **treasa/treise** strong, brave, valiant
trì *n, a* three
triall *v* go, journey, depart
trian *n m* third (*part*)
Trianaid *n f* Trinity
triantan *n* **-ain, -ain/-an** *m* triangle
triath *n* **-a, -an** *m* lord, chief
trì-bhileach *n* **-lich** *m* trefoil
tric *a, adv* **-e** often, frequent
trì-cheàrnach *a* triangular
trì-cheàrnag *n* **-aig, -an** *f* triangle
trìd *prep* (+ *gen*) through, by
trì-deug *n, a* thirteen **trì coin dheug** thirteen dogs
trì-dhualach *a* three-ply
trìd-shoilleir *a* **-e** transparent
trì fichead *n, a* sixty
trì-fillte *a* threefold, triple, treble
trìlleachan *n* **-ain, -ain** *m* oyster-catcher
trioblaid *n* **-e, -ean** *f* trouble, tribulation
trì-rothach *a* three-wheeled
trithead *n* **-eid, -an** *m* thirty
trìtheamh *a* third
triubhas *n* **-ais, -an** *m* trews, trousers
triùir *n f m* three (people) **t. ghillean** three boys
triuthach *n* **-aich** *f* **an t.** whooping cough
tro *prep* through
trobhad *def v* come, come on, come here
tròcair *n* **-e, -ean** *f* mercy
tròcaireach *a* **-riche** merciful
trod *n* **troid, troid/-an** *f m* quarrel; reproof
trod *aug prep* through your (*sg*)
troich *n* **-e, -ean** *f m* dwarf
troid *v* **trod** quarrel; scold
troigh *n* **-e, -ean** *f* foot (*on body & in length*)
troimh *prep See* **tro**
troimh-a-chèile *adv* mixed-up, confused
troimhe(san) *prep pron* through him/it
troimhpe(se) *prep pron* through her/it
trom *a* **truime** heavy, onerous; pregnant
trom *aug prep* through my; through their
tromalach *n* **-aich** *f* preponderance, majority
tromb *n* **-a, -an** *f* jew's harp
trombaid *n* **-e, -ean** *f* trumpet
tromhad(sa) *prep pron* through you (*sg*)
tromhaibh(se) *prep pron* through you (*pl & pol*)
tromhainn(e) *prep pron* through us
tromham(sa) *prep pron* through me
tromhpa(san) *prep pron* through them

trom-inntinneach *a* **-niche** depressed, melancholy
trom-laighe *n* **-an** *f m* nightmare
trom-neul *n* **-neoil, -neoil/-an** *m* coma
tron *aug prep* through the; through their
tror *aug prep* through our; through your
trosg *n* **truisg, truisg** *m* large cod
trotan *n* **-ain** *m* trot, trotting **dèan t.** *v* trot
truacanta *a* compassionate, merciful, pitying
truacantas *n* **-ais** *m* pity, compassion
truagh *a* **-aighe** miserable, wretched, pitiful, poor (*unfortunate*)
truaghag *n* **-aig, -an** *f* wretch (*female*), poor soul **A thruaghag bhochd!** You poor soul!
truaghan *n* **-ain, -ain/-an** *m* wretch (*male*), poor soul
truaighe *n* **-an** *f* misery, woe **mo thruaighe!** Oh dear!, Alas!
truaill *n* **-e, -ean** *f* scabbard
truaill *v* **-eadh** pollute, contaminate, defile; corrupt
truailleadh *n* **-lidh** *m* pollution, contamination; corruption
truaillte *a* polluted, contaminated, defiled; corrupt
truas *n* **truais** *m* pity, compassion, sympathy **gabh t. ri** *v* pity **tha t. agam rithe** I am sorry for her
truasail *a* **-e** compassionate, sympathetic
truileis *n f* trash, junk
truinnsear *n* **-eir, -an** *m* plate
trus *v* **-adh** gather, collect
trusgan *n* **-ain, -an** *m* garb, clothes, clothing, apparel, garment
trustar *n* **-air, -airean** *m* rotter, scoundrel
tu(sa) *pron* you
tuagh *n* **tuaigh(e), -an** *f* axe
tuaileas *n* **-eis, -an** *m* scandal, slander
tuaileasach *a* **-aiche** defamatory, slanderous, scurrilous
tuaineal *n* **-eil** *m* dizziness, giddiness
tuainealach *a* **-aiche** dizzy, giddy
tuainealaich *n* **-e** *f* dizziness, giddiness
tuaiream *n* **-eim, -an** *f* guess, conjecture **air thuaiream** at random **mu thuaiream** about
tuairisgeul *n* **-eil, -an** *m* description, report
tuairisgeulach *a* **-aiche** descriptive
tuairmeas *n* **-eis, -an** *m* guess, conjecture
tuairmse *n* **-an** *f* guess, estimate, conjecture **dèan t.** *v* guess
tuam *n* **tuaim, -an** *m* tomb
tuar *n* **tuair, -an** *m* hue, complexion
tuarastal *n* **-ail, -ail/-an** *f* wages, salary, earnings *Formerly* **tuarasdal**
tuasaid *n* **-e, -ean** *f* quarrel, squabble, fight
tuath *n* **-a** *f* tenantry, country people **air an t.** in the countryside
tuath *n*, *a* north, northern **t. air ...** north of ... **mu thuath** in the north, northwards **an ceann a tuath** the north end
tuathal *a* **-aile** anti-clockwise; confused
tuathanach *n* **-aich, -aich** *m* farmer
tuathanachas *n* **-ais** *m* agriculture, farming
tuathanas *n* **-ais, -an** *m* farm
tuba *n* **-nnan** *f m* tub
tubaist *n* **-e, -ean** *f* accident, mishap
tubhailte *n* **-an** *f* towel; tablecloth **t.-shoithichean** dish towel **t.-bùird** tablecloth
tùchadh *n* **-aidh** *m* hoarseness **tha an t. air** he is hoarse
tùchan *n* **-ain** *m* hoarseness; cooing
tùchanach *a* **-aiche** hoarse
tud *interj* tut!
tug *irr v* gave, brought (*See irr v* **thoir** *in Grammar*)
tugainn *def v* come, come on *pl* **tiugainnibh**
tugh *v* **-adh** thatch

tughadair *n* **-ean** *m* thatcher
tughadh *n* **-aidh** *m* thatch, thatching
tuig *v* **-sinn** understand, comprehend
tuigse *n f* understanding, insight
tuigseach *a* **-siche** understanding, perceptive
tuil *n* **-e, -ean/-tean** *f* flood, deluge, downpour
tuilleadh *adv* more, any more; again **a thuilleadh air** in addition to, as well as
tuilleadh *n m* more, additional quantity/number **t. 's a' chòir** too much
tuireadh *n* **-ridh, -ridhean** *m* lament, mourning
tui(r)neap *n* **-an** *m* turnip
tuirt *irr v* said (*See irr v* **abair** *in Grammar*)
tùis *n* **-e, -ean** *f* incense
tuiseal *n* **-eil, -an** *m* case (*gram*) **an t. ainmneach** the nominative case **an t. ginideach** the genitive case **an t. tabhartach** the dative case
tuisleadh *n* **-lidh, -lidhean** *m* stumbling, stumble, fall; (*met*) mistake, lapse
tuislich *v* **-leachadh** stumble, fall; (*met*) make a mistake, lapse
tuit *v* **-eam** fall
tuiteamach *a* **-aiche** fortuitous, contingent; epileptic
tuiteamas *n* **-ais, -an** *m* chance
tulach *n* **-aich, -aichean** *m* hillock, knoll
tulg *v* **-adh** rock (to and fro)
tulgach *a* **-aiche** rocking
tum *v* **-adh** dip, immerse, plunge
tunail *n* **-ean** *f m* tunnel
tunna *n* **-chan** *m* ton
tunnag *n* **-aig, -an** *f* duck
tùr *n* **tùir, tùir** *m* sense **duine gun t.** *a* reckless man
tùr *n* **tùir, tùir** *m* tower
tur *a* complete, whole, absolute **gu t.** entirely, completely, absolutely
turadh *n* **-aidh** *m* dry weather, dry spell **tha t. ann** it's dry **tha i air t. a dhèanamh** the rain has stopped
turaid *n* **-e, -ean** *f* turret
tùrail *a* **-e** sensible
turas *n* **-ais, tursan/-an** *m* journey, trip; time, occasion **t. malairt** trade mission **aon t.** once **t. eile** another time
turasachd *n f* tourism
Turcach *n* **-aich, -aich** *m* Turk *a* Turkish
tursa *n* **-chan** *m* standing stone **Tursachan Chalanais** the Callanish Stones
tùrsach *a* **-aiche** sad, sorrowful
tùs *n* **tùis** *m* start, beginning, origin **(bh)o thùs** from the beginning, originally
tùsaire *n* **-an** *m* pioneer, innovator
tùsanach *n* **-aich** *m* aborigine
tuthag *n* **-aig, -an** *f* patch

U

uabhar *n* **-air** *m* pride, haughtiness
uabhas *n* **-ais** *m* a lot; terror, dread, horror **bha an t-uabhas dhaoine ann** there were an awful lot of people there
uabhasach *a* **-aiche** terrible, dreadful *adv* very, terribly **u. math** very/terribly good
uachdaran *n* **-ain, -ain** *m* landlord, laird; governor, superior
uachdranachd *n f* landlordism; sovereignty, superiority, presidency
uachdranas *n* **-ais** *m* sovereignty, jurisdiction
uaibh(se) *prep pron* from you (*pl & pol*)
uaibhreach *a* **-riche** proud, haughty
uaibhreas *n* **-eis** *m* pride, haughtiness
uaigh *n* **-e/uaghach, -ean** *f* grave, tomb
uaigneach *a* **-niche** lonely, solitary, remote, secret
uaigneas *n* **-eis** *m* loneliness, solitude, secrecy, privacy
uaill *n* **-e** *f* pride, vanity; dignity

uaim *n* **-e** *f* alliteration
uaimh *n* **-e/uamha, -ean/uamhan** *f* cave
uaine *a* green
uainn(e) *prep pron* from us
uaipe(se) *prep pron* from her
uair *n* **uarach, -ean** *f* hour, time **u. an uaireadair** an hour **tha e u.** it is one o'clock **u. is u.** time and time again, repeatedly **u. dhan robh saoghal** once upon a time
uaireadair *n* **-ean** *m* watch **u.-grèine** sundial
uaireannan *adv* sometimes, at times
uaireigin *adv* sometime
uaisle *n f* nobility (*of nature*)
uaithe(san) *prep pron* from him
uallach *n* **-aich, -aichean** *m* concern, worry, burden; responsibility (*duty*) **na gabh u.** don't be concerned
uàlras *n* **-ais, -asan** *m* walrus
uam(sa) *prep pron* from me
uamh *n See* **uaimh**
uamhann *n* **-ainn** *m* dread, terror, horror
uamhas *n See* **uabhas**
uamhasach *a See* **uabhasach**
uan *n* **uain, uain** *m* lamb
uanfheòil *n* **-òla** *f* lamb (*meat*)
uapa(san) *prep pron* from them
uasal *a* **uaisle** noble
uasal *n* **-ail, uaislean** *m* nobleman, gentleman **na h-uaislean** the nobility, aristocracy
uat(sa) *prep pron* from you (*sg*)
ubhal *n* **-ail, ùbhlan** *f m* apple
ubhalghort *n* **-oirt, -an** *m* orchard
ucas *n* **ucais, ucais** *m* coalfish
uchd *n* **-a, -an** *m* chest, breast, bosom; brow of ... **ri u. bàis** at the point of death **u.-leanabh** *m* adopted child
uchd-mhacachd *n f* adoption
uchd-mhacaich *v* **-achadh** adopt
ud *dem a* that, yon, yonder
ud *exclam* away!, get away! (*dismissive*)
udalan *n* **-ain** *m* swivel **air u.** moving to and fro
ùdlaidh *a* **-e** gloomy
uèir *n* **-ichean** *f* wire **u.-bhiorach** barbed wire
ugan *n* **-ain, -nan** *m* upper breast
ugh *m* **uighe, uighean** *m* egg
ughach *m* **-aiche** oval
ughagan *n* **-ain** *m* custard
ùghdar *n* **-air, -an** *m* author
ùghdarras *n* **-ais, -an/-ais** *m* authority, mandate **u. ionadail** local authority
ùghdarrasail *a* **-e** authoritative
Uibhisteach *n* **-tich, -tich** *m* someone from Uist *a* from, or pertaining to, Uist
ùidh *n* **-e, -ean** *f* interest, desire
uidh *n* **-e** *f* degree, gradation **u. air n-u.** bit by bit, gradually
uidheam *n* **-eim, -an** *f* machine, utensil; gear, apparatus, equipment
uidheamachd *n* **-an** *f* equipment, apparatus
uidheamaich *v* **-achadh** equip; get ready
uidheamaichte *a* equipped, geared up
ùidheil *a* **-e** interesting, interested
uile *a* every, each, all **u.-gu-lèir** *adv* all, altogether, completely **a h-uile duine** everyone **na h-eòin uile** all the birds
uilebheist *n* **-ean** *f m* monster
uile-chumhachdach *a* **-aiche** all-powerful, almighty, omnipotent
uilinn *n* **uilinn/uilne, uilnean** *f* elbow *Also* **uileann**
uill *interj* well, indeed
uime(san) *prep pron* about him
uime sin *adv* therefore, thereupon
uimhir *n f* number, quantity; certain amount, measure
uimpe(se) *prep pron* about her
ùine *n* **ùinichean/-achan** *f* time (*span of*), period **anns an u. fhada** in the long term
uinneag *n* **-eige, -an** *f* window
uinnean *n* **-ein, -an** *m* onion
uinnseann *n* **-sinn, -an** *m* ash tree
ùir *n* **-e/ùrach** *f* soil, earth
uircean *n* **-ein, -an** *m* piglet
uiread *n f* a certain amount, measure, so much, as much

uireasbhach *a* **-aiche** suffering discomfort, sore; defective, inadequate
uireasbhaidh *n* **-ean** *f* deficiency, want, need, lack, inadequacy
uirsgeul *n* **-eil, -an** *f m* fable, legend; novel
uirsgeulach *a* **-aiche** fabulous, legendary
uiseag *n* **-eig, -an** *f* lark, skylark
uisge *n* **-achan/-gichean** *m* water; rain **a bheil an t-u. ann?** is it raining?
uisge-beatha *n m* whisky
uisgich *v* **-geachadh** water, irrigate
ulaidh *n* **-e, -ean** *f* treasure **m' u.** my dear, my precious one
ulbhag *n* **-aig, -an** *f* boulder
ulfhart *n* **-airt** *m* howl (*as dog*)
ullachadh *n* **-aidh** *m* preparation
ullaich *v* **-achadh** prepare
ullamh *a* ready, prepared; finished
ultach *n* **-aich, -aichean** *m* armful, lapful, load
umad(sa) *prep pron* about you (*sg*)
umaibh(se) *prep pron* about you (*pl & pol*)
ùmaidh *n* **-e, -ean** *f* blockhead, dolt, boor
umainn(e) *prep pron* about us
umam(sa) *prep pron* about me
umha *n m* brass; bronze **Linn an U.** the Bronze Age
umhail *a* **-e** obedient; humble
ùmhlachd *n f* obedience; humility; obeisance, homage **dèan u.** *v* pay homage
ùmhlaich *v* **-achadh** (*intrans*) obey, submit; (*trans*) humble, subdue
umpa(san) *prep pron* about them
uncail *n* **-ean** *m* uncle
ung *v* **-achadh/-adh** anoint
ungadh *n* **-aidh** *f* anointing, unction, ointment
Ungaireach *n* **-rich** *m* Hungarian *a* Hungarian
unnsa *n* **-chan/-idhean** *m* ounce
ùpag *n* **-aig, -an** *f* push, elbowing
ùpraid *n* **-e, -ean** *f* uproar, confusion, bustle
ùr *a* **ùire** new, fresh **a bheil càil às ùr?** anything fresh? **tòisich às ùr** *v* start again **talc-ùr** brand new
ur *poss pron* your (*pl & pol*)
ùrachadh *n* **-aidh** *m* renewal, refreshment; modernization
ùraich *v* **ùrachadh** renew, refresh; modernize
urchair *n* **-e/urchrach, -ean** *f* bullet, shot, report of gun
urchasg *n* **-aisg, -an** *m* antibiotic, antidote
ùr-fhàs *n* **-ais** *m* bloom, fresh growth
ùr-fhàs *v* **ùr-fhàs** grow afresh
ùr-ghnàthach *a* **-aiche** innovative
ùr-ghnàthaich *v* **-achadh** innovate
ùrlar *n* **-air, -an** *m* floor
ùrnaigh *n* **-ean** *m* prayer **Ù. an Tighearna** the Lord's Prayer **dèan ù.** *v* pray *Also vn* **ag ù.**
urra *n* **-cha(n)** *f* person **not an u.** a pound each **tha sin an u. riut fhèin** that is up to you **na h-urracha mòra** those and such as those, the high heid yins **gun u.** anonymous
urrainn *n* ability **is u. dhomh** I can
urram *n* **-aim** *m* honour, respect, reverence **cuir u. air** *v* honour
urramach *a* **-aiche** honourable, revered, venerable **an t-Urr** the Rev
urras *n* **-ais, -an** *m* surety, security, bond; trust **cha rachainn an u.** *v* I wouldn't bet against it, I bet
urrasair *n* **-ean** *m* trustee; sponsor
ursainn *n* **-ean** *f* doorpost, jamb
ùruisg *n* **-e, -ean** *m* water spirit; diviner
usgar *n* **-air/-grach, -an/ usgraichean** *m* bracelet, necklace, ornament, jewel
uspag *n* **-aig, -an** *f* light gust
ùth *n* **-a, -an/-annan** *m* udder
ùtraid *n* **-e, -ean** *f* access road, track

English–Gaelic dictionary

A

abandon *v* trèig, fàg
abate *v* lùghdaich, sìolaidh, lasaich
abbey *n* abaid *f*
abbot *n* aba *m*
abbreviation *n* giorrachadh *m*
abdicate *v* leig dheth/dhith *etc*, dìobair
abdomen *n* brù *f*, balg *m*
abduct *v* goid air falbh
abhor *v* **she abhors it** is lugha oirre e/tha dubh-ghràin aice air
abhorrent *a* gràineil, sgreamhail
abide *v* fuirich; (*tolerate*) fuiling
ability *n* comas *m*
abject *a* truagh, dìblidh
able *a* comasach **are you a. to ...?** an urrainn dhut ...? an tèid agad air ...?
abnormal *a* mì-nàdarra, neo-àbhaisteach, às a' chumantas, annasach
abnormality *n* mì-ghnàthas *m*, meang *f*
aboard *adv* air bòrd
abolish *v* cuir às (do)
abolition *n* cur às (do) *m*
aborigine *n* tùsanach *m*
abortion *n* casg-breith *m*
about *prep* mu, mu dheidhinn (+ *gen*), mu thimcheall (+ *gen*) mun cuairt air, timcheall air *adv* timcheall, mun cuairt **a. to** gus
above *prep* os cionn (+ *gen*) **a. all** gu seachd àraidh *adv* shuas, gu h-àrd
abrasive *a* sgrìobach; (*nature*) ceacharra, amh
abreast *adv* gualainn ri gualainn
abroad *adv* thall thairis **going a.** a' dol a-null thairis
abrupt *a* cas, aithghearr
abscess *n* neasgaid *f*
absence *n* neo-làthaireachd *f* **in the a. of** às aonais (+ *gen*)
absent *a* neo-làthaireach, nach eil an làthair
absolute *a* làn- (*precedes & len n)*, iomlan
absolutely *adv* gu tur, gu h-iomlan
absolve *v* math, saor (o)
absorb *v* sù(i)gh, deothail, gabh a-steach
abstain (from) *v* seachain; (*eg drink*) na gabh
abstemious *a* stuama
abstinence *n* stuamachd *f*, seachnadh *m*
abstract *a* eas-chruthach
absurd *a* gun toinisg/chiall
abundance *n* pailteas *m*, (*in numbers*) lìonmhorachd *f*
abundant *a* pailt, lìonmhor
abuse *n* mì-bhuileachadh *m*, ana-caitheamh *f m*; (*phys*) droch dhìol *f*, (*verbal*) càineadh *m*, droch bheul *m*
v mì-bhuilich; (*phys*) dèan droch dhìol air; (*verbally*) càin, thoir droch bheul do
abysmal *a* sgriosail, muladach
academic *a* sgoilearach
academy *n* acadamaidh *f*, àrd-sgoil *f*
accelerate *v* luathaich, greas
accent *n* (*voice*) blas *m*; (*stress*) buille *f*; (*speech mark*) stràc *f m*
accept *v* gabh ri
acceptable *a* iomchaidh, furasta gabhail ris
access *n* (*phys*) rathad *m*, slighe *f*; (*opportunity*) cothrom (air) *m* *v* ruig air
accessible *a* ruigsinneach, so-ruigsinn, fosgailte
accident *n* tubaist *f*, sgiorradh *m*; (*chance*) tuiteamas *m*
accidental *a* tuiteamach
accidentally *adv* gun fhiosta
accommodate *v* thoir àite-fuirich do; (*hold*) gabh
accommodation *n* àite-fuirich *m*, rùm *m*; (*abstr*) còrdadh *m*
accompany *v* rach còmhla ri, còmhdhalaich; (*mus*) thoir taic do
accompanying *a* an cois (+ *gen*) **a. the letter** an cois na litreach
accomplish *v* coilean, thoir gu buil
accomplished *a* coileanta, deas
accord *n* aonta *m*, co-chòrdadh *m* **in a. with** a rèir (+ *gen*)
accordingly *adv* mar sin, uime sin

according to *prep phr* a rèir (+ *gen*)
accordion *n* bogsa(-ciùil) *m*
account *n* iomradh *m*; (*fin*) cunntas *f m*
accountable *a* cunntachail
accountant *n* cunntasair *m*, neach-cunntais *f m*
accumulate *v* cruinnich
accurate *a* neo-mhearachdach, ceart
accusation *n* casaid *f*
accuse *v* tog casaid an aghaidh, cuir às leth, fàg air
accused *a* fo chasaid
accustomed *a* gnàthach, àbhaisteach **a. to** cleachdte ri
ace *n* an t-aon *m* *a* (*colloq*) sgoinneil
ache *n* cràdh *m*, goirteas *m*, pian *f* *v* **it aches** tha cràdh ann **my back aches** tha cràdh nam dhruim
achieve *v* coilean, thoir gu buil
achievement *n* euchd *m*
acid *n* searbhag *f* **a. rain** uisge-searbhaig *m*, uisge searbhagach *m* *a* searbh, geur
acknowledge *v* aithnich; (*admit*) aidich, gabh ri
acknowledgement *n* aithneachadh *m*; (*admission*) aideachadh *m*; (*reply*) freagairt *f*, fios-freagairt *m*
acquaint *v* cuir eòlas air, thoir eòlas do
acquainted *a* eòlach **a. with** eòlach air
acquire *v* faigh, coisinn
acre *n* acair(e) *f m*
across *adv* tarsainn, thairis, a-null *prep* tarsainn air, thairis air, thar (+ *gen*)
act *n* gnìomh *m*; (*legal*) achd *f*; (*in play*) earrann *f* *v* obraich, dèan gnìomh; (*conduct oneself*) giùlain thu fhèin *etc*; (*in a play*) cluich
action *n* gnìomh *m*; (*legal*) cùis-lagha *f* **a. plan** plana-gnìomha *m*
active *a* gnìomhach, dèanadach; (*gram*) spreigeach
activity *n* gnìomhachd *f*, obair *f*; (*pastime*) cur-seachad *m*
actor *n* cleasaiche *m*, actair *m*
actress *n* bana-chleasaiche *f*, ban-actair *f*
actual *a* dearbh, fìor (*both precede & lenite n*)
acute *a* geur; (*intense*) dian **a. accent** stràc gheur *f*
adapt *v* atharraich, ceartaich, dèan freagarrach **a. to** fàs suas ri
add *v* cuir ri, meudaich
adder *n* nathair(-nimhe) *f*
addict *n* tràill *f*
addicted *a* (**to**) fo smachd, na t(h)ràill do *etc*
addiction *n* tràilleachd *f*
addition *n* meudachadh *m*; (*sum*) cur-ris *m* **in a. to** a bharrachd/thuilleadh air
additional *a* a bharrachd, a thuilleadh
address *n* seòladh *m*; (*talk*) òraid *f* *v* cuir seòladh air; (*talk*) dèan òraid, labhair ri; (*tackle*) cuir aghaidh air
adept *a* sgileil, ealanta, teòma
adequate *a* gu leòr, iomchaidh
adhesive *n* tàthair *m* *a* leanailteach **a. tape** teip-tàthaidh *f*
adjacent (**to**) *a* faisg (air), dlùth (do/ri), ri taobh (+ *gen*)
adjective *n* buadhair *m*
adjourn *v* cuir dàil an, sgaoil, sguir de
adjust *v* ceartaich, rèitich, atharraich
administration *n* rianachd *f* **this A.** an Riaghaltas seo
administrator *n* rianadair *m*, rianaire *m*, neach-riaghlaidh *m*
admirable *a* ionmholta
admiration *n* meas *m*, sùim *f*
admire *v* saoil mòran de **I a. her** tha mi saoilsinn mòran dhith **I a. them** tha meas agam orra
admission *n* leigeil a-steach *m*; (*confession*) aideachadh *m*
admit *v* leig a-steach; (*confess*) aidich
adolescent *n* òigear *m*

adopt *v* uchd-mhacaich; (*policy*) gabh ri
adoption *n* uchd-mhacachd *f*; (*policy*) gabhail ri *m*
adore *v* bi fo throm-ghaol; (*relig*) dèan adhradh do **she adored him** bha gaol a cridhe aice air
adult *n*, *a* inbheach *m*
adultery *n* adhaltranas *m* **commit a.** dèan adhaltranas
advance *n* dol air adhart *m*, ceum air thoiseach *m*; (*of money*) eàrlas *m* *v* rach air adhart; (*rank*) àrdaich; (*money*) thoir eàrlas
advanced *a* adhartach
advantage *n* buannachd *f* **she took a. of me** ghabh i brath orm
advantageous *a* buannachdail
adventure *n* dàn'-thuras *m*
adventurous *a* dàna
adverb *n* co-ghnìomhair *m*
adverse *a* mì-fhàbharach, calltach
adversity *n* cruaidh-chàs *m*, teinn *f*
advertise *v* cuir sanas, sanasaich
advertisement *n* sanas *m*, sanas-reic *m*
advice *n* comhairle *f*
advise *v* comhairlich, earalaich **be advised** gabh comhairle
adviser *n* comhairleach *m*, neach-comhairleachaidh *m*
advocate *n* neach-tagraidh *m* *v* mol
aesthetic *a* tarraingeach, maiseach
affable *a* aoigheil, ceanalta
affair *n* gnothach *m*, cùis *f* **he had an a.** bha e a' falbh le tèile
affect *v* thoir buaidh air, drùidh air; (*pretend*) leig air/oirre *etc*
affection *n* gaol *m*, spèis *f*
affectionate *a* gaolach, teò-chridheach
affirm *v* dearbh, daingnich
affliction *n* doilgheas *m*, àmhghar *f m*
affluent *a* beairteach, saidhbhir
afford *v* ruig air; (*provide*) builich **I can't a. the time** chan urrainn dhomh ùine a chosg air
afloat *adv* air bhog, air flod
afraid *a* fo eagal, eagalach
African *n, a* Afraganach *m*, (*female*) ban-Afraganach *f*
after *prep* (+ *gen*) an dèidh, às dèidh *adv* an dèidh làimhe **a. all** an dèidh a h-uile rud/càil
afternoon *n* feasgar *m* **in the a.** feasgar
afterwards *adv* an dèidh sin
again *adv* a-rithist
against *prep* an aghaidh (+ *gen*)
age *n* aois *f*; (*period*) linn *f m* **it took ages** thug e ùine chianail *v* fàs sean/aosta
aged *a* sean, aosta
agency *n* (*body*) buidheann *f m*
agenda *n* clàr-gnothaich *m*
agent *n* àidseant *m*, neach-ionaid *m*; (*means*) dòigh *f*
aggravate *v* dèan nas miosa
aggregate *n* iomlan *m* *v* cuir còmhla
aggression *n* ionnsaigh *f m*
aggressive *a* ionnsaigheach
agile *a* sùbailte, subailte
agitate *v* cuir troimh-a-chèile, luasganaich; (*polit*) piobraich
ago *adv* o chionn; ... air ais **five years ago** o chionn c(h)òig bliadhna **long ago** o chionn f(h)ada **a short time ago** o chionn ghoirid
agony *n* dòrainn *f*
agree *v* aontaich, còrd, rach le
agreeable *a* taitneach, ciatach
agreement *n* aonta *m*, còrdadh *m*, cùmhnant *m*
agriculture *n* àiteachas *m*
aground *adv* air tìr
ahead *adv* air adhart **a. of** *prep phr* air thoiseach air
aid *n* cobhair *f*, cuideachadh *m*, còmhnadh *m* *v* cuidich, dèan cobhair air **First Aid** Ciad Fhuasgladh *m*
aim *n* cuimse *f*; (*intention*) amas *m*, rùn *m* *v* cuimsich (+ air); (*intend*) amais
air *n* àile *m*, èadhar *f*; (*breath of*) deò *f*; (*mus*) fonn *m* *v* leig an t-àile gu; (*opinion*) cuir an cèill
airline *n* companaidh phlèanaichean *f m*

airmail *n* post-adhair *m*
airport *n* port-adhair *m*
aisle *n* trannsa *f*
ajar *adv* leth-fhosgailte
alarm *n* rabhadh *m* **a. clock** cloc-rabhaidh *m*
alarming *a* eagalach, draghail
alas *exclam* Och!, Mo chreach!, Mo thruaighe!
alcohol *n* alcol *m*, deoch-làidir *f*
alcoholic *n* alcolach *m* *a* alcolach
ale *n* leann *m*
alert *a* furachail, forail, deas *v* **(to)** cuir na f(h)aireachadh (mu)
alien *n* coigreach *m*, neach-fuadain *m* *a* coimheach
alienate *v* gràinnich
alight *a* na t(h)eine
alike *adv* co-ionann, coltach ri chèile
alive *a* beò
all *a* uile, iomlan, gu h-iomlan, gu lèir
allegation *n* cur às leth *m* **a serious a.** casaid chudromach *f*
allege *v* cuir às leth, fàg air
alleviate *v* aotromaich, lùghdaich
alliance *n* caidreachas *m*, co-chòrdadh *m*
allocate *v* suidhich, sònraich; (*distribute*) riaraich
allow *v* leig le, ceadaich
allowance *n* cuibhreann *f m*
allude (to) *v* thoir tarraing/iomradh (air)
ally *n* caraid *m*, caidreabhach *m*; (*mil*) co-chòmhragaiche *m*
almost *adv* gu bhith, an ìre mhath, gu ìre bhig, cha mhòr nach, theab **it is a. finished** tha e gu bhith ullamh, tha e an ìre mhath ullamh, cha mhòr nach eil e ullamh **I a. fell** cha mhòr nach do thuit mi, theab mi tuiteam
alone *a* na (h-)aonar, leis/leatha fhèin *etc*
along (*with*) *adv* còmhla ri, cuide ri, maille ri, le, an cois (+ *gen*)
aloud *adv* gu h-àrd-ghuthach **read a.** leugh a-mach
alphabet *n* aibidil *f*
alphabetical *a* a rèir na h-aibideil **in a. order** an òrdugh na h-aibideil
already *adv* mar thà, mu thràth, cheana
also *adv* cuideachd, mar an ceudna
alter *v* atharraich; (*intrans*) caochail
alteration *n* atharrachadh *m*
alternate *a* mu seach
alternative *n* roghainn eile *f* *a* eile, eadar-roghnach
alternatively *adv* air an làimh eile
although *conj* ged; (*before a*) ge
altitude *n* àirde *f*
altogether *adv* gu lèir, uile-gu-lèir, gu h-iomlan, gu tur
always *adv* an còmhnaidh, daonnan
am *v* tha **am not** chan eil (*See verb* **to be** *in Grammar*)
amalgamate *v* cuir ri chèile, amalaich, measgaich; (*intrans*) rach còmhla
amateur *n* neo-dhreuchdair *m* *a* neo-dhreuchdail
amaze *v* cuir iongnadh air
amazement *n* iongantas *m*, iongnadh *m*
amazing *a* iongantach **amazingly good** iongantach fhèin math
ambassador *n* tosgaire *m*
ambiguous *a* dà-sheaghach
ambition *n* glòir-mhiann *f m*, miann-adhartais *f m* **I have an a. to ...** tha miann agam ...
ambitious *a* glòir-mhiannach, miannach air adhartas
ambulance *n* carbad-eiridinn *m*, ambaileans *f*
ambush *n* feall-fhalach *m* *v* dèan feall-fhalach
amenable *a* fosgailte (ri, do)
amend *v* atharraich, leasaich
amendment *n* atharrachadh *m*, leasachadh *m*
amenity *n* goireas *m*
American *n*, *a* Ameireaganach *m*, (*female*) ban-Ameireaganach *f*
amiable *a* càirdeil, bàidheil, ceanalta
amicable *a* càirdeil, suairce, geanail

amid(st) *prep* am measg, am meadhan (*both + gen*)
amiss *adv* gu h-olc, ceàrr
ammunition *n* connadh làmhaich *m*; (*met*) cothrom-losgaidh *m*
among(st) *prep* am measg, air feadh (*both + gen*)
amount *n* meud *m*, uimhir *f*; (*money*) sùim *f*
ample *a* pailt; (*in size etc*) mòr, tomadach
amplify *v* meudaich, leudaich air
amputate *v* geàrr dheth *etc*, sgath
amuse *v* toilich, thoir gàire air
amusing *a* èibhinn, ait
anaesthetic *n* an-fhaireachair *m*
analyze *v* mion-sgrùd, sgrùd
analysis *n* mion-sgrùdadh *m*, sgrùdadh *m*, anailis *f*
anarchy *n* ain-riaghailt *f*, ceannairc *f*
anatomy *n* (*body*) bodhaig *f*; (*science*) eòlas bodhaig *m*, corp-eòlas *m*
ancestor *n* sinnsear *m*
anchor *n* acair(e) *f m* **at a.** air (an) acair(e) *v* acraich
anchorage *n* acarsaid *f*
ancient *a* àrsaidh
and *conj* agus, is, 's
anecdote *n* naidheachd *f*, sgeula *f*
angel *n* aingeal *m*
anger *n* fearg *f*, corraich *f* *v* cuir fearg air
angle *n* uilinn *f*, ceàrn *f m*
angry *a* feargach **he was a.** bha an fhearg air
anguish *n* àmhghar *f m*, dòrainn *f*
animal *n* ainmhidh *m*, beathach *m*
animated *a* beothail, meanmnach
animosity *n* gamhlas *m*, mì-rùn *m*
ankle *n* adhbrann *f m*
annihilate *v* sgrios, cuir às do
anniversary *n* ceann-bliadhna *m*, cuimhneachan bliadhnail *m*
announce *v* ainmich, cuir an cèill, leig fhaicinn
announcement *n* teachdaireachd *f*, fios *m*
annoy *v* cuir dragh air, leamhaich
annoyance *n* dragh *m*, buaireas *m*
annoyed *a* diombach, mì-thoilichte
annoying *a* leamh, buaireanta
annual *a* bliadhnail **a. report** aithisg bhliadhnail *f* **A. General Meeting** Coinneamh Bhliadhnail *f*
annually *adv* gach bliadhna
anonymous *a* gun ainm, gun urra(inn)
another *pron* neach/tè eile *a* eile **one a.** a chèile
answer *n* freagairt *f* *v* freagair, thoir freagairt (do)
ant *n* seangan *m*
antagonize *v* dèan nàmhaid de
anthem *n* laoidh *f m* **national a.** laoidh nàiseanta/na rìoghachd
antibiotic *n* antibiotaig *f*
anticipate *v* sùilich; (*prepare for*) deasaich airson
anti-clockwise *a* tuathal
antidote *n* urchasg *m*
antipathy *n* fuath *m*
antique *n* seann rud *m* *a* àrsaidh
antler *n* cabar (fèidh) *m*
anxiety *n* dragh *m*, iomagain *f*, imcheist *f*
anxious *a* draghail, iomagaineach, fo imcheist
any *a* sam bith, air bith; (*pron*) aon/fear/tè sam bith, aon, gin **any at all** gin idir **any other business** gnothach sam bith eile
anyone *n* neach/duine sam bith *m*
anything *n* dad/sìon/rud/nì (sam bith) *m*, càil (sam bith) *f*
anywhere *adv* àite sam bith
apart *adv* air leth; (*distance, motion*) (bh)o chèile
apartment *n* (*suite*) àros *m*; (*room*) seòmar *m*
apathy *n* cion ùidh *m*
ape *n* apa *f*
apologize *v* dèan leisgeul, iarr do/a *etc* leisgeul a ghabhail
apology *n* leisgeul *m*
apostrophe *n* asgair *m*
appal *v* cuir uabhas air
appalling *a* sgriosail, cianail, eagalach
apparent *a* soilleir, follaiseach, faicsinneach

appeal *n* tarraing *f*; (*leg*) ath-agairt *m*, ath-thagradh *m* *v* tarraing; (*leg*) ath-agair **a. against** tagair an aghaidh
appear *v* nochd, thig am fianais/follais
appearance *n* (*phys*) coltas *m*, dreach *m*, aogas *m*
appendicitis *n* an grèim mionaich *m*
appetite *n* càil *f*, càil bìdh *f*; (*desire*) miann *f m*
applause *n* bualadh bhas *m*; (*met*) moladh *m*
apple *n* ubhal *f m* **a. of eye** dearc na sùla *m* **a.-tree** craobh-ubhail *f*
appliance *n* uidheam *f*, inneal *m*
applicant *n* tagraiche *m*
application *n* iarrtas *m*, tagradh *m*; (*use*) cur an sàs *m* **a. form** foirm/clàr-iarrtais *m*
apply (for) *v* cuir a-steach (airson); (*use*) cuir gu feum, cuir an gnìomh **a. to/with** (*phys*) cuir air
appoint *v* suidhich, cuir an dreuchd
appointment *n* coinneamh *f*, àm suidhichte *m*; (*to post*) cur an dreuchd *m*
apposite *a* freagarrach, iomchaidh
appraise *v* meas, dèan measadh air, thoir beachd air
appreciate *v* cuir luach air; (*understand*) tuig gu math; (*fin*) meudaich, rach suas an luach
apprehensive *a* gealtach, draghail
apprentice *n* preantas *m*, foghlamaiche-ciùird *m*
approach *n* dòigh *f*; (*entry*) slighe *f* *v* dlùthaich ri, teann ri
appropriate *a* freagarrach, iomchaidh, cubhaidh
approval *n* riarachadh *m*, toileachadh *m*; (*official*) aonta *m*, ceadachadh *m* **win a. of ...** riaraich
approve *v* gabh beachd math air; (*of plan etc*) aontaich ri, ceadaich
approximately *adv* timcheall air, mu thuairmeas, faisg air
April *n* an Giblean *m*
apron *n* aparan *m*
apt *a* deas **a. to** buailteach ri/do
aptitude *n* alt *m*, sgil *m* **an a. for ...** alt air ...
Arab *n* Arabach *m*, (*female*) ban-Arabach *f*
Arabic *a* Arabach **a. numerals** figearan Arabach *n m pl*; (*lang*) Arabais *f*
arable *a* àitich **a. land** talamh àitich *m*
arbitrary *a* neo-riaghailteach, neo-chunbhalach
arbitration *n* eadar-bhreith *f*, breith-rèite *f*
arch *n* stuagh *f*, bogha *m*
archaeologist *n* arc-eòlaiche *m*, àrsair *m*
archaeology *n* arc-eòlas *m*, àrsaidheachd *f*
architect *n* ailtire *m*
architecture *n* ailtireachd *f*
archive(s) *n* tasglann *f*
arduous *a* doirbh, cruaidh, spàirneil
are *v* tha **are not** chan eil (*See verb* **to be** *in Grammar*)
area *n* farsaingeachd *f*; (*topic*) raon *m*; (*geog*) ceàrnaidh *f*
argue *v* dèan argamaid, connsaich *Also vn* ag argamaid
argument *n* argamaid *f*, connsachadh *m*
argumentative *a* connspaideach, connsachail, aimhreiteach
arise *v* èirich
aristocracy *n* na h-uaislean *pl*
arithmetic *n* àireamhachd *f*, cunntas *m*
arm *n* gàirdean *m*
armed *a* fo armachd, armaichte
armful *n* achlasan *m*, ultach *m*
armour *n* armachd *f*
armpit *n* achlais *f*, lag na h-achlaise *f*
army *n* arm *m*, armailt *m*, feachd *f m*
aroma *n* boladh *m*
around *prep* timcheall, mu chuairt, mu thimcheall (*all + gen*) *adv* mun cuairt
arouse *v* dùisg

arrange *v* suidhich, cuir air dòigh; (*put in order*) cuir rian air
arrangement *n* òrdachadh *m*; (*met*) aonta *m*; (*mus*) rian *m*
arrest *v* cuir an grèim, cuir an sàs
arrival *n* teachd *m*, tighinn *m*, ruighinn *m* **on my a.** nuair a ràinig mi
arrive *v* ruig, thig
arrogance *n* àrdan *m*, ladarnas *m*
arrogant *a* àrdanach, ladarna
arrow *n* saighead *f*
art *n* ealain *f*; (*pictorial*) dealbhadaireachd *f* **the arts** na h-ealain(ean)
artery *n* cuisle *f*
arthritis *n* tinneas nan alt *m*
article *n* (*lit, gram*) alt *m*, artaigil *m*; (*of clothing*) ball aodaich *m*; (*leg*) bonn *m*
articulate *a* pongail, deas-bhriathrach, siùbhlach
artificial *a* brèige, fuadain
artist *n* dealbhadair *m*; (*performer*) neach-ealain *m*
artistic *a* ealanta
as *adv* cho ... ri (+ *n*), cho ... (+ *v*) is **as white as snow** cho geal ris an t-sneachda **as long as you like** cho fad' 's a thogras tu *conj* mar; (*time*) nuair
ascend *v* dìrich, streap, rach suas
ascent *n* dìreadh *m*
ascertain *v* faigh a-mach, fiosraich
ash(es) *n* luath *f*, luaithre *f*
ashamed *a* air mo/a *etc* nàrachadh, nàraichte
ashore *adv* air tìr
ashtray *n* soitheach-luaithre *f m*
Asian *n, a* Àisianach *m*, (*female*) ban-Àisianach *f*
aside *adv* gu aon taobh, an dàrna taobh, air leth
ask *v* (*request*) iarr; (*enquire*) faighnich, feòraich, farraid
asleep *adv* nam chadal, na c(h)adal *etc*
aspect *n* snuadh *m*, aogas *m*; (*of topic*) taobh *m*; (*view*) sealladh *m*
aspiration *n* miann *f m*, rùn *m*; (*ling*) analachadh *m*
aspire *v* rùnaich, miannaich
ass *n* asal *f m*
assassinate *v* murt
assault *n* ionnsaigh *f m* *v* thoir ionnsaigh air
assemble *v* cruinnich
assembly *n* co-chruinneachadh *m*, tional *m*; (*eccl*) àrd-sheanadh *m*; (*polit*) seanadh *m*
assent *n* aonta *m*, aontachadh *m*
assess *v* meas
assessment *n* meas *m*, measadh *m*
asset *n* maoin *f*
assiduous *a* dìcheallach, leanmhainneach
assign *v* cuir air leth, sònraich
assignment *n* obair shònraichte *f*, dleastanas sònraichte *m*
assist *v* cuidich, dèan cobhair air
assistance *n* cuideachadh *m*, cobhair *f*
assistant *n* neach-cuideachaidh *m*
association *n* comann *m*, caidreabh *m*
assume *v* bi dhen bheachd; (*take control*) gabh sealbh air
assurance *n* dearbhachd *f*, cinnt *f*; (*insurance*) àrachas *m* **self-a.** dànachd *f*
assure *v* dearbh, dèan cinnteach do **I a. you he'll come** thèid mi an urras dhut gun tig e
asthma *n* a' chuing *f*, an sac *m*
astonish *v* cuir iongnadh air
astonishment *n* mòr-iongnadh *m*, mòr-iongantas *m*
astray *adv* air seachran, air iomrall
astride *adv* casa-gòbhlach
astrology *n* reuladaireachd *f*
astronaut *n* speuradair *m*, speurair *m*
astronomy *n* reul-eòlas *m*
asylum *n* comraich *f*, tèarmann *m*; (*instit*) ospadal inntinn *m*
at *prep* aig **a. all** idir
atheism *n* neo-dhiadhachd *f*
atheist *n* neo-dhiadhaire *m*, ana-creidmheach *m*
athlete *n* lùth-chleasaiche *m*
athletic *a* (*person*) lùthmhor; (*game, feat*) lùth-chleasach
athletics *n* lùth-chleasachd *f*

atlas *n* atlas *m*
atmosphere *n* àile *m*; (*met*) faireachdainn *f*
atom *n* dadam *m*, smùirnean *m*, atam *m*
atomic *a* dadamach, smùirneach, atamach
atrocious *a* uabhasach, eagalach, cianail, sgriosail
atrocity *n* buirbe *f*
attach *v* ceangail, greimich air/ri
attached *a* ceangailte, an lùib (+ *gen*), an cois (+ *gen*) **very a. to ...** fìor mheasail air ...
attachment *n* dàimh *f m*, ceangal *m*; (*document*) faidhle *m*
attack *n* ionnsaigh *f m* **she had an attack of ...** bhuail ... i *v* thoir ionnsaigh (air)
attain *v* ruig, coisinn, faigh
attainable *a* ruigsinneach, so-ruighinn, a ghabhas f(h)aighinn
attempt *n* oidhirp *f* *v* dèan oidhirp, feuch ri
attend *v* fritheil **a. to** dèan, gabh os làimh
attendant *n* neach-frithealaidh *m*
attention *n* aire *f*, feairt *f* **pay a. to** thoir an aire do
attentive *a* furachail, suimeil
attic *n* seòmar-mullaich *m*
attitude *n* seasamh *m*, beachd *m*
attract *v* tarraing, tàlaidh
attraction *n* tarraing *f*, tàladh *m*
attractive *a* tarraingeach, tlachdmhor, bòidheach
auburn *a* buidhe-ruadh
auction *n* rup *f* **up for a.** ga reic
audible *a* osgarra, ri chluinntinn
audience *n* luchd-èisteachd *m*; (*a hearing*) èisteachd *f*
audit *n* sgrùdadh *m* *v* sgrùd, dèan sgrùdadh air
auditor *n* sgrùdaire *m*, neach-sgrùdaidh *m*
August *n* an Lùnastal *m*
aunt *n* piuthar-athar/màthar *f*, antaidh *f* **my a.** piuthar m' athar/mo mhàthar, m' antaidh
auspicious *a* gealltanach, fàbharach, rathail
austere *a* teann, cruaidh
Australian *n*, *a* Astràilianach *m*, (*female*) ban-Astràilianach *f*
authentic *a* fìor (+ *len*), cinnteach, dearbhte, dhà-rìribh
author *n* ùghdar *m*
authority *n* ùghdarras *m*, smachd *m*; (*warrant*) barantas *m* **the Local A.** an t-Ùghdarras Ionadail
authorize *v* thoir ùghdarras, ceadaich
autobiography *n* fèin-eachdraidh *f*
automatic *a* fèin-ghluasadach
autonomous *a* neo-eisimeileach
autumn *n* am foghar *m*
auxiliary *n* neach-cuideachaidh *m*, neach-taic(e) *m* *a* taiceil
available *a* ri fhaighinn/fhaotainn
avenge *v* dìol
average *n* cuibheas *m*, meadhan *m* *a* cuibheasach, gnàthach **on a.** anns a' chumantas
avoid *v* seachain
await *v* fuirich ri
awake *a* na d(h)ùisg *etc*
award *n* duais *f* *v* thoir duais
aware *a* mothachail, forail
awareness *n* mothachadh *m*
away *adv* air falbh
awful *a* eagalach, uabhasach, sgràthail
awkward *a* leibideach, clobhdach
axe *n* tuagh *f*, làmhagh *f*, làmhag *f*
axle *n* aiseal *f m*
aye *interj* seadh, aidh!

B

baby *n* leanabh *m*, bèibidh *m*
bachelor *n* baidsealair *m*, fleasgach *m*, seana-ghille *m*
back *n* cùl *m*, cùlaibh *m* *v* rach air ais; (*support*) seas, cuidich; (*bet on*) cuir airgead air *adv* air ais
background *n* cùl-raon *m*, bun-fhiosrachadh *m*
backside *n* tòn *f*, màs *m* *Also* tòin
backward(s) *adv* an comhair a c(h)ùil *etc*
backward *a* fad' air ais

bacon *m* muicfheòil *f*
bad *a* dona, droch (*precedes & len n*), olc **bad-tempered** *a* greannach, eangarra
badge *n* suaicheantas *m*, baidse *m*
badger *n* broc *m*
baffle *v* dubh-fhaillich air, fairtlich air **b. someone** dèan a' chùis air
bag *n* baga *m*, màileid *f*; (*sack*) poca *m*
baggage *n* bagaichean *m pl*
bagpipe *n* pìob *f* **great Highland b.** pìob-mhòr
bail *n* urras *m* **on b.** air urras *v* fuasgail air urras, thoir urras air
balllle *n* bàillidh *m*
bait *n* biathadh *m*, baoit *f*, maghar *m* *v* biadh, cuir biathadh/maghar air; (*taunt*) leamhaich, mag air
bake *v* fuin; (*in oven*) bruich san àmhainn
baker *n* bèicear *m*, fuineadair *m*
bakery *n* taigh-fuine *m*
baking *n* bèicearachd *f*, fuine *m* **b. powder** pùdar/fùdar-fuine *m*
balance *n* meidh *f*; (*abstr*) cothrom *m*, co-chothrom *m*; (*fin*) còrr *m* **b. sheet** clàr cothromachaidh *m* *v* cuir air mheidh; (*abstr*) cothromaich
balanced *a* cothromach
balcony *n* for-uinneag *f*
bald *a* maol, le sgall
ball *n* ball *m*, bàl(l)a *m*; (*wool*) ceirtle *f*; (*dance*) bàl *m*
ballast *n* balaist(e) *f m*
balloon *n* bailiùn *m*
ballot *n* baileat *m*, bhòtadh *m*
ban *n* toirmeasg *m*, casg *m*, bacadh *m* *v* toirmisg, caisg, bac
band *n* bann *m*; (*of people*) buidheann *f m*; (*mus*) còmhlan-ciùil *m*
bandage *n* bann *m*
bang *n* brag *m* *v* thoir brag air, buail
banish *v* fuadaich, fògair
bank *n* banca *m*; (*topog*) bruach *f m*, bac *m*
bank *v* cuir dhan bhanca **b. on** theirig an urras air
banker *n* bancair *m*
bankrupt *a* briste **the company went b.** bhris(t) air a' chompanaidh
banned *a* toirmisgte
banner *n* bratach *f*
banquet *n* fèist *f*, fleadh *m*, bangaid *f*
banter *n* tarraing-às *f*
baptism *n* baisteadh *m*
Baptist *n, a* Baisteach *m*
baptize *v* baist
bar *n* crann-tarsainn *m*; (*pub*) bàr *m*, taigh-seinnse *m*; (*hindrance*) bacadh *m* **b. chart** clàr-cholbh *m* **b. graph** graf-bann *m*
barbaric *a* borb
barbed *a* gathach **b. wire** uèir bhiorach/stobach *f*
barber *n* borbair *m*, bearradair *m*
bard *n* bàrd *m*, filidh *m*
bare *a* lom, rùisgte
bargain *n* bargan *f m*; (*agreement*) cùmhnant *m*
barge *n* bàirdse *f*
bark *n* rùsg *m*; (*of dog*) comhart *m*
barking *n* comhartaich *f* *Also vn* a' comhartaich
barley *n* eòrna *m*
barn *n* sabhal *m*
barnacle *n* giùran *m*, bàirneach *f*
barometer *n* glainne-sìde *f*
barrel *n* baraille *m* *Also* barailte
barren *a* neo-thorrach, seasg; (*land*) fàs
barrier *n* bacadh *m*, cnap-starra *m*
barrow *n* bara *m*
barter *n* malairt *f* *v* dèan malairt/iomlaid, malairtich
base *n* stèidh *f*, bonn *m*, bun *m*, bunait *f m*
bashful *a* nàrach, diùid
basic *a* bunaiteach, bunasach
basin *n* mias *f*
basis *n* bun *m*, bunait *f*, bun-stèidh *f*
bask *v* blian

basket *n* basgaid *f*
bass *a* beus
bat *n* slacan *m*, bat *m*; (*mammal*) ialtag *f*
batch *n* baidse *m*, grunn *m*, dòrlach *m*
bath *n* amar *m*
batter *v* liodraig, pronn
battery *n* bataraidh *f m*
battle *n* cath *m*, blàr *m*, batail *m*
bay *n* bàgh *m*, camas *m*, òb *m*
be *v* bi (*See verb* **to be** *in Grammar*)
beach *n* tràigh *f* **shingle b.** mol *m*
bead *n* grìogag *f* **beads** (*relig*) paidirean *m*
beak *n* gob *m*
beam *n* (*of wood*) sail *f*; (*of light*) gath *m*, boillsgeadh *m*; (*apparatus*) crann *m*
bean *n* pònair *f* (*normally used as coll*) **beans** pònairean
bear *n* mathan *m*
bear *v* giùlain; (*suffer*) fuiling; (*a child*) beir
beard *n* feusag *f*
beast *n* beathach *m*, ainmhidh *m*; (*pej*) biast *f*
beat *n* buille *f*
beautiful *a* brèagha, bòidheach, maiseach, riochdail
beauty *n* bòidhchead *f*, maise *f*, sgèimh *f*, àilleachd *f* **b. spot** ball-seirce *m*
because *conj* airson, a chionn, seach, ri linn **b. of** air sàillibh (+ *gen*)
become *v* fàs, cinn **b. a ...** rach na ... *etc*
bed *n* leabaidh *f* **bed and breakfast** leabaidh is bracaist **bedroom** rùm/seòmar-cadail *m*
bee *n* seillean *m*, beach *m*
beef *n* mairtfheòil *f*
beer *n* leann *m*
beetle *n* daolag *f*
beetroot *n* biotais *m*
before *prep* ro; (*in front of*) air beulaibh (+ *gen*) *adv* roimhe *conj* mus
beforehand *adv* ro-làimh
beg *v* guidh; (*for money etc*) iarr dèirc (air)
beggar *n* dèirceach *m*
begin *v* tòisich
beginner *n* neach-tòiseachaidh *m*
beginning *n* toiseach *m*, tòiseachadh *m*, tùs *m* **the very b.** toiseach tòiseachaidh
behalf *n* **on b. of** às leth (+ *gen*) **on my b.** às mo leth(-sa)
behave *v* bi modhail
behaviour *n* giùlan *m*
behind *adv* air d(h)eireadh *prep* air cùlaibh, air c(h)ùl (*both* + *gen*) **b. them** air an cùlaibh
belch *v* dèan brùchd
belief *n* (*relig*) creideamh *m*
believe *v* creid, thoir creideas do
bell *n* clag *m*
bellow *v* beuc, geum, dèan geum, bùir
belly *n* brù *f*, broinn *f*
belong *v* buin **b. to** buin do **that belongs to me** 's ann leamsa a tha sin
beloved *a* ionmhainn, gràdhach, gràdhaichte
below *adv* shìos; (*down here*) a-bhos; (*downwards*) sìos *prep* fo (+ *len*)
belt *n* crios *m*, bann *m*
bench *n* being(e) *f*
bend *n* lùb *m*, fiaradh *m* *v* lùb, aom, fiaraich; (*stoop*) crom
beneath *prep* fo (+ *len*)
beneficial *a* feumail, buannachdail
benefit *n* feum *m*, buannachd *f*, tairbhe *f*
benevolent *a* coibhneil, le deagh-ghean
benign *a* coibneil, fial; (*med*) neo-aillseach, neo-chronail
bent *a* lùbte, fiar, cam; (*stooped*) crom
bequest *n* dìleab *f*
berry *n* dearc *f*, dearcag *f*, sùbh *m*
beseech *v* guidh, dèan guidhe (ri)
beside *prep phr* ri taobh (+ *gen*), làimh ri
besides *adv* a bhàrr air, a bharrachd air, a thuilleadh air; (*anyway*) co-dhiù
best *a*, *adv* (as) fheàrr

bestow *v* builich
bet *n* geall *m* *v* cuir geall
betray *v* brath; (*feelings*) leig ris
better *a* nas fheàrr, (*past*) na b' fheàrr
between *prep* eadar *adv* eadar
beware *v* thoir an aire, bi air d' fhaiceall
beyond *prep* air taobh thall, thar (*both* + *gen*); (*time*) seachad air; (*exceeding*) os cionn (+ *gen*)
bias *n* leiteachas *m*; claon-bhàidh *f*; (*phys*) claonadh *m*
Bible *n* Bìoball *m*
bibliography *n* leabhar-chlàr *m*; (*activity*) leabhar-chlàradh *m*
bicycle *n* baidhsagal *m*, rothair *m*
bid *n* tairgse *f*, iarrtas *m* **bid for** dèan tairgse airson, cuir a-steach airson
big *a* mòr, tomadach
bigot *n* dalm-bheachdaiche *m*
bigotry *n* dalm-bheachd *m*
bile *n* domblas *m*
bilingual *a* dà-chànanach
bill *n* cunntas *f m*; (*of a bird*) gob *m*; (*leg*) bile *m*
billion *n* billean *m*
bin *n* biona *f m*
bind *v* ceangail, naisg; (*fetter*) cuibhrich
binoculars *n* prosbaig *f*, glainneachan *f pl*
biography *n* eachdraidh-beatha *f*
biology *n* bith-eòlas *m*
birch *n* beithe *f*
bird *n* eun *m*
birth *n* breith *f* **b. certificate** teisteanas-breith *m* **birthday** co-là-breith *m*, ceann-bliadhna *m*
biscuit *n* briosgaid *f*
bishop *n* easbaig *m*
bit *n* bìdeag *f*, mìr *m*, pìos *m*, criomag *f*; (*horse's*) cabstair *m*, mìreanach *m*
bitch *n* galla *f*, saigh *f*
bite *n* bìdeadh *m*, bìdeag *f*; (*of food*) grèim *m* *v* bìd, thoir grèim/bìdeag à
bitter *a* geur, searbh (*also met*)
black *a* dubh, dorch(a); (*mood*) gruamach **blackbird** lon-dubh *m* **blackboard** bòrd-dubh *m*
blacken *v* dubh, dèan dubh; (*reputation*) mill cliù
blacksmith *n* gobha *m*
bladder *n* aotroman *m*
blade *n* (*of knife*) lann *f*; (*on tool*) iarann *m*; (*of grass*) bileag *f*
blame *n* coire *f* *v* cuir coire air, coirich, faigh coire/cron do
blameless *a* neo-chiontach, gun choire
bland *a* mìn, tlàth, staoin
blank *a* bàn, falamh
blanket *n* plaide *f*, plangaid *f*
blatant *a* dalma, gun chleith
blaze *n* teine lasrach *m*, caoir *f*; (*domestic*) braidseal *m*
bleak *a* lom, aognaidh; (*met*) gun dòchas
bleat *v* dèan mèilich, dèan meigeadaich *Also vn* a' mèilich, a' meigeadaich
bleed *v* caill/sil fuil; (*drain*) leig
blemish *n* gaoid *f*, smal *m*
blend *n* coimeasgadh *m* *v* coimeasgaich
bless *v* beannaich
blessing *n* beannachd *f*, beannachadh *m*
blethering *n* bleadraich *f*, bleadaireachd *f*
blight *n* gaiseadh *m*
blind *n* sgàil(e) *f*
blind *a* dall **the b.** na doill *n m pl*
blindness *n* doille *f*
blink *v* caog, priob
bliss *n* sòlas *m*, sonas *m*, làn-aoibhneas *m*
blissful *a* sòlasach, sona, làn-aoibhneach
blister *n* builgean *m*, balg *m*, leus *m*
blizzard *n* cathadh-sneachda *m*
block *n* bloc *m*, sgonn *m*, ceap *m* *v* caisg, cuir bacadh air, dùin
blond(e) *a* bàn *n* tè bhàn *f*, fear bàn *m*
blood *n* fuil *f* **b. pressure** bruthadh-fala *m* **b. transfusion** leasachadh-fala *m* **bloodshed** dòrtadh-fala *m*
bloody *a* fuilteach **you b. idiot** amadain na mallachd/croiche *m*

bloom *n* blàth *m*, ùr-fhàs *m* *v* thig fo bhlàth
blossom *n* blàth *m*
blouse *n* blobhs(a) *f m*
blow *n* buille *f*, bualadh *m*, beum *m*; (*weather*) sèideadh *m* *v* sèid
blue *a* gorm **light blue** liath
bluff *v* meall, thoir an car à(s)
blunder *n* mearachd mhòr *f*
blunt *a* maol
blurred *a* doilleir, a-mach à fòcas
blush *n* rudhadh (gruaidhe) *m* *v* fàs dearg **she blushed** thàinig rudhadh na gruaidh
blushing *a* rudhach, ruiteach
boar *n* torc *m*
board *n* bòrd *m*, clàr *m*; (*plank*) dèile *f* *v* rach air bòrd
boast *n* bòst *m* *v* dèan bòst, bòstaich
boasting *n* bòstadh *m*
boat *n* bàta *m*; (*open*) eathar *f m* **fishing b.** bàt'-iasgaich **sailing b.** bàta-siùil
body *n* corp *m*, bodhaig *f*; (*of people*) buidheann *f m*, còmhlan *m*
bog *n* bog(l)ach *f*, fèithe *f*
boil *n* neasgaid *f*
boil *v* goil; (*food*) bruich **it's on the b.** tha e a' goil
boiled *a* bruich
boisterous *a* gailbheach; (*person*) iorghaileach
bold *a* dàna, tapaidh, dalma **b. type** (*liter*) clò trom *m*
boldness *n* dànadas *m*, dànachd *f*, tapachd *f*
bolster *v* cùm taic ri, misnich
bolt *n* bolt(a) *m*
bomb *n* bom(a) *m* *v* leag bom air, bom(aig)
bond *n* ceangal *m*, bann *m*, gealladh *m*
bone *n* cnàimh *m*
bonfire *n* tein-aighir *m*, tein-èibhinn *m*
bonnet *n* bonaid *f m*
bonny *a* bòidheach, brèagha, buaidheach
bonus *n* leasachadh (duaise) *m* **it was a real b.** 's e fìor bhuannachd a bh' ann
book *n* leabhar *m* **bookshop** bùth leabhraichean *f*
booklet *n* leabhran *m*
boot *n* bròg *f*
booth *n* bùth *f*, bothan *m*
booze *n* deoch-làidir *f* *v* òl, gabh steall
border *n* crìoch *f*; (*edge*) oir *f*, iomall *m*
bore *v* cladhaich, dèan toll; (*met*) bòraig, sàraich
boring *a* ràsanach, sàraichte
borrow *v* faigh (air) iasad
bosom *n* broilleach *m*
boss *n* ceannard *m*
botany *n* luibh-eòlas *m*
both *a* dà; (*of people*) dithis **with b. hands** leis an dà làimh **b. sons** an dithis mhac *adv* le chèile **b. great and small** eadar bheag is mhòr
bother *n* bodraigeadh *m*, dragh *m* *v* bodraig, cuir dragh air
bottle *n* botal *m*
bottom *n* ìochdar *m*, bonn *m*; (*sea*) aigeann *m*, grunnd *m*; (*of person*) màs *m*, tòn *f* **b. up** bhon bhonn suas
bounce *v* bunsaig, buns
bound *n* sìnteag *f*, cruinn-leum *m*
boundary *n* crìoch *f*
bow *n* bogha *m*; (*ship*) toiseach *m*; (*bending*) cromadh-cinn *m* *v* (*bend*) crom, lùb
bowel(s) *n* innidh *f*
bowl *n* bobhla *m*, cuach *f*
bowling *n* bòbhladh *m* **b. alley** ionad bòbhlaidh *m*
box *n* bogsa *m*, bucas *m*; (*blow*) buille *f* *v* cuir am bogsa; (*fight*) bogs(aig)
boxer *n* bogsair *m*
boxing *n* bogsadh *m*
boy *n* balach *m*, gille *m*
boycott *v* seachain, na gabh gnothach ri
boyfriend *n* carabhaidh *f m*, bràmair *m*
brace *n* uidheam-teannachaidh *m*; (*pair*) dithis *m*, càraid *f*, caigeann *f*
bracelet *n* bann-làimhe *m*
braces *n* gaileis *f*

bracken *n* raineach *f*
bracket *n* bracaid *f*; (*in writing*) camag *f*
brae *n* bruthach *f*, leathad *m*
brag *v* bòst, dèan bòst
brain *n* eanchainn *f*
brake *n* brèig *f*, casgan *m*
bramble *n* (*berry*) smeur *f*; (*bush*) dris *f*
branch *n* geug *f*, meangan *m*; (*abstr*) meur *f*
brand *n* seòrsa *m*; (*of fire*) aithinne *m* **b. new** talc-ùr, ùr nodha
brandy *n* branndaidh *f*
brass *n* pràis *f*
brat *n* isean *m*, peasan *m*
brave *a* gaisgeil, calma
bravery *n* gaisge *f*, gaisgeachd *f*, misneachd *f*
brawl *n* tuasaid *f*, còmhrag *f*
brazen *a* ladarna, gun nàire; (*metal*) pràiseach
breach *n* bris(t)eadh *m*, bealach *m*, beàrn *f m*
breach *v* dèan bris(t)eadh/beàrn
bread *n* aran *m*
breadth *n* leud *m*, farsaingeachd *f*
break *n* bris(t)eadh *m*; (*abstr*) fois *f* *v* bris(t); (*of word, promise*) rach air ais air
breakfast *n* bracaist *f*
breast *n* broilleach *m*, uchd *m* **a b.** cìoch *f*
breath *n* anail *f*, deò *f*
breathe *v* tarraing anail
breathless *a* gun anail, goirid san anail
breed *n* seòrsa *m*, gnè *f*, sìol *m* *v* gin, tàrmaich, briod(aich)
breeding *n* briodachadh *m*; (*met*) togail *f*, modh *f*
breeze *n* oiteag *f*, osag *f*, soirbheas *m*
brew *v* dèan grùdaireachd; (*tea*) tarraing
brewery *n* taigh-grùide *m*
bribe *n* brìb *f* *v* brìb
brick *n* breige *f m*
bride *n* bean-bainnse *f* **the b.** bean na bainnse
bridegroom *n* fear-bainnse *m* **the b.** fear na bainnse
bridesmaid *n* maighdeann-phòsaidh *f*, bean-chomhailteachd *f*
bridge *n* drochaid *f*
bridle *n* srian *f*
brief *v* leig brath gu, thoir fiosrachadh do
brief *a* goirid, geàrr
bright *a* soilleir; (*clever*) comasach
brighten *v* soillsich, soilleirich
brilliant *a* boillsgeach, lainnireach; (*very clever*) air leth comasach
brim *n* oir *f m*, bile *f* **full to the b.** làn gu bheul
bring *v* thoir, bheir **b. up** (family) àraich, tog (teaghlach)
brink *n* oir *f m*, bruach *f m*
brisk *a* beothail, sunndach, clis
bristle *n* calg *m*, frioghan *m* *v* cuir calg air, tog frioghan air
British *a* Breatannach
Briton *n* Breatannach *m*, (*female*) ban-Bhreatannach *f*
brittle *a* pronn, brisg
broad *a* leathan(n), farsaing
broadcast *n* craoladh *m* *v* craobh-sgaoil, craol
broadcaster *n* craoladair *m*
broadcasting *n* craoladh *m*
brochure *n* leabhran(-shanas) *m*
broken *past part* briste
bronchitis *n* at-sgòrnain *m*
bronze *n* umha *m* **B. Age** Linn an Umha *f m*
brooch *n* bràiste *f*, broidse *m*
brood *n* àl *m*, sìol *m*
brook *n* sruthan *m*, alltan *m*
broom *n* sguab *f*; (*bot*) bealaidh *m*
broth *n* brot *m*, eanraich *f*
brothel *n* taigh-siùrsachd *m*
brother *n* bràthair *m* **b.-in-law** bràthair-cèile *m*
brow *n* mala *f*, bathais *f*, maoil *f*; (*topog*) bruach *f m*
brown *a* donn, ruadh
bruise *n* bruthadh *m*, pat *m* *v* brùth
brunette *a* donn *n* tè dhonn *f*
brush *n* sguab *f*, bruis *f* *v* sguab, bruis(ig)

brutal *a* brùideil, garg
brutality *n* brùidealachd *f*
brute *n* brùid *f m*, beathach *m*
bubble *n* builgean *m*, gucag *f*
bucket *n* bucaid *f*, cuinneag *f*
buckle *n* bucall *m*
bud *n* gucag *f*
budge *v* caraich, gluais
budget *n* buidseat *m* **the B.** am Buidseat **b. for** comharraich ionmhas (airson)
budgie *n* buidsidh *m*
bug *n* (*illness*) treamhlaidh *f*; (*computer*) biastag *f*
build *v* tog
builder *n* neach-togail *m*
building *n* togalach *m*, aitreabh *m* **b. society** comann thogalach *m*
bulb *n* bolgan *m*; (*bot*) meacan *m*
bulge *v* brùchd a-mach
bulky *a* mòr, tomadach
bull *n* tarbh *m*
bullet *n* peilear *m*
bullock *n* damh *m*
bully *n* burraidh *m*
bullying *n* burraidheachd *f*
bungalow *n* bungalo *m*
buoy *n* puta *m*
burden *n* eallach *m*
bureaucracy *n* biurocrasaidh *m*
bureaucratic *a* biurocratach
burgh *n* baile *m*, borgh *m*
burglar *n* gadaiche *m*
burial *n* adhlacadh *m*, tiodhlacadh *m*, tòrradh *m*
burly *a* tapaidh, dòmhail
burn *n* losgadh *m*; (*stream*) sruthan *m*, alltan *m* *v* loisg **they suffered burns** chaidh an losgadh
bursary *n* bursaraidh *m*
burst *v* spreadh, sgàin
bury *v* adhlaic, tiodhlaic
bus *n* bus *m* **b. stop** stad-bus *m* **b. station** stèisean bhusaichean *m*
bush *n* preas *m*, dos *m*
business *n* gnothach *m*, gnothachas *f*, malairt *f* **it's none of your b.** chan e do ghnothach-sa e
businessman *n* neach-gnothaich *m*
bustle *n* drip *f*, trainge *f*
busy *a* trang, dripeil
but *conj*, *prep* ach **b. for that** mura b' e sin
butcher *n* bùidsear *m*, feòladair *m*
butler *n* buidealair *m*
butter *n* ìm *m* *v* cuir ìm air
buttercup *n* buidheag an t-samhraidh *f*
butterfly *n* dealan-dè *m*
buttermilk *n* blàthach *f*
buttock *n* màs *m*
button *n* putan *m* *v* dùin na putanan, putanaich
buy *v* ceannaich
buyer *n* ceannaiche *m*, neach-ceanna(i)ch *m*
buzz *n* srann *f*, crònan *m* **it gave me a real b.** thug e fìor thogail dhomh
buzzard *n* clamhan *m*
by *prep* le; (*near*) faisg air, ri taobh (+ *gen*) **by herself** leatha fhèin **by degrees** mean air mhean **by night** tron oidhche **by now** thuige seo **a picture by Picasso** dealbh le Picasso
by *adv* an dara taobh, seachad **we'll need to put a little money by** feumaidh sinn beagan airgid a chur an dara taobh **she went by** chaidh i seachad **by and by** a dh'aithghearr, ri ùine
by-election *n* fo-thaghadh *m*
bypass *n* seach-rathad *m*
byproduct *n* far-stuth *m*
byre *n* bàthach *f*
byway *n* frith-rathad *m*

C

cab *n* caba *m*; (*taxi*) tagsaidh *f m*
cabbage *n* càl *m*
cabin *n* bothan *m*; (*on ship*) cèaban *m*
cabinet *n* caibineat *m*, preasa *m* **the C.** an Caibineat
cable *n* càball *m*
cackle *n* glocail *f*
café *n* cafaidh *f m*
cage *n* cèidse *f*, eunlann *f*
cairn *n* càrn *m*

cajole *v* coitich, breug
cake *n* cèic *f m*
calamity *n* dosgainn *f*, mòr-chall *m*, truaighe *f*
calculate *v* meas, tomhais, obraich a-mach
calculator *n* àireamhair *m*
calendar *n* mìosachan *m*
calf *n* laogh *m*; (*of leg*) calpa *m*
calibre *n* cailibhear *m*, meudachd baraille *f*; (*of person*) stuth *m*, feartan *f pl*
call *n* èigh *f*, gairm *f*, glaodh *m* *v* èigh, glaodh, gairm; (*visit*) tadhail air; (*send for*) cuir fios air **they called her Jean** thug iad Sìne (mar ainm) oirre
calling *n* èigheach *f*; (*vocation*) dreuchd *f*, gairm *f*
callous *a* cruaidh(-chridheach), an-iochdmhor
calm *a* ciùin, sèimh *n* ciùine *f*; (*weather*) fèath *f m*
calorie *n* calaraidh *m*
calve *v* beir laogh
camel *n* càmhal *m*
camera *n* camara *m*
camp *n* campa *m* **c. site** àite-campachaidh *m* *v* campaich
campaign *n* iomairt *f*; (*in war*) còmhrag *f* *v* dèan iomairt
can *n* cana *m*, crogan *m*
can *v* is urrainn do; (*may*) faod **can you do that?** an urrainn dhut sin a dhèanamh? **can she go?** am faod i a dhol ann?
Canadian *n*, *a* Canèidianach *m*, (*female*) ban-Chanèidianach *f*
canal *n* clais-uisge *f*, canàl *m*, faoighteach *m*
cancel *v* dubh a-mach/às; (*event*) cuir dheth
cancer *n* aillse *f* **breast c.** aillse broillich
candid *a* fosgarra
candidate *n* tagraiche *m*
candle *n* coinneal *f* **candlestick** coinnlear *m*
candy *n* candaidh *m*, suiteis *m pl*
cane *n* cuilc *f*; (*stick*) bata *m*
canister *n* canastair *m*
canker *n* cnuimh *f*, cnàmhainn *f*
cannabis *n* cainb *f*, cainb-lus *m*
cannon *n* gunna-mòr *m*, canan *m*
canny *a* cùramach, gleusta
canoe *n* curachan *m*, curach Innseanach *f*
canopy *n* sgàil-bhrat *m*
canteen *n* biadhlann *f*, ionad bìdh *m*
canter *n* trotan *m*
canvas *n* canabhas *m*
canvass *v* (*views*) sir beachdan; (*votes*) sir bhòtaichean; (*support*) sir taic
cap *n* currac *m*, ceap *m*, bonaid *f m*; (*limit*) cuibhreachadh *m*, cuingealachadh *m* *v* (*cover*) còmhdaich; (*limit*) cuibhrich, cuingealaich; (*surpass*) thoir bàrr air
capability *n* comas *m*
capable *a* comasach
capacity *n* na ghabhas rud/ionad; (*role*) dreuchd *f*; (*mental*) comas *m*
cape *n* rubha *m*, maol *m*; (*cloak*) cleòc(a) *m*, guailleachan *m*
capital *n* prìomh-bhaile *m*, ceanna-bhaile *m*; (*fin*) calpa *m*; (*profit*) buannachd *f* *a* (*fin*) calpa **c. expenditure** caiteachas calpa *m* **c. letter** litir mhòr *f*
capitalism *n* calpachas *m*
capitalist *n* calpaire *m*
capsize *v* còp, cuir thairis
captain *n* caiptean *m*, sgiobair *m*
caption *n* fo-thiotal *m*, tiotal *m*
captive *n* prìosanach *m*, ciomach *m*, bràigh *f m*
captivity *n* ciomachas *m*, braighdeanas *m*
capture *n* glacadh *m*
car *n* càr *m* **car ferry** aiseag chàraichean *f* **car park** pàirc(e)-chàraichean *f*
caramel *n* carra-mheille *f*, caramail *m*
caravan *n* carabhan *f m* **c. site** ionad charabhanaichean *m*
caraway *n* lus MhicCuimein *m*, carabhaidh *f m*
carbohydrate *n* gualaisg *m*
carbon *n* gualan *m* **c. dioxide** gualan dà-ogsaid *m*
carbuncle *n* guirean *m*
carcase *n* closach *f*, cairbh *f*

card *n* cairt *f* **cardboard** cairt-bhòrd *m*
cardiac *a* cridhe **c. arrest** stad cridhe *m*
cardigan *n* càrdagan *m*, peitean *m*
cardinal *n* càirdineal *m*
cardinal *a* prìomh; (*numbers*) àrdail
care *n* cùram *m*, aire *f*, faiceall *f* **in my c.** air mo chùram(-sa) **take c.** thoir an aire **c. for** *v* gabh cùram (+ *gen*), gabh sùim (do)
career *n* cùrsa-beatha *m*, dreuchd *f* **careers convention** fèill-dhreuchdan *f*
careful *a* cùramach, faiceallach, furachail
careless *a* mì-chùramach, mì-fhaiceallach; (*indifferent*) coma
carelessness *n* mì-chùram *m*, cion cùraim *m*, dìth cùraim *f m*
caress *v* cnèadaich, cionacraich
caretaker *n* neach-aire *m*
cargo *n* luchd *m*, cargu *m* **c. boat** bàta cargu/bathair *m*
carnage *n* àr *m*, casgradh *m*
carnal *a* feòlmhor, corporra
carnation *n* càrnaid *f*
carnival *n* càrnabhail *m*, àrd-fhèill *f*
carol *n* laoidh *f m*, coireal *m*
carpenter *n* saor *m*
carpentry *n* saorsainneachd *f*
carpet *n* brat-ùrlair *m*, tapais *f*
carriage *n* (*person*) giùlan *m*; (*vehicle*) carbad *m*
carrier *n* neach-giùlain *m*; (*company*) buidheann giùlain *f m*
carrot *n* curran *m*
carry *v* giùlain, iomchair **c. out** (*fulfil*) coilean **c. over** thoir air adhart
cart *n* cairt *f*
cartilage *n* maoth-chnàimh *m*
carton *n* cartan *m*
cartoon *n* cartùn *m*, dealbh-èibhinn *f m*
cartridge *n* catraids(e) *f*
carve *v* snaigh; (*meat*) geàrr
carving *n* gràbhaladh *m*, snaigheadh *m;* (*meat etc*) gearradh *m*
case *n* màileid *f*, ceas *m*; (*abstr*) staid *f*, cor *m*; (*leg*) cùis(-lagha) *f*; (*gram*) tuiseal *m* **nominative c.** an tuiseal ainmneach **gen c.** an tuiseal ginideach **dat c.** an tuiseal tabhartach **if that is the c.** mas ann mar sin a tha **in any c.** co-dhiù
cash *n* airgead ullamh *m*, airgead làimhe *m*
cask *n* buideal *m*, baraille *m*
cassette *n* cèiseag *f* **c. recording** clàradh cèiseig *m*
cast *n* (*performers*) sgioba *f*; (*plaster*) còmhdach plàsta *v* caith/tilg (air falbh); (*moult*) cuir; (*mould*) molldaich **c. lots** tilg croinn
castigate *v* cronaich
castle *n* caisteal *m*
castrate *v* spoth
casual *a* tuiteamach; (*employment*) sealach
casualty *n* leòinteach *m*
cat *n* cat *m*
catalogue *n* catalog *f m*
catapult *n* tailm *f*, lungaid *f*
cataract *n* eas *m*; (*on eye*) meamran sùla *m*
catarrh *n* an galar smugaideach *m*
catastrophe *n* mòr-chreach *f*, lèirsgrios *m*
catch *n* glacadh *m*; (*latch*) claimhean *m* **a good c.** deagh mhurrag *f*, deagh iasgach *m* *v* glac, beir air, greimich air
catchy *a* tarraingeach, fonnmhor
categorical *a* deimhinnte, mionnaichte
category *n* gnè *f*, seòrsa *m*
cater *v* thoir biadh do, solair, ullaich
catering *n* solarachd *f*
caterpillar *n* burras *m*, bratag *f*
cathedral *n* cathair-eaglais *f*, àrd-eaglais *f*
Catholic *n*, *a* Caitligeach *m*, (*female*) ban-Chaitligeach *f*
catholic *a* coitcheann
cattle *n* crodh *m*, sprèidh *f* **c. grid** cliath chruidh *f* **c. show** fèill-chruidh *f*
cauliflower *n* colag *f*, càl-colaig *m*
cause *n* adhbhar *m*

v adhbhraich
causeway *n* cabhsair *m*
caustic *a* loisgeach; (*wit*) geur, guineach
caution *n* faiceall *f*, cùram *m*; (*warning*) rabhadh *m* *v* thoir rabhadh, cuir air *etc* fhaicill, earalaich
cautious *a* faiceallach, cùramach
cavalry *n* eachraidh *m*, marc-shluagh *m*
cave *n* uaimh *f*
cavern *n* uaimh *f*, talamh-toll *m*
cavity *n* sloc *m*, toll *m*, lag *f m*
cease *v* sguir, stad
cease-fire *n* fois-losgaidh *m*
ceaseless *a* gun sgur/stad/abhsadh
ceiling *n* mullach *m*, mullach rùm/seòmair
celebrate *v* dèan subhachas; (*mark*) comharraich, cùm; (*laud*) cuir an cèill cliù; (*sacrament*) cuartaich
celebrated *a* iomraiteach, cliùiteach
celebration *n* subhachas *m*; (*marking*) comharrachadh *m*
celebrity *n* neach iomraiteach *m*; (*fame*) iomraiteachd *f*
celery *n* soilire *m*
celestial *a* nèamhaidh
cell *n* (*church*) cill *f*; (*biol*) cealla *f*; (*prison*) cealla prìosain *f*
cellar *n* seilear *m*
cello *n* beus-fhidheall *f*
cellular *a* ceallach
Celt *n* Ceilteach *m*
Celtic *a* Ceilteach
cement *n* saimeant *m* *v* tàth, cuir ri chèile; (*met*) neartaich
cemetery *n* cladh *m*
censor *v* caisg
censorious *a* achmhasanach, coireachail, cronachail
censure *n* achmhasan *m*, cronachadh *m* *v* cronaich, coirich
census *n* cunntas *m*; (*pop*) cunntas-sluaigh *m*
cent *n* seant *m* **it didn't cost me a c.** cha do chosg e sgillinn (ruadh) dhomh
centenary *n* ceud *m*, ceud bliadhna *f*, cuimhneachan ceud *m*
centimetre *n* ceudameatair *m*
centipede *n* ceud-chasach *m*
central *a* meadhain, meadhanach, anns a' mheadhan
centralize *v* cuir/thoir dhan mheadhan
centre *n* meadhan *m*
century *n* linn *f m*, ceud *m*, ceud bliadhna *f*
cereal *n* gràn *m*; (*food*) biadh gràanach *m*
cerebral *a* eanchainneach
ceremony *n* deas-ghnàth *m*; (*event*) seirbheis *f*
certain *a* cinnteach, deimhinnte **absolutely c.** mionnaichte
certainly *adv* gu cinnteach, gu deimhinn, dha-rìribh
certainty *n* cinnt *f*, dearbhadh *m*
certificate *n* teisteanas *m*, barantas *m*
certify *v* teistich, dearbh
chaff *n* moll *m*, càth *f*
chain *n* sèine *f*, slabhraidh *f*, cuibhreach *m* *v* cuibhrich, cuir slabhraidh air
chair *n* cathair *f*, sèithear *m*; (*person*) cathraiche *m* **chairlift** beairt-dhìridh *f* **chairman** fear-cathrach *m*, fear na cathrach *m* **chairperson** neach-cathrach *m*, cathraiche *m* **chairwoman** bean-chathrach *f*, bean na cathrach *f* *v* gabh cathair
chalk *n* cailc *f*
challenge *n* dùbhlan *m* *v* thoir dùbhlan do; (*oppose*) cuir an aghaidh
chamber *n* seòmar *m*
champion *n* gaisgeach *m*, curaidh *m*, laoch *m*; (*winner*) buadhaiche *m*
chance *n* cothrom *m*, seansa/teans *m* **c. event** tuiteamas *m* **by c.** le turchairt/tuiteamas
chancellor *n* seansalair *m*
change *n* atharrachadh *m*, caochladh *m*; (*money*) iomlaid *f*, airgead pronn *m* *v* atharraich, caochail, mùth

changeable *a* caochlaideach
channel *n* cladhan *m*, clais *f*; (*topog*) caolas *m*; (*means*) modh *f m*
chant *v* seinn
chanter *n* (*of pipes*) feadan *m*, sionnsar *m*
chaos *n* mì-riaghailt *f*
chapel *n* caibeal *m*
chaplain *n* seaplain *m*; (*mil*) ministear-feachd *m*
chapter *n* caibideil *f m*
character *n* beus *f*, mèinn *f*, nàdar *m*; (*liter*) caractar *m*, pearsa *m*; (*typ*) litir *f* **he's a real c.** 's e cinneach a th' ann
characteristic *n* feart *m*, dual-nàdair *m* *a* coltach, samhlachail
charge *n* (*cost*) prìs *f*, cosgais *f*; (*attack*) ionnsaigh *f m*; (*accusation*) casaid *f* **in c. of** air ceann (+ *gen*) *v* (*attack*) dèan/thoir ionnsaigh; (*accuse*) cuir às leth, fàg air **how much did they c. for it?** dè na chuir iad ort e? **take c. of** gabh os làimh
charisma *n* tarraing pearsa *f*
charitable *a* carthannach, coibhneil
charity *n* carthannas *m*, coibhneas *m*; (*alms*) dèirc *f*; (*agency*) buidheann carthannais *f m*
charm *v* cuir seun air, cuir fo dhraoidheachd
charming *a* taitneach, meallach
chart *n* cairt-iùil *f*; (*mus*) clàr *m*
charter *n* cairt *f*, còir-sgrìobhte *f*; (*hire*) fastadh *m* *v* fastaidh
chase *n* sealg *f*, tòir *f*, faghaid *f* *v* ruith (às dèidh) **c. away** ruaig, fuadaich
chasm *n* mòr-bheàrn *m*
chat *n* còmhradh *m*, crac *m* *v* dèan còmhradh/crac/conaltradh
cheap *a* saor; (*remark*) suarach
cheat *n* mealltair *m* *v* meall, thoir an car à, dèan foill air
check *v* dèan cinnteach, thoir sùil air; (*stop*) caisg, bac; (*reprove*) cronaich
checklist *n* liosta-sgrùdaidh *f*
cheek *n* gruaidh *f*, lethcheann *m*; (*met*) mì-mhodh *m* **some cheek!** abair aghaidh!
cheeky *a* aghach, mì-mhodhail
cheer *v* tog spiorad, dèan sunndach **c. on** brosnaich, misnich
cheerful *a* sunndach, aighearach, ait
cheese *n* càise *f m*; (*one*) mulchag *f* **cheesecake** càis-chèic *f*
chef *n* còcaire *m*
chemical *n* ceimig *f* *a* ceimigeach
chemist *n* ceimigear *m*; (*pharmacist*) cungaidhear *m* **c.'s shop** bùth-cungaidheir *f*
chemistry *n* ceimigeachd *f*, ceimig *f*
cheque *n* seic *f* **c.-book** leabhar-sheicichean *m*
cherry *n* siris(t) *f*
chess *n* tàileasg *m*, fidhcheall *m*
chest *n* ciste *f*; (*human*) cliabh *m*, broilleach *m* **c. of drawers** ciste-dhràthraichean *f*
chestnut *n* geanm-chnò *f*
chew *v* cagainn, cnàmh
chick(en) *n* isean *m*; (*pullet*) eireag *f*; (*food*) cearc *f*, sitheann *f m*
chickenpox *n* a' bhreac-òtraich *f*
chief *n* ceannard *m*; (*clan*) ceann-feadhna *m* **c. executive** àrd-oifigear *m* *a* prìomh, àrd (*precedes n*)
chieftain *n* ceann-feadhna/cinnidh *m*
child *n* leanabh *m*, pàiste *m* **c. benefit** sochair chloinne *f* **c. care** cùram-chloinne *m*
childhood *n* leanabas *m*
childish *a* leanabail, leanabaidh
children *n* clann *f*
chill(y) *a* fuar, aognaidh
chimney *n* similear *m*, luidhear *m*
chin *n* smig *f m*, smiogaid *f m*
Chinese *n*, *a* Sìonach *m*, (*female*) ban-S(h)ìonach *f*
chip *n* mìr *m*, sgealb *f*, sliseag *f* **chips** sliseagan (buntàta) *f pl* *v* sgealb, snaigh

chisel *n* (s)geilb *f*, sgathair(e) *m*
chlorine *n* clòrain *m*
chocolate *n* seoclaid *f*, teòclaid *f*
choice *n* roghainn *m*, taghadh *m*
choir *n* còisir(-chiùil) *f*
cholesterol *n* coileastarail *m*
choke *v* tachd, mùch
choose *v* tagh, roghnaich
chop *v* sgud
chord *n* còrd(a) *m*
chore *n* car-obrach *m*
chorus *n* sèist *f m*, co-sheirm *f*
Christ *n* Crìosd(a) *m*
christen *v* baist
christening *n* baisteadh *m*
Christian *n* Crìosdaidh *m* *a* Crìosdail **C. name** ainm baistidh *m*
Christianity *n* Crìosdaidheachd *f*, Crìosdalachd *f*, an creideamh Crìosdaidh/Crìosdail *m*
Christmas *n* Nollaig *f* **C. Day** Là/Latha na Nollaig(e) *m* **C. Eve** Oidhche Nollaig *f* **Merry C.!** Nollaig Chridheil!
chronic *a* fìor dhona, trom; (*med*) buan, leantalach; (*slang*) cianail
chum *n* companach *m*, caraid *m*
chunk *n* caob *m*, cnap *m*
church *n* eaglais *f* **C. of Scotland** Eaglais na h-Alba **Catholic C.** an Eaglais Chaitligeach **Episcopal C.** an Eaglais Easbaigeach **Baptist C.** an Eaglais Bhaisteach **Free C.** an Eaglais Shaor **Free Presbyterian C.** an Eaglais Shaor Chlèireach **churchyard** cladh *m*, cill *f*
churlish *a* mosach, neo-fhialaidh
churn *n* crannachan *m*, muidhe *m*
cider *n* leann-ubhal *m*
cigar *n* siogàr *m*
cigarette *n* toitean *m*, siogarait *f*
cinder *n* èibhleag *f*
cinema *n* taigh-dhealbh *m*
cinnamon *n* caineal *m*
circle *n* cearcall *m*, cuairt *f*, buaile *f* *v* cuairtich, cuartaich, iadh
circuit *n* cuairt *f*
circular *n* cuairt-litir *f* *a* cruinn, cearclach, cuairteagach
circulate *v* cuir mun cuairt, cuir timcheall, cuairtich
circumference *n* cearcall-thomhas *m*
circumspect *a* faiceallach, aireach
circumstance *n* cùis *f*, cor *m*, staid *f*, suidheachadh *m*
circus *n* soircas *m*
cistern *n* tanca *f m*
cite *v* ainmich, tog; (*leg*) thoir sumanadh do, gairm
citizen *n* saoranach *m*, neach-àiteachaidh *m*, neach-dùthcha *m*
city *n* cathair-bhaile *f*, cathair *f*, baile-mòr *m*
civic *a* cathaireach, catharra
civil *a* catharra; (*behaviour*) sìobhalta, modhail, rianail **the Civil Service** an t-Seirbheis Chatharra *f* **c. servant** seirbheiseach catharra *m* **c. rights** còraichean catharra *f pl* **c. war** cogadh catharra *m*
civilian *n* sìobhaltach *m*, neach nach eil san Arm *m* *a* sìobhaltach
civilization *n* sìobhaltachd *f*
civilize *v* sìobhailich, cuir fo rian
claim *n* tagradh *m*, còir *f* **c. form** foirm-tagraidh *m* *v* (t)agair
clam *n* creachan(n) *m*
clamour gleadhraich *f*, othail *f*
clan *n* fine *f*, cinneadh *m* **clansman** fear-cinnidh *m*
clap *n* bas-bhualadh *m*; (*of thunder*) brag *m* *v* buail boisean, bas-bhuail
clarify *v* soilleirich, dèan soilleir
clarinet *n* clàirneid *f*
clarity *n* soilleireachd *f*
clash *n* (*dispute*) connsachadh *m*; (*sound*) glagadaich *f*
clasp *n* cromag *f*, dealg *m*; (*embrace*) cnèadachadh *m*
class *n* (*educ*) clas *m*; (*type*) seòrsa *m* **social c.** eagar sòisealta *m* **classroom** rùm/seòmar-teagaisg *m*
classic(al) *a* clasaigeach
classified *a* (*information*) dìomhair, glaiste

classify *v* seòrsaich
clause *n* (*gram*) clàs *m*; (*condition*) cumha *f m*
claw *n* spuir *m*, ionga *f*
clay *n* crèadh *f*, crè *f*
clean *a* glan *v* glan
cleaner *n* glanadair *m*, neach-glanaidh *m*
cleanliness *n* glainead *m*
cleanse *v* glan, ionnlaid
clear *v* (*clarify*) soilleirich; (*tidy*) rèitich, sgioblaich; (*free*) saor *a* soilleir
clearance *n* fuadach *m* **the Highland Clearances** na Fuadaichean
cleg *n* creithleag *f*
clemency *n* tròcair *f*, iochd *f*
clench *v* teannaich, dùin
clergy *n* clèir *f* **clergyman** pears-eaglais *m*
clerk *n* clèireach *m* **township c.** clàrc a' bhaile *m*
clever *a* deas, clis
click *v* gliog; (*met*) thig air a chèile
client *n* neach-dèiligidh *m*
cliff *n* creag *f*, bearradh *m*
climate *n* gnàth-shìde *f*
climax *n* àirde *f*
climb *v* dìrich, streap
climber *n* streapadair *m*
climbing *n* dìreadh *m*, streap *m*
clinch *v* daingnich, teannaich, dùin
cling *v* claon (ri)
clinic *n* clionaig *f*
clink *v* dèan gliong
clip *n* cliop *m* *v* geàrr, beàrr; (*sheep*) rùisg; (*shorten*) giorraich
cloak *n* cleòc(a) *m*, fallainn *f*
clock *n* cloc *m*
clockwise *a* deasail, deiseil
close *n* (*closure*) dùnadh *m*, crìoch *f*, ceann *m*; (*in tenement*) clobhsa *m* *v* dùin; (*end*) crìochnaich
close *a* faisg, teann, dlùth; (*atmos*) dùmhail, murtaidh
closed *a* dùinte
closing *n* dùnadh **c. date** ceann-latha *m*
cloth *n* aodach *m* **dish-c.** searbhadair-shoithichean *m*, tubhailt(e)-shoithichean *f m* **table-c.** tubhailt(e)-bùird *f m*
clothe *v* còmhdaich, èid
clothes *n* aodach *m* **c.-peg** bioran-anairt *m*, cnag-aodaich *f*
clothing *n* aodach *m*, èideadh *m*, trusgan *m*
cloud *n* sgòth *f*, neul *m*
cloudy *a* sgòthach, neulach
clover *n* clòbhar *m*; (*single plant*) seamrag *f*
clown *n* tuaistear *m*; (*met*) amadan *m*
club *n* cuaille *m*; (*in sport*) caman *m*; (*association*) club *m* **clubhouse** taigh-club *m*
cluck *v* dèan gogail
clue *n* tuairmse *f* **he hasn't a c.** chan eil sgot/poidhs aige
clump *n* bad *m*
clumsy *a* cliobach, cearbach, liobasta
cluster *n* bagaid *f*, cluigean *m*
clutch *v* greimich (air), glac
clutter *n* frachd *m*
coach *n* coidse *f*, bus *m*; (*instructor*) oide *m* *v* oidich, teagaisg, ionnsaich
coal *n* gual *m* **c. mine** mèinn(e)-guail *f*, toll-guail *m*
coalition *n* co-bhanntachd *f*; aonachadh *m*, tàthadh *m* **c. government** riaghaltas co-bhanntachd *m*
coarse *a* (*texture*) garbh; (*manners*) curs, neo-fhìnealta, amh
coast *n* oirthir *f*, costa *m* **coastguard** maor-cladaich *m*
coat *n* còta *m* **c. of arms** gearradh arm *m* *v* còmhdaich, cuir còta air
coax *v* coitich, tàlaidh
cobweb *n* eige *f*, lìon damhain-allaidh *m*
cocaine *n* coicèan *m*
cock *n* (*bird*) coileach *m* **c.-crow** gairm coilich *f* **haycock** coc fheòir *f*
cockle *n* coilleag *f*, srùban *m*
cocktail *n* earball a' choilich *m*, geinealag *f*

cocky *a* bragail
cocoa *n* còco *m*
coconut *n* cnò-còco *f*
cod *n* bodach(-ruadh) *m*, (*large*) trosg *m*
code còd *m*, riaghailt *f*; (*rule*) **c. of conduct** riaghailt obrach *f*
coerce *v* èignich, ceannsaich
co-exist *v* bi beò le
coffee *n* cofaidh *f m*
coffin *n* ciste(-laighe) *f*
cog *n* fiacail *f*, roth *f m*
cogent *a* làidir, cumhachdach
coherent *a* pongail, rianail, ciallach
cohesion *n* co-cheangal *m*, leantalachd *f*, co-thàthadh *m*
cohesive *a* co-cheangailte, leantalach, co-thàthach
coil *n* cuibhle *f*, cuairteag *f*
coin *n* bonn (airgid) *m*
coincide *v* co-thuit; (*agree*) co-aontaich, thig ri chèile
coincidence *n* tuiteamas *m*, co-thuiteamas *m*; (*agreement*) co-aontachadh *m*
coke *n* còc *m*
cold *n* fuachd *m*; (*common*) cnatan *m* **she had the c.** bha an cnatan oirre *a* fuar
colic *n* grèim-mionaich *m*
collaborate *v* co-obraich
collaboration *n* co-obrachadh *m*
collapse *v* tuit (am broinn a chèile); (*of person*) rach ann an laig(s)e
collar *n* coilear *m*; (*on horse*) braighdean *m* **c.-bone** ugan *m*, cnàimh an uga *m*
collate *v* cuir ri chèile
colleague *n* co-obraiche *m*, companach *m*
collect *v* cruinnich, tionail, trus; (*money*) tog
collection *n* cruinneachadh *m*, tional *m*
collector *n* cruinniche *m*, neach-tionail *m*
college *n* colaiste *f m*
collision *n* bualadh *m*, sgleog *f*
colon *n* caolan mòr *m*; (*gram*) còilean *f*
colonel *n* còirneal *m*, còirnealair *m*
colonial *a* colòiniach
colony *n* coloinidh *m*, eilthir *f*
colossal *a* àibheiseach
colour *n* dath *m* **c.-blind** dath-dhall *v* dath, cuir dath air; (*blush*) rudhadh *m*
coloured *a* dathte
colourful *a* dathach
column *n* colbh *m*; (*rock formation*) stac *m*
coma *n* trom-neul *m*, còma *m*
comb *n* cìr *f*; (*coxcomb*) cìrean *m* **honeycomb** cìr-mheala *f* *v* cìr
combine *v* cuir/rach còmhla
come *v* thig, ruig **where do you c. from?** cò às a tha thu? **if it comes to the bit** ma thig e gu h-aon 's gu dhà **c. on!** trobhad! t(h)ugainn! **c. to pass** tachair
comedy *n* comadaidh *m*, mear-chluich *f*
comet *n* reul chearbach *f*, rionnag an earbaill *f*
comfort *n* cofhurtachd *f* *v* cofhurtaich
comfortable *a* cofhurtail, socair
comic *n* comaig *f m*
comic(al) *a* èibhinn, ait, comaig
comma *n* cromag *f* **inverted commas** cromagan turrach
command *n* òrdugh *m*; (*authority*) ùghdarras *m*, smachd *f* *v* thoir òrdugh (seachad), òrdaich, àithn, bi an ceann; (*eg respect*) dleas
commander *n* ceannard *m*
commandment *n* òrdugh *m*; (*Bibl*) àithne *f*
commemorate *v* cuimhnich, comharraich
commence *v* tòisich
commend *v* mol
commendable *a* ionmholta, ri mholadh, airidh air moladh
comment *n* iomradh *m*, facal *m*, luaidh *m*, aithris *f* *v* thoir tarraing (air), dèan luaidh/aithris (air)
commentary *n* cunntas *m*, aithris *f*
commentator *n* neach-aithris *m*
commerce *n* malairt *f*
commercial *a* malairteach

commiserate *v* nochd co-fhaireachdainn/truas ri
commission *n* coimisean *m*; (*warrant*) barantas *m* **the European C.** an Coimisean Eòrpach *m* *v* barantaich
commissioner *n* coimiseanair *m*
commit *v* cuir an gnìomh; (*undertake*) cuir roimhe/roimhpe *etc*; (*entrust*) earb (ri)
committed *a* dealasach, daingeann **c. to/for ...** (*fin*) air a ghealltainn airson ...
commitment *n* dealas *m*
committee *n* comataidh *f* **sub-c.** fo-chomataidh
common *a* cumanta, coitcheann
common sense *n* toinisg *f*
commonwealth *n* co-fhlaitheas *m*
commotion *n* ùpraid *f*
communal *n* coitcheann
communicant *n* comanaiche *m*, neach-comanachaidh *m*
communicate *v* compàirtich, aithris, cuir an cèill, dèan conaltradh
communication *n* compàirteachadh *m*, conaltradh *m*
communion *n* co-chomann *m*; (*relig*) comanachadh *m*, comain *m* **take c.** comanaich *v*
communism *n* comannachas *m*, co-mhaoineas *m*
communist *n* comannach *m*, co-mhaoineach *m* *a* comannach, co-mhaoineach
community *n* coimhearsnachd *f*, co-chuideachd *f* **c. centre** ionad coimhearsnachd *m* **c. council** comhairle coimhearsnachd *f* **c. service** seirbheis coimhearsnachd *f*
commute *v* (*travel*) siubhail
compact *a* teann, dùmhail, daingeann
compact disc *n* meanbh-chlàr *m*
companion *n* companach *m*
company *n* cuideachd *f*, comann *m*; (*firm*) companaidh *f m*
comparable *a* cosmhail, a ghabhas coimeas **they're not c.** chan ionann iad
compare *v* coimeas, dèan coimeas (ri/eadar)
comparison *n* coimeas *m*
compartment *n* earrann *f*; (*room*) seòmar *m*
compass *n* combaist *f*, cairt-iùil *f*; (*ambit*) raon *m*
compassion *n* truas *m*, iochd *f*
compassionate *a* truasail, iochdmhor
compatible *a* co-chòrdail, co-fhreagarrach
compel *v* co-èignich, thoir air
compensate *v* dìol, ìoc, cuidhtich
compensation *n* dìoladh *m*, cuidhteachadh *m*
compete *v* strì, dèan farpais
competent *a* comasach
competition *n* co-fharpais *f*, farpais *f*
competitive *a* farpaiseach, strìtheil **c. tendering** tairgseachadh farpaiseach *m*
competitor *n* farpaiseach *m*
compile *v* cuir ri chèile, co-chruinnich
complacency *n* somaltachd *f*
complacent *a* somalta
complain *v* gearain, dèan gearan, dèan casaid
complaint *n* gearan *m*, casaid *f*; (*med*) treamhlaidh *f*
complement *n* làn *m* **a full c. of staff** làn-sgioba *f m*
complete *v* crìochnaich; (*form etc*) lìon *a* iomlan, coileanta
completely *adv* gu h-iomlan, gu tur, buileach
complex *a* iomadh-fhillte, casta
complexion *n* tuar *m*, dreach *m*
complicated *a* toinnte
compliment *n* moladh *m* **with compliments** le dùrachd *f* *v* mol, dèan moladh
comply *v* thig/dèan a rèir, cùm ri
component *n* pàirt *f m*, pìos *m*
compose *v* dèan, cuir ri chèile, sgrìobh; (*oneself*) socraich/stòldaich (e/i *etc* fhèin)
composed *a* socraichte, ciùin, stòlda
composer *n* (*mus*) sgrìobhaiche

ciùil *m*; (*liter*) ùghdar *m*
composition *n* sgrìobhadh *m*; (*essay*) aiste *f*
compost *n* todhar gàrraidh *m*
composure *n* suaimhneas *m*, socrachd *f*
compound *n* coimeasgadh *m*, co-thàthadh *m*
comprehend *v* tuig
comprehension *n* tuigse *f*
comprehensive *a* coitcheann, farsaing, iomlan, ioma-chuimseach **c. education** foghlam coitcheann *m* **c. school** sgoil choitcheann *f*
compromise *n* co-rèiteachadh *m*
compulsory *a* èigeantach, èigneachail **c. purchase** ceannach èigneachail *m*
compute *v* coimpiut, àireamhaich
computer *n* coimpiutair *m*
computing *n* coimpiutaireachd *f*
comrade *n* companach *m*
concave *a* fo-chearclach
conceal *v* ceil, cleith, falaich
concede *v* gèill, aidich, strìochd
conceit *n* fearas-mhòr(a) *f*, mòrchuis *f*
conceited *a* baralach, mòrchuiseach
conceive *v* fàs torrach/trom; (*think*) gabh a-steach, tuig
concentrate *v* thoir dlùth-aire do
concentration *n* (*heed*) dlùth-aire *f*; (*density*) dùmhlachd *f*
concentric *a* co-mheadhanach
concept *n* bun-bheachd *m*, smaoineas *m*
conception *n* gineamhainn *m*; (*thought*) beachd *m*
concern *n* cùram *m*, iomagain *f*; (*business*) gnothach *m* *v* cuir uallach/iomagain air; (*oneself with*) gabh gnothach ri
concerning *prep* mu, mu thimcheall (+ *gen*), mu dheidhinn (+ *gen*)
concert *n* cuirm-chiùil *f*, consairt *f* **c.-hall** talla-ciùil *m*
concession *n* strìochdadh *m*; (*fin*) lasachadh *m*; (*licence etc*) ceadachd *f*
conciliation *n* rèiteachadh *m*
concise *a* sgiobalta, goirid, geàrr
conclude *v* co-dhùin; (*finish*) crìochnaich
conclusion *n* co-dhùnadh *m*; (*finish*) crìoch *f*
concoct *v* dèan suas; (*mix*) measgaich
concord *n* còrdadh *m*, co-chòrdadh *m*
concrete *n* cruadhtan *m*, concrait *f m* *a* rudail, nitheil; (*substance*) concrait, de chruadhtan
concur *v* aontaich
concurrent *a* co-cheumnach, co-ruitheach
concussion *n* criothnachadh-eanchainn *m*
condemn *v* dìt
condensation *n* (*moisture*) taise *f*
condense *v* co-dhlùthaich, sùmhlaich
condescend *v* deònaich, irioslaich; (*be patronizing*) bi mòrchuiseach
condescending *a* neo-uallach; (*patronizing*) mòrchuiseach
condition *n* cùmhnant *m*, cumha *f*; (*state*) cor *m*, staid *f* **on c. that** air chùmhnant gu
conditional *a* air chùmhnant; (*gram*) cumhach **c. tense** an tràth cumhach *m*
condom *n* casgan-gin *m*
condone *v* leig seachad
conduct *n* giùlan *m*, dol-a-mach *m* *v* stiùir, treòraich; (*oneself*) giùlain
conductor *n* stiùiriche *m*; (*agent*) stuth-giùlain *m*
conduit *m* cladhan-uisge *m*
cone *n* còn *m*; (*pine*) durcan *m*
confederation *n* co-chaidreachas *m*
confer *v* cuir comhairle ri; (*grant*) builich
conference *n* co-labhairt *f*
confess *v* aidich; (*relig*) faoisidich
confession *n* aideachadh *m*, aidmheil *f*; (*relig*) èisteachd *f*, faoisid *f*
confide *v* leig rùn ri
confidence *n* misneachd *f*, dànadas *m*, earbsa *f*

confident *a* misneachail, dàna, bragail
confidential *a* dìomhair, fo rùn
confine *v* cùm a-staigh, cuir crìochan ro
confinement *n* cùbadh *m*, braighdeanas *m*; (*pregnancy*) ùine air leabaidh-shiùbhla *f*
confirm *v* daingnich, dearbh
confirmation *n* daingneachadh *m*; (*relig*) dol fo làimh easbaig *m*
conflict *n* strì *f*, còmhstri *f*, còmhrag *f*
conform *v* rach le, co-fhreagair, gèill, dèan/rach a rèir
confront *v* seas mu choinneimh, còmhlaich, cuir aghaidh air
confrontation *n* cur aghaidh air *m*
confuse *v* cuir troimh-a-chèile
confused *a* troimh-a-chèile
confusion *n* breisleach *m*, troimh-a-chèile *m*
congeal *v* reoth
congenial *a* taitneach, ri a c(h)àil *etc*
congestion *n* dùmhlachd *f*
congratulate *v* cuir meal-a-naidheachd air
congratulation(s) *n* co-ghàirdeachas *m* **c.!** meal do naidheachd!
congregate *v* cruinnich
congregation *n* coitheanal *m*, co-chruinneachadh *m*
congress *n* còmhdhail *f*
conifer *n* craobh-durcain *f*
conjecture *n* barail *f*, tuairmeas *m*
connect *v* ceangail
connected *a* ceangailte
connection *n* ceangal *m*, co-bhann *f* **in c. with** a thaobh (+ *gen*)
conquer *v* ceannsaich, cìosnaich
conquest *n* buaidh *f*, ceannsachadh *m*
conscience *n* cogais *f*, cuinnseas *f*
conscientious *a* cogaiseach
conscious *a* mothachail
consecrate *v* coisrig
consecration *n* coisrigeadh *m*
consecutive *a* co-leantaileach, às dèidh a chèile
consensus *n* co-aontachd *f*
consent *n* aonta *m*, cead *m* *v* aontaich
consequence *n* buil *f*, buaidh *f*, toradh *m*
consequently *adv* uime sin, ri linn sin
conservation *n* glèidhteachas *m*, gleidheadh *m*, dìon *m*
conservationist *n* neach-glèidhteachais *m*
Conservative *n* Tòraidh *m* **the C. Party** am Partaidh Tòraidheach *m*
conservative *a* caomhnach, glèidhteach, stuama
conserve *v* glèidh, taisg, dìon
consider *v* smaoinich, beachdaich, meòraich
considerable *a* cudromach, fiùghail
considerate *a* suimeil, mothachail, coibhneil
consideration *n* suimealachd *f*, coibhneas *m*; (*of matter*) beachdachadh *m*
consistency *n* cunbhalachd *f*
consistent *a* cunbhalach **c. with** co-chòrdail (ri)
consolation *n* furtachd *f*
consolidate *v* daingnich, neartaich
consonant *n* connrag *f*
consortium *n* co-bhanntachd *f*
conspicuous *a* follaiseach, nochdte
conspiracy *n* co-fheall *f*, gùim *m*
conspire *v* dèan co-fheall/gùim
constable *n* constabal *m*, maor-sìthe *m*
constant *a* seasmhach, daingeann, cunbhalach, dìleas
consternation *n* clisgeadh *m*, uabhas *m*
constituency *n* roinn-phàrlamaid *f*
constitution *n* (*phys*) aorabh *m*, dèanamh *m*; (*org*) bonn-stèidh *m*; (*polit*) bun-reachd *m*
constrain *v* co-èignich, thoir air
constrict *v* teannaich, tachd
construct *v* dèan, tog, cuir ri chèile

construction *n* cur ri chèile *m*; (*building*) togail *f*, togalach *m* **under c.** ga t(h)ogail, gan togail
constructive *a* cuideachail, adhartach
consul *n* consal *m*
consult *v* cuir comhairle ri, gabh comhairle
consultant *n* co-chomhairliche *m*
consultation *n* co-chomhairle *f* **c. paper** pàipear co-chomhairleachaidh *m*
consultative *a* co-chomhairleachaidh **c. committee** comataidh co-chomhairleachaidh *f*
consume *v* (*use*) caith; (*food*) ith; (*burn*) loisg
consumer *n* neach-cleachdaidh *m*, caitheadair *m* *pl* luchd-caitheimh/cleachdaidh
consummate *a* barraichte
consumption *n* caitheamh *f*; (*med*) a' chaitheamh *f*
contact *n* (*abstr*) co-cheangal *m*; (*phys*) suathadh *m*, beantainn *m* *v* cuir fios gu, bi an tobha ri
contagious *a* gabhaltach
contain *v* cùm; (*keep in check*) bac, caisg
container *n* soitheach *f m*; (*for cargo*) bogsa-stòraidh *m*
contaminate *v* truaill, salaich, gànraich
contemplate *v* beachd-smaoinich, meòraich, gabh beachd air
contemporary *a* co-aimsireil; (*in age*) co-aoiseach *n* comhaois *m*
contempt *n* tàir *f*, tarcais *f* **he was held in c.** bha e air a chur ann an suarachas
contemptible *a* suarach
contemptuous *a* tàireil, tarcaiseach
contend *v* cathaich, dèan strì an aghaidh (+ *gen*); (*maintain*) cùm a-mach
content *n* susbaint *f*
content(ed) *a* riaraichte, toilichte
contention *n* còmhstri *f*, connspaid *f*, aimhreit *f*, argamaid *f*
contentious *a* connspaideach
contentment *n* toileachas (-inntinn) *m*, riarachadh *m*
contents *n* na tha ann, na tha am broinn ... **list of c.** clàr-innse *m*
contest *n* strì *f*, farpais *f* *v* dèan strì; (*election*) seas
contestant *n* farpaiseach *m*
context *n* co-theacs(a) *m*
continent *n* mòr-thìr *f*
continually *adv* gun sgur, a-ghnàth **c. asking** a' sìor fhaighneachd
continue *v* lean (air)
continuing *a* leantainneach, a' leantainn
continuity *n* leantalachd *f*
continuous *a* leantainneach **c. assessment** measadh leantainneach *m*
contraception *n* casg-gin(eamhainn) *m*
contraceptive *a* casg-gineamhainneach
contract *n* cùmhnant *m*, cunnradh *m* **c. of employment** cùmhnant-obrach *m* *v* (*lessen*) lùghdaich; (*enter into*) dèan cùmhnant; (*illness*) gabh
contraction *n* teannachadh *m*, crìonadh *m*, giorrachadh *m*, lùghdachadh *m*
contractor *n* cunnradair *m*
contradict *v* cuir an aghaidh (+ *gen*)
contrary *a* an aghaidh (+ *gen*)
contrast *n* eadar-dhealachadh *m*, ao-coltas *m* *v* cuir an aghaidh a chèile, dèan iomsgaradh eadar
contravene *v* bris(t), rach an aghaidh
contribute *v* cuir ri, cuidich le **c. to** thoir ... do
contribution *n* tabhartas *m*, cuideachadh *m*
contrite *a* fo aithreachas
control *n* (*abstr*) smachd *m*, ùghdarras *m* **controls** uidheam-stiùiridh *f* *v* ceannsaich **gain c.** faigh smachd air
controller *n* neach-riaghlaidh *m*, rianadair *m*
controversial *a* connspaideach, connsachail

controversy *n* connspaid *f*, connsachadh *m*
conundrum *n* tòimhseachan (toinnte) *m*
convene *v* tionail, cruinnich, gairm
convener *n* neach-gairm *m*
convenience *n* goireas *m* **public c.** goireasan poblach
convenient *a* goireasach
convent *n* taigh-cràbhaidh *m*, clochar *m*
convention *n* (*norm*) cleachdadh *m*, gnàthas *m*; (*body*) co-chruinneachadh *m*; (*agreement*) cùmhnant *m*
conventional *a* gnàthach
conversant with *a* fiosrach (mu), eòlach (air)
conversation *n* còmhradh *m*
converse *v* dèan còmhradh
conversion *n* (*relig*) iompachadh *m*; (*building*) atharrachadh *m*
convert *n* iompachan *m*
convert *v* (*relig*) iompaich; atharraich
convex *a* os-chearclach
convey *v* giùlain, iomchair
convict *v* dìt
conviction *n* dìteadh *m*; (*feeling*) faireachdainn làidir *f*
convince *v* dearbh (do)
convivial *a* cuideachdail
convoy *n* comhailteachd *f*; (*naut*) luing-dhion *f pl*
coo *v* dèan dùrdail/tùchan
cook *n* còcaire *m* *v* còcairich, deasaich biadh, bruich
cooker *n* cucair *m*
cookery, cooking *n* còcaireachd *f*
cool *a* fionnar; (*colloq*) smodaig *v* fuaraich, fionnaraich
co-operate *v* co-obraich
co-operation *n* co-obrachadh *f*
co-operative *a* co-obrachail, cuideachail
co-opt *v* co-thagh
co-opted *a* co-thaghte
co-option *n* co-thaghadh *m*
co-ordinate *v* co-òrdanaich
co-ordinated *a* co-òrdanaichte
co-ordination *n* co-òrdanachadh *m*
co-ordinator *n* co-òrdanaiche *m*
cope *v* dèan an gnothach/a' chùis
copious *a* lìonmhor, pailt
copper *n* copar *m*
copse *n* badan *m*, frith-choille *f*
copulate *v* cuplaich
copy *n* lethbhreac *m*, copaidh *f m* *v* copaig, dèan lethbhreac, ath-sgrìobh
copyright *n* còraichean (foillseachaidh) *f pl*, dlighe-sgrìobhaidh *f*
coral *n* corail *m*
cord *n* còrd *m*, bann *m*
cordial *a* cridheil, càirdeil
core *n* cridhe *m*, eitean *m*
cork *n* àrc *f*, corcais *f*
corkscrew *n* sgriubha-àrc *m*
cormorant *n* sgarbh *m*
corn *n* arbhar *m*; (*on foot*) còrn *m* **c. on the cob** dias Innseanach *f*
corncrake *n* traon *m*, ràc an arbhair *m*
corner *n* oisean *m*, cùil *f*, còrnair *m* **c. kick** breab-oisein *f* **c. stone** clach-oisein/-oisne *f*
cornflakes *n* bleideagan coirce *f*
Cornish *a* Còrnach **C. person** *n* Còrnach *m*, (*female*) ban-Chòrnach *f*
coronation *n* crùnadh *m*
corporal *n* corpailear *m*
corporal *a* corporra, bodhaige
corporate *a* corporra
corporation *n* corporaid *f*, comhairle baile-mòr *f*
corpse *n* corp *m*, marbhan *m*
correct *v* ceartaich *a* ceart
correction *n* ceartachadh *m*
correlation *n* co-dhàimh *f*
correspond *v* co-fhreagair; (*write*) sgrìobh
correspondence *n* litrichean *f pl*, sgrìobhadh *m*; (*match*) co-fhreagradh *m*
corridor *n* trannsa *f*
corroborate *v* daingnich, co-dhearbh
corrode *v* meirg
corrosion *n* meirg *f*, meirgeadh *m*
corrugated *a* preasach **c. iron** iarann liorcach *m* **c. paper**

pàipear preasach *m*
corrupt *a* coirbte, breun, truaillte *v* coirb, truaill
corrupted *a* coirbte, truaillte
corruption *n* coirbeachd *f*, truaillidheachd *f*
cosmetic *n* cungaidh maise *f* **c. surgery** lannsaireachd cruth *f* *a* (*met*) air an uachdar
cosmonaut *n* speur(ad)air *m*
cosmopolitan *a* os-nàiseanta
cost *n* cosgais *f* **c. of living** cosgais bith-beò *f* *v* cosg
costly *a* cosgail, daor
costume *n* culaidh *f*
cosy *a* seasgair
cot *n* cot *m*
cottage *n* taigh-còmhnaidh beag *m*
cotton *n* cotan *m* **bog-c.** an canach *m* **c.-wool** snàth-cotain *m* *a* cotain
couch *n* sèidhs(e) *f*, langasaid *f*
cough *n* casad *m* *v* dèan casad
coughing *n* casadaich *f* *Also vn* a' casadaich
council *n* comhairle *f* **C. of Europe** Comhairle na h-Eòrpa *f* **C. Tax** Cìs Comhairle *f*
councillor *n* comhairliche *m*
counsel *v* comhairlich
counsellor *n* neach-comhairle *m*, comhairleach *m*
count *v* cunnt, cunntais, àireamh(aich)
countenance *n* gnùis *f*
counter *n* cuntair *m*
counter *v* rach an aghaidh (+ *gen*)
countess *n* ban-iarla *f*
counting *n* cunntadh *m*, cunntais *f m*
countless *a* gun àireamh, do-àireamh
country *n* dùthaich *f*, tìr *f*, rìoghachd *f*
countryside *n* dùthaich *f* **in the c.** air an dùthaich/tuath
county *n* siorrachd *f*, siorramachd *f*
couple *n* càraid *f*, dithis *f* **a c. of hours** dà uair
courage *n* misneach(d) *f*, smior *m*
courageous *a* misneachail, smiorail, tapaidh
courier *n* teachdaire *m*
course *n* cùrsa *m*; (*route*) slighe *f*, cùrsa *m*
court *n* cùirt *f* **courthouse** taigh-cùirte/cùrtach *m*
court *v* dèan suirghe *vn* a' suirghe
courteous *a* cùirteil, modhail, suairce
courtesy *n* modh *f m*, modhalachd *f*
courtship *n* suirghe *f*, leannanachd *f*
cousin *n* co-ogha *m*
covenant *n* cùmhnant *m*
cover *n* còmhdach *m*, brat *m*; (*for bed*) cuibhrig(e) *f m* *v* còmhdaich; (*deal with*) dèilig ri
covering *n* còmhdach *m*, brat *m*
covert *a* dìomhair, falaichte, os ìosal
covet *v* sanntaich
cow *n* bò *f*, mart *m*
coward *n* gealtaire *m*, cladhaire *m*
cowardice *n* gealtachd *f*, cladhaireachd *f*
coy *a* nàrach, màlda
crab *n* crùbag *f*, partan *m*
crabbed/crabbit *a* greannach
crack *n* sgàineadh *m*, sgoltadh *m* *v* sgàin, sgoilt
cradle *n* creathail *f*
craft *n* ceàird *f*; (*cunning*) seòltachd *f*; (*boat*) bàta *m* **craftsman** neach-ceàirde *m*
crafty *a* seòlta, carach
crag *n* creag *f*, stalla *f*, carraig *f*
cram *v* dinn
crammed *a* dinnte, dùmhail
cramp *n* an t-orc *m*, cramb *f*
crane *n* crann *m*; (*bird*) corra-mhonaidh *f*
cranny *n* cùil *f*, fròg *f*
crash *n* stàirn *f*, bualadh *m* *v* buail na chèile, craisig
crate *n* cliath-bhogsa *m*, creat *m*
craving *n* cìocras *m*, miann *f m*
crawl *v* snàig, crùb
crayon *n* creidhean *m*, cailc dhathte *f*

craze *n* fasan *m*, annas *m*
crazy *a* cracte, às a c(h)iall *etc*
creak *n* dìosgan *m* *v* dìosg, dèan dìosgan *Also vn* a' diòsganaich
cream *n* uachdar *m*, bàrr *m*; (*cosmetic*) cè *m*
crease *n* filleadh *m*, preas *m* *v* preas(aich)
create *v* cruthaich
creation *n* cruthachadh *m* **Creation** an Cruthachadh *m*, a' Chruthaigheachd *f*
creative *a* cruthachail
creator *n* neach-cruthachaidh *m* **the C.** an Cruthaighear *m*
creature *n* creutair *m*
credibility *n* creideas *m*
credible *a* creideasach, a ghabhas creidsinn
credit *n* creideas *m* **c. card** cairt-creideis *f* **that's to his c.** tha e ri mholadh airson sin *v* creid
creditable *a* teisteil, measail
creditor *n* neach-fiach *m*, creideasaiche *m*
creed *n* creud *f*, creideamh *m*
creek *n* geodha *m*, òb *m*, òban *m*
creel *n* cliabh *m*
creep *v* snàig, èalaidh, liùg
cremate *v* luaithrich
crematorium *n* luaithreachan *m*
crescent *n* corran *m*; (*of moon*) corran-gealaich *m*
cress *n* biolair *f*
crest *n* suaicheantas *m*; (*bird*) cìrean *m*; (*topog*) mullach *m*, bàrr *m*
crevice *n* sgoltadh *m*, sgàineadh *m*
crew *n* sgioba *f m*, criutha *m*
cricket *n* (*game*) criogaid *m*
crime *n* eucoir *f*
criminal *n*, *a* eucorach *m*
crimson *n*, *a* crò-dhearg *m*
cringe *v* crùb, gìog
cripple *n* crioplach *m*, bacach *m*
crippled *a* bacach, na c(h)rioplach *etc*
crisis *n* càs *m*, èiginn *f*, gàbhadh *m*
crisp *n* brisgean *m* *pl* brisgeanan *a* brisg
criterion *n* slat-t(h)omhais *f*
critic *n* sgrùdair *m*, breithniche *m*
critical *a* (*vital*) deatamach, èiginneach; (*liter*) sgrùdail, breitheach; (*adversely*) beumach
criticism *n* càineadh; (*liter*) sgrùdadh *m*, breithneachadh *m*
criticize *v* càin
croak *v* dèan gràgail
crockery *n* soithichean *m pl*
crocodile *n* crogall *m*
croft *n* croit *f*, lot(a) *m*
crofter *n* croitear *m* **Crofters Commission** Ùghdarras nan Croitearan
crony *n* seann charaid *m*, dlùth-chompanach *m*
crook *n* cromag *f*; (*person*) rògaire *m*
crooked *a* cam, crom, fiar
crop *n* (*harvest*) bàrr *m*; (*of bird*) sgròban *m*; (*haircut*) bearradh *m* *v* geàrr, buain; (*hair etc*) beàrr
cross *n* crois *f*; (*crucifixion*) crann-ceusaidh *m* **the Red C.** a' Chrois Dhearg *a* crosta *v* rach tarsainn/thairis **c. oneself** dèan comharra na croise **c. a cheque** cros seic
cross-beam *n* spàrr *f*, trastan *m*
cross-examine *v* cruaidh-cheasnaich
cross-eyed *a* cam, cam-shùileach, fiar-shùileach
crossfire *n* eadar-theine *m*
cross-legged *a* casa-gòbhlach
crossroads *n* crois (an) rathaid *f*
crossword *n* tòimhseachan-tarsainn *m*
crotch *n* gobhal *m*
crouch *v* crom, crùb
crow *n* feannag *f*, starrag *f*
crowbar *n* geimhleag *f*
crowd *n* sluagh *m*; (*pej*) gràisg *f*
crowded *a* dùmhail
crowdie *n* gruth *m*
crown *n* crùn *m*; (*of head*) mullach a' chinn *m*, bàrr a' chinn *m* *v* crùn
crucial *a* deatamach
crucifix *n* crois *f*
crucify *v* ceus
crude *a* amh; (*met*) drabasta,

curs(a)
cruel *a* an-iochdmhor, neo-thruacanta
cruelty *n* an-iochd *f*, neo-thruacantachd *f*
cruise *n* cuairt-mara *f*, turas-cuain *m*
crumb *n* criomag *f*, sprùilleag *f*, mìr *m* **crumbs** sprùilleach *m*
crumple *v* rocaich
crunch *n* **when it comes to the c.** nuair a thig e gu h-aon 's gu dhà
crusade *n* iomairt *f* **the Crusades** Cogaidhean na Croise *m pl*
crush *n* bruthadh *m* *v* pronn; (*met*) ceannsaich, mùch
crust *n* rùsg *m*, plaosg *m*
crutch *n* crasg *f*, croitse *f*
crux *n* cnag (na cùise) *f*
cry *n* èigh *f*, glaodh *f m*, gairm *f*; (*tears*) ràn *m* *v* èigh, glaodh, gairm; (*shed tears*) caoin, guil
crying *n* èigheach(d) *f*, glaodhaich *f*; (*tears*) caoineadh, gal/gul *m*, rànaich *f*
crystal *n* criostal *m* *a* criostail
cube *n* ciùb *m*
cubic *a* ciùbach
cuckoo *n* cuthag *f*
cucumber *n* cularan *m*
cuddle *v* dèan cionacraich air
cue *n* (*sport*) slat-chluiche *f*, ciù *m*; (*stage*) cagar *m*; (*hair*) ciutha *m*
cuisine *n* modh còcaireachd *m*
cull *v* tanaich
culpable *a* ciontach, coireach **c. homicide** marbhadh le coire *m*
culprit *n* ciontach *m*
cultivate *v* àitich
cultivation *n* àiteach *m*
cultural *a* cultarach
culture *n* cultar *m*
cumbersome *a* trom, liobasta
cunning *a* seòlta, carach
cup *n* cupa *m*, copan *m* **cup final** cuairt dheireannach a' chupa *f*
cupboard *n* preas(a) *m*
curb *v* ceannsaich, bac, cuir srian air
curdle *v* binndich
cure *n* leigheas *m*; (*specific*) cungaidh-leigheis *f* *v* leighis, slànaich; (*fish*) saill, ciùraig
curious *a* ceasnachail, farraideach, feòrachail; (*odd*) annasach, neònach
curl *n* dual *m*, bachlag *f*, cam-lùb *f* *v* bachlaich, caisich
curlew *n* guilbneach *f m*
curling *n* (*sport*) curladh *m*
curly *a* dualach, bachlagach, camagach
currant *n* dearc(ag) thiormaichte *f*
currency *n* airgead *m*
current *n* sruth *m*, buinne *f* **electric c.** sruth-dealain *m*
current *a* gnàthaichte, làithreach **c. account** cunntas làitheil *m*, cunntas-ruith *m* **c. affairs** cùisean an latha *f pl*
currently *adv* an-dràsta, an ceartuair
curriculum *n* curraicealam *m*, clàr-oideachais *m* **c. vitae** cunntas-beatha *m*
curry *n* coiridh *m*
curse *n* mallachd *f* *v* mallaich; (*swear*) mionnaich, bi ri na mionnan/guidheachan
cursory *a* cabhagach, gun aire
curtail *v* giorraich
curtain *n* cùirtear *m*, cùirtean *m*
curve *n* lùb *f*, camadh *m*
curved *a* lùbte, le camadh
cushion *n* cuisean *f m*, pillean *m*
custard *n* ughagan *m*
custody *n* grèim *m*, cùram *m*
custom *n* cleachdadh *m*, àbhaist *f*, gnàths *m*, nòs *m*
customary *a* àbhaisteach, gnàthach
customer *n* neach-ceanna(i)ch *m*
Customs *n* seirbheis na Cusbainn *f* **C. duty** cìs Cusbainn *f*
cut *n* gearradh *m* *v* geàrr, giorraich **cut hair** beàrr **his work is cut out for him** tha a dhìol/leòr aige ri dhèanamh
cutlery *n* uidheam-ithe *f*
cycle *n* cuairt *f*, cùrsa *m*; (*bicycle*) baidhsagal *m*, rothair *m*
cyclist *n* baidhsaglair *m*, rothaiche *m*

cyclone *n* toirm-ghaoth *f*, cuairt-gaoithe *f*
cygnet *n* isean eala *m*
cylinder *n* siolandair *m*
cymbal *n* tiompan *m*, ciombal *m*
cynic *n* sgaitear *m*, searbh-neach *m*
cynical *a* sgaiteachail, searbhasach
cyst *n* ùthan *m*, balgan *m*
Czech *n, a* Seiceach *m*, (*female*) ban-S(h)eiceach *f*

D

dab *v* suath
dad *n* dadaidh *m*
daffodil *n* lus a' chrom-chinn *m*
daft *a* gòrach, baoghalta
dagger *n* biodag *f*
daily *a* làitheil *adv* gach latha, gu làitheil
dainty *n* grinn, mìn
dairy *n* taigh-bainne *m* **d.-farm** tuathanachas bainne *m*
daisy *n* neòinean *m*
dale *n* dail *f*, gleann *m*
dam *n* dam *m*
damage *n* dìol *m*, dochann *m*, milleadh *m* *v* dèan dìol air, dèan dochann air, mill
damn! *interj* daingit!, gonadh!
damnable *a* damainte, mallaichte
damnation *n* dìteadh (sìorraidh) *m*, sgrios *m* *interj* daingit!
damp *a* tais
dampness *n* fuarachd *f*; (*weather*) taiseachd *f*
dance *n* dannsa *m* *v* danns, dèan dannsa
dancer *n* dannsair *m*
dancing *n* dannsa(dh) *m*
dandelion *n* beàrnan-brìde *m*
dandruff *n* sgealpaich *f*, càrr *f*
dandy *n* spaidire *m*
danger *n* cunnart *m*, gàbhadh *m*
dangerous *a* cunnartach
dangle *v* bi air bhogadan/udalan
Dane *n* Danmhairgeach *m*, (*female*) ban-D(h)anmhairgeach *f*
Danish *a* Danmhairgeach
dank *a* tungaidh
dapper *a* speiseanta
dare *v* dùraig; (*challenge*) thoir dùbhlan do **don't you d.** na gabh ort
daring *a* dàna
dark *a* dorch(a), doilleir **d. blue** dubh-ghorm
darken *v* dorchnaich
darkness *n* dorchadas *m*
darling *n* gaol *m*, gràdh *m*, eudail *f*, luaidh *f m* **my d.** a ghaoil, m' eudail *a* gaolach, gràdhach
darn *v* càirich
dart *n* gath *m*; (*move*) siorradh *m*
dash *n* ruith *f*, leum *m*, ruith is leum; (*punct*) strìochag *f*, sgrìob *f* *v* ruith, leum; (*break*) spealg, buail air **d. to pieces** spealt
data *n* dàta *m*
date *n* latha *m*; (*deadline*) ceann-latha *m*; (*appointment*) deit *f*; (*fruit*) deit *f* **up-to-d.** ùr-nòsach **to d.** gu ruige seo **d. of birth** latha-breith **out-of-d.** seann-fhasanta **past sell-by d.** seach an ceann-latha **she had a d. with Allan** bha deit aice fhèin 's Ailean *v* cuir latha air, comharraich an latha; (*intrans*) fàs seann-fhasanta
dative *a* tabhartach **the d. case** an tuiseal tabhartach *m*
daub *v* smeur, buaic
daughter *n* nighean *f* **d.-in-law** ban(a)-chliamhain *f*
dawn *n* camhana(i)ch *f*, beul an latha *m*
day *n* latha *m*, là *m* **the day after tomorrow** an-earar **the day before yesterday** a' bhòn-dè **d. centre** ionad latha *m* **daybreak** bris(t)eadh an latha *m* **daylight** solas an latha *m*
daze *v* cuir bho mhothachadh
dazzle *v* deàrrs, boillsgich
deacon *n* deucon *m*
dead *a* marbh **d. centre** teis-meadhan *m*
deadly *a* marbhtach
deaf *a* bodhar **d.-mute** balbhan *m*
deafen *v* bodhair, dèan bodhar
deafness *n* buidhre *f*
deal *n* cùmhnant *m*, cunnradh *m*

a great d. (*much*) tòrr *m* **a good d.** deagh bhargan *m* *v* dèilig (ri); (*in business*) dèan gnothach ri; (*cards*) roinn
dealer *n* neach-malairt *m*; (*of cards*) neach-roinn *m*
dean *n* deadhan *m*
dear *a* ionmhainn, gràdhach, gaolach; (*expensive*) daor *n* luaidh *f m*, gràdh *m*, eudail *m*
dearth *n* gainnc *f*, dìth *f m*
death *n* bàs *m*, caochladh *m*, eug *m*, aog *m*
debate *n* deasbad *f*, deasbaireachd *f* *v* bi a' deasbad, deasbair
debauched *a* neo-mheasarra, stròdhail
debauchery *n* neo-mheasarrachd *f*, mì-gheanmnachd *f*, geòcaireachd *f*
debility *n* laige *f*, anfhainneachd *f*
debit(s) *n* fiachan *f pl* *v* thoir à (cunntas)
debris *n* sprùilleach *m*
debt *n* fiachan *m pl*; (*met*) comain *f* **in d.** ann am fiachan
debtor *n* neach-fhiach *m*
debut *n* ciad nochdadh *m*
decade *n* deichead *m*
decadence *n* claonadh *m*, coirbeachd *f*
decadent *a* coirbte
decant *v* taom; (*move*) gluais
decay *n* crìonadh *m*, seargadh *m*, lobhadh *m* *v* crìon, searg, caith
decayed *a* seargte, crìon, lobhte
decease *n* caochladh *m*, bàs *m* **the deceased** am fear/tè nach maireann
deceit *n* cealgaireachd *f*, cealg *f*, foill *f*
deceitful *a* cealgach, foilleil
deceive *v* meall, thoir an car à
December *n* an Dùbhlachd *f*
decency *n* beusachd *f*, cubhaidheachd *f*
decent *a* beusach, cubhaidh
decentralize *v* sgaoil a-mach, gluais (bh)on mheadhan
deception *n* mealladh *m*, foill *f*
deceptive *a* meallta
decide *v* socraich/suidhich (air), co-dhùin, cuir romhad
deciduous *a* seargach
decimal *n*, *a* deicheamh *m*
decipher *v* mìnich, fuasgail
decision *n* breith *f*, co-dhùnadh *m*
decisive *a* dearbhachail, cinnteach
deck *n* deic *f*, clàr-uachdair *m*; (*of cards*) paca *m*
declaration *n* cur an cèill *m*
declare *v* cuir an cèill, inn(i)s
declension *n* cromadh *m*, teàrnadh *m*; (*gram*) tuisealadh *m*
decline *n* cromadh *m*, crìonadh *m*, dol air ais *m*, dol sìos *m* *v* crom, crìon, rach air ais, rach sìos; (*gram*) claoin
decompose *v* lobh
decorate *v* sgeadaich, maisich
decoration *n* sgeadachadh *m*, maiseachadh *m*
decorator *n* sgeadaiche *m*
decorum *n* stuaim *f*, deagh-bheus *f*
decrease *n* lùghdachadh *m*, dol sìos *m* *v* lùghdaich, beagaich, rach sìos
decree *n* òrdugh *m*, reachd *m*, breith *f* *v* òrdaich, reachdaich, thoir breith
decrepit *a* breòite, anfhann
decry *v* cuir sìos air, càin
dedicate *v* coisrig **d. to** ainmich air
dedicated *a* coisrigte; (*committed*) dìcheallach
dedication *n* coisrigeadh *m*; (*commitment*) dìcheall *f m*
deduce *v* dèan a-mach, tuig
deduct *v* thoir air falbh (bh)o
deed *n* gnìomh *m*, euchd *m*; (*leg*) sgrìobhainn lagha *f*
deem *v* meas
deep *a* domhainn *n* doimhne *f*
deep-freeze *n* cruaidh-reothadair *m*
deer *n* fiadh *m* **d.-forest** frìth *f*
deface *v* mill
defamation *n* tuaileas *m*, mì-chliù *m*
defamatory *a* tuaileasach

defeat *n* call *m* *v* gabh air, faigh buaidh (air)
defect *n* easbhaidh *f*, uireasbhaidh *f*
defective *a* easbhaidheach, uireasbhach
defence *n* dìon *m*, dìdean *f*; (*excuse*) leisgeul *m* **d. mechanism** dòigh dèiligidh (ri) *f*
defend *v* dìon
defender *n* neach-dìon(a) *m*, dìonadair *m*
defensive *a* dìonadach
defer *v* cuir air dàil, dàilich **d. to** thoir inbhe/urram do
deference *n* ùmhlachd *f*, urram *m*
defiance *n* dùbhlan *m*
defiant *a* dùbhlanach
deficiency *n* easbhaidh *f*, dìth *f m*
deficient *a* easbhaidheach
deficit *n* easbhaidh *f*, call *m*
defile *v* salaich, truaill, gànraich
define *v* seall brìgh, mìnich
definite *a* cinnteach, deimhinn(t)e
definition *n* mìneachadh *m*, comharrachadh *m*; (*audio-visual*) gèire *f*, soilleireachd *f*
deflate *v* traogh, leig gaoth às; (*met*) thoir a' ghaoth à siùil
deflect *v* cuir air falbh bho; (*intrans*) aom, claon
deformity *n* mì-chumadh *m*, mì-dhealbh *f m*
defraud *v* dean foill (air)
deft *a* ealamh, deas
defunct *a* à bith, (bh)o fheum
defy *v* thoir dùbhlan do, cuir gu dùbhlan
degenerate *v* rach bhuaithe, meath
degrade *v* ìslich, truaill
degrading *a* maslach, truaillidh
degree *n* inbhe *f*, ìre *f*; (*acad*) ceum *m*; (*temp*) puing *f* **to some d.** gu ìre **by degrees** beag air bheag, mean air mhean
dehydration *n* sgreubhadh *m*
deity *n* diadhachd *f*; (*a god*) dia *m*
dejected *a* fo bhròn/phràmh/sprochd
dejection *n* sprochd *m*, smuairean *m*
delay *n* dàil *f*, maill(e) *f* *v* cuir dàil/maill(e) an/air, cùm air ais
delayed *a* (*late*) fadalach, air dheireadh
delegate *n* neach-ionaid *m*, teachdaire *m*
delegate *v* thoir ùghdarras do
delegation *n* buidheann-riochdachaidh *m*, luchd-tagraidh *m*
delete *v* dubh às/a-mach
deliberate *v* beachdaich, meòraich
deliberate *a* a dh'aon ghnotha(i)ch; (*pace*) mall
delicacy *n* fìnealtas *m*, grinneas *m*
delicate *a* fìnealta, grinn; (*health*) meata, lag
delicious *a* fìor bhlasta
delight *n* aighear *m*, aoibhneas *m*, sòlas *m* *v* toilich, dèan aoibhneach **d. in** gabh tlachd an
delightful *a* aoibhneach, sòlasach, ciatach
delineate *v* dealbh, dealbhaich, tarrainn crìoch eadar
delinquent *n* eucorach *m*, ciontach *m* *a* ciontach, coireach
delirious *a* breisleachail, bruailleanach
delirium *n* breisleach *f*, bruaillean *m*
deliver *v* (*save*) saor, fuasgail, teàrn; (*an address, services*) lìbhrig, liubhair; (*child*) asaidich
deliverance *n* saoradh *f*, fuasgladh *m*, teàrnadh *m*
delivery *n* teàrnadh *m*; (*an address, services*) lìbhrigeadh *m*, liubhairt *m*; (*manner of speech*) cainnt *f*, dòigh-labhairt *f*; (*childbirth*) asaid *f*; (*mail*) post *m*
delude *v* meall, thoir an car à
deluge *n* tuil *f*, dìle *f* *v* cuir fodha
delusion *n* mealladh *m*, dalladh *m*
delve *v* cladhaich, ruamhair, àitich

demand *n* iarrtas *m*, tagradh *m* *v* iarr, tagair
demanding *a* iarrtach
demean *v* ìslich, dìblich
demeanour *n* giùlan *m*, modh *f m*, beus *f*
demented *a* air bhoil(e), às a rian
dementia *n* boile *f*; (*senility*) seargadh-inntinn *m*
demise *n* deireadh *m*; (*gradual*) crìonadh; (*death*) bàs *m*
demit *v* leig dheth/dhith *etc*
democracy *n* deamocrasaidh *m*
democrat *n* deamocratach *m*
democratic *a* deamocratach
demolish *v* leag
demolition *n* leagail (gu làr) *f*
demon *n* deamhan *m*
demonstrate *v* seall, soilleirich, taisbean
demonstration *n* taisbeanadh *m*, soilleireachadh *m*; (*protest*) sluagh-fhianais *f*
demonstrative *a* comharraichte, suaicheanta
demoralize *v* mì-mhisnich gu tur, thoir an cridhe (bh)o
demur *v* cuir an aghaidh (+ *gen*), cuir teagamh an
demure *a* stuama
den *n* saobhaidh *m*, garaidh *m*, faiche *f*, còs *m*
denial *n* àicheadh *m*; (*withholding*) diùltadh *m*
denigrate *v* dì-mol, cuir sìos air
denomination *n* ainm *m*, ainmneachadh *m*; (*relig*) seòrsa *m*, buidheann *f m*
denote *v* comharraich
denounce *v* càin; (*accuse*) tog casaid an aghaidh (+ *gen*)
dense *a* dùmhail, tiugh; (*not intelligent*) maol
density *n* dùmhlachd *f*, dlùths *m*
dent *n* lag *f m* *v* dèan lag an
dental *a* fiaclach, deudach
dentist *n* fiaclair *m*
dentistry *n* fiaclaireachd *f*
dentures *n* fiaclan fuadain *f pl*
denunciation *n* càineadh *m*; (*accusation*) casaid *f*
deny *v* àich, rach às àicheadh; (*withhold*) diùlt, cùm (bh)o
depart *v* falbh, triall, tog air *etc*
department *n* roinn *f*
departure *n* falbh *m*, fàgail *f*
depend *v* bi an eisimeil/am freastal (+ *gen*) **d. on (someone)** cuir earbsa an, earb à **it depends on ...** tha e an crochadh air ... **you can d. on it** faodaidh tu bhith cinnteach às
dependent *a* eisimealach **d. on** an eisimeil (+ *gen*), an eisimeil air, an crochadh air, an urra ri
depict *v* dealbh, tarraing dealbh de
depleted *a* falmhaichte, falamh
deplorable *a* sgriosail, muladach, maslach
deplore *v* faic/meas maslach **we d. what you've done** tha an rud a rinn sibh a' cur uabhas oirnn
depopulation *n* fàsachadh *m*
deport *v* fuadaich, fògair, cuir às an tìr
deportment *n* giùlan *m*, gluasad *m*
depose *v* cuir à dreuchd
deposit *n* tasgadh *m* **d. account** cunntas tasgaidh *m* *v* taisg
depot *n* ionad-stòraidh *m*
depraved *a* aingidh, coirbte
depravity *n* truaill(idh)eachd *f*, aingidheachd *f*
depreciate *v* ìslich (ann an luach), rach sìos
depreciation *n* ìsleachadh (luach) *m*, tuiteam (ann an luach) *m*
depress *v* cuir trom-inntinn (air); (*phys*) brùth sìos
depressed *a* airtnealach, fo sprochd, dubhach, trom-inntinneach
depression *n* airtneal *m*, sprochd *m*, trom-inntinn *f*, smalan *m*
deprivation *n* easbhaidh *f*, toirt air falbh *m*
deprive *v* thoir (air falbh) (bh)o, cùm (bh)o
depth *n* doimhneachd *f*, doimhne *f*
deputation *n* buidheann-tagraidh *f m*
depute *a* iar- (+ *len*) **d. director** iar-stiùiriche

deputy *n* neach-ionaid *m* *a* iar- (+ *len*) **d. head** iar-cheannard *m*
derail *v* cuir bhàrr an rèile; (*met*) cuir drithleann
deranged *a* às a c(h)iall *etc*, air/fon chuthach
derelict *a* trèigte, fàs
deride *v* dèan fanaid air
derision *n* fanaid *f*, sgeig *f*
derivation *n* freumhachadh *m*, bun *m*
derive *v* freumhaich, bunaich
derogatory *a* tarcaiseach, suarach
descend *v* teirinn, crom, thig a-nuas
descendant *n* fear/tè de shliochd *f m* **descendants** (*coll*) sliochd *m*, sìol *m*
descent *n* teàrnadh *m*, cromadh *m*
describe *v* thoir tuairisgeul air, dèan dealbh (de)
description *n* tuairisgeul *m*
descriptive *a* tuairisgeulach
desecrate *v* mì-naomhaich, truaill
desert *n* fàsach *f m*
desert *v* trèig, dìobair **d. from** teich à, ruith à
deserter *n* neach-teichidh *m*, neach-trèigsinn *m*
deserve *v* coisinn, toill, bi airidh air
deserving *a* airidh, toillteanach
design *n* dealbh *f*, dealbhadh *m*; (*intent*) rùn *m* **by d.** a dh'aon ghnotha(i)ch
design *v* dealbhaich, deilbh; (*intend*) rùnaich
designate *v* sònraich, ainmich
designer *n* dealbhaiche *m*, neach-deilbh *m*
desirable *a* ion-mhiannaichte
desire *n* miann *f m*, dèidh *f*, toil *f*, iarrtas *m* *v* miannaich
desirous *a* miannach, dèidheil (air)
desk *n* deasg *m*
desolate *a* fàsail, aonranach
desolation *n* fàsalachd *f*, aonranachd *f*
despair *n* eu-dòchas *m* *v* leig/thoir thairis dòchas
despatch *v* cuir air falbh
desperate *a* èiginneach, nam/na èiginn, na h-èiginn *etc*
desperation *n* èiginn *f*
despicable *a* suarach
despise *v* dèan tàir air
despite *prep* a dh'aindeoin (+ *gen*)
despondency *n* eu-dòchas *m*, dubhachas *m*
despondent *a* eu-dòchasach, dubhach
despot *n* aintighearna *m*
despotism *n* aintighearnas *m*
dessert *n* mìlsean *m*
destination *n* ceann-uidhe *m*
destiny *n* dàn *m* **he was destined to ...** bha e/sin an dàn dha
destitute *a* falamh, ainniseach *n* dìol-dèirce *m*
destroy *v* mill, sgrios
destruction *n* milleadh *m*, sgrios *m*, lèirsgrios *m*
destructive *a* sgriosail, millteach
detach *v* dealaich, cuir air leth
detached *a* dealaichte, air leth
detail *n* mion-phuing *f* *v* thoir mion-chunntas air
detailed *a* mionaideach
detain *v* cùm air ais
detect *v* (*notice*) thoir an aire; lorg; (*discover*) faigh a-mach
detective *n* lorg-phoileas *m*
detention *n* cumail air ais *m*; (*imprisonment*) cumail an grèim *m*
deter *v* cuir bacadh ro
detergent *n* stuth-glanaidh *m*
deteriorate *v* rach bhuaithe
deterioration *n* dol bhuaithe *m*, dol am miosad *m*
determination *n* diongmhaltas *m*, cruaidh-bharail *f*
determine *v* cuir ro, faigh a-mach; (*decide*) cuir romhad
determined *a* diongmhalta, daingeann
deterrent *n* casg *m*, bacadh *m*
detest *v* fuathaich, dubh-ghràinich **I d. it** tha grain (an) uilc agam air
detonate *v* leig dheth, spreadh; (*intrans*) spreadh

detour *n* cam-rathad *m*
detract *v* thoir air falbh (bh)o (luach)
detrimental *a* cronail, millteach
devaluation *n* lùghdachadh luach *m*, dì-luachadh *m*
devalue *v* lùghdaich luach, dì-luachaich
devastate *v* lèirsgrios, dèan lèirsgrios air
devastation *n* lèirsgrios *m*
develop *v* (*trans*) leasaich; (*intrans*) fàs
development *n* leasachadh *m*; (*growth*) fàs *m*
deviate *v* claon (bho)
device *n* innleachd *f*, cleas *m*
devil *n* diabhal *m*, deamhan *m*, donas *m*
devilish *a* diabhlaidh, deamhnaidh
devious *a* carach
devise *v* dealbh, innlich
devoid (of) *a* falamh (de), às eugmhais (+ *gen*)
devolution *n* sgaoileadh-cumhachd *m*
devolved *a* tiomnaichte
devote *v* cosg, thoir (ùine) do
devotion *n* dìlseachd *f*, ionmhainneachd *f*; (*relig*) cràbhadh *m*; (*devotions*) adhradh *m*
devour *v* sluig, glamh
devout *a* cràbhach
dew *n* dealt *f m*, dr(i)ùchd *m*
dewy *a* dealtach, dr(i)ùchdach
dexterity *n* deisealachd *f*, làmhchaireachd *f*
diabetes *n* tinneas an t-siùcair *m*
diabetic *n* diabaiteach *m*
diabolical *a* diabhlaidh, deamhnaidh
diagnose *v* lorg adhbhar
diagnosis *n* lorg-adhbhair *m*
diagonal *a* trasta(nach)
diagram *n* diagram *m*
dial *n* (*watch*) aodann (uaireadair) *m* **sun-d.** uaireadair-grèine *m*
dialect *n* dualchainnt *f*
dialogue *n* còmhradh *m*
diameter *n* trast-thomhas *m*
diamond *n* daoimean *m*
diaper *n* badan *m*
diaphragm *n* sgairt *f*
diarrhoea *n* an spùt *m*, a' bhuinneach *f*
diary *n* leabhar-latha *m*
dice *n* dìsinn *m pl* dìsnean
dictate *v* deachd, òrdaich
dictator *n* deachdaire *m*
dictatorial *a* ceannsalach, deachdaireach
dictatorship *n* deachdaireachd *f*
diction *n* modh-cainnt *f m*
dictionary *n* faclair *m*
die *v* caochail, bàsaich, eug, siubhail
diesel *n* dìosail *m*
diet *n* daithead *f* **regular d.** riaghailt bìdh *f*
differ *v* bi eadar-dhealaichte; (*disagree*) eas-aontaich
difference *n* eadar-dhealachadh *m*, diofar *m*, caochladh *m*
different *a* eadar-dhealaichte, diofraichte, air leth, air a' chaochladh
differentiate *v* diofaraich, eadar-sgar, dèan sgaradh eadar
differentiation *n* eadar-sgarachdainn *f*, eadar-dhealachadh *m*
differing *a* diofraichte
difficult *a* doirbh, duilich
difficulty *n* duilgheadas *m*, dorradas *m*
diffident *a* socharach, mì-mhisneachail, eu-dàna
diffuse(d) *a* sgaoilte *v* sgaoil
dig *v* cladhaich, ruamhair
digest *v* cnàmh, cnuasaich
digestion *n* (an) cnàmh *m*
digger *n* ruamhaire *m*, digear *m*
digit *n* meur *f m*; (*number*) figear *m*
digital *a* meurach; (*number*) figearail, didsiotach
dignified *a* le uaisleachd
dignify *v* urramaich, àrdaich
dignity *n* urram *m*, inbhe *f*
digress *v* rach a thaobh, rach thar sgeula
digression *n* fiaradh-sgeula *m*
digs *n* taigh/àite-loidsidh *m*

dilapidated *a* air a dhol bhuaithe
dilatory *a* màirnealach
dilemma *n* imcheist *f*, ceist *f*
diligence *n* dìcheall *f m*
diligent *a* dìcheallach, dèanadach
dilute *v* tanaich, lagaich
diluted *a* tanaichte, lagaichte
dim *v* doilleirich, duibhrich
dimension *n* tomhas *m*, meud *m*; (*aspect*) modh *f m*, taobh *m*
diminish *v* lùghdaich, beagaich (air); (*intrans*) lùghdaich
diminutive *a* meanbh, bìodach, beag bìodach
dimple *n* lagan-maise *m*
din *n* gleadhraich *f m*, toirm *f*, othail *f*
dine *v* gabh dìnnear/biadh
dinghy *n* geòla-bheag *f*
dingy *a* duainidh, gruamach
dining-room *n* seòmar-bìdh *m*
dinner *n* dìnnear *f*, diathad *f* **d.-time** àm dìnnearach *m*
dinosaur *n* dìneasair *m*
diocese *n* sgìr-easbaig *f*
dip *n* tumadh *m*, bogadh *m*; (*for sheep*) dup *m* *v* tùm, bog, dup
diploma *n* teisteanas *m*
diplomacy *n* gleustachd *f*; (*polit*) dioplòmasaidh *f m*
diplomat *n* gleustair *m*; (*polit*) riochdaire dioplòmasach *m*
diplomatic *a* gleusta, faiceallach; (*polit*) dioplòmasach
dire *a* eagalach, uabhasach, cianail **in d. straits** ann an cruaidh-chàs
direct *a* dìreach *v* stiùir, seòl
direction *n* stiùireadh *m*; (*point of compass*) àird *f*
directive *n* òrdugh *m*
directly *adv* air ball, dìreach
director *n* stiùiriche *m*, neach-stiùiridh *m*
dirt *n* salchar *m*
dirty *a* salach *v* salaich
disability *n* ciorram *m*
disabled person *n* ciorramach *m*
disadvantage *n* anacothrom, mì-leas *m*
disadvantaged *a* beag cothrom **the d.** na feumaich *m pl*
disaffected *a* diombach, mì-riaraichte
disagree *v* rach an aghaidh, eas-aontaich
disagreeable *a* mì-thaitneach, mì-thlachdmhor
disagreement *n* eas-aonta *f*, mì-chòrdadh *m*
disallow *v* diùlt, na ceadaich
disappear *v* rach à sealladh
disappoint *v* bris(t) dùil, leig sìos
disappointment *n* bris(t)eadh-dùil *m*
disapprove *v* bi an aghaidh **her parents d. of him** chan eil a pàrantan air a shon
disarm *v* dì-armaich
disarmament *n* dì-armachadh *m*
disaster *n* mòr-thubaist *f*, calldachd *f*
disastrous *a* sgriosail
disband *v* (*intrans*) sgaoil; (*trans*) leig mu sgaoil
disbelief *n* eas-creideamh *m*
disburse *v* caith/cuir a-mach airgead
disc *n* clàr *m*
discard *v* cuir dheth, dhith *etc*/bhuaithe, bhuaipe *etc*
discerning *a* lèirsinneach, tuigseach, geurchuiseach
discernment *n* lèirsinn *f*, tuigse *f*
discharge *n* sileadh *m*; (*release*) leigeil mu sgaoil *m*, fuasgladh *m*; (*debt*) ìoc *m*, pàigheadh *m* *v* sil; (*release*) leig mu sgaoil, fuasgail; (*debts*) ìoc, pàigh; (*obligation*) coilean; (*cargo*) falmhaich, cuir air tìr
disciple *n* deisciobal *m*
discipline *n* smachd *m*; (*acad*) cuspair *m* *v* smachdaich
disclose *v* foillsich, leig ris
disco *n* diosgo *m*
discomfort *n* mì-chofhurtachd *f*, anshocair *f*
disconcerting *n* buaireasach
disconnect *v* fuasgail, dealaich (bh)o chèile
disconsolate *a* brònach, dubhach, tùrsach
discontent *n* mì-riarachadh *m*, mì-thoileachadh *m*
discontented *a* mì-riaraichte, mì-

thoilichte
discontinue *v* leig seachad, sguir de, cuir stad air
discord *n* mì-chòrdadh *m*, aimhreit *f*; (*mus*) dì-chòrdadh *m*, eas-aonta *m*
discount *n* lasachadh (prìse) *m*
discourage *v* mì-mhisnich
discouragement *n* mì-mhisneachadh *m*
discourteous *a* mì-spèiseil, eas-urramach, gun mhodh
discourtesy *n* cion modh(a) *m*, cion spèis *m*
discover *v* faigh a-mach, lorg
discovery *n* lorg *f*
discredit *v* mì-chliùthaich, thoir creideas (bh)o
discreet *a* faiceallach, cùramach
discrepancy *n* diofar *m*
discrete *a* air leth
discretion *n* faiceall *f*, cùram *m*; (*judgement*) toil *f*, toinisg *f* **at your d.** a rèir do thoil (fhèin)
discriminate *v* dèan dealachadh eadar **d. in favour of** dèan leth-bhreith air
discrimination *n* eadar-dhealachadh *m*, leth-bhreith *f*
discuss *v* deasbair, bi a' deasbad, beachdaich (air/mu)
discussion *n* deasbaireachd *f*, deasbad *m*, cnuasachadh *m*, beachdachadh *m*
disdain *n* tàir *f*, dìmeas *m*
disease *n* tinneas *m*, galar *m*
disembark *v* rach air tìr, thig bhàrr/far (+ *gen*)
disengage *v* dealaich ri, fuasgail
disentangle *v* fuasgail, rèitich
disfigure *v* mill (cruth), cuir à cruth
disgrace *n* masladh *m*, tàmailt *f*, cùis-mhaslaidh *f* *v* maslaich, nàraich
disgraceful *a* maslach, nàr
disgruntled *a* mì-riaraichte, diombach
disguise *n* breug-riochd *m* **in d.** ann an riochd ... *v* cuir breug-riochd air/oirre *etc*
disgust *n* sgreamh *m*, gràin *f* *v* sgreamhaich, gràinich
disgusting *a* sgreamhail, gràineil
dish *n* soitheach *f m* **washing the dishes** a' nighe nan soithichean
dishearten *v* mì-mhisnich
disheartening *a* mì-mhisneachail
dishevelled *a* mì-sgiobalta
dishonest *a* eas-onarach
dishonesty *n* eas-onair *f*
dishonour *n* eas-onair *f*, eas-urram *m*, mì chliù *m*
dishwasher *n* nigheadair-shoithichean *m*
disillusion *n* bris(t)eadh-dùil *m*, fosgladh sùla *m*
disinclined *a* neo-thoileach, leisg (gu)
disinfectant *n* dì-ghalaran *m*
disingenuous *a* carach, neo-fhosgarra
disintegrate *v* rach às a chèile
disinterested *a* gun fhèin-chùis
disjointed *a* (*met*) neo-thàthach, briste
disk *n* clàr *m*
dislike *v* **dislikes** cha toigh/toil (le), cha chaomh (le), is beag air
dislocate *v* cuir à(s) àite, cuir às an alt
dislodge *v* cuir à(s) àite, fuasgail
disloyal *a* neo-dhìleas
dismal *a* dubhach, gruamach; (*poor*) truagh, leibideach
dismantle *v* thoir às a chèile
dismay *n* uabhas *m*
dismiss *v* cuir air falbh, cuir à dreuchd
dismissal *n* cur à dreuchd *m*
dismount *v* teirinn (bh)o, thig de
disobedience *n* eas-ùmhlachd *f*
disobedient *a* eas-umhail
disobey *v* bi eas-umhail do, rach an aghaidh
disorder *n* mì-rian *m*, buaireas *m*, troimh-a-chèile *f m*
disorderly *a* mì-rianail
disorganized *a* mì-dhòigheil, gun rian
disown *v* diùlt gabhail ri, cuir cùl ri
disparage *v* cuir sìos air, dì-mol
disparate *a* diofraichte, neo-ionann

disparity *n* diofar *m*, neo-ionannachd *f*
dispassionate *a* ceart-bhreitheach, neo-chlaon
dispatch *v* cuir air falbh
dispel *v* sgaoil, fògair
dispensary *n* ìoclann *f*
dispense *v* (*issue*) riaraich; (*drugs etc*) dèan suas cungaidh **d. with** faigh cuidhteas
dispersal *n* sgapadh *m*, sgaoileadh *m*
disperse *v* sgap, sgaoil
dispersed *a* sgapte, sgaoilte
dispirited *a* neo-shunndach, gun s(h)unnd
displace *v* cuir à àite, fògair
display *n* taisbeanadh *m*, foillseachadh *m* *v* taisbean, foillsich
displease *v* mì-thoilich
displeased *a* mì-thoilichte, diombach
displeasure *n* mì-thoileachas *m*, diomb *f m*
disposal *n* toirt seachad *f*, riarachadh *m* **d. of** faighinn cuidhteas *f*
dispose *v* thoir seachad, riaraich **d. of** faigh cuidhteas
dispossess *v* cuir à seilbh
disproportionate *a* neo-chuimseach, mì-chothromach
disprove *v* breugnaich
dispute *n* connspaid *f*, aimhreit *f* *v* connsaich, tagair
disqualify *v* dì-cheadaich, cuir à (farpais)
disquiet *n* iomagain *f*, iomnaidh *f*
disregard *v* cuir an neo-shùim, dèan dìmeas air
disrepair *n* droch c(h)àradh *m* **in a state of d.** feumach air a c(h)àradh
disreputable *a* le droch ainm
disrepute *n* droch ainm *m*, mì-chliù *m*
disrespect *n* dìmeas *m*, eas-urram *m*
disrespectful *a* eas-urramach
disrupt *v* cuir troimh-a-chèile; (*break up*) bris(t)
disruption *n* cur troimh-a-chèile *m*; (*breaking up*) bris(t)eadh *m* **the Disruption** Bris(t)eadh na h-Eaglaise
dissatisfaction *n* mì-riarachadh *m*
dissatisfied *a* mì-riaraichte
dissect *v* sgrùd; (*phys*) geàrr às a chèile
disseminate *v* sgaoil
dissent *n* eas-aonta *m*
dissertation *n* tràchdas *m*
disservice *n* cron *m*
dissident *n* eas-aontaiche *m*
dissimilar *a* eu-coltach (ri)
dissimilarity *n* eu-coltas *m*
dissociate *v* sgar, na gabh gnotha(i)ch ri
dissolute *a* stròdhail
dissolution *n* leaghadh *m*, eadar-sgaoileadh *m*; (*eg Parliament*) sgaoileadh *m*
dissolve *v* leagh, eadar-sgaoil; (*eg Parliament*) sgaoil
dissuade *v* thoir à beachd
distance *n* astar *m*, fad *m*
distant *a* fad' air falbh, cian; (*manner*) fad' às; (*relationship*) fada a-mach
distaste *n* mì-thlachd *f*
distasteful *a* mì-chàilear, mì-thaitneach
distil *v* tarraing, dèan grùdaireachd
distillery *n* taigh-staile *m*
distinct *a* eadar-dhealaichte; (*clear*) soilleir
distinction *n* eadar-dhealachadh *m*; (*quality*) cliù *m*
distinctive *a* sònraichte, eadar-dhealaichte
distinguish *v* dèan dealachadh eadar, aithnich (bh)o chèile
distinguished *a* òirdheirc, cliùiteach
distort *v* fiaraich
distorted *a* fiar
distortion *n* fiaradh *m*
distract *v* tarraing aire (bh)o, buair
distress *n* àmhghar *f m*, teinn *f*, sàrachadh *m*
distressing *a* àmhgharach
distribute *v* sgaoil, roinn, riaraich
distribution *n* sgaoileadh *m*,

riarachadh *m*
district *n* ceàrn *m*, sgìre *f*
distrust *n* cion earbsa *m*, mì-earbsa *f*, amharas *m*
distrustful *a* mì-earbsach, amharasach
disturb *v* cuir dragh air, buair
disturbance *n* buaireadh *m*, aimhreit *f*
disturbing *a* draghail
disunity *n* eas-aonachd *f*
disuse *n* dìth cleachdaidh *f m* **it fell into d.** chaidh e à cleachdadh
ditch *n* clais *f*, dìg *f*
ditto *adv* mar an ceudna
dive *v* dàibhig, rach fon uisge
diver *n* dàibhear *m*; (*bird*) eun tumaidh *m*
diverge *v* gabh caochladh slighe
diverse *a* eugsamhail, eadar-mheasgte, de chaochladh sheòrsa
diversify *v* eugsamhlaich, sgaoil
diversion *n* claonadh *m*; (*detour*) cam(a)-rathad *m*; (*distraction*) tarraing aire *f*; (*pastime*) cur-seachad *m*
diversity *n* eugsamhlachd *f*, iomadachd *f*
divert *v* claon; (*detour*) gabh cam(a)-rathad
divide *v* roinn, pàirtich
divided *a* roinnte, air a/an roinn *etc*
dividend *n* earrann *f*, roinn *f*
divine *a* (*relig*) diadhaidh **the d. will** toil Dhè *f*
divinity *n* diadhachd *f*
division *n* roinn *f*, earrann *f*; (*act of*) pàirteachadh *m*
divorce *n* sgaradh-pòsaidh *m* *v* sgar o chèile
divot *n* ceap *m*, sgrath *f*
divulge *v* foillsich, leig ris, taisbean
dizziness *n* tuaineal *m*, tuainealaich *f*, luairean *m*
dizzy *a* ann an tuaineal/luairean
do *v* dèan **do away with** cuir às do **do your best** dèan do dhìcheall **do what you can** dèan na 's urrainn dhut
docile *a* soitheamh, solta
dock *n* doca *m*; (*plant*) copag *f*
docken *n* copag *f*, cuiseag ruadh *f*
docker *n* docair *m*
doctor *n* dotair *m*, lighiche *m*; (*acad*) ollamh *m*
doctrinaire *a* rag-bharaileach
doctrine *n* teagasg *m*
document *n* sgrìobhainn *f*
documentary *n* aithriseachd *f* *a* aithriseach
documentation *n* pàipearan *m pl*
dodge *n* cleas *m* *v* (*avoid*) seachain
doe *n* (*deer*) maoiseach *f*
dog *n* cù *m*, madadh *m* **dog-tired** cho sgìth ris a' chù **dogfish** biorach *f*
dogged *a* leanailteach, ruighinn
doggerel *n* rannghal *m*, rabhd(aireachd) *f*
dogma *n* gnàth-theagasg *m*
dogmatic *a* dìorrasach, baraileach
dole *n* dòil *m*
doll *n* liùdhag *f*, doile(ag) *f*
dollar *n* dolair *m*
dolphin *n* leumadair-mara *m*
dolt *n* burraidh *m*, ùmaidh *m*
domain *n* raon *m*
dome *n* cuach mhullaich *f*
domestic *a* dachaigheil
domesticate *v* callaich
domesticated *a* callaichte
dominance *n* làmh-an-uachdair *f*
dominant *a* ceannasach, smachdail
dominate *v* ceannsaich, smachdaich, faigh làmh-an-uachdair air
domination *n* ceannsachadh *m*, smachdachadh *m*, làmh-an-uachdair *f*
domineering *a* maigh(i)stireil, ceannsalach
dominion *n* uachdranachd *f*
donate *v* thoir tabhartas/tiodhlac
donation *n* tabhartas *m*, tiodhlac *m*
donkey *n* asal *f m*
donor *n* tabhartaiche *m*
doom *n* bàs *m*, sgrios *m*; (*judgement*) binn *f*, dìteadh *m*

doomsday *n* Latha Luain *m*
door *n* doras *m* **front d.** doras-aghaidh **back d.** doras-cùil **d.-handle** làmh dorais *f* **doorpost** ursainn *f* **doorstep** maide-buinn *m*, leac an dorais *f*
dormant *n* na c(h)adal *etc*, na t(h)àmh *etc*, falaichte
dormitory *n* seòmar-cadail *m*
dormouse *n* dall-luch *f*
dose *n* dòs *m*; (*measure*) tomhas *m*
dot *n* dotag *f*; (*punct*) puing *f*
dote *v* gabh mòr-mhiadh air
dotted *a* dotagach
double *n* a dhà uimhir *f*, uimhir eile *f*; (*person*) mac-samhail *m* **d. chin** sprogan *m*, sprogaill *f* **d.-decker bus** bus dà-ùrlair *m* **d. glazing** uinneag dhùbailte *f* *a* dùbailte, dà-fhillte *v* dùblaich
doubt *n* teagamh *m*, imcheist *f* *v* cuir an teagamh, cuir teagamh an
doubtful *a* teagmhach
doubtless *adv* gun teagamh, gu cinnteach
dough *n* taois *f*; (*slang*) airgead *m*
dour *a* dùr
douse *v* smàl
dove *n* calman *m*
dowdy *a* seann-fhasanta, sgleòideach, duainidh
down *n* clòimhteach *f*
down *prep* shìos; (*motion*) sìos, a-nuas **are they d. there?** a bheil iad shìos an sin? **come d. here** thig a-nuas an seo
downcast *a* smuaireanach, dubhach
downfall *n* tuiteam *m*, leagadh *m* **that was his d.** 's e sin a dh'fhoghain dha
downhill *adv* leis/sìos an leathad, leis a' bhrutha(i)ch
downpour *n* dìle (bhàthte) *f*, deàrrsach *f*
downright *adv* dìreach
downstairs *adv* shìos an staidhre; (*motion*) sìos an staidhre
downward(s) *adv* sìos, a-nuas **going d.** a' dol sìos **coming d.** a' tighinn a-nuas
dowry *n* tochradh *m*
doze *v* dèan norrag/snuachdan
dozen *n* dusan *m*
dozy *a* cadalach
drab *a* duainidh
draft *n* dreach *m*, (*mil*) foireann *m*
drag *v* slaod, dragh, tarraing
dragon *n* dràgon *m*
drain *n* drèana *f*, clais *f* *v* drèan, sìolaidh, traogh
drainage *n* drèanadh *m*
drake *n* (d)ràc *m*, ràcan *m*
dram *n* dram(a) *m*
drama *n* dràma *f m*
dramatic *a* dràmadach
drat (it)! *interj* gonadh air!
draught *n* gaoth *f*; (*of ship*) tarraing-uisge *f* **d.-beer** leann baraille *m*
draughts *n* dàmais *f*
draughtsman *n* neach-tarraing *m*
draw *v* (*pull*) tarraing, dragh, slaod; (*picture*) dèan dealbh **d. lots** cuir croinn
drawer *n* drathair *m*
drawing *n* dealbh *f m*
drawing-pin *n* tacaid *f*
drawl *v* bruidhinn gu slaodach/sgleogach
dread *n* oillt *f*, uamhann *m*, sgàth *m*
dreadful *a* eagalach, cianail
dream *n* aisling *f*, bruadar *m* *v* bruadair, faic aisling *Also vn* ag aisling
dreary *a* muladach, dorcha, gruamach
dredge *v* sgrìob/glan grunnd
dregs *n* druaip *f*, grùid *f*
drenched *a* bog fliuch
dress *n* dreasa *f m*; (*clothes*) aodach *m*
dress *v* cuir aodach air/oirre *etc*, cuir uime/uimpe *etc*
dresser *n* (*furniture*) dreasair *m*
dressing *n* (*med*) bann lota *m*; (*salad*) sùgh saileid *m*
dressing-table *n* bòrd-sgeadachaidh *m*
dribble *v* dèan ròill; (*in football*) drioblaig
drift *n* siabadh *m*; (*argument*)

brìgh *f* **sand-d.** siaban *m* **snow-d.** cuithe sneachd(a) *f* *v* siab, falbh le gaoith; (*of snow*) rach na chuithe
drill *n* (*tool*) snìomhaire *m*; (*mil*) drile *f*; (*veg*) sreath *m* *v* drilich, drilig
drink *n* deoch *f* *v* òl, gabh deoch
drinker *n* neach-òil *m*, pòitear *m*
drip *n* boinne *m*, sileadh *m*, snighe *m*
drive *v* dràibh; (*animals*) iomain **d. away** ruaig
drivel *n* sgudal *m*
driver *n* dràibhear *m*; (*of animals*) neach-iomain *m*
driving *n* dràibheadh *m*; (*of animals*) iomain *f*
drizzle *n* ciùthran *m*, ciùthranaich *f*, smugraich *f*
droll *a* neònach; (*amusing*) ait
droop *v* crom, aom
drop *n* boinne *f*, braon *m*, drudhag *f*, deur *m*; (*fall*) tuiteam *m*
drop *v* leig às; (*give up*) leig seachad; (*fall*) tuit; (*liquid*) sil **d. me a line** cuir sgrìobag thugam **d. in any time** tadhail uair sam bith
dross *n* (*coal*) smùr *m*; (*met*) smodal *m*
drought *n* mòr-thiormachd *f*, tartmhorachd *f*
drove *n* dròbh *m*, treud *m*
drover *n* dròbhair *m*
drown *v* bàth; (*intrans*) bi air a b(h)àthadh *etc*
drowning *n* bàthadh *m*
drowsy *a* cadalach
drudgery *n* dubh-chosnadh *m*, tràilleachd *f*
drug *n* droga *f*, cungaidh-leighis *f* **d. addict** tràill-dhrogaichean *f*
druid *n* draoidh *m*
drum *n* druma *f m*
drummer *n* drumair *m*
drunk *a* air an daoraich, air mhisg **he was d.** bha an deoch/daorach air
drunkard *n* drungair *m*, misgear *m*
drunkenness *n* misg *f*, daorach *f*
dry *a* tioram; (*thirsty*) pàiteach *v* tiormaich **dry-clean** tioram-ghlan
dryer *n* tiormadair *m*
drying *n* tiormachadh *m* **good d. weather** turadh math *m*
dry-rot *n* mosgan *m*
dual *a* dùbailte **d.-carriageway** rathad dùbailte *m*
dubious *a* teagmhach
duchess *n* ban-diùc *f*
duck *n* tunnag *f*, (*wild*) lach *f*
duct *n* pìob-ghiùlain *f*
dud *n* rud gun fheum *m*
due *n* còir *f*, dlighe *f* *a* (*deserved*) dligheach, cubhaidh; (*of debt*) ri phàigheadh **when is it d.?** cuin a tha dùil ris? **d. back** ri th(i)lleadh *etc*
duel *n* còmhrag-dithis *f*
duet *n* òran-càraid/dithis *m*
duke *n* diùc *m*
dulcet *a* binn, fonnmhor
dull *a* dorch(a), gruamach, doilleir; (*of hearing*) bodhar; (*personality*) trom, somalta
dulse *n* duileasg *m*
duly *adv* gu riaghailteach
dumb *a* balbh **d. person** balbhan *m*
dumbness *n* balbhachd *f*; (*silence*) tostachd *f*
dummy *n* neach-brèige *m*
dump *n* òtrach *m*, lagais *f*, sitig *f* *v* caith air falbh, cuir bhuat
dumpling *n* turraisg *f*, duf *m*
dun *a* ciar, odhar, lachdann
dung *n* innear *f*, buachar *m*, todhar *m* **dunghill** sitig *f*, dùnan *m*
dungeon *n* toll-dubh *m*, sloc *m*
duodenum *n* beul a' chaolain *m*
dupe *v* meall, thoir an car à
duplicate *n* lethbhreac *m*, mac-samhail *m*
durable *a* maireannach, buan, seasmhach
duration *n* ùine *f*, fad *m*
during *prep* rè (+ *gen*)
dusk *n* ciaradh (an fheasgair) *m*, beul na h-oidhche *m*, eadar-sholas *m*
dusky *a* ciar
dust *n* dust *m*, duslach *m*, stùr *m*; (*human remains*) dust *m* *v* dust(aig)

dustbin *n* soitheach-sgudail *f m*
duster *n* dustair *m*
dusting *n* dustadh *m*
dusty *a* dustach
Dutch *n* (lang) Dùitsis *f* *a* Dùitseach
Dutchman *n* Dùitseach *m* **Dutchwoman** ban-D(h)ùitseach *f*
duty *n* dleastanas *m*; (*excise*) cìs *f* **d.-free** saor o chìsean
dux *n* ducs *m*
dwarf *n* troich *f m*
dwelling *n* àite/ionad-còmhnaidh *m*, fàrdach *f* **d. house** taigh-còmhnaidh *m*
dye *n* dath *m* *v* dath
dyke *n* (*wall*) gàrradh *m*
dynamic *a* fiùghantach
dynamics *n* daineamaig *f*
dynamite *n* daineamait *m*
dynamo *n* daineamo *m*
dynasty *n* sliochd rìoghail *m*
dysentry *n* a' bhuinneach mhòr *f*

E

each *a* gach *adv* an urra, an duine, an ceann **e. other** a chèile **each one is different** tha gach fear/tè eadar-dhealaichte **they cost £20 each** tha iad a' cosg £20 am fear/an tè
eager *a* dealasach
eagerness *n* dealas *m*
eagle *n* iolair(e) *f*
ear *n* cluas *f*; (*of corn*) dias *f*
earl *n* iarla *m*
early *a* tràth, moch
earmark *v* (*met*) comharraich, sònraich; (*phys*) cuir comharra air
earphone *n* cluasan *m*, fòn-cluaise *m*
earn *v* coisinn
earnest *a* dùrachdach
earning(s) *n* tuarastal *m*, cosnadh *m*
earring *n* fàinne-cluaise *f m*
earth *n* talamh *f m*; (*soil*) ùir *f* **the E.** an Talamh, an Cruinne-cè *m* **where on e. were you?** càit air an t-saoghal an robh thu?
earthly *a* talmhaidh
earthquake *n* crith-thalmhainn *f*
earthworm *n* boiteag *f*
earwig *n* gòbhlag(-stobach) *f*, fiolan-gòbhlach *m*
ease *n* fois *f*, tàmh *m*
east *n* ear *f*, an àird an ear *f*
Easter *n* a' Chàisg *f* **e. egg** ugh Càisge *m*
easterly *a* an ear, (bh)on ear
easy *a* furasta, soirbh
eat *v* ith
eavesdropping *n* farchluais *f*
ebb *n* tràghadh *m* **ebb-tide** sruth-tràghaidh *m* *v* tràigh, traogh
eccentric *a* àraid, annasach, neònach
ecclesiastic *a* eaglaiseil
echo *n* mac-talla *m*
eclectic *a* roghainneach
eclipse *n* dubhadh grèine/gealaich *m*
ecology *n* eag-eòlas *m*
economic *a* eaconamach
economical *a* cùramach, caomhnach/cùmhnach
economics *n* eaconamas *m*, eaconamachd *f*
economist *n* eaconamair *m*
economize *v* caomhain/cumhain
economy *n* eaconamaidh *m*
ecstasy *n* àrd-aoibhneas *m*, mire *f*; (*drug*) eacstasaidh *m*
ecstatic *a* àrd-aoibhneach, air mhire
ecumenical *a* uil-eaglaiseil, aont'-eaglaiseil
edge *n* oir *f m*, iomall *m*, bruach *m*; (*blade*) faobhar *m*; (*verge*) fàl *m*
edible *a* so-ithe, a ghabhas ithe
edict *n* reachd *m*
edit *v* deasaich
edition *n* deasachadh *m*, eagran *m*
editor *n* neach-deasachaidh *m*, deasaiche *m*
editorial *n* colbh deasaiche *m*
educate *v* foghlaim, teagaisg, ionnsaich
educated *a* foghlaim(ich)te **a well-e. person** neach a fhuair deagh fhoghlam

education *n* foghlam *m*, oideachas *m* **e. authority** ùghdarras foghlaim *m*
educational *a* oideachail, foghlaim
eel *n* easgann *f*
eerie *a* iargalta, gaoireil
effect *n* buaidh *f*, buil *f*, toradh *m* *v* thoir gu buil, coilean
effective *a* èifeachdach, buadhach
effectively *adv* gu h-èifeachdach, le èifeachd
effeminate *a* boireannta
effervescent *a* beothail, suigeartach, làn sunnd
efficacy *n* èifeachd *f*
efficiency *n* èifeachdas *f*
efficient *a* èifeachdach, (*person*) gnothachail
effort *n* oidhirp *f*, dìcheall *f m*, spàirn *f*
effrontery *n* bathais *f*, ladarnas *m*
egg *n* ugh *m* **boiled egg** ugh air a bhruich **egg-cup** glainne/gucag-uighe *f* **egg-white** gealagan *m* **egg-yolk** buidheagan *m*
ego *n* fèin *f*, an fhèin *f*
egotism *n* fèin-spèis *f*
egotist *n* fèin-spèisiche *m*, fèinear *m*
egotistical *a* fèin-spèiseach
Egyptian *n*, *a* Èipheiteach *m*, (*female*) ban-Èipheiteach *f*
eider duck *n* lach mhòr *f*
eight *n* a h-ochd *a* ochd **e. people** ochdnar *f m*
eighth *a* ochdamh
eighteen *n*, *a* ochd-deug **e. years** ochd bliadhna deug
eighty *n* ceithir fichead *f m*, ochdad *m*
either *a*, *pron*, *conj*, *adv* **on e. side of it** air gach taobh dheth/dhith **e. of them** an dara/dàrna fear/tè dhiubh, fear seach fear dhiubh, tè seach tè dhiubh **e. go or stay** an dara cuid falbh no fuirich **that's not right e.** chan eil sin ceart a bharrachd/nas mò
eject *v* cuir/tilg a-mach
elaborate *a* mionaideach, toinnte *v* leudaich (air)
elapse *v* rach seachad
elastic *n*, *a* lastaig *f* (*supple*) sùbailte, subailte
elation *n* mòr-aoibhneas *m*
elbow *n* uileann *f*, uilinn *f*
elder *n* (*eccl*) èildear *m*, foirfeach *m*; (*tree*) droman *m* *a* nas/as sine, na/a bu shine
elderly *a* sean, aosta
elect *v* tagh
elected *a* air a t(h)aghadh, taghte
election *n* taghadh *m* **e. day** latha taghaidh *m*
elector *n* neach-taghaidh *m*, neach-bhòtaidh *m*
electorate *n* luchd-taghaidh *m*
electric(al) *a* dealain
electrician *n* dealanair *m*
electricity *n* dealan *m*
electronic *a* dealanta(ch), eileagtronaigeach
elegance *n* grinneas *m*, eireachdas *m*, snas *m*, loinn *f*
elegant *a* grinn, eireachdail, snasail, loinneil
elegy *n* marbhrann *m*, tuireadh *m*, cumha *f m*
element *n* eileamaid *f*; (*in nature*) dùil *f*
elementary *a* bunasach, sìmplidh
elephant *n* ailbhean *m*
elevate *v* àrdaich, tog suas
elevation *n* àrdachadh *m*; (*height*) àirde *f*; (*plan*) dealbh *f m*
elevator *n* àrdaichear *m*
eleven *n*, *a* aon-deug **e. men** aon duine deug
elf *n* màileachan *m*
elicit *v* faigh/lorg a-mach
eligible *a* airidh air roghainn, iomchaidh, dligheach
eliminate *v* cuir às do, geàrr às
elk *n* lon *m*
elm *n* leamhan *m*
elocution *n* deas-chainnt *f*, uirgheall *m*
elongate *v* fadaich, tarraing/sìn a-mach
elope *v* teich, ruith air falbh
eloquence *n* deas-bhriathrachd *f*
eloquent *a* deas-bhriathrach
else *a*, *adv* eile **or e.** air neo
elucidate *v* soilleirich

elude *v* seachain, èalaidh às
elusive *a* èalaidheach
emaciated *a* reangach, seargte
e-mail *n* post-dealain *m*
emanate *v* sruth/thig (bh)o
embargo *n* bacadh *m*
embark *v* (*board*) rach air bòrd
e. on tòisich air
embarrass *v* nàraich, tàmailtich
embarrassed *a* air mo/a *etc* nàrachadh
embarrassing *a* nàrach, tàmailteach
embarrassment *n* nàrachadh *m*, tàmailt *f*
embassy *n* ambasaid *f*
embellish *v* sgeadaich, sgèimhich
ember *n* èibhleag *f*
embezzle *v* dèan foill le airgead
embittered *a* searbh
emblem *n* suaicheantas *m*
embrace *v* glac nad ghàirdeanan; (*accept*) gabh ri
embroider *v* cuir obair-ghrèis air
embroidery *n* obair-ghrèis *f*
embryo *n* suth *m*, tùs-ghinean *m*
emerald *n* smàrag *f*
emerge *v* thig am bàrr/am follais
emergency *a* suidheachadh-èiginn *m*, èiginn *f* **e. exit** doras-èiginn *m*
emigrant *n* eilthireach *m*
emigrate *v* fàg an dùthaich, dèan eilthireachd
emigration *n* eilthireachd *f*, às-imrich *f*
eminent *a* àrd, inbheil, iomraiteach
emit *v* leig a-mach
emotion *n* faireachdainn làidir *f*
emotional *a* làn faireachdainn
empathy *n* co-fhaireachdainn *f*
emperor *n* ìmpire *m*
emphasis *n* cudrom *m*; (*in speech*) sìneadh *m*
emphasize *v* cuir cudrom air; (*in speech*) cuir sìneadh an
emphatic *a* neartmhor, làidir
empire *n* ìmpireachd *f*
employ *v* fastaidh, thoir obair do; (*use*) cleachd
employee *n* neach-obrach *m*, obraiche *m*, cosnaiche *m*
employer *n* fastaiche *m*
employment *n* obair *f*, cosnadh *m*
empower *v* thoir comas/ ùghdarras do
emptiness *n* falamhachd *f*
empty *a* falamh *v* falmhaich
emulate *v* bi a' comharspaidh ri
enable *v* dèan comasach, thoir comas do
enact *v* cuir an gnìomh, coilean; (*leg*) dèan lagh de
enamel *n* cruan *m*
enchanted *a* fo gheasaibh, seunta
encircle *v* cuartaich
enclose *v* cuartaich, iath mun cuairt; (*in letter etc*) cuir an cois
enclosed *a* cuartaichte; (*of document etc*) an cois ...
enclosure *n* crò *m*, geàrraidh *m*; (*document etc*) na tha an cois ...
encompass *v* cuartaich, iath; (*include*) gabh a-steach
encounter *n* coinneachadh *m*, tachairt *f* *v* coinnich (ri), tachair (ri)
encourage *v* misnich, brosnaich
encouragement *n* misneachadh *m*, brosnachadh *m*
encouraging *a* brosnachail
encyclopedia *n* leabhar mòr-eòlais *m*
end *n* deireadh *m*, crìoch *f*, ceann *m* **in the end** aig a' cheann thall **from end to end** (bh)o cheann gu ceann **we will never hear the end of it** cha chluinn sinn a dheireadh (gu bràth/sìorraidh) **come to an end** thig gu ceann/crìch *v* crìochnaich, cuir crìoch air, thoir gu ceann
endanger *v* cuir an cunnart
endangered *a* an cunnart
endear *v* coisinn meas/spèis
endeavour *n* spàirn *f*, oidhirp *f* *v* oidhirpich
endless *a* gun cheann, gun chrìoch, sìorraidh, neo-chrìochnach
endorse *v* (*support*) cuir aonta ri, thoir taic do; (*sign*) cuir ainm ri
endow *v* builich, bàirig
endowment *n* buileachadh *m*,

bàirigeadh *m*
endurance *n* fulang(as) *m*
endure *v* fuiling; (*last*) seas, mair
enemy *n* nàmhaid *m*, eascaraid *m*
energetic *a* lùthmhor, sgairteil
energize *v* cuir brìgh/spionnadh an
energy *n* lùth *m*, neart *m*, spionnadh *m*, brìgh *f*
enforce *v* cuir an gnìomh; (*compel*) spàrr (air)
enforcement *n* cur an gnìomh *m*, sparradh *m*
engage *v* (*hire*) fastaidh **e. with** rach an sàs an
engaged *a* (*to be married*) fo ghealladh-pòsaidh; (*of phone*) trang; (*of toilet*) ga c(h)leachdadh **e. in** an sàs an
engagement *n* (*marriage*) gealladh-pòsaidh *m*; (*commitment*) dleastanas *m*
engaging *a* taitneach, tarraingeach
engine *n* einnsean *m*, inneal *m*, beairt *f*
engineer *n* einnseanair *m*, innleadair *m* **chief e.** prìomh innleadair **civil e.** innleadair-togail
engineering *n* einnseanaireachd *f*, innleadaireachd *f*
English *n* (*lang*) Beurla (Shasannach) *f* *a* Sasannach
Englishman *n* Sasannach *m* **Englishwoman** ban-S(h)asannach *f*
engrave *v* gràbhail
engrossed *a* beò-ghlacte
enhance *v* leasaich, thoir feabhas air; (*add to*) cuir ris
enjoy *v* còrd (ri), gabh tlachd an, meal **they enjoyed the holidays** chòrd na làithean-saora riutha
enjoyment *n* tlachd *f*, toileachas *m*, toil-inntinn *f*
enlarge *v* leudaich, meudaich
enlargement *n* leudachadh *m*, meudachadh *m*; (*phot*) meudachadh *m*
enlighten *v* soilleirich (do), thoir soilleireachadh (do)
enlist *v* (*mil*) liost(aig), gabh san Arm; (*support*) sir
enliven *v* beothaich
enmity *n* nàimhdeas *m*
enormous *a* ana-mhòr, àibheiseach
enough *n* leòr *f* *a, adv* gu leòr **did you get e.?** an d' fhuair thu do leòr/gu leòr? **e. is e.** fòghnaidh na dh'fhòghnas **do you have e. money?** a bheil airgead gu leòr agaibh? **I wasn't fast e.** cha robh mi luath gu leòr
enquire *v* faighnich, feòraich
enquiry *n* ceist *f*
enrage *v* cuir caoch/fearg air
enrich *v* dèan beairteach; (*soil etc*) neartaich
enrol *v* clàraich
en route *adv* air an t-slighe, air an rathad
ensemble *n* (*mus*) co-cheòltairean *m pl*; (*dress*) èideadh *m*
ensign *n* (*flag*) bratach *f*
ensue *v* lean, tachair (ri linn)
ensure *v* dèan cinnteach
entangle *v* rib, cuir an sàs, amail, rocail
entangled *a* an grèim, air amaladh, air rocladh
enter *v* rach/thig a-steach, inntrig
enterprise *n* iomairt *f*
enterprising *a* adhartach, iomairteach
entertain *v* dèan cur-seachad do, dèan dibhearsain; (*hospitality*) thoir aoigheachd do
entertainer *n* fèistear *m*, aisteach *m*
entertainment *n* fèisteas *m*, cur-seachadachd *f*, dibhearsain *m*; (*hospitality*) aoigheachd *f*
enthusiasm *n* dealas *m*, dìoghras *m*
enthusiastic *a* dealasach, dìoghrasach
entice *v* tàlaidh, meall, thoir a thaobh, breug
enticing *a* tarraingeach, tàlaidheach
entire *a* iomlan, slàn, uile
entirely *adv* gu lèir, gu tur
entitlement *n* còir *f*, làn-chòir *f*

entrails *n* mionach *m*, caolain *m pl*; (*animals*) greallach *f*
entrance *n* dol/tighinn a-steach *m*, inntrigeadh *m*; (*way in*) slighe a-steach *f* **main e.** dorasmòr *m*, prìomh dhoras *m*
entreat *v* guidh (air)
entreaty *n* guidhe *f m*, achanaich *f*
entrepreneur *n* neach-tionnsgain *m*
entrust *v* fàg an urra ri, cuir air cùram
entry *n* teachd a-steach *m*, inntrigeadh *m*
enumerate *v* àirmhich, cunnt
enunciate *v* cuir an cèill, aithris
envelop *v* còmhdaich, cuartaich
envelope *n* cèis-litreach *f*
envious *a* farmadach
environment *n* àrainneachd *f*
environmentalist *n* neach-àrainneachd *m*
envoy *n* tosgaire *m*
envy *n* farmad *m*, eud *m* *v* bi ri farmad **I envied her** bha farmad agam rithe
epic *n* euchd-dhàn *m*, mòr-dhuan *m*
epidemic *n* galar sgaoilte *m*, ruathar *m*
epilepsy *n* an tinneas tuiteamach *m*
episcopal *a* easbaigeach
Episcopalian *n, a* Easbaigeach *m*
episode *n* eadar-sgeul *m*, tachartas *m*
epitome *n* sàr eisimpleir *f m* **the e. of laziness** dealbh na leisge *f m*
equable *a* cothrom, rèidh, ciùin
equal *a* ionann, co-ionann **e. opportunities** co-ionannachd chothroman *f* *n* seise *m* *v* bi co-ionann
equality *n* co-ionannachd *f*, cothromachd *f*
equalize *v* dèan co-ionann
equation *n* co-ionannachadh *m*; (*maths*) co-aontar *m*
equator *n* meadhan-chearcall (na talmhainn) *m*, Crios-meadhain *m*
equestrian *n* marcaiche *m*
equilateral *a* co-shliosach **e. triangle** triantan ionann-thaobhach *m*
equinox *n* co-fhreagradh nan tràth *m*
equip *v* uidheamaich, beairtich
equipment *n* uidheam *f*, acfhainn *f*
equipped *a* uidheamaichte, acfhainneach
equivalent *a* co-ionann
era *n* linn *f*
eradicate *v* cuir às do, spìon à bun
erase *v* dubh às/a-mach
erect *v* tog, cuir suas *a* dìreach
erode *v* creim, bleith; (*intrans*) cnàmh, crìon
erosion *n* (*act*) creimeadh *m*, bleith *f*; (*state*) cnàmh *m*, crìonadh *m*
erotic *a* earotach
err *v* rach ceàrr, dèan mearachd, rach air seachran
errand *n* gnothach *m*, ceann-gnothaich *m*
erroneous *a* mearachdach, iomrallach
error *n* mearachd *f*, iomrall *m*
eruption *n* brùchdadh *m*; (*volcanic*) spreadhadh *m*
escalator *n* streapadan *m*
escape *n* teicheadh *m*, tàrrsainn às *m* *v* teich, tàrr às
escort *n* coimheadachd *f*, freiceadan *m* *v* coimheadaich, bi mar chompanach
Eskimo *n, a* Easgiomach *m*, (*female*) ban-Easgiomach *f*
especially *adv* gu h-àraidh, gu sònraichte
espionage *n* beachdaireachd *f*
esplanade *n* àilean *m*
espouse *v* nochd/thoir taic do, taobh ri
essay *n* aiste *f*
essence *n* brìgh *f*, sùgh *m*
essential *a* deatamach
establish *v* stèidhich, suidhich, cuir air bhonn
establishment *n* stèidheachadh *m*, cur air bhonn *m* **the E.** na

h-urracha mòra *m pl*
estate *n* oighreachd *f* **e. agent** reiceadair thaighean *m*
esteem *n* meas *m*, spèis *f* *v* meas, cuir luach air
estimate *n* tuairmse *f* *v* thoir tuairmse air, meas luach
estuary *n* inbhir *m*
eternal *a* sìorraidh, maireannach, bith-bhuan, suthainn
eternally *adv* gu sìorraidh, gu bràth
eternity *n* sìorr(aidhe)achd *f*, bith-bhuantachd *f*, biothbhuantachd *f*
ether *n* adhar fìnealta *m*, èatar *m*
ethical *a* beusanta, modhannach; (*of conduct*) beusach
ethics *n* beus-eòlas *m*; (*personal*) beusan *m pl*
ethnic *a* cinneachail
ethos *n* nòs *m*, feallsanachd *f*
etiquette *n* modh *f m*, dòigh-giùlain *f*
eulogy *n* moladh *m*, òraid-mholaidh *f*; (*poem*) dàn molaidh *m*
euphemism *m* caomh-ràdh *m*, maoth-fhacal *m*
euro *n* euro *f m*, ìuro *f m*
European *n*, *a* Eòrpach *m* **E. Commission** an Coimisean Eòrpach *m* **E. Parliament** Pàrlamaid na h-Eòrpa *f* **E. Union** an t-Aonadh Eòrpach *m*
evacuate *v* falmhaich
evade *v* seachain, faigh às
evaluate *v* meas, tomhais luach
evaluation *n* measadh *m*, luachadh *m*, tomhas luach *m*
evangelical *a* soisgeulach
evaporate *v* deataich
evaporation *n* deatachadh *m*
evasion *n* seachnadh *m*
even *a* rèidh, còmhnard **e.-tempered** ciùin **e. number** àireamh chothrom *f*
even *adv* eadhon, fiù 's **he didn't e. have a coat** cha robh fiù 's còta aige **e. the old folk were there** bha na seann daoine fhèin ann
evening *n* feasgar *m* **early e.** fionnairidh *f*
event *n* tachartas *m*
eventually *adv* mu dheireadh thall
ever *adv* uair sam bith; (*past only*) riamh; (*fut only*) gu bràth, gu sìorraidh **he was as stubborn as e.** bha e cho rag 's a bha e riamh
everlasting *a* sìorraidh, bith-bhuan **e. life** a' bheatha mhaireannach *f*
every *a* a h-uile, gach
everyday *a* làitheil; (*routine*) àbhaisteach
everyone *pron* a h-uile duine/neach, gach duine/neach
everything *pron* a h-uile nì/rud, gach nì/rud
everywhere *pron* (anns) a h-uile (h-)àite, (anns) gach àite
evict *v* fuadaich, cuir à seilbh
eviction *n* fuadach *m*, cur à seilbh *m*
evidence *n* fianais *f*, teisteanas *m*
evident *a* soilleir, follaiseach
evil *n* olc *m*, aingidheachd *f* *a* olc, aingidh
evoke *v* thoir gu cuimhne
evolve *v* thoir gu bith; (*intrans*) thig gu bith
ewe *n* caora *f*
exacerbate *v* dèan nas miosa
exact *a* ceart, mionaideach, pongail
exactly *adv* dìreach, gu mionaideach
exaggerate *v* àibheisich, cuir ris (an fhìrinn)
examination *n* deuchainn *f*, ceasnachadh *m*; (*scrutiny*) sgrùdadh *m*
examine *v* ceasnaich; (*scrutinize*) sgrùd, dèan sgrùdadh air
examiner *n* neach-ceasnachaidh *m*; (*scrutineer*) neach-sgrùdaidh *m*, sgrùdaire *m*
example *n* eisimpleir *f m*, ball-sampaill *m*
excavate *v* cladhaich, ruamhair
exceed *v* rach thairis air

exceedingly *adv* glè (+ *len*), anabarrach
excel *v* dèan math (an), bi sònraichte/barraichte air; (*surpass*) thoir bàrr (air) **she excelled at music** bha i sònraichte/barraichte air ceòl
excellence *n* feabhas *m*, sàr-mhathas *m*
excellent *a* sàr-mhath, barrail, sgoinneil
except *prep* ach, a-mach air **e. for one or two** a-mach air fear/tè no dhà
exception *n* mura-bhith *f*, fàgail a-mach *f*, nì eadar-dhealaichte *m* **with the e. of** ach a-mhàin **everyone without e.** a h-uile duine riamh **take e. to** nochd diomb (mu) *v*
exceptional *a* air leth, sònraichte
excess *n* (*surplus*) còrr *m*; (*too much*) anabarr *m*, cus *m*, tuilleadh 's a' chòir *m*
excessive *a* neo-chuimseach, mì-choltach
exchange *n* iomlaid *f*, malairt *f* **e. rate** co-luach an airgid *m*, luach-iomlaid *m* *v* dèan iomlaid, malairtich
exchequer *n* stàit-chiste *f* **the E.** Roinn an Ionmhais *f*
excise *v* geàrr às/de
excite *v* brosnaich, gluais
excited *a* air bhioran, air bhoil
excitement *n* brosnachadh *m*, spreagadh *m*, boil *f*
exclaim *v* glaodh
exclamation *n* glaodh *m*, clisgeadh *m* **e. mark** clisg-phuing *f*
exclude *v* cùm a-muigh, dùin a-mach, toirmisg
exclusion *n* cumail a-muigh *m*, dùnadh a-mach *m*, toirmeasg *m*
exclusive *a* toirmeasgach; (*expensive*) fìor chosgail
excruciating *a* creadhnachail, fìor chràiteach
excursion *n* cuairt *f*, sgrìob *f*
excuse *n* leisgeul *m* *v* gabh leisgeul (+ *gen*)
execute *v* cuir an gnìomh, thoir gu buil; (*person*) cuir gu bàs
execution *n* cur an gnìomh *m*; (*person*) cur gu bàs *m*
executive *n* (*person*) neach-gnìomh *m*, gnìomhaiche *m*; (*body*) roinn-ghnìomha *f* **the Scottish E.** Riaghaltas na h-Alba
exemplar *n* eisimpleir *f m*
exemplify *v* bi mar/nad eisimpleir de
exempt *a* saor (bh)o, neo-bhuailteach
exemption *n* saoradh (bh)o *m*
exercise *n* eacarsaich *f* **e. book** leabhar-obrach *m* *v* gnàthaich, cleachd; (*work out*) dèan eacarsaich
exertion *n* spàirn *f*, dìcheall *f m*
exhaust *v* traogh; (*tire out*) claoidh
exhausted *a* traoghte, air teirigsinn; (*of person*) claoidhte
exhaustion *n* traoghadh *m*; (*of person*) claoidheadh *m*
exhaustive *a* iomlan, mion
exhibit *v* taisbean
exhibition *n* taisbeanadh *m*
exhilarating *a* meanmnach, aighearach
exhort *v* earalaich, brosnaich
exile *n* fògarrach *m*, eilthireach *m* *v* fògair, fuadaich
exist *v* bi beò, bi ann **it doesn't e.** chan eil e ann/ann am bith
exit *n* dol a-mach *m*; (*way out*) slighe a-mach *f*
exorbitant *a* mì-choltach, ana-cuimseach
exotic *a* cian-annasach, cian-thìreach
expand *v* sgaoil, meudaich, leudaich
expansion *n* sgaoileadh *m*, meudachadh *m*, leudachadh *m*
expect *v* bi an dùil (gu), sùilich **expects** tha dùil aig …
expectant *a* dòchasach, fiughaireach
expectation *n* dùil *f*, dòchas *m*, fiughair *f*
expedient *a* deiseil do, freagarrach san àm

expedite *v* luathaich, cuir cabhag air
expedition *n* turas *m*; (*speed*) cabhag *f*, luaths *m*
expel *v* cuir às, fògair, fuadaich
expend *v* caith, cosg
expenditure *n* caiteachas *m*, cosgais *f*
expense *n* cosgais *f*
expensive *a* cosgail, cosgaiseach, daor
experience *n* eòlas *m*, fiosrachadh *m*, fèin-fhiosrachadh *m* *v* fiosraich, fairich
experienced *a* eòlach
experiment *n* deuchainn *f*, dearbhadh *m*
expert *n* eòlaiche *m* *a* fiosrach, eòlach, ealanta, teòma
expertise *n* ealantas *m*, teòmachd *f*
explain *v* mìnich
explanation *n* mìneachadh *m*
explicit *a* soilleir, follaiseach, gun chleith
explode *v* spreadh
exploit *n* euchd *m* *v* gabh an cothrom air, cleachd airson prothaid **e. unfairly** gabh brath air
exploitation *n* gabhail a' chothruim air *m*, cleachdadh airson prothaid *m*; (*unfair*) gabhail brath air *f*
explore *v* rannsaich, lorg a-mach
explosion *n* spreadhadh *m*
explosive *n* stuth spreadhaidh *m* **e. device** inneal/uidheam spreadhaidh *m*
export *n* às-mhalairt *f*, às-bhathar *m* **e. market** margadh às-mhalairt *m* *v* cuir a-null thairis, às-mhalairtich
expose *v* leig ris, nochd, thoir am follais
exposed *a* am follais; (*skin*) ris; (*site*) fosgailte
expound *v* mìnich, soilleirich
express *v* cuir an cèill; (*send quickly*) luathaich
express *a* luath **e. train** trèan-luath *f* **with the e. purpose** a dh'aon ghnotha(i)ch
expression *n* dòigh/modh-labhairt *f*; (*phrase*) abairt *f*; (*facial*) coltas *m*, fiamh *m*
expulsion *n* fògradh *m*
exquisite *a* loinneil, fìor àlainn
extempore *a* an làrach nam bonn, gun ullachadh
extend *v* sìn, leudaich, cuir ri **e. to** ruig (air)
extension *n* sìneadh *m*, leudachadh *m* **e. work** obair-leudachaidh *f*
extensive *a* farsaing, leathan(n)
extent *n* farsaingeachd *f*, leud *m*, meud *m*
exterior *n* taobh a-muigh *m*
exterminate *v* cuir às do, sgrios
external *a* (bh)on/air an taobh a-muigh
extinct *a* à bith; (*volcano*) marbh
extinguish *v* cuir às, smàl, mùch
extol *v* àrd-mhol
extort *v* foireignich
extra *a* fìor (+ *len*), ro (+ *len*); (*additional*) a chòrr *adv* a bharrachd, a thuilleadh
extract *n* earrann *f*, cuibhreann *f m* *v* tarraing/thoir/tog à
extraordinary *a* anabarrach, iongantach (fhèin)
extravagance *n* ana-caitheamh *m*, stròdhalachd *f*
extravagant *a* ana-caithteach, stròdhail
extreme *a* fìor (+ *len*), ro (+ *len*), anabarrach *n* iomall *m*, ceann thall *m*
extremely *adv* dha-rìribh **e. good** math dha-rìribh
extricate *v* saor, fuasgail
extrovert *n* neach fosgarra *m*
eye *n* sùil *f*; (*of needle*) crò (snàthaid) *m* **eye-opener** fosgladh sùla *m*, sùileachan *m* **eyebrow** mala *f* **eyelash** fabhra *m*, rosg *m* **eyelid** sgàile sùla *f*, fabhra *m* **eyesight** fradharc *m*, lèirsinn *f* **eyesore** cùis sgreamh *f*
eyrie *n* nead iolaire *m*

F

fable *n* uirsgeul *m*, sgeulachd *f*
fabric *n* aodach *m*, eige *f*; (*structure*) dèanamh *m*
fabulous *a* uirsgeulach; (*wonderful*) iongantach, mìorbhaileach
face *n* aodann *m*, aghaidh *f*; (*human only*) gnùis *f* **f.-cloth** clobhd aodainn *m* *v* cuir/thoir aghaidh air; (*be opposite*) bi mu choinneamh
facet *n* taobh *m*
facetious *a* saobh-spòrsail, magail
facile *a* furasta; (*superficial*) staoin
facilitate *v* dèan nas fhasa do, dèan comasach, cuidich
facility *n* goireas *m* **f. in** alt (air) *m*
facing *adv* mu choinneamh (+ *gen*)
fact *n* fìrinn *f*
faction *n* buidheann *f m*
factor *n* adhbhar *m*, eileamaid *f*; (*agent*) bàillidh *m*, seumarlan *m*; (*math*) factar *m*
factory *n* factaraidh *f m*, ionad ceàirde *m*, ionad tionnsgain *m*
faculty *n* ciad-fàth *f*, comas *m*, bua(i)dh *f*; (*acad*) dàmh **she had all her faculties** bha a buadhan uile aice
fade *v* searg, crìon, meath
fail *v* fàillig; (*intrans*) fàilnich, dìobair
failing *n* fàilligeadh *m*, fàillinn *f*
failure *n* fàilligeadh *m*, fàilneachadh *m*
faint *n* neul *m*, laigse *f*, luairean *m* *v* fannaich, fanntaig, rach an laigse
faint *a* fann, lag; (*unclear*) neo-shoilleir **f.-hearted** lag-chridheach, meata
fair *n* fèill *f*, faidhir *f*
fair *a* bàn, fionn; (*beautiful*) maiseach; (*just*) ceart, cothromach
fairly *adv* an ìre mhath, gu math
fairness *n* bàinead *f*; (*beauty*) maisealachd *f*; (*justness*) ceartas *m*, cothromachd *f*
fairy *n* sìthiche *m*; (*female*) bean-shìth *f*
faith *n* creideamh *m*; (*trust*) earbsa *f*, muinighin *f*, creideas *m*
faithful *a* dìleas, treibhdhireach
faithfulness *n* dìlseachd *f*, treibhdhireas *m*
falcon *n* seabhag *f*
fall *n* tuiteam *m*, leagail *m* **f. out** dol a-mach air a chèile *m* *v* tuit; (*in level*) sìolaidh
fallow *a* bàn
false *a* meallta, brèige; (*wrong*) ceàrr **f. teeth** fiaclan fuadain *f pl*
falsehood *n* breug *f*
falter *v* lagaich, tuislich
fame *n* cliù *m*, ainm *m*
familiar *a* eòlach (air); (*manner*) faisg
familiarize *v* cuir eòlas air, cuir aithne air
family *n* teaghlach *m* **f. tree** craobh-teaghlaich *f*
famine *n* gort(a) *f*
famous *a* ainmeil, iomraiteach
fan *n* gaotharan *m*
fanatic *n* eudmhoraiche *m*, dìoghrasaiche *m*
fanatical *a* eudmhorach, dìoghrasach
fanaticism *n* eudmhorachd *f*, dìoghrasachd *f*
fancy *a* àraid, annasach
fancy *v* smaoinich, beachdaich; (*desire*) miannaich
fancy dress *n* aodach-brèige *m*, culaidh choimheach *f*
fank *n* (*agric*) faing *f*, fang *m*
fantastic *a* mìorbhaileach; (*incredible*) do-chreidsinn
fantasy *n* sgeul mhìorbhail *m*; (*delusion*) sgeul gun bhrìgh
far *a*, *adv* fada **f. away** fad' air falbh **f. more** tòrr a bharrachd **f.-fetched** ràbhartach **f.-sighted** fad-fhradharcach
farce *n* baoth-chluich *f*, sgeig-chluich *f*
fare *n* faradh *m*; (*food*) biadh *m*, lòn *m*

farewell *n* soraidh *f*, slàn *m*, beannachd (le) *f*
farm *n* tuathanas *f*, baile-fearainn *m* **farmhouse** taigh-tuathanais *m*
farmer *n* tuathanach *m*
farming *n* tuathanachas *m*
fart *n* braidhm *m*; (*soundless*) tùt *m* *v* dèan braidhm/tùt
farther *adv* nas fhaide, na b' fhaide *a* as fhaide, a b' fhaide
fascinate *v* tàlaidh, tog aire/ùidh
fascinating *a* tarraingeach, ùidheil
fascism *n* faisisteachd *f*
fascist *n, a* faisisteach *m*
fashion *n* fasan *m*; (*habit*) cleachdadh *m*, gnàths *m*, dòigh *f* **in f.** san fhasan **out of f.** às an fhasan *v* cum, dealbh
fashionable *a* fasanta, nòsail
fast *n* trasg *f*, trasgadh *m* **f.-day** latha-traisg/trasgaidh *m* *v* traisg
fast *a* luath; (*firm*) daingeann, teann
fasten *v* ceangail, dùin **f. on to** gabh grèim air
fat *n* saill *f*, sult *m*, geir *f*, blona(i)g *f*; (*state*) reamhrachd *f* *a* reamhar, tiugh
fatal *a* marbhtach, bàsmhor
fate *n* dàn *m*
father *n* athair *m* **F.** (*relig*) an t-Athair **F. Christmas** Bodach na Nollaig *m* **f.-in-law** athair-cèile
fathom *n* aitheamh *m*
fathom *v* (*understand*) tuig, ruig air, dèan a-mach
fatigue *n* sgìths *m*
fatten *v* reamhraich
fault *n* coire *f*, cron *m*, lochd *m*; (*geog*) sgàineadh *m* *v* faigh coire do
faultless *a* neo-choireach, gun mheang
faulty *a* easbhaidheach
fauna *n* ainmhidhean *m pl*
favour *n* fàbhar *m*, bàidh *f*; (*decoration*) suaicheantas *m* *v* bi fàbharach do, nochd fàbhar do
favourable *a* fàbharach
favourite *n* annsachd *f*, neach as annsa/docha (le) *m* *a* ... as annsa/docha (le)
fawn *n* mang *f*
fax *n* facs *m* *v* cuir facs (gu)
fear *n* eagal *m*, fiamh *m*
fear *v* gabh eagal, bi fo eagal
fearful *a* eagalach
fearless *a* gun eagal, gun athadh
feasibility *n* comasachd *f* **f. study** sgrùdadh comasachd *m*
feasible *a* comasach, a ghabhas dèanamh
feast *n* fèist *f*, fleadh *m*, cuirm *f*
feat *n* euchd *m*
feather *n* ite *f*, iteag *f*
feature *n* (*aspect*) comharra *m*; (*facial features*) aogas *m*; (*landscape*) feart-tìre *m*; (*article*) alt sònraichte *m*
February *n* an Gearran *m*
federal *a* feadarail
federation *n* caidreachas *m*
fee *n* (*payment*) duais *f*; (*charge*) cìs *f*
feeble *a* fann, anfhann, breòite
feed *v* biadh, beathaich
feedback *n* fios air ais *m*
feeding *n* beathachadh *m*; (*for animals*) fodradh *m*
feel *v* fairich, mothaich; (*touch*) làimhsich, feuch
feeling *n* faireachdainn *f*, mothachadh *m*
feign *v* leig air/oirre *etc*
fell *v* leag, geàrr sìos
fellow *n* companach *m*, duine *m*
fellow *pref* co-
fellowship *n* comann *m*, companas *m*, caidreabh *m*
felony *n* eucoir *f*
felt *n* teàrr-anart *m*
female *n* bean *f*, boireannach *m* *a* boireann
feminine *a* banail, màlda; (*gram*) boireannta
feminist *n* boireannaiche *m*
fence *n* feansa *f m*, callaid *f* *v* feans(aig)
ferment *n* (*confusion*) troimh-a-chèile *f m* *v* (*alcohol*) brach
fern *n* raineach *f*

ferocious *a* garg
ferocity *n* gairge *f*
ferret *n* feòcallan *m*, neas *f*
ferry *n* aiseag *m*; (*boat*) bàt'-aiseig *m*
fertile *a* torrach
fertility *n* torrachas *m*
fertilizer *n* todhar *m*, mathachadh *m* **artificial f.** todhar Gallda
fervent *a* dùrachdach, dian, eudmhor
fervour *n* dèine *f*, dùrachd *f*, dìoghras *m*, eud *m*
fester *v* lionnraich, grod
festival *n* fèis *f*, fèill *f*
festive *a* fleadhach, cuirmeach, meadhrach **f. season** àm a' ghreadhnachais *m*
festivity *n* subhachas *m*, greadhnachas *m*
fetch *v* faigh, thoir gu
fetching *a* tarraingeach, taitneach
fetter *n* cuibhreach *m*, geimheal *m*
feu *n* gabhail *m*
feud *n* falachd *f*, strì *f*, connsachadh *m* *v* connsaich
feudal *a* fiùdalach
feudalism *n* fiùdalachd *f*
fever *n* fiabhras *m*, teasach *f*
few *n* beagan *m*, deannan *m* *a* ainneamh, gann, tearc
fiance(e) *n* leannan *m*
fibre *n* (*textile*) snàithleach *m*; (*in diet*) freumhag *f*
fickle *a* caochlaideach, gogaideach, leam-leat
fiction *n* uirsgeul *m*, ficsean *m*
fictional *a* uirsgeulach, ficseanail
fiddle *n* fidheall *f* *v* bi ri fìdhlearachd, cluich air an fhidhill; (*be dishonest*) bi ri foill **don't f. with it** na bi a' fideis ris
fiddler *n* fìdhlear *m*
fidelity *n* dìlseachd *f*
fidgety *a* idrisgeach, fideiseach, beag-fois
field *n* achadh *m*, raon *m* **f.-mouse** luch-fheòir *f*
fiend *n* deamhan *m*
fierce *a* fiadhaich, garg
fiery *a* teinnteach, loisgeach *f*; (*temper*) sradagach, aithghearr/cas (san nàdar)
f. cross crann-tàra *m*
fifteen *n* còig-deug **f. pence** còig sgillinn deug
fifth *a* còigeamh
fiftieth *a* leth-cheudamh
fifty *n* leth-cheud *m*, caogad *m* **f. pounds** leth-cheud/caogad not
fight(ing) *n* sabaid *f*, còmhrag *f* *v* sabaidich, dèan sabaid, còmhraig
figure *n* figear *m*; (*shape*) cumadh *m*, cruth *m*; (*of speech*) samhla *m*, ìomhaigh *f*
file *n* (*tool*) eighe *f*; (*office*) faidhle *m* *v* lìomh; (*papers*) faidhl(ig), cuir ann am faidhle
filing *n* faidhleadh *m* **f. cabinet** preasa faidhlidh *m*
fill *n* lìon *m*, sàth *m* *v* lìon; (*intrans*) lìon, fàs làn
filling *a* sàthach
filling-station *n* stèisean connaidh/peatrail *m*
filly *n* loth *f m*
film *n* film *m*; (*membrane*) sgannan *m* **f.-star** reul *m*, reultag film *f*
filter *n* sìoltachan *m*
filth *n* salchar *m*
filthy *a* salach
fin *n* ite *f*
final *a* deireannach *n*; (*sport*) cuairt dheireannach *f*
finalize *v* thoir gu crìch, crìochnaich
finally *adv* mu dheireadh thall
finance *n* ionmhas *m*, maoineachas *m*, airgead *m* **F. Department** Roinn an Ionmhais *f* *v* maoinich, pàigh, ionmhasaich
financial *a* ionmhasail, ionmhasach **f. year** bliadhna-ionmhais *f*
financier *n* maoiniche *m*
find *v* faigh, lorg
fine *n* càin *f* *v* cuir càin (air)
fine *a* (*quality*) grinn; (*smooth*) mìn; (*weather*) brèagha **that's f.** tha sin taghta/glan
finesse *n* snas *m*, fìnealtachd *f*
finger *n* meur *f*, corrag *f* **f.-nail** ìne *f* **f.-print** lorg-meòire *f*

v làimhsich, cuir meur air
finish *n* crìoch *f*, ceann *m* *v* crìochnaich, cuir crìoch air
finished *a* crìochnaichte, deiseil, ullamh
Finn *n* Fionnlannach *m*, (*female*) ban-Fhionnlannach *f*
Finnish *a* Fionnlannach
fir *n* giuthas *m*
fire *n* teine *m* **f. alarm** inneal-rabhaidh teine *m*, clag teine *m* **f.-engine** einnsean-smàlaidh *m* **f.-escape** slighe teichidh *f* **f.-extinguisher** inneal-smàlaidh *m* **firefighter** neach-smàlaidh *m*, smàladair *m* **firework** teine-ealain *m* **fireworks** teintean-ealain **firelighter** lasadair-teine *m* **fireside** teallach *m* **firewood** fiodh-connaidh *m* **by the f.** an tac an teine *v* (*weapons*) loisg **set f. to** cuir teine ri, cuir na t(h)eine *etc*
firm *n* companaidh *f m*
firm *a* daingeann, cruaidh; (*steadfast*) seasmhach, diongmhalta
firmness *n* daingneachd *f*, cruas *m*; (*steadfastness*) seasmhachd *f*, diongmhaltas *m*, cruas *m*
first *a* ciad, a' chiad, prìomh **f. thing in the morning** a' chiad char sa mhadainn **First Minister** Prìomh Mhinistear *m* *adv* an toiseach, anns a' chiad àite **from f. to last** bho thùs gu èis
first aid *n* ciad-fhuasgladh *m*
firth *n* linne *f*, caol *m*, caolas *m*
fiscal *n* fiosgail *m* *a* fiosgail; (*fin*) ionmhasail
fish *n* iasg *m* **f.-farm** tuathanas-èisg *m* **f.-market** margadh-èisg *m* **f.-shop** bùth-èisg *f* *v* iasgaich, bi ag iasgach
fisherman *n* iasgair *m*
fishing *n* iasgach *m* **f.-line** driamlach *f m* **f.-rod** slat-iasgaich *f*
fishmonger *n* reiceadair èisg *m*
fissure *n* sgoltadh *m*, sgàineadh *m*
fist *n* dòrn *m*
fit *n* cuairt *f*, taom *m* **he took a fit** thàinig cuairt air
fit *a* fallain; (*suitable*) iomchaidh, cubhaidh *v* dèan freagarrach, cuir an òrdugh; (*suit*) freagair
fitful *a* plathach
fitness *a* fallaineachd *f*; (*suitability*) freagarrachd *f*
fitting *a* iomchaidh, cubhaidh
five *n*, a còig *a* còig **f. people** còignear *f m*
fix *v* suidhich, socraich; (*mend*) càirich **that'll fix him** bheir siud air
fixture *n* rud suidhichte *m*; (*sport*) gèam *m*, maids *m* **f. list** clàr-gheamannan *m*
flabby *a* plamach, bog
flag *n* bratach *f* **flagpole** brat-chrann *m*
flagrant *a* dalma, ladarna
flagship *n* prìomh long *f* *a* suaicheanta
flail *n* sùist *f*
flair *n* liut *m*, alt *m*
flake *n* bleideag *f*
flame *n* lasair *f*
flammable *a* lasanta
flan *n* flana *m*
flank *n* slios *m*, taobh *m*
flap *n* flapa *m* **in a f.** na b(h)oil *etc* *v* crath
flare *n* lasair-bhoillsg *m*
flash *n* lasadh *m*, boillsgeadh *m* *v* deàlraich, boillsg, las
flashback *n* ais-shealladh *m*
flashing *a* boillsgeach
flask *n* flasg *m*, searrag *f*, buideal *m*
flat *n* còmhnard *m*; (*residence*) flat *f m* **f. calm** fèath nan eun *f m* *a* còmhnard, rèidh; (*met*) neo-bheothail; (*mus*) maol, flat
flatten *v* dèan rèidh; (*mus*) maolaich
flatter *v* dèan brosgal/miodal/sodal
flattering *a* brosgalach, sodalach
flattery *n* brosgal *m*, miodal *m*, sodal *m*
flatulence *n* gaothaireachd *f*
flavour *n* blas *m*
flaw *n* meang *f*, gaoid *f*
flax *n* lìon *m*
flea *n* deargann *f*, deargad *f*
flee *v* teich, tàrr às

fleece *n* rùsg *m*; (*garment*) seacaid-bhlàth *f*
fleet *n* cabhlach *m*, loingeas *m*
flesh *n* feòil *f*
flex *n* fleisg *f*, càball *m*
flexibility *n* sùbailteachd *f*, subailteachd *f*
flexible *a* sùbailte, subailte, so-lùbach
flicker *v* priob
flight *n* (*in air*) iteag *m*, iteal(adh) *m*; (*on plane*) turas-adhair *m*; (*escape*) teicheadh *m*, ruaig *f*; (*of imagination*) ruith-inntinn *f*
flimsy *a* tana, lag **f. excuse** leisgeul bochd *m*
flinch *v* clisg
fling *v* tilg, caith
flint *n* ailbhinn *f*, spor *m*
flippant *a* beadaidh
flirt *n* beadrach *f*, gogaid *f* *v* beadraich, dèan beadradh
flit *v* èalaidh; (*move house*) dèan imrich
flitting *n* (*moving house*) imprig *f*, imrich *f*
float *n* puta *m*, fleòdragan *m*
float *v* flod, bi a'/air fleòdradh, bi air bhog
flock *n* treud *m*, (*birds*) ealt(a) *f*
flood *n* tuil *f*, dìle *f* **f.-gate** tuil-dhoras *m* *v* còmhdaich le uisge
flooded *a* fo uisge, bàthte
flooding *n* tuileachadh *m*
floor *n* làr *m*, ùrlar *m* **f.-board** clàr ùrlair *m*, bòrd an ùrlair *m*
floppy disc *n* clàr-bog *m*
floral *a* flùr(an)ach, dìtheanach
florid *a* ruiteach
florist *n* reiceadair-fhlùraichean *m*
flounder *n* lèabag *f*, leòbag *f*
flour *n* flùr *m*, min-fhlùir *f*
flourish *v* fàs, rach gu math le; (*brandish*) steòrn le
flow *n* sruth *m*, sileadh *m* **f. chart** sruth-chlàr *m*, clàr-ruith *m* **f.-tide** sruth-lìonaidh *v* sruth, ruith, sil
flower *n* flùr *m*, dìthean *m*, blàth *m*
flowery *a* flùr(an)ach, dìtheanach
flu *n* an cnatan mòr *m*
fluctuate *v* luaisg, atharraich (bho àm gu àm)
fluent *a* fileanta, siùbhlach **f. speaker** fileantach *m*
fluid *n* lionn *m*
fluke *n* (*chance*) turchairt *m*, tuiteamas *m*; (*of anchor*) fliùt *m*, pliuthan *m*; (*worm*) cnuimh *f*, cruimh *f*
fluoride *n* fluoraid *m*
flurry *n* othail *f*
flush *n* (*facial*) rudhadh *m* *v* fàs dearg; (*toilet*) sruthlaich
fluster *v* cuir an cabhaig, cuir troimh-a-chèile
flute *n* duiseal *f*, cuisle-chiùil *f*
flutter *v* (*fly*) dèan itealaich, sgiathalaich
flux *n* sruthadh *m*, ruith *f*
fly *n* cuileag *f*; (*fishing*) maghar *m*
fly *a* carach, seòlta
fly *v* rach/falbh air iteig, itealaich; (*escape*) teich
flying *n* itealaich *f*, sgiathalaich *f*
foal *n* searrach *m*, loth *f m*
foam *n* cop *m*, cobhar *m*
focus *n* fòcas *m* *v* dèan fòcas air, cuimsich air
fodder *n* fodar *m*
foe *n* nàmhaid *m*, eascaraid *m*
foetus *n* ginean *m*, toircheas *m*
fog *n* ceò *f m*
foggy *a* ceòthach
foible *n* laigse bheag *f*
foil *v* cuir casg air, bac
fold *n* filleadh *m*, preas *m*; (*animal*) buaile *f*, crò *m* *v* paisg, fill
folder *n* pasgan *m*
foliage *n* duilleach *m*
folk *n* muinntir *f*, sluagh *m*, poball *m*, daoine *m pl* **f. music** ceòl dùthchasach *m* **folksong** mith-òran *m* **folktale** mith-sgeul *m*, sgeulachd *f* **folklore** beul-aithris *f*
follow *v* lean, thig an dèidh **as follows** mar a leanas
following *a* **the f. ...** an/am/an t-/a' ... a leanas **a f. wind** gaoth na c(h)ùl *etc*
folly *n* gòraiche *f*, amaideas *m*
fond *a* (*of*) dèidheil/measail/

miadhail air **a f. mother** màthair chaomh *f*
fondle *v* cnèadaich, tataidh
font *n* amar(-baistidh) *m*; (*type*) clò *m*
food *n* biadh *m*, lòn *m*
fool *n* amadan *m*, gloidhc *f* **female f.** òinseach *f* *v* meall, thoir an car à
foolish *a* gòrach, amaideach
foot *n* cas *f*, troigh *f*; (*of hill*) bonn *m*, bun *m*; (*in length*) troigh *f* **f. and mouth disease** an galar roil(l)each/ronnach *m* **football** ball-coise *m* **footpath** frith-rathad *m* **footprint** lorg-coise *f* **footstep** cas-cheum *m*
for *prep* do, ri, airson (+ *gen*), fad **he left this for you** dh'fhàg e seo dhut **wait for me** fuirich rium **they'll be here for a week** bidh iad an seo airson/fad seachdain **we paid £100 for it** phàigh/thug sinn ceud not air
forbearance *n* foighidinn *f*
forbid *v* toirmisg
forbidden *a* toirmisgte
force *n* neart *m*, cumhachd *f m* **the Armed Forces** Feachdan na Dùthcha *f pl* **undue f.** làmhachas-làidir *m* *v* co-èignich, thoir air, spàrr (air) **she forced her to do it** thug i oirre a dhèanamh
forceful *a* neartmhor
ford *n* àth *m*; (*between islands*) fadhail *f*
forecast *n* ro-aithris *f*, ro-amas *m* **weather f.** tuairmse sìde *f* *v* dèan ro-aithris, dèan ro-amas; (*weather*) dèan tuairmse air an t-sìde
forefather *n* sinnsear *m* **forefathers** na h-athraichean *m pl*
forefront *n* fìor thoiseach *m* **in the f. of the campaign** air ceann na h-iomairt
forego *v* leig seachad, dèan às aonais
forehead *n* bathais *f*, maoil *f*, mala *f*
foreign *a* coimheach, cian **F. Office** Oifis nan Dùthchannan Cèin *f*
foreigner *n* coigreach *m*
forelock *n* dosan *m*, logan *m*
foreman *n* gafair *m*
foremost *a* prìomh *adv* air thoiseach
forenoon *n* ro mheadhan-latha *m*, ro-nòin *m*
forensic *a* foireansach
foresee *v* faic ro-làimh
foresight *n* ro-shealladh *m*; (*met*) lèirsinn *f*
forest *n* coille *f* **deer f.** frìth *f*
forester *n* forsair *m*, coillteear *m*
forestry *n* forsaireachd *f*, coillteareachd *f* **F. Commission** Coimisean na Coille *m*
foretaste *n* blasad ro-làimh *m*, ro-aithne *f*
foretell *v* fàisnich
forever *adv* gu bràth, gu sìorraidh, a-chaoidh **f. more** gu bràth tuilleadh
forewarn *v* cuir air earalas
foreword *n* ro-ràdh *m*
forfeit *v* caill (còir air)
forge *n* teallach *m*, ceàrdach *f* *v* dealbh à meatailt; (*document etc*) feall-dheilbh, sgrìobh gu fallsa; (*links etc*) stèidhich
forgery *n* fallsaidheachd *f*, meall-sgrìobhadh *m*
forget *v* dìochuimhnich
forgetful *a* dìochuimhneach
forgive *v* math, thoir mathanas
forgiveness *n* mathanas *m*
fork *n* forc(a) *f*, greimire *m*; (*in road*) gobhal *m*
form *n* cumadh *m*, cruth *m*, riochd *m*, dealbh *f m*; (*document*) foirm *m*; (*mood*) cor *m*, triom *f m*; (*seat*) furm *m* **in good f.** an deagh shunnd *v* dealbh, cum, cruthaich, cuir ri chèile
formal *a* foirmeil, riaghailteach
formality *n* foirmealachd *f*, deas-ghnàth *m* **a f.** gnàths *m*
format *n* cruth *m*
formation *n* cumadh *m*, eagar *m*
former *a* a chaidh seachad, a bha ann (roimhe)
formidable *a* foghainteach

formula *n* foirmle *f*
formulate *v* riaghailtich, cuir ri chèile
fornication *n* strìopachas *f*
forsake *v* trèig, dìobair, cuir cùl ri
fort *n* dùn *m*, daingneach *f*
forth *adv* a-mach, air adhart **from this time f.** o seo a-mach/suas
forthcoming *a* a' tighinn, ri teachd; (*open*) fosgarra
forthright *a* dìreach, fosgailte
forthwith *adv* gun dàil
fortieth *a* dà fhicheadamh
fortify *v* daingnich, neartaich
fortitude *n* tapachd *f*, fiùghantachd *f*
fortnight *n* cola-deug *f*, ceala-deug *f*
fortress *n* daingneach *f*
fortuitous *a* tuiteamach
fortunate *a* fortanach, sealbhach
fortune *n* fortan *m*, sealbh *m*, àgh *m*
forty *n*, *a* dà fhichead *m*, ceathrad *m* **f. winks** norrag *f*
forum *n* fòram *m*
forward *a* iarrtach, aghach
forward(s) *adv* air adhart *v* adhartaich, cuir air adhart
fossil *n* fosail *f* **f.-fuel** connadh-fosail *m*
foster *v* altraim, àraich
foster-father *n* oide *m*
fosterling *n* dalta *m*
foster-mother *n* muime *f*
foul *n* fealladh *m*
foul *a* salach, gràineil, breun *v* salaich, gànraich; (*sport*) dèan fealladh
found *v* stèidhich, suidhich, bunaitich
foundation *n* stèidh *f*, bunait *f m*; (*org*) stèidheachd *f*
founder *v* theirig fodha
foundry *n* leaghadair *m*, ionad leaghaidh *m*
fountain *n* fuaran *m*
four *n* a ceithir *a* ceithir **f. people** ceathrar *f m*
fourteen *n*, *a* ceithir-deug **f. fish** ceithir iasg deug
fourteenth *a* ceathramh deug
fourth *a* ceathramh
fowl *n* eun *m*
fox *n* sionnach *m*, madadh-ruadh *m*
foxglove *n* lus nam ban-sìth *m*
foyer *n* for-thalla *m*
fraction *n* mìr *m*, bloigh *f*
fracture *n* bris(t)eadh *m* *v* bris(t), bloighdich
fragile *a* brisg, lag
fragment *n* fuidheall *m*, bloigh *f*, criomag *f*, mìr *m*
fragmented *a* bìdeagach, às a chèile
fragrance *n* cùbhraidheachd *f*
fragrant *a* cùbhraidh
frail *a* lag, anfhann
frame *n* frèam *m*, cèis *f*; (*of mind*) staid-inntinn *f*
framework *n* frèam *m*
franchise *n* còir *f*, còrachd *f*, ceadachd *f*
frank *a* faoilidh, fosgailte
frantic *a* air bhoil(e), air chuthach
fraternal *a* bràithreil
fraud *n* foill *f*
fraudulent *a* foilleil, fealltach
fray *v* bleith, sgaoil
freak *n* cùis-iongnaidh *f* **a f. event** fìor thuiteamas *m*
freckled *a* breac-bhallach
freckles *n* breacadh-seunain *m*
free *a* saor; (*of charge*) an asgaidh *v* saor, leig fa sgaoil
freedom *n* saorsa *f*, saorsainn *f*, cead *m*
freelance *a* ag obair air a c(h)eann fhèin
freemason *n* saor-chlachair *m*
freeze *n* reothadh *m* *v* reoth; (*stop*) cuir casg air
freezer *n* reothadair *m*
freight *n* luchd *m*; (*charge*) faradh *m*
French *n* **the F.** na Frangaich *m pl* *a* Frangach; (*lang*) Fraingis *f*
Frenchman *n* Frangach *m* **Frenchwoman** ban-Fhrangach *f*
frenetic *a* air bhoil(e)
frenzy *n* boil(e) *f*
frequent *a* tric, minig, bitheanta
frequent *v* tadhail, tathaich
frequently *adv* gu tric, gu minig
fresh *a* (*produce*) ùr; (*atmos*) fionnar

freshen *v* ùraich
freshness *n* ùrachd *f*, ùralachd *f*
fret *v* luaisg, bi frionasach
friction *n* suathadh (ri chèile) *m*, bleith *f*; (*discord*) eas-aonta *m*
Friday *n* Dihaoine *m*
fridge *n* fuaradair *m*, frids *m*
friend *n* caraid *m* **female f.** banacharaid *f*
friendly *a* càirdeil, dàimheil
friendship *n* càirdeas *m*, dàimh *f m*
fright *n* eagal *m*, clisgeadh *m*
frighten *v* cuir eagal air **were you frightened?** an robh an t-eagal ort?
frightening *a* eagalach
frightful *a* eagalach, oillteil
frigid *a* fuar
frill *n* fraoidhneas *m* **without any frills** gun spaidealachd sam bith
fringe *n* fraoidhneas *m*, oir *f m*, iomall *m*; (*hair*) logaidh *f* **the Festival F.** Iomall na Fèise
frisky *a* mear, mireagach
frivolous *a* faoin, luideach
frock *n* froga *m*
frog *n* losgann *m*
from *prep* (bh)o, à **f. time to time** (bh)o àm gu àm **f. dawn till dusk** o mhoch gu dubh, **a man from Uist** fear à Uibhist
front *n* aghaidh *f*, aodann *m*, toiseach *m*, beulaibh *m* **in f.** air thoiseach **in f. of** air beulaibh (+ *gen*)
frontier *n* crìoch *f*
frost *n* reothadh *m*
frosty *a* reòthte **a f. reception** fàilte glè fhuar
froth *n* cop *m*
frown *n* gruaim *f*, sgraing *f*, greann *f*
frozen *a* reòthte, reothta
frugal *a* glèidhteach, caomhntach
fruit *n* meas *m*; (*produce*) toradh *m* **f.-cake** cèic-mheasan *f m* **f. juice** sùgh mheasan *m*
fruitful *a* torrach; (*successful*) soirbheachail
fruition *n* buil *f* **come to f.** thig gu buil *v*
fruitless *a* neo-thorrach; (*met*) gun tairbhe **a f. expedition/exercise** siubhal gun siùcar
frustrate *v* leamhaich; (*hinder*) cuir bacadh air
fry *v* ròst, fraighig, praighig
frying-pan *n* aghann *f*, praigheapan *m*
fuel *n* connadh *m*
fugitive *n* fògarrach *m*
fulfil *v* coilean
fulfilled *a* coilcanta, sàsaichte
full *a* làn, iomlan **f. to the brim** loma-làn **f. moon** gealach (sh)làn *f* **f.-time** làn-thìde, làn-ùine
full stop *n* (*punct*) stad-phuing *f*
fulmar *m* fulmair *m*
fumble *v* làimhsich gu cearbach, bi cliobach
fumes *n* deatach *f*, smùid *f*
fun *n* fealla-dhà *f*, dibhearsain *m*, spòrs *f*
function *n* feum *m*; (*of person*) dreuchd *f*; (*event*) cruinneachadh *m* *v* obraich
fund *n* maoin *f*, stòr *m* **funds** ionmhas *m*, airgead *m* *v* maoinich
fundamental *a* bunaiteach
fundraising *n* togail-airgid *f*
funeral *n* tiodhlacadh *m*, adhlacadh *m*, tòrradh *m* **f. procession** giùlan *m*
funnel *n* pìob-tharraing *f*; (*on ship*) luidhear *m*
funny *a* èibhinn, ait
fur *n* bian *m*
furious *a* fiadhaich, air/fon chuthach
furnace *n* fùirneis *f*
furnish *v* cuir àirneis an; (*provide*) thoir do, uidheamaich
furniture *n* àirneis *f* **item of f.** ball àirneis *m*
furrow *n* clais *f*, sgrìob *f*; (*wrinkle*) roc *f*, preas *m*
furry *a* molach, ròmach
further *v* cuir air adhart, adhartaich *a*, *adv* a bharrachd
further education *n* foghlam adhartach *m*
furthermore *adv* rud eile, a thuilleadh air sin, cho math ri sin, a bhàrr/bharrachd air sin

furtive *a* fàil(l)idh
fury *n* cuthach *m*
fuse *n* fiùs(a) *m*
fusion *n* leaghadh *m*, aonadh *m*
fuss *n* othail *f*, ùpraid *f*
fussy *a* àilgheasach, tàrmasach
futile *a* dìomhain, faoin
future *n* àm ri teachd *m* *a* ri teachd, teachdail **f. tense** an tràth teachdail *m*

G

gadget *n* uidheam *f*, magaid *f*
Gael *n* Gàidheal *m*, (*female*) bana-Ghàidheal *f*
Gaelic *n*, *a* Gàidhlig *f* (*usually with def art*) a' Ghàidhlig
gag *v* cuir glas-ghuib air
gain *n* buannachd *f* *v* buannaich, coisinn; (*reach*) ruig
gait *n* dòigh-gluasaid *f*
galaxy *n* Slighe Chlann Uisnich *f*, reul-chrios *m*
gale *n* gèile *m*, gaoth mhòr *f*
gallant *a* (*chivalrous*) flathail; (*spirited*) meanmnach **a g. effort** oidhirp thapaidh
gallery *n* gailearaidh *f m*, lobhta *m*
galley *n* birlinn *f*; (*kitchen*) cidsin *m*
galling *a* leamh, doimheadach
gallon *n* galan *m*
gallop *v* falbh aig roid; (*on horseback*) luath-mharcaich
gallows *n* croich *f*
galore *adv* gu leòr
gamble *v* cuir airgead air gheall, dèan ceàrrachas
gambler *n* ceàrraiche *m*
gambling *n* ceàrrachas *m*
game *n* gèam *m*, cluiche *f*; (*food etc*) sitheann *f*
gamekeeper *n* geamair *m*
gander *n* gànradh *m*, gèadh fireann *m*
gang *n* buidheann *m*, foireann *m*
gannet *n* sùlaire *m* **g. chick** guga *m*
gap *n* beàrn *f m*; (*topog*) bealach *m*
garage *n* garaids *f* *v* cuir ann an garaids
garbage *n* sgudal *m*
garbled *a* troimh-a-chèile
garden *n* gàrradh *m*, lios *m*
gardener *n* gàirnealair *m*, gàrradair *m*
gardening *n* gàirnealaireachd *f*, gàrradaireachd *f*
gargle *v* sruthail
garlic *n* creamh *m*
garment *n* bad aodaich *m*
garrison *n* gearastan *m*
garrulous *a* cabach, goileamach
gas *n* gas *m* **gas cooker** cucair gas *m* **gas fire** teine gas *m* *v* mùch le gas, sgaoil gas
gash *n* gearradh *m*, lot domhainn *m*, beum *m* *v* geàrr, sgor
gasp *n* plosg *m*, ospag *f* *v* plosg
gastric *a* meirbheach
gastronomic *a* sòghail
gate *n* geata *m*, cachaileith *f*
gather *v* cruinnich, tionail, trus; (*money*) tog
gathering *n* cruinneachadh *m*, co-chruinneachadh *m*
gaudy *a* bastalach
gauge *n* tomhas *m* *v* tomhais, meas
gaunt *a* caol, seang, tana, lom
gay *a* sunndach, sùgach, aighearach; (*homosexual*) co-ghnèitheach, co-sheòrsach
gaze *v* dùr-amhairc
gear *n* uidheam *f*, àirneis *f*; (*clothes*) trusgan *m*; (*in engine*) giodhar *f*
gem *n* seud *m*, neamhnaid *f*, leug *f*
gender *n* (*gram*) gnè *f*; (*sex*) gin *f*
gene *n* gine *f*
genealogical *a* sloinnteachail
genealogist *n* sloinntear *m*
genealogy *n* sloinntearachd *f*
general *n* seanailear *m*
general *a* coitcheann, cumanta **in g.** sa bhitheantas, sa chumantas **G. Election** Taghadh Coitcheann *m*, Taghadh Pàrlamaid *m*
generalize *v* coitcheannaich
generally *adv* am bitheantas, sa bhitheantas
generate *v* gin, tàrmaich
generation *n* ginealach *m*, glùn *f*;

(*creation*) gineamhainn *m*
g. gap sgaradh nan ginealach *m*
generator *n* gineadair *m*
generic *a* gnèitheach, coitcheann
generosity *n* còiread *f*, fialaidheachd *f*, fiùghantachd *f*
generous *a* còir, fialaidh, faoilidh
genesis *n* gineachas *m*, toiseach *m*
genetic *a* ginteil
genetics *n* ginntinneachd *f*
genial *a* dàimheil, cridheil, aoigheil
genitals *n* buill-gineamhainn *m pl*
genitive *a* ginideach **the g. case** an tuiseal ginideach/seilbheach *m*
genius *n* (*person*) sàr-ghin *m*; (*quality*) sàr-ghineachas *m*, sàr-chomas *m*
gentle *a* ciùin, socair, soitheamh
gentleman *n* duin(e)-uasal *m*
genuine *a* fìor, dha-rìribh
geography *n* cruinn-eòlas *m*
geologist *n* clach-eòlaiche *m*
geology *n* clach-eòlas *m*
geometry *n* geoimeatraidh *m*
germ *n* bitheag *f*
German *n*, *a* Gearmailteach *m*, (*female*) ban-Ghearmailteach *f*; (*lang*) Gearmailtis *f*
germinate *v* ginidich, thoir fàs; (*intrans*) fàs
get *v* faigh; (*grow*) fàs **g. away!** thalla! **get dressed** cuir aodach ort **get rid of** faigh cuidhteas **getting on for ...** a' streap ri ... **get the better of** faigh làmh-an-uachdair air **get used to** fàs cleachdte ri
ghastly *a* oillteil, sgriosail
ghost *n* taibhs(e) *f m* tannasg *m*, bòcan *m* **the Holy G.** an Spiorad Naomh *m*
ghostly *a* taibhseil
giant *n* famhair *m*, fuamhaire *m*
giddy *a* tuainealach; (*met*) guanach, faoin
gift *n* tiodhlac *m*, gibht *f*
gifted *a* comasach, tàlantach
gigantic *a* àibheiseach mòr
giggle *v* dèan braoisgeil *Also vn* a' braoisgeil, a' cireaslaich
gimmick *n* innleachd *f*
gin *n* (*drink*) sine *f*, Sineubhar *f*; (*trap*) ribe *m*
ginger *n* dinnsear *m*
gingerbread *n* aran-crì/cridhe *m*
giraffe *n* sioraf *m*
girl *n* caileag *f*, nighean *f*
girlfriend *n* leannan *f*, bràmair *m*
gist *n* brìgh *f*
give *v* thoir, tabhair **g. up** leig seachad/thoir thairis
glacier *n* eigh-shruth *m*
glad *a* toilichte, aoibhinn
gladden *v* toilich, dèan aoibhneach
gladness *n* toil-inntinn *f*, aoibhneas *m*, toileachas *m*
glamour *n* riochdalachd *f*
glance *n* sùil aithghearr *f* *v* grad-amhairc
gland *n* fàireag *f*
glare *n* deàrrsadh *m*, dalladh *m*; (*look*) sùil fhiadhaich *f*; (*of publicity*) làn-fhollais *f* *v* thoir sùil fhiadhaich
glaring *a* (*obvious*) làn-fhollaiseach
glass *n* glainne *f* **g.-house** taigh-glainne *m*
glasses *n* glainneachan *f pl*, speuclairean *m pl*, speuclair *m*
gleam *n* boillsgeadh *m* *v* boillsg, soillsich, deàrrs
gleaming *a* boillsgeach, deàrrsach
glee *n* mire *f*, cridhealas *m*
glen *n* gleann *m*
glib *a* mìn-chainnteach, cabanta
glide *v* sigh, gluais gu ciùin
glider *n* glaidhdear *m*, plèan-seòlaidh *m*
glimmer *n* fann-sholas *m*
glimpse *n* aiteal *m*, boillsgeadh *m*, plathadh *m* *v* faigh sealladh (aithghearr) de
glisten *v* deàlraich, boillsg
glitter *n* lainnir *f* *v* deàrrs, boillsg, dèan lainnir/drithleann
glittering *a* boillsgeach, lainnireach
global *a* domhanta, cruinne, cruinneil **g. warming** blàthachadh na cruinne *m*
globe *n* cruinne *m* (*f in gen*)
gloom *n* duibhre *f*; (*dejection*) gruaim *f*, smalan *m*

gloomy *a* doilleir, gruamach; (*dejected*) fo ghruaim, smalanach
glorious *a* glòrmhor, òirdheirc
glory *n* glòir *f*
gloss *n* lìomh *f*; (*explanation*) mìneachadh *m* *v* lìomh; (*explain*) mìnich
glossy *a* gleansach, lìomharra
glove *n* miotag *f*
glow *n* lasadh *f*, blàthachadh *m* *v* deàrrs, las
glue *n* glaodh *m* *v* glaodh, tàth
glum *a* tùrsach, gruamach
glut *n* cus *m*, tuilleadh 's a' chòir *m*
glutton *n* glutaire *m*, geòcaire *m*, craosaire *m*
gnarled *a* meallach, plucach
gnash *v* gìosg
gnat *n* corr-mhial *f*
gnaw *v* creim, cagainn
go *v* falbh, imich, rach, theirig **go away!** thalla! **let him go** leig às e **go on/ahead** siuthad
goad *v* brod, greas; (*met*) stuig, cuir thuige
goal *n* ceann-uidhe *m*; (*in sport*) gòil *m*; (*score*) tadhal *m*, gòil *m* **goalkeeper** neach-gleidhidh *m*
goat *n* gobhar *f m*
God, god *n* Dia, dia *m*
goddess *n* ban-dia *f*
godly *a* diadhaidh
gold *n* òr *m*
gold(en) *a* òir, òrail, òrdha, òr-bhuidhe
golden eagle *n* fìr-eun *m*, iolaire-bhuidhe *f*
goldfish *n* iasg òir *m*, òr-iasg *m*
golf *n* goilf *m* **g.-club** caman goilf *m*; (*org*) comann goilf *m* **g.-course** raon goilf *m*
golfer *n* goilfear *m*
good *a* math, deagh (*precedes & len n*) **g.-natured** dòigheil, mèinneil **g.-looking** brèagha, eireachdail *n* math *m*
goodbye *n*, *interj* slàn le, beannachd le **g. (to you)** slàn leat, beannachd leat **she said g. to them** dh'fhàg i slàn aca
Good Friday *n* Dihaoine na Ceusta/a' Cheusaidh/na Càisge *m*
goodness *n* mathas *m*, deagh-bheus *f* (**My**) **g.!** A chiall!
goods *n* bathar *m*, cuid *f*, maoin *f* **g. train** trèan bathair *m*
goodwill *n* deagh-ghean *m*, deagh mhèin *f*
goose *n* gèadh *m*
gorge *n* (*topog*) clais mhòr *f*, mòr-ghil *f*; (*gullet*) slugan *m* *v* lìon craos
gorgeous *a* eireachdail, greadhnach, rìomhach
gorse *n* conasg *m*
gospel *n* soisgeul *m*
gossip *n* geodal *m*, fothal *m*; (*person*) goistidh *m* *v* bi a' gobaireachd, bi a' fothal
gouge (out) *v* buin à, cladhaich à
govern *v* riaghail, seòl
government *n* riaghaltas *m*, riaghladh *m* **the G.** an Riaghaltas *m*
governor *n* riaghladair *m*
gown *n* gùn *m*
grab *v* faigh/gabh grèim air
grace *n* gràs *m*; (*prayer*) altachadh *m*; (*quality*) loinn *f*, eireachdas *m* *v* sgeadaich, maisich, cuir loinn air
graceful *a* grinn
grade *n* ìre *f* *v* cuir an òrdugh, rangaich
gradient *n* àrdachadh *m*, ìsleachadh *m*, caisead *m*
gradual *a* beag air bheag, ceum air cheum, mean air mhean
gradually *adv* beag air bheag, ceum air cheum, mean air mhean
graduate *v* ceumnaich
graft *n* nòdachadh *m*; (*fin*) slaightearachd *f* *v* nòdaich
grain *n* gràinne *f*, gràinnean *m*, sìlean *m*; (*coll*) gràn *m*, sìol *m*
gram *n* gram *m*
grammar *n* gràmar *m*
grammatical *a* gramataigeach, gràmarach
grand *a* mòr, prìomh (*precedes & len n*) **that's g.** tha sin gasta
grandchild *n* ogha *m*
grandfather *n* seanair *m*

grandmother *n* seanmhair *f*
granite *n* clach-ghràin *f*, eibhir *f*
grant *n* tabhartas *m* *v* (*allow*) ceadaich, deònaich; (*bestow*) builich **g. aid** thoir tabhartas-cuideachaidh
granule *n* gràinean *m*, gràineag *f*
grape *n* fìon-dhearc *f*
grapefruit *n* seadag *f*
graph *n* graf *m*
grasp *v* dèan grèim air, greimich, glac
grass *n* feur *m*
grasshopper *n* fionnan-feòir *m*
grassroots *n* ìre an t-sluaigh *f* **at the g.** aig ìre an t-sluaigh
grate *n* grèata *m* *v* sgrìob, thoir sgreuch air; (*met*) bi mì-thaitneach
grateful *a* taingeil
grater *n* sgrìoban *m*
gratify *v* toilich, sàsaich
gratifying *a* riarachail, sàsachail
grating *a* sgreuchach, sgreadach
gratitude *n* taingealachd *f*, buidheachas *m*
grave *n* uaigh *f* **graveyard** cladh *m*
grave *a* stòlda, suidhichte
grave accent *n* stràc fhada *m*
gravel *n* greabhal *m*, grinneal *m*, morghan *m*
gravity *n* (*force*) iom-tharraing *f*; (*mass*) dùmhlachd *f*; (*seriousness*) sòlaimteachd *f*
gravy *n* sùgh feòla *m*, grèibhidh *m*
graze *v* feuraich, ionaltraich, bi ag ionaltradh; (*touch*) suath (an)
grease *n* saill *f*, crèis *f*
greasy *a* crèiseach
great *a* mòr, àrd
great-grandchild *n* iar-ogha *m*
great-grandfather *n* sinn-seanair *m*
great-grandmother *n* sinn-seanmhair *f*
greatness *n* mòrachd *f*; (*size*) meudachd *f*
greed *n* sannt *m*, gionaiche *m*
greedy *a* sanntach, gionach
Greek *n*, *a* Greugach *m*, (*female*) ban-Ghreugach *f*; (*lang*) Greugais *f*
green *a* uaine; (*of grass*) gorm, glas; (*inexperienced*) gorm *n* (dath) uaine *m*; (*grass*) rèidhlean *m*, faiche *f* **G. Party** am Partaidh Uaine *m*
greenhouse *n* taigh-glainne *m*
greet *v* fàiltich, cuir fàilte air, beannaich do
greeting *n* fàilte *f*, beannachadh *m*
grey *a* glas, liath **g. area** cùis neo-chinnteach *f* **g.-haired** liath
grid *n* cliath *f*
grief *n* bròn *m*, mulad *m*
grievance *n* cùis-ghearain *f*
grieve *v* caoidh
grill *n* (*cooking*) grìosach *f* *v* grìosaich
grim *a* mùgach, gnù
grimace *n* drèin *f*, gruaim *f*, mùig *m*
grin *n* braoisg *f* *v* cuir braoisg air/oirre *etc*
grind *v* meil, bleith, pronn
grip *n* grèim *m*
grisly *a* oillteil, dèisinneach
grit *n* grinneal *m*, garbhan *m*; (*of character*) tapachd *f*
groan *n* cnead *m*, osann *m*, osna *f* *v* dèan cnead/osna
grocer *n* grosair *m*
groin *n* loch-bhlèin *f*
groom *n* gille-each *m*; (*bridegroom*) fear na bainnse *m*
groove *n* clais *f*, eag *f*
grope *v* fairich, rùraich
gross *a* garbh, dòmhail; (*whole*) iomlan; (*disgusting*) sgreamhail
grotesque *a* suaitheanta, mì-dhealbhach, mì-nàdarrach
ground *n* grunnd *m*, talamh *m*, fonn *m*; (*foundation*) (bonn-)stèidh *f*; (*in piping*) ùrlar *m* **grounds** adhbhar *m* **g. floor** làr ìosal *m* *a* pronn
groundwork *n* stèidh *f*, deasachadh *m*
group *n* buidheann *f m*, còmhlan *m* **g. work** obair-buidhne *f*
group *v* cuir am buidhnean
grouse *n* cearc-fhraoich *f*, coileach-fraoich *m*; (*complaint*) gearan *m*

grovel *v* snàig, liùg
grow *v* fàs, cinn, cinnich, meudaich; (*trans*) thoir fàs air
growl *n* dranndan *m*, grùnsgal *m* *v* dèan dranndan
growth *n* fàs *m*, cinneas *m*, toradh *m*
grudge *n* diomb *f m*, doicheall *m* *v* sòr, talaich
gruff *a* gnuadh, durg(h)a, neo-aoigheil; (*voice*) greannach
grumble *v* gearain, talaich, dèan cànran
grumbling *n* gearan *m*
grunt *n* gnòsail *f*, gnòsad *f* *v* dèan gnòsail/gnòsad
guarantee *n* urras *m*, barantas *m* *v* rach an urras, barantaich
guard *n* (*person*) geàrd *m*, freiceadan *m*; (*watch*) faire *f*, dìon *m* *v* geàrd, glèidh, dìon
guardian *n* neach-gleidhidh *m*, neach-cùraim *m*
guess *n* tomhas *m*, tuairmse *f*, tuaiream *f* *v* tomhais, thoir tuairmse/tuairmeas
guest *n* aoigh *m* **g.-house** taigh-aoigheachd *m*
guidance *n* stiùireadh *m*, iùl *m*, treòrachadh *m*, seòladh *m* **g. teacher** tidsear treòrachaidh *m*
guide *n* neach-iùil/treòrachaidh *m* **guide-book** leabhar-iùil *m* *v* seòl, stiùir, treòraich
guidelines *n* seòladh *m*, stiùireadh *m*
guile *n* foill *f*, cealg *f*
guilt *n* ciont(a) *m*
guilty *a* ciontach
guinea-pig *n* gearra-mhuc *f*; (*met*) ball-sampaill *m*
guise *n* riochd *m*
guitar *n* giotàr *m*
gulf *n* camas mòr *m*, bàgh mòr *m*; (*met*) astar mòr *m*
gull *n* faoileag *f*
gullet *n* goile *f*, sgòrnan *m*, slugan *m*
gullible *a* so-mheallta, furasta an car a thoirt às/aiste *etc*
gulp *n* slugadh *m*, glacadh *m* *v* sluig, glac, glut
gum *n* càirean *m*, bannas *m*; (*glue*) glaodh *m*, bìth *f* **chewing gum** guma cagnaidh *m*
gumption *n* ciall *f*, toinisg *f*
gun *n* gunna *m*
gunwale *n* beul(-mòr) *m*
gurgle *n* glugan *m* *v* dèan glugan/plubraich
gush *n* spùt, brùchd
gust *n* oiteag *f*, osag *f*, cuairt-ghaoth *f*
gusty *a* oiteagach, gaothar
gut *n* caolan *m* **you've got guts** tha misneach(d) agad *v* cut, thoir am mionach à
gutter *n* guitear *m*; (*of fish*) cutair *m*
guy *n* fear *m* **come on, guys** siuthadaibh, fhearaibh
gymnasium *n* lann lùth-chleas *f*, talla spòrs *m*
gymnast *n* lùth-chleasaiche *m*
gymnastics *n* lùth-chleasachd *f*
gynaecology *n* lèigh-eòlas bhan *m*
gypsy *n* siopsach *m*, giofag *f*, rasaiche *m*

H

habit *n* cleachdadh *m*, fasan *m*, àbhaist *f*, nòs *m*; (*clothing*) earradh *m*, èideadh *m*
habitable *a* freagarrach airson còmhnaidh
habitat *n* àrainn *f*
habitual *a* gnàthach *adv* daonnan, gu gnàthach
hack *v* geàrr, spòlt, sgolt, sgoch
haddock *n* adag *f*
haemorrhage *n* sileadh/dòrtadh-fala *m*
hag *n* badhbh *f*, sgroidhd *f*
haggis *n* taigeis *f*
haggle *v* barganaich, dèan còmhstri mu phrìs
hail *n* clach-mheallain *f*, (*hailstones*) clachan-meallain *pl*
hair *n* falt *m*, gruag *f*; (*one*) gaoisnean *m*, fuiltean *m*, ròineag *f*; (*of animals*) gaoisid *f*, fionnadh *m* **h.-brush** bruis-chinn/fhuilt *f* **h.-dryer** tiormadair gruaige *m*

haircut *n* cliop *m*, bearradh fuilt *m*
hairdresser *n* gruagaire *m*
hairy *a* gaoisideach, molach, ròmach, fionnach
hale *a* slàn, fallain **h. and hearty** slàn fallain
half *n* leth *m* **h. past one** leth-uair an dèidh uair **h. a pound** leth-phunnd **h. a dozen** leth-dusan **h.-bottle** leth-bhotal *m* **h.-hearted** meadh-bhlàth **h.-pint** leth-phinnt *m* **halfway** *a, adv* letheach-slighe **h.-wit** gloidhc *f*, lethchiallach *m* **six and a h.** sia gu leth
halibut *n* lèabag/leòbag leathan(n) *f*
hall *n* talla *f m*; (*hallway*) trannsa
hallmark *n* comharra *m*
hallow *v* coisrig, naomhaich
Halloween *n* Oidhche Shamhna *f*
hallucination *n* mearachadh *m*, breug-shealladh *m*
halo *n* fàinne solais *f*; (*eg round moon*) buaile *f*, roth *f*, riomball *m*
halt *n* stad *m* *v* stad
halter *n* aghastar *m*
halve *v* dèan dà leth air
ham *n* hama *f*
hamlet *n* clachan *m*
hammer *n* òrd *m* *v* buail le òrd
hamper *n* basgaid *f* **food h.** basgaid bìdh
hamper *v* bac, cuir bacadh air
hamster *n* hamstair *m*
hamstring *n* fèith na h-iosgaid *f*
hand *n* làmh; (*large*) cròg *f m* **handloom** beart-làimhe *f* **the upper h.** làmh-an-uachdair *f* *v* sìn (+ do)
handbag *n* baga-làimhe *m*
handcuff *n* glas-làmh *f* *v* cuir glas-làmh air
handful *n* làn dùirn *m*; (*number*) dòrlach *m*
handicap *n* bacadh *m*; (*phys*) ciorram *m*
handicapped *a* ciorramach, ana-cothromach
handicraft *n* ceàird *f*
handiwork *n* obair-làimhe *f*
handkerchief *n* nèapraige *f*, nèapraigear *f*
handle *n* (*of door etc*) làmh *f*; (*of impl*) cas *f*; (*of cup, dish*) cluas *f* *v* làimhsich
handless *a* (*met*) cliobach
handshake *n* crathadh-làimhe *m*
handsome *a* eireachdail, maiseach, riochdail
handwriting *n* làmh-sgrìobha(i)dh *m*
handy *a* deas, ullamh; (*good with hands*) làmhchair(each); (*nearby*) deiseil, goirid
hang *v* croch **h. on!** fuirich!, dèan air do shocair!
hanging *n* crochadh *m*
hangover *n* ceann-daoraich *m*, ceann goirt *m*
hanker *v* miannaich
haphazard *a* tuiteamach; (*untidy*) rù-rà
happen *v* tachair
happiness *n* sonas *m*, toileachas *m*, àgh *m*
happy *a* sona, toilichte, àghmhor
harangue *n* òraid-ghearain *f*
harass *v* sàraich, leamhaich
harassed *a* sàraichte
harassment *n* sàrachadh *m* **sexual h.** sàrachadh gnè *m*
harbour *n* caladh *m*, port *m* **h.-master** ceannard-calaidh/puirt *m* *v* thoir fasgadh do, ceil
hard *a* cruaidh; (*of understanding*) doirbh *adv* cruaidh, dian **h.-hearted** cruaidh-chridheach **h.-working** dìcheallach
harden *v* cruadhaich, fàs cruaidh
hardly *adv* (bi) gann; cha mhòr gu(n) **there was h. any food left** is gann gun robh biadh air fhàgail **she could h. reach it** cha mhòr gun ruigeadh i air
hardship *n* cruadal *m*, cruaidh-chàs *m*, teinn *f*
hardware *n* bathar cruaidh *m*
hardy *a* cruaidh, calma
hare *n* geàrr *f*, maigheach *f*
harm *n* cron *m*, milleadh *m*, beud *m* *v* mill, dèan cron/milleadh air

harmful *a* cronail, millteach
harmless *a* gun lochd, neo-lochdach, gun chron
harmonious *a* co-sheirmeach, co-chòrdach, leadarra
harmonize *v* cuir an co-chòrdachd, ceòl-rèim, dèan ceòl-rèimeadh
harmony *n* co-sheirm *f*, co-cheòl *m*, ceòl-rèimeadh *m*
harness *n* acfhainn *f*, uidheam *f* *v* beairtich; (*utilize*) dèan feum de
harp *n* clàrsach *f*
harper *n* clàrsair *m*
harpoon *n* mòr-ghath *m*
Harrisman *n* Hearach *m* **Harriswoman** ban-Hearach *f*
Harris Tweed *n* an Clò Mòr/ Hearach *m*
harrow *n* cliath *f* *v* cliath
harrowing *a* gaoirsinneach
harsh *a* garg, borb; (*sound*) neo-bhinn
harvest *n* buain *f*, foghar *m* **h. moon** gealach an abachaidh *f*
haste *n* cabhag *f*
hasten *v* greas, dèan cabhag; (*trans*) cuir cabhag air
hasty *a* cabhagach, bras, cas
hat *n* ad(a) *f*
hatch *n* gur *m*; (*on ship*) haidse *f* *v* guir; (*met*) tàrmaich
hatchet *n* làmhagh *f*, làmhag *f*, tuagh *f*
hate *n* fuath *m*, gràin *f* *v* fuathaich, gràinich **she hated them** bha gràin aice orra
hatred *n* fuath *m*, gràin *f*
haughtiness *n* àrdan *m*, uabhar *m*
haughty *a* àrdanach, uaibhreach
haul *n* tarraing *f* **a big h.** meall mòr *m* *v* tarraing, slaod
haulage *n* tarraing bathair *f*, gluasad bathair *m*
haunch *n* leis *f*, leth-deiridh *m*, ceathramh *m*
haunt *n* àite-tathaich *m* *v* tathaich, tadhal
have *v* bi aig, seilbhich; (*take*) gabh; (*must*) feumaidh **do you h. money?** a bheil airgead agad? **will you h. a drink?** an gabh thu deoch? **you'll h. to call** feumaidh tu tadhal
haven *n* caladh *m*, acarsaid *f*
havoc *n* sgrios *m*, miast(r)adh *m*
hawk *n* seabhag *f m*
hawthorn *n* sgitheach *m*
hay *n* feur *m* **haystack** cruach-fheòir *f* **haycock** coc *f*
hazard *n* cunnart *m*, gàbhadh *m*
hazardous *a* cunnartach
haze *n* ceò *f m*, smùid *f*
hazel *n* calltainn *m* **hazelnut** cnò-challtainn *f* *a* (*colour*) buidhe-dhonn
hazy *a* ceòthach, sgleòthach, culmach
he *pron* e, (*emph*) esan
head *n* ceann *m*; (*person*) ceannard *m* *a* àrd-, prìomh **h. office** prìomh oifis *f* *v* stiùir **h. for** dèan air **headfirst** an comhair a c(h)inn *etc* **headlong** an comhair a c(h)inn *etc*; (*met*) (gu) bras **headstrong** fada na c(h)eann (fhèin) *etc*, ceann-làidir, ceannasach
headache *n* ceann goirt *m*
header *n* (*football*) buille-cinn *f*
heading *n* ceann *m*
headland *n* rubha *m*
headline *n* ceann-naidheachd *m*
headmaster *n* maigh(i)stir-sgoile *m*, ceannard-sgoile *m*
headmistress *n* bana-mhaigh(i)stir-sgoile *f*, ceannard-sgoile *m*
headphone *n* fòn-cluaise *m*
headquarters *n* prìomh-oifis *f*
headsquare *n* beannag *f*
headteacher *a* ceannard-sgoile *m*
headway *n* adhartas *m*
heal *v* leighis, slànaich *Also intrans*
health *n* slàinte *f* **h. board** bòrd slàinte *m* **h. centre** ionad slàinte *m*
healthy *a* fallain, slàn
heap *n* tòrr *m*, càrn *m*, dùn *m* *v* càrn, cruach
hear *v* cluinn, èist
hearing *n* (*faculty*) claisneachd *f*; (*listening*) èisteachd *f* **h.-aid**

inneal claisneachd *m*
hearsay *n* fathann *m*, iomradh *m*
hearse *n* carbad-tiodhlacaidh *m*
heart *n* cridhe *m*; (*centre*) meadhan *m*; (*met*) spiorad *m* **h.-attack** grèim-cridhe *m* **heartbreak** bris(t)eadh-cridhe *m* **heartburn** losgadh-bràghad *m*
heartfelt *a* dùrachdach, (bh)on chridhe, dha-rìribh
hearten *v* misnich, cùm cridhe ri
hearth *n* cagailt *f*, teinntean *m*, leac an teinntein *f*
hearty *a* cridheil, sunndach
heat *n* teas *m* *v* teasaich
heated *a* teth, air a theasachadh
heater *n* teasadair *m*, uidheam teasachaidh *f*
heath *n* (*topog*) blàr-fraoich *m*; (*bot*) fraoch *m* **h. burning** falaisg *f*
heathen *n* cinneach *m*, pàganach *m* *a* pàganta
heather *n* fraoch *m*
heating *n* teasachadh *m*
heaven *n* nèamh *m*, flaitheanas *m* **the heavens** na speuran *m pl* **Good heavens!** Gu sealladh orm!
heavenly *a* nèamhaidh
heavy *a* trom; (*of spirit*) airtnealach
Hebrew *n*, *a* Eabhra(idhea)ch *m*; (*lang*) Eabhra *f*
Hebridean *n*, *a* Innse-Gallach *m*
heckle *v* buair, piobraich
heckler *n* buaireadair *m*
hectare *n* heactair *m*
hectic *a* riaslach
hedge *n* callaid *f*
hedgehog *n* gràineag *f*
heed *n* feart *f*, aire *f* **pay no h. to him!** na toir feart air! *v* thoir feart/aire
heel *n* sàil *f*, bonn(-dubh) *m* *v* cuir sàil air **h. (over)** rach air fiaradh
hefty *a* garbh, tapaidh
heifer *n* agh *f m*
height *n* àirde *f*; (*topog*) mullach *m*, binnean *m*
heighten *v* àrdaich, tog suas
heinous *a* aingidh, gràineil
heir *n* oighre *m* **heiress** ban-oighre *f*
heirloom *n* seud *m*, ball-sinnsearachd *m*
helicopter *n* heileacoptair *m*
helium *n* hilium *m*
hell *n* ifrinn *f*, iutharna *f*
hellish *a* ifrinneach, iutharnail, diabhlaidh
helm *n* falmadair *m*, stiùir *f* **helmsman** stiùireadair *m*
helmet *n* clogad *f m*
help *n* cuideachadh *m*, cobhair *f* **helpline** loidhne-taice *f* *v* cuidich, thoir cobhair (do)
helper *n* neach-cuideachaidh *m*, cuidiche *m*
helpful *a* cuideachail
helpless *a* gun chuideachadh, gun taic
helter-skelter *n* giorna-gùirne *m* **go h.** rach na ruith 's na leum
hem *n* fàitheam *m* *v* **hem in** crò, druid
hemisphere *n* leth-chruinne *m* (*f in gen sg*)
hemp *n* cainb *f*
hen *n* cearc *f* **hen-house** bothag-chearc *f*
hence *adv* (*time*) à seo suas; (*place*) às a seo; (*for that reason*) air an adhbhar sin, mar sin
henceforth *adv* o seo a-mach
henpecked *a* fon spòig
heptagon *n* seachd-shliosach *m*, seachd-cheàrnach *m*
her *pron* i, (*emph*) ise *poss pron* a, a h- (*before vowels*)
herald *n* teachdaire *m*, earraid *m*
heraldic *a* suaicheantach, earraideach
heraldry *n* earraideas *m*
herb *n* lus *m*, luibh *f m*
herbal *a* lusragach
herd *n* treud *m*, greigh *f*, buar *m*; (*person*) buachaille *m* *v* buachaillich
herdsman *n* buachaille *m*
here *adv* an seo, seo
hereafter *adv* (bh)o seo a-mach, san àm ri teachd
hereby *adv* le seo, leis a seo

hereditary *a* dùth, dùthchasach **h. right** còir oighre *f*
herein *adv* an seo
heresy *n* saobh-chreideamh *m*, eiriceachd *f*
heretic *n* saobh-chreidmheach *m*
heretical *a* saobh-chreidmheach
herewith *adv* seo, le seo, leis a seo
heritable *n* oighreachail
heritage *n* dualchas *m*, oighreachd *f*
hermit *n* aonaran *m*, dìthreabhach *m*
hernia *n* màm-sic(e) *m*
hero *n* laoch *m*, gaisgeach *m*, curaidh *m* **heroine** bana-ghaisgeach *f*, ban-laoch *f*
heroic *a* gaisgeil
heroin *n* hearoin *m*
heroism *n* gaisgeachd *f*
heron *n* corra-ghritheach *f*
herring *n* sgadan *m*
herself *pron* ise, i fhèin
hesitate *v* stad; (*mental*) bi teagmhach
hesitation *n* stad *f*; (*mental*) teagamh *m*
heterogeneous *a* iol-ghnèitheach, ioma-sheòrsach
hew *v* geàrr, snaigh
hexagon *n* sia-shliosach *m*, sia-cheàrnach *m*
hexameter *n* sia-chasach *m*, meadrachd shia-chasach *f*
hey! *interj* hoigh!
heyday *n* treise *f* **in his/her h.** an trèine a neairt
hiatus *n* beàrn *f*, bris(t)eadh *m*
hibernation *n* cadal a' gheamhraidh *m*
hiccup *n* (an) aileag *f*
hidden *a* falaichte, am falach
hide *n* seiche *f*, bian *m*; (*place*) àite-falaich *m* *v* cuir am falach, falaich, ceil, cleith; (*intrans*) rach am falach
hide-and-seek *n* falach-fead *m*
hideous *a* oillteil, gràineil
hiding *n* falach *m*; (*beating*) liodraigeadh *m*, loineadh *m* **in h.** am falach **h.-place** àite-falaich *m*
hierarchy *n* rangachd *f*, siostam rangachaidh *m*; (*eccl*) riaghladh eaglais *m* **the h.** na h-urracha mòra *pl*
higgledy-piggledy *adv* dromach-air-thearrach, triomach-air-thearrach, rù-rà
high *a* àrd **h. and dry** tioram tràighte **h. court** àrd-chùirt *f* **h. jump** leum-àrd *f m* **h. tide** làn-àrd/mòr *m* **at h. tide** aig muir-làn **h.-powered** mòr-chumhachdach **h. priest** àrd-shagart *m* **h.-profile** follaiseach **h. school** àrd-sgoil *f* **h.-spirited** aigeannach, sùrdail **h. spirits** àrd-aigne *f*, sùrd *m* **h. water** muir-làn *f m*
Higher *n* (*exam*) Àrd Ìre *f*
Highland *a* Gàidhealach **the H. Council** Comhairle na Gàidhealtachd *f*
Highlander *n* Gàidheal *m*, (*female*) ban-Ghàidheal *f*
Highlands, the *n* a' Ghàidhealtachd *f* **H. and Islands Enterprise** Iomairt na Gàidhealtachd is nan Eilean *f*
highlight *v* cuir/leig cudrom air, soillsich
highway *n* rathad-mòr *m*
hilarity *n* àbhachd *f*, àbhachdas *m*
hill *n* cnoc *m*
hillock *n* cnocan *m*, tulach *m*
hillside *n* taobh cnuic *m*, slios beinne *m*, leitir *f*, leacann *f*
hilly *a* cnocach, monadail
him *pron* e, (*emph*) esan
himself *pron* e fhèin
hind *n* eilid *f*
hinder *v* cuir bacadh air, bac
Hindi *n* (*lang*) Hindidh *f*
hindrance *n* bacadh *m*
Hindu *n*, *a* Hindeach *m*, (*female*) ban-Hindeach *f*
hinge *n* bann *m*, lùdag *f*
hint *n* sanas *m*, leth-fhacal *m*, oidheam *m* *v* thoir sanas, thoir tuairmeas
hip *n* cruachan(n) *f m*
hippopotamus *n* each-aibhne *m*
hippy *n* hipidh *m*
hire *n* fastadh *m* *v* fastaidh,

tuarastalaich **hire-purchase** ceannach-iasaid *m*, ceannach air dhàil *m*
hirsute *a* molach
his *poss pron* a (+ *len*)
Hispanic *a* Spàinn(t)each
hiss(ing) *n* siosarnaich *f*
historian *n* eachdraiche *m*, neach-eachdraidh *m*
historical *a* eachdraidheil
history *n* eachdraidh *f*
hit *n* buille *f*; (*on target*) bualadh *m* *v* buail
hitch *n* (*snag*) amaladh *m*, tuisleadh *m* *v* ceangail **h.-hike** sir lioft **h. up** slaod suas
hither *adv* an seo **h. and thither** an siud 's an seo, a-null 's a-nall
hitherto *adv* gu ruige seo, fhathast
hive *n* sgeap *f*, beachlann *f*
hoard *n* tasgaidh *f*; (*treasure*) ulaidh *f* *v* taisg, glèidh
hoar-frost *n* liath-reothadh *m*
hoarse *a* tùchanach **he was h.** bha an tùchadh air
hoarseness *n* tùchadh *m*
hoary *a* liath
hoax *n* cleas-meallaidh *m*
hobble *v* cuagail
hobby *n* cur-seachad *m*
hockey *n* hocaidh *m*
hoe *n* todha *m*, sgrìoban *m* *v* todhaig
Hogmanay *n* a' Challainn *f*, Oidhche Challainn *f*, a' Chullaig *f*
hoist *v* tog suas
hold *n* grèim *m*; (*of ship*) toll *m* *v* cùm, cùm grèim air **h. back** cùm air ais **h. on** (*wait*) fuirich tiotan
hole *n* toll *m* *v* toll, tollaich
holiday *n* latha-saor *m*, saor-latha *m*, latha-fèille *m*
holiness *n* naomhachd *f*
hollow *n* lag *f m*, còs *m* *a* falamh, fàs; (*met*) gun bhrìgh
holly *n* cuileann *m*
holy *a* naomh, coisrigte
homage *n* ùmhlachd *f*
home *n* dachaigh *f* **h.-help** cuidiche-taighe *m* *adv* dhachaigh
home economics *n* eaconamas dachaigh *m*
homeless *a* gun dachaigh *n* daoine gun dachaigh *m pl*
home rule *n* fèin-riaghladh *m*
homesick *a* leis a' chianalas **she was h.** bha an cianalas oirre
homesickness *n* cianalas *m*
homespun *a* gun leòm
homicide *n* murt *m*
homogeneous *a* aon-ghnèitheach, aon-sheòrsach
homosexual *n*, *a* co-ghnèitheach *m*, co-sheòrsach *m*
homosexuality *n* fearas-feise *f*
hone *v* faobhraich
honest *a* onarach, treibhdhireach, ionraic
honesty *n* onair *f*, treibhdhireas *m*, ionracas *m*
honey *n* mil *f* **honeycomb** cìr-mheala *f*
honeymoon *n* mìos nam pòg *f* **h. period** àm nam pòg *m*
honeysuckle *n* iadh-shlat *f*
honorary *a* urramach
honour *n* onair *f*, urram *m* *v* onaraich, cuir urram air; (*fulfil*) coilean
honourable *a* onarach, urramach
hoodie-crow *n* feannag *f*
hoodwink *v* meall, thoir an car às
hoof *n* ladhar *m*, crubh *m*
hook *n* dubhan *m*, cromag *f* *v* glac le/air dubhan
hooligan *n* miastair *m*, ùpraidiche *m*
hooliganism *n* miast(r)adh *m*
hoop *n* cearcall *m*
hoot *v* goir, glaodh; (*vehicle*) seinn dùdach
hoover *n* sguabadair *m*
hop *n* sìnteag *f* *v* geàrr sìnteag, falbh air leth-chois
hop(s) *n* lus an leanna *m*
hope *n* dòchas *m* *v* bi an dòchas **I h.** tha dòchas agam
hopeful *a* dòchasach
hopeless *a* eu-dòchasach, gun dòchas
horde *n* dròbh *m*, greigh dhaoine *f*

horizon *n* fàire *f*, am bun-sgòth *m* **on the h.** air fàire
horizontal *a* còmhnard
hormone *n* hòrmon *m*, brodag *f*
horn *n* adharc *f*, cabar *m*; (*drinking, mus*) còrn *m*; (*car*) dùdach *m*
hornet *n* connspeach *f*
horoscope *n* reul-fhrìth *f*
horrible *a* sgreamhail, oillteil
horrid *a* sgreataidh
horror *n* uamhann *m*, oillt *f*, cùis-uabhais *f*
horse *n* each *m* **h. racing** rèiseadh-each *m* **horseshoe** crudha (eich) *m* **on horseback** air muin eich
horse-fly *n* creithleag *f*
horseman *n* marcaiche *m*
horsemanship *n* marcachd *f*
horse-radish *n* meacan ruadh *m*, racadal *m*
horticulture *n* gàrradaireachd *f*, tuathanas gàrraidh *m*
hose *n* (*stocking*) osan *m*, stocainn *f*; (*for water*) pìob-uisge *f*
hospitable *a* aoigheil, fialaidh
hospital *n* ospadal *m*, taigh-eiridinn *m*
hospitality *n* aoigheachd *f*, fàilte 's furan
host *n* fear-an-taighe *m*, neach-aoigheachd *m*; (*of people*) sluagh *m*
hostage *n* bràigh *f m*, giall *m*, neach am bruid *m*
hostel *n* ostail *f*
hostess *n* bean-an-taighe *f*
hostile *a* nàimhdeil
hostility *n* nàimhdeas *m*
hot *a* teth **hot-water bottle** *n* botal-teth *m*
hotch-potch *n* brochan *m*, butarrais *f*
hotel *n* taigh-òsta *m*
hotelier *n* òstair *m*
hound *n* gadhar *m*, cù-seilge *m*
hour *n* uair *f*
hourly *adv* gach uair, san uair
house *n* taigh *m* **H. of Commons** Taigh nan Cumantan **H. of Lords** Taigh nam Morairean *v* thoir/faigh taigh do **housekeeping** banas-taighe *f* **housewife** bean-taighe *f* **housework** obair-taighe *f*
household *n* teaghlach *m*
householder *n* ceann-taighe *m*
housing *n* taigheadas *m* **h. scheme** sgeama-thaighean *f*
hovel *n* bruchlag *f*, bothan *m*
hovercraft *n* bàta-foluaimein *m*
how *adv, int part* ciamar, cionnas (*before a or adv*) **how are you?** ciamar a tha thu? dè (cho), cia **how old is she?** dè an aois a tha i? **how often?** dè cho tric? **how many are there?** cia mheud a th' ann?
however *adv* ge-ta, gidheadh; co-dhiù
howl *n* donnal *m*, ulfhart *m* *v* dèan donnalaich/ulfhart
hubbub *n* othail *f*, coileid *f*
huddle *v* crùb còmhla
hue *n* dath *m*, tuar *m*, snuadh *m* **hue and cry** othail is èigheach
huff *n* stuirt *f* **in the h.** ann an stuirt
hug *v* glac teann thugad
huge *a* ana-mhòr
hulk *n* (*naut*) bodhaig luinge *f*; (*person*) sgonn mòr (duine) *m*, liodar *m*
hull *n* slige soithich *f*
hum *n* srann *f*, crònan *m* *v* dèan torman/crònan
human *a* daonna **h. rights** còraichean daonna *f pl*
humane *a* caomh, truacanta, daonnadach
humanism *n* daonnachas *f*
humanist *n* daonnaire *m*
humanity *n* daonnachd *f*, nàdar a' chinne-daonna *m*
humble *a* iriosal *v* (*oneself*) irioslaich, ùmhlaich; (*subdue*) thoir fo smachd
humbug *n* amaideas *m*; (*person*) buamastair *m*
humid *a* bruthainneach, tais
humidity *n* bruthainneachd *f*, taiseachd *f*
humiliate *v* tàmailtich, nàraich
humiliating *a* tàmailteach
humiliation *n* irioslachadh *m*,

ùmhlachadh *m*
humility *n* irioslachd *f*
humorous *a* ait, àbhachdach, èibhinn
humour *n* àbhachdas *m*; (*mood*) sunnd *m*, càil *f* **in good h.** an deagh thriom/shunnd **to h. someone** airson neach a thoileachadh
hump *n* croit *f* **humpbacked** *a* crotach
hunch *n* giùig *f*, meall *m*; (*idea*) beachd *m*
hundred *n*, *a* ceud *m*
hundredth *a* ceudamh
Hungarian *n*, *a* Ungaireach *m*, (*female*) ban-Ungaireach *f*
hunger *n* acras *m* **h.-strike** *n* stailc acrais *f*, diùltadh-bìdh *m*
hungry *a* acrach
hunt *n* sealg *f* *v* sealg
hunter *n* sealgair *m*
hunting *n* sealg *f*, sealgaireachd *f*
hurdle *n* cliath *f*
hurl *v* tilg
hurley/hurling *n* iomain Èireannach *f*
hurly-burly *n* uirle-thruis *f*
hurricane *n* doineann *f*
hurried *a* cabhagach
hurry *n* cabhag *f* **they were in a h.** bha cabhag orra *v* cuir cabhag air, luathaich; (*intrans*) dèan cabhag, greas (ort/air/oirre *etc*)
hurt *n* goirteachadh *m*, leòn *m* *v* goirtich, leòn
hurtful *a* goirt, cronail
husband *n* fear-pòsta *m*, cèile *m*
husbandry *n* àiteachas *m*
hush *v* sàmhaich, tostaich *interj* ist!
husk *n* cochall *m*, plaosg *m*
husky *a* plaosgach; (*voice*) tùchanach
hustle *n* drip *f* *v* cuir cabhag air, spursaig
hut *n* bothan *m*
hutch *n* bothag coineanaich *f*
hydrant *n* tobar-sràide *f m*
hydro-electric *a* dealan-uisgeach
hydro-electricity *n* dealan-uisge *m*
hydrogen *n* hàidridean *m*
hyena *n* hièna *m*
hygiene *n* slàinteachas *m*
hygienic *a* slàinteachail
hymn *n* laoidh *f m*, dàn spioradail *m* **hymnbook** laoidheadair *m*
hype *n* haidhp *f*
hyperbole *n* spleadhachas *m*, àibheiseachadh *m*
hypercritical *a* trom-bhreitheach
hyphen *n* sgrìob-cheangail *f*, tàthan *m*
hypnosis *n* suainealas *m*
hypnotic *a* suainealach
hypnotism *n* suainealachadh *m*
hypnotist *n* suainealaiche *m*
hypochondriac *a* leann-dubhach
hypocrisy *n* breug-chràbhadh *m*, cealg *f*, gò *m*
hypocrite *n* breug-chràbhaiche *m*, cealgair(e) *m*
hypocritical *a* breug-chràbhach, dà-aodannach, cealgach
hypothesis *n* beachd-bharail *f*
hypothetical *a* baralach
hysterical *a* r(e)achdail
hysterics *n* r(e)achd *f*

I

I *pron* mi, (*emph*) mise
ice *n* deigh *f*, eigh *f*, eighre *f* **the Ice Age** Linn na Deighe *f* **iceberg** beinn-deighe *f*, cnoc-eighre *m* **ice-cream** reòiteag *f* **ice-rink** rinc-deighe *f* **ice-skating** spèileadh-deighe *m*
Icelander *n* Innis-Tìleach *m*, (*female*) ban Innis-Tìleach *f*
Icelandic *a* Innis-Tìleach
icicle *n* caisean-reòthta *m*, stob reòthta *f*
icing *n* còmhdach-siùcair *m*
icon *n* ìomhaigh *f*
icy *a* reòthte, deighe
idea *n* smaoineas *m*, smaoin *f*, smuain *f* **I've no i.!** chan eil càil/sìon a dh'fhios agam!
ideal *a* taghta, sàr, barrail, sàr-inbheach
identical *a* ionann, co-ionann, ceudna
identification *n* aithneachadh *m*, dearbhadh-ionannachd *m*

identify *v* comharraich, dearbh-aithnich
identity *n* dearbh-aithne *f*, ionannachd *f* **i. card** cairt-aithneachaidh *f*
ideology *n* smaoineasachd *f*, creud *f*
idiom *n* gnàthas-cainnt *m*
idiosyncracy *n* nòsarachd *f*
idiosyncratic *a* nòsarach
idiot *n* amadan *m*, gloidhc *f*
idiotic *a* amaideach
idle *a* dìomhain; (*lazy*) leisg; (*at rest*) na t(h)àmh *etc*; (*thought*) faoin
idol *n* iodhal *m*, ìomhaigh *f*
idolize *v* dèan iodhal de, bi ag adhradh do
idyllic *a* eireachdail
if *conj* ma, nan, nam; (*if not*) mur(a); (*whether*) a/an/am **if they come** ma thig iad **if she does not come** mur(a) tig i **if you had come earlier** nan robh sibh air tighinn na bu tràithe **ask him if he is playing** faighnich dha/dheth a bheil e a' cluich
igloo *n* taigh-sneachda *m*
ignite *v* cuir teine ri, las
ignition *n* lasadh *m*, losgadh *m*; (*car*) adhnadh *m*
ignoble *a* suarach, neo-uasal
ignorance *n* aineolas *m*
ignorant *a* aineolach
ignore *v* leig seachad
ill *a* tinn, bochd, meadhanach; (*bad*) olc, dona **ill-informed** aineolach, beag-fios **ill-natured** droch-nàdarrach **ill-health** euslaint *f* **ill-treatment** droch làimhseachadh *m*
illegal *a* mì-laghail
illegible *a* do-leughadh, nach gabh leughadh
illegitimate *a* neo-dhligheil; (*person*) dìolain
illiberal *a* (*mean*) neo-fhialaidh; (*met*) cumhang
illicit *a* neo-cheadaichte, mì-laghail
illiterate *a* neo-litearra
illness *n* tinneas *m*, euslaint *f*
illogical *a* mì-sheaghach
illuminate *v* soilleirich
illumine *v* soillsich, soilleirich
illusion *n* mealladh *m*, mearachadh *m*
illustrate *v* dealbhaich; (*show*) seall, nochd
illustrated *a* dealbhaichte
illustration *n* dealbh *f m*; (*example*) eisimpleir *f*
illustrator *n* dealbhadair *m*
illustrious *a* cliùiteach, òirdheirc
image *n* ìomhaigh *f*; (*liter only*) samhla *m*
imagery *n* ìomhaigheachd *f*
imaginary *a* mac-meanmnach, ìomhaigheach
imagination *n* mac-meanmna *m*, mac-meanmainn *m*
imaginative *a* mac-meanmnach
imagine *v* smaoinich, smuainich (air); (*wrongly*) gabh na c(h)eann *etc*
imbecile *n* lethchiallach *m*
imbibe *v* òl, deothail
imbue *v* lìon
imitate *v* (*mimic*) dèan atharrais air; (*follow*) lean (eisimpleir, dòigh *etc*)
imitation *n* atharrais *f*, breug-shamhail *m*; (*copying*) leantainn *f m*
immaculate *a* gun smal, fìorghlan
immaterial *a* coma **it is i.** chan eil e gu diofar; (*without matter*) neo-nitheach
immature *a* an-abaich; (*person*) leanabail
immaturity *n* an-abaichead *m*; (*person*) leanabalachd *f*
immediate *a* grad, ealamh
immediately *adv* gun dàil, anns a' bhad, air ball
immense *a* àibheiseach, ana-mhòr
immerse *v* cuir am bogadh, tùm, bog
immersion *n* tumadh *m*, bogadh *m*, cur am bogadh *m* **i. course** cùrsa bogaidh *m*
immigrant *n* in-imrich *m*
immigration *n* in-imriche *f*, imrich a-steach *f*

imminent *a* gus teachd, an impis (+ *vn*)
immobile *a* neo-ghluasadach
immodest *a* mì-nàrach, mì-bheusach
immoral *a* mì-mhoralta
immorality *n* mì-mhoraltachd *f*
immortal *a* neo-bhàsmhor
immovable *a* neo-ghluasadach, nach gabh gluasad
immune *a* saor (bh)o, air a d(h)ìon (bh)o *etc*
immunisation *n* banachdach *f*
immunity *n* (*med*) dìonachd *f*, dìon *m*; (*leg*) saorsa *f*
immunize *v* dìon (bh)o ghalar, cuir a' bhanachdach air
imp *n* peasan *m*, deamhain *m*, spealg (dhen donas) *f*
impact *n* buaidh *f* *v* **i. on** thoir buaidh air
impair *v* mill, lùghdaich
impart *v* compàirtich
impartial *a* ceart-bhreitheach, cothromach, gun leth-bhreith
impasse *n* staing *f*
impassioned *a* lasanta, dùrachdach
impassive *a* do-fhaireachadh, socair, a' cleith faireachdainn
impatience *n* mì-fhoighidinn *f*, cion na foighidinn *m*
impatient *a* mì-fhoighidneach
impeach *v* casaidich (às leth na Stàite)
impeccable *a* gun smal, gun mheang, foirfe
impede *v* bac, cuir maill air
impediment *n* bacadh *m*, cnap-starra *m*
impenetrable *a* do-inntrig; (*met*) do-thuigsinn
imperative *n* (*command*) cruaidh-òrdugh *m*; (*urgency*) deatamas *m* **the i. mood** am modh àithneach *f* *a* (*urgent*) deatamach; (*gram*) àithneach
imperfect *a* neo-choileanta, easbhaidheach
imperial *a* ìmpireil
impersonal *a* neo-phearsanta
impersonate *v* gabh riochd (cuideigin)
impertinent *a* mì-mhodhail, beadaidh, bleideil
imperturbable *a* ciùin, somalta, sona
impetuous *a* bras, cas
impetus *n* gluasad *m*, sitheadh *m*
impinge *v* buail (air), suath (ri)
implacable *a* do-rèiteachail, neo-thruacanta
implant *v* suidhich, cuir a-steach
implausible *a* mì-choltach
implement *n* inneal *m*, uidheam *f*
implement *v* thoir gu buil, cuir an sàs
implicate *v* cuir an lùib
implication *n* (*impact*) buaidh *f* *m*, buil *f*
implicit *a* fillte, a' gabhail a-steach
implied *a* fillte, air a ghabhail a-steach, ri thuigsinn
implore *v* guidh, aslaich
imply *v* ciallaich, gabh a-steach
impolite *a* mì-mhodhail
import *n* brìgh *f*, ciall *f*; (*imports*) bathar a-steach *m*, in-mhalairt *f* *v* thoir a-steach bathar
importance *n* cudrom/cuideam *m*
important *a* cudromach, brìoghmhor
impose *v* cuir air, leag air, spàrr air
imposition *n* leagail *f*, sparradh *m*
impossible *a* do-dhèanta, eu-comasach
impostor *n* mealltair *m*
impotence *n* eu-comas *m*
impotent *a* eu-comasach
impound *v* punnd
impoverish *v* dèan/fàg bochd
impractical *a* nach obraich; (*person*) mì-dhòigheil
impress *v* (*someone*) fàg làrach air, coisinn deagh bheachd, drùidh air
impression *n* (*view*) beachd *m*; (*mark*) làrach *f m*; (*book*) deargadh *m*
impressive *a* ri m(h)oladh *etc*, drùidhteach
imprison *v* cuir dhan phrìosan
improbable *a* mì-choltach
impromptu *a* gun ullachadh, an làrach nam bonn

improper *a* mì-iomchaidh
improve *v* leasaich, cuir am feabhas; (*intrans*) tog air/oirre *etc*, thig air adhart, rach am feabhas
improvement *n* leasachadh *m*, feabhas *m*, piseach *f*
improvise *v* dèan gun ullachadh
impudence *n* beadaidheachd *f*, ladarnas *m*
impudent *a* beadaidh, ladarna
impulse *n* spreigeadh *m*, togradh *m*
impulsive *a* spreigearra, bras
impurity *n* neòghlaine *f*, truailleadh *m*
impute *v* cuir às leth
in *prep* ann, an, am, ann an/am/a **in the** anns an/a'/na, sa *adv* (*inside*) a-staigh; (*at home*) a-staigh, aig an taigh; (*motion*) a-steach
inability *n* neo-chomas *m*, dìth comais *f m*
inaccessible *a* do-ruigsinn, do-ruighinn
inaccurate *a* mearachdach
inactive *a* neo-ghnìomhach, na t(h)àmh *etc*
inadequate *a* easbhaidheach
inadvertently *adv* gun fhiosta
inane *a* faoin
inanimate *a* marbh, gun bheatha
inappropriate *a* mì-choltach, mì-fhreagarrach, neo-iomchaidh
inarticulate *a* mabach, gagach
inattention *n* cion aire *m*, neo-aire *f*
inattentive *a* neo-aireil, cion-aireachail
inaudible *a* nach gabh cluinntinn
inaugurate *v* tòisich; (*with ceremony*) coisrig
inauspicious *a* bagarrach
inbred *a* eadar-ghinte; (*ingrained*) nàdarra, dualchasach
incalculable *a* do-àireamh, thar tomhais
incapable *a* neo-chomasach
incapacity *n* neo-chomas *m*
incendiary *a* loisgeach
incense *n* tùis *f*
incense *v* cuir an cuthach/fhearg air
incentive *n* brosnachadh *m*
inception *n* tùs *m*, toiseach *m*
incessant *a* sìor, daonnan, gun sgur/stad
incessantly *adv* gun sgur/stad
incest *n* col *m*
inch *n* òirleach *f*; (*island*) innis *f*
incident *n* tachartas *m*
incinerate *v* dubh-loisg
incision *n* gearradh *m*
incisive *a* geur, geurchuiseach
incite *v* brosnaich, gluais, spreig
incitement *n* brosnachadh *m*, piobrachadh *m*
incivility *n* mì-shìobhaltachd *f*, mì-mhodhalachd *f*
inclement *a* an-iochdmhor; (*weather*) mosach
inclination *n* (*tendency*) aomadh *m*, claonadh *m*; (*desire*) iarraidh *m*, togradh *m*, deòin *f*
incline *n* leathad *m* *v* aom, claon; (*desire*) togair
inclined (to) *a* buailteach
include *v* gabh/thoir a-steach
inclusion *n* gabhail a-steach *m*, in-ghabhail *m* **social i.** in-ghabhail sòisealta
inclusive *a* a ghabhas a-steach, in-ghabhalach
incoherent *a* neo-leanailteach, sgaoilte, mabach
income *n* teachd-a-steach *m* **i. support** taic teachd-a-steach *f* **i. tax** cìs cosnaidh *f*
incomparable *a* gun choimeas
incompatible *a* nach freagair, nach tig air a chèile
incompetence *n* neo-chomasachd *f*
incompetent *a* neo-chomasach
incomplete *a* neo-choileanta, neo-iomlan
incomprehensible *a* do-thuigsinn
inconceivable *a* do-smaoineachaidh, thar tuigse
inconclusive *a* neo-chinnteach, neo-dhearbhte
incongruous *a* mì-fhreagarrach, mì-choltach
inconsiderate *a* beag-diù, neo-shuimeil, neo-mhothachail
inconsistency *n* neo-

chunbhalachd *f*
inconsistent *a* neo-chunbhalach
inconsolable *a* nach gabh cofhurtachadh
incontinent *a* (*phys*) neo-dhìonach
inconvenience *n* neo-ghoireasachd *f*
inconvenient *a* mì-ghoireasach
incorporate *v* co-cheangail, gabh a-steach
incorporation *n* co-cheangal *m*, gabhail a-steach *m*
incorrect *a* mearachdach, ceàrr
incorrigible *a* thar leasachaidh
incorruptible *a* neo-thruaillidh, do-choirbte, nach gabh coirbeadh/truailleadh
increase *n* meudachadh *m*, cinntinn *m* *v* meudaich, cuir am meud; (*intrans*) fàs lìonmhor, rach am meud
incredible *a* do-chreidsinn(each)
incredulity *n* cion creidsinn *m*
increment *n* leasachadh *m*, meudachadh *m*
incremental *a* beag air bheag, mean air mhean
incriminate *v* cuir ciont(a) air
incubate *v* guir
incubation *n* gur *m*
incumbent (on) *a* mar fhiachaibh (air)
incur *v* tarraing (air/oirre fhèin *etc*), bi buailteach do
incurable *a* do-leigheas, thar leigheas, nach gabh leigheas
indebted *a* an comain (+ *gen*), fo fhiachan (do)
indecency *n* mì-chuibheasachd *f*, mì-bheus *m*, drabastachd *f*
indecent *a* mì-chuibheasach, mì-bheusach, drabasta
indecision *n* neo-dheimhinnteachd *f*
indecisive *a* neo-dheimhinnte, eadar dà bheachd
indeed *adv* gu dearbh(a), gu deimhinne
indefensible *a* neo-leisgeulach, nach gabh dìon
indefinite *a* neo-shònraichte, neo-chinnteach
indelible *a* nach gabh dubhadh/suathadh às
indelicate *a* neo-ghrinn, neo-cheanalta
indented *a* eagach, gròbach
independence *n* neo-eisimeileachd *f*; (*polit*) saorsa *f*
independent *n* neo-eisimeileach *m* *a* neo-eisimeileach; (*polit*) saor
indescribable *a* do-aithris **It's i.** cha ghabh cachdraidh/luaidh dèanamh air
indestructible *a* nach gabh sgrios
indeterminate *a* neo-chinnteach, gun sònrachadh
index *n* clàr-amais *m* **i. finger** sgealbag/calgag *f* **i.-card** cairt-comharrachaidh *f*
Indian *n*, *a* Innseanach *m*, (*female*) ban-Innseanach *f*
indicate *v* comharraich, taisbean
indication *n* comharra *m* **there is every i. that ...** tha a h-uile coltas gu ...
indicator *n* taisbeanair *m*
indict *v* cuir às leth, tog casaid an aghaidh (+ *gen*)
indifference *n* neo-shùim *f*, cion-diù *m*
indifferent *a* coma, neo-shuimeil, coingeis
indigenous *a* dùthchasach
indigent *a* ainniseach
indigestion *n* cion-cnàmh *m*, dìth-cnàmhaidh *f*
indignant *a* diombach, feargach
indignation *n* diomb *f m*, corraich *f*
indignity *n* tàmailt *f*
indigo *n* guirmean *m*
indirect *a* neo-dhìreach, fiar
indiscipline *n* cion smachd *m*, mì-rian *m*
indiscreet *a* neo-chrìonna, mì-chùramach
indiscretion *n* neo-chrìonnachd *f*
indiscriminate *a* (*random*) neo-chuimsichte; (*jumbled*) am measg a chèile
indispensable *a* riatanach, neo-sheachanta
indisposed *a* tinn, bochd

indistinct *a* neo-shoilleir
indistinguishable *a* nach gabh aithneachadh/dealachadh (bh)o chèile; (*vision*) doilleir
individual *n* urra *f*, neach (air leth) *m*, pearsa *m* *a* fa leth, air leth, pearsanta
individually *adv* air leth, fa leth
indolent *a* leisg, dìomhain
indomitable *a* do-chlaoidhte
indoor(s) *a, adv* a-staigh
induce *v* adhbhraich, thoir air; (*birth*) thoir air adhart
inducement *n* brosnachadh *m*
induct *v* (*educ*) oidich; (*eccl*) pòs (ri coitheanal)
induction *n* (*educ*) oideachadh *m*, inntrigeadh *m*; (*eccl*) pòsadh *m*
indulge *v* leig le, toilich
indulgence *n* gèilleadh *m*, toileachadh *m*; (*favour*) cead *m* **i. in** tromachadh air
industrial *a* tionnsgalach, gnìomhachasach **i. estate** raon gnìomhachais *m*
industrialist *n* tionnsgalaiche *m*, neach-gnìomhachais *m*
industrious *a* dèanadach, gnìomhach
industry *n* gnìomhachas *m*, tionnsgal *f*; (*effort*) saothair *f*
inebriated *a* air mhisg, fo/air dhaorach
inedible *a* nach gabh ithe
ineffective *a* neo-èifeachdach, neo-bhuadhach
ineffectual *a* neo-tharbhach
inefficiency *n* neo-èifeachdas *m*
inefficient *a* neo-èifeachdach/tharbhach
inelegant *a* mì-loinneil
ineligible *a* neo-cheadaichte, neo-iomchaidh
inept *a* leibideach
inequality *n* neo-ionannachd *f*
inequitable *a* mì-cheart, mì-chothromach
inert *a* na t(h)àmh *etc*, marbhanta
inertia *n* tàmhachd *f*; (*in person*) leisg(e) *f*
inestimable *a* os cionn luach, nach gabh a luach
inevitable *a* do-sheachanta
inexcusable *a* neo-leisgeulach
inexpensive *a* saor
inexperience *n* cion eòlais *m*
inexperienced *a* neo-eòlach, gun eòlas, neo-chleachdte
inexplicable *a* do-thuigsinn, nach gabh tuigsinn
infallible *a* neo-mhearachdach
infamous *a* maslach, mì-chliùiteach
infamy *n* masladh *m*, mì-chliù *m*
infant *n* naoidhean *m*, pàiste beag *m*, leanaban *m*
infantry *n* coisridh *f*, saighdearan-coise *m pl*
infatuation *n* dalladh *m*, cur fo gheasaibh *m* **he had an i. for her** bha e air a dhalladh leatha
infect *v* cuir galar/tinneas air, truaill
infection *n* galar-ghabhail *m*
infectious *a* gabhaltach **i. disease** tinneas gabhaltach *m*
infer *v* co-dhùin
inference *n* co-dhùnadh *m*
inferior *a* nas miosa; (*in quality*) bochd, truagh; (*in status*) ìochdarach
infertile *a* neo-thorrach, aimrid
infidel *n* ana-creidmheach *m*
infidelity *n* neo-dhìlseachd *f*
infiltrate *v* eàlaidh (a-steach)
infinite *a* neo-chrìochnach, suthainn
infinity *n* neo-chrìochnachd *f*
infinitive *n* neo-fhinideach *m* **the i. mood** am modh neo-fhinideach *f m*
infirm *a* anfhann
infirmary *n* taigh-eiridinn *m*
infirmity *n* laige *f*, anfhannachd *f*, breòiteachd *f*
inflame *v* (*met*) fadaidh, cuir suidse ri; (*lit*) cuir teine ri
inflammable *a* lasarra, lasanta
inflammation *n* (*med*) at *m*, teas-at *m*, ainteas *m*; (*lit*) lasadh *m*
inflammatory *a* (*met*) buaireasach; (*med*) le at; (*lit*) loisgeach
inflate *v* sèid (suas), cuir gaoth an; (*intrans*) at

inflated *a* air at
inflation *n* sèideadh *m*; (*fin*) atmhorachd *f*
inflexible *a* rag, neo-lùbach
inflict *v* leag ... air
influence *n* buaidh *f* **under the i. of alcohol** fo bhuaidh na dibhe, fon mhisg *v* thoir buaidh air, buadhaich air
influential *a* buadhach, aig a bheil buaidh
influenza *n* an cnatan mòr *m*
influx *n* sruth (a-steach) *m*
inform *v* innis (do), thoir brath (do), cuir/leig/thoir fios (gu/do)
informal *a* neo-fhoirmeil
information *n* fiosrachadh *m*, brath *m* **i. centre** ionad fiosrachaidh *m* **i. and communications technology (ICT)** teicneòlas fiosrachaidh agus conaltraidh (TFC) *m*
informed *a* fiosrach, fiosraichte
informer *n* neach-brathaidh *m*, brathadair *m*
infrastructure *n* bun-structair/eagar *m*
infrequent *a* ainneamh
infringe *v* bris(t) a-steach air
infringement *n* bris(t)eadh a-steach *m*
infuriate *v* cuir air bhoil(e), cuir corraich/cuthach air
infuse *v* lion (le), cuir ... air feadh
ingenious *a* innleachdach, teòma
ingenuity *n* innleachd *f*, teòmachd *f*
ingrained *a* fuaighte
ingratiate *v* lorg fàbhar
ingredient *n* tàthchuid *f*
inhabit *v* àitich, tuinich, tàmh (an)
inhabitant *n* neach-àiteachaidh *m* *pl* luchd-àiteachaidh, muinntir (an àite) *f*
inhale *v* tarraing anail, gabh a-steach leis an anail
inherent *a* dualach, in-ghnèitheach
inherit *v* sealbhaich/faigh mar oighreachd
inheritance *n* oighreachd *f*, sealbh *m*; (*cult*) dualchas *m*
inhibit *v* caisg, cùm air ais, cuir stad air
inhibition *n* casg *m*, bacadh *m*, cuing (san nàdar) *f* **she had no inhibitions about singing on stage** cha robh leisge sam bith oirre seinn air àrd-ùrlar
inhospitable *a* mosach, neo-fhialaidh
inhuman *a* mì-dhaonna
inhumane *a* an-iochdmhor
inhumanity *n* an-iochdmhorachd *f*
inimitable *a* gun choimeas
iniquitous *a* aingidh
iniquity *n* aingidheachd *f*, olc *m*
initial *n* ciad litir *f* **my initials** ciad litrichean m' ainm *a* ciad, tùsail
initially *adv* sa chiad dol a-mach, aig toiseach gnothaich
initiate *v* tòisich, cuir air bhonn/chois; (*into an order*) gabh a-steach; (*into a skill*) teagaisg, oidich
initiative *n* iomairt *f*, tionnsgnadh *m*
inject *v* (*med*) sàth-steallaich; (*met*) cuir a-steach do, cuir ri
injection *n* sàth-stealladh *m* **i. of** cur a-steach *m*, cur ris *m*
injunction *n* àithne *f*, òrdugh *m*
injure *v* goirtich, ciùrr, dèan dochann air, leòn
injury *n* goirteachadh *m*, dochann *m*, leòn *m*
injustice *n* ana-ceartas *m*
ink *n* dubh *m*, inc *f m*
inland *a* a-staigh san tìr
inmate *n* neach fo chùram/ghlais *m*
inn *n* taigh-seinnse/òsta *m*
innate *a* dualach, nàdarra
inner *a* as fhaide/a b' fhaide a-staigh
innocence *n* neo(i)chiontachd *f*, ionracas *m*
innocent *a* neo(i)chiontach, ionraic
innocuous *a* neo-lochdach, neo-choireach
innovation *n* ùr-ghnàthachadh *m*, nuadhas *m*
innovative *a* ùr-ghnàthach

innovator *n* ùr-ghnàthadair *m*, nuadhasair *m*
innuendo *n* fiar-shanas *m*, leth-iomradh *m*
innumerable *a* gun àireamh, do-àireamh
inoculate *v* cuir a' bhreac air
inoculation *n* cur na brice *m*
inoffensive *a* neo-lochdach
inoperable *a* (*med*) do-leigheas, nach gabh leigheas
inopportune *a* mì-thràthail
inordinate *a* neo-chuimseach **an i. length of time** ùine gun chiall *f*
input *n* cur a-steach *m* *v* cuir a-steach
inquest *n* rannsachadh *m*, sgrùdadh *m*
inquire *v* feòraich, faighnich
inquiring *a* rannsachail
inquiry *n* rannsachadh *m*; (*query*) ceist *f* **public i.** rannsachadh poblach
inquisitive *a* ceasnachail, farraideach
insane *a* às a c(h)iall *etc*, às a rian *etc*
insanity *n* cuthach *m*, dìth-cèille *f m*; (*slang*) crac *m*
insatiable *a* nach gabh sàsachadh/riarachadh
inscribe *v* sgrìobh air
inscription *n* sgrìobhadh *m*; (*statue etc*) snaigheadh *m*
insect *n* biastag *f*, meanbh-fhrìde *f*
insecure *a* neo-thèarainte
insecurity *n* neo-thèarainteachd *f*
insemination *n* sìolachadh *m*
inseparable *a* do-sgaradh, nach gabh dealachadh
insert *v* cuir a-steach
inside *n* an taobh/leth a-staigh *m* **i.-out** caoin air ascaoin, an taobh a-staigh a-muigh *prep* am broinn (+ *gen*) *adv* a-staigh
insidious *a* lìogach, sniagach; (*dangerous*) cunnartach
insight *n* lèirsinn *f*
insignia *n* suaicheantas *m*
insignificant *a* suarach, beag-seagh
insincere *a* neo-threibhdhireach, neo-dhùrachdach
insincerity *n* neo-threibhdhireas *m*, neo-dhùrachd *f*
insinuate *v* leth-thuaileasaich
insipid *a* blian, gun bhlas
insist *v* cùm a-mach **i. on** sìor iarr **he insists on a dram every night** feumaidh e drama fhaighinn a h-uile h-oidhche
insolence *n* stràicealachd *f*
insolent *a* stràiceil
insoluble *a* do-sgaoilte; (*problem*) do-rèite, nach gabh rèiteach/f(h)uasgladh
insolvent *a* briste, air bris(t)eadh air/oirre *etc*
insomnia *n* bacadh-cadail *m*
inspect *v* sgrùd
inspection *n* sgrùdadh *m*
inspector *n* neach-sgrùdaidh *m*, sgrùdaire *m*
inspiration *n* sàr-smaoin *f*; (*source of*) brosnachadh *m*
inspire *v* brosnaich, spreag
inspiring *a* brosnachail, spreagail
instability *n* cugallachd *f*, neo-sheasmhachd *f*
instal *v* (*object*) cuir a-steach; (*person*) cuir an dreuchd, suidhich
installation *n* (*of object*) cur a-steach *m*; (*person*) cur an dreuchd *m*, suidheachadh *m*
instalment *n* cuibhreann *f m*, earrann *f*
instance *n* eisimpleir *f m* **for i.** mar eisimpleir **in the first i.** anns a' chiad àite **in this i.** an turas seo
instant *n* tiota *m* *a* grad, an làrach nam bonn
instantly *adv* sa bhad, san spot
instead *adv* an àite, an àite sin
instigate *v* cuir air bhonn, tòisich; (*incite*) piobraich
instigation *n* cur air bhonn *m*, tòiseachadh *m*; (*incitement*) piobrachadh *m*
instil *v* teagaisg, cuir an inntinn
instinct *n* gnèithealachd *f*, nàdar *m*
instinctive *a* gnèitheach, nàdarrach, a rèir gnè

institute *n* stèidheachd *f* *v* cuir air chois, stèidhich
institution *n* (*act of*) stèidheachadh *m*; (*place*) ionad *m*, stèidheachd *f*; (*practice*) riaghailt *f*
instruct *v* teagaisg, ionnsaich
instruction *n* teagasg *m*, ionnsachadh *m*; (*order*) òrdugh *m*, stiùireadh *m*
instructor *n* neach-teagaisg *m*
instrument *n* (*tool*) inneal *m*; (*mus*) ionnsramaid *f*, inneal-ciùil *m*; (*means*) meadhan *m*
instrumental *a* (*mus*) ionnsramaideach **i. in** mar mheadhan air
insubordinate *a* eas-umhail
insufferable *a* doirbh a ghiùlan, doirbh cur suas leis; (*met*) maslach
insufficient *a* goirid, geàrr, gann
insular *a* eileanach; (*met*) cumhang
insulate *v* còmhdaich **i. from** dealaich, cuir air leth
insulated *a* còmhdaichte **i. from** dealaichte, air a chur air leth
insult *n* ailis *f*, beum *m* *v* ailisich, thoir beum/droch bheul do
insulting *a* beum(n)ach, tàireil
insurance *n* àrachas *m* **i. claim** tagradh àrachais *m* **i. company** companaidh àrachais *f m* **i. policy** poileasaidh àrachais *m*
insure *v* thoir àrachas air, faigh/thoir urras air
insured *a* fo àrachas
insurrection *n* ar-a-mach *m*
intact *a* slàn, iomlan
intake *n* gabhail a-steach *f*
intangible *a* nach gabh làimhseachadh/fhaicinn, do-bheantainn
integral *a* slàn, coileanta, riatanach
integrate *v* aonaich **i. with** fill a-steach còmhla ri
integrated *a* aonaichte, fighte-fuaighte
integrity *n* treibhdhireas *m*, ionracas *m*; (*wholeness*) iomlanachd *f*
intellect *n* inntinn *f*
intellectual *a* inntleachdail *n* innleachdach *m*
intelligence *n* tuigse *f*; (*report*) aithris *f*, fiosrachadh *m*; (*covert*) fàisneis *f*
intelligent *a* inntleachdach, tùrail
intelligible *a* so-thuigsinn
intemperate *a* mì-stuama, ana-measarra
intend *v* dùilich, cuir roimhe/roimhpe *etc*, rùnaich
intended *a* san amharc
intense *a* dian, teann
intensify *v* teinnich, geuraich
intensity *n* dèine *f*, teinne *f*
intensive *a* dian **i. care** dlùth-chùram *m*
intent *n* rùn *m*
intention *n* rùn *m*
intentional *a* a dh'aon obair/ghnotha(i)ch
intentionally *adv* a dh'aon ghnotha(i)ch
inter *v* adhlaic, tiodhlaic
inter- *pref* eadar-
interaction *n* eadar-obrachadh *m*
intercede *v* dèan eadar-ghuidhe
intercept *v* ceap, stad san t-slighe
interchange *n* iomlaid *f*, malairt *f*
interchangeable *a* co-iomlaideach, co-mhalairteach, a ghabhas iomlaid/malairt
intercourse *n* (*social*) co-chomann *m*, comhluadar *m*; (*sexual*) feis(e) *f*
interdependent *a* eadar-eisimeileach, an eisimeil a chèile
interdict *n* toirmeasg/bacadh (lagha) *m*
interest *n* ùidh *f*; (*fin*) riadh *m*; (*stake*) earrann *f*, pàirt *f m* **i. rate** ìre an rèidh *f* *v* gabh/tog ùidh
interesting *a* ùidheil, inntinneach
interface *n* eadar-aghaidh *f*
interfere *v* gabh gnotha(i)ch ri, buin ri
interference *n* gabhail gnotha(i)ch ri *m*, buntainn ri *m*; (*atmos*) riasladh *m*
interim *n* eadar-àm *m* *a* eadar-amail **in the i.** anns an eadar-àm
interior *n* an leth/taobh a-staigh *m*

interject *v* geàrr a-steach, caith a-steach
interlacing *a* eadar-fhighte
interlink *v* naisg, ceangail ri chèile
interlocking *a* co-naisgte, co-cheangailte
interlude *n* eadar-chluiche *f*
intermediate *a* eadar-mheadhanach, meadhanach
interment *n* adhlacadh *m*, tiodhlacadh *m*
interminable *a* neo-chrìochnach, gun chrìoch
intermittent *a* (bh)o àm gu àm, air is dheth
internal *a* a-staigh
international *n* eadar-nàiseanail *m* *a* eadar-nàiseanta
internecine *a* co-sgriosail
internet *n* eadar-lìon *m* **the I.** an t-Eadar-lìon
interpret *v* mìnich; (*translate*) eadar-theangaich
interpretation *n* mìneachadh *m*; (*translation*) eadar-theangachadh *m*
interpreter *n* neach-mìneachaidh *m*, mìniche *m*; (*translator*) eadar-theangaiche *m*
interrogate *v* cruaidh-cheasnaich
interrogation *n* cruaidh-cheasnachadh *m*
interrupt *v* bris(t) a-steach (air); (*halt*) cuir casg/stad air
interruption *n* bris(t)eadh a-steach *m*; (*halting*) casg *m*, stad *m*
intersect *v* geàrr tarsainn (a chèile), trasnaich
intersperse *v* sgap am measg
intertwined *a* eadar-thoinnte
interval *n* eadar-ùine *f*, eadar-àm *m*; (*school*) àm-cluiche *m*, pleidhe *m*
intervene *v* rach san eadraiginn, thig eadar
intervention *n* tighinn eadar *m*
interview *n* agallamh *m* *v* dèan agallamh le
interviewer *n* agallaiche *m*, ceasnaiche *m*, neach-ceasnachaidh *m*
intestine(s) *n* caolan(an) *m*; (*animal only*) greallach *f*
intimacy *n* dlùth-chaidreabh *m*
intimate *a* dlùth-chaidreach, fìor eòlach
intimate *v* ainmich, inn(i)s
intimation *n* ainmeachadh *m*, fios *m*
intimidate *v* cuir fo eagal
into *adv* do, a-steach do
intolerable *a* do-ghiùlan, nach gabh fhulang **i. pain** cràdh eagalach/thar tomhais *m*
intolerant *a* neo-fhulangach, cumhang na s(h)ealladh *etc*
intonation *n* fonn cainnt *m*
intoxicated *a* air mhisg, air an daoraich, fo bhuaidh na dibhe
intoxication *n* misg *f*, daorach *f*
intractable *a* nach gabh f(h)uasgladh, neo-fhuasglach
intrepid *a* dàna, gaisgeil, tapaidh
intricate *a* toinnte, mion
intrigue *n* cluaineas *m*, cuilbheart *f*
intrinsic *a* gnèitheach, ann fhèin *etc*
introduce *v* cuir an aithne; (*subject*) tog, thoir iomradh air
introduction *n* cur an aithne *m*; (*of subject*) togail *f*; (*in book*) ro-ràdh *m*
introvert *a* neo-fhosgarra, dùr
intrude *v* bris(t)/brùth a-steach
intuition *n* im-fhios *m*
inundate *v* cuir fo uisge **we were inundated with requests** bha sinn a' dol fodha le iarrtasan
invade *v* thoir ionnsaigh air, bris(t) a-steach
invalid *n* euslainteach *m*
invalid *a* neo-bhrìgheil, neo-dhligheach
invalidate *v* cuir an neo-bhrìgh
invaluable *a* thar luach, nach gabh luach a chur air
invariably *adv* an còmhnaidh, daonnan; (*very frequently*) mar as trice
invasion *n* ionnsaigh *f*, bris(t)eadh a-steach *m*
inveigle *v* meall, thoir a thaobh
invent *v* innlich, tionnsgail
invention *n* innleachd *f*, tionnsgal *m*

inventive *a* innleachdach, tionnsgalach
inventor *n* innleadair *m*, tionnsgalair *m*
inventory *n* cunntas *f m*, clàr-seilbhe/stuthan *m*
invert *v* cuir bun-os-cionn, tionndaidh
invest *v* (*fin*) cuir an seilbh, cuir airgead an
investigate *v* rannsaich, sgrùd
investigation *n* rannsachadh *m*, sgrùdadh *m*
investment *n* (*fin*) cur an seilbh *m*, airgead-seilbhe/tasgaidh *m*
investor *n* neach-tasgaidh *m*
invidious *a* fuath-dhùsgach; (*unfair*) mì-cheart
invigilate *v* cùm sùil air, bi ri faire
invincible *a* do-cheannsachail, nach gabh ceannsachadh
invisible *a* neo-fhaicsinneach
invitation *n* cuireadh *m*, fiathachadh *m*
invite *v* iarr, thoir cuireadh (do), thoir fiathachadh (do)
inviting *a* tarraingeach
invoice *n* cunntas *f m*
involuntary *a* neo-shaor-thoileach, an aghaidh toil
involve *v* gabh a-steach **were you involved in it?** an robh thusa na lùib/an sàs ann?
irascible *a* crosta, feargach, greannach
irate *a* feargach, fiadhaich
ire *n* fearg *f*, corraich *f*
iris *n* (*of eye*) cearcall na sùla *m*; (*plant*) sealastair *f m*, seileastair *f m*
Irish *n* (*lang*) a' Ghaeilge *f*, Gàidhlig na h-Èireann *f* *a* Èireannach
Irishman *n* Èireannach *m* **Irishwoman** ban-Eireannach *f*
irksome *a* leamh, sàraichte
iron *n* iarann *m* *a* iarainn **I. Age** Linn an Iarainn *f* **i. ore** clach-iarainn *f* *v* iarnaig
ironic(al) *a* ìoranta
irony *n* ìoranas *m*
irrational *a* neo-reusanta
irreconcilable *a* do-rèiteachail, nach gabh toirt gu chèile
irregular *a* neo-chunbhalach, neo-riaghailteach **i. verb** gnìomhair neo-riaghailteach *m*
irregularity *n* neo-chunbhalachd *f*, neo-riaghailteachd *f*
irrelevant *a* nach buin dhan/ris a' ghnothach, neo-bhointealach, mì-fhreagarrach
irreparable *a* nach gabh càradh/leasachadh
irrepressible *a* nach gabh casg(adh)
irresistible *a* nach gabh diùltadh
irrespective *adv* a dh'aindeoin
irresponsible *a* neo-chùramach, gun chùram
irresponsibility *n* cion cùraim *m*, dìth cùraim *f*
irretrievable *a* nach gabh lorg/sàbhaladh
irreverence *n* eas-urram *m*
irreverent *a* eas-urramach
irreversible *a* nach gabh atharrachadh
irrevocable *a* nach gabh tilleadh/atharrachadh
irrigation *n* uisgeachadh *m*
irritable *a* crosta, frionasach, greannach
irritate *v* cuir caise/frionas air
irritation *n* crostachd *f*, frionas *m*
is *v* tha, is (*See verb* **to be** *in Grammar*)
Islam *n* an creideamh Ioslamach *m*; (*people*) a' mhuinntir Ioslamach *f*
Islamic *a* Ioslamach
island *n* eilean *m*, innis *f*
islander *n* eileanach *m*
Islay person *n* Ìleach *m*, (*female*) ban-Ìleach *f*
isolated *a* air leth, iomallach, lethoireach
isolation *n* aonarachd *f*, lethoireachd *f* **in i.** leis fhèin
Israeli *n*, *a* Israelach/Iosaraileach *m*
issue *n* ceist *f*, cùis *f*; (*offspring*) clann *f*, sliochd *m*; (*liter*) iris *f* *v* bris(t)/thig/cuir a-mach, lìbhrig
isthmus *n* tairbeart *f*, aoidh *f*

it *pron* e, i
Italian *n*, *a* Eadailteach *m*, (*female*) ban-Eadailteach *f*; (*lang*) Eadailtis *f*
italics *n* clò eadailteach *m*
itch *n* tachas *m*; (*desire*) miann *f m*
itchy *a* tachasach
item *n* nì *m*, rud *m*
itinerant *a* siùbhlach, siubhail
itinerary *n* clàr-siubhail *m*
its *poss pron* a
itself *pron* e/i fhèin
ivory *n* ìbhri *f*
ivy *n* eidheann *f*

J

jackdaw *n* cathag *f*
jacket *n* seacaid *f*
Jacobite *n* Seumasach *m* **J. Rebellion/Rising** Ar-a-mach nan Seumasach *m*
jade *n* sèad *f*
jaded *a* seachd sgìth
jag *n* briogadh *m*; (*notch*) eag *f*
jagged/jaggy *a* eagach
jail *n* prìosan *m*
jam *n* silidh *m*; (*congestion*) dùmhlachd *f* **in a jam** ann an staing **jam-jar** crogan-silidh *m*, sileagan *m* *v* brùth, dùmhlaich **my fingers got jammed** chaidh mo mheòirean a ghlacadh
jangle *v* dèan gleadhraich/gliongadaich
janitor *n* dorsair *m*, neach-cùraim sgoile *m*
January *n* am Faoilleach/Faoilteach *m*
Japanese *n, a* Iapanach, (*female*) ban-Iapanach *f*
jar *n* crogan *m*, sileagan *m*
jargon *n* ceàird-chainnt *f*
jaundice *n* a' bhuidheach *f*, an tinneas buidhe *m*
jaunt *n* sgrìob *f*, splaoid *f*
javelin *n* sleagh *f*
jaw *n* peirceall *m*, giall *f*
jealous *a* eudmhor **she was j. of her** bha i ag eudach rithe
jealousy *n* eud *m*, eudmhorachd *f*
jeans *n* dinichean *f pl*
jeer *v* mag (air), dèan magadh (air)
Jehovah *n* Iehòbhah *m*
jelly *n* slaman-milis *m*
jellyfish *n* muir-tiachd *f m*
jeopardy *n* cunnart *m*, gàbhadh *m*
jerk *n* tarraing obann *f*, tulgag *f* *v* tarraing gu h-obann
jersey *n* geansaidh *m*
jest *n* abhcaid *f*, fealla-dhà *f*
jet *n* steall *m*; (*plane*) seit (-phlèan) *m*
jettison *v* tilg a-mach, cuir bhuat
jetty *n* cidhe *m*, laimrig *f*
Jew *n* Iùdhach *m* **Jewess** ban-Iùdhach *f*
jewel *n* seud *m*, leug *f*, àilleag *m*
jeweller *n* seudair *m*
jewellery *n* seudraidh *f*
Jewish *a* Iùdhach
jig *n* (*tune*) port-cruinn *m*; (*dance*) sige *f*
jigsaw *n* mìrean-measgaichte *f pl*
jilt *v* trèig, faigh cuidhteas (leannan)
jingle *n* gliong *m*; (*ad*) rannag *f*
job *n* obair *f*, cosnadh *m* **job-centre** ionad obrach *m* **job description** dealbh-obrach *f m*
jockey *n* marcach *m*, marcaiche *m*
jocular *a* spòrsail, abhcaideach
jog *v* bi a' trotan, ruith; (*nudge*) put; (*memory*) brod cuimhne
join *v* ceangail, aonaich, cuir ri chèile, tàth; (*eg club*) gabh ballrachd an
joiner *n* saor *m*
joinery *n* saorsainneachd *f*
joint *n* alt *m*; (*of meat*) spòlt *m* *a* co-, coitcheann, co-phàirteach
jointly *adv* cuideachd, le chèile, an co-bho(i)nn
joist *n* sail *f*, spàrr *m*, cas-ceangail *f*
joke, joking *n* abhcaid *f*, fealla-dhà *f* **I was only joking** cha robh mi ach ri spòrs
jolly *a* cridheil, aighearach
jolt *n* crathadh *m*, tulgadh *m*
jostle *v* put, brùth (a-null 's a-nall)

jotter *n* diotar *m*, leabhran-sgrìobhaidh *m*
journal *n* (*diary*) leabhar-latha *m*; (*magazine*) iris *f*
journalism *n* naidheachdas *m*
journalist *n* neach-naidheachd *m*, naidheachdair *m*
journey *n* turas *m*, cuairt *f*
jovial *a* fonnmhor, suilbhir
jowl *n* giall *f*, bus *m*
joy *n* aoibhneas *m*, gàirdeachas *m*, sòlas *m*
joyful *a* aoibhneach, ait, sòlasach
jubilant *a* lùth-ghaireach
jubilee *n* iubailidh *f*
judge *n* britheamh *m* *v* thoir breith, breithnich, meas
judgement *n* breith *f*, breithneachadh *m*, binn *f* **J. Day** Latha a' Bhreitheanais *m*, Latha Luain *m*
judicial *a* laghail, a rèir an lagha, breitheach
judicious *a* tuigseach, geurchuiseach
jug *n* siuga *f m*
juggle *v* làmh-chleasaich
jugular *n* fèith sgòrnain *f*
juice *n* sùgh *m*; (*essence*) brìgh *f*
juicy *a* sùghmhor; (*pithy*) brìoghmhor
July *n* an t-Iuchar *m*
jumble *n* measgachadh *m*, brochan *m* **j. sale** reic treal(l)aich *m* *v* cuir troimh-a-chèile, measgaich
jump *n* leum *m*, sùrdag *f* **standing j.** cruinn-leum *m* *v* leum
jumper *n* (*sport*) leumadair *m*; (*garment*) geansaidh *m*
junction *n* snaidhm *m*, comar *m*, ceangal *m*
June *n* an t-Ògmhios *m*
jungle *n* dlùth-choille *f*
junior *a* as òige, a b' òige
juniper *n* aiteann *m*
junk *n* smodal *m*, truileis *f*; (*naut*) long Shìonach *f*
Jupiter *n* Iupatar *m*
jury *n* diùraidh *m*
just *a* cothromach, ceart, fìrinneach *adv* (*recently*) dìreach; (*with difficulty*) air èiginn **j. now** an-dràsta, an ceartuair **it is j. amazing** tha e dìreach iongantach **the shop has j. closed** tha a' bhùth dìreach air dùnadh **they only j. escaped** 's ann air èiginn a thàrr iad às
justice *n* ceartas *m*
justifiable *a* reusanta, a ghabhas scasamh/dìon
justify *v* seas, dìon; (*relig*) fìreanaich
juvenile *n* òganach *m* *a* òigridh

K

kangaroo *n* cangarù *m*
keel *n* druim *m*
keen *a* dian, dealasach; (*sharp*) geur
keenness *n* dealas *m*, eudmhorachd *f*
keep *v* cùm, glèidh
keeper *n* neach-gleidhidh *m*
keepsake *n* cuimhneachan *m*
kelpie *n* each-uisge *m*, ùruisg *m*
kennel *n* taigh-chon *m*
kerb *n* oir a' chabhsair *f m*, cabhsair *m*
kernel *n* eitean *m*
kestrel *n* speireag ruadh *f*, clamhan ruadh *m*
kettle *n* coire *m*
key *n* iuchair *f*; (*mus*) gleus *f m*; (*on keyboard*) meur *f*; (*solution*) fuasgladh *m* *a* cudromach, prìomh (*precedes n*)
keyboard *n* meur-chlàr *m*
kick *n* breab *f m* *v* breab
kid *n* meann *m*; (*child*) pàiste *m*
kidnap *v* goid air falbh
kidney *n* dubhag *f*, àra *f*, àirne *f*
kill *v* marbh, cuir gu bàs
killer *n* murtair *m*
killing *n* marbhadh *m*, spadadh *m*
kilogram(me) *n* cileagram *m*
kilometre *n* cilemeatair *m*
kilowatt *n* cileabhat *m*
kilt *n* (f)èileadh *m*
kin(dred) *n* dàimhean *f m pl*, càirdean *m pl*
kind *n* gnè *f*, seòrsa *m*

kindle *v* las, fadaich; (*met*) beothaich, brosnaich
kind(ly) *a* coibhneil, còir, bàidheil
kindness *n* coibhneas *m*, caomhalachd *f*, bàidhealachd *f*
kindred *a* co-aigneach **they were k. spirits** bha iad a dh'aon aigne
kinetic *a* gluaiseach
king *n* rìgh *m*
kingdom *n* rìoghachd *f*
kinsman *n* fear-dàimh *m* **kinswoman** bean-dàimh *f*
kipper *n* ciopair *m*, sgadan rèisgte *m*
kirk *n* eaglais *f*
kiss *n* pòg *f* *v* pòg, thoir pòg
kit *n* acfhainn *f*, uidheam *f*; (*clothes*) èideadh *m*
kitchen *n* cidsin *m*
kite *n* iteileag *f*; (*bird*) clamhan *m*
kitten *n* piseag *f*
knack *n* alt *m*, liut *f*
knead *v* fuin, taoisnich
knee *n* glù(i)n *f* **k.-cap** failmean (na glùine) *m*
kneel *v* lùb glù(i)n, sleuchd
knickers *n* drathais/drathars *f*
knife *n* sgian *f*
knight *n* ridire *m*
knit *v* figh **k. together** (*after injury*) ceangail, slànaich
knitting-needle *n* bior-fighe *m*
knob *n* cnap *m*, cnag *f*
knock *n* buille *f*, sgailc *f*, sgleog *f*; (*at door*) gnogadh *m* *v* (*door*) gnog **k. down** leag
knocking *n* gnogadh *m*
knoll *n* tom *m*, tolman *m*, tulach *m* **fairy k.** sìthean *m*
knot *n* snaidhm/snaoim *m*; (*nautical mile*) mìle mara *m*; (*in wood*) meuran *m* *v* snaidhmich/snaoimich, cuir snaidhm/snaoim air
know *v* **knows** tha fios aig; (*person*) is aithne do; (*recognize*) aithnich **k. well** bi eòlach air
knowledge *n* eòlas *m*, aithne *f*
knowledgeable *a* fiosrach
knuckle *n* rùdan *m*
kyle *n* caol(as) *m*

L

label *n* bileag *f* *v* cuir bileag air
laboratory *n* obair-lann *f*, deuchainn-lann *f*
laborious *a* saothrachail, deacair
labour *n* saothair *f*, obair *f*; (*med*) saothair chloinne *f* **in l.** air leabaidh-shiùbhla **the L. Party** am Partaidh Làbarach *m* *v* saothraich, obraich
labourer *n* obraiche *m*, dubh-chosnaiche *m*
labyrinth *n* ioma-shlighe *f*
lace *n* sròl *m*; (*shoe*) barrall *m* *v* ceangail
lack *n* easbhaidh *f*, dìth *f m*, cion *m* *v* bi a dh'easbhaidh **he lacks ...** tha ... a dhìth air
lacklustre *a* marbhanta, gun spionnadh
laconic *a* geàrr-bhriathrach
lad *n* gille *m*, balach *m*
ladder *n* (f)àradh *m*
ladle *n* ladar *m*, liagh *f*
lady *n* bean-uasal *f*, baintighearna *f*, leadaidh *f*
ladybird *n* an daolag dhearg-bhreac *f*
lager *n* làgar *m*
lair *n* saobhaidh *f*, garaidh *m*; (*grave*) rèilig *f*
laird *n* uachdaran *m*
lake *n* loch *m*
lamb *n* uan *m*; (*meat*) uanfheòil *f*, feòil uain *f*
lame *a* cuagach, bacach, crùbach
lament *n* cumha *m*, tuireadh *m*, caoidh *f* *v* caoidh, dèan tuireadh
lamentable *a* cianail, tùrsach, muladach
laminated *a* lannaichte
lamp *n* lampa *f m* **l.-post** post-lampa *m* **l.-shade** sgàil-lampa *f*
lampoon *n* aoir *f* *v* aoir
lance *n* sleagh *f*; (*med*) lannsa *f* *v* leig fuil, geàrr le lannsa
land *n* fearann *m*, talamh *m*; (*country*) tìr *f*, dùthaich *f* **the L. Court** Cùirt an Fhearainn *f* *v* (*go ashore*) rach air tìr; (*of plane*) laigh; (*goods*) cuir air tìr

landlady *n* bean an taighe *f*
landlord *n* (*estate*) uachdaran *m*; (*property, pub etc*) fear an taighe *m*
landmark *n* comharra-stiùiridh *m*
landowner *n* uachdaran *m*
landscape *n* dealbh-tìre *f m*, cruth tìre *m*; (*picture*) sealladh tìre *m*
landslide *n* maoim-slèibhe *f*, maoim-talmhainn *f*
lane *n* frith-rathad *m*, caolshràid *f*; (*on motorway*) sreath *f m*
language *n* cànan *f m*; (*speech*) cainnt *f*
languid *a* anfhann, gun sunnd
languish *v* fannaich, crìon
lanky *a* fada caol
lantern *n* lanntair *f m*, lainntear *f m*, lòchran *m*
lap *n* uchd *m*, sgùird *f*; (*sport*) cuairt *f* *v* (*slurp*) slupairich, bileagaich; (*waves*) sruthail
lapel *n* liopaid *f*, fillteag *f*
lapse *n* sleamhnachadh *m*, mearachd *f* *v* sleamhnaich, tuislich, dèan mearachd; (*expire*) thig gu ceann **she lapsed into English** thionndaidh i gu Beurla
lapwing *n* curracag *f*
larceny *n* goid *f*, gadachd *f*
larch *n* learag *f*
lard *n* blona(i)g *f*
larder *n* preas/seòmar-bìdh *m*
large *a* mòr, tomadach
lark *n* uiseag *f*, topag *f*; (*play*) cleas *m*
larynx *n* bràigh an sgòrnain *m*
laser *n* leusair *m* **l. beam** gath leusair *m* **l. printer** clò-bhualadair leusair *m*
lash *v* sgiùrs, stiall
lass *n* nighean *f*, caileag *f*
last *a* deireannach, mu dheireadh **l. week** an t-seachdain seo chaidh **l. night** a-raoir **the night before l.** a' bhòn-raoir **l. year** an-uiridh **the l. person** an duine mu dheireadh *adv* air deireadh **at (long) l.** mu dheireadh (thall) *v* mair, seas
lasting *a* maireannach, buan
latch *n* clàimhean *m*, dealan-dorais *m*
late *a* anmoch, fadalach, air deireadh; (*evening, night*) anmoch; (*deceased*) nach maireann **they arrived l.** bha iad fada gun tighinn
lately *adv* o chionn ghoirid
latent *a* falaichte, neo-fhollaiseach
lateral *a* taobhach, leth-taobhach
lathe *n* beairt-thuairnearachd *f*
lather *n* cop *m*
Latin *n* Laideann *f*
latitude *n* domhan-leud *m*; (*scope*) saorsa *f*
latter *a* deireannach, mu dheireadh
laud *v* àrd-mhol
laudable *a* ionmholta, ri m(h)oladh *etc*
laugh *n* gàire *f m* **loud l.** lachan *m*, lasgan *m* *v* gàir, dèan gàire
laughing-stock *n* culaidh/cùis-mhagaidh *f*
laughter *n* gàireachdaich *f* **loud l.** lasganaich *f*
launch *n* cur air bhog *m*; (*product*) foillseachadh *m* *v* cuir air bhog; (*product*) foillsich; (*begin*) tòisich air
laundry *n* taigh-nighe *m*
lava *n* làbha *f*
lavish *a* fialaidh, strùidheil, cosgail
law *n* lagh *m* **lawsuit** cùis-lagha *f*
lawful *a* laghail
lawless *a* mì-riaghailteach, gun spèis do lagh
lawn *n* rèidhlean *m*, faiche *f* **l.-mower** lomaire-feòir *m*
lawyer *n* neach-lagha *m*
lax *a* slac, sgaoilte, gun chùram
laxative *n* purgaid *f*
lay *v* càirich, cuir **lay egg** breith ugh **lay foundation** leag stèidh **lay off** (*staff*) leig mu sgaoil **lay wager** cuir geall **lay waste** sgrios, cuir fàs
layer *n* filleadh *m*, sreath *f m*
layout *n* cruth *m*; (*of page*) coltas-duilleig *m*
laziness *n* leisg(e) *f*

lazy *a* leisg
lazybones *n* leisgeadair *m*
lead *n* (*metal*) luaidhe *f m*
lead *n* stiùir *f*; (*dog's*) taod *m* *v* stiùir, treòraich
leader *n* ceannard *m*, ceannbhair *m*
leadership *n* ceannas *m*
leaf *n* duilleag *f*
leaflet *n* duilleachan *m*, bileag *f*
league *n* dionnasg *m*; (*sport*) lìog *f* **the Premier L.** a' Phrìomh Lìog
leak *n* aoidion *m* *v* leig a-steach/a-mach; (*intrans*) bi aoidionach; (*reveal*) leig mu sgaoil
leaking, leaky *a* aoidionach
lean *v* leig do thaic air, leig cudrom air
lean *a* caol, tana
leap *n* leum *m* **standing l.** cruinn-leum *m* **l. year** bliadhna-lèim *f* *v* leum, thoir leum
learn *v* ionnsaich, foghlaim
learned *a* foghlaim(ich)te, ionnsaichte
learner *n* neach-ionnsachaidh *m* *pl* luchd-ionnsachaidh
lease *n* gabhail *m*, còir *f* *v* gabh air mhàl
leash *n* iall *f*
least *sup a* as lugha **at l.** co-dhiù, aig a' char as lugha
leather *n* leathar *m* *a* leathair
leave *n* (*permission*) cead *m*; (*from duty*) fòrladh *m*
leave *v* fàg, trèig **l. alone** leig le **l. off** sguir de
lecherous *a* drùiseil
lecture *n* òraid *f* *v* dèan òraid, thoir (seachad) òraid; (*tell off*) cronaich
lecturer *n* òraidiche *m*
ledge *n* leac *f*; (*topog*) palla *m*
ledger *n* leabhar-cunntais *m*
lee *n* taobh an fhasgaidh *m*
leek *n* creamh-gàrraidh *m*
leer *v* claon-amhairc
left *n* an taobh clì/ceàrr *m*, an làmh chlì/cheàrr *f* **the l. hand** an làmh chlì *f*, a' chearrag *f* **l.-handed** ciotach, cearragach *a* clì **l. over** air fhàgail **leftovers** corran *m pl*
leg *n* cas *f*; (*of meat*) ceathramh feòla *m*
legacy *n* dìleab *f*
legal *a* laghail, dligheach, ceadaichte
legalize *v* dèan laghail
legend *n* uirsgeul *m*, fionnsgeul *m*
legendary *a* uirsgeulach; (*famous*) iomraiteach
legible *a* so-leughte, a ghabhas leughadh
legislate *v* dèan lagh(an), reachdaich
legislation *n* reachdas *m*
legitimate *a* dligheach
leisure *n* saor-ùine *f* **l. activity** cur-seachad *m*
lemon *n* liomaid *f* **l. sole** lèabag cheàrr *f*
lemonade *n* liomaineud *m*
lend *v* thoir iasad (de), thoir an iasad
length *n* fad *m*, faid *f*
lengthen *v* cuir fad ri/às, dèan nas fhaide, sìn; (*intrans*) fàs nas fhaide, sìn
leniency *n* tròcair *f*, iochdalachd *f*, iochd *f*
lenient *a* tròcaireach, iochdail
lenition *n* sèimheachadh *m*
lens *n* lionsa *f*
Lent *n* an Carghas *m*
lentil *n* leantail *m*, peasair nan luch *f*
leopard *n* liopard *m*
leper *n* lobhar *m*
leprosy *n* luibhre *f*
lesbian *n*, *a* leasbach *f*
less *comp a* nas lugha, na bu lugha
lessen *v* lùghdaich, beagaich (air); (*intrans*) lùghdaich
lesson *n* leasan *m*
let *v* leig le, ceadaich; (*property*) thoir air ghabhail **let go** leig às **let on** leig ort/air/oirre *etc*
lethal *a* marbhtach, bàsmhor
lethargic *a* trom, slaodach
letter *n* litir *f* **capital l.** litir mhòr **l.-box** bogsa-litrichean *m*
lettuce *n* leatas *f*
leukaemia *n* bànachadh-fala *m*

level *n* còmhnard *m*; (*grade*) inbhe *f*, ìre *f* *a* còmhnard, rèidh *v* dèan còmhnard/rèidh **l. an accusation at** cuir às leth (+ *gen*)
lever *n* geimhleag *f*, luamhan *m* **gear l.** stob nan giodhraichean *m*
levy *n* cìs *f* *v* (*tax etc*) leag
lewd *a* draosta
Lewis person *n* Leòdhasach *m*, (*female*) ban-Leòdhasach *f*
liability *n* (*fin*) fiach *m*; (*tendency*) buailteachd *f* **it was just a l.** cha robh ann ach call
liable *a* buailteach (do), dualtach
liaise *v* dèan ceangal (ri)
liaison *n* ceangal *m*, co-cheangal *m*
liar *n* breugaire *m*, breugadair *m*
libel *n* tuaileas *m*, cliù-mhilleadh *m* *v* cuir tuaileas air, mill cliù **he libelled me** chuir e na breugan orm
libellous *a* tuaileasach
liberal *a* fial, fialaidh; (*phil*) libearalach
Liberal *n, a* Libearalach *m* **L. Democratic Party** am Partaidh Libearalach Deamocratach *m*
liberate *v* saor, cuir mu sgaoil
liberation *n* saoradh *m*, leigeil/cur mu sgaoil *m*
liberty *n* saorsa *f*
libidinous *a* ana-miannach, drùiseil
librarian *n* leabharlannaiche *m*
library *n* leabharlann *f m*
licence *n* cead *m*
license *v* ceadaich, thoir cead do/seachad
licensed *a* fo cheadachd, le cead, ùghdarraichte
licentious *a* mì-bheusach
lick *v* imlich
lid *n* ceann *m*, mullach *m*
lie *n* breug *f* **I had a lie-down** chaidh mi nam shìneadh *v* (*tell untruth*) inn(i)s breug; (*phys*) laigh
lieutenant *n* leifteanant *m*; (*associate*) neach-ionaid *m*
life *n* beatha *f*; (*vitality*) beothalachd *f* **l.-insurance** àrachas beatha *m* **l.-style** dòigh-beatha *f* **lifebelt** crios teasairginn *m* **lifeboat** bàta-teasairginn *m* **lifeguard** neach-teasairginn *m* **l.-jacket** seacaid-teasairginn *f* **lifeline** loidhne-teasairginn *f*; (*met*) cothrom eile *m*
lifeless *a* marbh, gun deò; (*met*) trom
lifetime *n* rè *f*, beò *m*, saoghal *m*
lift *n* togail *f*; (*elevator*) àrdaichear *m* *v* tog
ligament *n* ball-nasg *m*, ceanglachan *m*
light *n* solas *m*; (*daylight*) soilleireachd *f* **l.-house** taigh-solais *m* *v* las **l. up** (+ *met*) soillsich
light *a* aotrom; (*of daylight*) soilleir **l.-headed** aotrom, mear **l.-hearted** sunndach, suigeartach, aighearach
lighten *v* deàlraich, soillsich; (*weight*) aotromaich
lighter *n* lasadair *m*
lightning *n* dealanach *m*
like *v* **likes** is toigh/toil (le), is caomh le **be l.** bi coltach ri
like *n* leithid *f*, samhail *f*, mac-samhail *m* *a* coltach (ri), mar (+ *len*) *adv* mar
likelihood *n* coltas *m*
likely *a* coltach, dòcha
liken *v* samhlaich, coimeas
likeness *n* (*similarity*) coltas *m*, ìomhaigh *f*; (*picture*) dealbh *f m*
likewise *adv* cuideachd, mar an ceudna
lilac *n* liath-chorcra *f* *a* bàn-phurpaidh
lily *n* lilidh *f*
limb *n* ball *m*
lime *n* aol *m*; (*fruit/tree*) teile *f*
limit *n* crìoch *f*, iomall *m* *v* cuingealaich, cuir crìoch ri
limited *a* cuingealaichte, cuibhrichte **l. company** companaidh earranta *f m*
limp *n* ceum *m* **he has a l.** tha ceum ann, tha e cuagach *a* bog *v* bi bacach/cuagach/crùbach

limpet *n* bàirneach *f*
line *n* loidhne *f*; (*in writing*) sreath *f m*; (*clothes*) ròp anairt; (*fishing*) driamlach *f*; (*geneal*) sìol *m*, gineal *f m* **l.-fishing** dorghach *m* **on-l.** air loidhne *v* lìnig
linear *a* sreathach, loidhneach
linen *n* anart *m*, lìon-aodach *m*
ling *n* (*fish*) langa *f*
linger *v* dèan dàil, rongaich, gabh ùine
lingerie *n* aodach-cneis *m*
linguistic *a* cànanach
lining *n* lìnig(eadh) *m*
link *n* ceangal *m*; (*in chain*) tinne *f*, dul *m* **linkspan** alt-aiseig *m* *v* dèan co-cheangal
lint *n* lìon *m*, caiteas *m*
lintel *n* àrd-doras *m*
lion *n* leòmhann *m* **the l.'s share** an ceann reamhar *m*
lip *n* bile *f*, lip *f*; (*geog*) oir *f m* **lip-service** beul bòidheach *m* **lipstick** dath-lipean *m*, peant bhilean *m*
liqueur *n* liciùr *m*
liquid *n* lionn *m* *a* lionnach, sruthach
liquidate *v* (*company*) sgaoil; (*kill*) cuir às do
liquidation *n* (*of company*) sgaoileadh *m*
liquidize *v* lionnaich
liquor *n* deoch(-làidir) *f*
liquorice *n* carra-mheille *m*
lisp *n* liotaiche *m*, liotachas *m* *v* bi liotach
lisping *a* liotach
list *n* liosta *f*; (*to side*) fiaradh *m* *v* dèan liosta; (*of ship*) liost(aig)
listen *v* èist (ri)
listening *n* èisteachd *f*
listless *a* gun lùths/sunnd
literacy *n* litearrachd *f*, litearras *m*
literal *a* litireil
literary *a* litreachail
literate *a* litearra
literature *n* litreachas *m* **oral l.** litreachas beòil
lithe *a* sùbailte, subailte
litigate *v* rach gu lagh, agair lagh air
litigation *n* agartachd *f*, cùis-lagha *f*
litre *n* liotair *m*
litter *n* sgudal *m*; (*of animals*) cuain *f*, iseanan *m pl* *v* fàg na bhùrach **discard l.** fàg sgudal
little *n* beagan *m*, rud beag *m* *a* beag, meanbh
liturgy *n* ùrnaigh choitcheann *f*
live *v* bi beò
live *a* beò
livelihood *n* beòshlaint *f*, teachd-an-tìr *m*, bith-beò *m*
lively *a* beothail, frogail, sunndach
liver *n* adha *m*, grùthan *m*
livid *a* (*met*) **he was l.** bha an cuthach dearg air
living *n* beòshlaint *f*, teachd-an-tìr *m*, bith-beò *m* *a* beò
lizard *n* laghairt *f m*, dearc-luachrach *f*
load *n* luchd *m*, eallach *m*; (*on mind*) uallach *m* *v* luchdaich, lìon; (*gun*) cuir urchair an
loaf *n* lof *f m*
loan *n* iasad *m* **loanword** facal-iasaid *m* *v* thoir iasad do, thoir ... air iasad
loath *a* ain-deònach
loathe *v* fuathaich **I loathed it** bha gràin (an) uilc agam air
loathing *n* gràin uilc *f*, sgreamh *m*
loathsome *a* gràineil, sgreamhail, sgreataidh
lobby *n* lobaidh *f*, trannsa *f*; (*pressure group*) luchd-coiteachaidh *m* *v* coitich
lobster *n* giomach *m* **l.-pot** cliabh-ghiomach *f*
local *a* ionadail **l. authority** ùghdarras ionadail *m* **l. government** riaghaltas ionadail *m*
locality *n* àite *m*, coimhearsnachd *f*, sgìre *f*
locate *v* suidhich, cuir na àite
location *n* suidheachadh *m*, àite *m*
loch *n* loch *m*
lock *n* glas *f*; (*of hair*) dual *m*, ciabh *f*, cuailean *m* *v* glas
locker *n* preasa glaiste *m*

locus *n* lòcas *m*, àite *m*
locust *n* lòcast *m*
lodge *n* loidse *f m*, taigh-geata *m*
lodge *v* (*submit*) cuir a-steach, càirich; (*stay*) gabh còmhnaidh
lodger *n* loidsear *m*
lodging *n* loidseadh *m* **l. house** taigh-loidsidh *m*
loft *n* lobhta *m*
log *n* sail *f*, loga *f m*; (*book*) leabhar-aithris *m*; (*math*) log *m*
logic *n* loidsig *f*
logical *a* loidsigeach
log off *v* thig dheth, tarraing às
log on *v* rach air, dèan ceangal
loin *n* blian *m* **the loins** an leasraidh *f*
loiter *v* dèan màirneal, rongaich
lollipop *n* loiliopop *f*
Londoner *n* Lunnainneach *m*, neach à Lunnainn *m*
lone *a* aonarach, na (h-)aonar *etc*, leis/leatha fhèin *etc*
loneliness *n* aonaranachd *f*
lonely *a* aonaranach
loner *n* aonaran *m*
long *a* fada **l. ago** o chionn f(h)ada **l.-lasting** buan, maireannach **l.-suffering** fad-fhulangach **l.-term** fad-ùine *v* **l. for** miannaich; (*weary for*) gabh fadachd ri
long division *n* roinn fhada *f*
longing *n* miann *f m*, togradh *m*, fadachd *f*
longitude *n* domhan-fhad *m*
long jump *n* leum-fada *m*, leum-fhada *f*
look *n* sùil *f;* (*appearance*) coltas *m*, fiamh *m v* seall, coimhead, amhairc **l. for** coimhead airson, lorg, sir
loom *n* beairt(-fhighe) *f*
loop *n* lùb *f*
loophole *n* beàrn *f*, dòigh às *f*
loose *a* fuasgailte, sgaoilte, gun cheangal **l. change** airgead pronn *m*
loose(n) *v* fuasgail, cuir/leig mu sgaoil
loot *n* creach *f* *v* creach
lop *v* sgud, sgath, geàrr
lopsided *a* leathoireach, gu aon taobh
loquacious *a* briathrach
lord *n* tighearna *m*, triath *m*, morair *m* **House of Lords** Taigh nam Morairean *m* **the Lord's Prayer** Ùrnaigh an Tighearna *f*
lorry *n* làraidh *f*
lose *v* caill
loss *n* call *m*
lost *a* air chall, caillte
lot *n* (*amount*) mòran *m*, tòrr *m*; (*in life*) crannchur *m* **cast lots** tilg croinn
lotion *n* cungaidh *f*
lottery *n* crannchur *m* **the National L.** an Crannchur Nàiseanta
loud *a* àrd, faramach
loudspeaker *n* glaodhaire *m*
lounge *n* rùm-suidhe *m* *v* sìn
louse *n* mial *f*
lousy *a* grod; (*with lice*) mialach
lout *n* burraidh *m*
love *n* gaol *m*, gràdh *m*; (*tennis*) neoni *m* **my l.** m' eudail *v* gràdhaich, thoir gaol **I l. you** tha gaol agam ort **we l. skiing** 's fìor thoigh leinn sgitheadh, tha sinn fìor dhèidheil/mhiadhail air sgitheadh
lovely *a* bòidheach, àlainn, lurach, maiseach
lover *n* leannan *m*
lovesick *a* an trom-ghaol
loving *a* gràdhach, ionmhainn
low *a* ìosal, ìseal
low *v* geum, bi a' geumnaich
lower *v* ìslich, lùghdaich
lowing *n* geumnaich *f*
Lowlander *n* Gall *m*, (*female*) bana-Ghall *f pl* Goill
low water *n* muir-tràigh *f*
loyal *a* dìleas
loyalist *n* dìlseach *m*
loyalty *n* dìlseachd *f*
lubricate *v* lìomh, dèan sleamhainn, cuir ola air/an
lucid *a* soilleir
luck *n* sealbh *m*, fortan *m*, rath *m* **Good l.!** Gur(a) math a thèid dhut/leat!
lucky *a* sealbhach, fortanach
lucrative *a* airgeadach

ludicrous *a* amaideach, gòrach
luggage *n* bagaichean *m pl*, màileidean *f pl*
lukewarm *a* meadh-bhlàth, flodach
lull *v* meall; (*to sleep*) cuir a chadal
lullaby *n* tàladh *m*
lumbago *n* leum-droma *m*
lumber *n* treal(l)aich *f*, seann àirneis *f*
luminous *a* soillseach, deàlrach
lump *n* cnap *m*; (*geog*) meall *m* **a l. sum** cnap airgid *m*
lumpy *a* cnapach
lunacy *n* euslaint-inntinn *f*; (*met*) mullach an amaideis *m*
lunatic *n* euslainteach-inntinn *m*
lunch *n* lòn *m*, diathad *f* **l. break** tràth-bìdh *m*, biadh meadhain-latha *m*
lung *n* sgamhan *m*
lurch *n* tulgadh *m*, siaradh *m* *v* dèan tulgadh/siaradh
lure *v* buair, breug
lurid *a* eagalach, sgràthail, oillteil
lurk *v* falaich, siolp
luscious *a* sòghmhor
lush *a* mèath
lust *n* ana-miann *f m*, drù(i)s *f* *v* **l. after/for** sanntaich, miannaich
lustre *n* deàlradh *m*, gleans *m*, lainnir *f*; (*met*) mòr-chliù *m*
luxurious *a* sòghail
luxury *n* sògh *m*, sòghalachd *f*
lying *n* (*phys*) laighe *f*; (*telling lies*) innse bhreug *f* *a* (*untruthful*) breugach
lynch *v* croch (gun chùirt)
lyric *n* liric *f*, ealaidh *f*
lythe *n* liugha *f*, liùgh *f*

M

machination *n* innleachd *f*
machine *n* inneal *m*
machinery *n* innealradh *m*; (*met*) modhan-obrach *f pl*
mackerel *n* rionnach *m*
mad *a* às a c(h)iall/rian *etc*; (*slang*) cracte **he was mad** (*angry*) bha an cuthach air
madam *n* bean-uasal *f*
madden *v* (*anger*) cuir an cuthach air
madness *n* dìth-cèille *f m*; (*slang*) crac *m*
magazine *n* iris *f*; (*quarterly*) ràitheachan *m*; (*arms store*) armlann *f*; (*of gun*) cèis-bhiathaidh *f*
maggot *n* cnuimh *f*
magic *n* draoidheachd *f* *a* draoidheil
magician *n* draoidh *m*
magistrate *n* bàillidh *m*, maigh(i)stir-lagha *m*
magnanimous *a* fial-inntinneach, fialaidh
magnet *n* magnait *m*, clach-iùil *f*
magnificent *a* òirdheirc
magnify *v* meudaich; (*extol*) àrdaich
magpie *n* pitheid *f*, pioghaid *f*
maid(en) *n* maighdeann *f*, gruagach *f*; (*servant*) searbhanta *f*
mail *n* post *m*, litrichean *f pl* **m.-order** òrdugh tron phost *m* *v* post(aig), cuir sa phost
maim *v* ciorramaich, leòn, ciùrr
main *a* prìomh **m. road** rathad-mòr *m*
mainland *n* tìr-mòr *f m*, mòr-thìr *f*
mainly *adv* anns a' mhòr-chuid, gu beagnaich
maintain *v* (*keep*) glèidh, cùm; (*support*) cùm suas; (*in argument*) cùm a-mach, tagair
maintenance *n* gleidheadh *m*, cumail suas *f*; (*of person*) beathachadh *m*
maize *n* cruithneachd Innseanach *f m*
majestic *a* flathail
majesty *n* mòrachd *f*, rìoghachd *f*
major *n* (*mil*) màidsear *m*; (*sport*) prìomh fharpais *f*
major *a* mòr, cudromach; (*greater*) … as/a bu motha
majority *n* mòr-chuid *f*, tromlach *f*, a' chuid as/a bu motha *f*
make *n* seòrsa *m* **m.-up** rìomhadh (gnùis(e)) *m*; (*met*) dèanamh *m*, nàdar *m* *v* dèan; (*compel*) thoir

air, co-èignich; (*bed*) càirich **m. for** (*head for*) dèan air **m. believe** leig air/oirre *etc* **we'll m. it** nì sinn a' chùis
male *n* fireannach *m* *a* fireann
malevolent *a* gamhlasach, le droch rùn
malice *n* mì-rùn *m*, droch rùn *m*, droch mhèinn *f*
malicious *a* droch-rùnach, droch-mhèinneach
malign *v* mì-chliùthaich
malignant *a* millteach; (*of cancer*) cronail, nimheil
mallard *n* lach riabhach *f*
malleable *a* so-chumte, a ghabhas cumadh
malnutrition *n* dìth beathachaidh *f m*, cion a' bhìdh *m*
malpractice *n* mì-chleachdadh *m*, droch ghiùlan *m*
malt *n* braich *f* **m. whisky** mac na braiche *m*
maltreat *v* droch-làimhsich, dèan droch ghiollachd air
maltreatment *n* droch-làimhseachadh *m*, droch ghiollachd *m*
mammal *n* sineach *m*, mamal *m*
man *n* duine *m*, fear *m*, fireannach *m*; (*husband*) duine
manage *v* stiùir; (*be able to*) dèan a' chùis
manageable *a* so-riaghladh, so-stiùireadh, a ghabhas dèanamh
management *n* stiùireadh *m*, riaghladh *m*; (*personnel*) luchd-stiùiridh *m*
manager *n* manaidsear *m*, ceannbhair *m*
manageress *n* bana-mhanaidsear *f*, bana-cheannbhair *f*
mandate *n* òrdugh *m*, àithne *f*; (*electoral*) ùghdarras *m*
mandatory *a* do-sheachanta, èigneachail
mane *n* muing *f*
manfully *adv* gu duineil, gu dian
mangle *v* reub, dèan ablach de
manhood *n* fearalas *m*
mania *n* boile-cuthaich *f*
maniac *n* neach-cuthaich *m*, caochanach *m*
manic *a* fon chuthach
manicure *n* grinneachadh làimhe *m* *v* grinnich làmhan
manifest *a* follaiseach, soilleir *v* taisbean, nochd, foillsich
manipulate *v* obraich
mankind *n* an cinne-daonna *m*
manliness *n* duinealas *m*, fearalachd *f*
manly *a* duineil, fearail
manner *n* modh *f m*, seòl *m*, dòigh *f*
mannerism *n* cleachdadh *m*, cleas *m*, cuinse *f*
mannerly *a* modhail
manners *n* modh *f m*
manoeuvre *n* eacarsaich *f*; (*mil*) gluasad (airm) *m*; (*met*) innleachd *f*, cleas *m*
manpower *n* sgiobachd *f*
manse *n* mansa *m*
mansion *n* taigh/aitreabh mòr *m*, àros *m*
mantlepiece *n* breus *m*
manual *a* làimhe **m. work** obair làimhe *f* *n* leabhar-làimhe/mìneachaidh *m*
manufacture *v* dèan
manure *n* todhar *m*, mathachadh *m*, innear *f*
manuscript *n* làmh-sgrìobhainn *f*
Manx *n* Gàidhlig Mhanainneach *f* *a* Manainneach
Manxman *n* Manainneach *m* **Manxwoman** ban-Mhanainneach *f*
many *n* mòran *m* *a* iomadh, iomadach **m. people** mòran dhaoine **m. a time ...** 's iomadh uair ... **as m. again** uiread eile **so m.** a leithid de, uiread de **twice as m.** a dhà uimhir
map *n* map(a) *m*, clàr-dùthcha *m*
mar *v* mill
marble *n* màrmor *m*; (*ball*) marbal *m*, mìrleag *f*
March *n* am Màrt *m*
march *n* màrsail *f*, mèarrsadh *m*; (*tune*) caismeachd *f* *v* dèan màrsail/mèarrsadh, mèarrs
mare *n* làir *f*
margarine *n* margarain *m*

margin *n* oir *f m*, iomall *m*
marginal *a* iomallach, leathoireach
marigold *n* a' bhile bhuidhe *f*
marine *a* mara
mariner *n* maraiche *m*
maritime *a* cuantach
mark *n* comharra *m*; (*trace*) làrach *f m*, lorg *f*; (*currency*) marc *m* *v* comharraich; (*notice*) thoir fa-near, gabh beachd air
market *n* fèill *f*, margadh *f m*, margaid *f m* **m. place** ionad margaidh *m*
marketing *n* margaideachd *f*
marmalade *n* marmalaid *m*
marquee *n* puball *m*, pàillean *m*
marquis *n* marcas *m*
marriage *n* pòsadh *m*
married *a* pòsta **m. couple** càraid phòsta *f*
marrow *n* smior *m*; (*veg*) mearag *f*
marry *v* pòs
marsh *n* boglach *f*, fèith *f* **m.-marigold** lus buidhe Bealltainn *m*
marshal *v* cuir an òrdugh, trus
mart *n* ionad margaidh *m*
martial *a* gaisgeanta
Martinmas *n* an Fhèill M(h)àrtainn *f*, Latha Fhèill Màrtainn *m*
martyr *n* martarach *m*
marvel *n* iongnadh *m*, mìorbhail *f* *v* gabh iongnadh
marvellous *a* mìorbhaileach, iongantach
Marxist *n, a* Marcsach *m*
mascot *n* suaichnean *m*
masculine a fearail; *(gram)* fireannta
mash *v* pronn
mashed *a* pronn
mask *n* aghaidh-choimheach *f*, aodannan *m*
mason *n* clachair *m*
masonry *n* clachaireachd *f*
mass *n* tomad *m*; (*great quantity*) meall *m*, tòrr *m*; (*majority*) mòr-chuid *f*; (*relig*) aifreann *f m*
massacre *n* casgradh *m* *v* casgair, murt
massage *n* suathadh/taosgnadh-bodhaig *m*
massive *a* tomadach, àibheiseach
mast *n* crann *m*
master *n* maigh(i)stir *m*; (*of ship*) sgiobair *m* **m. of ceremonies** fear an taighe *m* *v* (*subdue*) ceannsaich; (*become proficient in*) fàs suas ri
masterly *a* ealanta, sgaiteach
masterpiece *n* sàr obair *f*, euchd *m*
mat *n* brat *m*
match *n* maids(e) *m*, lasadair *m*; (*sport*) maids(e) *m*; (*equal*) seise *m*, samhail *m* **m.-box** bogsa/bucas-mhaidseachan *m* *v* freagair, co-fhreagair, maids
mate *n* cèile *m*, companach *m*; (*rank*) meat(a) *m*
material *n* stuth *m*
materialistic *a* saoghalta
maternal *a* màithreachail
maternity *a* màthaireil **m. hospital** ospadal mhàthraichean *m* **m. leave** fòrladh màthaireil *m*
mathematical *a* matamataigeach
mathematics *n* matamataig *m*
matrimony *n* dàimh-pòsaidh *f m*
matrix *n* machlag *f*; (*maths*) meatrags *f*
matron *n* bean-phòsta *f*; (*rank*) ban-cheannard *f*
matter *n* stuth *m*, brìgh *f*; (*affair*) gnothach *m*, cùis *f* **what's the m.?** dè tha ceàrr? *v* **it does not m.** chan eil e gu diofar
mattress *n* bobhstair *m*
mature *a* abaich, inbheach, air tighinn gu ìre *v* abaich
maturity *n* abaichead *m*, ìre *f*
maul *v* pronn, lidrig
mauve *n* liath-phurpaidh *m*
maximize *v* barraich
maximum *a* … as motha **the m.** a' chuid as motha *n* os-mheud *m*
May *n* an Cèitean *m*, a' Mhàigh *f* **May Day** Latha (Buidhe) Bealltainn *m*
may *v* (*permission*) faod; (*perhaps*) faod, 's dòcha **may I go?** am faod mi falbh? **they**

may not chan fhaod iad **she may come** faodaidh i tighinn; (*perhaps*) faodaidh gun tig i, 's dòcha gun tig i
mayday *n* gairm èiginn *f*
mayor *n* àrd-bhàillidh *m*, ceannard baile *m*
maze *n* ioma-shlighe *f*
me *pron* mi, (*emph*) mise
meadow *n* lòn *m*, faiche *f*, dail *f*, lèana *f*
meagre *a* gann, lom
meal *n* biadh *m*; (*flour*) min *f*
mean *a* spìocach; (*of spirit*) suarach, tàireil; (*stat*) meadhanail
mean *v* ciallaich; (*intend*) cuir romhad
meaning *n* ciall *f*, seagh *m*, brìgh *f*
meaningful *a* ciallach, brìoghmhor
meanness *n* spìocaireachd *f*; (*of spirit*) suarachas *m*
meantime *adv* an-dràsta **in the m.** anns an eadar-àm
meanwhile *adv* aig a' cheart àm
measles *n* a' ghriùthrach *f*, a' ghriùthlach *f*
measure *n* tomhas *m*; (*portion*) cuid *f*, roinn *f*; (*action*) ceum *m* *v* tomhais
measurement *n* tomhas *m*
meat *n* feòil *f*
mechanic *n* meacanaig *f*
mechanical *a* meacanaigeach
mechanism *n* uidheam *f*; (*means*) meadhan *m*, dòigh *f*
medal *n* bonn *m* **gold medal** bonn òir
meddle *v* buin ri, cuir làmh an, gabh gnothach ri
media, the *n* na meadhanan *m pl*
mediate *v* rèitich, rach san eadraiginn, eadar-mheadhanaich
mediation *n* eadraiginn *f*, eadar-ghuidhe *f*
mediator *n* eadar-mheadhanair *m*
medical *a* lèigh, meidigeach
medication *n* cungaidh leighis *f*
medicine *n* ìocshlaint *f*, cungaidh *f*; (*science*) eòlas-leighis *m*
medieval *a* meadhan-aoiseil
mediocre *a* meadhanach
meditate *v* beachdaich, beachd-smaoinich, meòraich
Mediterranean *n* a' Mhuir Mheadhan-thìreach *f* *a* Meadhan-thìreach
medium *a* meadhanach **m.-sized** meadhanach mòr **m. wave** bann meadhanach *m* *n* meadhan *m*
meek *a* macanta, ciùin
meet *v* coinnich, tachair; (*gather*) cruinnich; (*fulfil*) coilean
meeting *n* coinneamh *f*; (*act of*) coinneachadh *m*
melancholy *n* leann-dubh *m* *a* dubhach, fo leann-dubh
mellifluous *a* binn, milis
mellow *a* tlàth, làn-abaich
melodic/melodious *a* binn, fonnmhor
melody *n* fonn *m*
melon *n* meal-bhuc *m*
melt *v* leagh
member *n* ball *m* **MP** BP (Ball Pàrlamaid) *m* **MSP** BPA (Ball Pàrlamaid na h-Alba) **MEP** BPE (Ball Pàrlamaid Eòrpach)
membership *n* ballrachd *f*
membrane *n* meamran *m*
memento *n* cuimhneachan *m*
memoir(s) *n* eachdraidh-beatha *f*
memorable *a* ainmeil, fada air chuimhne
memorandum/memo *n* meòrachan *m*
memorial *n* cuimhneachan *m* **m. stone** clach-chuimhne *f* **m. cairn** càrn cuimhne *m* **m. service** seirbheis cuimhneachaidh *f*
memorize *v* cùm air chuimhne
memory *n* cuimhne *f*
menace *n* bagradh *m*, maoidheadh *m* **he's a m.** 's e plàigh a th' ann *v* bagair, maoidh
mend *v* càirich **be on the m.** rach am feabhas, thig air adhart
menial *a* sgalagail, seirbheiseil
meningitis *n* fiabhras eanchainn(e) *m*, teasach eanchainn *f*

mental *a* inntinneil **m. hospital** ospadal inntinn *m*
mention *n* iomradh *m*, luaidh *m* *v* ainmich, thoir iomradh/tarraing air, dèan luaidh air
menu *n* clàr-bìdh *m*, cairt-bìdh *f*; (*computer*) clàr-iùil *m*
mercenary *n* (*mil*) amhasg *m*, buanna *m*
mercenary *a* sanntach, miannach air airgead
merchandise *n* bathar *m*
merchant *n* ceannaiche *m*, marsanta *m* **the M. Navy** an Cabhlach Marsantach *m*
merciful *a* tròcaireach, iochdmhor
merciless *a* gun tròcair, an-iochdmhor
mercury *n* airgead-beò *m*
mercy *n* tròcair *f*, iochd *f*
merely *adv* a-mhàin, dìreach
merge *v* rach còmhla, coimeasg, dèan cothlamadh
merger *n* coimeasg(adh) *m*, aonadh *m*
meringue *n* mearang *m*
merit *n* luach *m*, airidheachd *f* *v* toill, bi airidh air
mermaid *n* maighdeann-mhara *f*
merriment *n* aighear *m*, mire *f*
merry *a* aighearach, mear
mesh *n* mogal *m*
mesmerize *v* dian-ghlac, cuir fo gheas
mess *n* bùrach *m*, butarrais *f*; (*staff*) seòmar-comaidh *m*
message *n* teachdaireachd *f*
messenger *n* teachdaire *m*
metabolism *n* meatabolachd *f*, fàs-atharrachadh *m*
metal *n* meatailt *f* **m. work** obair mheatailt *f*
metamorphose *v* cruth-atharraich
metaphor *n* meatafor *m*
metaphorical *a* meataforach
metaphysical *a* feallsanachail
meteor *n* dreag *f*, rionnag-earbaill *f*
meteorite *n* aileag *f*, sgeith-rionnaig *f*
meteorological *a* dreagach **Met. Office** Oifis na Sìde *f*
meteorology *n* eòlas-sìde *m*
meter *n* inneal-tomhais *m*
method *n* dòigh *f*, seòl *m*, modh *f m*; (*order*) rian *m*
methodical *a* òrdail, rianail
methodology *n* dòigh-obrach *f*, modh-obrach *f m*
metre *n* meatair *m*; (*of poetry*) rannaigheachd *f*, meadrachd *f*
metric *a* meatrach
metrical *a* rannaigheachd, meadrachail
metro *n* trèan fo thalamh *m*
metropolitan *a* prìomh-bhailteach
mettle *n* smioralachd *f*
mew *v* dèan miathalaich/miamhail
Michaelmas *n* an Fhèill M(h)ìcheil *f*, Latha Fhèill Mìcheil *m*
microbe *n* bitheag *f*, meanbhag *f*
microbiology *n* meanbh-bhith-eòlas *m*
microphone *n* maicreafòn *m*
microscope *n* maicreasgop *m*
microwave *n* meanbh-thonn *f*; (*oven*) àmhainn mheanbh-thonnach *f*
midday *n* meadhan-latha *m*
midden *n* sitig *f*, òcrach *f*, òtrach *f*
middle *n* meadhan *m* **m.-aged** sa mheadhan-latha **(the) M. Ages** na Meadhan-Aoisean *f pl* **m.-class** eagar meadhanach *m* *a* meadhan, meadhanach
midge *n* meanbh-chuileag *f*
midnight *n* meadhan-oidhche *m*
midriff *n* (an) sgairt *f*
midsummer *n* meadhan (an t-) samhraidh *m*; (*St John's Day*) Latha Fèill Eòin *m*
midway *adv* letheach-slighe, sa mheadhan
midwife *n* bean-ghlùine *f*
midwifery *n* banas-glùine *m*
might *n* cumhachd *m*, neart *m*, spionnadh *m*
might *v* faod, 's dòcha; (*ought*) bu choir dhut **a seat belt m. have saved his life** dh'fhaodadh gum biodh/gun robh crios-

sàbhalaidh air a chumail beò **you m. have apologized to her** bha coir agad a bhith air mathanas iarraidh oirre

mighty *a* cumhachdach, foghainteach

migrate *v* dèan imrich

migration *n* imrich *f*; (*overseas*) imrich cuain

mild *a* màlda, ciùin, tlàth

mildew *n* clòimh-liath *f*

mile *n* mìle *f m* **mileage** astar mhìltean *m* **milestone** clach-mhìle *f*

militant *n* mìleantach *m*, cathach *m* *a* mìleanta, cathachail

military *a* cogail, armailteach

militate *v* (*against*) obraich an aghaidh

militia *n* mailisidh *m*

milk *n* bainne *m* *v* bleoghain(n)

mill *n* muileann *f m* **millstone** clach-mhuilinn *f*; (*met*) eallach *m*

millennium *n* mìle bliadhna *f m*

milligram *n* mìlegram *m*

millilitre *n* mìleliotair *m*

millimetre *n* mìlemeatair *m*

million *n* millean *m*

millionaire *n* milleanair *m*

mime *n* mìm *f* *v* dèan mìm

mimic *v* dèan atharrais (air)

mince *n* mions *m*

mind *n* inntinn *f*, aigne *f*, ciall *f* **keep in m.** cuimhnich *v* **what did you have in m.?** dè bh' agad san amharc? **he is out of his m.** tha e às a chiall *v* thoir an aire, thoir fa-near; (*remember*) cuimhnich

mindful *a* cuimhneachail, cùramach

mine *n* mèinn *f* **coal m.** toll-guail *m* *v* cladhaich; (*plant mines*) cuir mèinnean (an)

mine *pron* leamsa, agamsa **that's m.** 's ann leamsa a tha sin **this memory of m.** a' chuimhne seo agamsa

miner *n* mèinneadair *m*, mèinnear *m*

mineral *n* mèinnir *m* *a* mèinnireach **m. water** uisge mèinnireach *m*

mingle *v* measgaich, coimeasg, cuir an ceann a chèile; (*with people*) rach an lùib

minibus *n* bus beag *m*

minimal *a* fìor bheag; (*least*) as/a bu lugha

minimize *v* lùghdaich, ìslich

minimum *n* a' chuid as/a bu lugha *f*, ìos-mheud *m* *a* as/a bu lugha

minister *n* ministear *m* *v* fritheil, ministrealaich

ministry *n* ministre(al)achd *f* **the M. of Defence** Ministre(al)achd an Dìon *f*

mink *n* minc *m*

minor *a* beag, as lugha, fo- *n* òg-aoisear *m*

minority *n* mion/beag-chuid *f*; (*age*) òg-aois *f* **m. language** mion-chànan *f m*

mint *n* meannt *m*; (*place*) taigh-cùinnidh *m* **he made a m.** rinn e fortan

minus *prep* às aonais (+ *gen*); (*math*) thoir air falbh

minute *n* mionaid *f*; (*of meeting*) geàrr-chunntas *m*

minute *a* meanbh, mion, beag bìodach

miracle *n* mìorbhail *f*

miraculous *a* mìorbhaileach

mirage *n* mearachadh sùla *m*

mire *n* poll *m*, eabar *m*

mirror *n* sgàthan *m*

mirth *n* mire *f*, sùgradh *m*

misadventure *n* mì-shealbh *m*, sgiorradh *m*

misbehave *v* bi ri mì-mhodh, bi mì-mhodhail

misbehaviour *n* mì-mhodh *m*, droch ghiùlan *m*

miscalculate *v* àireamhaich ceàrr; (*met*) dèan co-dhùnadh ceàrr

miscall *v* càin

miscarriage *n* (*med*) asaid anabaich *f*; (*general*) dol a dhìth *m* **m. of justice** iomrall ceartais *m*

miscarry *v* asaid an-abaich; (*general*) rach a dhìth

miscellaneous *a* measgaichte, eugsamhail

miscellany *n* measgachadh *m*

mischief *n* luathaireachd *f*; (*serious*) aimhleas *m*, miastadh *m*
mischievous *a* luathaireach
misconception *n* mì-thuigsinn *f*, claon-bheachd *m*
misconduct *n* mì-mhodh *m*, droch ghiùlan *m*
misdemeanour *n* eucoir *f*, mì-ghnìomh *m*
miser *n* spìocaire *m*
miserable *a* truagh, brònach
misfit *n* faondraiche *m*
misfortune *n* mì-fhortan *m*, mì-shealbh *m*
misgiving(s) *n* teagamh(an) *m* (*pl*)
misguided *a* neo-ghlic, cearbach
mishap *n* mì-thapadh *m*, tubaist *f*
misinform *v* thoir fios meallta/ceàrr
misinterpret *v* mì-bhreithnich, tog ceàrr
misjudge *v* thoir mì-bhreith (air), tuig ceàrr
mislay *v* caill
mislead *v* meall, mì-threòraich, cuir ceàrr/air seachran
misleading *a* meallta
mismatch *n* neo-ionannachd *f*
misplace *v* caill
misprint *n* mearachd clò *f*
misrepresent *v* thoir claon-aithris
misrule *n* mì-riaghladh *m*; (*anarchy*) mì-riaghailt *f*
Miss *n* A' Mhaighdeann *f* (*abb*) A' Mh.
miss *v* ionndrainn; (*train etc*) caill; (*target etc*) ana-cuimsich
missile *n* tilgean *m*, astas *m*
missing *a* a dhìth, a dh'easbhaidh; (*person*) air chall, gun lorg
mission *n* misean *f*; (*purpose*) rùn *m* **m. statement** aithris rùin *f*
missionary *n* miseanaraidh *m*
mist *n* ceò *f m*, ceathach *m*
mistake *n* mearachd *f*, iomrall *m*
Mister (Mr) *n* Maigh(i)stir (Mgr) *m*
mistletoe *n* uil-ìoc *m*
mistress *n* bana-mhaighstir *f*; (*lover*) coimhleapach *f m*, boireannach eile *m* **Mrs** A' Bh.
misty *a* ceòthach, ceòthar
misunderstand *v* tog ceàrr
misunderstanding *n* mì-thuigse *f*, togail ceàrr *f*
misuse *n* mì-bhuileachadh *m*
mite *n* fìneag *f*
mitigating *a* lasachaidh, maothachaidh
mitigation *n* lasachadh *m*, maothachadh *m*
mix *v* measgaich, cuir an lùib a chèile, cothlaim
mixed *a* measgaichte, measgte
mixer *n* measgaichear *m*, inneal-measgachaidh *m*
mixture *n* measgachadh *m*
moan *n* gearan *m*; (*sound*) acain *f*, osna *f* *v* gearain; (*sound*) dèan acainn/osna
mob *n* gràisg *f*
mobile *a* gluasadach **m. phone** *n* fòn-làimhe *f m*
mobility *n* gluasadachd *f*, cothrom gluasaid *m*
mock *v* mag (air), dèan fanaid (air)
mockery *n* magadh *m*, fanaid *f*
mod *n* mòd *m* **the National Mod** am Mòd Nàiseanta **local m.** mòd ionadail
mode *n* modh *f m*, dòigh *f*, seòl *m*, rian *m*
model *n* modail *m*, cruth *m*, samhail *m*; (*make*) seòrsa *m*; (*fashion*) modail *m* *a* **m. employee** brod an obraiche *v* deilbh, cum, dealbhaich **m. oneself on** lean eisimpleir (+ *gen*)
modem *n* mòdam *m*
moderate *a* cuibheasach, meadhanach; (*disposition*) stuama, riaghailteach *v* (*of weather*) ciùinich; (*exams*) co-mheas
moderation *n* stuaim *f*, riaghailteachd *f*; (*of exams*) co-mheasadh *m*
moderator *n* co-mheasadair *m*; (*eccl*) moderàtor *m*
modern *a* ùr, nuadh, nodha
modernize *v* ùraich, nuadhaich
modest *a* nàrach, màlda, socharach

modesty *n* beusachd *f*, màldachd *f*, socharachd *f*
modify *v* atharraich, leasaich
module *n* modal *m*
moist *a* tais, bog
moisten *v* taisich, bogaich
moisture *n* taiseachd *f*, fliche *f*
mole *n* (*animal*) famh *f*; (*on skin*) ball-dòrain *m*; (*insider*) ruamharaiche *m* **molehill** dùnan-faimh *m*
molecule *n* moileciuil *m*
molest *v* (*accost*) thoir ionnsaigh air; (*annoy*) cuir dragh air
mollify *v* maothaich, ciùinich
molten *a* leaghte
moment *n* tiota(n) *m*, mòmaid *f*
momentary *a* car tiota
momentous *a* fìor chudromach
momentum *n* cumhachd gluasaid *m*; (*velocity*) luaths *m*
monarch *n* monarc *m*
monarchist *n* monarcach *m*
monarchy *n* monarcachd *f*
monastery *n* manachainn *f*
Monday *n* Diluain *m*
monetary *a* ionmhasail
money *n* airgead *m*
mongol *n* mongolach *m*
mongrel *n*, *a* eadar-ghnè *f*
monitor *v* cùm sùil air, sgrùd
monk *n* manach *m*
monkey *n* muncaidh *m*
mono- *pref* aon-
monopolize *v* lèir-shealbhaich, gabh thairis
monopoly *n* monopolaidh *f m*, lèir-shealbhachd *f*
monotonous *a* aon-duanach, liosta
monotony *n* an aon duan *m*, liostachd *f*
monster *n* uilebheist *f m*
monstrous *a* sgriosail, oillteil
month *n* mìos *f m*
monthly *a* mìosail
monument *n* carragh-cuimhne *f*, càrn-cuimhne *m*
mood *n* sunnd *m*, gleus *f m*, triom *f*; (*gram*) modh *f m*
moody *a* caochlaideach, greannach, frionasach
moon *n* gealach *f m* **moonlight** solas na gealaich *m* **the man in the m.** bodach na gealaich *m*
moor *n* mòinteach *f*, monadh *m* **m. fire** falaisg *f*
moor *v* acraich
moorhen cearc-fhraoich *f*
moose *n* lon *m*
mop *n* mop *m*, sguab-fhliuch *f*
mope *v* bi fo ghruaimean
moral *a* moralta, beusach *n* (*of story*) teagasg *m*, teachdaireachd *f* **morals** *n* beusan *f pl*
morale *n* misneachd *f*, spiorad *m*
morality *n* moraltachd *f*
morass *n* bog(l)ach *f*
morbid *a* mì-fhallain, dubhach
more *n* tuilleadh *m*, barrachd *f* *adv* **any m.** tuilleadh, nas mò
morning *n* madainn *f*
moron *n* lethchiallach *m*
morose *a* gruamach, mùgach
morphia, morphine *n* moirfin *f*
morsel *n* mìr *f*, criomag *f*, bìdeag *f*
mortal *a* bàsmhor
mortar *n* aol-tàthaidh *m*
mortgage *n* morgaids(e) *m*
mosaic *n* breac-dhualadh *m*
Moslem *n*, *a See* Muslim
mosque *n* mosg *m*
mosquito *n* mosgìoto *f*
moss *n* (*bot*) còinneach *f*; (*topog*) bog(l)ach *f*
most *n* a' mhòr-chuid *f*, a' chuid as motha *f* *a* as motha/a bu mhotha, a' chuid as motha/a bu mhotha
mostly *adv* mar as trice, sa mhòr-chuid
moth *n* leòmann *m*
mother *n* màthair *f* **m.-in-law** màthair-chèile *f*
motion *n* gluasad *m*; (*at meeting*) moladh *m* **set in m.** cuir a dhol *v*
motivate *v* spreag, brod
motivation *n* togradh *m*
motive *n* adhbhar *m*, ceann-fàth *m*
motley *a* ioma-sheòrsach, ioma-dhathach
motor *n*, *a* motair *m* **m. bicycle** motair-baidhsagal *m* **m.-cycle** motair-rothair *m*

motorist *n* motairiche *m*
motorway *n* mòr-rathad *m*
motto *n* faca(i)l-suaicheantais *m*
mould *n* molldair *m*; (*form*) cruth *m* **blue m.** clòimh-liath *f* *v* com
moult *v* cuir/tilg na h-itean, cuir fionnadh/gaoisid
mound *n* tom *m*, tòrr *m*
mount *v* dìrich, streap; (*horse*) rach air muin eich; (*set up*) cuir air dòigh
mountain *n* beinn *f*, monadh *m*
mountaineer *n* streapadair (beinne) *m*
mountaineering *n* streapadaireachd *f*, streap nam beann *m*
mourn *v* caoidh
mournful *a* brònach, tiamhaidh
mourning *n* bròn *m*, caoidh *f*, tuireadh *m* **in m.** a' caoidh, ri bròn
mouse *n* luch *f*
moustache *n* stais *f*
mouth *n* beul *m*; (*large*) craos *m* **m.-music** port-à-beul *m* **m.-organ** òrgan-beòil *m*
mouthful *n* làn-beòil *m*, balgam *m*
move *v* gluais, caraich; (*propose*) cuir air adhart, mol **m. house** dèan imrich/imprig
movement *n* gluasad *m*
moving *a* (*emotion*) drùidhteach
mow *v* geàrr, buain
mower *n* lomaire *m*
much *adv* mòran; (*with a*) fada **as m. again** uimhir eile **as m. as** uiread ri/agus **too m.** cus **that is m. better** tha sin fada/cus/mòran nas fheàrr *n* mòran *m*
muck *n* salchar *m*, eabar *m*; (*manure*) buachar *m*, innear *f*
mucky *a* salach
mucus *n* ronn *m*
mud *n* poll *m*, eabar *m*
muddle *n* bùrach *m*, troimh-a-chèile *f m* *v* cuir troimh-a-chèile
muddy *a* eabarach, fo eabar/pholl
muffle *v* (*wrap up*) còmhdaich; (*deaden*) mùch
mug *n* muga *f m*; (*fool*) gloidhc *f*
mug *v* dèan braid-ionnsaigh
mugging *n* braid-ionnsaigh *f*
muggy *a* bruthainneach
Mull person *n* Muileach *m*, (*female*) ban(a)-Mhuileach *f*
multi- *pref* ioma-
multicoloured *a* ioma-dhathach
multicultural *a* ioma-chultarach
multilateral *a* ioma-thaobhach
multilingual *a* ioma-chànanach
multimedia *n* ioma-mheadhan *m*
multinational *a* ioma-nàiseanta
multiple *a* ioma-sheòrsach, iomadach
multiplication *n* iomadachadh *m*, meudachadh *m*
multiply *v* iomadaich, meudaich; (*genetically*) sìolaich, fàs lìonmhor
multitude *n* mòr-shluagh *m*
mum(my) *n* mamaidh *f*
mumble *v* bi a' brunndail
mumps *n* an t-at-busach *m*, an tinneas-plocach *m*
munch *v* cagainn
mundane *a* àbhaisteach, làitheil
mural *n* dealbh-balla *m*
murder *n* murt *m* *v* dèan murt
murderer *n* murtair *m*
murmur *n* (*of nature*) monmhar *m*, torman *m*, crònan *m*; (*person*) brunndail *f*
muscle *n* fèith *f*
muscular *a* fèitheach
museum *n* taigh-tasgaidh *m*
mushroom *n* balgan-buachair *m*
music *n* ceòl *m*
musical *a* ceòlmhor, binn; (*person*) math air ceòl **m. instrument** *n* inneal-ciùil *m*
musician *n* neach-ciùil *m*
Muslim *n, a* Muslamach *m*, (*female*) ban-Mhuslamach *f*
mussel *n* feusgan *m*
must *v* feumaidh, bi aig … ri, 's èiginn do, 's fheudar do
mustard *n* (*bot*) sgeallan *m*; (*condiment*) mustard *m*
muster *v* cruinnich, trus
musty *a* tungaidh, fuaraidh
mutation *n* mùthadh *m*, atharrachadh *m*
mute *a* balbh, tostach
mutilate *v* ciorramaich, geàrr

mutiny *n* ceannairc *f*, ar-a-mach *m* *v* dèan ceannairc/ar-a-mach
mutter *v* dèan dranndan/gearan
mutton *n* muilt-fheòil *f*, feòil caorach *f*
mutual *a* co-aontach, a rèir a chèile
muzzle *v* cuir glas-ghuib air
my *poss pron* mo, (*before vowels*) m', agam(sa) **my key** an iuchair agam
myself *pron* mi fhèin/fhìn
mysterious *a* dìomhair
mystery *n* dìomhaireachd *f*, rùn dìomhair *m*
mystical *a* fàidheanta
mystify *v* cuir an imcheist
myth *n* miotas *m*, uirsgeul *m*
mythical *a* miotasach
mythology *n* miotas-eòlas *m*

N

nag *v* dèan cànran
nail *n* tarrag *f*; (*finger/toe*) ìne *f* **n.-file** lìomhan-ìnean *m* **n. varnish** bhàrnais ìnean *f*
naive *a* neo(i)chiontach, sìmplidh
naked *a* lomnochd, rùisgte
name *n* ainm *m*; (*reputation*) cliù *m* *v* ainmich **give a n. to** thoir ainm air
nap *n* norrag *f*, snuachdan *m*, cadalan *m*; (*on cloth*) caitean *m*
napkin *n* nèapaigin *m*
nappy *n* badan *m*
narrate *v* aithris
narration *n* aithris *f*, iomradh *m*, seanchas *m*
narrator *n* neach-aithris *m*, seanchaidh *m*
narrow *a* cumhang, caol **n.-minded** cumhang
nasty *a* mosach, suarach
nation *n* nàisean *m*, dùthaich *f*, rìoghachd *f*
national *a* nàiseanta **n. insurance** *n* àrachas nàiseanta *m* **the N. Health Service** Seirbheis Nàiseanta na Slàinte *f*
nationalism *n* nàiseantachas *m*
nationalist *n, a* nàiseantach *m*
nationality *n* nàiseantachd *f*
nationalize *v* stàit-shealbhaich, cuir an seilbh na stàite
native *n* dùthchasach *m* **n. of** neach a mhuinntir ... *m* (+ *gen*) *a* dùthchasach, san dualchas **n. speaker** fileantach ((bh)o dhùthchas) *m*
natural *a* nàdarra(ch)
naturalist *n* neach-eòlais-nàdair *m*
naturally *adv* gu nàdarra(ch)
nature *n* nàdar *m*, gnè *f*, seòrsa *m* **n. reserve** tèarmann nàdair *m*
naught *n* neoni *m*
naughty *a* dona, mì-mhodhail
nausea *n* òrrais *f*, neoshannt *m*
nautical *a* seòlaidh, maraireachd
navel *n* imleag *f*
navigate *v* (*plot course*) tog cùrsa; (*make passage*) seòl
navigation *n* mara(irea)chd *f*
navy *n* cabhlach *m*, nèibhidh *m*
navy-blue *a* dubh-ghorm
neap-tide *n* conntraigh *f*
near *a* faisg (air), dlùth (air), teann (air)
nearly *adv* faisg/dlùth air; (*almost*) cha mhòr nach (+ *v*)
neat *a* grinn, sgiobalta, cuimir
necessary *a* riatanach, deatamach, do-sheachanta
necessity *n* riatanas *m*, deatamachd *f* **dire n.** an dubh-èiginn *f*
neck *n* amha(i)ch *f*, muineal *m*
necklace *n* seud-muineil *m*, usgar-bràghad *m*, paidirean *m*
need *n* feum *m*; (*want*) dìth *f m*, easbhaidh *f*; (*poverty*) airc *f* *v* bi feumach air; (*must*) feum(aidh); (*want*) bi a dhìth air **we n. money** tha sinn feumach air airgead **we'll n. to go** feumaidh sinn falbh **what do you n.?** dè tha dhìth ort? **you n. not do that** cha leig/ruig thu a leas sin a dhèanamh
needle *n* snàthad *f*
needless *a* gun adhbhar
needy *a* ainniseach, easbhaidheach *n* **the n.** na feumaich *m pl*
negative *a* àicheil

neglect *n* dearmad *m* *v* dèan dearmad (air), bi gun diù (mu)
negligence *n* dearmadachd *f*, mì-chùram *m*, cion diù *m*
negligent *a* dearmadach, mì-chùramach
negligible *a* suarach, neonitheach
negotiate *v* barganaich, dèan gnothach (ri), co-rèitich
negotiation *n* barganachadh *m*, co-rèiteachadh *m*
neigh *v* dèan sitir/sitrich, sitrich
neighbour *n* nàbaidh *m*, coimhearsnach *m*
neighbourhood *n* nàba(idhea)chd *f*, coimhearsnachd *f*
neither *a, pron* a h-aon *conj* cha mhò *adv* nas mò **n. of them stayed** cha do dh'fhuirich a h-aon aca/fear seach fear aca/tè seach tè aca **she doesn't drive and n. does he** cha dèan ise dràibheadh 's cha mhò a nì esan
neo- *pref* nuadh-
nephew *n* mac peathar/bràthar *m*
nerve *n* fèith-mhothachaidh *f*, nearbh *f* **what a n.!** abair aghaidh! **he lost his n.** chaill e a mhisneachd
nervous *a* iomagaineach, nearbha(sa)ch
nest *n* nead *f m* *v* neadaich
net *n* lìon *m* **the Net** an Lìon
netball *n* ball-lìn *m*
nettle *n* deanntag *f*, feanntag *f*
network *n* lìon *m*, lìonra *m* *v* dèan lìonra; (*met*) dèan eadar-cheanglaichean
neuter *a* (*gram*) neodrach
neutral *a* neo-phàirteach, gun taobh
never *adv* (*with neg v*) a-chaoidh, gu bràth, uair sam bith; (*in past*) (a-)riamh **n. mind!** *interj* coma leat!
nevertheless *adv* an dèidh sin, a dh'aindeoin sin
new *a* ùr, nuadh **New Year** a' Bhliadhn' Ur *f* **N. Year's Day** Latha na Bliadhn' Uire *m* **Happy New Year!** Bliadhna Mhath Ùr!
news *n* naidheachd *f*, fios *m*
newspaper pàipear-naidheachd *m*
next *a* an ath (+ *len*), ... as fhaisge/a b' fhaisge *adv* a-nis **n. week** an ath sheachdain **what next!** dè nis!, dè an ath rud!
nibble *v* criom, creim
nice *a* gasta, laghach, snog
niche *n* cùil *f*, oisean *m*
nick *n* eag *f* **in the n. of time** dìreach na uair/ann an tide *v* eagaich; (*steal*) goid
nickname *n* far-ainm *m*, frith-ainm *m*
niece *n* nighean peathar/bràthar *f*
night *n* oidhche *f* **all n.** fad na h-oidhche **at n.** air an oidhche **the n. before last** a' bhòn-raoir **last n.** a-raoir **tonight** a-nochd **tomorrow n.** an ath-oidhch'
nightgown/nightie *n* gùn-oidhche *m*
nightmare *n* trom-laighe *f m*
nil *n* neoni *m*
nimble *a* clis, sgiobalta
nine *n* a naoi *a* naoi, naodh **n. people** naoinear, naodhnar *f m*
nineteen *n, a* naoi-deug, naodh-deug **n. points** naoi puingean deug
ninety *n, a* ceithir fichead 's a deich, naochad *m*
ninth *a* naoidheamh, naodhamh
nip *n* bìdeadh *m*, teumadh *m*; (*of whisky*) tè bheag *f* *v* bìd, teum
nit *n* mial *f*
no *neg response* cha/chan *plus verb used in question* **will you be there? no** am bi thu ann? cha bhi **will she tell him? no** an innis i dha? chan innis *a* sam bith, gin, sgath **it was of no benefit to him** cha robh buannachd sam bith ann dha **we have no milk** chan eil sgath bainne againn **there were no children** cha robh gin a chloinn ann *adv* càil/dad nas ... (*with neg v*) **he is no better** chan eil e càil/dad nas fheàrr
nobility *n* uaislean *m pl*, maithean *m pl*; (*quality*) uaisleachd *f*
noble *n, a* uasal *m*

nobody/no one *n* (*after neg v*) aon *m*, duine *m* **there was n. to be seen** cha robh duine/neach (sam bith) ri fhaicinn
nod *n* gnogadh cinn *m* *v* gnog/crom (do cheann) **she nodded off** rinn i norrag
noise *n* fuaim *f m*
noisy *a* fuaimneach, gleadhrach, faramach
nominal *a* san ainm
nominate *v* ainmich
nomination *n* ainmeachadh *m*
nominative *a* ainmneach **the n. case** an tuiseal ainmneach *m*
non- *pref* neo-
non-stop *a*, *adv* … gun stad
nonchalant *a* gun chùram
none *pron* (*after neg v*) aon duine *m*, neach (sam bith) *m*, gin *f*, sgath *m*
nonsense *n* amaideas *m*
nook *n* cùil *f*, iùc *f*
noon *n* nòin *m*, meadhan-latha *m*
nor *conj* no, cha mhò
norm *n* àbhaist *f*
normal *a* riaghailteach, àbhaisteach, gnàthach
normally *adv* am bitheantas, anns a' chumantas
Norse *a* Lochlannach
north *n, a* (an) tuath *m*, an àird a tuath *f* **in the n.** mu thuath **n. of** tuath air **n.-east** (an) ear-thuath *m* **n.-west** (an) iar-thuath *m*
Norwegian *n*, *a* Nirribheach *m*, (*female*) ban-Nirribheach *f*
nose *n* sròn *f* **nosebleed** leum-sròine *m*
nostalgia *n* cianalas *m*
not *adv* cha, chan, na, nach **we will not go there** cha tèid sinn ann **I will not leave it** chan fhàg mi e **do not move it** na gluais e **he said that he would not do that** thuirt e nach dèanadh e sin
notable *a* ainmeil, sònraichte
notch *n* eag *f*
note *n* nota *f*; (*letter*) sgrìobag *f*; (*mus*) pong *m* *v* thoir fa-near, comharraich
noted *a* ainmeil, cliùiteach
nothing *n* neoni *m*; (*with neg*) nì/rud sam bith **she would think n. of it** cha shaoileadh i dad dheth
notice *n* fios *m*, brath *m*; (*written*) sanas *m*; (*warning*) rabhadh *m* *v* mothaich, thoir fa-near, thoir an aire
notify *v* leig fhaicinn do, thoir fios (do)
notion *n* beachd *m*, smaoin *f*; (*concept*) bun-bheachd *m*
notorious *a* suaicheanta, le droch cliù
noun *n* ainmear *m* **verbal n.** ainmear gnìomhaireach
nourish *v* àraich, beathaich, tog
nourishment *n* beathachadh *m*
novel *n* nobhail *f*, uirsgeul *m*
novel *a* nuadh, annasach
novelty *n* annas *m*
November *n* an t-Samhain *f*
now *adv* a-nis(e), an-dràsta, an ceartuair
nowadays *adv* an-diugh, san là an-diugh
nowhere *adv* (*after neg v*) an àite sam bith
nozzle *n* soc *m*, smeachan *m*
nuclear *a* niùclasach **n. power** cumhachd niùclasach *f m* **n. waste** sgudal niùclasach *m* **n. weapons** armachd niùclasach *f*
nucleus *n* niùclas *m*
nude *a* rùisgte, lomnochd
nudge *v* put
nuisance *n* dragh *m*
null *a* gun stàth, gun bhrìgh **n. and void** falamh gun èifeachd
numb *a* meilichte, rag le fuachd, anns an eighealaich **n. with cold** air a lathadh *etc* *v* meilich, ragaich
number *n* àireamh *f* **phone n.** àireamh-fòn *v* cunnt(ais), àireamhaich
numeral *n* figear *m*
numerate *a* àireamhachail
numerical *a* àireamhach
numerous *a* lìonmhor, iomadach (*precedes n*)
nun *n* bean-chràbhaidh *f*, cailleach-dhubh *f*

nurse *n* banaltram *f*, nurs *f m*, *v* nurs(aig), altraim
nursery *n* seòmar-altraim *m*; (*school*) sgoil-àraich *f*; (*bot*) planntlann *f*
nursing *n* banaltramachd *f*, nursadh *m*; (*of child*) altramas *m* **n.-home** taigh-altraim *m*
nurture *v* àraich, oileanaich
nut *n* (*food, mech*) cnò *f*
nutrition *n* beathachadh *m*, mathas *m*
nylon *n* nàidhlean *m*

O

oak *n* darach *m* *a* daraich
oar *n* ràmh *m*
oasis *n* innis-fàsaich *f*
oatcake *n* aran-coirce *m*
oath *n* bòid *f* **oaths** mionnan *f m pl*
oatmeal *n* min-choirce *f*
oats *n* coirce *m*
obdurate *a* rag-mhuinealach
obedience *n* ùmhlachd *f*
obedient *a* umhail
obese *a* reamhar, tiugh, sultmhor
obey *v* bi umhail (do)
obituary *n* iomradh-bàis *m*; (*death notice*) sanas bàis *m*
object *n* nì *m*, rud *m*; (*objective*) adhbhar *m* **o. of ...** cùis- ... *f*, cuspair *m* (+ *gen*); (*gram*) cuspair *m*
object *v* cuir an aghaidh
objection *n* cur an aghaidh *m*, gearan *m*
objective *n* amas *m*, ceann-uidhe *m* *a* cothromach, neo-eisimeileach
obligation *n* comain *f*, dleastanas *m*
oblige *v* (*require*) cuir mar fhiachaibh air; (*do a favour to*) cuir fo chomain
obliging *a* èasgaidh, deònach
obliterate *v* dubh a-mach
oblong *a* cruinn-fhada
obnoxious *a* gràineil
obscene *a* draosta, drabasta
obscure *a* doilleir; (*met*) dìomhair *v* dèan doilleir, cuir fo sgleò, falaich
observant *a* forail, mothachail, aireil
observatory *n* amharclann *f*
observe *v* amhairc, coimhead, thoir an aire; (*keep*) cùm, glèidh
observer *n* neach-coimhid *m*, neach-amhairc *m*
obsession *n* beò-ghlacadh *m*
obsolete *a* à cleachdadh, (bh)o fheum
obstacle *n* cnap-starra *m*, bacadh *m*
obstinate *a* rag-mhuinealach, fada na c(h)eann fhèin *etc*
obstruct *v* bac, cuir bacadh air
obstruction *n* cnap-starra *m*, bacadh *m*
obtain *v* faigh
obvious *a* follaiseach, soilleir, nochdte
occasion *n* (*event*) tachartas *m*; (*reason*) adhbhar *m*; (*time*) uair *f*, turas *m* **on one o.** aon uair/turas
occasionally *adv* corra uair, an-dràsta 's a-rithist, (bh)o àm gu àm
occupation *n* obair *f*, dreuchd *f*; (*of property*) gabhail thairis *m*
occupy *v* gabh sealbh/còmhnaidh; (*space*) lìon; (*time*) cuir seachad tìde; (*property*) gabh thairis
occur *v* tachair **o. to** thig a-steach air
occurrence *n* tachartas *m*
ocean *n* cuan *m*, fairge *f*
octagon *n* ochd-shliosach *m*
octave *n* ochdad *m*
October *n* an Dàmhair *f*
octopus *n* ochd-chasach *m*, gibearnach-meurach *m*
odd *a* neònach, àraid; (*number*) còrr **o. one out** (an) conadal *m*
odds *n* còrrlach *m*; (*leftovers*) fuidheall *m* **against the o.** an aghaidh an t-sruth **it makes no o.** is coma, chan eil e gu diofar
ode *n* duan *m*
odour *n* boladh *m*, boltradh *m*
of *prep* de/dhe, à **one of these days** latha dhe na lathaichean

many of us mòran againn/dhinn **think of it** smaoinich air/mu dheidhinn (*often conveyed by gen form*) **a sum of money** sùim airgid) **of course it is** nach eil fhios gu bheil
off *prep* de, dhe, bhàrr/far (+ *gen*) **the car went off the road** chaidh an càr bhàrr an rathaid/dhen rathad *adv* dheth **he put off the light** chuir e dheth an solas **they made off** rinn iad às **come off it!** thalla is thoir ort! **it's gone off** (*gone bad*) tha e air fàs grod
offence *n* oilbheum *m*, coire *f*; (*criminal*) eucoir *f*
offend *v* dèan/thoir oilbheum do; (*criminally*) dèan eucoir
offender *n* eucorach *m*, ciontach *m*
offensive *a* oilbheumach; (*attacking*) ionnsaigheach
offer *n* tairgse *f*, tathann *m* *v* tairg, dèan/thoir tairgse, tathainn
offhand *a* coma, beag-sùim
office *n* oifis *f*, oifig *f*; (*role*) dreuchd *f*
officer *n* oifigear *m*
official *n* oifigeach *m* *a* oifigeil **o. opening** fosgladh oifigeil *m*
offspring *n* sliochd *m*, àl *m*
often *adv* (gu) tric, (gu) minig
oil *n* ola *f* *v* cuir ola air **oilfield** raon-ola *m* **oilrig** crann-ola *m* **oil-tanker** tancair ola *m*
oily *a* olach, ùilleach
ointment *n* acfhainn *f*, aolmann *m*
old *a* sean, aosta **old-fashioned** seann-fhasanta **old man** bodach *m* **old woman** cailleach *f*
olive *n* (*tree*) crann-ola *m*; (*fruit*) meas a' chroinn-ola *m*, dearc-ola *m* **o.-oil** ola a' chroinn-ola *f*
omen *n* manadh *m*
ominous *a* droch-fhàistinneach
omission *n* dearmad *m*
omit *v* dèan dearmad, fàg às
omnipotent *a* uile-chumhachdach
on *prep* air; (*after*) an dèidh *adv* air; (*onwards*) air adhart **off and on** air is dheth, thuige 's bhuaithe
once *adv* uair, aon uair/turas
one *n* a h-aon; (*person*) neach *m*, fear *m*, tè *f*; (*one thing*) aon(an) *m*
one *a* aon **one-way** aon-shligheach
onerous *a* trom, sàrachail
onion *n* uinnean *m*
on-line *n* air loidhne
only *a* aon **the o. way** an aon dòigh *adv* a-mhàin *conj* (*after neg v*) ach **he o. wanted to help her** cha robh e ach airson a cuideachadh
onus *n* uallach *m*
onward *adv* air adhart
ooze *v* sil
opaque *a* doilleir, do-lèirsinneach
open *v* fosgail *a* fosgailte; (*frank*) fosgarra
opener *n* fosglair *m*
opening *n* fosgladh *m*, beàrn *f m*
openly *adv* gu fosgailte
opera *n* opara *f pl* oparathan
operate *v* obraich; (*med*) dèan opairèisean, cuir fon sgithinn
operation *n* obair *f*, gnìomhachd *f*; (*med*) opairèisean *f m*
opinion *n* barail *f*, beachd *m* **o. poll** cunntas-bheachd *m*
opinionated *a* rag-bharalach, fada na c(h)eann fhèin *etc*
opponent *n* cuspairiche *m*, neach-dùbhlain *m*
opportune *a* fàbharach
opportunity *n* cothrom *m*
oppose *v* cuir an aghaidh
opposite *n* ceart-aghaidh *f* *prep* (+ *gen*) fa chomhair, mu choinneamh
opposition *n* cur an aghaidh *m*, dùbhlan *m*; (*polit*) **the O.** am Partaidh Dùbhlanach *m*
oppress *v* claoidh, dèan fòirneart air
oppression *n* ainneart *m*, fòirneart *m*
oppressive *a* ainneartach, fòirneartach; (*weather*) trom, murtaidh
opt for *v* tagh **opt out** tarraing a-mach/às

optician *n* fradhairciche *m*, neach nan sùilean *m*
optimism *n* so-aigne *f*
optimistic *a* so-aigneach
option *n* roghainn *f m*
optional *a* roghnach, ri roghnachadh
opulence *n* saidhbhreas *m*, toic *f*
or *conj* no, air neo
oral *a* labhairteach, beòil **o. tradition** beul-aithris *f*
orange *n* orainsear *m* **o. juice** sùgh orains *m* *a* orains
orator *n* òraidiche *m*
orbit *a* reul-chuairt *f*, cuairt *f*
Orcadian *n*, *a* Arcach *m*, (*female*) ban-Arcach *f*
orchard *n* ubhal-ghort *m*
orchestra *n* orcastra *f*
ordain *v* socraich, sònraich; (*relig*) cuir an dreuchd
ordeal *n* cruaidh-dheuchainn *f*
order *n* òrdugh *m*, òrdan *m*; (*relig*) riaghailt *f* **in o. that** air chor ('s gu) **out of o.** briste; (*met*) mì-iomchaidh
order *v* òrdaich; (*arrange*) cuir an òrdugh
orderly *a* òrdail, riaghailteach
ordinary *a* àbhaisteach, cumanta
ore *n* clach-meinnir *f*
organ *n* (*body*) ball *m*; (*mus*) òrgan *m*
organic *a* fàs-bheairteach
organist *n* òrganaiche *m*
organization *n* buidheann *f m*; (*act of*) eagrachadh *m*
organize *v* cuir air dòigh, eagraich
organizer *n* neach-eagrachaidh *m*, eagraiche *m*
orgy *n* ruidhtearachd *f*
oriental *a* earach
orifice *n* fosgladh *m*
origin *n* tùs *m*, bun *m*, màthair-adhbhar *f*
original *a* tùsail, prìomh, bun-
originate *v* tàrmaich, tòisich
ornament *n* òrnaid *f*
ornamental *a* òrnaideach
ornate *a* mòr-mhaisichte, mòr-sgeadaichte
ornithology *n* eun-eòlas *m*
orphan *n* dìlleachdan *m*
orthodox *a* gnàthach; (*relig*) ceart-chreideach
osprey *n* iolair-uisge *f*
ostrich *n* struth *m*
other *pron* eile **the o. day** an latha roimhe **one after the o.** fear/tè às dèidh fir/tè **the others** càch **they gave each o. gifts** thug iad tiodhlacan dha chèile
otherwise *adv* a chaochladh, air mhodh eile; (*or else*) no
otter *n* biast-dhubh *f*, dòbhran *m*
ouch! *exclam* aobh!, aobhag!
ought *v* is còir, tha còir aig **she o. to do it** is còir dhi a dhèanamh/ tha còir aice a dhèanamh **you o. to have done it** bu chòir dhut a bhith air a dhèanamh/bha còir agad a bhith air a dhèanamh
ounce *n* unnsa *m*
our *poss pron* ar, ar n- (*before vowels*), againne **our father** ar n-athair **our house** an taigh againne
ourselves *pron* sinn fhèin/fhìn
oust *v* cuir às
out *adv* a-muigh; (*motion outwards*) a-mach **O. you/we go!** Mach à seo!
outcast *n* dìobarach *m*
outcome *n* buil *f*, toradh *m*
outcry *n* iolach *f*, gàir *m*
outdoors *adv* a-muigh, air a' bhlàr a-muigh
outer *a* a-muigh, a-mach
outfit *n* trusgan *m*, aodach *m*
outing *n* splaoid *f*, cuairt *f*
outlaw *n* neach-cùirn *m*, neach fon choill *m* *v* cuir fon choill
outline *n* dealbh-iomaill *f m*; (*met*) cnàmhan *m pl* *v* thoir cunntas air
outlook *n* sealladh *m*
out-of-date *a* à fasan, às an fhasan; (*past sell-by date*) seachad air a' cheann-latha
output *n* cur a-mach *m*, toradh *m*
outrage *n* cùis-uabhais *f*
outrageous *a* uabhasach
outright *adv* (gu) buileach, (gu) tur
outset *n* fìor thoiseach *m*, ciad

dol a-mach *m*
outside *n* an taobh/leth a-muigh *m* *adv* a-muigh; (*motion*) a-mach
outsize *n*, *a* mòr-thomhas *m*, mòr-mheud *m*
outskirts *n* iomall (baile) *m*
outspoken *a* fosgarra, a-mach leis
outstanding *a* barraichte, air leth ...
outward *a* air an taobh a-muigh; (*met*) faicsinneach
outwardly *adv* (bh)on taobh a-muigh, (bh)o shealladh dhaoine
outwit *v* thoir an car à/às
oval *a* air chumadh uighe, ugh-chruthach *n* ugh-chruth *m*
ovation *n* mòr-bhualadh-bhas *m*
oven *n* àmhainn *f*
over *prep* (*above*) os cionn (+ *gen*); (*beyond*) thar (+ *gen*); (*across*) thairis air, tarsainn air *adv* (*hither*) a-null; (*yonder*) a-nall; (*past*) seachad; (*additional*) a bharrachd, a bhàrr air; (*left over*) a chòrr *pref* ro- (+ *len*)
overall *a* iomlan
over-anxious *a* ro chùramach
overcharge *v* iarr/cuir tuilleadh 's a' chòir (+ air)
overcome *v* thoir buaidh air, ceannsaich
overdo *v* dèan tuilleadh 's a' chòir
overdraft *n* for-tharraing *f*
overdue *a* fadalach
overflow *n* cur thairis *m* *v* cuir thairis
overhead *adv* os cionn, gu h-àrd
overheads *n* cosgaisean a bharrachd *f pl*
overhear *v* dèan farchluais
overload *v* an-luchdaich, cuir cus air
overlook *v* seall thairis air; (*forget*) dèan dearmad air
overnight *a* tron oidhche
overrule *v* bac, diùlt
overrun *v* cuir fo smachd; (*time*) ruith thairis air ùine
overseas *a* thall thairis *adv* thall thairis; (*motion*) a-null thairis
overshadow *v* cuir fo sgàil
oversight *n* dearmad *m*; (*supervision*) stiùireadh *m*
overt *a* nochdte, follaiseach
overtake *v* beir air, rach seachad air
overthrow *v* tilg sìos, cuir às do
overtime *n* ùine a bharrachd *f*, còrr ùine *f*
overturn *v* cuir car de, cuir bun-os-cionn
overweight *a* ro throm
owe *v* bi fo fhiachan aig; (*gratitude*) bi an comain (+ *gen*) **I o. him £20** tha fichead not aige orm **he owes me £20** tha fichead not agam air
owl *n* cailleach-oidhche *f*, comhachag *f*
own *pron* fhèin/fèin
own *v* sealbhaich; (*admit*) gabh ri, aidich
owner *n* neach-seilbhe *m*, sealbhadair *m*
ownership *n* sealbh *m*
ox *n* damh *m*
oxter *n* achlais *f*
oxygen *n* ogsaidean *m*
oyster *n* eisir *m*
oystercatcher *n* trìlleachan *m*
ozone *n* òson *m*, àile *m*

P

pace *n* ceum *m*; (*speed*) astar *m* *v* ceumnaich, spaidsirich
pacifist *n* sìochantair *m*
pacify *v* sìthich, ciùinich
pack *n* paca *m*; (*a large number of*) dròbh *f m* **a pack of lies** tòrr bhreug(an) *v* pacaig; (*fill up*) lìon
package *n* pasgan *m*, pacras *m* **p. deal** tairgse iomlan *f*
packaging *n* pacaigeadh *m*, còmhdach *m*
packet *n* pacaid *f*
packing *n* pacadh *m*, pacaigeadh *m*
pact *n* cùmhnant *m*, còrdadh *m*
pad *n* pada *f*; (*residence*) cùil *f*

paddle *n* pleadhag *f*, pleadhan *m* *v* grunnaich, plubraich; (*boat*) pleadhagaich
pagan *n*, *a* pàganach *m*
paganism *n* pàganachd *f*
page *n* duilleag *f*, taobh-duilleig(e) *m*; (*boy*) gille-frithealaidh *m*
pageant *n* taisbeanadh-gluasaid *m*
pail *n* peile *m*, cuinneag *f*
pain *n* cràdh *m*, pian *m*
painful *a* cràiteach, piantach
painstaking *a* saothrachail, mionaideach
paint *n* peant(a) *m* *v* peant
painter *n* peantair *m*; (*boat's rope*) ball *m*
painting *n* peantadh *m*; (*a picture*) dealbh *f m*
pair *n* càraid *f*, paidhir *f m* *v* dèan càraid/paidhir
Pakistani *n*, *a* Pagastànach *m*, (*female*) ban-Phagastànach *f*
pal *n* companach *m*
palace *n* lùchairt *f*
palatable *a* blasta
palate *n* càirean *m*, mullach-beòil *m*; (*met*) càil *f*
pale *a* bàn
palm *n* bas/bois *f*; (*tree*) craobh-phailm *f*
palpable *a* follaiseach; (*tangible*) a ghabhas fhaireachdainn
palpitation *n* plosgartaich *f*
paltry *a* suarach
pamper *v* dèan cus de, peataich
pamphlet *n* duilleachan *m*, bileag *f*
pan *n* pana *m* **p. loaf** lof(a)-phan(a) *f*
pan- *pref* uil(e)-
panacea *n* uil-ìoc *m*
pancake *n* foileag *f*
pancreas *n* am brisgean milis *m*
pander (to) *v* riaraich
pane *n* l(e)òsan *m*, glainne *f*
panel *n* pannal *m*; (*section*) clàr *m*
pang *n* biorgadh *m*, guin *m*
panic *n* clisgeadh *m*, breisleach *m*
pant *v* plosg
panther *n* pantar *m*
panting *n* plosgartaich *f* **he was p.** bha anail na uchd, bha aonach air
pantomime *n* pantomaim *m*
pantry *n* stòr-bìdh *m*, preas(a)-bìdh *m*
pants *n* drathais *f*, pants *f pl*; (*trousers*) briogais *f*
papal *a* pàpach
paper *n* pàipear *m* **p.-clip** greimear-pàipeir *m* *v* pàipearaich, boltaig
par *n* co-ionannachd *f*; (*golf*) an cuibheas *m* **feeling below par** gun a bhith gu math
parable *n* cosamhlachd *f*
parachute *n* paraisiut *m*
parade *n* (*march*) caismeachd *f* *v* spaidsir
Paradise *n* Pàrras *m*
paradox *n* frith-bharail *f*, dubh-fhacal *m*
paraffin *n* paireafain *m*
paragon *n* sàr-eisimpleir *f m*
paragraph *n* paragraf *m*
parallel *n* (*line*) sgrìob cho-shìnte *f*; (*met*) samhailt *f* *a* co-shìnte; (*met*) ionann
paralysis *n* pairilis *f m*
parameter *n* paraimeatair *m*, crìoch *f*
paramount *a* os cionn gach nì, fìor chudromach
parapet *n* uchd-bhalla *m*
paraphrase *n* ath-innse *f*; (*relig*) laoidh *m*
parasite *n* dìosganach *m*, faoighiche *m*
parasol *n* sgàilean-grèine *m*
paratrooper *n* saighdear paraisiuit *m*
parcel *n* parsail *m*, pasgan *m*, trusachan *m*
parched *a* pàiteach, gus teuchdadh/tiachdadh
pardon *n* mathanas *m* *v* math, thoir mathanas **p. me** gabh mo leisgeul
pare *v* beàrr, snaigh
parent *n* pàrant *m*
parish *n* sgìre *f*, paraiste *f*
parity *n* co-ionannachd *f*
park *n* pàirc(e) *f* **car p.** pàirc(e)

chàraichean *f* *v* parc; (*set down*) càirich
parking place *n* ionad/àite-parcaidh *m*
Parliament *n* Pàrlamaid *f*
parochial *a* sgìreachdail, sgìreil; (*met*) beag-seallaidh
parody *n* atharrais *f*
parole *n* paròil *m*
parrot *n* pitheid *f*, pearraid *f*
parry *v* dìon o bhuille; (*met*) cuir seachad
parsimonious *a* cruaidh, spìocach
parsley *n* peirsill *f*
parsnip *n* curran geal *m*
part *n* pàirt *f m*, cuid *f*, roinn *f*, cuibhreann *f m*; (*in drama*) pàirt *m* **for my p.** air mo shon-sa *v* sgar, dealaich, tearb
partake *v* compàirtich
partial *a* ann an cuid; (*biased*) leth-bhreitheach **p. to** dèidheil/titheach air
participant *n* compàirtiche *m*
participate *v* compàirtich, gabh pàirt (an)
particle *n* gràinean *m*, mìrean *m*; (*gram*) mion-fhacal *m*
particular *a* àraidh, sònraichte; (*fastidious*) faiceallach
parting *n* dealachadh *m*
partisan *a* aon-taobhach, leth-bhreitheach
partition *n* balla-tarsainn *m*, tallan *m*, cailbhe *m*; (*polit*) roinn *f* *v* roinn
partly *adv* gu ìre, ann an cuid
partner *n* companach *m*; (*in business*) neach-compàirt *m* *v* rach cuide ri, rach an co-bhonn ri
partnership *n* companas *m*; (*in business*) compàirteachas *m*
partridge *n* cearc-thomain *f*
party *n* partaidh *m*; (*group*) buidheann *f m*
pass *n* (*topog*) bealach *m*; (*in games*) pas *m*
pass *v* rach/gabh seachad; (*in sport*) pas(aig); (*exam*) dèan a' chùis, pas(aig); (*eg salt*) thoir/sìn do; (*law*) dèan lagh **p. away** eug, siubhail **p. the time** cuir seachad ùine
passage *n* turas *m*, slighe *f*; (*text*) earrann *f* **passageway** trannsa *f*
passenger *n* neach-siubhail *m* *pl* luchd-siubhail
passing place *n* àite-seachnaidh *m*
passion *n* boile *f*, dìoghras *m*; (*of Christ*) fulangas (Chrìosd) *m*
passionate *a* dìoghrasach
passive *a* neo-ghnìomhach; (*gram*) fulangach
passport *n* cead-siubhail *f*
password *n* facal-faire *m*
past *a* seachad **p. tense** an tràth caithte *m* *n* an t-àm a dh'fhalbh *m* *prep* seach, seachad air
paste *n* taois *f*; (*glue*) glaodh *m* *v* glaodh
pasteurize *v* paistiuraich
pastime *n* cur-seachad *m*
pastor *n* aoghair *m*
pastoral *a* (*relig*) aoghaireil; (*way of life*) treudach
pastry *n* pastraidh *m*
pasture *n* ionaltradh *m*, feurach *m*
pat *v* clapranaich
patch *n* brèid *m*, tuthag *f* *v* cuir tuthag air, cuir pìos ùr air
patently *adv* gu follaiseach
paternal *a* athaireil
path *n* starran *m*, ceum *m*, frith-rathad *m*
pathetic *a* truagh; (*awful*) cianail **a p. soul** culaidh-thruais *f*
pathology *n* galar-eòlas *m*
pathos *n* drùidhteachd *f*, truasachd *f*
patience *n* foighidinn *f*
patient *n* euslainteach *m* *a* foighidneach
patiently *adv* gu foighidneach
patriotism *n* gràdh-dùthcha *m*
patrol *n* freiceadan-faire *m*
patron *n* neach-taice *m*
patronymic *n* sloinneadh *m*
patter *n* briog-brag *m*; (*talk*) goileam *m*
pattern *n* pàtran *m*
paucity *n* gainne *f*
paunch *n* maodal *f*

pauper *n* ainnis *m*, bochd *m*
pause *n* stad *m*, anail *f* *v* stad, fuirich
pavement *n* cabhsair *m*
pavilion *n* pàillean *m*
paw *n* spòg *f*, màg *f*
pawn *v* cuir dhan phàn
pay *n* pàigheadh *m*, tuarastal *m* *v* pàigh; (*met*) dìol **p. attention to** thoir aire (do) **you'll pay for it yet** dìolaidh tu air fhathast
payable *a* ri p(h)àigheadh
payment *n* pàigheadh *m*
pea *n* peasair *f pl* peasraichean
peace *n* sìth *f*, fois *f*, tàmh *m*
peaceful *a* sìtheil, ciùin
peach *n* peitseag *f*
peacock *n* peucag *f*, coileach-peucaig *m*
peak *n* (*hill*) stùc *f*, binnean *m*; (*summit*) mullach *m*
peal *n* torrann *m*, bualadh *m*
peanut *n* cnò-thalmhainn *f*
pear *n* peur *f*
pearl *n* neamhnaid *f*
peasant *n* neach-tuatha *m*
peat *n* mòine *f*; (*single*) fàd *m* **p.-bank** poll-mòna(ch)/mòna(dh) *m* **p.-stack** cruach-mhòna(ch)/mhòna(dh) *f*
pebble *n* molag *f*
peck *v* pioc; (*kiss*) thoir pògag
peculiar *a* àraid, neònach
pedal *n* casachan *m*, troighean *m*
pedantic *a* rag-fhoghlamach
peddle *v* reic, malairtich
pedestal *n* bun-carraigh *m*, bonn *m*
pedestrian *n* coisiche *m* **p. precinct** àrainn-choisichean *f* *a* coise; (*uninspiring*) mu làimh **p. way** ceum coise *m*
pedigree *n* sinnsearachd *f*
peel *n* rùsg *m*, plaosg *m* *v* rùisg
peeled *a* air a rùsgadh
peep *n* caogadh *m*, dìdeadh *m* *v* caog, dìd
peer *n* (*noble*) morair *m*; (*in age*) comhaois *m*; (*equal*) seise *m*, co-inbheach *m*
peeved *a* leamh, tàmailteach
peewit *n* curracag *f*
peg *n* cnag *f*, ealchainn *f*
pelican *n* peileagan *m*
pellet *n* gràinnean *m*
pelt *n* bian *m*, seiche *f*
pelt *v* caith ... air
pen *n* peann *m*; (*fold*) crò *m*, buaile *f*
penalize *v* peanasaich, cuir peanas air
penalty *n* peanas *m* **p. kick** breab peanais *f*
pence *n* sgillinnean *f pl*
pencil *n* peansail *m* **p. sharpener** geuraiche peansail *m*
pendant *n* crochadan *m*
pending *a* a' feitheamh, ri t(h)ighinn
pendulum *n* cudrom-siùdain *m*
penetrate *v* drùidh, faigh tro
penetrating *a* drùidhteach; (*met*) geurchuiseach
penguin *n* ceann-fionn *m*
penicillin *n* peinisilean *m*
peninsula *n* leth-eilean *m*
penis *n* bod *m*
penitence *n* aithreachas *m*
penitent *a* aithreachail
penknife *n* sgian-p(h)òcaid *f*
pennant *n* bratachag *f*
penniless *a* gun sgillinn
penny *n* sgillinn *f*
pension *n* peinnsean *m*
pensioner *n* peinnseanair *m*, neach-peinnsein *m*
pensive *a* fo throm-smaoin
pentagon *n* còig-cheàrnach *m*
Pentecost *n* a' Chaingis *f*
penthouse *n* bàrr-àros *m*
penultimate *a* leth-dheireannach
people *n* sluagh *m*, muinntir *f*
pepper *n* piobar *m*
per capita *adv* gach pearsa/neach
perceive *v* mothaich, thoir fa-near
per cent *adv* sa cheud
percentage *n* ceudad *m*, ìre sa cheud *f*
perceptible *a* nochdte
perception *n* tuigse *f*, lèirsinn *f*
perceptive *a* lèirsinneach, breithneachail, geurchuiseach
perch *n* spiris *f*, spàrr *m*; (*fish*) creagag *f* *v* rach air spiris
percolate *v* sìolaidh

percolator *n* sìol(t)achan *m* **coffee p.** sìol(t)achan cofaidh
percussion *n* bualadh *m*, faram *m*
peremptory *a* obann, sparrail; (*decisive*) do-atharraichte
perennial *a* bliadhnail; (*long-lasting*) maireannach
perfect *a* coileanta, foirfe *v* dèan coileanta/foirfe
perfection *n* foirfeachd *f*, coileantachd *f*
perfectionist *n* foirfiche *m*
perforate *v* toll, cuir tuill an
perform *v* (*carry out*) dèan, coilean; (*in play*) cluich; (*stage*) cuir air àrd-ùrlar
performance *n* (*execution*) coileanadh *m*, cur an gnìomh *m*; (*on stage etc*) cluich *f* **p. indicator** comharra coileanaidh *m*
performer *n* cluicheadair *m*, cleasaiche *m*
perfume *n* cùbhrachd *f*
perhaps *adv* is dòcha (gu), math dh'fhaodte/is mathaid (gu)
peril *n* gàbhadh *m*
perilous *a* gàbhaidh
perimeter *n* cuairt-thomhas *m*
period *n* ùine *f*; (*era*) àm *m*; (*punct*) stad-phuing *f*; (*menstruation*) fuil-mìos *f*
periodically *adv* (bh)o àm gu àm
periodical *n* ràitheachan *m*, iris *f*
peripheral *a* iomallach, air an oir; (*met*) neo-chudromach
periphery *n* iomall *m*, oir *f m*
periscope *n* pearasgop *m*
perish *v* rach a dhìth, rach às an rathad
perjure *v* thoir fianais-bhrèige/mionnan-eithich
perjury *n* eitheach *f m* **commit p.** *v* thoir fianais-bhrèige/mionnan-eithich
perky *a* bideanach
perm *n* pearm *m*
permanent *a* buan, maireannach
permeate *v* rach air feadh, rach tro
permissible *a* ceadaichte
permission *n* cead *m*
permit *n* bileag-cead *f*, ceadachd *f* *v* ceadaich, leig le
permutation *n* iomlaid *f*, mùthadh *m*
pernicious *a* millteach
perpendicular *a* inghearach, dìreach suas/sìos
perpetrate *v* dèan, cuir an gnìomh
perpetual *a* sìor-mhaireannach
perpetuate *v* cùm a' dol, sìor chleachd
perplex *v* cuir imcheist air
perplexed *a* imcheisteach, an imcheist
perquisite *n* frith-bhuannachd *f*
persecute *v* geur-lean, dèan geur-leanmhainn air
persecution *n* geur-leanmhainn *m*
perseverance *n* leanaltas *m*, cumail aige *f*
persevere *v* lean air, cùm aig/ri
persist *v* lean air/ri, cùm a' dol
persistent *a* leanailteach, sìor-
person *n* neach *m*, pearsa *m* **spokesperson** neach-labhairt *m*
personable *a* tlachdmhor
personal *a* pearsanta
personality *n* pearsantachd *f* **a p.** pearsa ainmeil *m*
personification *a* pearsachadh *m*
personify *v* pearsaich
personnel *n* luchd-obrach *f*, sgioba *f*, sgiobachd *f* **P. Dept** Roinn na Sgiobachd *f*
perspective *n* (*standpoint*) sealladh *m*, beachd *m*; (*in art*) buaidh-astair *f* **from my p.** na mo shealladh-sa
perspiration *n* fallas *m*
perspire *v* cuir fallas de **he was perspiring** bha fallas air/bha e a' cur falla(i)s dheth
persuade *v* cuir ìmpidh air, thoir … a thaobh, thoir air
persuasion *n* ìmpidh *f*, toirt … a thaobh *m*; (*creed*) creideamh *m*; (*values*) feallsanachd *f*
persuasive *a* buadhmhor, a bheir neach a thaobh
pervasive *a* lìonsgarach, fad' is farsaing
pertain *v* buin do
pertinent *a* iomchaidh

perturb *v* buair, cuir dragh air
perturbed *a* draghail
peruse *v* leugh; (*scrutinise*) sgrùd, rannsaich
pervade *v* lìon, rach air feadh
perverse *a* claon
pervert *n* claonaire *m* *v* claon, cuir fiaradh an
pessimism *n* eu-dòchas *m*
pessimist *n* neach gun dòchas *m*
pessimistic *a* eu-dòchasach
pest *n* plàigh *f* **he's a p.** 's e plàigh a th' ann
pester *v* cuir dragh air
pesticide *n* puinnsean bhiastagan *m*
pet *n* peata *m*
petal *n* flùr-bhileag *f*
petition *n* athchuinge *f*, tagradh *m*, guidhe *f m* *v* dèan athchuinge, guidh, aslaich
petrified *a* a' dol à cochall mo chridhe, eagal mo bheatha orm
petrol *n* peatrail *m* **p.-pump** pump(a) peatrail *m*
petticoat *n* còta-bàn *m*
petty *a* beag, suarach
petulant *a* bleideil
pew *n* suidheachan *m*, treasta *m*
pewter *n* feòdar *m*
phallic *a* bodail, mar bhod
phantom *n* taibhs(e) *m*, tannasg *m*
pharmacy *n* eòlas-leigheasan *m*; (*shop*) bùth ceimigeir *f*
phase *n* ìre *f* **p. in** *v* thoir a-steach mean air mhean **p. out** *v* cuir às mean air mhean
pheasant *n* easag *f*
phenomenon *n* iongantas *m*, rud air leth *m*
phial *n* meanbh-bhotal *m*
philanthropy *n* deagh euchdachd *f*
philology *n* eòlas chànan *m*
philosopher *n* feallsanach *m*
philosophical *a* feallsanachail; (*stoical*) leagte ri
philosophy *n* feallsanachd *f*
phlegm *n* ronn *m*
phone *n* fòn *f m* *v* fòn(aig)
phonetic *a* fogharach
phoney *a* fallsa, breugach, gun bhrìgh *n* mealltaire *m*
phosphate *n* fosfat *m*
phosphorescence *n* caile-bianain *m*, teine-sionnachain *m*
phosphorus *n* fosfor *m*, sionn *m*
photocopier *n* lethbhreacadair *m*, copaidhear *m*
photocopy *n* lethbhreac *m*, copaidh *f* *v* dèan lethbhreac/copaidh
photograph *n* dealbh camara *f m* *v* tog dealbh
photographer *n* neach-togail-dhealbh *m*
photography *n* togail dhealbh *f*
phrase *n* abairt *f*
physical *a* corporra **p. education** foghlam corporra *m*
physician *n* lèigh *m*, lighiche *m*
physics *n* fiosaig *f*
physiotherapist *n* anaclair-cuirp *m*
physiotherapy *n* anacladh-cuirp *m*
physique *n* dèanamh *m*
pianist *n* cluicheadair piàna *m*
piano *n* piàna *m*
pibroch *n* ceòl-mòr *m*
pick *n* taghadh *m*; (*pickaxe*) pic *m*, piocaid *f* *v* (*choose*) tagh, roghnaich; (*lift*) tog; (*meat off bones*) pioc, spiol
picket *n* piceid *m*
pickle *n* picil *f* *v* saill, cuir ann am picil
pickpocket *n* mèirleach-pòcaid *m*
picky *a* àilgheasach
picnic *n* cuirm-chnuic *f*
Pict *n* Cruithneach *m*
picture *n* dealbh *f m*, pioctar *m*
picturesque *a* àillidh, mar dhealbh
pie *n* paidh *m* **pie chart** clàr-cearcaill *m*
piece *n* pìos *m*, mìr *m*, earrann *f*, bìdeag *f*; (*sandwich*) pìos *m*
piecemeal *a* (*unsystematic*) bìdeagach *adv* (*gradually*) mean air mhean
pier *n* cidhe *m*
pierce *v* toll
piercing *a* (*sound*) biorach
piety *n* cràbhadh *m*
pig *n* muc *f* **piglet** uircean *m*

pigsty fail-mhuc *f*
pigeon *n* calman *m*
pig-headed *a* ceann-dàna, rag
pike *n* pìc *f*; (*fish*) geadas *m*
pile *n* dùn *m*, càrn *m*, tòrr *m* *v* càrn, cruach
pilfer *v* dèan braide, goid
pilgrim *n* taistealach *m*
pilgrimage *n* taistealachd *f*, taisteal *m*
pill *n* pile *f m*, gràinnean *m*
pillage *v* creach, spùill
pillar *n* carragh *f*, colbh *m*
pillow *n* cluasag *f* **p.-case** cuibhrig(e)-cluasaig *f m*
pilot *n* neach-iùil *m*, paidhleat *m* **p. scheme** sgeama dearbhaidh *m* *v* (*guide*) treòraich, stiùir; (*try out*) dèan dearbhadh air, feuch
pimple *n* guirean *m*, plucan *m*
pin *n* prìne *m*, dealg *f* **pin cushion** prìneachan *m* **pins and needles** cadal-deilgneach *m*
pincers *n* teanchair *m*
pinch *n* bìdeag *f*, gòmag *f*; (*small quantity*) gràinnean *m* *v* thoir bìdeag/gòmag à
pine *n* giuthas *m* **p. forest** giùthsach *m*
pine *v* searg, caith **p. for** gabh fadachd airson
pineapple *n* anann *m*
pink *a* pinc, ban-dhearg
pinky *n* lùdag *f*
pinnacle *n* binnean *m*, bidean *m*
pint *n* pinnt *m* **a p. of beer** pinnt leann(a)
pioneer *n* tùsaire *m*
pious *a* cràbhach, diadhaidh
pipe *n* pìob *f* *v* cluich/seinn a' phìob
pipeline *n* loidhne phìoban *f* **in the p.** sa bheairt
piper *n* pìobaire *m*
piping *n* pìobaireachd *f*
pirate *n* spùinneadair-mara *m*
pistol *n* daga *m*
piston *n* loinid *f*
pit *n* toll *m*, sloc *m*
pitch *n* (*tar*) bìth *f*; (*sound*) àirde *f*; (*sport*) raon-cluiche *m*
pitch *v* suidhich; (*throw*) tilg; (*target*) amais **p. tent** cuir suas teanta
pitfall duilgheadas *m*
pith *n* glaodhan *m*; (*met*) spionnadh *m*, brìgh *f*
pitiful *a* truagh
pittance *n* sùim shuarach *f*
pity *n* truas *m*, iochd *f*, truacantas *m* **what a p.!** 's mòr am beud! *v* gabh truas de/ri
pivot *n* maighdeag *f*
pizza *n* piotsa *m*
placate *v* ciùinich
place *n* àite *m*, ionad *m* **p. name** ainm-àite *m* *v* suidhich, socraich, càirich, cuir
placid *a* ciùin, sèimh
plagiarism *n* mèirle-sgrìobhaidh *f*
plague *n* plàigh *f*
plaice *n* lèabag/leòbag-mhòr *f*
plaid *n* breacan *m* *a* breacain
plain *n* còmhnard *m*, faiche *f* *a* rèidh, còmhnard; (*clear*) soilleir, plèan; (*ordinary*) plèan
plaintive *a* tiamhaidh
plait *n* figheachan *m*
plan *n* plana *m*, innleachd *f* **development p.** plana leasachaidh *v* dealbh, innlich, planaig
plane *n* plèan(a) *m*, itealan *m*; (*tool*) locair *f*; (*abstr*) raon *m* *v* locair, locraich
planet *n* planaid *f*
plank *n* clàr *m*, dèile *f*
planner *n* neach-dealbh(ach)aidh *m*
planning *n* dealbh(ach)adh *m*, planadh *m* **p. permission** cead-dealbh(ach)aidh *m*
plant *n* lus *m*, luibh *f m*, planntrais *f*; (*mech*) uidheam *m*; (*factory*) factaraidh *f m* *v* cuir, planntaich; (*place*) suidhich
plantation *n* (*place*) ionad cuir/cura *m*; (*trees etc*) planntachas *m*
plaster *n* plèastar *m*, sglàib *f*; (*med*) plàst *m*
plaster *v* plèastair
plasterer *n* plèastair *m*
plastic *n* plastaig *f* **p. surgery** *n* ath-dhealbhadh bodhaig *m* *a* plastaig

plasticine *n* plastasan *m*
plate *n* truinnsear *m*; (*sheet*) pleit *f*
platform *n* àrd-ùrlar *m*
platter *n* truinnsear mòr *m*
plausible *a* beulach, beulchar
play *n* cluich(e) *m*, cleas *m*; (*stage*) dealbh-chluich *f m* *v* cluich
player *n* cluicheadair *m*
playful *a* beadrach, sùgrach
playground *n* raon-cluiche *m*
playgroup *n* cròileagan *m*
playleader *n* stiùiriche-cluiche *m*
playwright *n* sgrìobhaiche dràma *m*, dràmadaiche *m*
plea *n* guidhe *f m*; (*law*) tagradh *m*
plead *v* guidh air; (*in law*) tagair; (*excuse*) thoir mar leisgeul
pleasant *a* taitneach, tlachdmhor
please *v* toilich, riaraich; (*intrans*) còrd, taitinn **if you p.** mas e do thoil e, (*pl & pol*) mas e ur toil e
pleased *a* toilichte
pleasing *a* tlachdmhor, càilear
pleasure *n* tlachd *f*, toileachadh *m*
pleat *n* filleadh *m*, pleat *f* *v* figh, cuachaich, pleat
pleated *a* cuachach, pleatach
pledge *n* geall *m*, gealladh *m*, barantas *m* *v* geall, rach an geall, thoir barantas
plenary *a* làn-, iomlan **p. session** làn-sheisean *m*
plentiful *a* pailt, lìonmhor
plenty *n* pailteas *m* *adv* gu leòr
pleurisy *n* an grèim mòr *m*, pliùrais *m*
pliable *a* sùbailte, subailte, so-lùbte
pliers *n* greimire *m*
plight *n* cor *m*, càradh *m*
plod *v* saothraich, imich gu trom
plot *n* (*of ground*) goirtean *m*, pìos talmhainn *m*; (*scheme*) innleachd *f*, guim *m;* (*lit*) plot(a) *m* *v* dèan innleachd/gùim; (*track*) lorg/lean slighe
plough *n* crann *m* **the P.** an Crann *v* treabh
ploughman *n* treabhaiche *m*
plover *n* feadag *f*
ploy *n* plòidh *f*; (*tactic*) cleas *m*
pluck *v* spìon, buain
plucky *a* tapaidh
plug *n* plucan *m*, pluga *m*, cnag *f*; (*in boat*) tùc *m* **plughole** toll-sìolaidh *m* *v* dùin, plucaich; (*of product*) put
plum *n* pluma(i)s *m*
plumb *v* feuch doimhneachd
plumb *a* dìreach **p.-line** sreang-dhìreach *f*
plumber *n* plumair *m*
plummet *v* tuit gu grad
plump *a* reamhar, tiugh, sultmhor
plunder *n* creach *f*, cobhartach *f m* *v* spuinn, creach
plunge *n* tumadh *m* *v* tùm; (*thrust*) sàth
plural *a* iomarra *n*, *a* iolra *m*
plus *prep* agus, le, a thuilleadh air
ply *v* saothraich; (*supply*) cùm ... ri; (*shipping*) ruith
pneumonia *n* am fiabhras-clèibhe *m*, teasach sgamhain *f*
poach *v* poidsig; (*food*) slaop
poacher *n* poidsear *m*
pocket *n* pòcaid *f* **p.-money** airgead-pòcaid *m* *v* cuir na p(h)òcaid *etc*, pòcaidich
pod *n* plaosg *m*
poem *n* dàn *m*, duan *m*
poet *n* bàrd *m*, filidh *m*
poetess *n* bana-bhàrd *f*
poetry *n* bàrdachd *f*
poignant *a* tiamhaidh
point *n* puing *f*; (*headland*) rubha *m*; (*of pencil*) gob *m*; (*of view*) barail *f*, sealladh *m* **what's the p.?** dè am feum a th' ann? *v* comharraich, seall
pointed *a* biorach; (*remark*) geur
poise *n* giùlan grinn *m*; (*balance*) co-chothrom *m*
poised *a* an co-chothrom, air mheidh **p. to ...** deiseil gu ...
poison *n* puinnsean *m*, nimh *m* *v* puinnseanaich
poisonous *a* puinnseanach, puinnseanta, nimheil
poke *n* (*bag*) poca *m*

poke *v* brod(an)aich; (*prod*) stob **p. about** rùraich
poker *n* brod-teine *m*, pòcair *m*
polar bear *n* mathan bàn *m*
polarize *v* pòlaraich, cuir calg-dhìreach an aghaidh a chèile
pole *n* pòla *m*, pòile *m*, cabar *m* **the North P.** am Pòla a Tuath **the South Pole** am Pòla a Deas
Pole *n* Pòlainneach *m*, (*female*) ban-Phòlainneach *f*
polecat *n* taghan *m*
police *n* poileas *m* **p. car** càr poilis *m* **p. officer** oifigear poilis *m* **p. station** stèisean poilis *m*
policeman *n* poileas *m*, poileasman *m*
policewoman *n* ban-phoileas *f*
policy *n* poileasaidh *m*
polish *n* lìomh *f*, lìomhadh *m* *v* lìomh, cuir lìomh air, lìomhaich
Polish *a* Pòlainneach
polished *a* lìomhte
polite *a* modhail
politic *a* glic, gleusta
political *a* poilitigeach **p. asylum** comraich phoilitigeach *f* **p. party** partaidh poilitigeach *m*
politically correct *a* ceart gu poilitigeach
politician *n* neach-poilitigs *m*
politics *n* poilitigs *f*
poll *n* cunntas cheann *m*; (*vote*) bhòtadh *m*; (*election*) taghadh *m* **p. tax** *n* cìs cheann *f*
pollen *n* poilean *m*
pollute *v* truaill, salaich
polluted *a* truaillte, air a t(h)ruailleadh *etc*
pollution *n* truailleadh *m*
polygon *n* ioma-cheàrnach *f*
pomp *n* greadhnachas *m*
pomposity *n* mòrchuis *f*
pompous *a* mòrchuiseach
pond *n* linne *f*, lòn *m*
ponder *v* beachd-smaoinich, cnuasaich, meòraich
ponderous *a* trom
pontificate *v* cuir às do chorp, dèan searmon de
pontoon *n* pontùn *m*
pony *n* pònaidh *m*
pool *n* linne *f*, glumag *f*, lòn *m*
poor *a* bochd, truagh
pop *n* (*sound*) brag *m* **p. music** ceòl pop *m*
Pope *n* am Pàp(a) *m*
poplar *n* pobhlar *m*
poppy *n* crom-lus *m*
popular *a* measail (aig daoine)
popularity *n* measalachd *f*
population *n* sluagh *m*; (*number*) àireamh-sluaigh *f*
porch *n* poirdse *m*
porcupine *n* gràineas *m*
pore *n* pòr *m*
pork *n* muicfheòil *f*, feòil muice *f*
pornography *n* drùiseantachd *f*
porous *a* pòrach, còsach
porpoise *n* pèileag *f*, cana *m*
porridge *n* lite *f*, brochan *m*
port *n* port *m*, caladh *m*, baile-puirt *m*; (*wine*) fìon-poirt *m*; (*naut*) clì *m*, an taobh clì *m*
portable *a* so-ghiùlan, a ghabhas giùlan
portent *n* comharra *m*, manadh *m*
porter *n* portair *m*, dorsair *m*; (*drink*) portair *m*
portion *n* earrann *f*, roinn *f*, cuid *f*
portrait *n* dealbh (neach) *f m*
portray *v* dèan cunntas/dealbh
Portuguese *n* Portagaileach *m*, (*female*) ban-Phortagaileach *f*; (*lang*) Portagaileis *f* *a* Portagaileach
pose *v* suidhich (thu *etc* fhèin), rach ann an cruth/riochd; (*question*) cuir ceist; (*problem*) adhbhraich; (*impersonate*) leig air/oirre a bhith na *etc*
posh *a* spaideil
position *n* suidheachadh *m*; (*in contest*) àite *m*; (*rank*) inbhe *f*, ìre *f*
positive *a* dòchasach, deimhinneach; (*certain*) dearbh-chinnteach; (*genuine*) dìreach, sònraichte **p. discrimination** leth-bhreith thaiceil *f*
possess *v* sealbhaich, gabh seilbh (de) **I don't even p. a watch** chan eil fiù 's uaireadair agam
possession *n* seilbh *f* **my possessions** mo chuid *f*

possessive *a* seilbheach
possibility *n* comas *m*, comasachd *f*, cothrom *m*
possible *a* comasach **it is not p. to do that** cha ghabh sin dèanamh, tha sin do-dhèanta
possibly *adv* is dòcha (gu), math dh'fhaodte (gu)
post *n* post *m*; (*position*) dreuchd *f* **postcode** còd puist *m* **p. office** oifis/oifig a' phuist *f* *v* post, cuir sa phost
postage *n* postachd *f*
postal *a* puist **p. vote** bhòt tron phost *f*
postcard *n* cairt-p(h)uist *f*
poster *n* postair *m*
postgraduate *n* iar-cheumnaiche *m* *a* iar-cheumnach
posthaste *adv* an làrach nam bonn
postman/postwoman *n* post(a) *m*
postpone *v* cuir dàil an, cuir dheth
postscript *n* fo-sgrìobhadh *m*
posture *n* giùlan *m*; (*polit*) seasamh *m*
pot *n* poit *f*, prais *f*
potassium *n* potasaidheam *m*
potato *n* buntàta *m*
potbellied *a* bronnach
potent *a* cumhachdach, làidir
potential *n* comas *m* *a* comasach air a bhith, san t-sealladh
potion *n* deoch *f*
potter *n* crèadhadair *m*
pottery *n* crèadhadaireachd *f*; (*place*) ionad-crèadhaidh *m*
pouch *n* pòcaid *f* **tobacco p.** spliùchan *m*
poultice *n* fuar-lit *f*
poultry *n* cearcan *f pl*
pounce *v* leum air
pound *n* punnd *m*; (*money*) nota *m* **p. sterling** punnd Sasannach *m*
pound *v* pronn; (*impound*) punnd, cuir ann am punnd; (*strike*) buail
pour *v* (*trans*) dòirt **it poured with rain** bha dìle uisge ann
pout *v* cuir bus/gnoig air/oirre *etc*
poverty *n* bochdainn *f*
powder *n* fùdar *m*, pùdar *m* *v* cuir fùdar air; (*pulverize*) min-phronn
power *n* cumhachd *f m*; (*authority*) ùghdarras *m*
powerful *a* cumhachdach
powerless *a* gun chumhachd, lag
practical *a* practaigeach; (*skilled*) deas-làmhach
practice *n* cleachdadh *m*; (*performance*) cur an gnìomh *m*; (*instrument etc*) dol thairis air *m*
practise *v* bi ri ...; (*perform*) cuir an gnìomh; (*instrument etc*) rach thairis air
pragmatic *a* pragmatach
pragmatism *n* pragmatachas *m*
prairie *n* prèiridh *m*
praise *n* moladh *m*, cliù *m* *v* mol
praiseworthy *a* ionmholta, ri m(h)oladh *etc*
pram *n* pram *m*
prance *v* leum, geàrr sùrdag
prank *n* cleas *m*
prattle *v* dèan cabadaich/gobaireachd
prawn *n* muasgan-caol *m*
pray *v* dèan ùrnaigh *Also vn* ag ùrnaigh
prayer *n* ùrnaigh *f* **p. meeting** coinneamh-ùrnaigh *f*
pre- *pref* ro-
preach *v* searmonaich, teagaisg
preacher *n* searmonaiche *m*
preamble *n* facal-toisich *m*
precarious *a* cugallach
precaution *n* earalas *m*
precede *v* rach/thig ro
precedent *n* ro-shampall *m*, eisimpleir *f m*
preceding *a* roimhe
precentor *n* neach togail fuinn *m*, neach cur a-mach na loidhne *m*
precept *n* àithne *f*, reachd *m*
precinct *n* crìoch(an) *f pl*, àrainn *f*; (*district*) ceàrn *f* **shopping p.** àrainn bhùthan
precious *a* prìseil, luachmhor **p. stone** seud *m*
precipice *n* bearradh *m*, stùc *f*
precipitate *v* (*hasten*) cabhagaich; (*cause*) adhbhraich

precipitate *a* bras, cabhagach
precipitous *a* cas
precise *a* pongail, mionaideach
precisely *adv* gu cruinn ceart
precision *n* pongalachd *f*, mionaideachd *f*
preclude *v* bac, dùin a-mach
precocious *a* ro-abaich, comasach ron àm
preconception *n* ro-bheachd *m*
predator *n* sealgair *m*
predatory *a* creachach, reubainneach
predecessor *n* neach a bh' ann roimhe *m*
predetermine *v* ro-rùnaich
predicament *n* càs *m*, teinn *f*
predict *v* ro-inn(i)s, dean fàisneachd air
predictable *a* ro-innseach, ris a bheil dùil
prediction *n* fàisneachd *f*
predominant *a* as bitheanta, buadhach
pre-empt *v* caisg ro-làimh
prefabricated *a* togte ro-làimh
preface *n* ro-ràdh *m* *v* can sa chiad dol a-mach
prefer *v* **prefers** 's fheàrr le ...
preferable *a* nas fheàrr
preference *n* roghainn *m*
preferential *a* am fàbhar (neach)
prefix *n* ro-leasachan *m*
pregnancy *n* leatrom *m*
pregnant *a* trom, torrach, air turas
prehistoric *a* ro-eachdraidheil
prejudge *v* ro-bhreithnich, thoir ro-bhreith air
prejudice *n* claon-bhàidh/bhreith *f* *v* claon-bharailich; (*damage case etc*) dochainn, mill
prejudiced *a* le claon-bharail
preliminary *a* tòiseachail
prelude *n* ro-thachartas *m*
premature *a* an-abaich, ron àm
premeditated *a* ro-bheachdaichte
premier *n* prìomhaire *m* *a* prìomh (+ *len*)
premiere *n* ciad shealladh *m*
premise *n* tùs-bheachd *m*
premises *n* aitreabh *f*, togalach *m* **on the p.** san àite (fhèin)
premium *n* (*eg insurance*) tàilleabh *m*
premonition *n* ro-fhaireachdainn *f*, rabhadh *m*
prenatal *a* ro bhreith
preoccupation *n* cùram *m*
pre-ordain *v* ro-òrdaich
preparation *n* ullachadh *m*, deasachadh *m*
prepare *v* ullaich, deasaich
prepared *a* ullaichte, deasaichte
preposition *n* roimhear *m*
prepositional pronoun *n* ro-riochdair *m*
preposterous *a* gun sgot/chiall
prerequisite *n* riatanas *m*
Presbyterian *n*, *a* Clèireach *m*
presbytery *n* clèir *f*
prescribe *v* òrdaich, comharraich
prescribed *a* òrdaichte, comharraichte
prescription *n* òrdugh *m*, riaghailt *f*; (*med*) òrdugh-cungaidh *m*
prescriptive *a* òrdachail
presence *n* làthaireachd *f*
present *n* (*time*) an t-àm (a) tha (an) làthair *m*; (*gift*) tiodhlac *m* **at p.** an ceartuair **the p. day** an là an-diugh *m* **the p. tense** an tràth làthaireach *m* *a* an làthair, làthaireach
present *v* nochd, taisbean; (*give*) thoir do, thoir seachad do, builich (air)
presentation *n* taisbeanadh *m*; (*gift*) tabhartas *m*
preservation *n* gleidheadh *m*
preserve *v* glèidh, cùm; (*food*) grèidh
presidency *n* uachdranachd *f*
president *n* ceann-suidhe *m*
press *n* (*printing*) clò *m*; (*newspapers*) na pàipearan *m*; (*journalists*) luchd-naidheachd *m*; (*cupboard*) preas *m* **p. conference** coinneamh naidheachd *f* **p. release** fios naidheachd *m* **p. statement** brath naidheachd *m*
press *v* fàisg, brùth, put; (*point*) leig cuideam air; (*urge*) cuir ìmpidh air, spàrr (air)

pressing *a* deatamach
pressure *n* bruthadh *m*, teannachadh *m*; (*stress*) èiginn *f*, eallach *m*; (*atmos*) tomhas-bruthaidh *m* **p. group** buidheann-tagraidh *f m*
pressurize *v* cuir/leig cuideam air
prestige *n* cliù *m*, ainm *m*, teist *f*
prestigious *a* cliùiteach, a sheallas inbhe
presumably *adv* 's fheudar (gu), a rèir coltais
presume *v* gabh air/oirre *etc*, rach dàn; (*assume*) bi dhen bheachd
presumptuous *a* ladarna, dalma
presuppose *v* bi dhen bheachd; (*imply*) gabh ris gu bheil
pretence *n* leisgeul *m*, leigeil air *m*
pretend *v* leig air/oirre *etc*, cuir an ìre
pretext *n* leisgeul *m*
pretty *a* brèagha, bòidheach *adv* an ìre mhath
prevail *v* buadhaich **p. upon** thoir air
prevailing *a* (*usual*) àbhaisteach **p. wind** gnàth-ghaoth *f*
prevalent *a* cumanta, bitheanta
prevaricate *v* dèan breug, bi ri mealltaireachd
prevent *v* bac, caisg
prevention *n* bacadh *m*, casg *m*
preview *n* ro-shealladh *m*
previous *a* eile
previously *adv* mu thràth, mar tha, ro-làimh
pre-war *a* ron chogadh
prey *n* creach *f*, cobhartach *f m* *v* spùinn, creach **p. upon** gabh brath air
price *n* prìs *f* **p. list** liosta phrìsean *f* *v* cuir prìs air
priceless *a* thar luach, prìseil thar tomhais
prick *v* bior, cuir bior an; (*met*) bior, brod, stuig
prickly *a* biorach; (*irritable*) calgach, crosta
pride *n* pròis *f*, uaill *f*, àrdan *m*; (*justified*) moit *f*
priest *n* sagart *m*
prim *a* ro ghrinn, ro fhìnealta
primarily *adv* sa chiad àite, gu h-àraid
primary *a* ciad, prìomh **p. school** bun-sgoil *f*
primate *n* àrd-easbaig *m*; (*biol*) prìomhaid *m*
prime *a* prìomh (+ *len*) **p. example** fìor dheagh eisimpleir *f m* **P. Minister** Prìomhaire *m* *n* làn-bhlàth *m*; (*phys*) trèine a neairt *f*
prime *v* cuir air ghleus
primitive *a* prìomhadail
primrose *n* sòbhrach *f*, sòbhrag *f*
prince *n* prionnsa *m*
princess *n* bana-phrionnsa *f*
principal *n* prionnsapal *m*, ceann(ard) *m* *a* prìomh (+ *len*)
principally *adv* gu sònraichte, gu h-àraid
principle *n* prionnsapal *m*
principled *a* prionnsapalta, le prionnsapail
print *n* clò *m*; (*footprint*) lorg *f* *v* clò-bhuail, cuir an clò
printer *n* clò-bhualadair *m*
prior *a* ro-làimh *adv* roimhe **p. to their arrival** mun do ràinig iad
prioritize *v* prìomhaich, dèan prìomhachas air
priority *n* prìomhachas *m*
prison *n* prìosan *m*
prisoner *n* prìosanach *m*
pristine *a* fìorghlan, gun mheang
privacy *n* uaigneas *m*
private *a* uaigneach, dìomhair, prìobhaideach **p. eye** lorgaire *m* **p. sector** roinn phrìobhaideach *f* *n* saighdear cumanta *m* **in p.** ann an dìomhaireachd
privately *adv* gu dìomhair, os ìosal, gu prìobhaideach
privilege *n* sochair *f*
privileged *a* fo shochair
prize *n* duais *f* *v* meas, cuir luach air
proactive *a* for-ghnìomhach
probable *a* coltach
probably *adv* is dòcha (gu/gun/gum/nach)
probation *n* pròbhadh *m*; (*period*)

àm dearbhaidh *m*
probationer *n* neach fo dhearbhadh *m*
probe *n* (*implement*) bior-tomhais *m*; (*inquiry*) rannsachadh *m*; (*space*) sireadh *m* *v* rannsaich, sir
problem *n* ceist *f*, duilgheadas *m*; (*maths*) cuistean *m*
problematic *a* na cheist/dhuilgheadas
procedure *n* modh *f m*, dòigh *f*, dòigh-obrach *f*
proceed *v* rach air adhart, gluais, lean (air/oirre *etc*)
proceedings *n* dol air adhart *m*, cùisean *f pl*; (*leg*) cùis-lagha *f*
proceeds *n* teachd a-steach *m*, toradh *m*
process *n* giullachd *f*, modh-obrachaidh *f m*, cùrsa *m* *v* làimhsich, dèilig ri
procession *n* caismeachd *f*, triall *m*
proclaim *v* aithris gu follaiseach
proclamation *n* aithris fhollaiseach *f*
procrastinate *v* dèan maill(e), màirnealaich, cuir dheth
procrastination *n* dàil *f*, maill(e) *f*, màirneal *m*
procreate *v* gin, sìolaich
procurator *n* procadair *m* **p. fiscal** neach-casaid a' Chrùin *m*, fiosgal *m*
procure *v* faigh, solaraich
prod *v* brod, stob; (*encourage*) brosnaich
prodigal *a* strùidheil, stròdhail **the P. Son** am Mac Stròdhail *m*
prodigious *a* anabarrach
produce *n* toradh *m*, cinneas *m*
produce *v* dèan; (*show*) nochd, taisbean, thoir am follais; (*eg film*) riochdaich
producer *n* (*eg film*) riochdaire *m*
product *n* toradh *m*; (*result*) buil *f*
production *n* dèanamh *m*; (*artistic*) riochdachadh *m*
productive *a* torrach, tarbhach
profane *a* mì-naomha
profess *v* cuir an cèill, aidich
profession *n* dreuchd *f*, obair *f*; (*relig*) aidmheil *f*
professional *a* dreuchdail, proifeiseanta
professor *n* (àrd-)ollamh *m*, proifeasair *m*
proficiency *n* comas *m*, alt *m*, liut *m*
proficient *a* comasach, ealanta
profile *n* leth-aghaidh *f*; (*article*) geàrr-iomradh *m*; (*image*) ìomhaigh *f* **she has a high p.** tha i gu mòr san fhollais
profit *n* prothaid *f*, buannachd *f* *v* prothaidich, dèan prothaid à, faigh buannachd à
profitable *a* prothaideach, buannachdail
profligate *a* ana-caithteach, mì-stuama
profound *a* domhainn
profuse *a* pailt
profusion *n* mòr-phailteas *m*, sgaoilteach *f*
prognosis *n* fàisneas *m*, ro-thuaiream *f*
programme *n* prògram *m* *v* prògram
progress *n* adhartas *m* **p. report** aithisg adhartais *f* *v* rach air adhart
progression *n* gluasad *m*; (*continuity*) leantainneachd *f*
progressive *a* adhartach
progressively *adv* mean air mhean
prohibit *v* toirmisg
prohibited *a* toirmisgte
prohibition *n* toirmeasg *m*, bacadh *m*
prohibitive *a* toirmeasgach; (*price*) ro dhaor
project *n* pròiseact *f m*
project *v* stob a-mach; (*on screen*) tilg; (*estimate*) dèan ro-mheasadh
projection *n* stob *m*; (*on screen*) tilgeil *f*; (*estimate*) ro-mheasadh *m*
projector *n* proiseactair *m*
proliferate *v* sìolaich, fàs lìonmhor
prolific *a* torrach; (*rich in*) beairteach

prolong *v* sìn a-mach, cuir dàil an
promenade *n* promanàd *m*; (*walk*) sràidireachd *f*
prominent *a* follaiseach, nochdte; (*to the fore*) inbheach
promiscuous *a* iol-fheiseach
promise *n* gealladh *m*, gealltanas *m* *v* geall, thoir gealladh
promising *a* gealltanach
promontory *n* rubha *m*, sròn *f*, àird *f*
promote *v* cuir air adhart/aghaidh; (*at work*) àrdaich, thoir àrdachadh do
promotion *n* cur air adhart *m*; (*at work*) àrdachadh (inbhe) *m*
prompt *a* clis, sgiobalta *v* spreig; (*remind*) cuir an cuimhne
prone *a* dual, buailteach do; (*lying*) air a b(h)eul fodha *etc*
pronoun *n* riochdair *m* **personal p.** riochdair pearsanta
pronounce *v* fuaimnich; (*leg*) thoir a-mach binn
pronunciation *n* fuaimneachadh *m*
proof *n* dearbhadh *m*
prop *n* taic *f*, cùl-taic *f* *v* cùm suas, thoir taic do, cuir taic ri
propaganda *n* propaganda *m*
propel *v* iomain
propeller *n* proipeilear *m*
proper *a* iomchaidh, cubhaidh, dòigheil, ceart
properly *adv* gu cubhaidh, gu dòigheil, (gu) ceart
property *n* cuid *f*, seilbh *f*; (*attribute*) buadh *f*
prophecy *n* fàisneachd *f*, fàidheadaireachd *f*
prophesy *v* fàisnich, dèan fàidheadaireachd
prophet *n* fàidh *m*
propitious *a* fàbharach
proportion *n* cuid *f*, earrann *f*; (*symmetry*) cumadh *m*, cunbhalachd *f*, co-rèir *m* **in p. to** a rèir
proportional *a* co-rèireach, co-roinneil **p. representation** riochdachadh co-roinneil *m*
proposal *n* (*offer*) tairgse *f*; (*motion*) moladh *m*; (*of marriage*) tairgse-pòsaidh *f*
propose *v* tairg; (*motion*) mol
proposition *n* tairgse *f*; (*phil*) smaoineas *m* *v* (*sexual*) tairg feis
proprietor *n* sealbhadair *m*
propriety *n* freagarrachd *f*, iomchaidheachd *f*
propulsion *n* iomain *f*
prosaic *a* lom, tioram, neo-bheothail
proscribe *v* toirmisg, caisg
proscribed *a* toirmisgte
prose *n* rosg *m*
prosecute *v* tog casaid an aghaidh, cuir casaid às leth
prosecution *n* casaideachadh *m*; (*service*) luchd-casaid *m*
prospect *n* (*view*) sealladh *m*; (*met*) dùil *f* **in p.** san amharc
prospective *a* san amharc, ri teachd
prospectus *n* ro-shealladh *m*; (*institutional*) leabhran-iùil oilthigh/colaiste/sgoile *m*
prosper *v* soirbhich
prosperity *n* soirbheachadh *m*
prosperous *a* soirbheachail
prostitute *n* siùrsach *f*, strìopach *f*
prostitution *n* siùrsachd *f*, strìopachas *m*; (*of talents*) mì-bhuileachadh *m*
prostrate *a* sleuchdte, sìnte
protect *v* dìon, teasraig
protection *n* dìon *m*
protective *a* dìona
protein *n* pròtain *m*
protest *n* gearan *m*, casaid *f* *v* gearain, tog casaid; (*against*) tog fianais an aghaidh (+ *gen*)
Protestant *n*, *a* Pròstanach *m*, (*female*) ban-Phròstanach *f*
protester *n* neach-togail-fianais *m*, casaidiche *m*
protocol *n* pròtacal *m*
protractor *n* protractair *m*
protrude *v* bi na stob a-mach, bi faicsinneach
proud *a* pròiseil, uailleil, àrdanach; (*justifiably*) moiteil
prove *v* dearbh; (*test*) feuch
proved, proven *a* dearbhte

proverb *n* seanfhacal *m*, gnàth-fhacal *m*
provide *v* solair, solaraich
providence *n* freastal *m*
province *n* roinn *f*
provincial *a* roinneil, a bhuineas dhan tuath; (*attitude*) beag-sheallach
provision *n* ullachadh *m*, solar *m* **provisions** lòn *m*
provisional *a* (*temporary*) sealach, car ùine; (*conditional*) air chùmhnant
proviso *n* cumha *f*, cùmhnant *m*
provocation *n* buaireadh *m*, stuigeadh *m*, cùis-fheirge *f*
provocative *a* buaireasach, buaireanta
provoke *v* cuir thuige, cuir conas air, stuig; (*engender*) adhbhraich
provost *n* pròbhaist *m*
prowess *n* comas *m*; (*in battle*) gaisge *f*
prowl *v* liùg
proximity *n* fagasachd *f*
proxy *n* neach-ionaid *m*, neach a ghabhas àite *m*
prude *n* neach nàrach *m*
prudence *n* crìonnachd *f*, faiceall *f*
prudent *a* crìonna, faiceallach, ciallach
prune *n* prùn *m*
prune *v* sgath, beàrr
psalm *n* salm *f m*
psalmody *n* salmadaireachd *f* **p. class** sgoil fhonn *f*
psalter *n* salmadair *m*
psyche *n* aigne *f*
psychiatrist *n* lighiche-inntinn *m*
psychiatry *n* leigheas-inntinn *m*
psychic *a* leis an dà shealladh; (*of psyche*) aignidheil
psychological *a* inntinn-eòlach
psychologist *n* eòlaiche-inntinn *m*
psychology *n* eòlas-inntinn *m*
ptarmigan *n* tàrmachan *m*
pub *n* taigh-seinnse *m*
puberty *n* inbhidheachd *f*
public *n* poball *m*, mòr-shluagh *m* *a* poblach **p. conveniences** goireasan poblach *m pl* **p. holiday** saor-latha poblach *m*, latha fèille *m* **p. house** taigh-seinnse *m* **p. inquiry** rannsachadh poblach *m*
publican *n* òstair *m*
publication *n* foillseachadh *m*
publicity *n* follaiseadh *m*
publicize *v* thoir am follais
publish *v* foillsich, cuir a-mach
publisher *n* foillsichear *m*
publishing *n* foillseachadh *m*
pudding *n* (*sweet*) mìlsean *m* **black/white p.** marag dhubh/gheal *f*
puddle *n* lòn *m*
puff *n* (*of wind*) osag *f*, oiteag *f*
puffin *n* buthaid *f*
pugnacious *a* buaireanta, cogail
puke *v* sgeith, cuir a-mach
pull *n* tarraing *f*, slaodadh *m*, draghadh *m* *v* tarraing, slaod, dragh
pullet *n* eireag *f*
pulley *n* ulag *f*
pulp *n* glaodhan *m*, taois *f*, pronnach *f*
pulpit *n* cùbaid *f*
pulse *n* (*med*) buille cuisle *f*
pulverize *v* mìn-phronn
pump *n* pump(a) *m*; (*dancing shoe*) bròg-dannsa *f* *v* tarraing, pump
pun *n* cainnt-chluich *f m*, geàrr-fhacal *m*
punch *n* dòrn *m*, buille *f*; (*tool*) tollair *m*; (*drink*) puinnse *m*
punctual *a* pongail, na uair, ris an uair
punctuation *n* puingeachadh *m*, pungadh *m*
puncture *n* toll *m*, tolladh *m* *v* toll
pungent *a* searbh, geur, guineach
punish *v* peanasaich, cronaich
punishment *n* peanas *m*, cronachadh *m*
punitive *a* peanasach
puny *a* crìon, beag
pup *n* cuilean *m*
pupil *n* sgoilear *m*; (*of eye*) clach na sùla *f*
puppet *n* pupaid *f m*, gille-mirein *m*

puppy *n* cuilean *m*
purchase *v* ceannaich
pure *a* fìorghlan
purgative *n* purgaid *f*
purge *v* glan, cairt, purgaidich
purification *n* glanadh *m*
purify *v* glan
purity *n* fìorghlaine *f*
purple *a* purpaidh, corcair
purport *v* leig ort, cùm a-mach
purpose *n* adhbhar *m*, rùn *m*
purposely *adv* a dh'aon ghnotha(i)ch
purr *v* dèan crònan
purse *n* sporan *m*
pursue *v* rach às dèidh/air tòir (+ *gen*); (*met*) lean
pursuit *n* tòir *f*, ruaig *f*; (*pastime*) cur-seachad *m* **in p. of** air tòir (+ *gen*)
pus *n* iongar *m*, brachadh *m*
push *n* putag *f* *v* put; (*press*) brùth
pushchair *a* carbad-leanaibh *m*
pushy *a* aghach
put *v* cuir **put aside** cuir mu seach, cuir an dàrna taobh **put off (the light)** cuir às/dheth (an solas) **put on clothes** cuir ort/umad *etc* aodach
putrid *a* grod, lobhte
putt *v* (*golf*) amais **putting the shot** putadh na cloiche *m*
putty *n* potaidh *m*, botaidh *f*
puzzle *n* tòimhseachan *m*, dubh-fhacal *m* *v* cuir fo imcheist; (*intrans*) bi an imcheist
pygmy *n* luchraban *m*, troich *f m*
pyjamas *n* deise-leapa *f*
pylon *n* crann-dealain *m*
pyramid *n* pioramaid *f*

Q

quadrangle *n* ceithir-cheàrnag *f*
quadruple *v* ceathraich
quadruplets *n* ceathrar (san aon bhrcith) *m*
quagmire *n* bog(l)ach *f*, sùil-chritheach/chruthaich *f*
quaich *n* cuach *f*
quaint *a* neònach, seann-fhasanta
quake *v* rach air chrith, criothnaich
qualification *n* (*formal*) teisteanas *m*; (*attribute*) feart *m*; (*caveat*) ceist *f*, teagamh *m*
qualified *a* (*formally*) le teisteanas; (*equipped*) uidheamaichte; (*with caveat*) le ceist/teagamh
qualify *v* thoir a-mach teisteanas; (*be eligible*) bi freagarrach (airson)
quality *n* buadh *f*, feart *m*, gnè *f*
quandary *n* imcheist *f* **in a q.** fo imcheist, eadar dhà bharail
quango *n* cuango *m*
quantify *v* àirmhich, tomhais meud
quantity *n* meud *m*, uiread *m*, uimhir *f*
quarrel *n* aimhreit *f*, còmhstri *f*, trod *f m* *v* rach far a chèile, troid, bi ag aimhreit
quarrelsome *a* aimhreiteach, connspaideach
quarry *n* cuaraidh *f m*; (*prey*) creach *f*
quarter *n* cairteal *m*, ceathramh *m*; (*of year*) ràith(e) *f*; (*area*) ceàrn *m*; (*mercy*) tròcair *f* **q. past one** cairteal/ceathramh an dèidh uair
quarterly *n* (*magazine*) ràitheachan *m* *adv* ràitheil, gach ràith(e), uair san ràith(e)
quarters *n* àite-fuirich *m*, cairtealan *m pl*
quartet(te) *n* (*group*) ceathrar *m*; (*mus piece*) ceòl-ceathrar *m*
quash *v* mùch, caisg, cuir an dara taobh
quatrain *n* ceathramh *m*, rann *m*
quaver *n* crith *f*; (*mus*) caman *m*
quay *n* cidhe *m*
queen *n* banrigh *f*
queer *a* neònach
quell *v* ceannsaich, mùch
quench *v* bàth, cuir às
quern *n* brà *f*
query *n* ceist *f*
quest *n* tòir *f*, iarraidh *m*, sireadh *m*
question *n* ceist *f*; (*doubt*) amharas *m* **q. mark** comharra-ceiste *m* *v* ceasnaich, faighnich,

feòraich; (*doubt*) cuir teagamh an
questionable *a* teagmhach, a' togail ceist
questioning *n* ceasnachadh *m*
questionnaire *n* ceisteachan *m*
queue *n* ciudha *f*
quibble *n* gearan beag-seagh *m* *v* gearain mu nithean beag-seagh
quick *a* luath, ealamh, clis
quickly *adv* gu luath, gu h-ealamh, gu clis
quid *n* nota *f*
quiet *a* sàmhach, tostach **be q.!** (e)ist! *n* sàmhchair *f*, tost *m*
quieten *v* ciùinich; (*intrans*) fàs sàmhach
quietness *n* sàmhchair *f*, ciùineas *m*
quilt *n* cuibhrig(e) *f m*
quit *v* sguir, falbh, leig seachad; (*place*) fàg
quite *adv* (*fairly*) gu math, rudeigin, lethchar; (*completely*) gu tur, gu lèir, gu h-iomlan, buileach (*with neg*) **it wasn't q. ready** cha robh e buileach deiseil
quiver *v* crith, dèan ball-chrith
quiz *n* ceasnachadh *m*, farpais-cheist *f*
quorum *n* àireamh riaghailteach *f*, cuòram *m*
quota *n* cuid *f*, cuota *m*
quotation *n* (*extract*) pìos air a thogail à *m*, às-earrann *f*; (*estimate*) tuairmeas *m*; (*valuation*) luach *m* **q. marks** cromagan turrach *f pl*
quote *n* briathran (a labhradh) *m pl*; (*estimate*) tuairmeas *m* *v* (*extract*) tog à; (*cite*) tog mar ùghdarras; (*estimate*) thoir tuairmeas

R

rabbit *n* coineanach *m*, rabaid *f*
rabble *n* gràisg *f*
rabid *a* (*lit*) cuthachail; (*met*) dearg (+ *n/a & len*)
rabies *n* fibin *f*
race *n* rèis *f*; (*ethnic*) cinneadh *m*; (*genetic*) gineal *f* **racecourse** cùrsa-rèis *m* **racehorse** steud-each *m* **r. relations** dàimh cinnidh *m* *v* ruith
racial *a* cinneadail **r. discrimination** leth-bhreith chinneadail *f*
racing *n* rèiseadh *m* **r. car** càr-rèisidh *m*
racism *n* gràin-cinnidh *f*
racist *n* neach a tha ri gràin-cinnidh *f* *a* gràin-c(h)innidheach
rack *n* ealchainn *f*; (*for torture*) inneal pianaidh *m* **going to r. and ruin** a' dol a Thaigh Iain Ghròt(a)
racket *n* (*noise*) gleadhraich *f*; (*sport*) racaid *f*
radar *n* rèidear *m*
radiant *a* lainnireach, boillsgeach, deàlrach
radiate *v* deàlraich
radiation *n* rèididheachd *f*
radical *a* radaigeach, freumhail, bunasach
radio *n* rèidio *m*, radio *m*
radioactive *a* rèidio-beò
radiography *n* rèidiografaidh *m*
radiology *n* rèidio-eòlas *m*
radiotherapy *n* gath-leigheas *m*
radish *n* meacan-ruadh *m*
radium *n* rèidium *m*
radius *n* rèidius *m*, spòg *f*
raffle *n* crannchur-gill *m*
raft *n* ràth *m*
rafter *n* cabar *m*, taobhan *m*, tarsannan *m*
rag *n* luideag *f*, clobhd(a) *m*
rage *n* boile *f*, cuthach *m*
ragged *a* luideagach
raging *a* fon chuthach, air bhoil(e)
raid *n* ruaig *f*, ionnsaigh *f*, creach *f* *v* ruag, thoir ionnsaigh (air)
raider *n* creachadair *m*, neach-ionnsaigh *m*
rail *n* rèile *f*
railway *n* rathad-iarainn *m* *a* rèile
rain *n* uisge *m* **raincoat** còta-froise *m* **rainfall** uisge *m* **rainforest** coille-uisge *f* *v* sil; (*heavily*) dòirt **it's raining** tha an t-uisge ann

rainbow *n* bogha-froise *m*
raise *v* tog, àrdaich **r. awareness** dùisg mothachadh, tog aire
raisin *n* rèiseid *f*
rake *n* ràcan *m*; (*person*) raidhc *m*, ràcaire *m* *v* ràc
rally *n* (*gathering*) cruinneachadh *m* *v* misnich, thoir cruinn; (*intrans*) ath-chruinnich; (*from illness*) ath-bheothaich
ram *n* reithe *m*, rùda *m*
ramble *n* cuairt *f*, fàrsan *m* *v* bi a' cuairtearachd/rèabhaireachd; (*in talk*) bi ri blabhdaireachd
rambler *n* ramalair *m*, fàrsanach *m*, rèabhair(e) *m*
rambling *a* fàrsanach; (*talk*) sgaoilte; (*bot*) streapach
ramification *n* ioma-bhuaidh *f*, buil *f*
ramp *n* ramp *m*
rampant *a* gun srian, gun cheannsachadh
ranch *n* rains(e) *f*
rancid *a* breun
rancour *n* gamhlas *m*
random *a* air thuaiream, tuaireamach
randy *a* macnasach
range *n* raon *m*; (*of mountains*) sreath bheanntan *f m*
rank *n* inbhe *f*; (*row*) rang *f m*, sreath *f m* **the r. and file** a' mhòr-chuid chumanta *f*, na mithean *m pl* *v* rangaich, cuir an òrdugh *a* (*intens*) tur, buileach; (*odour*) breun
rankle *v* fàg cais/ainmein air
ransack *v* rùraich; (*plunder*) creach
ransom *n* èirig *f* *v* saor/fuasgail (air èirig)
rant *v* bi ri blaomadaich **ranting and raving** ag èigheach 's ag uabhas
rap *n* buille *f*, sgailc *f*; (*on door*) gnogadh cruaidh *m* **take the rap** faigh/gabh a' choire
rape *n* èigneachadh *m* *v* èignich
rapid *a* bras, clis
rapids *n* bras-shruth *m*
rapport *n* co-bhàidh *f*
rapturous *a* mòr-aoibhneach
rare *a* tearc, ainneamh; (*in cooking*) gann-bhruich
rascal *n* blaigeard *m*, rasgal *m*
rash *n* broth *m* *a* bras, gun tùr
rasher *n* sliseag *f*
raspberry *n* subh-craoibh *m*
rat *n* radan *m*
rate *n* ìre *f*; (*speed*) astar *m* **r. of interest** ìre an rèidh *f* **the rates** na reataichean *m pl* *v* meas
rather *adv* rudeigin, car **r. than** seach, an àite (+ *gen*) **I'd r. go** b' fheàrr leam falbh
ratify *v* daingnich
ratio *n* co-mheas *m*
ration *n* cuibhreann *f m* *v* cùm ri cuibhreann
rational *a* ciallach, reusanta
rationale *n* feallsanachd *f*
rationalize *v* dèan leisgeul; (*operation etc*) cuir air stèidh ùr
rattle *n* gliogan *m*, glag *m*, glagadaich *f*; (*toy*) gliogan *m*
ravage *v* spùill, creach, cuir fàs
rave *n* hòro-gheallaidh *f m* *v* bi air bhoil(e) **r. about** dèan othail mu dheidhinn
raven *n* fitheach *m*
ravenous *a* cìocrach, gu fannachadh
ravine *n* mòr-ghil *f*
ravish *v* èignich
raw *a* amh **r. material** bun-stuth *m*
ray *n* gath *m*, leus *m*
raze *v* leag gu làr
razor *n* ealtainn *f*, ràsar *m* **r.-fish** muirsgian *f*
re- *pref* ath-
reach *v* ruig **r. for** sìn a dh'iarraidh (+ *gen*)
react *v* gluais, gabh ri, freagair **he reacted badly to it** chaidh e dona dha
reaction *n* gluasad *m*, gabhail ris *m*, freagairt *f*; (*chem*) iom-obrachadh *m*
reactor *n* reactar *m*
read *v* leugh
reader *n* leughadair *m*
readily *adv* gu toileach; (*quickly*) gu sgiobalta
reading *n* leughadh *m*

ready *a* deiseil, ullamh
reaffirm *v* daingnich
real *a* fìor
realistic *a* ciallach, practaigeach
reality *n* fìrinn *f*, fìorachd *f* **in r.** an dà-rìribh
realize *v* tuig; (*fulfil*) thoir gu buil; (*sell*) reic
really *adv* gu dearbh; (*sceptically*) seadh?
realm *n* rìoghachd *f*
reap *v* buain
reaper *n* buanaiche *m*; (*mech*) inneal-buana *m*
rear *n* deireadh *m*
rear *v* tog, àraich, altraim
reason *n* ciall *f*, reusan *m*; (*cause*) adhbhar *m*, fàth *m* *v* reusanaich
reasonable *a* reusanta, ciallach, coltach
reasoning *n* reusanachadh *m*
reassurance *n* fois-inntinn *f*
reassure *v* thoir fois-inntinn do
reassuring *a* fois-inntinneach
rebate *n* lasachadh *m*
rebel *n* reubaltach *m* *v* dèan ar-a-mach **r. against** rach an aghaidh (an t-sruth)
rebellion *n* ar-a-mach *m*
rebellious *a* ceannairceach
rebound *v* leum air ais **it will r. on him** thig e air ais air
rebuff *n* diùltadh *m*
rebuild *v* tog às ùr, ath-thog
rebuke *v* thoir achmhasan (do), cronaich
rebut *v* dearbh ceàrr, breugnaich
recall *v* cuimhnich air, bi cuimhn' aig; (*bring back*) thoir air ais
recap *n* ath-shùil *f*
recede *v* rach air ais, sìolaidh
receipt *n* (*written*) cuidhteas *m*
receive *v* faigh; (*react to*) gabh ri; (*welcome*) fàiltich
recent *a* ùr, o chionn ghoirid
recently *adv* o chionn ghoirid
reception *n* gabhail ri *m*; (*in hotel etc*) fàilteachadh *m*; (*event*) cuirm *f*
receptionist *n* fàiltiche *m*
receptive *a* fosgailte (ri)
recess *n* cùil *f*; (*vacation*) fosadh *m*
recession *n* crìonadh *m*, seacadh *m*
recipe *n* reasabaidh *m*
recipient *n* neach-faighinn *m*, neach a gheibh *m*
reciprocal *a* air gach taobh
reciprocate *v* dèan dha rèir
recitation *n* aithris *f*
recite *v* aithris
reckless *a* neo-chùramach
reckon *v* cunnt; (*consider*) meas
reclaim *v* thoir air ais; (*recover*) faigh/iarr air ais
recline *v* sìn, laigh
recluse *n* aonaran *m*
reclusive *a* aonaranach, leathoireach
recognize *v* aithnich; (*admit*) aidich
recoil *v* leum air ais **r. from** clisg (bh)o
recollect *v* cuimhnich
recollection *n* cuimhne *f*
recommend *v* mol
recommendation *n* moladh *m*
recommended *a* air a m(h)oladh *etc*
recompense *n* ath-dhìoladh *m*, èirig *f*
reconcile *v* (*bring together*) thoir gu chèile; (*figures etc*) rèitich **they were reconciled** thàinig iad gu rèite
reconciliation *n* (*bringing together*) toirt gu chèile *f*; (*figures etc*) rèite *f*
reconsider *v* ath-bheachdaich
reconstruction *n* ath-thogail *f*, ath-chruthachadh *m*
record *n* cunntas *m*, clàr *m*; (*disc*) clàr *m* *v* clàraich, cùm cunntas (air); (*express*) cuir an cèill; (*mus*) cuir air clàr
recorder *n* clàradair *m*; (*mus*) reacòrdair *m*
recording *n* clàr *m*, clàradh *m*
recount *v* aithris; (*vote*) ath-chunnt
recoup *v* faigh air ais
recover *v* (*get back*) faigh air ais; (*improve*) fàs nas fheàrr, rach am feabhas

recovery *n* faighinn/faotainn air ais *f*; (*in health*) fàs nas fheàrr *m*, dol am feabhas *m*
re-create *v* ath-chruthaich
recreation *n* cur-seachad *m*
recruit *v* tog
rectangle *n* ceart-cheàrnag *f*
rectangular *a* ceart-cheàrnach
rectify *v* ceartaich, cuir ceart
rector *n* (*educ*) ceannard *m*; (*university*) reachdair *m*; (*relig*) ministear *m*
recuperate *v* slànaich, rach am feabhas
recur *v* tachair a-rithist
recurrent *a* tillteach
recycle *v* ath-chleachd, ath-chuartaich
recycling *n* ath-chleachdadh *m*, ath-chuartachadh *m*
red *a* dearg; (*hair*) ruadh
redeem *v* (*save*) saor, fuasgail; (*fin*) ath-cheannaich
redirect *v* ath-sheòl
redistribute *v* ath-riaraich
redouble *v* (*efforts*) dèan spàirn is ath-spàirn
redraft *v* ath-dhreachd
redress *n* (*fin*) ath-dhìoladh *m*; (*leg*) furtachd *f*
reduce *v* lùghdaich, ìslich
reduced *a* lùghdaichte, air a lùghdachadh
reduction *n* lùghdachadh *m*, beagachadh *m*, ìsleachadh *m*
redundancy *n* pàigheadh dheth *m*; (*superfluity*) anbharr *m* **r. pay** airgead pàigheadh dheth *m*
redundant *a* anbharra, gun fheum; (*idle*) gun obair **they were made r.** chaidh am pàigheadh dheth
reed *n* cuilc *f*; (*mus*) ribheid *f*
reef *n* bodha *m*, sgeir *f*; (*a sail*) riof *f*
reek *v* (*smell*) cuir fàileadh dheth/dhith *etc*; (*smoke*) cuir smùid/toit dheth/dhith *etc*
reel *n* r(u)idhle *m*; (*of thread*) piorna *f m*
re-elect *v* ath-thagh
re-examine *v* ath-sgrùd
refectory *n* biadhlann *f*
refer (to) *v* thoir iomradh/tarraing air; (*pass to*) cuir gu; (*send back*) till air ais
referee *n* rèitire *m*; (*for job*) teistiche *m*
reference *n* iomradh *m*, tarraing *f*; (*testimonial*) teisteanas *f* **with r. to** a thaobh (+ *gen*) **r. book** leabhar-fiosrachaidh *m*
referendum *n* reifreann *m*, referendum *m*
refine *v* glan; (*met*) grinnich
reflect *v* tilg air ais; (*think*) meòraich, cnuasaich
reflection *n* faileas *m*; (*in mirror*) dealbh-sgàthain *f m*; (*thought*) meòrachadh *m*, cnuasachadh *m*
reflective *a* meòrachail, breithneachail
reflex *a* neo-shaor-thoileach
reform *n* leasachadh *m*, ath-leasachadh *m* *v* leasaich, ath-leasaich
reformation *n* ath-leasachadh *m* **the R.** an t-Ath-Leasachadh
refrain *v* cùm (bh)o, sguir
refresh *v* ùraich
refreshment *n* (*drink*) deoch *f*; (*renewal*) ùrachadh *m*
refrigerator *n* inneal-fionnarachaidh *m*, frids *m*
refuel *v* ath-chonnaich, lìon le connadh a-rithist
refuge *n* tèarmann *m*, dìdean *m*
refugee *n* fògarrach *m*
refund *n* airgead air ais *m* *v* pàigh air ais, ath-dhìol
refuse *n* sgudal *m*, sprùilleach *m*
refuse *v* diùlt
refute *v* dearbh ceàrr, breugnaich
regain *v* ath-choisinn, ath-shealbhaich
regal *a* rìoghail
regard *n* meas *m*, sùim *f*, spèis *f* **with kind regards** leis gach deagh dhùrachd **as regards** a thaobh (+ *gen*) *v* (*consider*) meas; (*esteem*) thoir spèis do; (*pay heed to*) thoir aire do
regardless *adv* a dh'aindeoin (sin)

regatta *n* rèisean shoithichean *f pl*
regenerate *v* ath-nuadhaich
regeneration *n* ath-nuadhachadh *m*
regime *n* riaghladh *m*; (*system*) rèim *f*
regiment *n* rèisimeid *f*
region *n* roinn *f*, ceàrn *f*
regional *a* roinneil, roinne
register *n* clàr *m* **cash r.** clàradair airgid *m* *v* clàraich; (*reveal*) leig ris; (*show up*) nochd
registrar *n* neach-clàraidh *m*
registration *n* clàradh *m*
registry *n* ionad-clàraidh *m*
regret *n* aithreachas *m*; (*sorrow*) duilichinn *f* *v* gabh aithreachas; (*be sorry*) bi duilich
regrettable *a* na adhbhar aithreachais; (*sad*) duilich
regular *a* cunbhalach, riaghailteach
regularity *n* cunbhalachd *f*
regulate *v* riaghlaich, rèitich
regulation *n* riaghailt *f*; (*act of*) riaghladh *m*
rehearsal *n* ruith thairis *f*
rehearse *v* ruith thairis air; (*go through*) ath-aithris
reign *n* rìoghachadh *m*
reimburse *v* pàigh air ais (airson)
rein *n* srian *f*
reindeer *n* rèin-fhiadh *m*
reinforce *v* daingnich, neartaich
reinstate *v* ath-shuidhich
reissue *v* cuir a-mach às ùr, ath-sgaoil
reiterate *v* ath-aithris
reject *v* diùlt
rejoice *v* dèan gàirdeachas/aoibhneas
rekindle *v* ath-bheothaich
relapse *n* tuiteam air ais *m*; (*med*) tilleadh tinneis *m*
relate *v* innis, aithris
related (to) *a* co-cheangailte ri; (*family*) càirdeach (do), an dàimh ri **r. by marriage** ann an cleamhnas
relation *n* co-cheangal *m*; (*relative*) neach-dàimh *m*, dàimh *m* **in r. to** ann an dàimh ri
relationship *n* càirdeas *m*, dàimh *m* **be in a r. with ...** a bhith a' falbh le ...
relative *n* neach-dàimh *m*, *pl* luchd-dàimh *m*, càirdean *m* *a* dàimheach **r. to** an coimeas ri
relaunch *v* cuir air bhog a-rithist
relax *v* gabh fois; (*rules etc*) lasaich, fuasgail
relaxation *n* fois *f*, tàmh m; (*pastime*) cur-seachad *m*
relaxed *a* socrach
relay *n* sreath (mu seach) *f m* **r. race** rèis phàirteach *f* *v* (*news etc*) sgaoil
release *v* fuasgail, leig às, cuir/leig mu sgaoil
relegate *v* cuir sìos
relent *v* taisich, gabh truas
relentless *a* gun sgur, gun abhsadh; (*implacable*) neo-thruacanta
relevance *n* buntainneas *m*
relevant *a* buntainneach, a' buntainn ri
reliable *a* earbsach
reliance *n* earbsa *f*, muinighin *f*
relief *n* fao(tha)chadh *m*, furtachd *f*; (*help*) cobhair *f*, cuideachadh *m*
relieve *v* furtaich, thoir fao(tha)chadh do; (*help*) cuidich **we were relieved** fhuair sinn fao(tha)chadh
religion *n* creideamh *m*
religious *a* cràbhach, diadhaidh
relinquish *v* leig/thoir seachad
relish *v* gabh fìor thlachd de/an
relocate *v* gluais (gu àite eile)
reluctant *a* ain-deònach **I was r. to do that** bha leisg(e) orm sin a dhèanamh
rely *v* cuir earbs(a) (an/ri)
remain *v* fuirich, fan
remainder *n* fuidheall *m*, còrr *m*
remains *n* fuidhleach *m*; (*corpse*) dust, duslach *m*
remark *n* iomradh *m*, facal *m* *v* thoir iomradh air; (*notice*) thoir fa-near
remarkable *a* sònraichte, suaicheanta, iongantach
remedial *a* leasachail

remedy *n* (*med*) leigheas *m*, ìocshlaint *f*; (*solution*) leasachadh *m* *v* leighis, slànaich; (*solve*) leasaich
remember *v* cuimhnich
remind *v* cuir an cuimhne, cuimhnich do
reminisce *v* cuimhnich (air)
remiss *a* dearmadach, neo-shuimeil
remit *n* raon-dleastanais/ ùghdarrais *m*
remit *v* cuir air falbh; (*refer back*) till, cuir air ais; (*cancel*) math
remittance *n* pàigheadh *m*, sùim airgid *f*
remnant *n* fuidheall *m*, iarmad *m*
remorse *n* dubh-aithreachas *m*, agartas-cogais *m*
remorseful *a* làn aithreachais
remote *a* iomallach, cian, fad' às
removal *n* gluasad *m*; (*flitting*) imrich *f*
remove *v* thoir air falbh; (*move*) gluais
remunerate *v* ìoc do, pàigh
renaissance *n* ath-bheothachadh *m* **the R.** Linn an Ath-Bheothachaidh *f m*
rend *v* srac, reub
render *v* (*pay*) ìoc, liubhair; (*make*) dèan
rendezvous *n* àite-coinneachaidh *m*
renew *v* ath-nuadhaich, ùraich
renewal *n* ath-nuadhachadh *m*, ùrachadh *m*
rennet *n* binid *f*
renounce *v* leig bhuat, trèig, cuir cùl ri
renovate *v* ùraich, nuadhaich
renovation *n* nuadhachadh *m*, ùr-sgeadachadh *m*
renown *n* cliù *m*
renowned *a* cliùiteach, iomraiteach
rent *n* sracadh *m*, reubadh *m*; (*fin*) màl *m* *v* gabh air mhàl
rented *a* air mhàl
re-open *v* fosgail às ùr
reorganization *n* ath-eagrachadh *m*, ath-òrdachadh *m*
reorganize *v* ath-eagraich, cuir rian ùr air
repair *v* càirich **r. to** tog air/oirre *etc* gu
repay *v* pàigh air ais
repayment *n* pàigheadh air ais *m*
repeal *v* cuir à bith
repeat *v* can a-rithist, ath-aithris
repeatedly *adv* uair is uair
repel *v* till; (*be offensive to*) sgreamhaich, cuir sgàig air
repent *v* dèan/gabh aithreachas
repercussion *n* toradh *m*, buil *f*
repetition *n* ath-aithris *f*, ath-innse *f*
repetitive *a* a-rithist is a-rithist
replace *v* gabh àite (+ *gen*) **r. ... with ...** cuir ... an àite ...
re-plant *v* cuir a-rithist, ath-chuir
replay *n* ath-chluich *f* *v* ath-chluich
replenish *v* ath-lìon
replete *a* làn, buidheach
replica *n* mac-samhail *m*
reply *n* freagairt *f* *v* freagair
report *n* aithisg *f*, iomradh *m* *v* thoir cunntas/iomradh (air), dèan aithisg (air)
reporter *n* neach-naidheachd *m*
repossess *v* ath-shealbhaich, thoir air ais (bh)o
represent *v* riochdaich
representation *n* riochdachadh *m*
representative *n* riochdaire *m* *a* riochdachail, samhlach
repression *n* mùchadh *m*, ceannsachadh *m*
reprieve *n* allsachd *f*
reprimand *n* achmhasan *m* *v* cronaich, thoir achmasan do
reprint *v* ath-chlò-bhuail
reprisal *n* dìoghaltas *m*
reproach *n* cronachadh *m*; (*disgrace*) masladh *m* **beyond r.** gun choire sam bith
reproduce *v* gin; (*copy*) mac-samhlaich
reproduction *n* gintinn *m*; (*copy*) mac-samhlachadh *m*
reptile *n* pèist *f*, snàgair *m*
republic *n* poblachd *f*
republican *n, a* poblachdach *m*
repudiate *v* cuir cùl ri, diùlt gabhail ri

repulse *v* ruaig, cuir ruaig air
repulsive *a* gràineil, oillteil
reputable *a* le deagh chliù, measail
reputation *n* cliù *m*, ainm *m*
request *n* iarrtas *m* *v* iarr
require *v* feum; (*ask*) iarr
requirement *n* riatanas *m*, feumalachd *f*
requisite *a* riatanach, air a bheil feum
rescue *n* sàbhaladh *m*, teasairginn *f* *v* sàbhail, teasairg
research *n* rannsachadh *m*, sgrùdadh *m* *v* rannsaich, dèan sgrùdadh
researcher *n* neach-rannsachaidh *m*, rannsaiche *m*
resemble *v* bi coltach ri
resent *v* fairich searbh mu, gabh san t-sròin
resentful *a* searbh, tàmailteach
resentment *n* tàmailt *f*
reservation *n* (*doubt*) cumha *f m*, teagamh *m*; (*booking*) ro-chlàradh *m*
reserve *v* glèidh, taisg
reserved *a* fad' às, dùinte; (*place, polit*) glèidhte
reservoir *n* tasgadh-uisge *m*; (*met*) stòr *m*, stòras *m*
reside *v* fuirich, gabh còmhnaidh an
residence *n* àite/ionad-còmhnaidh *m*, àros *m*
resident *n* neach-còmhnaidh *m*
residential *a* còmhnaidheach
residue *n* fuidheall *m*, còrr *m*
resign *v* leig dheth/dhith *etc* dreuchd, thoir suas; (*yield*) gèill, bi leagte ri
resignation *n* leigeil dheth/dhith *etc* dreuchd *m*; (*yielding*) gèilleadh *m*
resilient *a* fulangach
resin *n* ròiseid *f*, bìth *f*
resist *v* strì, cuir an aghaidh
resistance *n* strì *f*, cur an aghaidh *m*
resolute *a* seasmhach, gramail
resolution *n* (*outcome*) fuasgladh *m*; (*decision*) rùn *m*; (*resolve*) seasmhachd *f*
resolve *n* rùn suidhichte *m* *v* cuir romhad, rùnaich; (*solve*) fuasgail, rèitich
resonant *a* ath-fhuaimneach; (*met*) a' dùsgadh ...
resort *n* baile turasachd *m*; (*recourse*) innleachd *f*, dòigh *f*
resource *n* goireas *m*, stòras *m*; (*ingenuity*) innleachd *f*; (*fin*) ionmhas *m* **r. centre** ionad ghoireasan *m*
resourceful *a* innleachdach
respect *n* spèis *f*, urram *m* **with r. to** a thaobh (+ *gen*) *v* thoir spèis/urram do
respectable *a* measail, coltach
respectful *a* modhail, suimeil
respectively *adv* fa leth
respite *n* fao(tha)chadh *m*, anail *f* **r. care** cùram fao(tha)chail *m*
respond *v* (*answer*) freagair; (*act on*) dèilig ri
response *n* freagairt *f*
responsibility *n* dleastanas *m*, cùram *m*, uallach *m*
responsible *a* cùramach; (*accountable*) cunntachail; (*behaviour*) ciallach **r. for** an urra ri
responsive *a* freagairteach, mothachail
rest *n* fois *f*, tàmh *m*; (*mus*) clos *m* **the r.** (*persons*) càch; (*things*) an còrr *v* gabh fois, leig anail
restaurant *n* taigh-bìdh *m*
restful *a* socair, foiseil
restless *a* an-fhoiseil, mì-stòlda, luasganach, idrisgeach
restore *v* dèan suas às ùr; (*give back*) thoir air ais; (*of health*) aisig gu slàinte
restrain *v* bac, caisg, ceannsaich
restrained *a* sriante, fo srian
restraint *n* (*curb*) bacadh *m*, casg *m*; (*self-control*) smachd *m*
restrict *v* cuingealaich, cuibhrich
restricted *a* cuingealaichte
restriction *n* cuingealachadh *m*, cuibhreachadh *m*
result *n* buil *f*, toradh *m* **you'll see the r.!** bidh a' bhuil ann!
resume *v* tòisich a-rithist; (*recover*) gabh air ais

resurgence *n* ath-bheothachadh *m*, dùsgadh *m*
resurrection *n* aiseirigh *f*
resuscitate *v* ath-bheothaich
retail *a* bùtha
retailer *n* ceannaiche *m*, marsanta *m*
retain *v* cùm, glèidh
retaliate *v* dìoghail, sabaidich air ais
retaliation *n* dìoghaltas *m*, sabaid air ais *f*
retard *v* bac, cùm air ais
retch *v* sgeith
retention *n* cumail *f*, gleidheadh *m*
retentive *a* glèidhteach
reticent *a* dùinte, diùid
retire *v* rach air chluainidh, leig dheth/dhith dreuchd *etc* **I retired** leig mi dhìom mo dreuchd
retired *a* air chluaineas/ chluainidh
retirement *n* cluaineas *m*, leigeil dheth/dhith *etc* dreuchd *m*
retort *n* freagairt gheur *f* *v* freagair gu geur/bras
retrace *v* rach air ais air
retract *v* tarraing air ais
retreat *n* ionad dìomhair *m*; (*eccl*) tèarmann *m*; (*mil*) ratreut *m* *v* teich, tarraing air ais
retrieve *v* faigh air ais; (*met*) leasaich
retrograde *a* ais-cheumach **a r. step** ceum air ais *m*
retrospect *n* coimhead/sealltainn air ais *m* **in r.** le sùil air ais
retrospective *a* ais-sheallach
return *n* tilleadh *m*; (*fin*) prothaid *f* **r. fare** faradh gach rathad *m* *v* till; (*give back*) cuir/thoir air ais
reunion *n* ath-choinneachadh *m*
reveal *v* nochd, taisbean, foillsich, leig ris
revealing *a* nochdte, follaiseach
revelation *n* taisbeanadh *m*; (*eye-opener*) sùileachan *m* **Book of Revelations** Leabhar an Taisbeanaidh *m*
revelry *n* fleadhachas *m*
revenge *n* dìoghaltas *m* **take r. on** *v* dèan dìoghaltas air
revenue *n* teachd a-steach *m* **Inland R.** Oifis nan Cìsean *f*
reverberate *v* ath-ghairm; (*affect*) thoir buaidh air
reverence *n* urram *m*, ùmhlachd *f*
reverend *a* urramach **the Rev** an t-Urramach (an t-Urr)
reverent *a* a' nochdadh spèis/ urraim
reverse *v* rach air ais; (*overturn*) cuir car de
revert *v* till (gu)
review *n* breithneachadh *m*; (*arts*) lèirmheas *m*, sgrùdadh *m* *v* dèan breithneachadh air; (*arts*) dèan lèirmheas air, sgrùd
reviewer *n* lèirmheasaiche *m*
revise *v* ath-sgrùd, thoir sùil air ais air
revision *n* ath-sgrùdadh *m*, sùil air ais *f*
revitalise *v* ath-bheothaich
revival *n* ath-bheothachadh *m*; (*relig*) dùsgadh *m*
revive *v* ath-bheothaich, dùisg; (*trans*) ùraich
revoke *v* tarraing air ais
revolt *n* ar-a-mach *m*
revolting *a* gràineil, sgreamhail
revolution *n* car *m*, cuairt iomlan *f*; (*polit*) reabhlaid *f*, ar-a-mach *m*; (*met*) cruth-atharrachadh *m*, làn-thionndadh *m*
revolutionary *n* reabhlaideach *m*, neach ar-a-mach *m* *a* gu tur ùr; (*polit*) reabhlaideach
revolve *v* rach mun cuairt
revulsion *n* sgàig *f*
reward *n* duais *f* *v* thoir duais
rewrite *v* ath-sgrìobh
rhetoric *n* ùr-labhairt *f*, deas-chainnt *f*; (*pej*) glòireis *f*
rhetorical *a* ùr-labhrach, deas-chainnteach; (*pej*) glòireiseach
rheumatism *n* lòinidh *f m*
rhinoceros *n* sròn-adhairceach *m*
rhododendron *n* ròs-chraobh *f*
rhubarb *n* rùbarab *m*, ruadh-bhàrr *m*
rhyme *n* comhardadh *m* **internal r.** uaithne *m* *v* dèan comhardadh; (*compose a verse*) dèan rann

rhythm *n* ruitheam *m*, ruith *f*
rib *n* asna *f m pl* asnaichean, aisean *f pl* aisnean
ribbon *n* ribean *m*, ribinn *f*
rice *n* rus *m*
rich *a* beairteach, saidhbhir; (*soil*) torrach
riches *n* beairteas *m*, saidhbhreas *m*
rick *n* coc *f m*, cruach *f*
rid *v* saor, fuasgail **get r. of** faigh cuidhteas (+ *nom*)
riddle *n* tòimhseachan *m*; (*agric*) ruideal *m*, criathar garbh *m*
ride *v* marcaich
rider *n* marcaiche *m*
ridge *n* druim *m*
ridicule *n* sgeig *f*, fanaid *f* *v* dèan fanaid air, dèan cùis-bhùirt de
ridiculous *a* gòrach, amaideach, luideach
riding *n* marcachd *f*
rife *a* pailt, lìonmhor
rifle *n* raidhfil *f*, isneach *f*
rift *n* sgoltadh *m*; (*between people*) sgaradh *m*
rig *n* rioga *f*; (*agric*) feannag *f* **oilrig** crann-ola *m* *v* (*equip*) uidheamaich, beartaich; (*manipulate*) claon
right *n* còir *f*, dlighe *f*; (*justice*) ceartas *m* *a* ceart; (*hand etc*) deas **r. away** sa bhad *v* cuir ceart
righteous *a* ionraic, fìreantach
rightful *a* dligheach
rights *n* còraichean *f pl* **civil r.** còraichean catharra
rigid *a* rag, do-lùbaidh
rigorous *a* cruaidh, mion
rigour *n* cruas *m*
rim *n* oir *f m*, bile *f*, iomall *m*
rind *n* rùsg *m*
ring *n* fàinne *f m*; (*area*) cearcall *m*, buaile *f* **r. finger** mac an aba *m* **r.-road** cuairt-rathad *m* *v* seirm **r. the bell** brùth an clag
rink *n* rinc *m* **ice r.** rinc deighe *m*
rinse *v* sgol, sruthail
riot *n* ùpraid *f*, iorghail *f*
riotous *a* ùpraideach, iorghaileach; (*prodigal*) stròdhail
rip *v* srac, reub
ripe *a* abaich
ripen *v* abaich
ripple *n* crith *f*, luasgan *m*, caitean *m*
rise *v* èirich
risk *n* cunnart *m* *v* feuch; (*put at risk*) cuir an cunnart
risky *a* cunnartach
ritual *n* deas-ghnàth *m*
rival *n* co-dheuchainniche *m*, co-fharpaiseach *m*
rivalry *n* còmhstri *f*, farpais *f*
river *n* abhainn *f*
riveting *a* aire-tharraingeach, drùidhteach
road *n* rathad *m* **r. sign** soidhne rathaid *f*
roam *v* rach air fàrsan
roar *n* beuc *m*, glaodh *m*, bùirean *m* *v* beuc, glaodh
roast *n* ròst *f m* **r. beef** mairtfheòil ròsta *f* *v* ròist
rob *v* robaig, creach, goid air
robber *n* robair *m*, gadaiche *m*
robbery *n* goid *f*, robaireachd *f*, gadachd *f*
robe *n* fallaing *f*, trusgan *m*
robin redbreast *n* brù-dhearg *m*
robust *a* calma, làidir, foghainteach
rock *n* creag *f*, carraig *f*; (*substance*) clach *f*
rock *v* luaisg, tulg
rocket *n* rocaid *f*
rocking chair *n* sèithear-tulgaidh *m*
rocking horse *n* each-tulgach *m*
rock music *n* ceòl rog *m*
rocky *a* creagach
rod *n* slat *f*
rodent *n* criomach *m*
roe *n* earb *f*, ruadhag *f*; (*of fish*) iuchair *f*, glasag *f* **roebuck** boc-earba *m*
rogue *n* slaightear *m*, rògaire *m*
role *n* pàirt *f m*; (*in org*) dreuchd *f*; (*in society*) àite *m* **r.-play** gabhail riochd *m*
roll *n* roile *f m* *v* roilig, cuir car air char; (*fold*) paisg, fill
roller *n* roilear *m* **r.-coaster** roilear-còrsair *m* **r.-skate** bròg-roth *f*

Roman *n*, *a* Ròmanach *m*, (*female*) ban-Ròmanach *f*
Roman Catholic *n*, *a* Caitligeach *m*, (*female*) ban-Chaitligeach *f*
romance *n* romansachd *f*; (*story*) sgeul romansach *m*; (*love affair*) suirghe *f*
romantic *a* romansach
romp *v* bi a' ruideal
rone *n* guitear *m*, ròn *f*
roof *n* mullach *m*
rook *n* ròca(i)s *f*
room *n* rùm *m*, seòmar *m*; (*space*) àite *m*, rùm *m*
roomy *a* rùmail, farsaing
roost *n* spàrr *m*, spiris *f*
root *n* freumh *m*, bun *m*
rope *n* ròp(a) *m*, ball *m*
rosary *n* a' chonair(e) *f*, paidirean *m*
rose *n* ròs *m*
rot *n* grodadh *m*, lobhadh *m* *v* grod, lobh
rota *n* clàr-dleastanais *m*
rotate *v* cuir mun cuairt; (*intrans*) rach mun cuairt
rotten *a* grod, lobhte, breun
rotter *n* trustar *m*
rotund *a* cruinn
rough *a* garbh; (*hairy*) molach; (*temper*) garg
roughness *n* gairbhead *m*, gairge *f*
round *n* cuairt *f*, car *m* *a* cruinn *adv* mun cuairt, timcheall
roundabout *n* timcheallan *m*, cearcall-rathaid *m*
rouse *v* dùisg; (*stimulate*) brosnaich, piobraich
rousing *a* brosnachail, spreigearra
rout *n* ruaig *f*, sgiùrsadh *m* *v* rua(i)g, sgiùrs
route *n* rathad *m*, slighe *f*
routine *n* gnàth-chùrsa *m* *a* gnàthach
rove *v* bi a' ruagail, bi a' rèabhaireachd
row *n* (*line*) sreath *f m*
row *n* (*quarrel*) sabaid *f*, trod *m* *v* trod
row *v* (*boat*) iomair
rowan *n* caorann *m*
rowdy *a* gleadhrach
rowing *n* iomradh *m* **r. boat** bàta-ràmh *m*, geòla *f*
royal *a* rìoghail **the R. Family** an Teaghlach Rìoghail *m*
royalty *n* rìoghalachd *f*; (*fin*) dleasadh ùghdair *m*
rub *v* suath
rubber *n* rubair *m*
rubbish *n* sgudal *m*, treal(l)aich *f* **it's just r.** chan eil ann ach frachd **r. bin** biona-sgudail *m* **r. dump** lagais *f*, òtrach *m*
ruby *n* ruiteachan *m*, rùbaidh *f*
rucksack *n* màileid-droma *f*
rudder *n* stiùir *f*, falmadair *m*
ruddy *a* ruiteach, ruadh
rude *a* mì-mhodhail
rudeness *n* mì-mhodh *m*
rudimentary *a* tòiseachail
rue *v* gabh aithreachas mu
rueful *a* dubhach, brònach, leamh
ruffian *n* brùid *f m*
ruffle *v* dèan ain-rèidh; (*met*) cuir colg air
rug *n* ruga *m*, brat-ùrlair *m*
rugby *n* rugbaidh *m*
rugged *a* garbh, corrach
ruin *n* sgrios *m*; (*site*) làrach *f m*, tobhta *f* *v* sgrios, mill
rule *n* riaghailt *f*; (*exercise of*) ceannas *m* **as a r.** mar as trice *v* riaghail, riaghlaich
ruler *n* riaghladair *m* **rulers** luchd-riaghlaidh *m pl*; (*measuring*) rùilear *m*
rum *n* ruma *m*
rumble *v* dèan torrann; (*stomach*) bi a' rùchdail
rumbling *n* torrann *m*, brùnsgal *f*; (*stomach*) rùchdail *f*
rummage *v* rùraich
rumour *n* fathann *m*
rump *n* dronn *f*, rumpall *m*
run *n* ruith *f*; (*transport*) slighe *f* *v* ruith; (*flee*) teich; (*melt*) leagh
runner *n* neach-ruith *m*
running *n* ruith *f* **r. costs** cosgais ruith *f*
runway *n* raon-laighe *m*
rupture *v* bris(t), sgàin, sgaoil
rural *a* dùthchail
ruse *n* innleachd *f*, clìc *f*

rush *n* dian-ruith *f*, sitheadh *m*, roid *f* *v* dèan cabhag/sitheadh **r. out** brùchd a-mach
rushes *n* luachair *f*
Russian *n*, *a* Ruiseanach *m*, (*female*) ban-Ruiseanach *f*; (*lang*) Ruisis *f*
rust *n* meirg *f* *v* meirg(ich)
rustic *a* dùthchail
rustling *n* siosarnaich *f*
rusty *a* meirgeach
rut *n* clais *f*; (*of deer*) dàmhair (nam fiadh) *f* **in a rut** san aon imire/eag
ruthless *a* cruaidh; (*pitiless*) gun iochd
rye *n* seagal *m*

S

Sabbath *n* an t-Sàbaid *f* **S. Day** Latha na Sàbaid *m*
sabotage *n* sabotàis *f*
sack *n* poca *m*, sac *m* **s.-race** rèis a' phoca *f*
sack *v* (*from work*) cuir à obair; (*destroy*) sgrios, creach
sacred *a* naomh, coisrigte
sacrifice *n* ìobairt *f* *v* ìobair
sacrilege *n* ceall-shlad *m*, airchealladh *m*
sad *a* brònach, dubhach, muladach; (*pitiful*) truagh
sadden *v* cuir bròn air, dèan dubhach
saddle *n* dìollaid *f*
sadness *n* bròn *m*, mulad *m*
safe *a* sàbhailte, tèarainte **s. and sound** slàn sàbhailte *n* ciste-tasgaidh *f*
safeguard *n* dìon *m* *v* dìon, geàrd
safety *n* sàbhailteachd *f*, tèarainteachd *f* **s.-belt** crios-sàbhalaidh *m* **s.-pin** prìne (banaltraim) *m*
sag *v* tuit
saga *n* sgeulachd *f*, mòr-sgeul *m*
sage *n* (*bot*) slàn-lus *m*; (*person*) saoi *m*
sail *n* seòl *m* *v* seòl, bi a' seòladh
sailor *n* seòladair *m*, maraiche *m*
saint *n* naomh *m*
saithe *n* saoithean *m*
sake *n* sgàth *m* **for the s. of** air sgàth (+ *gen*)
salad *n* sailead *m* **s. dressing** annlann saileid *m*
salary *n* tuarastal *m*
sale *n* reic *m*; (*reduced prices*) reic-saor *m* **s. of work** fèill-reic *f* **salesman** fear-reic *m* **salesperson** neach-reic *m*
saliva *n* seile *m*
salivate *v* seilich
sallow *a* lachdann
salmon *n* bradan *m*
salon *n* ionad *m* **beauty s.** ionad maise
salt *n* salann *m* **s. cellar** saillear *m* **s.-water** sàl *m* *a* saillte *v* saill
saltire *n* bratach na croise *f*
salty *a* saillte
salubrious *a* greadhnach
salutary *a* tairbheach **a s. warning** rabhadh feumail *m*
salute *n* (*mil*) nochdadh urraim *m* *v* nochd urram; (*acknowledge*) fàiltich, cuir fàilte air
salvage *v* dèan sàbhaladh air
salvation *n* teàrnadh *m*, saoradh *m*, slàinte *f* **Salvation Army** Arm an t-Saoraidh *m*
same *a* ionann, ceudna, ceart, aon
sameness *n* co-ionannachd *f*
sample *n* eisimpleir *f m*, sampall *m*; (*abstr*) taghadh *m* *v* feuch, blais
sanctify *v* naomhaich
sanctimonious *a* feall-chràbhach
sanction *n* (*approval*) aontachadh *m*, ùghdarras *m*; (*ban*) smachd-bhann *m*, òrdugh *m* *v* (*approve*) ceadaich, ùghdarraich; (*ratify*) daingnich
sanctuary *n* (*relig*) ionad coisrigte *m*; (*refuge*) comraich *f*, tèarmann *m*
sand *n* gainmheach *f* **s. dune** coilleag *f*, dùn gainmhich *m* **sandbank** oitir-ghainmhich *f*, banca-gainmhich *m* **sandpaper** pàipear-gainmhich *m* **sandstone** clach-ghainmhich *f*

sandal *n* cuaran *m*
sandpiper *n* fìdhlear *m*
sandwich *n* ceapaire *m*
sandy *a* gainmheil, gaineamhach
sane *a* ciallach
sanguine *a* dòchasach
sanitary *a* slàinteil, slàinte
sanitation *n* slàintealachd *f*
sanity *n* ciall *f*
Santa Claus *n* Bodach na Nollaig *m*
sap *n* snodhach *m*, sùgh *m* *v* sùgh, traogh
sapphire *n* gorm-leug *f*
sarcasm *n* searbhas *m*, searbh-chainnt *f*, leamhachas *m*
sarcastic *a* searbh, leamh, beumnach
sardine *n* sàrdain *m*
sardonic *a* sgaiteach
sash *n* crios *m*, bann *m*
Satan *n* Sàtan *m*, an Donas *m*, an Droch Fhear *m*
satanic *a* diabhlaidh, deamhnaidh
satellite *n* saideal *m*
satin *n* sròl *m* *a* sròil
satire *n* aoir *f*
satirical *a* aoireil
satirize *v* aoir, dèan aoireadh
satisfaction *n* riarachadh *m*, sàsachadh *m*, toileachadh *m*
satisfactory *a* dòigheil, mar as còir
satisfied *a* riaraichte, sàsaichte, toilichte
satisfy *v* riaraich, sàsaich, toilich
satisfying *a* sàsachail
saturate *v* trom-fhliuch; (*met*) lèir-sgaoil
saturated *a* bog fliuch, trom-fhliuch; (*met*) loma-làn
Saturday *n* Disathairne *m*
sauce *n* sabhs *m*, leannra *m*
saucepan *n* sgeileid *f*
saucer *n* sàsar *m*, flat *m*
saucy *a* beadaidh
sauna *n* teaslann (smùide) *f*
saunter *v* spaidsirich
sausage *n* isbean *m*
savage *a* allaidh, borb
savagery *n* buirbe *f*
save *v* sàbhail, caomhain
saved *a* saorte, air a s(h)àbhaladh
saving(s) *n* sàbhaladh *m*, tasgadh *m* **s. bond** bann tasgaidh *m*
Saviour *n* an Slànaighear *m*
savour *v* feuch blas
savoury *a* blasta
saw *n* sàbh *m* **sawdust** min-sàibh *f* **sawmill** muileann-sàbhaidh *f m* *v* sàbh(aig)
saxifrage *n* lus nan cluas *m*
saxophone *n* sagsafòn *m*
say *v* can, abair
saying *n* ràdh *m*, facal *m*
scab *n* sgreab *f*, càrr *f*
scabies *n* am piocas *m*
scaffolding *n* sgafallachd *f*
scald *v* guail, sgald
scale *n* tomhas *m*; (*size*) meud *m*; (*mus, geog*) sgèile *f*; (*on fish*) lann *f*
scale *v* (*climb*) streap
scallop *n* creachan(n) *m*
scalp *n* craiceann a' chinn *m*
scalpel *n* sgian lèigh *f*, lannsa *f*
scamper *n* ruith, thoir ruaig, teich
scampi *n* muasgain-chaola *m*
scan *v* sgrùd; (*metr*) bi a rèir meadrachd, meadaraich
scandal *n* sgainneal *m*, tuaileas *m*
scandalize *v* sgainnealaich
scandalous *a* maslach, tàmailteach, sgainnealach
Scandinavian *n*, *a* Lochlannach *m*
scanner *n* sganair *m*
scant(y) *a* gann, tearc
scapegoat *n* cùis-choireachaidh *f*
scar *n* làrach *f m*, leòn *m*
scarce *a* gann, tearc, ainneamh
scarcely *adv* air èiginn, is gann gu
scarcity *n* gainnead *m*, teirce *f*
scare *n* eagal *m* *v* cuir eagal air
scarecrow *n* bodach-ròcais/feannaig/starraig *m*
scarf *n* sgarfa *f*, stoc *m*
scarlet *n* sgàrlaid *f* **s. fever** an teasach sgàrlaid *f*
scatter *v* sgap, sgaoil
scattered *a* sgapte
scene *n* (*view, drama*) sealladh *m*; (*place*) ionad *m*
scenery *n* sealladh *m*
scent *n* fàileadh *m*, boladh *m*,

cùbhras *m*
scented *a* cùbhraidh
sceptic *n*, *a* eas-creidmheach *m*
sceptical *a* eas-creidmheach
scepticism *n* eas-creideamh *m*
schedule *n* clàr(-ama) *m* **ahead of s.** ron àm, tràth **on s.** ris an uair **behind s.** fadalach, air d(h)eireadh *v* cuir air clàr(-ama)
scheme *n* sgeama *m*, innleachd *f*, dòigh *f* *v* dèan sgeama/innleachd
schism *n* sgaradh *m*
scholar *n* sgoilear *m*
scholarship *n* sgoilearachd *f*, foghlam *m*
school *n* sgoil *f* **s.house** taigh-sgoile *m* **s.master** maigh(i)stir-sgoile *m* **s.mistress** ban-sgoilear, bana-mhaigh(i)stir-sgoile *f*
sciatica *n* siataig *f*
science *n* saidheans *m*
scientific *a* saidheansail
scientist *n* neach-saidheans *m*
scissors *n* siosar *m*
sclerosis *n* sglearòis *f*
scoff *v* mag, dèan fanaid (air)
scold *v* càin, cronaich
scone *n* sgona *f m*, bonnach *m*
scoop *n* liagh *f*, ladar *m*, taoman *m* *v* cladhaich a-mach, tog a-mach
scope *n* comas *m*; (*opportunity*) cothrom *m*; (*extent*) raon *m*, farsaingeachd *f*
score *n* (*sport*) sgòr *m*; (*twenty*) fichead *m*; (*cut*) sgrìob *f* *v* (*sport*) cuir/faigh tadhal; (*cut*) sgrìob
scorn *n* tàir *f*, dìmeas *m* *v* dèan tàir/dìmeas air; (*opportunity*) leig seachad
scornful *a* tàireil
scorpion *n* sgairp *f*
Scot *n* Albannach *m*
Scots *n* (*language*) Albais *f*, Beurla Ghallda *f*
Scottish *a* Albannach **S. Arts Council** Comhairle Ealain na h-Alba **S. Executive** Riaghaltas na h-Alba **S. Parliament** Pàrlamaid na h-Alba
scoundrel *n* balgaire *m*
scour *v* sgùr
scourge *v* sgiùrs
scout *n* beachdair *m*
scowl *v* bi fo ghruaim, cuir drèin/mùig air/oirre *etc*
scraggy *a* reangach
scramble *v* bi a' sporghail; (*climb*) streap
scrap *n* criomag *f*, mìr *f*; (*fight*) sabaid *f*, tuasaid *f*
scrape *v* sgrìob **s. together** trus le èiginn
scratch *n* sgrìobadh *m*, sgrìob *f*, sgrìoch *f* *v* sgròb, sgrìob; (*itch*) tachais
scrawl *n* sgròbaireachd *f* *v* dèan sgròblaich
scream *n* sgiamh *f m*, sgreuch *m* *v* dèan sgiamh/sgreuch
screech *n* sgread *m*, sgreuch *m* *v* dèan sgread/sgreuch
screen *n* sgàilean *m*, sgrion *m* *v* (*shelter*) dìon, sgàilich; (*examine*) cuir fo sgrùdadh
screw *n* sgriubha *m* *v* sgriubh(aig)
screwdriver *n* sgriubhaire *m*
scribble *n* sgròbail *m* **a. quick s.** sgrìobag ghoirid *f* *v* dean sgròbail
scribe *n* sgrìobhaiche *m*
script *n* sgrìobhadh *m*, clò *m*; (*handwriting*) làmh-sgrìobha(i)dh *f*
scripture *n* sgriobtar *m*
scroll *n* rolla *f* *v* roilig
scrub *v* sgùr, nigh gu math
scruffy *a* piollagach, loireach
scruple *n* teagamh *m*, imcheist *f*
scrupulous *a* fìor chùramach, mion-fhaiceallach
scrutinize *v* sgrùd
scrutiny *n* sgrùdadh *m*
scuffle *n* buaireas *m*
scullery *n* sguilearaidh *f m*, cùlaist *f*
sculptor *n* snaigheadair *m*
sculpture *n* snaigheadh *m*; (*a piece of*) ìomhaigh shnaighte *f*
scum *n* rèim *m*, sgùm *m*; (*slang*) salchair *m pl*
scurrilous *a* sgainnealach, tuaileasach

scythe *n* speal *f* *v* speal
sea *n* muir *f m*, cuan *m*, fairge *f*
seabed *n* grunnd na mara *m*, aigeann *m*
seagull *n* faoileag *f*
seal *n* ròn *m*; (*document*) seula *m* *v* seulaich; (*close*) dùin
seam *n* (*clothing*) dùnadh *m*, fuaigheal *m*
seaman *n* maraiche *m*, seòladair *m*
search *n* lorg *m*, sireadh *m* **searchlight** solas-siridh *m* *v* lorg, sir
seashore *n* cladach *m*, tràigh *f*
seasick *a* leis an tinneas-mhara, le cur na mara
seasickness *n* an tinneas-mara *m*, cur na mara *m*
season *n* ràith(e) *f*, seusan *m*; (*time*) aimsir *f*, tràth *m*
season *v* (*wood etc*) seusanaich, grèidh; (*food*) cuir blas ri
sea-spray *n* siaban *m*, marcan-sìne *m*
seat *n* suidheachan *m*, cathair *f*, àite-suidhe *m*; (*residence*) àros *m*; (*in Parliament*) seat *f* **s. belt** crios-suidheachain *m*
sea trout *n* bànag *f*, gealag *f*
seaweed *n* feamainn *f*
secede *v* bris(t) air falbh, trèig
secluded *a* uaigneach, leathoireach
second *n* diog *m*
second *a* dara, dàrna
second *v* cuir taic ri; (*to post*) fo-fhastaich
secondary *a* dàrnacha, dhen dàrna ìre **s. school** àrd-sgoil *f*
seconder *n* neach-taice *m*
secondhand *a* ri/air ath-reic
secondly *adv* anns an dara h-àite, anns an dàrna àite
secrecy *n* dìomhaireachd *f*, cleith *f*
secret *n* rùn-dìomhair *m*, sgeul-rùin *m* *a* dìomhair, falaichte, falchaidh
secretariat *n* clèireachas *m*, rùnachas *m*
secretary *n* clèireach *m*, ban-chlèireach *f*; (*personal*) rùnaire *m* **S. of State** Rùnaire (na) Stàite *m*
secretive *a* falchaidh, ceilteach
secretly *adv* os ìosal, gun fhiosta (do dhaoine)
sect *n* dream *m*, treubh *f*
sectarian *a* dreamail, treubhail
section *n* roinn *f*, earrann *f*
sector *n* roinn *f*, raon *m*
secular *a* saoghalta
secure *a* tèarainte, seasgair *v* dèan cinnteach; (*lock*) gla(i)s; (*obtain*) faigh
security *n* (*abstr*) tèarainteachd *f*, dìon *m*; (*personnel*) luchd-dìon *m* **s. of tenure** còir-gabhaltais *f* **s. guard** geàrd-faire *m*
sedate *a* ciùin, stòlda
sedative *n* cungaidh stòlaidh *f*
sedge *n* seisg *f*
sediment *n* grùid *f*
seduce *v* thoir a thaobh, breug
seduction *n* toirt a thaobh *f*, breugadh *m*
see *v* faic **see you soon** chì mi (a) dh'aithghearr thu
seed *n* sìol *m*, fras *f*; (*offspring*) sliochd *m*, gineal *m*, iarmad *m* *v* sìolaich, cuir fras de
seek *v* iarr, sir, lorg
seem *v* bi mar ... , leig air/oirre *etc* (a bhith)
seemly *a* iomchaidh, cubhaidh, coltach
seep *v* sìolaidh tro
seer *n* fiosaiche *m*, fàidh *m*
seethe *v* (*met*) bi fo chuthach
segment *n* gearradh-cuairteig *m*, roinn *f*
segregate *v* dealaich, sgar, tearb
segregation *n* dealachadh *m*, sgaradh *m*, tearbadh *m*
seize *v* glac, cuir làmh an, greimich air
seizure *n* glacadh *m*, grèim *m*
seldom *adv* ainneamh, gu tearc, gu h-ainmig
select *v* tagh, roghnaich
selection *n* taghadh *m*, roghainn *f m*
selective *a* roghnach
self *pron* fhèin, fèin
self-confidence *n* fèin-mhisneachd *f*
self-confident *a* fèin-mhisneachail

self-denial *n* fèin-àicheadh *m*
self-employed *a* ag obair air a c(h)eann fhèin *etc*, fèin-fhastaichte
self-explanatory *a* fèin-mhìneachail
self-government *n* fèin-riaghladh *m*
self-interest *n* fèin-bhuannachd *f*
selfish *a* fèineil, fèinchuiseach
selfishness *n* fèinealachd *f*
self-respect *n* fèin-mheas *m*
self-satisfied *a* fèin-riaraichte
self-service *n* fèin-fhrithealadh *m*
self-same *a* ceart, ionann
sell *v* reic
seller *n* reiceadair *m*, neach-reic *m*
semblance *n* samhla *m*, coltas *m*
semi- *pref* leth-
semi-circle *n* leth-chearcall *m*
semi-colon *n* leth-chòilean *m*, leth-stad *m*
semi-detached *a* leth-dhealaichte
seminal *a* mòr-bhuadhach; (*phys*) sìolach
seminar *n* co-chonaltradh *m*
senate *n* seanadh *m*
senator *n* seanadair *m*
send *v* cuir **s. word** cuir fios (gu) **s. for** cuir a dh'iarraidh
senile *a* seanntaidh
senior *a* as sine, nas sine, àrd- (+ *len*), prìomh (+ *len*)
sensation *n* mothachadh *m*, faireachdainn *f m*
sense *n* (*wits*) ciall *f*, toinisg *f*; (*meaning*) brìgh *f*, seagh *m*; (*faculty*) ceudfath *f*, mothachadh *m*
senseless *a* gun chiall/sgot; (*phys*) gun mhothachadh
sensibility *n* mothachas *m*
sensible *a* ciallach, tùrail
sensitive *a* mothachail; (*contentious*) frionasach
sensory *a* mothachaidh
sensual *a* feòlmhor, collaidh
sensuous *a* ceudfathach
sentence *n* seantans *f*, rosgrann *m*; (*leg*) binn *f*, breith *f* *v* thoir binn, dìt
sentiment *n* (*thought*) smaoin *f*; (*emotion*) faireachdainn *f m*
sentimental *a* maoth-inntinneach
separate *a* dealaichte, sgaraichte, air leth, leis fhèin *v* dealaich, sgar, tearb, roinn
separation *n* dealachadh *m*, sgaradh *m*
sept *n* fine *f*
September *n* an t-Sultain *f*
septic *a* lionnraichte, iongarach
sequel *n* na leanas **the s. to** a leanas
sequence *n* leanmhainn *m*, ruith *f* **in s.** an sreath a chèile
serene *a* soineannta, ciùin, suaimhneach
serenity *n* soineanntachd *f*, ciùineas *m*, suaimhneas *m*
sergeant *n* sàirdseant *m*
serial *n* leansgeul *m*
series *n* sreath *f m*
serious *a* cudromach, trom-chuiseach; (*person*) dùrachdach
seriously *adv* an da-rìribh
sermon *n* searmon *m* **preach s.** searmonaich, dèan searmon
serpent *n* nathair *f*
serrated *a* eagach
servant *n* searbhanta *f*, seirbheiseach *m*, sgalag *f*
serve *v* (*food*) frithcil, riaraich; (*in office*) dèan seirbheis **s. one's time** thoir a-mach ceàird
service *n* seirbheis *f*, frithealadh *m*; (*relig*) seirbheis *f*; (*dom*) muinntireas *f m* **s.-station** stèisean-frithealaidh *m*
serviceable *a* feumail, iomchaidh
serviette *n* nèapaigin-bùird *f m*
servile *a* tràilleil
session *n* seisean *m*
set *n* seat(a) *m* *a* suidhichte, stèidh(ich)te; (*usual*) gnàthach; (*ready*) deiseil
set *v* suidhich, socraich, stèidhich, cuir; (*sun*) laigh, rach fodha **s. apart** cuir air leth **s. fire to** cuir na theine, cuir teine ri **s. off/out** tog air/oirre *etc* **s. out** (*outline*) mìnich; (*resolve*) cuir roimhe/roimhpe *etc* **s. up** cuir air bhonn/chois **s. table** deasaich/seat am bòrd

settee *n* seidhs(e) *f m*
setter *n* cù-eunaich/luirg *m*
setting *n* suidheachadh *m*, seatadh *m* **s. of sun** dol fodha na grèine *m*
settle *v* seatlaig, socraich; (*intrans*) sìolaidh; (*argument*) rèitich; (*inhabit*) tuinich, àitich
settled *a* stèidhichte, seatlaigte
settlement *n* socrachadh *m*; (*resolution*) rèite *f*, rèiteachadh *m*; (*habitation*) tuineachadh *m*
settler *n* tuiniche *m*, neach-tuineachaidh *m*
seven *n* a seachd *a* seachd **s. people** seachdnar *m*
seventeen *a* seachd-deug **s. cards** seachd cairtean deug
seventh *a* seachdamh
seventy *n* trì fichead 's a deich *m*, seachdad *m*
sever *v* sgar, dealaich
several *a* iomadh, iomadach
severe *a* cruaidh; (*intense*) dian; (*of person*) gnù, gnuath, gruamach; (*criticism*) feanntach
severity *a* cruas *m*, teinne *f*
sew *v* fuaigh, fuaigheil
sewage *n* giodar *m*, òtrachas *m*
sewer *n* sàibhear *m*
sewing *n* fuaigheal *m* **s. machine** beairt-fuaigheil *f*
sex *n* gnè *f*, cineal *m*; (*act*) feis(e) *f* **sex appeal** tarraing chorporra *f* **sex discrimination** leth-bhreith (a thaobh) gnè *f*
sexist *a* gnè-thaobhach
sexual *a* gnèitheasach, gnèitheach
sexy *a* seagsaidh
shabby *a* robach; (*treatment*) suarach
shack *n* bothag *f*
shackle *n* geimheal *m*, ceangal *m* *v* geimhlich, cuingealaich
shade *n* sgàil *f*, dubhar *m*
shadow *n* faileas *m*, sgàil *f*, dubhar *m*
shadowy *a* faileasach, sgàileach
shady *a* dubharach; (*met*) a' togail amharais/teagaimh, mì-chneasta
shaft *n* cas *f*, samhach *f*; (*mech*) crann *m*; (*of light*) gath *m*; (*lift, mine*) toll *m*
shaggy *a* molach, ròmach
shake *n* crith *f* *v* crath, luaisg; (*intrans*) crith **s. hands with** beir/breith air làimh air
shaky *a* critheanach
shallow *a* ao-domhainn, tana; (*met*) staoin
sham *n* mealladh *m*
shambles *n* bùrach *m*
shame *n* nàire *f*, masladh *m*, tàmailt *f* **it's a s.** 's e call a th' ann *v* nàraich, maslaich
shameful *a* nàr, maslach
shameless *a* lugha-nàire, beag-nàrach
shampoo *n* siampù *m*, failcean *m* *v* failc
shamrock *n* seamrag *f*
shank *n* lurg(a) *f*, cas *f*
shape *n* cumadh *m*, cruth *m* *v* cum, dealbh, thoir cumadh air
shapeless *a* gun chumadh; (*not shapely*) neo-chuimir
shapely *a* cuimir, cumadail
share *n* roinn *f*, cuid *f*, cuibhreann *f m*, earrann *f* *v* roinn, pàirtich, riaraich **s. in** gabh pàirt an **s. and s. alike** dèan roinn a' mhic is an athar air **shareholder** neach-earrannan *m* *pl* luchd-earrannan
shark *n* siorc *m* **basking s.** cearban *m*
sharp *a* geur, biorach; (*of person*) geurchuiseach; (*of practice*) carach
sharpen *v* geuraich, faobharaich
shatter *v* bris(t) na mhìrean, bloighdich
shave *n* bearradh *m*, lomadh *m* **he had a close s.** (*met*) chaidh fìor shàbhaladh air *v* beàrr, lom(aich)
shawl *n* seàla *f*, guailleachan *m*
she *pron* i, (*emph*) ise
sheaf *n* sguab *f m*
shear *v* rùisg, lomair, beàrr
shearing *n* rùsgadh *m*, lomadh *m*, bearradh *m*
shears *n* deamhais *f m*
sheath *n* truaill *f*, duille *f*

shed *n* bothan *m*, sead(a) *f m*
shed *v* dòirt, sil; (*staff*) leig dheth
sheen *n* lainnir *f*
sheep *n* caora *f* **sheepdog** cù-chaorach *m* **sheepskin** craiceann-caorach *m*
sheepish *a* (*met*) similidh
sheer *a* fìor; (*steep*) cas
sheet *n* siota *m*; (*bed*) braith-lìn *f*; (*of paper*) duilleag *f*; (*sail*) sgòd-siùil *m* **ice-s.** clàr-deighe *m*
shelduck *n* cràdh-ghèadh *m*
shelf *n* sgeilp *f*; (*of rock*) sgeir *f*
shell *n* slige *f*, plaosg *m*
shellfish *n* maorach *m*
shelter *n* fasgadh *m*, dìon *m* **bus s.** ionad-fasgaidh bus *m* *v* (*take*) gabh fasgadh; (*give*) thoir fasgadh do
sheltered *a* fasgach
shepherd *n* cìobair *m*
sheriff *n* siorram *m*, siorraidh *m* **s. court** cùirt an t-siorraim *f*
sherry *n* searaidh *m*
shield *n* sgiath *f* *v* dìon, glèidh
shift *v* caraich, gluais
shifty *a* seòlta, carach
shilling *n* tastan *m*
shin *n* lurg *f*, lurgann *f*
shine *n* deàlradh *m*, gleans(a) *m* *v* deàlraich, soillsich, deàrrs
shingle *n* mol *m*, morghan *m*
shingles *n* deir *f*
shining *a* deàlrach, deàrrsach, boillsgeach
shinty *n* iomain *f*, camanachd *f* **s. stick** caman *m*
shiny *a* deàlrach, gleansach
ship *n* bàta *m*, soitheach *f m*, long *f* *v* (*load*) cuir air bòrd; (*transport*) giùlain; (*water*) leig a-steach uisge
shipbuilding *n* togail shoithichean *f*
shipyard *n* gàrradh-iarainn *m*
shire *n* siorr(am)achd *f*
shirk *v* seachain
shirt *n* lèine *f* **s.-sleeve** muilicheann lèine *m*
shiver *n* crith *f*, gaoir *f* *v* crith, bi air chrith; (*with cold*) bi ga lathadh *etc*
shivering *a* air chrith
shoal *n* tanalach *m*; (*of fish*) sgaoth *m*
shock *n* clisgeadh *m*, sgànradh *m*; (*horror*) oillt *f*; (*of hair*) cnuaic *f*, cràic *f* *v* (*startle*) cuir clisgeadh air, sgànraich; (*horrify*) uabhasaich
shocking *a* sgriosail
shoddy *a* bochd, suarach, mu làimh
shoe *n* bròg *f*; (*horse*) crudha (eich) *m*
shoelace *n* barrall *m*
shoemaker *n* greusaiche *m*
shoot *n* faillean *m*, ògan *m*
shoot *v* (*gun*) loisg; (*in game*) srad, amais air an lìon
shooting *n* losgadh *m*
shop *n* bùth *f*
shopkeeper *n* neach-bùtha *m*
shopping centre *n* ionad bhùthan *m*
shore *n* cladach *m*, tràigh *f*
short *a* goirid, geàrr **s.-cut** aithghearrachd *f* **s. leet** liosta thaghte *f* **shortlived** diombuan **s.-sighted** geàrr-sheallach **s. story** sgeulachd ghoirid *f* **s.-tempered** cas, aithghearr (san nàdar) **s.-term** *n* geàrr-ùine *f* *a* geàrr-ùineach
shortage dìth *f m*, gainne *f*
shortbread *n* aran-milis *m*
shortcoming *n* easbhaidh *f*
shorten *v* giorraich
shorthand *n* geàrr-sgrìobhadh *m*
shortly *adv* a dh'aithghearr
shorts *n* briogais ghoirid *f*
shot *n* (*of gun*) urchair *f*
shotgun *n* gunna-froise *m*
shoulder *n* gualainn *f*, slinnean *m*
shout *n* èigh *f*, glaodh *m* *v* èigh, glaodh
shove *n* putadh *m*, putag *f* *v* put
shovel *n* sluasaid *f* *v* obraich le sluasaid/spaid
show *n* sealladh *m*, taisbeanadh *m*; (*entertainment*) cuirm-chluich *f* *v* seall, nochd, foillsich, taisbean
shower *n* fras *f*, meall *m*; (*appliance*) frasair *m* **what a s.!** abair seat! *v* fras, dòirt, sil

showery *a* frasach
showroom *n* seòmar-taisbeanaidh *m*
shred *n* mìr *m*, bìdeag *f*, criomag *f* *v* cuir na stiallan
shrewd *a* glic, teòma, gleusta, geurchuiseach
shriek *n* sgread *m*, sgreuch *m* *v* dèan sgread/sgreuch
shrill *a* sgalanta, sgairteil
shrimp *n* carran *m*
shrine *n* ionad coisrigte *m*
shrink *v* seac; (*recoil*) bi fo gheilt, tarraing air ais (bh)o
shrivel *v* crìon, searg
shrivelled *a* seargte
shroud *n* marbhphaisg *f*; (*naut*) cupaill *m pl*
shrub *n* preas *m*
shrubbery *n* preasarnach *f*
shrug *n* crathadh guailne *m* *v* crath guailnean
shudder *n* ball-chrith *f*, criothnachadh *m* *v* criothnaich
shuffle *v* (*cards etc*) measgaich; (*gait*) dragh do chasan
shun *v* seachain
shut *v* dùin *a* dùinte
shutter *n* còmhla (uinneige) *f*
shuttle *n* spàl *m* **shuttlecock** gleicean *m*
shy *a* diùid, socharach
sick *a* tinn, bochd, meadhanach
sicken *v* fàs tinn/bochd, gabh tinneas; (*trans*) dèan tinn
sickle *n* corran *m*
sickness *n* tinneas *m*, bochdainn *f* **s. benefit** sochair tinneis *f*
side *n* taobh *m*, cliathach *f* **s.-road** frith-rathad *m* **s.-street** frith-shràid **sidewalk** cabhsair *m f* *v* **s. with** gabh taobh (+ *gen*) **sidetrack** thoir a thaobh
sideboard *n* preasa-tasgaidh *m*
sideline *n* iomall *m*; (*another activity*) frith-obair *f* *v* cuir gus an oir/an t-iomall
sidestep *v* (*met*) seachain; (*phys*) gabh ceum às an rathad
sideways *adv* air fiaradh, an comhair a t(h)ao(i)bh *etc*
sidle *v* siolp
siege *n* sèist *f m*
sieve *n* criathar *m*
sift *v* criathraich, rèitich
sigh *n* osna *f*, osann *f* *v* leig osna/osann, osnaich
sight *n* sealladh *m*; (*faculty*) fradharc *m* **out of s.** às an t-sealladh **second s.** an dà shealladh
sightseeing *n* siubhal sheallaidhean *m*
sign *n* comharra *m*, soidhne *m* **signpost** post-seòlaidh *m*, post-soidhne *m* *v* soidhnig, cuir ainm ri; (*indicate*) dèan comharra
signal *n* comharra *m*, soidhne *m*
signature *n* ainm-sgrìobhte *m*
signet *n* fàinne seula *f*
significance *n* brìgh *f*; (*importance*) cudromachd *f*
significant *a* brìgheil; (*important*) cudromach
signify *v* comharraich, ciallaich
Sikh *n* Siog *m*, (*female*) ban-Siogach *f* *a* Siogach
silence *n* sàmhchair *f*, tost *m*
silent *a* sàmhach, na t(h)ost *etc*
silhouette *n* sgàil-riochd *m*
silicon *n* sileagon *m*
silk *n*, *a* sìoda *m*
silk(y)/silken *a* sìodach
sill *n* sòl *f*
silliness *n* gòraiche *f*, faoineas *f*
silly *a* gòrach, faoin
silt *n* eabar *m*
silver *n* airgead *m* *a* airgid, airgeadach
similar *a* coltach, ionann
similarity *n* coltas *m*, ionannachd *f*; (*resemblance*) suaip *f*
simile *n* samhla *m*
simmer *v* earr-bhruich
simple *a* sìmplidh; (*in mind*) slac, baoth
simplify *v* sìmplich
simplistic *a* ro shìmplidh
simply *adv* dìreach
simulate *v* leig ort
simultaneous *a* còmhla, mar-aon, aig an aon àm, co-amail
sin *n* peacadh *m* *v* peacaich
since *adv* (bh)o *conj* a chionn

gu(n) *prep* (bh)o, o chionn (+ *gen*)
sincere *a* treibhdhireach, dùrachdach
sincerity *n* treibhdhireas *m*, dùrachd *f*
sinew *n* fèith *f*
sing *v* seinn, gabh òran
singe *v* dàth
singer *n* seinneadair *m*; (*female*) ban-sheinneadair *f*
single *a* singilte; (*not married*) gun phòsadh **s.-handed** leis/leatha (*etc*) fhèin, gun chuideachadh
singular *a* singilte; (*unusual*) sònraichte, àraid
sinister *a* (*threatening*) bagarrach; (*evil*) olc
sink *n* sinc(e) *f m*
sink *v* (*trans*) cuir fodha; (*intrans*) rach fodha
sinner *n* peacach *m*
sinuous *a* lùbach
sip *n* balgam *m*, drudhag *f* *v* gabh balgam/drudhag
siphon *n* pìob-èalaidh *f*
sir *n* an ridire *m*, sir *m*
siren *n* (*hooter*) dùdach *f m*, conacag *f*
sister *n* piuthar *f* **s.-in-law** piuthar-chèile *f*
sit *v* suidh, dèan suidhe
site *n* làrach *f m*, ionad *m* *v* suidhich
sitting-room *n* seòmar-suidhe *m*, rùm-suidhe *m*
situated *a* suidhichte, air a s(h)uidheachadh **well s.** air a dheagh shuidheachadh
situation *n* suidheachadh *m*
six *n*, *a* sia **s. people** sianar *m*
sixteen *n* a sia, *a* sia-deug *m* **s. letters** sia litrichean deug
sixth *a* siathamh
sixty *n*, *a* trì fichead *m*, seasgad *m*
sizeable *a* meadhanach mòr, meudmhor
size *n* meud *m*, meudachd *f*, tomhas *m*
skate *n* (*fish*) sgait *f*; (*ice*) spèil *f*, bròg-spèilidh *f* *v* spèil
skating *n* spèileadh *m*
skeleton *n* cnàimhneach *m*
skelp *n* sgailc *f*
skerry *n* sgeir *f*
sketch *n* sgeidse *f* *v* dèan sgeidse
ski *n* sgì *f pl* sgithean *v* sgì
skid *v* sleamhnaich
skiff *n* coit *f*, sgoth *m*
skiing *n* sgitheadh *m*
skilful *a* sgileil, ealanta
skill *n* sgil *f m*
skilled *a* sgileil, ealanta
skim *v* (*eg milk*) thoir uachdar de; (*intrans*) falbh air uachdar/bàrr (+ *gen*); (*read*) dèan bloigh leughaidh (air)
skin *n* craiceann *m*; (*of animals*) bian *m*, seiche *f* **by the s. of one's teeth** dìreach air èiginn *v* feann, thoir an craiceann de
skinny *a* caol, tana
skip *n* leum *m*, sùrdag *f*; (*rubbish*) tasgan sgudail *m* *v* leum, dean sùrdag
skipper *n* sgiobair *m*
skipping *n* sgiob(aige)adh *m* **s. rope** ròp(a)-sgiobai(gi)dh *m*
skirt *n* sgiort(a) *f*
skulk *v* bi a' cùiltearachd
skull *n* claigeann *m*
sky *n* adhar *m*, speur *m* **skylight** fàirleus *f m* **skyline** fàire *f*
Skyeman *n* Sgitheanach *m* **Skyewoman** ban-Sgitheanach *f*
skylark *n* uiseag *f*
slab *n* leac *f*
slack *a* slac, flagach; (*not busy*) sàmhach, slac; (*lax*) lag
slacken *v* slac, lasaich
slam *v* slàraig, thoir slaic air; (*met*) càin, thoir slaic air
slander *n* cùl-chàineadh *m*, tuaileas *m* *v* cùl-chàin, sgainnealaich
slanderous *a* sgainnealach
slang *n* mith-chainnt *f*
slant *n* (*phys, met*) claonadh *m*, fiaradh *m*
slanted *a* air a chlaonadh, le fiaradh ann; (*biased*) claon, fiar
slap *n* sgailc *f*, pais *f* *v* thoir sgailc/pais do
slapdash *a* leibideach, gun diù

slash *n* gearradh *m*, sgath *f* *v* geàrr, sgath
slate *n* sglèat *m* *v* sglèat, cuir sglèat air
slater *n* sglèatair *m*
slaughter *n* marbhadh *m*, casgairt *f* **slaughterhouse** taigh-spadaidh *m* *v* spad, casgair, marbh
Slav/Slavonic *n, a* Slàbhach *m*, (*female*) ban-Slàbhach *f*
slave *n* tràill *f m*
slavery *n* tràillealachd *f*, braighdeanas *m*
slay *v* marbh
sledge *n* càrn-slaoid *m*, slaodan *m*
sleek *a* slìom, mìn
sleep *n* cadal *m* **short s.** norrag *f* *v* caidil, dèan cadal
sleeping bag *n* poca-cadail *m*
sleepless *a* gun chadal
sleepy *a* cadalach
sleet *n* flin(ne) *m*
sleeve *n* muilicheann *m*, muinichill *m*
slender *a* tana, seang
slice *n* slis *f*, sliseag *f* *v* slis, slisnich
sliced *a* sliseagach
slick *a* ealanta, le liut
slide *n* sleamhnag *f* *v* slaighd, sleamhnaich
slight *n* dìmeas *m*, tàire *f* *a* beag, aotrom
slim *a* tana, seang, caol *v* fàs seang/caol, caill cuideam
slime *n* làthach *f m*, clàbar *m*
sling *n* (*med*) iris gàirdein *f*; (*weapon*) crann-tabhaill *m*
slink *v* siap
slip *n* (*phys, met*) tuisleadh *m*; (*error*) mearachd *f* *v* tuislich **s. up** dèan mearachd
slipper *n* sliopair *f m*, slapag *f*
slippery *a* sleamhainn
slipshod *a* mu làimh
slipway *n* cidhe m; (*for launching*) leathad cur air bhog *m*
slit *n* sgoltadh *m* *v* sgoilt, geàrr
slogan *n* sluagh-ghairm *f*
slope *n* leathad *m*, bruthach *f m*
sloping *a* ag aomadh
sloppy *a* bog; (*untidy*) mì-sgiobalta; (*shoddy*) leibideach, lapach
slot *n* beulag *f*
sloth *n* leisg(e) *f*
slothful *a* leisg
slovenly *a* robach, rapach
slow *a* slaodach, màirnealach
sludge *n* eabar *m*, làthach *f m*
slug *n* seilcheag *f*
sluggish *a* slaodach, trom, gun sgoinn
slum *n* sluma *m*, bochd-cheàrn *f*
slump *v* tuit nad chnap; (*fin*) tuit gu mòr
slur *n* (*insult*) aithis *f*; (*of speech*) slugadh *m*, mabladh *m* *v* (*of speech*) sluig facail/faclan **cast a s.** aithisich
slush *n* sneachd(a) leaghte *m*
slut *n* luid *f*, sgliùrach *f*
sly *a* carach, slìogach
smack *n* dèiseag *f*
small *a* beag
smallpox *n* a' bhreac *f*
smart *a* grinn, spaideil; (*clever*) geur
smash *n* bris(t)eadh *m*; (*accident*) bualadh na chèile *m* *v* bris(t); (*tennis*) smoidsig
smashing *a* (*met*) sgoinneil
smear *v* smeur, liacair, smiùr
smell *n* fàileadh *m*, boladh *m* *v* (*trans*) feuch/tog fàileadh **it smells** tha fàileadh dheth
smelt *v* leagh
smile *n* fiamh-ghàire *m*, snodha-gàire *m*, faite-gàire *f* *v* dèan fiamh-ghàire, dèan snodha/faite-gàire
smirk *n* plìon(as) *m* *v* **he smirked** thàinig plìonas air
smith *n* gobha *m*
smock *n* lèine *f*
smoke *n* ceò *f m*, toit *f*, deatach *f* *v* (*tobacco*) gabh ceò/smoc, smoc(aig)
smoky *a* ceòthach
smooth *a* mìn, rèidh, còmhnard
smoothe *v* dèan rèidh
smother *v* mùch, tachd
smoulder *v* cnàmh-loisg

smudge *n* smal *m*, spuaic *f* *v* smalaich, cuir spuaic air
smug *a* riaraichte (leis/leatha fhèin *etc*)
smuggle *v* dèan cùl-mhùtaireachd
smuggler *n* cùl-mhùtaire *m*
smut *n* drabastachd *f*
smutty *a* drabasta
snack *n* blasad bìdh *m*, greimeag *f*
snag *n* duilgheadas *m*
snail *n* seilcheag *f*
snake *n* nathair *f*
snap *v* bris(t) le brag; (*bite*) dèan glamhadh
snapshot *n* mion-dhealbh *f m*; (*met*) dealbh aithghearr *f m*
snare *n* ribe *f* *v* rib
snarl *v* dèan dranndan
snatch *v* glac, beir (air)
sneak *n* sniag *m*, lìogaire *m* *v* sniag, liùg, èalaidh
sneaky *a* sniagach, lìogach
sneer *v* dèan fanaid, cuir an neo-shùim
sneeze *n* sreothart *m* *v* dèan sreothart
sniff *n* boladh *m*, fàileadh *m* *v* gabh fàileadh/boladh **s. at** dèan tarcais air
snigger *n* siot-ghàire *f*
snip *v* geàrr le siosar
snipe *n* naosg *f m*
snob *n* sodalan *m*, mòrchuisiche *m*
snobbery *n* sodalachd *f*, mòrchuiseachd *f*
snobbish *a* mòrchuiseach, sodalach
snooze *n* norrag *f*, snuachdan *m* *v* dèan norrag/snuachdan
snore *n* srann *f m* *v* dèan srann
snort *n* srannartaich *f* *v* bi a' srannartaich
snotty *a* spliugach
snout *n* soc *m*, sròn *f*
snow *n* sneachd(a) *m* **snowball** ball-sneachd(a) *m* **snowdrift** cith(e) *m* **snowflake** pleòideag *f*, bleideag *f*, lòineag *f* **snowman** bodach-sneachd(a) *m* **snowstorm** stoirm s(h)neachd(a) *f m* *v* cuir sneachd(a)
snowdrop *n* gealag-làir *f*
snuff *n* snaoisean *m* **s. box** bogsa/bucas snaoisein *m*
snug *a* seasgair, clùthmhor
snuggle *v* teann dlùth ri
so *adv* cho; (*like this*) mar seo; (*therefore*) mar sin **so long as** cho fad 's a **so-and-so** a leithid seo a dhuine **s. much** uimhir *interj* seadh
soak *v* drùidh; (*eg clothes*) cuir am bogadh
soaking/soaked *a* bog fliuch
soap *n* siabann *m* **TV s.** siabann telebhisein
soar *v* itealaich gu h-àrd; (*fin*) àrdaich gu mòr
sob *n* glug caoinidh *m*
sober *a* sòbarra; (*moderate*) stuama, measarra *v* sòbraich, fuaraich, dèan/fàs sòbarra
soccer *n* ball-coise *m*
sociable *a* cuideachail, càirdeil
social *a* sòisealta, caidreabhach, comannach **S. Democrat** Deamocratach Sòisealta *m* **s. security** tèarainteachd shòisealta *f* **s. work** obair shòisealta *f*
socialism *n* sòisealachd *f*
socialist *n, a* sòisealach *m*
society *n* an comann-sòisealta *m*, sòisealtas *m*; (*body*) comann *m*
sociology *n* eòlas sòisealtais *m*
sock *n* stocainn *f*, socais *f*; (*blow*) sgleog *f*
socket *n* socaid *f* **electrical s.** bun-dealain *m*
sod *n* fòid *f*, sgrath *f*
soda *n* sòda *f m*
sodden *a* bog fliuch
sodium *n* sòidium *m*
sofa *n* sòfa *f*, langasaid *f*
soft *a* bog, maoth, socair **s.-hearted** tais-chridheach
soften *v* bogaich, maothaich
softness *n* buige *f*, maothachd *f*
software *n* bathar bog *m*
soggy *a* bog fliuch
soil *n* ùir *f*, talamh *m*
soil *v* salaich, truaill
soiled *a* loireach

solace *n* cofhurtachd *f*, furtachd *f*
solan goose *n* sùlaire *m* **young s.g.** guga *m*
solar *a* na grèine
sold *a* air a reic *etc*
solder *v* sobhdraich, solldraig
soldier *n* saighdear *m*
sole *n* bonn na coise *m*; (*fish*) lèabag/leòbag-cheàrr *f*
sole *a* aon
solely *adv* a-mhàin
solemn *a* sòlaimte
solicit *v* (*request*) iarr
solicitor *n* neach-lagha *m*
solid *n* teann-stuth *m* *a* teann, cruaidh, daingeann; (*sound*) susbainteach
solidarity *n* dlùth-phàirteachas *m*, dìlseachd *f*
solidify *v* cruadhaich
solitary *a* aonranach, uaigneach
solitude *n* uaigneas *m*
solo *n* (*song*) òran aon-neach *m*, (*instrumental*) cluich aon-neach *f* *a* leis/leatha *etc* fhèin
soloist *n* òranaiche *m*, neach-ciùil aona(i)r *m*
soluble *a* so-sgaoilte
solution *n* fuasgladh *m*; (*substance*) eadar-sgaoileadh *m*
solve *v* fuasgail
solvent *n* lionn-sgaoilidh *m*
solvent *a* comasach air pàigheadh
sombre *a* dubhach, gruamach; (*of dress*) dorch(a)
some *n* cuid *f*, roinn *f*, pàirt *f m*; (*people*) feadhainn *f*, cuid *f*
somebody *pron* cuideigin *f*, neacheigin *m*
somehow *adv* air dòigh air choreigin, air dòigheigin
someone *n* cuideigin *f*, neacheigin *m*
somersault *n* car a' mhuiltein *m* *v* dèan car a' mhuiltein
something *pron* rudeigin *m*, nìtheigin *m*
sometime *adv* uaireigin
sometimes *adv* uaireannan
somewhat *adv* rudeigin, beagan, car, lethchar
somewhere *adv* an àiteigin, am badeigin
son *n* mac *m*, gille *m* **son-in-law** cliamhainn *m*
song *n* òran *m*, amhran *m*
soon *adv* a dh'aithghearr, gu grad, an ùine ghoirid/gheàrr
soot *n* sùith(e) *f m*
soothe *v* (*calm*) ciùinich; (*assuage*) thoir fao(tha)chadh do
soothing *a* sèimheachail
sophisticated *a* soifiostaigeach
sordid *a* suarach, salach
sore *a* goirt, cràiteach; (*resentful*) leamh *n* creuchd *f*, lot *m*
sorrow *n* bròn *m*, mulad *m*, tùrsa *f*
sorrowful *a* brònach, muladach, tùrsach
sorry *a* duilich
sort *n* seòrsa *m*, gnè *f* *v* cuir an òrdugh, seòrsaich; (*fix*) cuir air dòigh
so-so *a*, *adv* mu làimh, meadhanach
soul *n* anam *m* **we didn't see a s.** chan fhaca sinn duine beò
sound *n* fuaim *m*; (*topog*) caolas *m* *a* (*healthy*) slàn, fallain; (*reliable*) earbsach; (*advice*) glic **s. asleep** na s(h)uain *etc* chadail **s.-proof** fuaim-dhìonach *v* dèan fuaim; (*alarm*) gairm rabhadh; (*instrument*) sèid, seinn **s. out** faigh beachd (bh)o **that sounds fine/reasonable** tha sin taghta/reusanta
soup *n* brot *m*, eanraich *f*
sour *a* goirt, geur, searbh
source *n* màthair-adhbhar *m*, bun *m*, freumh *m* **s. of river** bun aibhne *m*
south *n*, *a* deas *f* **the s.** an (àird a) deas *f* **the s.-east** an (àird an) ear-dheas *f* **the s.-west** an (àird an) iar-dheas *f*
southerly *a*, *adv* deas, à deas
southern *a* mu dheas, a deas
souvenir *n* cuimhneachan *m*
sovereign *n* rìgh *m* àrd-uachdaran *m*; (*coin*) sòbhran *m* *a* uachdarail, neo-eisimeileach
sovereignty *n* uachdaranachd *f*

sow *n* muc *f*, cràin *f*
sow *v* cuir (sìol)
space *n* rùm *m*, rèidhleach *m*, farsaingeachd *f*; (*atmos*) fànas *m*; (*gap*) beàrn *f* **spaceship** soitheach-fànais *f m* **s. shuttle** spàl-fànais *m*
spacious *a* farsaing, mòr, rùmail
spade *n* spaid *f*, caibe m
span *n* rèis *f*; (*lifetime*) rèis *f*, saoghal *m*; (*interval*) greis *f*
Spaniard *n* Spàinn(t)each *m*, (*female*) ban-Spàinn(t)each *f*
spaniel *n* cù-eunaich *m*
Spanish *n* (*lang*) Spàinn(t)is *f* *a* Spàinn(t)each
spanner *n* spanair *m*
spare *a* a chòrr, a bharrachd **s. part** pàirt-càraidh *f*
spare *v* caomhain, cumhain
spared *a* air a s(h)àbhaladh *etc* **if we are s.** ma bhios sinn air ar caomhnadh/cùmhnadh
spark *n* sradag *f*
sparkle *n* lainnir *f*, deàlradh *m* *v* lainnrich, deàlraich
sparkling *a* deàlrach, drìlseach
sparrow *n* gealbhonn *m*
sparrow-hawk *n* speireag *f*
sparse *a* gann
spasm *n* crupadh fèithe *m*
spasmodic *a* an-dràsta 's a-rithist
spastic *n, a* spastach *m*
spate *n* lighe *f*; (*met*) meall *m*
spawn *n* sìol *m*, cladh *m* *v* sìolaich, cladh
speak *v* abair, bruidhinn, labhair
speaker *n* neach-labhairt *m*, òraidiche *m*; (*mus etc*) labhradair *m* **the S.** an Labhraiche *m*
spear *n* sleagh *f*, gath *m*
special *a* àraidh, sònraichte
specialism *n* speisealachd *f*
specialist *n* speisealaiche *m*, fìor-eòlaiche *m* *a* speisealta
specialize *v* speisealaich
specialized *a* speisealaichte
species *n* seòrsa *m*, gnè *f*
specific *a* sònraichte, àraid
specification *n* sònrachadh *m*, mion-chomharrachadh *m*
specified *a* sònraichte, comharraichte
specify *v* sònraich, comharraich
specimen *n* sampall *m*, ball-sampaill *m*
specious *a* meallta
speck *n* smùirnean *m*, sal *m*, smal *m*
speckled *a* breac, ballach
spectacle *n* sealladh *m*
spectacles *n* speuclairean *m pl*, speuclair *m*, glainneachan *f pl*
spectator *n* neach-amhairc/coimhid *m*
spectre *n* tannasg *m*
spectrum *n* speactram *m*
speculate *v* beachdaich, dèan tuairmeas air; (*fin*) cuir airgead sa mhargadh
speculation *n* beachdachadh *m*, tuairmeas *m*
speculative *a* beachdachail, tuairmeasach
speech *n* cainnt *f*; (*oration*) òraid *f* **s. therapy** leasachadh cainnt *m*
speechless *a* gun chainnt, balbh
speed *n* luaths *m*, astar *m* **s. limit** casg astair *m* *v* rach luath, greas
spell *n* (*of time*) greis(eag) *f*; (*charm*) seun *m*
spell *v* litrich
spelling *n* litreachadh *m*
spend *v* caith, cosg
spendthrift *n* caithtiche *m* *a* caithteach
sperm *n* sìol(-ginidh) *m*
spew *v* cuir a-mach, sgeith
sphere *n* cruinne *m*; (*met*) raon *m*
spherical *a* cruinn
spice *n* spìosradh *m* *v* spìosraich, dèan spìosrach
spicy *a* spìosrach
spider *n* damhan-allaidh *m*
spike *n* spìc *f*, bior *m*
spill *v* dòirt
spin *v* snìomh; (*wheel*) cuir caran **s. around** grad-thionndaidh *n* (*met*) snìomh *m*
spinach *n* bloinigean-gàrraidh *m*
spindle *n* dealgan *m*, fearsaid *f*
spindrift *n* cathadh-mara *m*, siaban *m*

spine *n* cnàimh-droma *m*
spinner *n* (*person*) snìomhadair *m*; (*mech*) uidheam-snìomh *f*
spinning *n* snìomh *m*, calanas *m* **s.-wheel** cuibheall-shnìomh *f*
spinster *n* maighdeann *f*, boireannach gun phòsadh *m*
spiral *n* snìomhan *m* *a* snìomhanach
spire *n* stìopall *m*, binnean *m*
spirit *n* spiorad *m*, aigne *f*; (*mettle*) meanmna *m*, misneachd *f*; (*ghost*) tannasg *m*
spirited *a* aigeannach, misneachail, meanmnach
spirits *n* (*drink*) deoch-làidir *f*
spiritual *a* spioradail
spit *n* smugaid *f*; (*roasting*) bior-ròstaidh *m* *v* tilg smugaid
spite *n* gamhlas *m*, miosgainn *f* **in s. of** a dh'aindeoin (+ *gen*)
spiteful *a* gamhlasach
spittle *n* seile *m*, ronn *m*
splash *n* steall *f*, splais *f* *v* steall, splaisig
splay-footed *a* spleadhach, pliutach
spleen *n* (*anat*) an dubh-chlèin *f*; (*spite*) gamhlas *m*
splendid *a* gasta, taghta; (*imposing*) greadhnach
splendour *n* greadhnachas *m*
splice *v* spla(o)idhs
splint *n* cleithean *m*
splinter *n* sgealb *f*, spealg *f* *v* spealg
split *n* sgoltadh *m* *v* sgoilt
splutter *v* (*person*) bi a' sgeamhadaich
spoil *v* mill, cuir a dholaidh
spoils *n* creach *f*, cobhartach *f m*
spoilt *a* air a m(h)illeadh *etc*, millte
spoke *n* spòg *f*, tarsannan *m*
spokesperson *n* neach-labhairt *m*, labhraiche *m* **spokesman** fear-labhairt *m* **spokeswoman** tè-labhairt *f*
sponge *n* spong *m*; (*cake*) spuinnse *f*
sponsor *n* neach-urrais *m*, goistidh *m* *v* rach mar neach-urrais, bi mar ghoistidh
sponsorship *n* urrasachd *f*, goistidheachd *f*
spontaneous *a* saor-thoileach, deònach
spoon *n* spàin *f*
sporadic *a* corra uair
spore *n* spòr *m*
sport *n* spòrs *f*
sporting *a* spòrsach
sports *n* lùth-chleasan *m pl*, geamachan *m pl* **s. centre** ionad spòrs *m*
sportsman *n* neach-spòrs *m*
spot *n* spot *f m*; (*place*) àite *m*, bad *m*; (*stain*) smal *m* **on the s.** (*time*) an làrach nam bonn *v* (*notice*) mothaich do
spotless *a* gun smal
spotted *a* ballach, breac
spotty *a* guireanach
spouse *n* cèile *f m*, cèile-p(h)òsta *f m*
spout *n* srùb *m*, spùt *m* *v* spùt; (*whale*) sèid; (*hold forth*) cuir dheth/dhith *etc*
sprain *n* snìomh *m*, sgochadh *m*, siachadh *m* *v* cuir snìomh an, sgoch
sprawl *v* sìn a-mach; (*of person*) bi nad shlèibhtrich
spray *n* (*sea*) cathadh-mara *m*; (*water*) sradadh *m*; (*aerosol*) frasadair *m*; (*bot*) fleasg *f* *v* srad (air)
spread *v* sgaoil, sgap, sìn a-mach
spreadsheet *n* cliath-dhuilleag *f*
spree *n* (*drinking*) daorach *f* **shopping s.** splaoid ceannaich *f*
sprig *n* faillean *m*
sprightly *a* (*of mood*) beothail, suigeartach; (*phys*) frogail, spraiceil
spring *n* earrach *m*; (*water*) fuaran *m*; (*leap*) grad-leum *m*; (*mech*) sprionga *m*, cuairteag *f* **s.-tide** reothart *m* *v* grad-leum **s. from** thig/sruth (bh)o
springboard *n* (*met*) stèidh *f*
sprinkle *v* crath
sprinkling *n* craiteachan *m*
sprint *n* roid *f*, deann-ruith *f*; (*race*) dian-rèis *f* *v* dian-ruith, ruith le roid

sprout *n* buinneag *f* **Brussels sprouts** buinneagan Bruisealach *f pl*
spruce *n* giuthas Lochlannach *m*
spruce *a* deas, speiseanta
spur *n* spor *m*, brod *m*; (*met*) spreigeadh *m* *v* brod, stuig; (*met*) spursaig, spreig, piobraich
spurious *a* breugach
spurn *v* diùlt le tàir
spurt *n* briosgadh *m*, cabhag *f*; (*of liquid*) stealladh *m*
spy *n* beachdair *m*, neach-brathaidh *m*, brathadair *m* *v* bi ri beachdaireachd
squabble *n* connsachadh *m*, tuasaid *f*
squad *n* sguad *m*
squalid *a* robach, salach
squall *n* sgal/cnap-gaoithe *m*
squander *v* caith, dèan ana-caitheamh air, mì-bhuilich
square *n* ceàrnag *f* *a* ceithir-cheàrnach, ceàrnagach
squash *v* brùth, pronn
squat *v* crùb
squatter *n* sguatair *m*
squeak *n* bìog *m* *v* bi a' bìogail
squeal *n* sgiamh *f* *v* dèan sgiamh
squeamish *a* òrraiseach
squeeze *n* fàsgadh *m*, bruthadh *m* *v* fàisg, brùth
squid *n* gibearnach *m*
squint *n* claonadh *m*, fiaradh *m* *a* claon, fiar **s.-eyed** cam/fiar-shùileach **it is s.** tha e cam, tha fiaradh ann *v* seall claon
squirrel *n* feòrag *f*
squirt *v* steall, spùt
stab *v* sàth, stob
stabbing *n* sàthadh *m*, stobadh *m*
stabilize *v* bunailtich, cùm air bhunailt
stable *a* bunailteach, seasmhach
stable *n* stàball *m*
stack *n* stac(a) *m*, càrn *m*; (*of hay, peat etc*) cruach *f* *v* cruach, càrn; (*shelves*) cuir air sgeilp
stadium *n* lann-cluiche *f*
staff *n* luchd-obrach *m*; (*stick*) bata *m* **staffroom** seòmar luchd-obrach *m*
stag *n* damh (fèidh) *m*
stage *n* àrd-ùrlar *m*; (*in process*) ìre *f*
stagger *v* rach mu seach; (*amaze*) cuir fìor iongnadh air
staggering *a* (*met*) iongantach
stagnant *a* marbh, neo-ghluasadach
stagnate *v* bi/fàs marbhanta
staid *a* stòlda, suidhichte
stain *n* sal *m*, smal *m* *v* salaich, cuir/fàg smal air
stair *n* staidhre *f*
stake *n* post *m*; (*betting wager*) airgead-gill *m*
stalactite *n* aol-chluigean *m*
stalagmite *n* aol-charragh *f*
stale *a* sean, goirt
stalemate *n* clòsadh *m*, glasadh *m*
stalk *n* gas *f*
stalk *v* bi a' stalcaireachd **s. person** lean neach mun cuairt
stalker *n* stalcaire *m*; (*of person*) lorgair *m*
stall *n* stàile *f*
stall *v* cuir maill air
stallion *n* àigeach *m*
stalwart *a* sgairteil, calma, làidir
stamina *n* cùl *m*, smior *m*, cumail ris *m*
stammer *n* (s)gagachd *f*, stad *m* **she has a s.** tha stad na cainnt *v* bi (s)gagach
stamp *n* stamp(a) *f*; (*met*) comharra *m* *v* (*feet*) stamp; (*of letters*) cuir stampa air **s. out** cuir às do
stance *n* (*met*) seasamh *m*; (*phys*) dòigh-seasaimh *f*; (*site*) làrach *f m*
stand *n* seasamh *m*; (*stance*) ionad *m*; (*display*) taisbeanadh *m* *v* seas; (*endure*) fuiling, cuir suas ri; (*in election*) seas san taghadh
standard *n* inbhe *f*, ìre *f*, bun-tomhas *m*; (*flag*) meirghe *f* **s. of living** cor beòshlaint *m* *a* cumanta, cunbhalach, coitcheann **S. Grade** an Ìre Choitcheann *f*
standardize *v* cunbhalaich, dèan cunbhalach

standing *n* (*met*) seasamh *m*, inbhe *f* *a* na s(h)easamh *etc* **s. committee** gnàth-chomataidh *etc f* **s. orders** gnàth-riaghailtean *f pl* **s. stones** tursachan *m pl*
standstill *n* stad *m* **at a s.** na stad/t(h)àmh *etc*
stanza *n* rann *m*
staple *n* stìnleag *f*
staple *a* prìomh
star *n* rionnag *f*, reul *f* *v* comharraich le reul; (*in performance*) gabh prìomh phàirt
starboard *n* deas-bhòrd *m*
starch *n* stalc *m*, stuthaigeadh *m* *v* stalcaich, stuthaig
stare *v* geur-amhairc, spleuchd
starfish *n* crosgan *m*
stark *a* rag; (*absolute*) tur, fìor **s. naked** dearg-rùisgte
starling *n* druid *f*
starry *a* rionnagach, làn rionnagan
start *n* toiseach *m* **a sudden s.** clisgeadh *m* *v* tòisich; (*be startled*) clisg; (*sudden move*) leum
starter *n* neach-tòiseachaidh *m*; (*in engine*) inneal-spreigidh *m*
startle *v* clisg, cuir clisgeadh air
starvation *n* gort(a) *f*
starve *v* leig gort(a) air **s. to death** (*intrans*) bàsaich leis a' ghort **we were starving** bha an t-acras gar tolladh
state *n* staid *f*, cor *m*; (*country*) stàit *f*
state *v* can, cuir an cèill
stately *a* stàiteil
statement *n* aithris *f*, cunntas *m*
statesman *n* stàitire *m*
static *a* na stad, gun ghluasad
station *n* stèisean *m*; (*in life*) staid *f*, inbhe *f*
stationary *a* na stad, gun ghluasad
stationery *n* stuth-sgrìobhaidh *m*, pàipearachd *f*
statistical *a* staitistigeil, àireamhail
statistics *n* staitistearachd *f*
statue *n* ìomhaigh *f*
stature *n* àird *f*
status *n* inbhe *f*
statute *n* reachd *m*
statutory *a* reachdail, a rèir an lagha
staunch *a* daingeann, dìleas
staunch *v* caisg
stay *v* fuirich, fan
steadfast *a* daingeann, dìleas
steady *a* seasmhach, daingeann, socraichte *v* socraich, daingnich
steak *n* staoig *f*
steal *n* goid *f*, mèirle *f* *v* goid, dèan mèirle **s. away** (*intrans*) liùg air falbh
stealing *n* goid *f*, mèirle *f*
steam *n* toit *f*, smùid *f*
steed *n* steud *f*, steud-each *m*
steel *n* cruaidh *f*, stàilinn *f* *a* dhen chruaidh, dhen stàilinn
steep *a* cas; (*price*) anabarrach daor
steep *v* bog, cuir am bogadh, tùm
steeple *n* stìopall *m*
steer *v* stiùir, treòraich **s. clear of** cùm clìoras (+ *nom*)
steering *n* stiùireadh *m* **s. committee** comataidh stiùiridh *f*
stem *n* (*bot*) gas *f*
stench *n* boladh *m*, breuntas *m*
step *n* step *m*; (*a pace*) ceum *m* **s. by s.** ceum air cheum **take steps** (*met*) cuir mu dheidhinn
step *a* leth- **s.-brother** leth-bhràthair *m* **s.-sister** leth-phiuthar *f* **s.-daughter** nighean-cèile *f* **s.-son** dalta *m* **s.-father** oide *m* **s.-mother** muime *f*
stereotype *n* gnàth-iomhaigh *f*
sterile *a* seasg, aimrid; (*ground*) fàs; (*med*) sgaldach
sterilize *v* seasgaich; (*ground*) fàsaich; (*med*) sgald
sterling *n* airgead Bhreatainn *m* **a pound s.** not(a) Breatannach *m*
sterling *a* fìor, foghainteach
stern *n* deireadh *m*
stern *a* gruamach, dùr
stethoscope *n* steatasgop *m*
stew *n* stiubha *f* *v* stiubhaig
steward *n* stiùbhard *m*

stewardess ban-stiùbhard *f*
stick *n* maide *m*, bioran *m* **walking s.** bata *m*
stick *v* (*adhere to*) steig; (*become caught*) rach an sàs; (*endure*) fuiling
sticker *n* steigear *m*
sticky *a* steigeach; (*problem*) righinn
stiff *a* rag
stiffen *v* ragaich
stiffness *n* raige *f*
stifle *v* mùch
stigma *n* adhbhar nàire *m*; (*bot*) stiogma *m*
stigmatize *v* dèan cùis-nàire de
still *n* poit-dhubh *f*, stail *f*
still *a* sàmhach, balbh; (*weather*) ciùin, fèathach
still *adv* an dèidh sin, a dh'aindeoin sin; (*of time*) fhathast
stimulant *n* stuth beothachaidh *m*
stimulate *v* brosnaich, spreig
stimulating *a* brosnachail, togarrach
stimulus *n* brosnachadh *m*, spreagadh *m*
sting *n* gath *m*, guin *m* *v* cuir gath ann, guin
stinginess *n* spìocaireachd *f*
stingy *a* spìocach
stink *n* tòchd *m*, samh *m*
stinking *a* breun, malcaidh
stipend *n* tuarastal *m*
stipulate *v* sònraich, cùmhnantaich
stir *n* othail *f*, ùinich *f*
stir *v* (*food*) cuir mun cuairt; (*move*) gluais; (*stimulate*) brosnaich **s. up** dùisg
stirk *n* gamhainn *m*
stirring *a* togarrach, brosnachail
stitch *n* (*med, sewing*) grèim *m*; (*knitting*) lùb *f*; (*pain*) grèim *m*; (*of clothing*) stiall *f* *v* fuaigh, fuaigheil
stoat *n* neas gheal *f*
stock *n* stoc *m* **s.-taking** cunntas stoc *m* *v* stocaich
stock exchange *n* margadh nan earrannan *m*
stockbroker *n* margaiche earrannan *m*
stocking *n* stocainn *f*
stocks *n* (*fin*) earrannan *f pl*
stodgy *a* trom
stoical *a* strìochdte
stoke *v* cùm connadh ri
stolen *a* air a g(h)oid *etc*
stomach *n* stamag *f*, goile *f*, maodal *f*
stone *n* clach *f* **S. Age** Linn na Cloiche *m* *a* cloiche
stonechat *n* clacharan *m*
stonemason *n* clachair *m*
stook *n* adag *f*, suidheachan *m*
stool *n* stòl *m*, furm *m*
stoop *v* crom, lùb, crùb
stooped *a* crom
stop *n* stad *m*; (*ban*) toirmeasg *m* **s.-cock** goc *m* **s.-gap** neach/nì a lìonas beàrn *m* *v* stad, cuir stad air; (*cease*) sguir, stad
stoppage *n* stad *m*, stopadh *m*, grabadh *m*
stopper *n* àrc *f*, ceann *m*
storage *n* stòradh *m*, tasgadh *m*
store *n* stòr *m*; (*resources*) stòras *m* *v* stòir, taisg
storey *n* lobhta *f m*, làr *m*
stork *n* corra-bhàn *f*
storm *n* stoirm *f m*, doineann *f*, gailleann *f* *v* thoir ionnsaigh air
stormy *a* stoirmeil, doineannach, gailbheach
story *n* sgeul *m*, sgeulachd *f*, stòiridh *f* **s.-teller** sgeulaiche *m*, seanchaidh *m*
stout *n* leann dubh *m*
stout *a* garbh, tiugh; (*brave*) tapaidh
stove *n* stòbh(a) *f m*
straddle *v* rach gòbhlachan/casa-gòbhlagain air
straggler *n* slaodaire *m*
straight *a* dìreach **s. away** *adv* sa mhionaid, gun dàil
straighten *v* dìrich
strain *n* strèan *m*; (*phys*) teannachadh *m*, snìomh *m*; (*mental*) uallach *m* *v* strèan; (*phys*) teannaich, snìomh; (*filter*) sìolaidh
strainer *n* sìol(t)achan *m*; (*for fence*) strèanair *m*

straitjacket *n* cuing-cuirp *f*
strait(s) *n* caol *m*, caolas *m*; (*distress*) cruaidh-theinn *f*
stramash *n* hù-bhitheil *f m*, ùpraid *f*
strand *n* dual *m*; (*shore*) tràigh *f*
strange *a* neònach, iongantach, coimheach
stranger *n* coigreach *m*, srainnsear *m*
strangle *v* tachd, mùch
strap *n* strap *m*, iall *f* *v* strapaig, cuir strap/bann air
strapping *a* tapaidh, mòr, calma
stratagem *n* cuilbheart *f*
strategic *a* ro-innleachdail
strategy *n* ro-innleachd *f*
strath *n* srath *m*
straw *n* connlach *f*, fodar *m*; (*for drinking*) sràbh *m* **s. poll** beachd air thuairmse *m*
strawberry *n* sùbh-làir *m*
stray *a* conadail, fuadain; (*wayward*) air seachran *v* rach air seachran
streak *n* stiall *f*, srianag *f*
stream *n* sruth *m*
streamline *v* sìmplich
street *n* sràid *f*
strength *n* neart *m*, spionnadh *m*, lùths *m*
strengthen *v* neartaich
strenuous *a* dian, saothrachail
stress *n* (*phys*) cuideam *m*; (*mental*) uallach *m*, eallach *m* *v* cuir/leig cuideam air
stretch *v* sìn, sgaoil, leudaich
strict *a* teann, cruaidh
stride *n* sìnteag *f*, searradh *m* *v* sìnteagaich, dèan searradh
strife *n* strì *f*, còmhstri *f*
strike *n* (*ind*) stailc *f* *v* buail; (*go on strike*) rach air stailc
striker *n* stailcear *m*; (*football*) neach-ionnsaigh *m*
striking *a* comharraichte, sònraichte
string *n* sreang *f*; (*mus*) teud *m*
stringent *a* teann
strip *n* stiall *f* *v* thoir dheth/dhith *etc* d' aodach
stripe *n* srianag *f*, sgrìob *f*
striped *a* srianach, sgrìobach
stripped *a* rùisgte, lomnochd
strive *v* dèan spàirn/strì
stroke *n* stràc *f m*, buille *f*; (*med*) stròc *m* *v* slìob
stroll *v* gabh cuairt/ceum, spaidsir
strong *n* làidir, treun
structure *n* structair *m*, dèanamh *m*, togail *f* *v* structair
struggle *n* gleac *m*, spàirn *f*, strì *f* *v* gleac, dèan spàirn/strì
strut *v* falbh gu stràiceil
stub *n* bun *m*
stubble *n* asbhuain *f*; (*facial*) bun feusaig *m*
stubborn *a* rag, rag-mhuinealach
stubbornness *n* raigeann *m*, rag-mhuinealas *m*
stubby *a* cutach, bunach
stuck *a* an sàs, steigte
stud *n* stud *f*; (*horses*) greigh *f*
student *n* oileanach *m*
studio *n* stiùidio *f*
studious *a* dèidheil air foghlam
study *n* ionnsachadh *m*; (*room*) seòmar-sgrùdaidh *m* *v* ionnsaich (mu); (*research*) sgrùd, cnuasaich; (*consider*) beachdaich (air)
stuff *n* stuth *m* *v* lìon, dinn
stumble *n* tuisleadh *m* *v* tuislich
stumbling-block *n* ceap-tuislidh *m*, cnap-starra *m*
stump *n* bun *m*, stoc *m*
stun *v* cuir an tuaineal, cuir tuainealaich air
stunt *n* cleas *m*
stupid *a* amaideach, gòrach
stupidity *n* amaideas *m*, gòraiche *f*
stupor *n* tuaineal *m*, neul *m*
sturdy *a* bunanta, gramail
stutter *v* bi manntach/gagach
stye *n* (s)leamhnagan *m*
style *n* stoidhle *f*, modh *f m*; (*fashion*) fasan *m*, stoidhle *f*; (*title*) tiotal *m* **with s.** le snas/loinn
stylish *a* fasanta, spaideil
sub- *pref* fo- (+ *len*)
sub-committee *n* fo-chomataidh *f*
subconscious *n* fo-mhothachadh *m*
sub-contract *v* fo-chunnraich

subdivide *v* fo-roinn
subdue *v* ceannsaich, cìosnaich
sub-heading *n* fo-thiotal *m*
subject *n* cuspair *m*; (*of talk etc*) ceann-labhairt/teagaisg *m*, cuspair *m*; (*citizen*) ìochdaran *m*
subject *v* ceannsaich, cuir fo smachd (+ *gen*) **s. to ...** cuir fo ...
subjective *a* pearsanta, suibseigeach
subject to *a* umhail do, fo smachd (+ *gen*), an urra ri
subjugate *v* ceannsaich
subjunctive *a* (*gram*) eisimeileach
sublime *a* òirdheirc
submarine *n* bàta-aigeil *m*
submerge *v* tùm; (*trans*) cuir fodha; (*intrans*) rach fodha
submission *n* (*lodged*) tagradh *m*; (*yielding*) ùmhlachd *f*, gèill *f*
submissive *a* umha(i)l
submit *a* (*lodge, argue*) cuir a-steach, (t)agair; (*yield*) gèill, strìochd
subordinate *a* ìochdarach, fo- (+ *len*)
subscribe *v* fo-sgrìobh **s. to** gabh/thoir taic do
subscription *n* fo-sgrìobhadh *m*, sìnteas *m*
subsequent *a* a leanas, an dèidh làimhe
subsequently *adv* mar sin, na dhèidh sin, an dèidh làimhe
subside *v* sìolaidh, traogh, tràigh
subsidence *n* dol sìos *m*, traoghadh *m*, ìsleachadh *m*, fo-thuiteam *m*
subsidiary *a* ìochdaireil, cuideachail, fo- (+ *len*)
subsidize *v* thoir subsadaidh/tabhartas do
subsidy *n* subsadaidh *m*, tabhartas *m*
subsistence *n* teachd-an-tìr *m*
substance *n* susbaint *f*, brìgh *f*; (*material*) stuth *m*
substantial *a* susbainteach, làidir, tàbhachdach
substantiate *v* dearbh, fìrinnich
substitute *n* stuth/nì-ionaid *m* (an) ionad *m*; (*person*) neach-ionaid *m*, riochdaire *m* *v* cuir an àite **s. for** gabh àite (+ *gen*)
sub-title *n* fo-thiotal *m*
subtle *a* seòlta
subtlety *n* seòltachd *f*
subtract *v* thoir (air falbh) (bh)o
suburb *n* iomall baile *m*
subversive *a* ceannairceach
subway *n* fo-shlighe *f*
succeed *v* soirbhich, rach le; (*follow*) lean
success *n* soirbheachadh *m*, buaidh *f*
successful *a* soirbheachail
successive *a* leantainneach, an dèidh a chèile
successor *n* neach-ionaid *m*, neach a thig an àite/às dèidh ... *m* (+ *gen*)
succinct *a* geàrr, cuimir
succulent *a* brìoghmhor, blasta
succumb *v* gèill, strìochd
such *a*, *pron* (a) leithid, mar, dhen t-seòrsa **as s.** ann/innte fhèin
suck *v* deothail, deoc, sùigh
sudden *a* obann, grad, aithghearr
suddenly *adv* gu h-obann, gu grad, gu h-aithghearr
sue *v* thoir gu lagh
suet *n* geir *f*
suffer *v* fuiling; (*permit*) ceadaich
suffering *n* fulangas *m*
suffice *v* foghain
sufficient *a* leòr, cuibheasach
suffix *n* (iar-)leasachan *m*
suffocate *v* mùch
suffuse *v* sgaoil air feadh
sugar *n* siùcar *m*
suggest *v* mol, comhairlich, cuir an inntinn (+ *gen*)/air shùilibh do
suggestion *n* moladh *m*, cur an inntinn (+ *gen*)/air shùilibh *m*
suicide *n* fèin-mhurt *m* **commit s.** cuir às dhut fhèin
suit *n* deise *f*; (*law*) cùis(-lagha) *f*
suit *v* freagair
suitable *a* freagarrach, iomchaidh
suitcase *n* màileid *f*, baga *m*
suite *n* (*rooms*) sreath *f m*; (*furniture*) suidht *f*; (*mus*) sreath *f m*

suitor *n* suirghiche *m*
sullen *a* dùr, gnù
sully *v* salaich, truaill, cuir smal air
sulphur *n* pronnasg *m*
sulphuric *a* pronnasgach
sultry *a* bruthainneach
sum *n* àireamh *f*, sùim *f*
summarize *v* thoir geàrr-chunntas air, giorraich
summary *n* geàrr-chunntas *m*, giorrachadh *m*
summer *n* samhradh *m* **s. school** sgoil shamhraidh *f*
summit *n* mullach *m*, bàrr *m* **s. meeting** àrd-choinneamh *f*
summon *v* gairm; (*leg*) sumain
summons *n* gairm *f*; (*leg*) bàirlinn *f*, sumanadh *m*
sumptuous *a* sòghail
sums *n* cunntadh *m*
sun *n* grian *f* **sundial** uaireadair-grèine *m* **sunflower** neòinean-grèine *m* **sunrise** èirigh na grèine *f* **sunset** dol fodha na grèine *m*, laighe na grèine *f m* **sunshine** deàrrsadh na grèine *m* **sunbathe** *v* gabh a' ghrian, blian (thu/e/i *etc* fhèin) **sunburnt** *a* loisgte aig a' ghrèin
Sunday *n* Didòmhnaich *m*, Latha/Là na Sàbaid *m*
sundry *a* iomadaidh, measgaichte
sunk *a* air a dhol fodha
sunny *a* grianach
super *a* sgoinneil, barraichte *pref* os-, an(a)-
superannuation *n* peinnseanachadh *m*
superb *a* barraichte, sgoinneil
superficial *a* staoin, gun doimhneachd
superfluous *a* iomarcach, thar a' chòrr
superhuman *a* os-daonna
superintendent *n* stiùireadair *m*, àrd-neach-stiùiridh *m*
superior *n* uachdaran *m* *a* uachdarach, àrd
superiority *n* uachdarachd *f*, bàrr *m*, ceannas *m*
superlative *a* còrr, barraichte; (*gram*) feabhasach
supermarket *n* mòr-bhùth *f*
supernatural *a* os-nàdarra(ch)
supersede *v* gabh àite (+ *gen*), cuir às àite
superstition *n* saobh-chràbhadh *m*
superstitious *a* saobh-chràbhach
supervise *v* stiùir, cùm sùil air
supervision *n* stiùireadh *m*, cumail sùil air *f*
supervisor *n* neach-stiùiridh/coimhid *m*
supper *n* suipear *f*
supple *a* sùbailte, subailte
supplement *n* leasachadh *m*
supplementary *a* a bharrachd, leasachail **s. benefit** sochair-leasachaidh *f*
supplier *n* solaraiche *m*
supply *n* solarachadh *m*, solar *m* *v* solaraich, cùm ri **do s. work** obraich an àite cuideigin
support *n* taic *f*, tacsa *m*, cùl-taic *m* *v* thoir taic do, cuir/cùm taic ri, cuidich
supporter *n* neach-taic(e) *m*; (*sport*) neach-leantail/leantainn *m*
supportive *a* taiceil
suppose *v* saoil
suppress *v* cùm fodha, mùch
suppression *n* cumail fodha *f*, mùchadh *m*
supremacy *n* ceannasachd *f*, àrd-cheannas *m*
supreme *a* àrd-, sàr, barraichte
supremo *n* àrd-cheannard *m*
surcharge *n* for-chìs *f* *v* leag for-chìs air
sure *a* cinnteach, deimhinnte
surely *adv* is cinnteach, gu fìrinneach
surf *n* ròd *m*, rùid *m* *v* marcaich tuinn **s. the net** tràl an lìon
surface *n* uachdar *m*, leth a-muigh *m*
surfeit *n* sàth *m*, cus *m*
surge *n* onfhadh *m* *v* at, bòc
surgeon *n* lannsair *m*
surgery *n* obair-lannsa *f*; (*place*) ionad an dotair *m*; (*polit*) freastal-lann *f*
surly *a* gnù, greannach

surmise *v* saoil, bi dhen bharail
surmount *v* rach/faigh os cionn (+ *gen*)
surname *n* cinneadh *m*, sloinneadh *m*
surpass *v* thoir bàrr air
surplus *n* còrr *m*
surprise *n* iongnadh *m*, iongantas *m* *v* cuir iongnadh/iongantas air **s. someone** thig gun fhios air
surprising *a* iongantach, neònach
surrender *v* (*intrans*) strìochd, gèill; (*trans*) thoir suas
surround *v* cuartaich, iadh mu thimcheall
survey *n* tomhas *m*, sgrùdadh *m* *v* tomhais, sgrùd; (*look at*) gabh beachd air
surveyor *n* neach-tomhais/ sgrùdaidh *m*
survive *v* mair beò, tàrr às **s. on** thig beò air
survivor *n* neach a tha beò/ maireann *m*, neach a thàrr às *m*
susceptible *a* buailteach (do)
suspect *n* neach fo amharas *m* *v* bi/cuir an amharas **I s.** tha amharas agam (gu)
suspected *a* fo amharas
suspend *v* (*hang*) croch; (*defer*) cuir dàil an; (*from work*) cuir à dreuchd rè ùine
suspense *n* teagamh *m* **in s.** fo theagamh, a' feitheamh, air bhioran
suspension *n* crochadh *m*; (*from work*) cur à dreuchd rè ùine *m* **s. bridge** drochaid crochaidh *f*
suspicion *n* amharas *m*
suspicious *a* amharasach
sustain *v* cùm suas; (*suffer*) fuiling
sustainable *a* buan, seasmhach
sustenance *n* lòn *m*, beathachadh *m*
swallow *n* gòbhlan-gaoithe *m*
swallow *v* sluig
swamp *n* fèith *f*, bog(l)ach *f*
swan *n* eala *f*
swarm *n* sgaoth *m*
swarthy *a* doimhearra, ciar
sway *n* riaghladh *m*, seòladh *m* *v* luaisg; (*opinion*) gluais, buadhaich
swear *v* (*vow*) mionnaich, thoir mionnan, bòidich; (*curse*) bi ri guidheachan/mionnan
swearing *n* (*avowing*) mionnachadh *m*; (*cursing*) guidheachan *f m pl*
sweat *n* fallas *m* *v* cuir fallas (dheth/dhith *etc*)
sweatshirt *n* lèine spòrs *f*
sweaty *a* fallasach
Swede *n* Suaineach *m*, (*female*) ban-S(h)uaineach *f*
Swedish *a* Suaineach *n* (*lang*) Suainis *f*
sweep *v* sguab
sweeper *n* sguabaire *m*
sweet *n* mìlsean *m* *a* milis; (*scent*) cùbhraidh; (*sound*) binn
sweeten *v* mìlsich, dèan milis
sweetheart *n* leannan *m*, eudail *f*
sweets *n* suiteis *m pl*, siùcaran *m pl*
swell *v* at, sèid, bòc
swelling *n* at *m*, cnap *m*, bòcadh *m*
sweltering *a* brothallach, bruthainneach
swerve *v* claon, lùb, rach a thaobh
swift *n* gobhlan-gainmhich *m*
swift *a* luath, grad, siùbhlach, ealamh
swim *n* snàmh *m* *v* snàmh
swimmer *n* snàmhaiche *m*
swimming *n* snàmh *m* **s.-pool** amar-snà(i)mh *m*
swindle *v* thoir an car à, dèan foill (air)
swine *n* mucan *f pl*; (*slang*) trustar *m*
swing *n* (*action*) luasgadh *m*; (*for playing*) dreallag *f*; (*pendulum*) siùdan *m*; (*polit*) gluasad *m*; (*golf*) dòigh-bualaidh *f* **in full s.** fo làn-sheòl *v* luaisg; (*of pendulum*) dean siùdan; (*polit*) gluais
swingeing *a* cruaidh
swipe *n* sgailc *f*
Swiss *n, a* Eilbheiseach *m*, (*female*) ban-Eilbheiseach *f*
switch *n* suidse *f m*; (*wand*) slat *f*

switch *v* atharraich
swivel *n* udalan *m*, fulag *f*
swollen *a* air at/sèid
swoon *v* rach an neul, rach am paiseanadh
swoop *v* thig le roid/sitheadh **s. for** sguab leat, grad-ghlac
sword *n* claidheamh *m* **s.-dance** danns a' chlaidheimh *m*
swot *v* ionnsaich gu dian
syllable *n* lideadh *m*
syllabus *n* clàr-obrach *m*
symbol *n* samhla *m*
symbolical *a* samhlachail
symbolism *n* samhlachas *m*
symbolize *v* samhlaich, riochdaich
symmetrical *a* ceart-chumadail, cothromaichte
sympathetic *a* co-fhaireachail, truasail
sympathize *v* nochd co-fhaireachdainn
sympathy *n* co-fhaireachdainn *f*
symphony *n* (*mus piece*) siansadh *m*
symptom *n* comharra *m*
synchronize *v* co-thìmich
syndicate *n* comann iomairt *m*; (*media*) buidheann naidheachdais *f m*
synod *n* seanadh *m*
synonym *n* co-fhacal *m*
synopsis *n* geàrr-iomradh *m*, giorrachadh *m*
syntax *n* co-chàradh *m*
synthesis *n* co-chur *m*, co-thàthadh *m*
synthetic *a* co-thàthte; (*artificial*) fuadain
syphon *n* sùghachan *m*, lìonadair *m*
syringe *n* steallair(e) *m*
syrup *n* siorap *f m*
system *n* siostam *m*, seòl *m*
systematic *a* rianail, òrdail, eagarach

T

table *n* bòrd *m*; (*figures*) clàr *m* **t.-tennis** teanas-bùird *m* **tablecloth** anart-bùird *m*, tubhailt(e) *f m*
tablet *n* pile *f*; (*block*) clàr *m*
tacit *a* gun ainmeachadh, gun a ràdh
tack *n* tacaid *f*; (*naut*) tac(a) *f*; (*lease*) tac *f*
tackle *n* acfhainn *f*, uidheam *f*; (*in sport*) dol an sàs *m*
tactic *n* innleachd *f*, seòl *m*
tactical *a* innleachdail
tactile *n* beantainneach, beanailteach
tadpole *n* ceann-phollan *m*, ceann-simid *m*
tail *n* earball *m*, eàrr *f m*, feaman *m* **tailback** ciudha charbadan *m*
tailor *n* tàillear *m*
tainted *a* trothach, air a t(h)ruailleadh *etc*, millte
take *v* gabh, thoir **it takes a long time** tha e a' toirt ùine mhòr **t. a photograph** tog dealbh
takeover *n* gabhail thairis *m*
takings *n* teachd-a-steach *m*
tale *n* sgeulachd *f*, sgeul *m*
talent *n* tàlant *m*, comas *m*, buadh *f*
talented *a* tàlantach, comasach
talk *n* bruidhinn *f*, cainnt *f*; (*chat*) còmhradh *m*; (*lecture*) òraid *f* *v* bruidhinn; (*chat*) dèan còmhradh
talkative *a* còmhraideach, bruidhneach, cabach
talking *n* bruidhinn *f*, labhairt *f*
tall *a* àrd
tallow *n* geir *f*, blona(i)g *f*, crèis *f*
tally *n* cunntas *m*, àireamh *f*
talon *n* spuir *m*, ionga *f*
tame *a* soitheamh, call(d)a, ceannsaichte *v* callaich, ceannsaich
tamper *v* buin/bean ri, mill
tan *n* dubhadh (-grèine) *m* *v* gabh a' ghrian; (*leather*) cairt
tang *n* blas geur *m*
tangent *n* beantan *m* **going off at a t.** a' dol bhàrr do sgeòil
tangible *a* so-bheantainn, susbainteach, a ghabhas làimhseachadh
tangle *n* troimh-a-chèile *f m*; (*fishing line*) rocladh *m*;

(*seaweed*) stamh *m* *v* rach an sàs/an lùib a chèile; (*fishing line*) rocail
tank *n* tanca *f m*
tanker *n* tancair *m*
tantalize *v* cùm air bhioran, leamhaich
tantamount *a* co-ionann, ionann
tantrum *n* prat *m*, dod *m*
tap *n* goc *m*, tap *f m*; (*sound*) gnogag *f* *v* (*sound*) thoir gnogag do; (*access*) tarraing air/à
tape *n* teip *f* **t.-measure** teip-tomhais *f* **t.-recorder** teip-chlàradair *m* *v* teip, cuir teip air; (*record*) cuir air teip, clàraich
taper *v* (*intrans*) fàs barra-chaol; (*trans*) dèan caol
tapestry *n* brat-grèise *m*
tar *n* teàrr *f*, bìth *f* *v* teàrr
tardy *a* athaiseach, màirnealach, slaodach
target *n* targaid *f* **t. audience** luchd-amais sònraichte *m* *v* cuimsich air
tariff *n* cìs *f*; (*prices*) clàr-phrìsean *m*
tarnish *v* smalaich, dubhaich
tarpaulin *n* cainb-thearra *f*
tart *n* pigheann *m*
tart *a* searbh, geur
tartan *n* tartan *m*, breacan *m*
task *n* obair *f*, gnìomh *m* **t.-force** buidheann-gnìomha *f m*
tassel *n* cluigean *m*, babag *f*
taste *n* blas *m*; (*judgement*) breithneachadh *m* *v* blais, feuch
tasteless *a* neo-bhlasta, gun bhlas; (*met*) neo-chubhaidh, mì-chiatach
tasty *a* blasta
tattle *n* goileam *m*
tattoo *n* tatù *m*
taunt *n* beum *m*, magadh *m*, tilgeil air *f* *v* beum, mag, tilg air
taut *a* teann
tawdry *a* suarach, gun snas
tawny *a* lachdann, ciar
tawse *n* strap *m*, stràic *f*
tax *n* cìs *f*, càin *f* **income tax** cìs cosnaidh **tax office** oifis chìsean *f* *v* leag cìs, cuir cìs air
taxation *n* leagail cìse *m*, cìs *f*
taxi *n* tagsaidh *f m*
taxman *n* cìs-mhaor *m*
taxpayer *n* neach-pàighidh cìse *m*
tea *n* tì *f*, teatha *f* **teacup** cupa tì *m*, copan teatha *m* **teapot** poit-tì/teatha *f* **teaspoon** spàin-tì/teatha *f*
teach *v* teagaisg, ionnsaich
teacher *n* tidsear *f m*, neach-teagaisg *f*
teaching *n* teagasg *m*
teal *n* crann-lach *f*
team *n* sgioba *f m*
tear *n* deur *m*; (*rent*) sracadh *m* *v* srac, reub
tease *v* tarraing à, farranaich; (*comb out*) cìr
teat *n* sine *f*
technical *a* teicneòlach, teicnigeach
technician *n* teicneòlaiche *m*
technique *n* alt *m*, dòigh *f*
technological *a* teicneòlach
technology *n* teicneòlas *m*
tedious *a* sàrachail, sgìtheil, ràsanach
teeming *a* loma-làn, a' cur thairis
teenager *n* deugaire *m*
telecommunications *n* tele-chonaltradh *m*
telephone *n* fòn *f m*, teilefòn *m* **t. directory** leabhar a'/na fòn *m* *v* fòn(aig)
telephonist *n* neach-freagairt fòn *m*
telescope *n* prosbaig *f*, teileasgop *f*
teletext *n* tele-theacsa *m*
television *n* telebhisean *f m*
tell *v* innis, abair
telltale *n* cabaire *m*
temerity *n* ladarnas *m*
temper *n* nàdar *m*
temperament *n* nàdar *m*, càil *f*
temperance *n* measarrachd *f*, stuamachd *f*
temperate *a* measarra, stuama; (*atmos*) eadar-mheadhanach
temperature *n* teòthachd *f*

temple *n* teampall *m*; (*head*) lethcheann *m*
tempo *n* luaths *m*
temporarily *adv* airson ùine ghoirid, rè tamaill
temporary *a* sealach, airson ùine ghoirid, rè seal
tempt *v* buair, tàlaidh
temptation *n* buaireadh *m*
ten *n* a deich *a* deich **ten people** deichnear *f m*
tenable *a* reusanta, a ghabhas seasamh
tenacious *a* leanailteach, righinn, greimeil
tenacity *n* leanailteachd *f*, rìghneas *m*
tenancy *n* gabhaltas *m*
tenant *n* neach-gabhail *m*
tend *v* fritheil, àraich; (*incline*) aom, bi buailteach
tendency *n* aomadh *m*, buailteachd *f*
tender *n* tairgse *f* *v* tairg, tabhann
tender *a* maoth, caoin
tenderness *n* maothalachd *f*, caomhalachd *f*
tenement *n* teanamaint *m*
tennis *n* teanas *m*
tenor *n* brìgh *f*, seagh *m*; (*mus*) teanor *m*
tense *n* tràth *m* **present/future/past t.** an tràth làthaireach/teachdail/caithte
tense *a* teann, rag
tension *n* teannachadh *m*, ragachadh *m*; (*stress*) strì *f*
tent *n* teant(a) *f m*
tentacle *n* greimiche *m*
tentative *a* teagmhach, mì-chinnteach
tenth *n* deicheamh *m*, an deicheamh cuid *f* *a* deicheamh
tenuous *a* (*flimsy*) lag; (*fine*) tana
tenure *n* còir-fearainn *f*, gabhaltas *m*
tepid *a* flodach; (*met*) meadh-bhlàth
term *n* (*of time*) teirm *f*; (*end*) crìoch *f*, ceann *m*; (*condition*) cùmhnant *m*, cumha *f m*; (*verbal*) facal *m*, briathar *m*
terminal *a* (*med*) crìche
terminate *v* cuir crìoch air, crìochnaich
termination *n* crìochnachadh *m*; (*med*) casg-breith *f*
terminology *n* briathrachas *m*
tern *n* steàrnan *m*
terrible *a* eagalach, uabhasach, sgràthail
terrier *n* abhag *f*
terrify *v* oilltich, cuir oillt/eagal air
terrifying *a* eagalach, oillteil
territory *n* tìr *f*, fonn *m*, fearann *m*
terror *n* eagal *m*, oillt *f*; (*person*) cùis-eagail *f*
terrorism *n* ceannairc *f*
terse *a* geàrr, cuimir
test *n* deuchainn *f*, ceasnachadh *m*
testament *n* tiomnadh *m* **the Old T.** an Seann Tiomnadh **the New T.** an Tiomnadh Nuadh
testicle *n* magairle *f m*, magairlean *m*, clach *f*
testify *v* thoir fianais
testimonial *n* teisteanas *m*
testimony *n* teisteas *m*, fianais *f*
tetchy *a* frionasach
tether *n* teadhair *f*, feist(e) *f*
text *n* teacsa *m*; (*sermon*) ceann-teagaisg *m* **textbook** teacs-leabhar *m*
textile *n* aodach fighte *m*
texture *n* dèanamh *m*, inneach *m*
than *conj* na **more t.** barrachd air **other t.** ach, a thuilleadh air
thank *v* thoir taing/buidheachas
thankful *a* taingeil, buidheach
thankless *a* gun taing; (*ungrateful*) mì-thaingeil, neo-ar-thaingeil
thanks *n* tapadh leat/leibh *m* **many t.** mòran taing
that *dem a* sin, siud *dem pron* sin, ud *rel pron* a **all t.** na *conj* gu, gum, gun *adv* cho **is it that late?** a bheil e/i cho anmoch sin?
thatch *n* tughadh *m* *v* tugh
thaw *n* aiteamh *m* *v* bi ag aiteamh, leagh

the *def art* (*singular forms*) an, am (+ *b, f, m, p*), a' (+ *len*), an t- (+ *vowels*); (*plural*) na, na h- (+ *vowels*) (*See Forms of the article in Grammar*)
theatre *n* taigh-cluiche *m*
theft *n* mèirle *f*, goid *f*, braide *f*
their *poss pron* an, am, ... aca
them *pers pron* iad, (*emph*) iadsan
theme *n* cuspair *m*; (*mus*) ùrlar *m*
themselves *emph pron* iad fhèin
then *adv* an sin, an uair sin; (*afterwards*) an dèidh sin; (*in that case*) mar sin, a-rèist(e)
thence *adv* às a sin, às an àite sin, (bh)o sin
theology *n* diadhachd *f*
theoretical *a* teòiridheach, beachdail
theory *n* teòiridh *f*, beachd *m*, beachd-smuain *m*
therapist *n* neach-slànachaidh *m*, leasaiche *m* **speech t.** leasaiche cainnt *m*
therapy *n* slànachadh *m*, leasachadh *m*
there *adv* an sin, an siud
thereabouts *adv* mu thimcheall sin
thereafter *adv* an dèidh sin, an uair sin
thereby *adv* le sin, leis a sin
therefore *adv* mar sin, air an adhbhar sin
thermal *a* tearmach
thermometer *n* teas-mheidh *f*
these *dem pron* iad seo
thesis *n* tràchdas *m*
they *pers pron* iad, (*emph*) iadsan
thick *a* tiugh, garbh
thicken *v* dèan nas tighe; (*intrans*) fàs nas tighe
thicket *n* doire d(h)ùmhail *f m*
thickness *n* tighead *m*
thief *n* mèirleach *m*, gadaiche *m*
thieve *v* goid, dèan mèirle
thigh *n* sliasaid *f*
thimble *n* meuran *m*
thin *a* tana, caol; (*scarce*) gann *v* tanaich
thing *n* nì *m*, rud *m* **how are things?** ciamar a tha cùisean?
think *v* smaoinich, saoil, meas
thinness *n* tainead *m*, caoilead *m*
third *n* trian *m*, treas cuid *f* *a* treas, tritheamh
thirdly *adv* san treas àite
thirst *n* pathadh *m*, tart *m*, iota(dh) *m*
thirsty *a* pàiteach, tartmhor, ìotmhor **are you t.?** a bheil am pathadh ort?
thirteen *n, a* trì-deug **t. minutes** trì mionaidean deug
thirteenth *a* treas ... deug
thirty *n, a* deich air fhichead, trithead *m*
this *dem a* seo
thistle *n* cluaran *m*, fòghnan *m*
thole *v* fuiling
thong *n* iall *f*
thorn *n* dris *f*, droigheann *m*
thorny *a* driseach, droighneach; (*difficult*) connspaideach, ciogailteach
thorough *a* mionaideach, domhainn; (*complete*) fìor
those *dem pron* iad sin, iad siud
though *conj* ge, ged **as t.** mar gu/gun/gum
thought *n* smaoin *f*, smuain *f*
thoughtful *a* smaointeach; (*considerate*) tuigseach
thoughtless *a* beag diù, gun smaoin(eachadh)
thousand *n, a* mìle *m*
thrash *v* slaic, sgiùrs; (*grain*) buail
thread *n* snàthainn *m*, snàithlean *m*
threadbare *a* lom
threat *n* bagairt *f*, maoidheadh *m*
threaten *v* bagair, maoidh
threatening *a* bagarrach
three *n* a trì *a* trì **t. people** triùir *m* **t.-legged** trì-chasach **t.-quarters** trì chairteil *m pl*
thresh *v* buail
threshold *n* stairs(n)each *f*, maide-buinn *m*
thrift *n* cùmhntachd *f*
thrifty *a* cùmhntach, glèidhteach
thrill *n* gaoir *f* *v* cuir gaoir an
thriller *n* gaoir-sgeul *m*
thrilling *a* fìor thogarrach, gad chur nad b(h)oil *etc*

thrive *v* soirbhich
throat *n* amha(i)ch *f*, sgòrnan *m*
throb *v* dèan plosgartaich
thrombosis *n* trombòis *f*, cleiteachd-fala *f*
throne *n* rìgh-chathair *f*
throng *n* sluagh mòr *m*, co-long *f* *v* dùmhlaich/lìon àite **t. to** còmh(dha)laich
throttle *v* tachd, mùch
through *prep* tro, tre, trìd **t. other** troimh-a-chèile
throughout *adv* o cheann gu ceann, feadh gach àite
throw *n* tilgeadh *m*, tilgeil *m*, sadail *m*, caitheamh *m* *v* tilg, sad, caith **t. up** dìobhair
thrush *n* smeòrach *f*; (*med*) craos-ghalar *m*
thrust *n* sàthadh *m*, sparradh *m*; (*of argument*) prìomh phuing *f* *v* sàth, spàrr
thud *n* turtar *m*
thug *n* ùmaidh *m*
thumb *n* òrdag *f*
thump *n* buille *f*, slaic *f*; (*noise*) trost *m* *v* buail, thoir slaic do
thunder *n* tàirneanach *m* **t. and lightning** tàirneanaich is dealanaich
thunderbolt *n* beithir *f m*
Thursday *n* Diardaoin *m*
thus *adv* mar seo, air an dòigh seo
thwart *v* cuir bacadh air
thyme *n* lus an rìgh *m*
tick *n* (*sound*) diog *m*, buille *f*; (*moment*) diog *m*; (*mark*) strìochag *f*; (*insect*) gartan *m*, mial-chaorach *f*
ticket *n* tiogaid *f*, tigead *f*
tickle *v* diogail
tide *n* làn *m*, seòl-mara *m*, tìde-mhara *f* **high t.** muir-làn *f m* **low t.** muir-tràigh *f m*
tidy *a* sgiobalta *v* sgioblaich
tie *n* bann *m*; (*necktie*) tàidh *f* *v* ceangail
tier *n* sreath *f m*, ìre *f*
tiger *n* tìgear *m*
tight *a* teann
tighten *v* teannaich
tights *n* stocainnean-teann *f pl*
tile *n* leacag *f*, tàidhl *f* *v* leacaich, tàidhl
till *prep* gu, gu ruig(e) *conj* gus
tiller *n* (f)ailm *f*, falmadair *m*; (*of soil*) treabhaiche *m*
tilt *v* aom
timber *n* fiodh *m* *a* fiodha
time *n* àm *m*, uair *f*; (*period of*) ùine *f*, tìde *f*; (*abstr*) tìm *f* **a long t. ago** o chionn f(h)ada **any t.** uair sam bith **for a long t.** airson ùine mhòir **from t. to t.** b(h)o àm gu àm **in a week's t.** an ceann seachdain **in t.** na uair **it's high t. you ...** tha làn-àm/thìde agad ... **on t.** ris an uair **plenty of t.** ùine/tìde gu leòr **what's the t.?** dè 'n uair a tha e? **at times** uaireannan *v* tomhais an ùine
timely *adv* an deagh àm
timetable *n* clàr-ama *m* *v* dèan clàr-ama
timid *a* gealtach, meata
timing *n* tomhas-ama *m*
timorous *a* eagalach, sgeunach, sgàthach
tin *n* staoin *f*; (*can*) tiona *m*, canastair *m* **tin-opener** fosglair chanastairean *m*
tinge *n* lìth *f*, fiamh *m* *v* dath
tingle *n* biorgadaich *f* *v* (*feel a tingling*) fairich biorgadh
tinker *n* ceàrd *m*
tinkle *v* dèan/thoir gliong
tinsel *n* tionsail *f*
tint *n* fiamh-dhath *m*, bàn-dhath *m*, tuar *m* *v* dath
tiny *a* bìodach, meanbh, crìon
tip *n* bàrr *m*; (*money*) bonn-boise *m*
tipple *v* dèan pòit, gabh deoch
tipsy *a* air leth-mhisg, froganach
tiptoe *n* corra-biod(a) *m* **on t.** air chorra-biod(a)
tirade *n* sruth-cainnt *m*
tire *v* sgìthich, sàraich; (*intrans*) fàs sgìth, sgìthich
tired *a* sgìth
Tiree person *n* Tiristeach *m*, (*female*) ban-Thiristeach *f*
tiresome *a* sàrachail, leamh
tiring *a* sgìtheil

tissue *n* (*cell*) stuth (cealla) *m*; (*muscle*) maothran *m* **paper t.** nèapaigin pàipeir *m*
tit *n* (*bird*) gocan *m*, smutag *f*; (*slang*) cìoch *f*
tit-bit *n* grèim blasta *m*
title *n* tiotal *m*; (*leg*) còir *f*, dlighe *f*
to *prep* do (+ *len*), (*to a*) gu, (*to the*) chun (+ *gen*); (*before verbs and place names*) a (+ *len*); (*after verbs*) ri **are you going to the shop?** a bheil thu a' dol dhan bhùtha? **she went to a meeting** chaidh i gu coinneimh **are they going to the wedding?** a bheil iad a' dol chun na bainnse? **we are going to play football** tha sinn a' dol a chluich ball-coise **she spoke to him** bhruidhinn i ris *adv* **to and fro,** a-null 's a-nall
toad *n* muile-mhàgag *f*
toast *n* tost *m*; (*drink*) deoch-slàinte *f* *v* tost(aig); (*drink*) òl deoch-slàinte
toaster *n* tostair *m*
tobacco *n* tombaca *m*
today *adv* an-diugh
toddler *n* pàiste *m*
toe *n* òrdag coise *f*
toffee *n* tofaidh *m*
together *adv* còmhla, le chèile
toil *n* saothair *f*, dubh-chosnadh *m* *v* saothraich
toilet *n* taigh-beag *m* **t. roll** roile toidhleit *f m*
token *n* comharra *m*; (*memento*) cuimhneachan *m*
tolerable *a* a ghabhas fhulang; (*fairly good*) meadhanach math
tolerance *n* fulangas *m*; (*patience*) foighidinn *f*
tolerant *a* fosgailte; (*patient*) foighidneach
tolerate *v* fuiling, ceadaich, bi fosgailte do
toll *n* cìs *f*
tomato *n* tomàto *m*
tomb *n* uaigh *f*, tuam *m*
tomcat *n* cat fireann *m*, cullach *m*
tome *n* leabhar mòr *m*
tomorrow *adv* a-màireach
ton *n* tunna *m*
tone *n* (*sound*) fuaim *m*; (*mus*) tòna *f*; (*of voice*) dòigh-labhairt *f* **t.-deaf** *a* ceòl-bhodhar
tongs *n* clobha *m*
tongue *n* teanga *f*; (*lang*) cainnt *f*, cànan *f m*
tonic *n* ìocshlaint *f*; (*uplift*) togail *f*
tonight *adv* a-nochd
tonsil *n* tonsail *f*
too *adv* ro (+ *len*); (*also*) cuideachd, mar an ceudna **too black** ro dhubh **too much** cus, tuilleadh 's a' chòir
tool *n* inneal *m*, ball-acfhainn *m*
tooth *n* fiacail *f* **back t.** fiacail-cùil **toothache** an dèideadh *m* **toothbrush** bruis-fhiaclan *f* **toothpaste** uachdar-fhiaclan *m*
top *n* mullach *m*, bàrr *m*, uachdar *m* **spinning t.** dòtaman *m* **on t. of** air muin (+ *gen*) **top-heavy** bàrr-throm *v* thoir bàrr air
topic *n* cuspair *m*, ceann(-còmhraidh) *m*
topical *a* àmail, sna naidheachdan
topsy-turvy *a*, *adv* bun-os-cionn, dromach-air-thearrach
torch *n* toirds *f m*, biùgan *m*
torment *n* àmhghar *f m*, dòrainn *f* *v* lèir
torpedo *n* spaileart *m*
torrent *n* tuil *f*, bras-shruth *m*, beum-slèibhe *m*
torrid *a* loisgeach; (*met*) fìor dhian
torso *n* colann *f*, com *m*
tortoise *n* sligeanach *m*
tortuous *a* snìomhach, toinnte, lùbach
torture *n* cràdh *m*, pianadh *m* *v* cràidh, ceus
Tory *n* Tòraidh *m* **the T. Party** am Partaidh Tòraidheach *m*
toss *v* luaisg; (*throw*) tilg; (*of a coin*) cuir croinn
total *a* iomlan, uile *n* sùim (iomlan) *f*
totally *adv* gu lèir, gu h-iomlan, gu tur
touch *v* bean do, suath an, buin ri, làimhsich; (*with emotion*) drùidh air, maothaich

touching *a* (*emotive*) drùidhteach, maothach
touchy *a* frionasach
tough *a* cruaidh, righinn; (*of meat etc*) righinn
toughen *v* cruadhaich, rìghnich
tour *n* turas *m*, cuairt *f*
tourism *n* turasachd *f*
tourist *n* neach-turais *m pl* luchd-turais **t. information centre** ionad fiosrachaidh turasachd *m* **t. office** oifis turasachd *f*
tow *v* slaod, dragh
towards *prep* a dh'ionnsaigh (+ *gen*); gu, chun (+ *gen*); (*purpose*) a chum (+ *gen*)
towel *n* searbhadair *m*, tubhailt(e) *f m*
tower *n* tùr *m*
town *n* baile *m*, baile-mòr *m* **t. council** comhairle baile *f* **t. hall** talla baile *m*
township *n* baile *m*
toy *n* dèideag *f v* cluich
trace *n* lorg *f v* lorg
track *n* lorg *f*; (*path*) frith-rathad *m*, ceum *m*
tracksuit *n* deise-spòrs *f*
tract *n* leabhran *m*, tràchd *f m*; (*of land*) raonach *m*
tractor *n* tractar *m*
trade *n* malairt *f*; (*craft*) ceàird *f* **t. fair** fèill-mhalairt *f* **t. mark** comharra malairt *m* **t. union** aonadh-ciùird *m v* dèan malairt, malairtich
trader *n* neach-malairt *m*
tradition *n* dualchas; (*oral*) beul-aithris *f*
traditional *a* dualchasach, traidiseanta, beul-aithriseach
traffic *n* trafaig *f* **t. jam** stopadh trafaig *m*
traffic *v* dèan malairt
tragedy *n* cùis-mhulaid *f*; (*liter*) bròn-chluich *f*
tragic *a* muladach, cianail, dòrainneach
trail *n* lorg *f*, slighe *f v* bi air lorg (+ *gen*); (*drag*) slaod; (*intrans*) bi slaodach **t. after** triall às dèidh (+ *gen*)
trailer *n* trèilear *m*
train *n* trèan(a) *f*; (*bride*'s) sguain *f v* trèan(aig), teagaisg, ionnsaich; (*intrans*) trèanaig, ionnsaich
trainee *n* foghlamach *m*, neach fo thrèanadh *m*
trainer *n* neach-trèanaidh *m*
trainers *n* brògan-trèanaidh *f pl*
training *n* trèanadh *m*, ionnsachadh *m*
trait *n* stil *f*
traitor *n* neach-brathaidh *m*, brathadair *m*
tramp *n* (*person*) deòra(i)dh *m*; (*walk*) ruaig *f v* coisich le ceum trom
trample *v* saltair, stamp
trance *n* neul *m*
tranquil *a* ciùin, sìochail, sèimh
tranquillity *n* ciùineas *m*, sìth-thàmh *m*
tranquillizer *n* ciùineadair *m*, tàmhadair *m*
transaction *n* gnothach *m*
transcend *v* rach thairis air, thoir bàrr air
transcribe *v* cuir an sgrìobhadh
transcript *n* riochd sgrìobhte *m*
transfer *n* gluasad *f*, aiseag *m v* gluais, aisig; (*intrans*) gluais gu
transfix *v* (*met*) beò-ghlac
transform *v* cruth-atharraich
transformation *n* cruth-atharrachadh *m*
transgress *v* bris(t) riaghailt/lagh, peacaich
transgression *n* bris(t)eadh riaghailt/lagh(a) *m*, peacadh *m*
transient *a* diombuan, neo-mhaireann
transition *n* caochladh *m*, eadar-ghluasad *f*
transitional *a* trastach, san eadar-àm, eadar-amail
translate *v* eadar-theangaich; (*move*) gluais
translation *n* eadar-theangachadh *m* **simultaneous t.** eadar-theangachadh mar-aon
translator *n* eadar-theangair *m*
transmission *n* sgaoileadh *m*; (*broadcast*) craobh-sgaoileadh *m*, craoladh *m*
transmit *v* sgaoil; (*broadcast*)

craobh-sgaoil, craol
transmitter *n* uidheam-sgaoilidh *m*; (*mast*) crann-sgaoilidh *m*
transparency *n* trìd-shoilleireachd *f*; (*met*) follaiseachd *f*
transparent *a* trìd-shoilleir; (*met*) follaiseach
transpire *v* thig am follais; (*happen*) tachair
transplant *n* ath-chur *m* **liver t.** ath-chur air grùthan *v* ath-chuir
transport *n* giùlan *m*, còmhdhail *f* **T. Dept** Roinn na Còmhdhail *v* giùlain, iomchair
transpose *v* atharraich òrdugh; (*mus*) cuir an gleus eile
transverse *a* tarsainn, trasta
trap *n* ribe *f* *v* rib, glac
trash *n* sgudal *m*, smodal *m*
travel *n* siubhal *m*, taisteal *m* **t. agency** buidheann-siubhail *f m* **t. centre** ionad siubhail *m* *v* siubhail
traveller *n* neach-siubhail *m*, taistealaiche *m*
travelling *n* siubhal *m* *a* siùbhlach **t.-people** luchd-siubhail *m pl*
traverse *v* triall, rach tarsainn
trawl *n* lìon-sguabaidh *f* *v* sgrìob, tràl(aig); (*search*) dèan sireadh farsaing
trawler *n* tràlair *m*, bàta-sgrìobaidh *m*
tray *n* treidhe *m*, sgàl *m*
treacherous *a* cealgach, foilleil; (*dangerous*) cunnartach
treachery *n* cealg/ceilg *f*, foill *f*
treacle *n* trèicil *m*
tread *v* saltair
treason *n* brathadh *m*, feall *f*
treasure *n* ionmhas *m*, ulaidh *f* *v* cuir luach mòr air **he treasured her** bha meas a chridhe aige oirre
treasurer *n* ionmhasair *m*
treat *n* treat *f*, sòlas *m*; (*event*) cuirm *f* *v* thoir aoigheachd do; (*deal with*) dèilig ri, làimhsich; (*med*) thoir aire do **t. someone to ...** seas do làmh
treatment *n* làimhseachadh *m*, giullachd *f*
treaty *n* cùmhnant *m*, còrdadh *m*, cunnradh *m*
treble *a* trì-fillte; (*of voice*) àrd
tree *n* craobh *f*
trefoil *n* trì-bhileach *m*
tremble *v* criothnaich, bi air chrith
trembling *a* critheanach
tremendous *a* àibheiseach, sgoinneil **a t. loss** call cianail *m* **a t. help** cuideachadh mòr *m*
tremor *n* crith *f*
tremulous *a* critheanach; (*anxious*) iomagaineach
trench *n* clais *f*; (*in war*) trainnse *f*
trenchant *a* geur, cumhachdach
trend *n* claonadh *m*, gluasad *m*
trepidation *n* geilt *f*; (*phys*) crith-eagail *f*
trespass *v* rach thar chrìochan; (*sin*) peacaich
trial *n* deuchainn *f*, dearbhadh *m*; (*leg*) cùirt *f*
triangle *n* triantan *m* **equilateral t.** triantan ionann-thaobhach **isosceles t.** triantan co-chasach
triangular *a* triantanach
tribe *n* treubh *f*, sliochd *m*
tribulation *n* trioblaid *f*, àmhghar *f m*
tribunal *n* tribiùnal *m*
tribute *n* moladh *m*; (*payment*) càin *f*
trick *n* car *m*, cleas *m* *v* thoir an car à/às, meall
trickle *n* beag-shileadh *m*, beag-shruth *m* *v* sil, sruth
tricycle *n* trì-rothach *m*, traidhsagal *m*
trifle *n* faoineas *m*, rud beag *m*; (*sweet*) mìlsean-measgaichte *m*, traidhfeal *m*
trifling *a* beag, suarach
trigger *n* iarann-leigidh *m*
trim *a* sgiobalta, cuimir, grinn *v* geàrr, lomaich; (*decorate*) snasaich
Trinity *n* Trianaid *f* **T. College** Colaiste na Trianaid *f*
trinket *n* faoin-sheud *m*
trio *n* triùir *f m*; (*mus*) ceòl-triùir *m*
trip *n* turas *m*, cuairt *f*, sgrìob *f*; (*stumble*) tuisleadh *m* *v* tuislich

triple *a* trì-fillte *v* trìoblaich
triplets *n* triùir *f m*
tripod *n* trì-chasach *m*
trite *a* beag seagh
triumph *n* buaidh *f*; (*exultation*) buaidh-chaithream *m* *v* thoir buaidh, buadhaich
triumphant *a* (*victorious*) buadhmhor; (*exultant*) caithreamach
trivial *a* suarach, gun fhiù
trolley *n* troilidh *f*
trombone *n* trombòn *m*
troop *n* buidheann *f m*, cuideachd *f*, trùp *m* **t. of horses** greigh each *f* *v* triall
trophy *n* cuach buaidhe *f*
tropic *n* tropaig *f* **the Tropics** na Tropaigean *f pl*
tropical *a* tropaigeach
trot *v* dèan trotan, trot
trouble *n* dragh *m*, saothair *f*; (*dispute*) trioblaid *f*, buaireas *m* *v* cuir dragh air, buair
troublemaker *n* buaireadair *m*, neach-buairidh *m*
troublesome *a* draghail; (*causing trouble*) buaireasach
trough *n* amar *m*
trounce *v* liodraig
trousers *n* briogais *f*
trout *n* breac *m* **sea t.** bànag *f*
trowel *n* sgreadhail *f*
truancy *n* seachnadh-sgoile *m*
truant *n* seachnaiche(-sgoile) *m*
truce *n* fosadh (còmhraig) *m*
truck *n* truga *f* **have no t. with** na gabh gnothach ri
truculent *a* ceacharra
trudge *v* ceumnaich gu trom
true *a* fìor, fìrinneach; (*faithful*) dìleas; (*right*) ceart **a t. understanding** fìor thuigse
truly *adv* gu fìrinneach, gu dearbh, gu deimhinn(e) **yours t.** le dùrachd
trumpet *n* trombaid *f*
truncate *v* giorraich
truncheon *n* plocan *m*
trunk *n* stoc *m*, bun-craoibhe *m*; (*for storage*) ciste *f*; (*of animal*) sròn *f*, gnos *m*; (*anat*) com *m* **t. road** prìomh-rathad *m*
trust *n* earbsa *f*, creideas *m*; (*company*) urras *m* **the National T.** an t-Urras Nàiseanta *v* earb à, cuir muinighin an, thoir creideas do
trustee *n* urrasair *m*
trusting *a* earbsail
trustworthy *a* earbsach
truth *n* fìrinn *f* **in t.** gu fìrinneach **to tell the t.** a dh'innse na fìrinn
try *v* feuch
trying *a* deuchainneach
tryst *n* dàil *f*, coinneamh *f*; (*place*) àite-coinneachaidh *m*
tub *n* tuba *f m*, ballan *m*
tube *n* pìoban *m*, feadan *m*, tiùb *f*
tuberculosis *n* a' chaitheamh *f*
tuck *v* trus
Tuesday *n* Dimàirt *m*
tuft *n* dos *m*, topan *m*
tug *n* tarraing *f*, draghadh *m*; (*naut*) tuga *f* *v* tarraing, dragh, spìon
tuition *n* teagasg *m*, oideachadh *m*, ionnsachadh *m*
tulip *n* tiuilip *f*
tumble *n* tuiteam *m* **t. dryer** *n* car-thiormaichear *m* *v* tuit
tummy *n* brù *f*
tumour *n* at *m*, màm *m*, meall *m*
tumult *n* iorghail *f*, onghail *f*
tumultuous *a* iorghaileach, onghaileach
tune *n* fonn *m*, port *m* *v* gleus, cuir air ghleus
tuneful *a* ceòlmhor, fonnmhor
tuner *n* neach-gleusaidh *m*
tunnel *n* tunail *f m*
tup *n* reithe *m*, rùda *m*
turbine *n* roth-uidheam *f*
turbot *n* turbaid *f*
turbulence *n* buaireas *m*, luaisgeachd *f*
turbulent *a* buaireasach, luaisgeach
turf *n* (*ground*) bàrr-talmhainn *m*; (*a sod*) sgrath *f*, fò(i)d *f*
turgid *a* air at; (*style*) trom, iom-fhaclach
Turk *n* Turcach *m*, (*female*) ban-T(h)urcach *f*
turkey *n* eun-Frangach *m*, cearc

Fhrangach *f*
Turkish *a* Turcach; (*lang*) Turcais *f*
turmoil *n* troimh-a-chèile *f m* ùpraid *f*
turn *n* tionndadh *m*, car *m*, lùb *f*; (*in sequence*) cuairt *f* **she took a t.** thàinig cuairt oirre *v* tionndaidh, cuir mun cuairt
turnip *n* tui(r)neap *m*, snèap *f*
turnout *n* na nochd
turnover *n* luach na malairt *m*; (*of staff etc*) atharrachadh *m*
turquoise *a* tuirc-ghorm
turret *n* turaid *f*
turtle *n* turtar *f*
tusk *n* starr-fhiacail *f*, tosg *m*
tussle *n* tuasaid *f*, strì *f*
tut! *interj* t(h)ud!
tutor *n* oide *m*
tutorial *n* tràth-oideachaidh *m*
twang *n* gliong *m*; (*lang*) blas *m*
tweak *v* cuir car de; (*met*) dèan atharrachadh beag air
tweed *n* clò (mòr) *m* **Harris T.** an Clò Mòr/Hearach *m*
tweezers *n* greimiche *m*
twelfth *a* dara ... deug
twelve *n* a dhà-dheug *a* dà ... dheug **t. disciples** dà dheisciobal dheug *m*
twentieth *a* ficheadamh
twenty *n*, *a* fichead *m*
twice *adv* dà uair, dà thuras
twig *n* faillean *m*, slat *f*
twilight *n* eadar-sholas *m*, camhanaich *f*, ciaradh *m*
twin *n* leth-aon *m* *pl* leth-aonan, càraid *f*
twine *v* toinn
twinge *n* biorgadh *m*
twinkle/twinkling *n* priobadh *m*; (*in eye*) drithleann *m* **in the t. of an eye** ann am priobadh na sùla *v* priob
twirl *n* roithleagan *m*; (*act*) ruidhleadh *m* *v* ruidhil mun cuairt
twist *n* toinneamh *m*, car *m*, snìomh *m* *v* toinn; (*story*) cuir car an; (*ankle*) cuir snìomh an
twisted *a* snìomhte, toinnte; (*nature*) coirbte
twit *n* amadan *m*, gloidhc *f*
twitch *n* spadhadh *m*, strangadh *m*
twitter *v* ceilearaich
two *n* a dhà *a* dà **two people** dithis *f* **two-dimensional** dà-sheallach **two-faced** dà-aodannach, leam-leat **two-fold** dà-fhillte, dùbailte **two-ply** dà-dhualach
tycoon *n* toicear *m*, saidhbhriche *m*
type *n* seòrsa *m*; (*typ*) clò *m* *v* clò-sgrìobh, taidhp
typhoid *n* am fiabhras breac *m*
typhus *n* am fiabhras ballach *m*
typical *a* coltach, dualach **that's t. of him** tha sin cho coltach ris
typify *v* riochdaich, bi na (h-) *etc* eisimpleir dc
typing *n* clò-sgrìobhadh *m*
typographical *a* clò-bhualaidh **t. error** mearachd clò-bhualaidh *f*
tyrannical *a* aintighearnail
tyrannize *v* dèan ainneart air
tyranny *n* aintighearnas *m*
tyrant *n* aintighearna *m*
tyre *n* tàidhr *f*, taidhear *f*

U

ubiquitous *a* sa h-uile h-àite, uile-làthaireach
ugly *a* grànda
Uist person *n* Uibhisteach *m*, (*female*) ban-Uibhisteach *f*
ulcer *n* neasgaid *f*
ulterior *a* ìochdarach; (*met*) neo-fhollaiseach
ultimate *a* deireannach, mu dheireadh
ultimatum *n* rabhadh deireannach *m*
ultra *a* ro, sàr-, fìor, buileach
umbrage *n* oilbheum *m*
umbrella *n* sgàilean *m*
umpire *n* rèitire *m*, britheamh *m*
unable *a* eu-comasach **u. to** gun chomas
unacceptable *a* ... ris nach fhaodar gabhail
unaccompanied *a* na (h-)aonar *etc*; (*mus*) gun taic-ciùil
unaccustomed *a* neo-chleachdte (ri)

unadulterated *a* neo-thruaillte
unaided *a*, *adv* gun chuideachadh
unambiguous *a* (*lit*) aon-seaghach; (*met*) gun cheist
unanimous *a* aon-ghuthach, a dh'aon inntinn
unanimously *adv* gu h-aon-ghuthach
unappetizing *a* neo-bhlasta, mì-chàilear
unarmed *a* gun armachd, neo-armaichte
unassuming *a* iriosal
unattainable *a* do-ruighinn, thar ruigse
unattended *a* gun neach na c(h)ois *etc*
unauthorized *a* gun ùghdarras, neo-cheadaichte
unavailing *a* gun tairbhe
unavoidable *a* do-sheachanta
unaware *a* gun fhios/mhothachadh
unbalanced *a* mì-chothromach
unbearable *a* do-fhulang
unbeatable *a* nach gabh beatadh
unbecoming *a* mì-chneasta
unbelief *n* eas-creideamh *m*
unbiased *a* gun chlaonadh
unborn *a* gun bhreith
unbreakable *a* nach gabh bris(t)eadh
unbroken *a* gun bhris(t)eadh
unbutton *v* fuasgail
unceasing *a* gun sgur/stad/abhsadh
uncertain *a* mì-chinnteach
uncertainty *n* mì-chinnt *f*
unchanging *a* neo-chaochlaideach
uncivil *a* gun mhodh
uncivilized *a* neo-shìobhalta, borbarra
uncle *n* bràthair-athar/màthar *m*, uncail *m*
unclean *a* neòghlan
uncombed *a* gun chìreadh
uncomfortable *a* mì-chofhurtail
uncommon *a* neo-àbhaisteach, neo-chumanta
uncomplaining *a* neo-ghearaineach
unconcerned *a* gun chùram, gun dragh
unconditional *a* gun chùmhnantan/chumhachan
unconfirmed *a* gun daingneachadh
unconnected *a* gun cheangal, neo-cheangailte
unconscious *a* gun mhothachadh/fhaireachadh
unconstitutional *a* neo-reachdail
uncontested *a* gun fharpais
uncontrollable *a* thar smachd(achaidh)
uncooked *a* amh, gun chòcaireachd
uncouth *a* neo-ghrinn, amh
uncover *v* rùisg; (*met*) thoir gu follais
undecided *a* mì-chinnteach
undeniable *a* do-àicheadh
under *prep* fo *adv* fodha **it went u.** chaidh e/i fodha
undercurrent *n* fo-shruth *m*; (*met*) faireachdainn *f m*
undercut *v* cuir air prìs nas ìsle
underestimate *v* meas fo luach
undergo *v* rach/theirig tro, fuiling
underground *a* fo thalamh **u. train** trèan(a) fo thalamh *f*
underhand *a* cealgach, clìceach
underline *v* (*lit*) cuir sgrìob/loidhne fo; (*met*) comharraich, dearbh
undermine *v* (*lit*) cladhaich fo; (*met*) lagaich
underneath *prep* fo *adv* shìos, gu h-ìosal/ìseal
underpass *n* bealach fo thalamh *m*
underskirt *n* cota-bàn *m*
underspend *n* caiteachas fon t-sùim shuidhichte *m* *v* caith fon t-sùim shuidhichte
understand *v* tuig
understanding *n* tuigse *f*, breithneachadh *m*; (*accord*) còrdadh *m*
understanding *a* tuigseach
undertake *v* gabh os làimh
undertaker *n* neach-adhlacaidh *m*, adhlaicear *m*
undertaking *n* gnothach *m*, iomairt *f*
underway *a* fo sheòl, ga c(h)ur an

gnìomh
underwear *n* fo-aodach *m*
undeserved *a* neo-thoillte
undisputed *a* gun chonnspaid, gun cheist, dearbhte
undo *v* fuasgail; (*unpick*) sgaoil; (*abstr*) mill
undoubtedly *adv* gun teagamh
undress *v* cuir/thoir aodach dheth, dhith *etc* **I undressed** chuir mi dhìom (m' aodach)
undue *a* neo-dhligheach; (*excessive*) cus
uneasy *a* mì-shaorsainneil
uneconomic *a* neo-eaconamach
uneducated *a* neo-fhoghlaim(ich)te, gun fhoghlam
unemployed *a* gun obair
unemployment *n* cion cosnaidh *m*, dìth obrach *f m* **u. benefit** sochair cion cosnaidh *f*
unequal *a* neo-ionann
uneven *a* mì-chothrom, mì-chòmhnard
unexpectedly *adv* gun dùil ris/rithe *etc*
unfair *a* mì-cheart, mì-chothromach
unfaithful *a* mì-dhìleas, neo-dhìleas
unfamiliar *a* coimheach **u. surroundings** àite far nach eil/robh mi *etc* eòlach
unfashionable *a* neo-fhasanta
unfasten *v* fuasgail
unfavourable *a* neo-fhàbharach
unfinished *a* neo-chrìochnaichte, gun chrìochnachadh
unfit *a* (*phys*) gun spionnadh; (*unsuitable*) mì-fhreagarrach, neo-iomchaidh; (*unworthy*) neo-airidh
unforeseen *a* gun dùil ris/rithe *etc*
unfortunate *a* mì-fhortanach, mì-shealbhach
unfortunately *adv* gu mì-fhortanach, gu mì-shealbhach
unfriendly *a* neo-chàirdeil, fad' às
ungainly *a* liobasta, cliobach, spàgach
ungodly *a* ain-diadhaidh
ungrateful *a* mì-thaingeil
unhappy *a* mì-thoilichte, mì-shona
unhealthy *a* mì-fhallain
unholy *a* mì-naomh(a); (*met*) mì-chneasta
uniform *n* èideadh *m*, deise dreuchd *f* **firefighter's u.** èideadh smàladair *m* *a* aon-fhillte; (*consistent*) cunbhalach
unify *v* co-aonaich
unilateral *a* aon-taobhach
unimportant *a* neo-chudromach **that is u.** chan fhiach sin bruidhinn air
uninformed *a* aineolach, gun eòlas
uninspired *a* neo-thogarrach, marbhanta
unintentionally *adv* gun fhiosta, gun a bhith an rùn
uninterested *a* gun ùidh
uninvited *a* gun chuireadh/fhiathachadh
union *n* aonadh *m* **trade u.** aonadh luchd-ciùird
unique *a* gun choimeas, air leth **it was u.** cha robh a leithid ann
unison *a* aon-ghuthach
unit *n* aonad *m*
unite *v* aonaich
united *a* aonaichte **the U. Kingdom** an Rìoghachd Aonaichte *f* **the U. States** na Stàitean Aonaichte *f pl* **the U. Nations** na Dùthchannan Aonaichte *f pl*
unity *n* aonachd *f*
universal *a* uile-choitcheann, coitcheann
universe *n* cruinne *m* (*f in gen*), cruinne-cè *m* (*f in gen*), domhan *m*
university *n* oilthigh *m*
unjust *a* mì-cheart
unkind *a* mosach, gun choibhneas
unknown *a* neo-aithnichte
unlawful *a* mì-laghail
unleaded *a* gun luaidhe (ann/innte) **u. petrol** peatrail gun luaidhe *m*
unless *conj* mur(a), nas lugha na
unlicensed *a* gun cheadachd
unlike *a* ao-coltach (ri)
unlikely *a* mì-choltach

unlimited *a* gun chrìoch, neo-chrìochnach
unload *v* thoir an luchd de
unlock *v* fosgail (glas)
unlucky *a* mì-shealbhach
unmarried *a* gun phòsadh
unmistakable *a* do-àicheanta
unnatural *a* mì-nàdarra(ch)
unnecessary *a* neo-riatanach, gun fheum air
unobtainable *a* nach gabh faighinn, do-ruighinn
unobtrusive *a* neo-fhollaiseach/nochdte
unoccupied *a* falamh, bàn
unofficial *a* neo-oifigeil
unorthodox *a* neo-ghnàthach
unpack *v* falmhaich, thoir às
unpaid *a* gun phàigheadh/tuarastal
unpalatable *a* mì-bhlasta/chàilear
unpardonable *a* nach fhaodar a mhathadh
unplayable *a* nach gabh cluich(e), do-chluiche
unpleasant *a* mì-thlachdmhor
unpopular *a* gun mheas air/oirre *etc*
unprecedented *a* gun choimeas, nach do thachair roimhe
unprepared *a* mì-dheiseil, neo-ullaichte
unproductive *a* gun tairbhe, neo-thorrach, neo-tharbhach
unprofessional *a* mì-phroifeiseanta
unprofitable *a* gun bhuannachd, neo-phrothaideach
unprotected *a* gun dìon
unqualified *a* gun teisteanas; (*total*) iomlan, fìor
unquestionably *adv* gun cheist
unravel *v* (*trans*) rèitich; (*intrans*) sgaoil
unreal *a* neo-fhìor
unrealistic *a* neo-phractaigeach
unreasonable *a* mì-reusanta
unrelated *a* gun bhuntainneas/cheangal
unreliable *a* neo-earbsach
unrest *n* an-fhois *f*; (*civil*) buaireadh *m*
unrestricted *a* gun bhacadh/chuing
unripe *a* an-abaich
unrivalled *a* gun choimeas, gun samhail
unruly *a* mì-rianail, tuasaideach; (*of children*) luathaireach
unsafe *a* mi-shàbhailte, cunnartach
unsatisfactory *a* neo-iomchaidh **I found it u.** cha robh mi riaraichte leis
unsavoury *a* (*taste*) mì-bhlasta; (*met*) mì-chneasta
unseemly *a* mì-chiatach
unselfish *a* neo-fhèineil
unsettled *a* neo-shuidhichte, mì-sheatlaigte
unsightly *a* grànda, mì-mhaiseach
unsophisticated *a* sìmplidh
unspecified *a* neo-ainmichte
unspoiled *a* gun mhilleadh
unstable *a* cugallach, neo-sheasmhach
unsteady *a* cugallach, mì-chothromach
unsuccessful *a* neo-shoirbheachail
unsuitable *a* mì-fhreagarrach
unsuspecting *a* gun amharas
unsympathetic *a* neo-fhaireachail, neo-thruasail, gun cho-fhaireachdainn
untested *a* gun dearbhadh/fheuchainn
unthinkable *a* nach gabh smaoineachadh (air)
untidy *a* mì-sgiobalta
untie *v* fuasgail
until *prep* gu *conj* gus **u. she returns** gus an till i
unto *prep* gu, do, chun (+ *gen*)
untrue *a* neo-fhìrinneach, fìor (*preceded by neg v*) **that's quite u.** chan eil sin idir fìor
untruth *n* breug *f*
untruthful *a* neo-fhìrinneach, neo-fhìor
unusual *a* neo-àbhaisteach, annasach
unused *a* gun chleachdadh, nach deach a chleachdadh
unveil *v* leig ris, taisbean

unwanted *a* gun iarraidh
unwarranted *a* gun adhbhar cothromach
unwell *a* tinn, bochd, meadhanach
unwieldy *a* doirbh a ghiùlain, lòdail, liobasta
unwilling *a* ain-deònach, mì-dheònach
unwind *v* thoir às an toinneamh, fuasgail; (*relax*) gabh fois
unwise *a* neo-ghlic, gòrach
unworthy *a* (*person*) neo-airidh; (*motive*) suarach
unwrap *v* thoir còmhdach de
up *prep* suas *adv* shuas **up the hill** suas an cnoc **were you up?** an robh thu shuas? **we were up until 2 o'clock** bha sinn an-àird(e) gu dà uair
upbringing *n* togail *f*, àrach *m*
update *n* cunntas às ùr *m* *v* ùraich, clàraich às ùr, thoir cunntas as ùr do
uphold *v* glèidh, thoir taic do, cùm suas
uplift *v* (*phys*) tog (suas); (*mental*) tog inntinn/meanmna
uplifting *a* brosnachail, a thogas meanmna
upon *prep* air, air muin (+ *gen*), air uachdar (+ *gen*)
upper *a* shuas, uachdrach
upright *a* dìreach; (*met*) dìreach, treibhdhireach, ceart
uproar *n* ùpraid *f*
uproot *v* spìon on fhreumh/bhun
upset *n* troimh-a-chèile *f m*, bun-os-cionn *m* *v* cuir troimh-a-chèile/bun-os-cionn
upshot *n* bun a bh' ann *m*, buil *f*
upside-down *adv* bun-os-cionn, a c(h)asan os a c(h)ionn *etc*
upstairs *a, adv* shuas an staidhre *adv* shuas an staidhre **going u.** a' dol suas an staidhre
up-to-date *a* an là an-diugh **u. fashions** fasain an là an-diugh
upwards *adv* suas
urban *a* baile
urbane *a* furm(h)ailteach
urge *n* miann *f m* *v* brosnaich, spàrr, cuir ìmpidh air
urgency *n* deatamachd *f*, èiginneachd/èigeannachd *f*, cabhag *f*
urgent *a* èiginneach/èigeannach
urgently *adv* gu cabhagach, na (h-)èiginn *etc*
urine *n* mùn *m*
us *pron* sinn, *emph* sinne
usage *n* cleachdadh *m*, gnàths *m*
use *n* cleachdadh *m*, ùisneachadh *m*; (*usefulness*) feum *m* **what use is it?** dè am feum a th' ann? *v* cleachd, cuir gu feum, cuir an sàs, ùisnich
useful *a* feumail, gu feum
useless *a* gun fheum
user *n* neach-cleachdaidh *m*
usher *n* treòraiche *m* *v* treòraich a-steach
usual *a* àbhaisteach **as u.** mar as àbhaist, (*past tense*) mar a b' àbhaist
usually *adv* gu h-àbhaisteach, mar as/(a) bu trice
usurp *v* gabh/glèidh gun chòir
utensil *n* soitheach *f m*, uidheam *f*, inneal *m*
uterus *n* machlag *f*
utility *n* goireas *m*, feum *m*
utilize *v* cleachd, cuir gu feum, cuir an sàs, ùisnich
utmost *a* as fhaide a-mach **I will do my u.** nì mi m' uile dhìcheall
utter *v* abair, can, labhair
utterly *adv* gu tur, uile-gu-lèir
U-turn *n* làn-char *m*, tur-atharrachadh *m*

V

vacancy *n* àite bàn/falamh *m*, beàrn *f m*
vacant *a* falamh, bàn, fàs
vacate *v* falmhaich, fàg
vacation *n* saor-làithean *m pl*, làithean-saora *m pl*
vaccination *n* banachdach *f*
vaccinate *v* thoir banachdach do
vacillate *v* bi eadar dhà bharail, bi sa bhonnalaich
vacuous *a* falamh, baoth
vacuum *n* falamhachd *f*

vacuum-cleaner *n* glanadair-sùghaidh *m*
vagina *n* faighean *m*
vagrant *n* siùbhlach *m*, faondrach *m*
vague *a* neo-shoilleir
vain *a* (*futile*) dìomhain, faoin; (*proud*) mòr às/aiste *etc* fhèin
valiant *a* calma, treubhach, foghainteach
valid *a* dligheach; (*of time*) a' seasamh
validate *v* dearbh
valley *n* gleann *m*; (*wide, with river*) srath *m*
valour *n* gaisge *f*
valuable *a* luachmhor, prìseil
valuation *n* meas *m*, luachadh *m*
value *n* luach *m*, fiach *m* *v* meas, cuir luach air, luach
valve *n* còmhla *f*, bhalbh *f m*
van *n* bhan(a) *f*; (*front*) toiseach *m*, tùs *m*
vandal *n* milltear *m*, sgriosadair *m*
vandalism *n* milleadh *m*, sgriosadh *m*
vanish *v* rach às an t-sealladh
vanity *a* dìomhanas *m*, faoineas *m*
vapour *n* deatach *f*, smùid *f*
variable *a* caochlaideach *n* caochladair *m*
variant *n* riochd eile *m*
variation *n* atharrachadh *m*, caochladh *m*; (*mus*) tionndadh *m*
varicose veins *n* fèithean borrach *f pl*
varied *a* eadar-dhealaichte
variety *n* (*mixture*) measgachadh *m*, caochladh *m*; (*kind*) seòrsa *m*, gnè *f*
various *a* iomadh, iomadach, eug-samhail
varnish *n* falaid *m*, bhàrnais *f* *v* cuir falaid/bhàrnais air, falaidich
vary *v* atharraich, caochail
vase *n* bhàs(a) *f*
vaseline *n* bhasailin *m*
vast *a* ro mhòr, àibheiseach
vault *n* (*cellar*) seilear *m*; (*tomb*) tuam *m*
vault *v* leum thairis air, geàrr sùrdag
veal *n* feòil-laoigh *f*
veer *v* gabh fiaradh, tionndaidh
vegetable(s) *n* glasraich *f*
vegetarian *n* glasraichear *m*, feòil-sheachnair *m*
vegetation *n* fàs-bheatha *f*
vehemence *n* dèineas *m*
vehement *a* dian, dealasach
vehicle *n* carbad *m*; (*means*) seòl *m*
veil *n* (*on person*) sgàile *f*, brat-gnùise *m* *v* còmhdaich, ceil, cuir fo sgàil
vein *n* cuisle *f*, fèith-fala *f* **in that v.** air a' mhodh sin
velvet *n* meileabhaid *f*
veneer *n* snas-chraiceann *m*; (*met*) còmhdach uachdair *m*, sgeadachadh *m*
venerate *v* thoir mòr-spèis do
venereal *a* muineil **v. disease** a' bhreac Fhrangach *f*
vengeance *n* dìoghaltas *m*
venison *n* sitheann(-fèidh) *f m*
venom *n* nimh *m*, puinnsean *m*
venomous *a* nimheil
vent *n* fosgladh *m*, luidhear *m* *v* leig a-mach, leig ruith le
ventilate *v* fionnaraich, èadhraig
ventilation *n* fionnarachadh *m*, èadhraigeadh *m*
venture *n* iomairt *f*, oidhirp *f* *v* meantraig
venue *n* àite *m*, ionad *m*
Venus *n* Bheunas *f*
verb *n* gnìomhair *m*
verbatim *adv* facal air an fhacal
verbose *a* briathrach, ro bhriathrach, cabach
verdant *a* gorm, feurach
verdict *n* breith *f*
verge *n* oir *f m*; (*of road*) fàl *m* **on the v. of ...** an impis ... (+ *vn*)
verify *v* dearbh, fìrinnich, dèan cinnteach
veritable *a* fìor, cinnteach
vermin *n* (*lice*) mialan *f pl*; (*rodents*) criomairean *m pl*
versatile *a* iol-chomasach, làmhcharach
verse *n* rann *m*, earrann *f*;

(*poetry*) bàrdachd *f*
version *n* (*draft*) dreach *m*; (*of events*) cunntas *f m*; (*alternative*) tionndadh *m*
versus *prep* an aghaidh (+ *gen*)
vertebrae *n* cnàmhan an droma *m pl*
vertebrate *n* druim-altach(an) *m*
vertical *a* dìreach
vertigo *n* tuaineal *m*, tuainealaich *f*
very *a* fìor (+ *len*), anabarrach; (*same*) ceart, dearbh (*both* + *len*) *adv* glè, fìor, ro (*all* + *len*)
vessel *n* soitheach *f m* **blood v.** balg fala *m*
vest *n* fo-lèine *f*; (*waistcoat*) siosacot *m*
vestibule *n* for-dhoras *m*
vestige *n* lorg *f*, comharra *m*
vet *n* lighiche-sprèidh *m*, bheat *m*
vet *v* sgrùd, breithnich
veteran *n* seann eòlach *m*; (*soldier*) seann saighdear *m* *a* seann, sean, eòlach
veto *n* crosadh *m*, bacadh *m*, bhèato *m* *v* cros, bac, dèan bhèato air
vex *v* leamhaich, buair, sàraich
vexation *n* leamhachas *m*, buaireadh *m*, sàrachadh *m*
via *prep* taobh (+ *gen*), tro
viability *n* comas obrachaidh *m*
viable *a* a ghabhas obrachadh
vial *n* searrag ghlainne *f*, meanbh-bhotal *m*
vibrate *v* crith, cuir air chrith, triob(h)uail
vibration *n* crith *f*, triob(h)ualadh *m*
vicar *n* piocair *m*, biocair *m*
vice *n* dubhailc *f*; (*tool*) bithis *f*, teanchair *m*
vice- *pref* iar-, leas- **vice-president** iar-cheann-suidhe *m* **vice-versa** *adv* agus a chaochladh
vicinity *n* àrainn *f*, nàbachas *m*
vicious *a* guineach, garg
victim *n* fulangaiche *m*, neach a dh'fhuiling(eas) *m*
victorious *a* buadhach, buadhmhor
victory *n* buaidh *f*
video *n* bhidio *f* **videotape** teip bhidio *f* **v. conference** co-labhairt bhidio *f*
vie *v* strì (ri)
view *n* sealladh *m*; (*opinion*) beachd *m* *v* seall air, faic
viewer *n* neach-amhairc/coimhid *m*
viewpoint *n* àite-seallaidh/ amhairc/coimhid *m*; (*opinion*) beachd *m*
vigil *n* faire *f* **keeping a v.** ri faire
vigilant *a* furachail
vigorous *a* sgairteil, calma
vigour *n* spionnadh *m*, sgairt *f*, treòir *f*
vile *a* gràineil, sgreataidh
vilify *v* màb, dubh-chàin
villa *n* taigh mòr *m*, taigh air leth *m*
village *n* baile beag *m*, clachan *m*
villain *n* slaightear *m*, eucorach *m*; (*liter*) droch fhear *m*
vindicate *v* dearbh; (*justify*) fìreanaich
vindictive *a* dìoghaltach
vine *n* fìonan *f m*, crann-fìona *m* **vineyard** fìon-lios *m*
vinegar *n* fìon geur *m*
violate *v* mill, bris(t)
violation *n* milleadh *m*, bris(t)eadh *m*; (*of person*) èigneachadh *m*
violence *n* fòirneart *m*, ainneart *m*
violent *a* fòirneartach, ainneartach **v. storm** gailleann *f*, doinnean *f* **he has a v. temper** tha leum eagalach na nàdar
violet *n* sail/dail-chuach *f*, bròg na cuthaige *f*
violin *n* fidheall *f*
violinist *n* fìdhlear *m*
viper *n* nathair-nimhe *f*
virgin *n* òigh *f*, maighdeann *f*
virginity *n* òigheachd *f*, maighdeannas *m*
virile *n* fearail, duineil
virtual *a* mas fhìor **v. reality** mas-fhìorachd *f*
virtually *adv* an impis (+ *vn*) **it's v. finished** cha mhòr nach eil e ullamh

virtue *n* subhailc *f*, deagh-bheus *f*, feart *m*
virtuous *a* subhailceach, beusach
virulent *a* nimhneach, geur
virus *n* bhìoras *m*
visa *n* bhìosa *f*
visage *n* aghaidh *f*, gnùis *f*
vis-à-vis *prep* a thaobh (+ *gen*); (*opposite*) aghaidh ri aghaidh
visibility *n* faicsinneachd *f*
visible *a* faicsinneach
vision *n* (*sight*) fradharc *m*, lèirsinn *f*; (*insight*) sealladh *m*, lèirsinn *f*; (*dream*) bruadar *m*, aisling *f*
visionary *n* neach le lèirsinn *m* *a* lèirsinneach
visit *n* tadhal *m*, cèilidh *f m* *v* tadhail, dèan cèilidh
visitor *n* neach-tadhail *m*, aoigh *m*, cèiliche *m*
visor *n* cidhis *f*
vista *n* sealladh *m*
visual *a* fradharcach, lèirsinne
visualize *v* dèan samhla sùla, dèan dealbh san inntinn
vital *a* beò, beathail; (*important*) ro chudromach
vitality *n* beathalachd *f*
vitamin *n* beothaman *m*
vitriol *n* (*acid*) searbhag loisgeach *f*; (*rancour*) nimhealachd *f*
vituperation *n* aithiseachadh *m*
vivacious *a* aigeannach, beothail
vivid *a* beò, boillsgeanta
vixen *n* sionnach boireann *m*
viz *adv* is e sin, 's e sin ri ràdh
vocabulary *n* (*of person*) stòr fhaclan *m*, (*glossary*) faclair *m*
vocal *a* guthach; (*outspoken*) àrd-ghuthach
vocation *n* (*work*) dreuchd *f*, ceàird *f*; (*calling*) gairm beatha *f*
vocative *a* gairmeach **v. case** an tuiseal gairmeach *m*
vociferous *a* sgairteach
vodka *n* bhodca *m*
vogue *n* fasan *m* **in v.** san fhasan
voice *n* guth *m* *v* cuir am briathran/an cèill
void *n* fàsalachd *f*; (*outer space*) fànas *a* falamh, fàs
volatile *a* cugallach, caochlaideach, luaineach
volcano *n* beinn-theine *f*, b(h)olcàno *m*
volition *n* toil *f*
volley *n* (*of gun*) làdach *m*; (*sport*) bhòilidh *f*
volleyball *n* ball-làmhaich *m*
volt *n* bholt(a) *m*
voltage *n* bholtaids *f*, bholtachd *f*
voluble *a* sruth-chainnteach
volume *n* (*book*) leabhar *m*; (*capacity*) tomhas-lìonaidh *m*; (*size*) tomad *m*
voluntary *a* saor-thoileach **v. organization** buidheann s(h)aor-thoileach *f m*
volunteer *n* saor-thoileach *m* *v* tairg
voluptuous *a* (*shape*) làn-chumadail
vomit(ing) *n* cur a-mach *m*, sgeith *m*, dìobhairt *m* *v* cuir a-mach, sgeith, dìobhair
voracious *a* cìocrach, gionach, craosach
vote *n* bhòt(a) *f* **postal v.** bhòt(a) tron phost *v* bhòt
voter *n* neach-bhòtaidh *m*, bhòtair *m*
voting *n* bhòtadh *m* **v. system** siostam/modh bhòtaidh *m*
vouch *v* dearbh, thoir fianais
voucher *n* bileag fianais *f*, bileag-theist *f*
vow *n* bòid *f*, gealladh *m* *v* bòidich, mionnaich
vowel *n* fuaimreag *f*
voyage *n* turas-mara *m*, bhòidse *f*
vulgar *a* mì-chneasta, gràisgeil
vulnerable *a* (*to attack*) fosgailte (gu ionnsaigh); (*person*) so-leònte, dualach a g(h)oirteachadh *etc*
vulture *n* fang *f*

W

wade *v* grunnaich
wafer *n* abhlan *m*, slisneag *f*
waffle *n* (*met*) baoth-chòmhradh *m*, cainnt gun bhrìgh *f*
wag *n* àbhachdaiche *m*, sgeigire *m*

wage(s) *n* tuarastal *m*, duais *f*
wager *n* geall *m* *v* cuir geall, rach an urras
wagtail *n* breac-an-t-sìl *m*, breacan-buidhe *m*
wail(ing) *n* caoineadh *m*, gal *m*, burralaich *f*
waist *n* meadhan *m*
waistcoat *n* siosacot *m*, peitean *m*
wait *n* feitheamh *m*, stad *m* **they had a long w.** bha iad fada a' feitheamh *v* fuirich, feith, fan; (*serve*) fritheil
waiting-list *n* liosta-feitheimh *f*
waiting-room *n* seòmar-feitheimh *m*
waiter *n* fear-frithealaidh *m*
waitress *n* tè-fhrithealaidh *f*
waive *v* cuir an dàrna taobh
wake *n* faire *f*, taigh-fhaire *m*
wake(n) *v* dùisg
walk *n* cuairt *f*, ceum *m* *v* coisich, gabh ceum
walking-stick *n* bata *m*
wall *n* balla *m*; (*dyke*) gàrradh *m*
wallet *n* leabhar-pòcaid *m*
wallpaper *n* pàipear(-balla) *m*, bolt *m* *v* pàipearaich, boltaig
walnut *n* gall-chnò *f*
walrus *n* each-mara *m*, uàlras *m*
wand *n* slat *f*, slatag *f*
wander *v* rach air shiubhal; (*go astray*) rach air seachran; (*in mind*) rach iomrall
wanderer *n* siùbhlaiche *m*
wane *v* lùghdaich, crìon, searg
want *n* (*lack*) easbhaidh *f*, dìth *f m*; (*poverty*) bochdainn *f* *v* iarr; (*lack*) bi a dh'easbhaidh (+ *gen*)
wanton *a* drùiseil; (*reckless*) dalma
war *n* cogadh *m* **war memorial** cuimhneachan-cogaidh *m* *v* cog, cathaich
ward *n* (*hospital*) uàrd *m*; (*division*) roinn *f* **w. of court** neach fo chùram (cùrtach) *m*
warden *n* neach-gleidhidh *m*
warder *n* neach-faire *m*
wardrobe *n* preas-aodaich *m*
warehouse *n* taigh-bathair *m*
warfare *n* cogadh *m*
warm *a* blàth; (*personality*) coibhneil *v* blàthaich, gar
warmth *n* blàths *m*; (*personality*) tlàths *m*
warn *v* thoir rabhadh (do)
warning *n* rabhadh *m*
warp *v* claon, seac
warrant(y) *n* barantas *m*
warren *n* broclach *f*, toll *m*
warrior *n* laoch *m*, gaisgeach *m*, curaidh *m*
warship *n* long-chogaidh *f*
wart *n* foinne *f m*
wary *a* faiceallach, cùramach
was *v* bha (*See verb* **to be** *in Grammar*)
wash *n* nighe *m*, glanadh *m*, ionnlad *m* *v* nigh, ionnlaid
washer *n* (*mech*) cearclan *m*
washing *n* nigheadaireachd *f* **w. machine** inneal nigheadaireachd *m* **w.-powder** fùdar nigheadaireachd *m* **w.-up-liquid** stuth-nighe shoithichean *m*
wasp *n* speach *f*, connspeach *f*
waste *n* (*misuse*) ana-caitheamh *m*; (*destruction*) sgrios *m*; (*rubbish*) sgudal *m* **w. of time** cosg tìde/ùine *m* **w.-paper basket** basgaid sgudail *f* *a* fàs *v* dèan mì-fheum de, dèan ana-caitheanaich; (*spoil*) mill
wasteful *a* caithteach, strùidheil
wasteland *n* talamh fàs *m*, àite fàsail *m*
waster *n* strùidhear *m*; (*slang*) duine gun fheum *m*
watch *n* faire *f*, caithris *f*; (*timepiece*) uaireadair *m* *v* cùm sùil air; (*TV etc*) coimhead; (*be careful*) thoir an aire **keep w.** *v* dèan/cùm faire, caithris
watchman *n* neach-faire *m*
water *n* uisge *m*, bùrn *m* **w. level** àird(e) an uisge *f* **w.-lily** duilleag-bhathte *f* **w.-mill** muileann-uisge *f m* **w.-pipe** pìob-uisge *f* *v* uisgich, fliuch
watercress *n* biolaire *f*
waterfall *n* eas *m*
waterproof *a* uisge-dhìonach
watershed *n* (*geog*) druim-uisge *m*; (*met*) àm/adhbhar-tionndaidh *m*

watertight *a* dìonach
waulking *n* luadh *m*, luadhadh *m*
w. song òran-luaidh *m*
wave *n* tonn *m*, stuagh *f*
wave *v* crath **w. (to)** smèid (ri)
waveband *n* bann *m* **Medium Wave** am Bann Meadhain
wavelength *n* bann *m* **on the same w.** air an aon ràmh
wavy *a* (*hair*) dualach
wax *n* cèir *f* *v* cèirich, cuir cèir air; (*grow*) fàs
way *n* (*route*) slighe *f*, rathad *m*; (*method*) dòigh *f* **w. of life** dòigh-beatha *f*
waylay *v* dèan feall-fhalach
wayward *a* claon, fiarach, frithearra
we *pron* sinn, (*emph*) sinne
weak *a* lag, fann, anfhann, lapach
weaken *v* lagaich; (*intrans*) fannaich
weakling *n* lagach *m*, meathach *m*
weakness *n* laigse *f*, anfhannachd *f*
wealth *n* beairteas *m*, saidhbhreas *m*, ionmhas *m*
wealthy *a* beairteach, saidhbhir
wean *v* cuir bhàrr na cìche
weapon *n* ball-airm *m*, inneal-cogaidh *m*
wear *v* (*clothes*) caith, cuir umad/ort **w. out** cosg
weariness *n* sgìths *f m*, claoidh *f*
weary *a* sgìth, claoidhte *v* sgìthich, claoidh, sàraich **w. for** gabh fadachd ri
weasel *n* neas *f*
weather *n* aimsir *f*, sìde *f* **w. forecast** tuairmse sìde *f* **under the w.** gun a bhith ann an sunnd *v* (*met*) seas ri, cùm ri; (*geol*) caith, caoinich
weave *v* figh
weaver *n* breabadair *m*, figheadair *m*
weaving *n* breabadaireachd *f*, figheadaireachd *f*
web *n* lìon *m*, eige *f* **the World-Wide Web** Lìon na Cruinne *m*
website *n* làrach-lìn *f m*
wed *v* pòs
wedder *n* molt *m*
wedding *n* banais *f*, pòsadh *m* **w. day** latha na bainnse *m*
wedge *n* geinn *m* *v* cuir geinn an
Wednesday *n* Diciadain *m*
wee *a* beag
weed *n* luibh *f m* *v* glan, priog
weedkiller *n* puinnsean luibhean *m*
week *n* seachdain *f* **this w. (coming)** an t-s. seo/sa (tighinn) **last w.** an t-s. seo/sa chaidh
weekend *n* deireadh seachdain *m*
weekly *a* gach seachdain, seachdaineach *adv* gach seachdain
weep *v* caoin, guil, dèan caoineadh/gal
weeping *n* caoineadh *m*, gal *m*, gul *m*
weigh *v* cothromaich, cuir air mheidh, tomhais **w. up** breithnich **w. anchor** tog acair
weight *n* cudthrom *m*, cuideam *m*, truimead *m* **lose w.** *v* caill cuideam
weird *a* air leth neònach
welcome *n* fàilte *f*, furan *m* *a* di-beathte; (*of development*) ris an dèanar toileachadh **you're w.** 's e do bheatha *v* (*person*) cuir fàilte air, fàiltich; (*development*(*s*)) dèan toileachadh ri
weld *v* tàth
welding *n* tàthadh *m*
welfare *n* sochair *f*, math *m* **w. state** stàit shochairean *f*
well *n* tobar *f m*, fuaran *m*
well *a* math, gasta; (*of health*) fallain *adv* gu math
well-behaved *a* modhail
well-dressed *a* spaideil, leòmach
well-informed *a* fiosrach
wellington *n* bòtann *f m*
well-known *a* ainmeil, iomraiteach
Welsh *a* Cuimreach *n* (*lang*) Cuimris *f*
Welshman *n* Cuimreach *m* **Welshwoman** ban-Chuimreach *f*
were *v* bha (*See verb* **to be** *in*

Grammar)
west *n* an iar *f*, an àird an iar *f*
the w. side an taobh siar *m*
a siar *adv* an iar
westerly *a* on iar, às an àird an iar
western *a* siar **the W. Isles** na h-Eileanan Siar/an Iar
wet *a* fliuch *v* fliuch
whale *n* muc-mhara *f*
what *int* dè? *rel pron* an rud a; (*all that*) na *exclam* abair ...!
w. a crowd! abair sluagh!
whatever *pron* às bith, ge b' e air bith, ge brith *a* sam bith
wheat *n* cruithneachd *f m*
wheel *n* cuibheall *f*, cuibhle *f*, roth *m* **w.-house** taigh-cuibhle *m*, taigh na cuibhle *m* *v* (*trans*) cuibhil, ruidhil; (*intrans*) tionndaidh mun cuairt
wheelbarrow bara(-roth) *m*
wheelchair sèithear-cuibhle *m*, cathair-chuibhle *f*
wheeze *n* pìochan, sèitean *m* *v* dèan pìochan, bi a' sèiteanaich
whelk *n* faochag *f*
when *int* cuin? *conj* nuair (a), an uair (a)
whence *adv* cò às, cò bhuaithe
whenever *adv* gach uair, ge b' e uair, àm sam bith
where *int* càite? *rel pron* far, san àite san
whereas *conj* ach; (*since*) a chionn ('s gu)
whereby *conj* leis, leis an do
wherever *adv* ge b' e càite, às bith càite, ge brith càite
whereupon *adv* le sin, leis a sin
whet *v* geuraich, faobharaich; (*appetite*) brod càil
whether *conj* co-dhiù, a/an/am (+ *v*)
which *int* cò, cò aca? *rel pron* a; (*neg*) nach
whichever *pron* ge b' e cò, às bith cò, ge brith cò
whiff *n* aithneachadh (fàil(e)idh) *m*; (*air*) oiteag *f*
while *n* treis *f*, greis *f*, tacan *m* *v* cuir seachad (an) ùine *adv* fhad 's, am feadh 's
whim *n* baog *f*, baogaid *f*, saobh-smaoin *f*
whimper *n* cnead *m*, sgiùgan *m*
whin *n* conasg *m*
whine *v* caoin, dèan caoidhearan; (*complain*) sìor ghearan
whinge *v* dèan cànran
whingeing *a* cànranach
whip *n* cuip *f* *v* cuip, sgiùrs
whiphand *n* làmh-an-uachdair *f*
whirl *n* cuairt *f*, cuartag *f*
whirligig *n* gille-mirein *m*
whirlpool *n* ioma-shruth *m*, cuairt-shruth *m*
whirlwind *n* ioma-ghaoth *f*
whisk *v* sguab, sgiot
whisky *n* uisge-beatha *m*
whisper *n* cagar *m*, sanais *m* *v* cagair, cuir cagar
whispering *n* cagarsaich *f*, sainnsearachd *f*
whistle *n* fead *f*; (*mus*) feadag *f*, fìdeag *f* *v* dèan fead/feadaraich
white *a* geal; (*pale*) bàn **w.-board** bòrd-geal *m* **W. Paper** Pàipear Geal *m*
whitewash *n* aol-uisg(e) *m*, gealachadh *m*; (*met*) dreach eile/glan *m* *v* gealaich; (*met*) cuir dreach eile/glan air
whiting *n* cuidhteag *f*
who *int pron* cò? *rel pron* a; (*neg*) nach
whoever *pron* ge b' e cò, às bith cò, ge brith cò; neach sam bith *int pron* cò idir?
whole *a* slàn, iomlan, uile, gu lèir; (*healthy*) fallain
wholehearted *a* làn-(+ *a*), le (h-) uile *etc* chridhe
wholesale *n* mòr-dhìol *m*, mòr-reic *m*
wholesome *a* slàn, fallain
wholly *adv* gu h-iomlan/buileach
whooping cough *n* an triuthach *f*
whose *int pron* cò leis?
why *int* carson? *adv* carson
wick *n* siobhag *f*, buaic *f*
wicked *a* olc, aingidh
wickedness *n* olc *m*, aingidheachd *f*
wide *a* farsaing, leathan(n)
w.-ranging farsaing
widely *adv* fad' is farsaing

widen *v* leudaich; (*intrans only*) fàs farsaing
widespread *a* (*common*) bitheanta, fad' is farsaing
widow(er) *n* bantrach *f* (*m*)
width *n* leud *m*
wield *v* làimhsich, obraich
wife *n* bean *f*, bean-phòsta *f*
wig *n* gruag *f*, pioraraig *f*
wild *a* fiadhaich, allaidh
wilderness *n* fàsach *m*
wildlife *n* fiadh-bheatha *f*
wile *n* cuilbheart *f*, car *m*
wilful *a* fada na c(h)eann *etc*, ceann-làidir
will *n* toil *f*, rùn *m*, deòin *f*; (*leg*) tiomnadh *m*
willing *a* deònach, toileach
willingly *a* gu deònach/toileach
willow *n* seileach *m*
willy-nilly *adv* a dheòin no (a) dh'aindeoin
wily *a* seòlta, carach
win *v* buannaich, coisinn, buinig
wind *n* gaoth *f*; (*breath*) anail *f* **w. direction** àird na gaoithe *f*
wind *v* (*around*) suain, toinn, fill; (*clock*) rothaig **w. up** thoir gu crìch; (*tease*) bi a' tarraing à
windfall *n* (*fin*) clabag *f*
winding *a* lùbach, cam, cama-lùbach
windmill *n* muileann-gaoithe *f m*
window *n* uinneag *f* **w.-pane** l(e)òsan (uinneige) *m* **w.-sill** sòl uinneige *m*
windpipe *n* pìob-sgòrnain *f*
windscreen *n* sgùl *m*, sgàile-gaoithe *m*
windsurfing *n* marcachd thonn *f*
windward *n* fuaradh *m*, taobh an fhuaraidh *m*
windy *a* gaothach, gailbheach, garbh
wine *n* fìon *m* **red w.** fìon dearg **white w.** fìon geal **w.-list** clàr-fìona *m*
wing *n* sgiath *f*
wink *n* priobadh *m*, caogadh *m*, sùil bheag *f* *v* priob, caog, dèan sùil bheag
winner *n* neach-buannachaidh *m*, buadhaiche *m*
winnow *v* fasgain
winter *n* an geamhradh *m* *v* geamhraich
wintry *a* geamhrachail
wipe *v* suath **w. off** glan dheth
wiper *n* suathair *m*
wire *n* uèir *f*, teud *m* **barbed w.** uèir-bhiorach/stobach *f*
wiry *a* seang
wisdom *n* gliocas *m*
wise *a* glic
wish *n* miann *f m*, toil *f*, togradh *m*, dùrachd *f* *v* miannaich, togair, luthaig, rùnaich
wisp *n* sop *m*
wistful *a* cianail, tiamhaidh
wit *n* eirmseachd *f*, geur-labhairt *f*; (*sense*) toinisg *f*
witch *n* bana-bhuidseach *f*
witchcraft *n* buidseachd *f*
with *prep* le, cuide ri, còmhla ri, leis (+ *art*)
withdraw *v* thoir air ais/falbh, tarraing a-mach/air ais
wither *v* searg, seac, crìon
withered *a* seargte, seacte, crìon
withhold *v* cùm air ais
within *adv* a-staigh *prep* taobh a-staigh (+ *gen*)
without *prep* gun, às aonais (+ *gen*)
withstand *v* seas ri
witness *a* (*abstr*) fianais *f* *v* thoir fianais
witty *a* eirmseach, geur
wizard *n* buidseach *m*, draoidh *m*
woeful *a* muladach, truagh
wolf *n* madadh-allaidh *m*
woman *n* bean *f*, boireannach *m*
womb *n* machlag *f*, bolg *f*, brù *f*
wonder *n* iongnadh *m*, iongantas *m* *v* gabh iongantas
wonderful *a* iongantach
woo *v* bi a' suirghe (air)
wood *n* fiodh *m*; (*forest*) coille *f*
wooden *a* fiodha
woodland *n* fearann coillteach *m*
woodpecker *n* snagan-daraich *m*
woodwork *n* saorsainneachd *f*
woodworm *n* (*insect*) raodan *m*; (*condition*) raodanas *m*
wool *n* clòimh *f*, olann *f*; (*knitting*) snàth *m*

woollen *a* clòimhe
woolly *a* clòimhe; (*met*) ceòthach, doilleir
word *n* facal *m*; (*promise*) gealladh *m* **w. for w.** facal air an fhacal **w. processing** rianachadh fhaclan *m* **w.-processor** rianadair fhaclan *m*
work *n* obair *f*, saothair *f* **workforce** luchd-obrach *m* **workshop** bùth-obrach *f* *v* obraich, saothraich
worker *n* obraiche *m*, neach-obrach *m*
working-party *n* buidheann-obrach *f m*
works *n* (*place*) ionad-obrach *m* **gasworks** ionad a' ghas *m*
world *n* saoghal *m*, cruinne *m* (*f in gen*)
worldly *a* saoghalta
worm *n* boiteag *f*, cnuimh *f*, durrag *f*
worn *a* caithte, breòite
worried *a* draghail, fo iomagain, fo chùram
worry *n* dragh *m*, iomagain *f*, cùram *m* *v* dèan dragh do, cuir dragh/iomnaidh air **I w. too much** bidh cus cùraim orm (mu rudan)
worse *a* nas miosa
worsen *v* fàs nas miosa
worship *n* adhradh *m* **family w.** adhradh teaghlaich, gabhail an Leabhair *m* *v* dèan adhradh *Also vn* ag adhradh
worst *a* as miosa
worth *n* fiach *m*, luach *m* *a* fiù, airidh air **it is not w. bothering about** chan fhiach/cha d' fhiach bodraigeadh mu dheidhinn
worthless *a* gun luach, gun fhiù
worthy *a* airidh, fiùghail, fiachail
wound *n* lot *m*, leòn *m*, creuchd *f* *v* leòn, lot
wounded *a* leònte
wounding *a* guineach
wrangle *v* connsaich, troid
wrap *v* paisg, fill **w. around** suain
wrapping paper *n* pàipear-còmhdaich *m*
wrath *n* corraich *f*, fearg *f*
wreath *n* blàth-fhleasg *f*
wreck *n* (*naut*) long-bhriste *f*; (*of a person or article*) ablach *m* *v* sgrios, mill
wren *n* dreathan-donn *m*
wrench *v* spìon
wrest *v* tarraing (bh)o
wrestle *v* bi a' carachd, gleac
wrestler *n* caraiche *m*, gleacadair *m*
wrestling *n* carachd *f*, gleac *m*
wretch *n* truaghan *m*
wretched *a* truagh, àmhgharach
wriggle *v* rach an lùban, toinneamhaich
wring *v* fàisg
wrinkle *n* preas *m*, roc *f*
wrinkled *a* preasach, liorcach, rocach
wrist *n* caol an dùirn *m* **wristband** bann dùirn *m* **wristwatch** uaireadair làimhe *m*
writ *n* sgrìobhainn-cùirte/cùrtach *f*
write *v* sgrìobh **w. up** dèan cunntas air **w. off** meas gun luach, dubh às
writer *n* sgrìobhadair *m*, sgrìobhaiche *m*
writhe *v* snìomh, bi gad aonagraich fhèin
writing *n* sgrìobhadh *m* **w.-paper** pàipear-sgrìobhaidh *m*
written *a* sgrìobhte
wrong *n* coire *f*, eucoir *f*, euceart *m* *a* ceàrr; (*culpable*) coireach, eucorach *v* dèan eucoir air
wry *a* cam, fiar, claon

X

xenophobia *n* gamhlas do choigrich *m*
Xmas *n* an Nollaig *f*
x-ray *n* x-ghath *m* *a* x-ghathach *v* x-ghathaich
xylophone *n* saidhleafòn *m*

Y

yacht *n* sgoth-seòlaidh *f*, gheat *f*
yak *n* iac *m*

yank *v* spìon
yap *v* (*dog*) dèan comhart; (*talk*) bleadraig
yard *n* slat *f*; (*enclosure*) gàrradh *m*, lios *f* **yardstick** slat-t(h)omhais *f*
yarn *n* snàth *m*; (*story*) sgeulachd *f*, naidheachd *f*
yawn *n* mèaran *m*, mèanan *m* *v* bi a'/dèan mèaranaich/ mèananaich *Also vn* a' mèaranaich, a' mèananaich
yawning *n* mèaranaich *f*, mèananaich *f*
year *n* bliadhna *f* **this y.** am-bliadhna **next y.** an ath-bhliadhna **last y.** an-uiridh **the y. before last** a' bhòn-uiridh
yearn *v* miannaich gu làidir, bi fo fhadachd airson
yearning *n* iarraidh *f m*, fadachd *f*
yeast *n* beirm *f*
yell *n* glaodh *m*, sgal *m*, sgairt *f* *v* glaodh
yellow *n*, *a* buidhe *m*
yelp *n* sgiamh *f m*; (*of dog*) tathann *m* *v* dèan sgiamh; (*dog*) dèan tathann
yes *adv a Yes answer is represented by the positive form of the verb used in a question, eg* a bheil thu sgìth? tha an e saor a th' ann? 's e am faca tu an gèam? chunnaic; (*in argument*) seadh
yesterday *adv* an-dè **the day before y.** a' bhòn-dè
yet *conj* an dèidh sin, ach *adv* fhathast **yet again** aon uair eile
yew *n* iubhar *m*
yield *n* toradh *m* *v* thoir a-mach toradh; (*submit*) gèill, strìochd
yoga *n* iòga *f*
yoghurt *n* iogart *m*
yoke *n* (*phys, met*) cuing *f* *v* (*ready*) beairtich; (*oppress*) cuingich
yolk (**of egg**) *n* buidheagan *m*
yon(der) *adv* thall, ud, an siud
you *pron* thu, (*emph*) thusa, (*pl & pol*) sibh, (*emph*) sibhse
young *a* òg **younger than** nas òige na **youngest** as òige *n* àl (òg) *m*; (*people*) òigridh *f*
youngster *n* òganach *m*
your *poss pron* do, d', t', (*pl & pol*) bhur, ur
yours *poss pron* leat, (*emph*) leatsa, (*pl & pol*) leibh, (*emph*) leibhse
yourself *pron* thu fhèin, (*pl & pol*) sibh fhèin, sib' fhèin
youth *n* (*abstr*) òige *f*; (*person*) òigear *m*, òganach *m*; (*coll*) òigridh *f* **y. centre** ionad òigridh *m* **y. club** club-òigridh *m*, buidheann-òigridh *f m* **y. hostel** ostail òigridh *m*
youthful *a* òg, ògail
Yuch/Yuck *exclam* (A) ghia!
Yule *n* Nollaig *f*

Z

zany *a* cleasach, àraid
zeal *n* eud *m*, dealas *m*
zealot *n* eudmhoraiche *m*
zealous *a* eudmhor, dealasach
zebra *n* seabra *m* **z. crossing** trast-rathad seabra *m*
zenith *n* bàrr *m*
zero *n* neoni *f* **z. tolerance** nach ceadaich an cron as lugha
zest *n* fonn *m*, sunnd *m*
zigzag *a* cam-fhiarach
zinc *n* sinc *m*
zip *n* siop *m*
zodiac *n* grian-chrios *m*, crios na grèine *m*
zone *n* raon *m*, ceàrn *m*, sòn *m*; (*geog*) bann *m*, crios *m* *v* suidhich raon/sòn
zoo *n* sù *m*, sutha *f*
zoologist *n* ainmh-eòlaiche *m*
zoology *n* ainmh-eòlas *m*
zoom *v* falbh le roid

Surnames *Sloinnidhean*

The forms of surnames for women and men differ from each other in Gaelic. Where a man's surname begins with **Mac**, a woman's begins with **Nic**. Thus, **Dòmhnall MacLeòid** (Donald MacLeod) but **Oighrig NicLeòid** (Effie MacLeod). With surnames other than those beginning with **Mac/Nic**, the female form of the noun is lenited. Thus, **Seumas Caimbeul** (James Campbell) but **Màiri Chaimbeul** (Mary Campbell).

As will be seen below, there is more than one Gaelic version of some names, one with **Mac/Nic** and one without, like **MacFhearghais/Fearghasdan** (Ferguson). In addition, a form in **-ach** is often used when the person's surname and not his personal name is being used, eg **'Chunnaic mi an Granndach an-diugh'** ('I saw Grant today'). This practice is much less common with the surnames of women, but on the rare occasions on which it would be used, the female equivalent would be **'a' bhan-Ghranndach'**. In the case of a few names, this form is as common or commoner in speech than the **Mac/Nic** form is, and so it has has been listed below in addition to the other form.

For convenience, the English names have all been spelt with a capital after Mac, but it is recognized that there are many variations on this, and also in other aspects (MacNeil/ MacNeill etc). The same is true of Gaelic names, especially those which have the element **gille** (lad, servant) in them. Here we have rendered that element as **Ille** or **Ill**.

Beaton	*Peutan*
Black	*MacIlleDhuibh*
Boyd	*Boidhd*
Bruce	*Brus, Brusach*
Buchanan	*Bochanan*
Cameron	*Camshron*
Campbell	*Caimbeul*
Chisholm	*Siosal, Siosalach*
Douglas	*Dùghlas*
Ferguson	*Fearghasdan, MacFhearghais*
Finlayson	*Fionnlasdan, MacFhionnlaigh*
Fraser	*Friseal*
Gillies	*MacIllIosa*
Graham	*Greum, Greumach*
Grant	*Grannd*
Johnson	*MacIain*
Kennedy	*Ceanadach, MacUalraig*
MacAllister	*MacAlasdair*
MacArthur	*MacArtair*
MacAskill	*MacAsgaill*
MacAulay	*MacAmhlaigh*
MacBain	*MacBheathain*
MacBeth	*MacBheatha*
MacCorquodale	*MacCòrcadail, MacThòrcadail*
MacCrimmon	*MacCruimein*
MacDonald	*MacDhòmhnaill, Dòmhnallach*
MacDougall	*MacDhùghaill, Dùghlach*
MacEachen	*MacEachainn*
MacEachern, MacKechnie	*MacEacharna*
MacFadyen	*MacPhàidein*
MacFarlane	*MacPhàrlain*
MacGregor	*MacGriogair*
MacInnes	*MacAonghais*
MacIntosh	*Mac an Tòisich*
MacIntyre	*Mac an t-Saoir*
MacIver	*MacÌomhair*
MacKay	*MacAoidh*
MacKenzie	*MacCoinnich*
MacKerlich	*MacTheàrlaich*
MacKinlay	*MacFhionnlaigh*
MacKinnon	*MacFhionghain*
MacLean	*MacIllEathain*
MacLellan	*MacIllFhaolain, MacIllFhialain*
MacLennan	*MacIllFhinnein*
MacLeod	*MacLeòid*
MacMillan	*MacIlleMhaoil, Mac a' Mhaoilein*
MacNab	*Mac an Aba*
MacNeil	*MacNèill*
MacPhail	*MacPhàil*
MacPhee	*Mac-a-phì*
MacPherson	*Mac a' Phearsain*
MacQuarrie	*MacGuaire*
MacRae	*MacRath*
MacRitchie	*MacRisnidh*
MacSween	*MacSuain*
MacTaggart	*Mac an t-Sagairt*
MacVicar	*Mac a' Phiocair*
MacVurich, Currie	*MacMhuirich*
Martin	*Màrtainn*
Montgomery	*MacGumaraid*
Morrison	*Moireasdan, MacIlleMhoire*
Munro	*Rothach, Mac an Rothaich*
Murray	*Moireach*
Nicolson, MacNicol	*MacNeacail*
Robertson	*Robasdan, MacDhonnchaidh*
Ross	*Ros*
Smith	*Mac a' Ghobhainn*
Thomson	*MacThòmais*
Whyte	*MacIlleBhàin*

First names *Ciad ainmean*

Some of the names below are not etymologically related in the way that Alan and **Ailean** are but are used as equivalents, eg Claire/**Sorcha** and Kenneth/**Coinneach**.

Agnes	*Ùna*
Alan	*Ailean*
Alasdair, Alexander	*Alasdair*
Alec, Alex, Alick	*Ailig*
Alice	*Ailis, Ailios*
Andrew	*Anndra*
Angus	*Aonghas*
Ann(e), Anna	*Anna, Annag*
Archibald	*Gilleasbaig*
Archie	*Eàirdsidh*
Arthur	*Artair*
Barbara	*Barabal*
Bessie	*Beasag*
Beth	*Beathag*
Betty	*Beitidh*
Cal(l)um, Malcolm	*Calum*
Catherine, Katherine	*Catrìona*
Cathleen, Kathleen	*Caitlin*
Charles	*Teàrlach*
Chrissie	*Criosaidh, Ciorstag*
Christine, Christina	*Cairistìona, Ciorstag*
Christoper	*Crìsdean*
Claire	*Sorcha*
Colin	*Cailean*
David	*Daibhidh*
Deirdre	*Deirdre*
Derek, Der(r)ick	*Ruairidh*
Diarmid, Dermot	*Diarm(a)id*
Dolina, Dolly	*Doileag, Doilìona, Doilidh*
Donald	*Dòmhnall*
Donnie	*Donaidh*
Douglas	*Dùghlas*
Duncan	*Donnchadh*
Edward	*Eideard, Ìomhar*
Effie, Euphemia	*Oighrig*
Elizabeth	*Ealasaid*
Ewan, Ewen	*Eògha(i)nn*
Farquhar	*Fearchar*
Fergus	*Fearghas*
Finlay	*Fionnlagh*
Flora	*Flòraidh, Fionnghal*
George	*Seòras, Deòrsa*
Gilbert	*Gille-Brìghde*
Gordon	*Gòrdan*
Graham	*Greum*
Hector	*Eacha(i)nn*
Helen	*Eilidh*
Henry	*Eanraig*
Hugh	*Ùisdean, Aodh, Eòghann*
Ia(i)n	*Iain*
Innes	*Aonghas*
Isobel, Ishbel	*Iseabail*
Ivor	*Ìomhar*
Jack, Jock	*Seoc*
James	*Seumas*
Jane	*Sìne*
Janet	*Seònaid*
Jessie	*Seasaidh*
Joan	*Seonag*
John	*Iain, Seonaidh*
Johnny	*Seonaidh*
Joseph	*Eòsaph, Iòsaph*
Julia	*Sìleas*
Kate	*Ceit, Ceiteag*
Katie	*Ceitidh, Ceiteag*
Kenna	*Ceana*
Kenneth	*Coinneach*
Kieran	*Ciaran*

Kirsty	*Ciorstaidh*
Lachlan	*Lachla(i)nn, Lachann*
Maggie	*Magaidh*
Margaret	*Mai(gh)read*
Marion	*Mòr*
Marjory	*Marsaili*
Mark	*Marc*
Mary	*Màiri*
May	*Màili*
Michael	*Mìcheal*
Morag	*Mòrag*
Murdo	*Murchadh*
Myles	*Maoilios, Maoileas*
Nancy	*Nansaidh*
Neil, Niall	*Niall*
Norman	*Tormod*
Patrick	*Pàdraig*
Paul	*Pòl*
Peggy	*Peigi*
Peter	*Peadar, Pàdraig*
Rachel	*Raonaid, Raghnaid*
Ranald, Ronald	*Raghnall*
Robert	*Raibeart, Rob*
Roderick	*Ruairidh*
Roy	*Ruadh*
Ruth	*Rut*
Samuel, Sorley	*Somhairle*
Sheena	*Sìne*
Sheila	*Sìle*
Stephen, Steven	*Steaphan*
Stewart	*Stiùbhart*
Susan	*Siùsaidh*
Thomas	*Tòmas*
Torquil	*Torca(i)ll*
Una	*Ùna*
William	*Uilleam*

place names

Aberdeen	*Obar Dheathain*
Aberfeldy	*Obar Pheallaidh*
Aberfoyle	*Obar Phuill*
Africa	*Afraga*
Airdrie	*Àrd Ruighe*
Albania	*Albàinia*
America	*Ameireaga(idh)*
Argyll	*Earra-Ghàidheal*
Arran	*Arainn*
Asia	*(An) Àisia*
the Atlantic Ocean	*An Cuan Siar*
Athens	*Baile na h-Àithne*
Australia	*Astràilia*
Austria	*An Ostair*
Aviemore	*An Aghaidh Mhòr*
Ayr	*Inbhir Àir*
Badenoch	*Bàideanach*
Ballachulish	*Bail' a' Chaolais*
Balmoral	*Baile Mhoireil*
Bannockburn	*Allt a' Bhonnaich*
Barra	*Barraigh*
Beauly	*A' Mhanachainn*
Belfast	*Beul Feirste*
Belgium	*A' Bheilg*
Benbecula	*Beinn na Fadhla/ Beinn a' Bhadhla*
Ben Nevis	*Beinn Nibheis*
Bernera(y)	*Beàrnaraigh*
Berwick	*Bearaig*
the Black Isle	*An t-Eilean Dubh*
Blair Atholl	*Blàr (an) Athaill*
the Borders	*Na Crìochan*
Bosnia	*Bosnia*
Bowmore	*Bogha Mòr*
Braemar	*Bràigh Mhàrr*
Britain	*Breata(i)nn*
Brittany	*A' Bhreata(i)nn Bheag*
Brussels	*A' Bhruiseal*
Bulgaria	*Bulgàiria*
Bute	*Bòd*
the Cairngorms	*Am Monadh Ruadh*
Caithness	*Gallaibh*
Callander	*Calasraid*
Campbeltown	*Ceann Loch (Chille Chiarain)*
Canada	*Canada*
Canna	*Canaigh*
Cape Breton	*Ceap Breatann*
Castlebay	*Bàgh a' Chaisteil*
Coll	*Col(l)a*
Colonsay	*Colbhasaigh*
China	*Sìona*
Cornwall	*A' Chòrn*
Craignure	*Creag an Iubhair*
Crieff	*Craoibh*
Croatia	*Croatia*
Cromarty	*Cromba(i)dh*
the Cuillins	*An Cuiltheann*
Culloden	*Cùl Lodair*
Cumbernauld	*Comar nan Allt*
Czech Republic	*Poblachd nan Seic*
Denmark	*An Danmhairg*
Dingwall	*Inbhir Pheofharain*

Dublin	*Baile Àtha Cliath*
Dumbarton	*Dùn Breatann*
Dunfermline	*Dùn Phàrlain*
Dumfries	*Dùn Phris*
Dunblane	*Dùn Blathain*
Dundee	*Dùn Dèagh*
Dunkeld	*Dùn Chailleann*
Dunoon	*Dùn Omhain*
Dunvegan	*Dùn Bheagain*
East Kilbride	*Cille Bhrìghde an Ear*
Edinburgh	*Dùn Èideann*
Egypt	*An Èipheit*
Eigg	*Eige*
Elgin	*Eilginn*
England	*Sasa(i)nn*
Eriskay	*Èirisgeigh*
Estonia	*Estòinia*
Europe	*An Roinn Eòrpa*
Falkirk	*An Eaglais Bhreac*
Fife	*Fìobha*
Finland	*Fionnlainn*
Forres	*Farrais*
Fort Augustus	*Cille Chuimein*
Fort William	*An Gearastan, An Gearasdan*
France	*An Fhraing*
Fraserburgh	*A' Bhrua(i)ch*
Gairloch	*Geàrrloch*
Galloway	*Gall-Ghàidhealaibh*
Germany	*A' Ghearmailt*
Gigha	*Giogha*
Glasgow	*Glaschu*
Glencoe	*Gleann(a) Comhann*
Glenfinnan	*Gleann Fhionghain*
Golspie	*Goillspidh*
Greece	*A' Ghrèig*
Greenock	*Grianaig*
Harris	*Na Hearadh*
the Hebrides	*Innse Gall*
Helmsdale	*Bun Ilidh*
the Highlands	*A' Ghàidhealtachd*
Holland	*An Òlaind*
Hungary	*An Ungair*
Huntly	*Hunndaidh*
Iceland	*Innis Tìle*
India	*Na h-Innseachan*
Inveraray	*Inbhir Aora*
Invergordon	*Inbhir Ghòrdain*
Inverness	*Inbhir Nis*
Iona	*Ì (Chaluim Chille)*
Iran	*Iran, Ioran*
Iraq	*Iraq, Iorag*
Ireland	*Èirinn*
Islay	*Ìle*
Isle of Man	*Eilean Mhanainn*
Isle of Skye	*An t-Eilean Sgitheanach*
Israel	*Israel, Iosarail*
Italy	*An Eadailt*
Japan	*Iapan*
Jerusalem	*Ierusalem*
Jordan	*Iòrdan*
Jura	*Diùra*
Kenya	*Ceinia*
Killin	*Cill Fhinn*
Kilmarnock	*Cille Mheàrnaig*
Kingussie	*Cinn a' Ghiùthsaich*
Kinlochleven	*Ceann Loch Lìobhann*
Kintyre	*Cinn Tìre*
Knoydart	*Cnòideart*
Kyle of Lochalsh	*Caol Loch Aills(e)*
Lanark	*Lannraig*
Largs	*Na Leargaidh Ghallda*
Latvia	*Latbhia*
Leith	*Lìte*
Lewis	*Leòdhas*
Libya	*Libia*
Lismore	*Lios Mòr*
Lithuania	*Lituàinia*
Lochaber	*Loch Abar*
Lochgilphead	*Ceann Loch Gilb*
Lochboisdale	*Loch Baghasdail*
Lochinver	*Loch an Inbhir*
Loch Lomond	*Loch Laomainn*
Lochmaddy	*Loch nam Madadh*

Loch Ness	*Loch Nis*
London	*Lunnainn*
Lothian	*Lodainn, Lobhdaidh*
the Lowlands	*A' Ghalldachd*
Luing	*Luinn*
Luxembourg	*Lugsamburg*
Mallaig	*Malaig*
the Mediterranean	*A' Mhuir Mheadhan-thìreach*
the Minch	*An Cuan Sgìth*
Moidart	*Mùideart*
Morvern	*A' Mhorbhairne*
Motherwell	*Tobar na Màthar*
Muck	*Eilean nam Muc*
Mull	*Muile*
Nairn	*Inbhir Narann*
Ness	*Nis*
the Netherlands	*An Tìr Ìosal*
Newtonmore	*Bail' Ùr an t-Slèibh*
the North Sea	*An Cuan a Tuath*
North Uist	*Uibhist a Tuath*
Norway	*Nirribhidh*
Nova Scotia	*Alba Nuadh*
Oban	*An t-Òban*
Orkney	*Arcaibh*
the Pacific Ocean	*An Cuan Sèimh*
Paisley	*Pàislig*
Pakistan	*Pagastan*
Perth	*Peairt*
Peterhead	*Ceann Phàdraig*
Pitlochry	*Baile Chloichrigh*
Plockton	*Am Ploc*
Poland	*A' Phòlainn*
Port Ellen	*Port Ilein*
Portree	*Port Rìgh, Port Ruighe*
Portugal	*Portagail*
Raasay	*Ratharsair, Ratharsaigh*
River Clyde	*Abhainn Chluaidh*
River Forth	*Abhainn Foirthe*
River Spey	*Abhainn Spè, Uisge Spè*
River Tay	*Abhainn Tatha*
River Tweed	*Abhainn Tuaidh*
Romania	*Romàinia*
Rome	*An Ròimh*
Ross	*Ros*
Rothesay	*Baile Bhòid*
Rum	*Rùm, Eilean Ruma*
Russia	*An Ruis, Ruisia*
Scalpay	*Sgalpaigh*
Scandinavia	*Lochlann*
Scotland	*Alba*
Serbia	*Serbia*
Shetland	*Sealtainn*
Sleat	*Slèite*
Slovakia	*Slobhagia*
Slovenia	*Slobhinia*
South Africa	*Afraga a Deas*
South Uist	*Uibhist a Deas*
Spain	*An Spàinn*
Staffin	*Stafainn, An Taobh Sear*
St Andrews	*Cill Rìmhinn*
Stirling	*Sruighlea*
Stornoway	*Steòrnabhagh*
Strathclyde	*Srath Chluaidh*
Strathspey	*Srath Spè*
Sweden	*An t-Suain*
Switzerland	*An Eilbheis*
Tain	*Baile Dhubhthaich*
Tarbert	*An Tairbeart*
Thurso	*Inbhir Theòrsa*
Tiree	*Tiriodh, Tiridhe*
Tobermory	*Tobar Mhoire*
Tongue	*Tunga*
Torridon	*Toirbheartan*
the Trossachs	*Na Tròiseachan*
Turkey	*An Tuirc*
Tyndrum	*Taigh an Droma*
Uig	*Ùige, Ùig*
Uist	*Uibhist*
Ullapool	*Ulapul*
the United States	*Na Stàitean Aonaichte*
Vatersay	*Bhatarsaigh*
Wales	*A' Chuimrigh*
Wick	*Inbhir Ùige*

Word order

In English, the subject precedes the verb. In Gaelic, the verb precedes the subject and is normally the first word in a sentence or question, eg

bha sinn anmoch	we were late
an glas mi an doras?	shall I lock the door?

In certain types of question, a question word precedes the verb:

cò bha siud?	who was that?

Another change in sequence between English and Gaelic arises with nouns and adjectives. Whereas in English the adjective precedes the noun, in Gaelic the noun generally precedes the adjective, eg

latha math	(a) good day

Adjectives are lenited if the noun they are qualifying is feminine in gender. Lenition is shown in the written form of a word by the insertion of an **h** after the first letter.

oidhche mhath	good night

There are a few exceptions to this convention. The adjectives **deagh** (good), **droch** (bad), **sàr** (excellent, supreme), **fìor** (true, absolute) and **seann** (old) are the main exceptions. These cause lenition, where applicable, of the following noun, eg

dcagh bhiadh	good food
droch shìde	bad weather
sàr sheinneadair	an excellent singer
fìor charaid	a true friend
seann chù	an old dog

Adverbs

An adverb is formed by putting **gu** or **gu h-** before an adjective. **gu h-** is used when the adjective begins with a vowel, eg

mòr (great)	**gu mòr** (greatly)
àrd (high)	**gu h-àrd** (above)

Forms of the article

There is no indefinite article in Gaelic – 'a window' is **uinneag,** 'a jacket' is **seacaid.** There are, however, several forms of the definite article (equivalent to 'the' in English). The form of article used varies according to the gender, number and case of the noun. The main forms of the article are set out in the table below:

(a) Forms of the article with nouns in the nominative case

Gender & number	First letter of noun	Form of article	Example
Masculine singular	b, f, m, p a, e, i, o, u other letters	am an t- an	am bòrd an t-ubhal an leabhar
Feminine singular	b, c, g, m, p	a' + (len)	a' bhròg a' chaileag
	f	an + (len)	an fhreagairt an fhairge
	sl, sn, sr, s + vowel	an t-	an t-sràid an t-seacaid
	other letters	an	an nighean an sgoil an uinneag
Masculine, feminine plural	consonant	na	na leabhraichean na sgoilearan
	vowel	na h-	na h-òrdagan na h-uinneagan

(b) Forms of the article with nouns in the genitive case

Gender & number	First letter of noun	Form of article	Example
Masculine singular	b, c, g, m, p	a' + (len)	am post → oifis a' phuist
	f	an + (len)	am fraoch → dath an fhraoich
	sl, sn, sr, s + vowel	an t-	an salann → blas an t-salainn
	other letters	an	an rathad → ceann an rathaid
Feminine singular	consonant	na	a' chailleach → còta na caillich
	vowel	na h-	an eaglais → doras na h-eaglaise
Masculine, feminine plural	b, f, m, p	nam	na bàird → obair nam bàrd
	other letters	nan	na leabhraichean → Comhairle nan Leabhraichean

(c) Forms of the article with nouns in the dative case

Gender & number	First letter of noun	Form of article	Example
Masculine singular	b, c, g, m, p	a' + (len)	am balach → leis a' bhalach
	f	an + (len)	am feur → anns an fheur
	sl, sn, sr, s + vowel	an t-	an salm → anns an t-salm
	other letters	an	an taigh → air an taigh
Feminine singular	b, c, g, m, p	a' + (len)	a' ghealach → air a' ghealaich
	f	an + (len)	an fheòrag → aig an fheòraig

	sl, sn, sr, s + vowel	an t-	an t-sràid → air an t-sràid
	other letters	an	an trèan → air an trèan an uinneag → air an uinneig
Masculine, feminine plural	consonant	na	na bùithean → anns na bùithean
	vowel	na h-	na h-òrain → ris na h-òrain

Regular verbs

Gaelic verbs have three forms:

- independent – normally the first word in a sentence
- dependent – used in subordinate clauses or after particles
- relative – used after relative pronouns

The root of the verb is the second person singular imperative, eg *seall* (look), literally, 'look you'.

The verb 'to be' apart, Gaelic verbs have no simple present tense. The present tense is formed by combining the verb 'to be' with the verbal noun of the verb being used.

eg *tha iad a' cluich* – they are playing

The verbal noun, as the name implies, can act both as noun or as verb. It is marked in English by the *-ing* ending.

eg *bha sinn a' snàmh* – we were swimming
tha snàmh math dhut – swimming is good for you

Root	Verbal Noun	Infinitive	Subjunctive/ Conditional
bris *break*	a' briseadh *breaking*	a bhriseadh *to break*	bhrisinn *I would break*
cuir *put*	a' cur *putting*	a chur *to put*	chuirinn *I would put*
dùin *close/shut*	a' dùnadh *closing/shutting*	a dhùnadh *to close/shut*	dhùineadh e *he would close/shut*

freagair *answer*	a' freagairt *answering*	a fhreagairt *to answer*	fhreagradh i *she would answer*
gabh *take*	a' gabhail *taking*	a ghabhail *to take*	ghabhadh tu *you would take*
las *light*	a' lasadh *lighting*	a lasadh *to light*	lasainn *I would light*
mill *spoil*	a' milleadh *spoiling*	a mhilleadh *to spoil*	mhilleadh tu *you would spoil*
nigh *wash/clean*	a' nighe *washing/ cleaning*	a nighe *to wash/clean*	nigheamaid *we would wash/clean*
pòs *marry*	a' pòsadh *marrying*	a phòsadh *to marry*	phòsadh iad *they would marry*
ruith *run*	a' ruith *running*	a ruith *to run*	ruitheadh sibh *you (pl) would run*
suidh *sit*	a' suidhe *sitting*	a shuidhe *to sit*	shuidheadh i *she would sit*
tog *lift*	a' togail *lifting*	a thogail *to lift*	thogadh iad *they would lift*
aithnich *recognize*	ag aithn-eachadh *recognizing*	a dh'aithn-eachadh *to recognize*	dh'aithn-icheadh sibh *you (pl) would recognize*
èirich *rise*	ag èirigh *rising*	a dh'èirigh *to rise*	dh'èireamaid *we would rise*
ith *eat*	ag ithe *eating*	a dh'ithe *to eat*	dh'itheadh e *he would eat*
òl *drink*	ag òl *drinking*	a dh'òl *to drink*	dh'òlainn *I would drink*
ullaich *prepare*	ag ullachadh *preparing*	a dh'ullachadh *to prepare*	dh'ullaicheadh i *she would prepare*
fuirich *stay/wait*	a' fuireach *staying/waiting*	a dh'fhuireach *to stay/wait*	dh'fhuiricheadh iad *they would stay/wait*

Notes

- there are different ways of forming verbal nouns
- verbal nouns beginning in consonants are preceded by *a'*
- verbal nouns beginning in vowels are preceded by *ag*
- the infinitive ('to') forms are related to the verbal noun forms
- there is no apostrophe after the *a* in the infinitive
- infinitive forms of verbs beginning in consonants are lenited where possible
- infinitive forms of verbs beginning in *f* followed by a vowel begin with *dh'* and are lenited. The *fh* combination is not pronounced and the verb is treated as if it began in a vowel
- subjunctive/conditional forms vary according to the person being referred to, or subject. The following is an example of the different forms of one verb:

chuirinn	I would put	*chuireamaid*	we would put
chuireadh tu	you would put	*chuireadh sibh*	you (pl) would put
chuireadh e	he would put	*chuireadh iad*	they would put
chuireadh i	she would put		

- the first person singular and plural forms have special forms which include the pronoun, while the pronoun is added separately in the second and third persons. However, in some areas *sinn* is retained in the first person plural, eg *chuireadh sinn*
- *thu* appears as *tu* in the subjunctive/conditional
- subjunctive/conditional forms of verbs beginning in consonants are lenited
- subjunctive/conditional forms of verbs beginning in vowels or *f* followed by a vowel begin with *dh'*

Regular verbs: past tense

Root	Positive	Negative	Interrogative
bris *break*	bhris *broke*	cha do bhris *did not break*	an do bhris? *did ... break?*
cuir *put*	chuir *put*	cha do chuir *did not put*	an do chuir? *did ... put?*
dùin *close/shut*	dhùin *closed/shut*	cha do dhùin *did not close/shut*	an do dhùin? *did ... close/shut?*

freagair *answer*	fhreagair *answered*	cha do fhreagair *did not answer*	an do fhreagair? *did ... answer?*
gabh *take*	ghabh *took*	cha do ghabh *did not take*	an do ghabh? *did ... take?*
las *light*	las *lit*	cha do las *did not light*	an do las? *did ... light?*
mill *spoil*	mhill *spoilt*	cha do mhill *did not spoil*	an do mhill? *did ... spoil?*
nigh *wash/clean*	nigh *washed/ cleaned*	cha do nigh *did not wash/clean*	an do nigh? *did ... wash/clean?*
pòs *marry*	phòs *married*	cha do phòs *did not marry*	an do phòs? *did ... marry?*
ruith *run*	ruith *run*	cha do ruith *did not run*	an do ruith? *did ... run?*
suidh *sit*	shuidh *sat*	cha do shuidh *did not sit*	an do shuidh? *did ... sit?*
tog *lift*	thog *lifted*	cha do thog *did not lift*	an do thog? *did ... lift?*
aithnich *recognize*	dh'aithnich *recognized*	cha do dh'aithnich *did not recognize*	an do dh'aithnich? *did ... recognize?*
èirich *rise*	dh'èirich *rose*	cha do dh'èirich *did not rise*	an do dh'èirich? *did ... rise?*
ith *eat*	dh'ith *ate*	cha do dh'ith *did not eat*	an do dh'ith? *did ... eat?*
òl *drink*	dh'òl *drank*	cha do dh'òl *did not drink*	an do dh'òl? *did ... drink?*
ullaich *prepare*	dh'ullaich *prepared*	cha do dh'ullaich *did not prepare*	an do dh'ullaich? *did ... prepare?*
fuirich *stay/wait*	dh'fhuirich *stayed/waited*	cha do dh'fhuirich *did not stay/wait*	an do dh'fhuirich? *did ... stay/wait?*

Notes

- positive forms of the past tense are derived by leniting the root form, where possible. Verbs beginning in *l, n, r* and *sg, sm, sp, st* retain the root form
- positive forms of verbs beginning in vowels begin with *dh'*
- negative forms of the past tense are marked by *cha do*
- interrogative (question) forms of the past tense are marked by *an do*
- the interrogative forms are answered, as appropriate, by the positive (yes) and negative (no) forms

  eg *an do dh'aithnich thu iad? dh'aithnich/cha do dh'aithnich*
  did you recognize them? yes no

Regular verbs: future tense

Root	Positive	Negative	Interrogative
bris *break*	brisidh *will break*	cha bhris *will not break*	am bris ...? *will ... break?*
cuir *put*	cuiridh *will put*	cha chuir *will not put*	an cuir ...? *will ... put?*
dùin *close/shut*	dùinidh *will close/ shut*	cha dhùin *will not close/shut*	an dùin ...? *will ... close/shut?*
freagair *answer*	freagraidh *will answer*	cha fhreagair *will not answer*	am freagair ...? *will ... answer?*
gabh *take*	gabhaidh *will take*	cha ghabh *will not take*	an gabh ...? *will ... take?*
las *light*	lasaidh *will light*	cha las *will not light*	an las ...? *will ... light?*
mill *spoil*	millidh *will spoil*	cha mhill *will not spoil*	am mill ...? *will ... spoil?*
nigh *wash/clean*	nighidh *will wash/ clean*	cha nigh *will not wash/ clean*	an nigh ...? *will ... wash/ clean?*
pòs *marry*	pòsaidh *will marry*	cha phòs *will not marry*	am pòs ...? *will ... marry?*
ruith *run*	ruithidh *will run*	cha ruith *will not run*	an ruith ...? *will ... run?*

suidh *sit*	suidhidh *will sit*	cha shuidh *will not sit*	an suidh ...? *will ... sit?*
tog *lift*	togaidh *will lift*	cha thog *will not lift*	an tog ...? *will ... lift?*
aithnich *recognize*	aithnichidh *will recognize*	chan aithnich *will not recognize*	an aithnich ...? *will ... recognize?*
èirich *rise*	èiridh *will rise*	chan èirich *will not rise*	an èirich ...? *will ... rise?*
ith *eat*	ithidh *will eat*	chan ith *will not eat*	an ith ...? *will ... eat?*
òl *drink*	òlaidh *will drink*	chan òl *will not drink*	an òl ...? *will ... drink?*
ullaich *prepare*	ullaichidh *will prepare*	chan ullaich *will not prepare*	an ullaich ...? *will ... prepare?*
fuirich *stay/wait*	fuirichidh *will stay/wait*	chan fhuirich *will not stay/wait*	am fuirich ...? *will ... stay/wait?*

Notes

- positive forms of the future are generally derived by adding *-idh* or *-aidh* to the root form. The former is added when the last vowel in the root is *i* or *e*, and *-aidh* is added when the last vowel is *a*, *o* or *u*
- a few verbs, eg *freagair*, drop part of the second syllable before adding the *-(a)idh* element
- negative forms are marked by *cha* or *chan*. *Chan* is used before vowels and before *f* followed by a vowel
- interrogative (question) forms are marked by *an* or *am*. *Am* is used before verbs beginning in *b, f, m, p*
- the interrogative forms are answered, as appropriate, by the positive (Yes) and negative (No) forms

  eg *an gabh thu cofaidh?* *gabhaidh/cha ghabh, tapadh leat*
  will you have a coffee? yes/no, thank you
- some alternative forms not involving lenition of *d*, *s* and *t* are not listed above eg *cha suidh*

Irregular verbs

Root	Verbal Noun	Infinitive	Subjunctive/ Conditional
abair	ag ràdh	a ràdh	theirinn
say	*saying*	*to say*	*I would say*
beir	a' breith/ a' beireachdainn	a bhreith/ a bheireachdainn	bheireadh i
catch	*catching*	*to catch*	*she would catch*
cluinn	a' cluinntinn	a chluinntinn	chluinneamaid
hear	*hearing*	*to hear*	*we would hear*
dèan	a' dèanamh	a dhèanamh	dhèanainn
do, make	*doing, making*	*to do, make*	*I would do, make*
faic	a' faicinn	a dh'fhaicinn	chitheadh tu
see	*seeing*	*to see*	*you would see*
faigh	a' faighinn	a dh'fhaighinn	gheibheadh iad
get	*getting*	*to get*	*they would get*
rach	a' dol	a dhol	rachainn
go	*going*	*to go*	*I would go*
ruig	a' ruighinn/ a' ruigsinn	a ruighinn/ a ruigsinn	ruigeadh sibh
arrive, reach	*arriving, reaching*	*to arrive, reach*	*you would arrive, reach*
thoir/tabhair	a' toirt/ a' tabhairt	a thoirt/ a thabhairt	thoireamaid
give, take, bring	*giving, taking, bringing*	*to give, take, bring*	*we would give, take, bring*
thig	a' tighinn	a thighinn	thigeadh e
come	*coming*	*to come*	*he would come*

Irregular verbs: past tense

Root	Positive	Negative	Interrogative
abair	thuirt/ thubhairt	cha tuirt/ tubhairt	an tuirt/ tubhairt ...?
say	*said*	*did not say*	*did ... say?*
beir	rug	cha do rug	an do rug ...?
catch	*caught*	*did not catch*	*did ... catch?*
cluinn	chuala	cha chuala	an cuala ...?
hear	*heard*	*did not hear*	*did ... hear?*

dèan *do, make*	rinn *did, made*	cha do rinn *did not do, make*	an do rinn ...? *did ... do, make?*
faic *see*	chunnaic *saw*	chan fhaca *did not see*	am faca ...? *did ... see?*
faigh *get*	fhuair *got*	cha d' fhuair *did not get*	an d' fhuair ...? *did ... get?*
rach *go*	chaidh *went*	cha deach *did not go*	an deach ...? *did ... go?*
ruig *arrive, reach*	ràinig *arrived, reached*	cha do ràinig *did not arrive, reach*	an do ràinig ...? *did ... arrive, reach?*
thoir/tabhair *give, take, bring*	thug *gave, took, brought*	cha tug *did not give, take, bring*	an tug ...? *did .... give, take, bring*
thig *come*	thàinig *came*	cha tàinig *did not come*	an tàinig ...? *did ... come?*

Irregular verbs: future tense

abair *say*	their *will say*	chan abair *will not say*	an abair ...? *will ... say?*
beir *catch*	beiridh *will catch*	cha bheir *will not catch*	am beir ...? *will ... catch?*
cluinn *hear*	cluinnidh *will hear*	cha chluinn *will not hear*	an cluinn ...? *will ... hear?*
dèan *do, make*	nì *will do, make*	cha dèan *will not do, make*	an dèan ...? *will ... do, make?*
faic *see*	chì *will see*	chan fhaic *will not see*	am faic ...? *will ... see?*
faigh *get*	gheibh *will get*	chan fhaigh *will not get*	am faigh ...? *will ... get?*
rach *go*	thèid *will go*	cha tèid *will not go*	an tèid ...? *will ... go?*
ruig *arrive, reach*	ruigidh *will arrive, reach*	cha ruig *will not arrive, reach*	an ruig ...? *will ... arrive, reach?*

thoir/tabhair *give, take, bring*	bheir *will give, take, bring*	cha toir/ tabhair *will not give, take, bring*	an toir/ tabhair ...? *will ... give, take, bring?*
thig *come*	thig *will come*	cha tig *will not come*	an tig ...? *will ... come?*

The verb 'to be'

There are two separate strands of the verb 'to be' in Gaelic. One is based on **bi** and the other, known as the assertive form, is based on **is**.

These strands are set out separately below:

bi forms

Root	**Present positive**	**Present negative**	**Present interrogative**
bi	tha *am, is, are*	chan eil *am not, is not, are not*	a bheil? *am?, is?, are?*
	Past positive	**Past negative**	**Past interrogative**
	bha *was, were*	cha robh *was not, were not*	an robh? *was ... not?, were ... not?*
	Future positive	**Future negative**	**Future interrogative**
	bidh/bithidh *will be*	cha bhi *will not be*	am bi? *will ... be?*
	Present relative	**Present dependent positive**	**Present dependent negative**
	a tha *who/which/ that is*	gu bheil *that ... is*	nach eil *that ... is not*
	Past relative	**Past dependent positive**	**Past dependent negative**
	a bha *who/which/ that was/were*	gun robh *that ... was/were*	nach robh *that ... was/ were not*
	Future relative	**Future dependent positive**	**Future dependent negative**
	a bhitheas/ a bhios *who/which/ that will be*	gum bi *that ... will be*	nach bi *that ... will not be*

2nd pl. imp.	Infinitive	Subjunctive/ conditional dependent	Subjunctive/ conditional
bithibh *be (pl)*	a bhith *to be*	bhithinn *I would be*	gum bithinn *that I would be*
		bhiodh/ bhitheadh ... *you/he/she/it/ they would be*	gum biodh/ bitheadh *that he/she/it/ they would be*
		bhitheamaid, bhitheadh sinn *we would be*	gum bitheamaid, gum bitheadh sinn *that we would be*

Assertive forms

Present positive	**Present negative**	**Present interrogative**
is/'s *am, is, are*	cha(n) *am not, is not, are not*	an, am *am?, is?, are?*
Past positive & Conditional positive	**Past negative & Conditional negative**	**Past interrogative & Conditional interrogative**
bu/b' *was, were, would be*	cha bu, cha b' *was not, were not, would not be*	am bu? am b'? *was?, were?, would ... be?*
Present relative	**Present dependent positive**	**Present dependent negative**
as *that am, that is, that are*	gur *that am, that is, that are*	nach *that am not, that is not, that are not*
Past relative & Conditional relative	**Past dependent positive & Conditional dependent positive**	**Past dependent negative & Conditional dependent negative**
(a) bu, b' *that was, that were, that would be*	gum bu, gum b' *that was, that were, that would be*	nach bu, nach b' *that was not, that were not, that would not be*

Is is often reduced to **'S** in pronunciation and in writing, while **Bu** becomes **B'** before a word beginning in a vowel.

The Assertive forms are used to highlight, identify and define a particular point, eg

's e àite snog a th' ann	*it's a nice place*
's ann à Ile a tha iad	*they are from Islay*
cha b' ise a bh' ann idir	*it wasn't her at all*
b' ann a-raoir a thachair e	*it was last night it happened*

'S and **B'** are followed by pronouns when the point being highlighted or identified is a person or thing. They are accompanied by **ann** when reference is being made to a place or time.

The various forms of **Is** and **Bu** feature in a number of phrases in combination with a noun or adjective and a prepositional pronoun. These phrases convey the meanings carried by certain verbs in English, eg

's toil/toigh leam	*I like*
's caomh leis	*he likes*
's fheàrr leatha	*she prefers*
's beag orm	*I dislike*
's lugha air	*he hates*
chan àbhaist dhomh	*I don't usually*
an urrainn dhut?	*can you?*
bu chòir dhi	*she should/ought to*
an aithne dhuibh?	*do you (pl) know?*

The prepositional pronouns

Preposition		Singular		
	1st	2nd	3rd Masc	3rd Fem
aig *at*	agam *at me*	agad *at you*	aige *at him/it*	aice *at her/it*
air *on*	orm *on me*	ort *on you*	air *on him/it*	oirre *on her/it*
ann *in*	annam *in me*	annad *in you*	ann *in him/it*	innte *in her/it*
às *out of*	asam *out of me*	asad *out of you*	às *out of him/it*	aiste *out of her/it*
bho *from* o	bhuam uam *from me*	bhuat uat *from you*	bhuaithe uaithe *from her/it*	bhuaipe uaipe *from her/it*
de *of, off*	dhìom *of me*	dhìot *of you*	dheth *of him/it*	dhith *of her/it*
do *to*	dhomh *to me*	dhut *to you*	dha *to him/it*	dhi *to her/it*

eadar *between*	-	-	-	-
fo *under*	fodham *under me*	fodhad *under you*	fodha *under him/it*	foidhpe/foipe *under her/it*
gu/chun *to*	thugam *to me*	thugad *to you*	thuige *to him/it*	thuice *to her/it*
le *with, by*	leam *with me*	leat *with you*	leis *with him/it*	leatha *with her/it*
mu *about*	umam *about me*	umad *about you*	uime *about him/it*	uimpe *about her/it*
ri *to*	rium *to me*	riut *to you*	ris *to him/it*	rithe *to her/it*
ro/roimh *before*	romham *before me*	romhad *before you*	roimhe *before him/it*	roimhpe *before her/it*
tro/troimh *through*	tromham *through me*	tromhad *through you*	troimhe *through him/it*	troimhpe *through her/it*
thar *over*	tharam *over me*	tharad *over you*	thairis (air) *over him/it*	thairte *over her/it*

Plural

	1st	**2nd**	**3rd**
aig *at*	againn *at us*	agaibh *at you*	aca *at them*
air *on*	oirnn *on us*	oirbh *on you*	orra *on them*
ann *in*	annainn *in us*	annaibh *in you*	annta *in them*
às *out of*	asainn *out of us*	asaibh *out of you*	asta *out of them*
bho *from* o	bhuainn *from us* uainn	bhuaibh *from you* uaibh	bhuat *from them* uat
de *of, off*	dhinn *of us*	dhibh *of you*	dhiubh *of them*
do *to*	dhuinn *to us*	dhuibh *to you*	dhaibh *to them*
eadar *between*	eadarainn *between us*	eadaraibh *between you*	eatarra *between them*
fo *under*	fodhainn *under us*	fodhaibh *under you*	fodhpa/fòpa *under them*
gu/chun *to*	thugainn *to us*	thugaibh *to you*	thuca *to them*
le *with, by*	leinn *with us*	leibh *with you*	leotha *with them*
mu *about*	umainn *about us*	umaibh *about you*	umpa *about them*
ri *to*	rinn/ruinn *to us*	ribh/ruibh *to you*	riutha *to them*
ro/roimh *before*	romhainn *before us*	romhaibh *before you*	romhpa *before them*
tro/troimh *through*	tromhainn *through us*	tromhaibh *through you*	tromhpa *through them*
thar *over*	tharainn *over us*	tharaibh *over you*	tharta *over them*

teach yourself

gaelic

boyd robertson & iain taylor

- Do you want to cover the basics then progress fast?
- Do you want to communicate in a range of situations?
- Do you want to reach a high standard?

Gaelic starts with the basics but moves at a lively pace to give you a good level of understanding, speaking and writing. You will have lots of opportunity to practise the kind of language you will need to be able to communicate with confidence and understand Gaelic culture.

teach yourself®

the A-Z of **teach yourself** language titles

Afrikaans
Arabic
Arabic Script, Beginner's
Bengali
Brazilian Portuguese
Bulgarian
Cantonese
Catalan
Chinese
Chinese, Beginner's
Chinese Script, Beginner's
Croatian
Czech
Danish
Dutch
Dutch, Beginner's
Dutch Dictionary
Dutch Grammar
English, American (EFL)
English as a Foreign Language
English, Correct
English Grammar
English Grammar (EFL)
English for International Business
English Vocabulary
Finnish
French
French, Beginner's
French Grammar
French Grammar, Quick Fix
French, Instant
French, Improve your
French, One-Day
French Starter Kit
French Verbs
French Vocabulary
Gaelic
Gaelic Dictionary
German
German, Beginner's
German Grammar
German Grammar, Quick Fix
German, Instant
German, Improve your
German Verbs
German Vocabulary
Greek
Greek, Ancient
Greek, Beginner's
Greek, Instant
Greek, New Testament
Greek Script, Beginner's
Gulf Arabic
Hebrew, Biblical
Hindi
Hindi, Beginner's
Hindi Script, Beginner's
Hungarian
Icelandic
Indonesian
Irish
Italian
Italian, Beginner's
Italian Grammar
Italian Grammar, Quick Fix
Italian, Instant
Italian, Improve your
Italian, One-Day
Italian Verbs
Italian Vocabulary
Japanese
Japanese, Beginner's
Japanese, Instant
Japanese Script, Beginner's
Korean
Latin
Latin American Spanish
Latin, Beginner's
Latin Dictionary
Latin Grammar
Nepali
Norwegian
Panjabi
Persian, Modern
Polish
Portuguese
Portuguese, Beginner's
Portuguese Grammar
Portuguese, Instant
Romanian
Russian
Russian, Beginner's
Russian Grammar
Russian, Instant
Russian Script, Beginner's
Sanskrit
Serbian
Spanish
Spanish, Beginner's
Spanish Grammar
Spanish Grammar, Quick Fix
Spanish, Instant
Spanish, Improve your
Spanish, One-Day
Spanish Starter Kit
Spanish Verbs
Spanish Vocabulary
Swahili
Swahili Dictionary
Swedish
Tagalog
Teaching English as a Foreign Language
Teaching English One to One
Thai
Turkish
Turkish, Beginner's
Ukrainian
Urdu
Urdu Script, Beginner's
Vietnamese
Welsh
Welsh Dictionary
World Cultures:
- China
- England
- France
- Germany
- Italy
- Japan
- Portugal
- Russia
- Spain
- Wales

Xhosa
Zulu

available from bookshops and on-line retailers